MICROECONOMICS
INDIVIDUAL CHOICE IN COMMUNITIES

SECOND EDITION

BY GERALD FRIEDMAN

MICROECONOMICS:

INDIVIDUAL CHOICE IN COMMUNITIES, SECOND EDITION

ISBN: 978-1-939402-17-2

Published by:

Economic Affairs Bureau, Inc. d/b/a *Dollars & Sense*

95 Berkeley Street, Boston, MA 02116

617-447-2177; dollars@dollarsandsense.org.

For order information, contact Economic Affairs Bureau or visit: www.dollarsandsense.org.

Cover image: Coit Tower, San Francisco (2013) - 08" by Another Believer - Own work. Licensed under Creative Commons Attribution-Share Alike 3.0 via Wikimedia Commons.

CONTENTS

FIGURES

TABLES

INTRODUCTION: WHY ECONOMICS?

THE QUEEN OF THE SOCIAL SCIENCES?

Economics studies the social construction of the material side of life. A focus on production and exchange distinguishes economics from other social studies focused on culture (the concern of anthropology), government and state policy (political science), or social networks (sociology). Focusing on the *social* organization of production and exchange distinguishes economics from engineering and psychology. Economics examines production as a social process where people work with each other, often exchanging or sharing the products of their labor. Social production requires two types of division of labor: *detailed*[1] division in production and *social* division in the exchange of different final products produced by different producers. Both require coordination between producers of *intermediate*[2] products and between different producers. Because production and material life are social, they require that people be able to communicate with others and that they be able to trust each other through the production and exchange process and later when different people hold different products. Because it begins with the division of labor, the foundation of rising production and the root of social exchange, economics is a *social science*[3] that connects each individual's work and consumption to the rest of the human community.

Social institutions and the rules governing them are fundamental for shaping economic behavior because they shape social interactions. This is what distinguishes economics from engineering, which is concerned with the production process between people (including individuals) and things; things do what we tell them to do without requiring any process of persuasion or social control. It also distinguishes economics from psychology, which is concerned with individual consciousness and the individual's decision making removed from either the material world or from other people in society. A social science, economics is about the way people create and change communities through collective action in the material world.

Economics has been called the "queen of the social sciences." With roots in the 18th century Enlightenment writings of David Hume (1711-1776), François Quesnay (1694-1774), and Adam Smith (1723-90), it is the oldest social science, the first systematic attempt to explain social life in terms of human choices. Rather than citing its antiquity, some now ascribe the field's prominence to its use of rigorous models and fancy mathematics. It is true that a good background in mathematics is helpful for understanding some economic models. Nonetheless, technique is always secondary and all important economic ideas can be expressed so that they can be understood by virtually anyone regardless of mathematical proficiency. Rather than claiming superiority for a rigorous method, economics is the premier social science because its content is central to understanding our lives

THE DIVISION OF LABOR: SOCIAL AND DETAILED

The social division of labor refers to the exchange of final products produced by different people, such as when a massage therapist and an auto mechanic trade a massage for a car tune-up. The social division of labor is often coordinated through markets although it is also common within households. The detailed division of labor involves breaking up the production process into tasks performed by individual workers where each worker produces only a part of the final product. A worker on an automobile assembly line responsible for shooting rivets into the panel of the car body is part of a detailed division of labor. Because it does not involve the production of final products, the detailed division of labor is outside commodity markets; instead it is usually coordinated by command where tasks are executed at the order of managers and other supervisors.

and our society. The social processes that make a society are rooted in economic concerns, including the economic division of labor. This claim would be understood by philosophers from Aristotle (384-322 BCE) through Voltaire (1694-1778) and Karl Marx (1818-83). If we believe that consciousness is shaped by participation in material life, then economics studies processes essential to understanding society and our culture.

THE POLITICS OF ECONOMIC THEORY

Economics is so central to our politics that when we choose an economic theory, we choose our politics. Because of its broad scope and central position within the social sciences, economics is a necessary guide to social policy and political action. Any coherent politics must rest on an economic theory of how economic policies will shape outcomes, including levels of production and the allocation of output. Politics makes economic theory into a battleground. On one side are those who would defend the existing distribution of wealth and power as *fair*, because they view the distribution of economic rewards through the market as reflecting merit, and as *efficient*, because it encourages maximum output at minimum cost. Against these defenders of the status quo stand those whose economic theory condemns the existing distribution as *unfair*, granting rewards according to chance, force, or other power, and as *inefficient*,[4] discouraging activity that would raise productivity.

In general, conservatives base their economics on individual action and view economic activity as reflecting individual choice, where individuals maximize their *welfare*[5] subject to the constraints imposed by a stingy nature. By associating economic outputs with individual choice, conservatives deny the legitimacy and even the effectiveness of political action. In this individualist approach, from the perspective of *methodological individualism*,[6] social regulations are necessarily bad because they interfere with individual choice, taking from individuals some of what they have chosen to produce through their own labor or have chosen to exchange. When individuals choose the best course for themselves and achieve for themselves as much well-being as is possible given the stinginess of nature, any social regulation that interferes with their choices *must* lower welfare that has been maximized by individual action.

Progressive politics rests on an economics that believes that social action can contribute to higher output and a more fair distribution of income. This approach is rooted in Adam Smith's observation that the division of labor is the root of higher productivity and, therefore, social regulations can improve economic outcomes by facilitating the division of labor. If we believe the division of labor is the root of high productivity, we can dismiss the argument that social action must lower output. On the contrary, in a world with the division of labor, it is wrong to attach any particular output to any particular individual because it is only by working together that all are able to produce more than they could as individuals; what we produce is a social product, the result of an entire community's collaboration, its social institutions, values, and history.

METHODOLOGICAL INDIVIDUALISM AND SOCIAL SCIENCE

Rejecting methodological individualism, a social perspective tilts towards an egalitarian distribution that gives all of us a more-or-less equal share in the wealth of our society. If we owe most of our output to living in a particular

---

NEOCLASSICAL ECONOMICS AND FREE-ENTERPRISE ECONOMISTS

While **Milton Friedman (1912-2006)** was a leading exponent of free-market capitalism and neoclassical orthodoxy, his own work showed the importance of non-monetary motivations. On the home page of the Friedman Foundation for Educational Choice, a foundation established by the late Milton Friedman and his wife Rose Friedman, there is a list of the awards granted this distinguished economist. In addition to the Nobel Prize for Economics (1976), Friedman was awarded the  John Bates Clark medal of the American Economic Association (1951), the National Medal of Science (1988), the Presidential Medal of Freedom (also 1988), 17 other medals, 18 honorary degrees, and was elected to 10 honorary societies. Together with a commitment to make the world better, these honors gave him as much motivation in his hard work as did any financial incentives he received.

community, in the United States rather than in Lesotho or Nepal, then one may reasonably argue that we should all share equally in this windfall. Distribution becomes a legitimate matter for political and social debate because it involves the allocation of social products; indeed, redistribution may be a necessary function to protect those, such as children and their care-givers, whose contribution to production is yet to come or is indirect. Methodological individualists, those who would explain social outcomes solely in terms of individuals and their motivations, would reject redistributive programs fearing that they reduce incentives to work hard or efficiently; they are, however, hard-pressed to explain the behavior of care-givers who provide goods and services to others without contract or market exchange. Yet, without care-givers, society would die out quickly, beginning with children and babies.

Against methodological individualism are economic theories where economics is a social science, the study of how people work together to produce their material world. Individuals are shaped by their community, their values, their work, and the way they conduct their lives. In the social approach, people are born into an existing society which gives them language, values, and training to participate productively. While people shape their society and change it, there is a society that exists independently of any individual or their perceptions, and it contributes to people's economic productivity, making us, for example, more productive than people in Senegal or Panama. Although he is best known for his argument that the profit motive can lead individuals "as if by an invisible hand" to advance society's best interests, Adam Smith (1723-1790) rejected methodological individualism. In his *Theory of Moral Sentiments*, Adam Smith did not rely on individual selfishness to explain social well-being. Instead, he concluded that people are shaped by their community and are naturally led to care for others: "How selfish so-ever man may be supposed, there are evidently some principles in his nature, which interest him in the fortune of others, and render their

WHY DO PEOPLE WORK HARD?

Does the possibility of making money lead people to work hard? Financial incentives are certainly important for some workers. But many work for nonfinancial rewards, including social esteem and even love. Your parents were not paid to raise you; friends often help each other without financial reward.

Recently, we have seen highly productive work performed without regard for financial compensation. The Linux operating system, much YouTube content, and the Open Office applications package have been developed and are maintained by volunteer work. Even popular music is often provided without financial reward. Radiohead eports that it made more from downloads of its "free"

Radiohead's Thom Yorke

album "In Rainbows" than it did in total for its previous album "Hail To The Thief." Apparently, a lot of talented people are willing to work without regard for financial incentives; and people are willing to contribute outside of the market system.

happiness necessary to him, though he derives nothing from it except the pleasure of seeing it." In his 1776 classic, *The Wealth of Nations*, Smith showed how society shaped individuals and their behavior in three fundamental ways: *values*,[7] *production*,[8] and the *rules of exchange*.[9] Individuals, Smith argued, draw their values from their community, including their tastes and preferences. Moreover, their productivity is shaped by their participation in production as a social process with the division of labor. Their exchanges are structured by laws governing property and shaping markets. In each of these dimensions of economic behavior—values, productivity, and exchange relations—society shapes individuals. It is therefore unreasonable to object to social regulation as violating the supposed free choices of individuals; and wrong to study economic behavior as if individuals were outside of society.

ECONOMIC THEORY AND POWER

If social organizations influence welfare, then better social organizations can increase welfare, raising productivity and improving the distribution of wealth so as to increase well-being and raise future productivity. On the other hand, worse social institutions can lower productivity and produce a less-fair distribution of income. Recognizing the social side of production also means acknowledging the danger of *power* in a society where one person has disproportionate influence over others, allowing some to *exploit*[10] others and take from them some of what they deserve. Methodological individualists regularly deny the significance of economic power, denying that any individual could hold power over others. But control over social organizations or the ability to manipulate socially constructed values gives some individuals power over others. Better social regulation can improve welfare and enhance freedom by reducing the scope for private power. Social regulation can also promote welfare by encouraging socially constructive values, much as we discourage drunk driving and the abuse of dangerous drugs, or even by lowering *transactions costs*[11] by discouraging dishonesty and theft. Social action can raise *productivity*[12] by improving the operation of the division of labor and by providing better education and training. Social action can also improve economic outcomes by reducing the power that some have over others.

ECONOMIC THEORY AND INDIVIDUALISM

Everyone has a point-of-view, an *ideology*, a common-sense view of the world, and an associated politics. The world is an infinite mass of information which we can make meaningful only if we have a way to structure our perceptions and limit what we observe. This is the role of an ideological system. A filter for our perceptions, an ideology is a system for organizing information, differentiating things from each other, and grouping things that are alike. More, it is a way to rank phenomena, to establish causal relationships, and to decide on one's political stance and actions.

Only through an ideology can we interpret the mass of otherwise random facts in the world. This means that we can be conscious of things only to the extent that our ideology allows us to assign meaning to them.[13] Our ideology frames our observations of the world even prior to our observing it. This creates a paradox: because we observe the world only within an ideological system, we can never evaluate that system empirically. The evidence that we might use to evaluate an ideological system, to question its causal connections, can only be gathered within a particular system and, therefore, can never challenge that system's assumptions.[14] The best we can do is to be aware of the limits of our understanding, and to be aware that others may legitimately differ with us on fundamental assumptions. For students of economics, this means that we might be able to understand alternative economic theories and associated politics, but we cannot expect to refute them. We have to choose a theory and a politics on the basis of our preferences, our own "common sense"

Economists who treat economics as a study of individual behavior subject to constraint focus on the ways individuals maximize their well-being when confronting a stingy material world. I reject this approach, methodological individualism, as appropriate only for asocial individuals living on isolated islands or psychotics isolated within their own neuroses. I believe the production process is social; we produce with the help of others and then we exchange what we make with others for different things and services that we need or want. To me, the economy is a social phenomenon, a *social fact*[15] that needs to be studied as the product of other social phenomena and social facts.

My social approach distinguishes this work from the many texts in microeconomics that are written from an individualist perspective. While this is the "orthodox" approach, popular with "neoclassical" economists, I question how useful can be a theory that assumes that people could survive as isolated individuals, and question how methodological individualists can *reasonably* explain such common phenomenon as parents caring for children or the readiness of people to sacrifice anonymously for each other. Instead, I assume that people are social animals who need social relations and are shaped by their involvement with others. Others would differ with my conception of "reasonably," and there is no simple empirical test to choose between a social view of economics and methodological individualism. All good theories are *ideologies*, sophisticated enough to explain all phenomena and open enough that any phenomenon can be fit within the parameters of their models. In the case of economic ideology, you will have to choose *your* theory, choosing between my social approach and other, individualist approaches, on the basis of which seems most reasonable to you, which seems to explain the world in the way that is most plausible to you. There is no other way to choose among social theories. Recognizing that economics is not a science, where major theories can be subjected to simple empirical tests, makes economics *an art as well as a science*, a discipline where methods of argument and discourse matter; and where the personality of the scholar matters. (This is why I include brief summaries of the contributions of major economists throughout the book.)

This work develops the social view of economic activity. Without discounting the importance of individual initiative, I argue that economic actions depend on the organization of society and are shaped by social life. Like methodological individualism, this social approach engenders a particular politics. Focusing on the individual's contribution, *orthodox neoclassical economics*[16] implies a *libertarian*[17] politics and *laissez faire*[18] economics. By contrast, social economics has a *statist* tilt, believing in a constructive role for government; economic life is a social product and, therefore, social action is needed to sustain the economy, and can improve it.

ALTERNATIVE ECONOMICS

I first wrote this book in frustration. Unhappy with introductory texts that presented the orthodox neoclassical model uncritically, I wanted a text that would delve deeply into the assumptions underlying the orthodox model, both to provide a better basis for understanding this model and to provide the foundation for alternative models.[19] Like everyone else, I have preferences for a particular type of economic theory; and I would prefer if everyone, including all who read this, would agree with me. That said, as a teacher, I feel that I have done right by you if you come away from this work with more appreciation of the diversity of economic models, and their points of disagreement. If you also leave believing that the orthodox neoclassical model is the best, *c'est la vie*.

While recognizing the variation within each approach, this book focuses on two broad classes of economic ideologies: those built on *methodological individualism* where social formations reflect the characteristics of individuals, and *social science* theories where social formations are independent of individuals and determine individual characteristics. Within each system, there are alternative variants, with different approaches and politics. While methodological individualism tilts towards *laissez faire* (hands off) economic policy and social science towards *public intervention*, there are arguments within both perspectives favoring either kind of economic policy.

For the last 50 years or so, the most common economic ideology in the United States, the orthodox economic theory taught in most textbooks is a version of neoclassical theory associated with *market fundamentalism*. Based in methodological individualism and associated with the writings of economists from the University of Chicago, including Milton Friedman,[20] this approach treats all social action as coming from the optimizing activities of individuals. It has, therefore, a strong presumption that these individuals should be left free to choose because by maximizing their own well-being, the sum of their optimizing behavior will bring the maximum possible benefit for the entire society.[21] Even the presence of *market imperfections* and *public goods* does not shake market fundamentalists; they argue that whatever the problems with the free market, government regulation will make them worse because regulatory agencies will inevitably be captured by special interests that will use them to further oppress the public.[22]

While methodological individualism may have a tilt towards *laissez faire*, not all go that far. Even while acknowledging the danger of regulatory capture, some argue for public regulation to correct *market failures* due to lack of competitive markets or the lack of markets at all, as is the case for some *public goods*.[23] Others question the market fundamentalists' assumption of individual hyper-rationality. Based on experimental data, *behavioral economists* argue that individuals regularly fail to optimize, and the social organization of markets can dramatically change outcomes.[24] These findings open new areas for public intervention, where individual and aggregate well-being can be raised by regulations that correct systemic mistakes that individuals make and provide constructive *nudges* to help individuals do what they would want to do on their own volition but do not because of mistakes and irrational choices.[25]

Another type of ideology goes beyond these critiques to challenge the politics of market fundamentalism. Instead of viewing society as the product of individual action, social scientists view it as prior to and separate from the individuals within. Treating economics as a *social science*, they argue that economic systems need to be studied as a result of group dynamics, including group conflicts that are worked out through political processes. In this social science category are *Marxists* and various types of *institutionalists* who emphasize different *social facts* as essential for understanding the economy, including economic interests, the distribution of property, the roles of race and gender, and the political structure of a society.[26]

In choosing among the various economic theories and ideologies discussed in this work, methodological individualism and market fundamentalism has an initial advantage. Based on a few axioms of individual behavior and the production process, such theories are simple and require minimal knowledge of the world. By contrast, theories involving social institutions not only take longer to explain but often appear as *ad hoc* or even *post hoc*, descriptive rather than predictive. When viewed as a result of institutions, history, and political and social conflict, social outcomes vary in ways that can be unique to a particular time and place, and so may be unpredictable.[27] To methodological individualists, society is the way it is because it must be that way as a result of individual choices, and the work of economists is to explain why these choices were optimal and should not be changed; in the social scientists, they are that way because of history and the outcomes of political conflict. And they can be made better.

ACKNOWLEDGMENTS

In preparing this work I have benefitted from comments from many past students and from teaching assistants, from Michael Ash, David Eisnitz, Nancy Folbre, Natasha Friedman, Rosa Friedman, Debra Jacobson, Esther Jacobson, David Kotz, Merrilee Mardon, Mark Paul, and Alejandro Reuss. I am grateful for research assistance from David Eisnitz, Mark Paul, Luke Pretz, Javed Kesselman, and Stedman Hood; and for expert copyediting by my daughters Natasha and Rosa. Alejandro Reuss provided superb editing, *comme d'habitude*.

I have enjoyed a life of the greatest privilege, the opportunity to develop my ideas freely and in the company of others who share my political and scholarly commitment to free inquiry. I owe much to my colleagues in the Economics Department at the University of Massachusetts who established and maintained our program, and to these colleagues and to our students who have pushed me to do my best work. I offer this in thanks to them.

DISCUSSION QUESTIONS

What is "methodological individualism"? What is a "social science"? Which one of these describes economics? Does one or the other approach necessarily imply a particular politics?

What is the "division of labor"? How does the division of labor impel one to approach economics as a social science or through methodological individualism?

What is "ideology"? How would you disprove an ideology?

ENDNOTES

[1]The detailed division of labor involves breaking up the production process into a set of smaller tasks. The social division of labor is where workers specialize in producing particular final products which they then exchange.

[2]Intermediate products are produced goods used in the further production of final consumer goods. Examples would include the steel or plastic used in making automobiles, or the cloth used in making dresses and other apparel.

[3]A social science studies human behavior as a product of a society and arrangements between individuals. This is in contrast with methodological individualism which studies behavior as a result of processes internal to individuals.

[4]"Inefficient" refers to activities where the means employed are wasteful or otherwise inappropriate to achieve the end. In such cases, the same end could be achieved with less expensive means.

[5]By "welfare" we mean the subjective perception of how well-off a person feels.

[6]Methodological individualists study human behavior from the perspective of individuals and their motivation independent of any community or society.

[7]Values refers to the preferences people have including their willingness to help others.

[8]Production is where labor is applied to transform nature or to provide human services for people.

[9]Rules specify the way exchanges are conducted, including the way the rate of exchange of one

product for another is set and the rights individuals have to their possessions.

[10]A controversial idea, exploitation is to take unfair advantage of the situation of others to make an exchange where what is given is of less value than what is received.

[11]Transactions costs are the costs of making exchanges including the costs of negotiating prices and protecting property.

[12]Productivity is the relationship between the amount produced and inputs, including human labor.

[13]A favorite trope in literature and video involves people who are unable to filter the world. In "Earshot" (season 3 episode 18), for example, Buffy the Vampire Slayer could read minds. Unable to filter the mass of information she was receiving, however, Buffy began to go crazy.

[14]See, for example, the discussion in Karl Mannheim, *Ideology and Utopia: An Introduction to the Sociology of Knowledge* (San Diego: Harcourt Brace Jovanovich, 1985); Thomas S. Kuhn, *The Structure of Scientific Revolutions*, 3rd ed (Chicago, IL: University of Chicago Press, 1996).

[15]Social facts are things external to and coercive to individuals that exist regardless of individual volition. The French sociologist Émile Durkheim viewed the study of social facts as the true provenance of the social sciences.

[16]Orthodox neoclassical economics is the economic theory developed in the late-19th century which views economic activity as the result of individuals, their preferences, the available technology (or methods) of production, and the supply of factor inputs, including labor, land, and other raw materials.

[17]Libertarianism is the social philosophy that states and other social bodies should not interfere with the choices and actions of individuals.

[18]Laissez faire economics is the economic equivalent of libertarianism, the view that government should not interfere with the economic choices of individuals.

[19]This, of course, is an argument in defense of free inquiry presented in John Stuart Mill, *On Liberty* (Indianapolis: Hackett Pub. Co, 1978) I should add as well that I am appalled at the high price of other textbooks.

[20]Milton Friedman, *Capitalism and Freedom* (Chicago: University of Chicago Press, 1962); Milton Friedman, *Price Theory, a Provisional Text* (Chicago: Aldine Pub. Co, 1962); also see Robert Van Horn, Philip Mirowski, and Thomas A. Stapleford, eds., *Building Chicago Economics: New Perspectives on the History of America's Most Powerful Economics Program*, Historical Perspectives on Modern Economics (Cambridge ; New York: Cambridge University Press, 2011).

[21]The "free to choose" reference is to Milton Friedman's popular statement published with his wife, Rose, at the beginning of the Reagan Administration in the United States and that of Margaret Thatcher in Britain; Milton Friedman, *Free to Choose: A Personal Statement*, 1st ed (New York: Harcourt Brace Jovanovich, 1980).

[22]James M. Buchanan and Gordon Tullock, *The Calculus of Consent: Logical Foundations of Constitutional Democracy*, The Selected Works of Gordon Tullock, v. 2 (Indianapolis: Liberty Fund, 2004); Mancur Olson, *The Rise and Decline of Nations: Economic Growth, Stagflation, and Social Rigidities* (New Haven: Yale University Press, 1982); George J. Stigler, "The Theory of Economic Regulation," *The Bell Journal of Economics and Management Science* 2, no. 1 (April 1, 1971): 3–21, doi:10.2307/3003160.

[23]Richard T Ely, *Monopolies and Trusts, Big Business* (New York: Arno Press, 1973); John Maurice Clark, *Social Control of Business* (Chicago, Ill: The University of Chicago Press, 1926); John Bates Clark, *The Control of Trusts*, Rewritten and enl. ed, Reprints of Economic Classics (New York: A. M. Kelley, 1971); John Bates Clark, *The Problem of Monopoly; a Study of a Grave Danger and of the Natural Mode of Averting It*, Columbia University Lectures. [Hewitt Foundation] (New York, London: The Columbia University Press, The Macmillan Company, agents; Macmillan & Co., Ltd, 1904); John Bates Clark, *Social Justice without Socialism*, Barbara Weinstock Lectures on the Morals of Trade (Boston, New York: Houghton Mifflin company, 1914).

[24]Wesley C Mitchell, *The Backward Art of Spending Money* (New Brunswick, N.J., U.S.A: Transaction Publishers, 1999); Daniel Kahneman, Ed Diener, and Norbert Schwarz, eds., *Well-Being: The Foundations of Hedonic Psychology* (New York: Russell Sage Foundation, 1999); Dan Ariely, *Predictably Irrational: The Hidden Forces That Shape Our Decisions*, 1st ed (New York, NY: Harper, 2008).

[25]Richard H. Thaler, *Nudge: Improving Decisions about Health, Wealth, and Happiness* (New Haven: Yale University Press, 2008).

[26]Émile Durkheim, *The Rules of Sociological Method*, 8th ed (Chicago, Ill: The University of Chicago press, 1938); Karl Marx, *Capital: A Critique of Political Economy* (London & Toronto: J. M. Dent & sons ltd, 1934); Nancy Folbre, *Valuing Children: Rethinking the Economics of the Family, The Family and Public Policy* (Cambridge, Mass: Harvard University Press, 2008).

[27]Compare Milton Friedman, *Essays in Positive Economics* (Chicago, London: University of Chicago Press, 1964); Émile Durkheim, *The Division of Labor in Society* (New York: Free Press of Glencoe, 1964); Durkheim, *The Rules of Sociological Method*; Richard T. Ely, *The Past and the Present of Political Economy* (Baltimore: N. Murray, publication agent, Johns-Hopkins university, 1884).

2

THE BEST OF ALL POSSIBLE WORLDS?

LEIBNIZ, CANDIDE, AND THE PRESUPPOSITIONS OF ECONOMIC THEORY

Some study economics from the sheer joy of understanding a complex system, a joy analogous to that of solving a difficult crossword puzzle or a particularly challenging mystery story. Alas, there are relatively few academic positions for puzzle masters and little government support for research in solving Rubik's Cubes. Economics is part of the *academy*[1] and receives government funding and social status because it has implications for how we organize our lives and our communities. Economics has *politics*; different economic theories have implications for the size and type of government and community we create. Debates in economic theory are really arguments about politics. Most economists became involved in economic theory to make political statements and their choice of economic theory and presuppositions reflect their politics.

Research on this is not like economic research because it has no political implications.

Speaking broadly, disputes in economic politics pit *individualists*[2] against *communitarians*[3] who believe in social action. On one side are those who believe that individual action will produce beneficent outcomes; against them are those who believe that some form of social or government intervention is needed, either because individuals are incapable of making good decisions, good individual choices do not aggregate to good social choices, or be individual action is incapable of addressing important social issues.

The popularity of methodological individualism reflects its association with a type of political *liberalism*[4] that traces back to the optimistic philosophy of the *Enlightenment*[5] and even of certain *theist*[6] philosophies. Perhaps the last "universal genius," Gottfried Wilhelm Leibniz (1646–1716) made deep and lasting contributions to the fields of metaphysics, epistemology, logic, philosophy of religion, as well as physics, geology, jurisprudence, and history. He was also a pioneering mathematician. After inventing calculus, contemporaneously with Sir Isaac Newton, he developed binary arithmetic and, in 1671, a simple computer, the nonprogrammable *step reckoner*, using technology still in use today. Even Denis Diderot (1713-1784), the eighteenth-century French atheist and *materialist*[7] who often disagreed with Leibniz, was awed by his achievement. Almost despairing at one point, he wrote that: "When one compares the talents one has with those of a Leibniz, one is tempted to throw away one's books and go die quietly in the dark of some forgotten corner."

Leibniz is well remembered today, as much for his work in philosophy as for his mathematics. Alas, as with many, his reputation has suffered from the enthusiasm of his followers. Beginning from the principle that God is an absolutely perfect being, and that power and knowledge are aspects of perfection, Leibniz concludes that God, possessing supreme and infinite wisdom, must act in the most perfect manner and, with infinite power, must always act for the best, including creating the best world. A perfect and all-powerful Deity, Leibniz argues, could do no less. That said, Leibniz *never* denies the existence of misery and suffering, or the pain inflicted on many innocent humans and

Gottfried Wilhelm Leibniz

Leibniz calculating machine, one of the first computers.

animals. Instead, in the tradition of Christian apologists like Augustine, he argues that such suffering is necessary for the realization of the greater beauty and perfection of the world. We may lack the capacity to understand, but suffering is necessary for the realization of God's essential goodness in the world. Our understanding may be deficient; but we know from the logic of Leibnitz's argument about the power and omniscience of God, that we do, indeed, live in the best of all *possible* worlds.

It is, of course, impossible to contradict a statement like this that depends on a comparison with an unobservable alternative. All the horrors of our world may pale before other worlds yet unknown! This may explain why Voltaire's trenchant *Candide* never could vanquish Leibnitz's *Panglossian*[8] interpretation of the world; at least for those who really want to believe. For us, Leibnitz is important because from him, and other Enlightenment-era social thinkers, came a persistent belief in a beneficent natural order that has endured over the centuries in economics as a form of *secular theology*.[9] More than wishful thinking may be involved here; belief in a beneficent natural order has buttressed classical liberals in their defense of individual autonomy against state oppression. A secular theist, Adam Smith rejected the Christian idea of original sin and the inherent evil of human nature. For him, belief in a beneficent nature allowed him to reject the statist conceptions of Thomas Hobbes and others who believed that a powerful authoritarian state was needed to defend against a war of all-against-all. Instead, Smith and others have argued that a benign nature had arranged the world, this "best of all possible worlds," to allow for a natural and spontaneous harmony without oppressive police or state powers.

Smith developed his social philosophy on the Panglossian notion that a benevolent Creator had so ordered the universe as to produce the greatest possible human happiness and that it is the task of *moral philosophy*,[10] including politics and economics, to discover the natural laws which make for the happiness of God's creatures. In his 1759 book, *The Theory of Moral Sentiments*, for example, Smith argues that humans have an intrinsic sense of "sympathy" with others, the ability to sense their feelings and to imagine ourselves in their situation. From this sympathetic sense comes our ability to form moral judgments, expressions of impartial sympathy with the motives and result of human action. Our sense of justice, Smith argues, derives from the "sympathy" we feel with the pleasures and pains of others, making sympathy, and natural justice, pillars of the social structure. Providence, Smith concludes, has so ordered the world that men, in pursuing their own welfare within the limits set by sympathy and justice, contribute to the general welfare regardless of their own intent. Having established this doctrine of a natural harmony of interests, Smith then argues in *Moral Sentiments* and his later *Wealth of Nations* for a theory of natural liberty where everyone is free to pursue his own welfare in his own way. Writing in the same year that Smith published *The Wealth of Nations*, another Enlightenment-era liberal wrote that people "are endowed by their Creator with certain unalienable Rights." Left to their own devices, individuals would arrange their affairs well. They organize governments not from necessity but convenience.

Here at the birth of modern economic theory, we have the orthodox tradition founded on two fundamentally conservative pillars: a Smithian belief in an intrinsically beneficent nature joined to a Panglossian sense that things could be worse.[11] Together, these enlightenment thinkers give us a vision of individual human nature that justifies a liberal social policy *against* a strong state and social regulation. To resist the oppression of state and clerical authorities, economics was developed as a secular religion, founded on the premises of *natural benevolence*[12] and methodological individualism, the idea that individuals exist *prior* to society, live peacefully and prosperously outside of

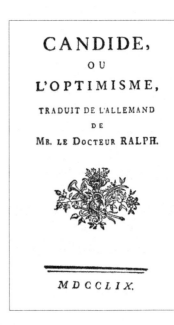

CANDIDE,
O U
L'OPTIMISME,
TRADUIT DE L'ALLEMAND
D E
MR. LE DOCTEUR RALPH.

MDCCLIX.

society, and choose to form society and government to achieve particular and restricted ends without surrendering any significant part of their *natural* independence. There are two crucial ideas here: individuals are *rational* in the sense that they act to pursue their own welfare; and society is unproductive, it adds nothing to the welfare produced by individual action and it is not needed to prevent conflict among different individuals. Here we have an economic theology, a vision of the world that supports a politics of *laissez faire* opposed to any political regulation of economic behavior. Orthodox economics advances a positive political program in defense of individual liberty by associating it with a particular economic methodology, methodological individualism.

Built into the very foundation of orthodox economic theory thus is a fundamental and, to my view, false dichotomy between the individual and the group, between individual development and social action. On one side, the Panglossian liberals posited a beneficent nature which creates inherently good individuals who produce, consume, and distribute economic goods. Acting independently, without the interference of community or government, they will "naturally" create "the best of all possible worlds". On the other side are social institutions like states and other community associations which are inherently suspect because they interfere with individuals. All good comes from individuals; all bad from social institutions that interfere with the workings of a beneficent nature. Bad people, greedy and selfish politicians, create governments and institutions as vehicles to exploit good individuals. Social institutions have no place within the orthodox Panglossian system *except* as restraints on individual development or self-expression.

Smith's confidence in a beneficent nature helps to form his value theory, or his theory of the rate of exchange between commodities. Without monopoly, Smith argues, workers will be paid the real value of their time and goods will exchange at their cost of production, or, ultimately, for the cost of the labor embodied in their production. Here we have the *labor theory of value*[13] as a theory of relative prices. Where the price of a commodity depends on the labor embodied within it, prices will reflect the real cost, the real human price of the commodity, and will, therefore, provide a fair gauge of the value that *should* be put on the commodities. In the absence of regulation or monopoly, Smith argues, market competition will ensure both that consumers pay the fair price for commodities and *with from* this normatively fair set of relative prices, competition will ensure a fair and equitable distribution of income.

Alas, even in this halcyon day of natural fair market competition, there was a problem, a darker side that was soon exposed by a group of English economists known as the *Ricardian socialists* because of their use of the labor theory of value in David Ricardo and Adam Smith. The problem was that when Smith developed the labor theory of value in the beginning of *The Wealth of Nations*, he left no place for capitalist profit beyond a return for supervisory and entrepreneurial labor. If the relative value of the beaver in terms of deer, the price of beaver, is set by the labor applied in hunting, then how do hunting capitalists extract a profit?[14] Later in *The Wealth of Nations*, Smith acknowledges rent and profit, recognizing that "this original state of things, in which the labourer enjoyed the whole produce of his own labour, could not last beyond the first intro-

---

SMITH AND SYMPATHY EXPLAINED: MIRROR NEURONS

In the early 1990s, Italian researchers found individual neurons in the brains of macaque monkeys that fired both when the monkeys performed an action and also when another monkey performed the same action. Scientists have since identified the same neurons in human brains and speculate that such "mirror neurons" could help explain how and why we "read" other people's minds and feel empathy for them. Studies have linked mirror neurons to the emergence of language, abstract reasoning and even self-awareness or consciousness. "The self and the other are just two sides of the same coin. To understand myself, I must recognize myself in other people," says Marco Iacoboni, a neuroscientist at UCLA.

ADAM SMITH'S THEORY OF VALUE

"In that early and rude state of society which precedes both the accumulation of stock and the appropriation of land, the proportion between the quantities of labour necessary for acquiring different objects seems to be the only circumstance which can afford any rule for exchanging them for one another. If among a nation of hunters, for example, it usually costs twice the labour to kill a beaver which it does to kill a deer, one beaver should naturally exchange for or be worth two deer. It is natural that what is usually the produce of two days or two hours labour, should be worth double of what is usually the produce of one day's or one hour's labour.".

duction of the appropriation of land and the accumulation of stock." Still, Smith includes rent and profit in value in a most unsatisfying manner, simply adding them to the labor value of the product without an explanation of the determination of either the rate of profit or why there should be profit at all in equilibrium? Why in equilibrium would prices diverge from embodied labor? Is there some value added by ownership? Or is the return to ownership simply a tribute paid by labor to those who have a monopoly over access to the means of production. Smith implicitly recognizes the role of historically and politically developed monopoly as a source of profit. This is why he devotes most of *The Wealth of Nations* to an analysis of how power and monopoly have been exercised by landlords and capitalists against labor and other producers. Believing in the iniquity of capital, especially when aligned with a repressive state, Smith famously argued that "[p]eople of the same trade seldom meet together, even for merriment and diversion, but the conversation ends in a conspiracy against the public or in some contrivance to raise prices." Employers, for their part, Smith finds

Adam Smith

are always and everywhere in a sort of tacit, but constant and uniform combination, not to raise the wages of labour above their actual rate. To violate this combination is everywhere a most unpopular action, and a sort of reproach to a master among his neighbours and equals. We seldom, indeed, hear of this combination, because it is the usual, and one may say, the natural state of things which nobody ever hears of. Masters too sometimes enter into particular combinations to sink the wage of labour even below this rate.

From this perspective, wages and the rate of profit do not depend only on economic circumstances but on history and on politics. In addition to such economic conditions as the rate of growth of the economy and the population, profit and wages, and relative prices in general, they depend on the organization of the employers and workers, and the political and historical institutions of the society that affect the bargaining position of labor and capital, the ability of each to maintain combinations against the other. These implications from Smith were developed by some of his most influential followers, including David Ricardo, and were picked up by the Ricardian socialists, including Thomas Hodgskin, John Bray, William Thompson, and John Gray. From them, these ideas shaped the thinking of a German philosopher and political activist turned economist, Karl Marx.[15] Yet, they have been ignored by most, including most economists, today who, as a result, have little to say about value theory and the determination of the rate of profit.

Instead of discussing the social factors determining profit and value, most orthodox economists have founded their work on the "early and rude state of society" where value depends only on labor without regard for profit. In effect, they have pursued economics as if there is no society, to interpret and guide the behavior of a Robinson Crusoe marooned by himself with only his own concerns. Founded in this way, on a basis of methodological individualism, orthodox economics looks towards psychology among the other human sciences. Oddly enough, modern economics has nothing to say to the other social sciences, including sociology, political science, or history, because it provides a theory of value and distribution that depends entirely on individual choice. A theory suited for an isolated individual

AN EXCERPT FROM DAVID RICARDO'S *PRINCIPLES OF POLITICAL ECONOMY*

"The produce of the earth—all that is derived from its surface by the united application of labour, machinery, and capital, is divided among three classes of the community; namely, the proprietor of the land, the owner of the stock or capital necessary for its cultivation, and the labourers by whose industry it is cultivated. .... But in different stages of society, the proportions of the whole produce of the earth which will be allotted to each of these classes, under the names of rent, profit, and wages, will be essentially different; depending mainly on the actual fertility of the soil, on the accumulation of capital and population, and on the skill, ingenuity, and instruments employed in agriculture. ...To determine the laws which regulate this distribution, is the principal problem in Political Economy: much as the science has been improved by the writings of Turgot, Stuart, Smith, Say, Sismondi, and others, they afford very little satisfactory information respecting the natural course of rent, profit, and wages."

Frédéric Bastiat

allocating his or her own time and labor, it was conceived without regard for any social relations. There is no place within a system like this, a system of methodological individualism, for groups or states *except* as obstacles to individual self-expression; there is nothing for economics to learn from studying the development of groups or states because it already knows that they are oppressive barriers to self-expression. Likewise, these orthodox economists have almost nothing to say about public policy because all state action interferes with individuals. All they have to say about public policy is the famous phrase: *laissez faire, laissez passer*.[16] With its optimism, this version of Smith provided a happy justification for the established order. And there were economists who were content to use the theory in this way, defending the established regime whatever its iniquities. But there were others, who realized that the labor theory of value Smith presents in the beginning of *The Wealth of Nations* is inadequate outside of the "early and rude state." And there were some who questioned the simple and happy conclusions Smith, and his followers, drew from labor theory of value. Modern orthodox economics, neoclassical theory,[17] was to develop from the conflict between the simple interpretation of Smith and the challenge posed by this more sophisticated and politically threatening version.

MICROECONOMICS AND THE DIVISION OF LABOR

Those who read beyond the first book of *The Wealth of Nations* know that Smith has a much more complicated, and less optimistic, vision than that which has usually been credited to him. Nonetheless—perhaps *because* so few ever read beyond that first book!—a Panglossian interpretation of Smith has remained central to economists. France's Frédéric Bastiat (1801-1850), for example, insisted that there is a basic harmony of interest between different individuals. He championed private property and limited government by arguing that voluntary exchange through markets would lead to peace and prosperity, "economic harmony," so long as government was restricted to protecting the lives and property of citizens. The America Francis Wayland (1796–1865) agreed. A Baptist minister and self-taught economist, Wayland was at Brown University as professor and president between pastorates. During his presidency, he wrote two of the most widely used and influential American textbooks of the nineteenth century, *The Elements of Moral Science* (1835) and *The Elements of Political Economy* (1837). Defending the freedom of autonomous individuals, he argued that "a man has an entire right to use his own body as he will, provided he do not so use it as to interfere with the rights of his neighbor." Similarly, he considered the right of property to be "the right to use something as I choose, provided I do not so use it as to interfere with the rights of my neighbor." Like Bastiat, he was comfortable with these libertarian positions. Economics, Wayland argued, is the "systematic arrangement of the laws which God has established" and "God intended that men should live together in friendship and harmony." Beginning with beneficent nature, it was a short step for Wayland to end with the conclusion that government interference is almost always a bad thing, detrimental as much to morals as to economic prosperity.

> "The greatest improvement in the productive powers of labour, and the greater part of the skill, dexterity, and judgment with which it is anywhere directed, or applied, seem to have been the effects of the division of labour."

Yet these ideas of natural harmony coming from a beneficent nature did not monopolize economic analysis in the century after the publication in 1776 of Smith's *The Wealth of Nations*. Instead, some of the most important economists after Smith were profound pessimists who believed that an inherent conflict between economic classes would lead inevitably to the progressive *immiseration*[18] of the poor. For the great "Classical" economists, Thomas Robert Malthus (1766-1834), David Ricardo (1772-1823), and even John Stuart Mill (1806-73), economics was a "dismal science." As Thomas Carlyle said of Malthus: "[n]owhere, in that quarter of his intellectual world, is there light; nothing but a grim shadow of hunger . . . Dreary, stolid, dismal, without hope for this world or the next." Malthusian demographics, the "natural" tendency of population growth to drive down wages and lower average productivity, accounts for the most dismal aspects of classical economics. Ricardo explains that when wages are high, population increases until "wages again fall to their natural price, and indeed from a reaction sometimes fall below it." But beyond the details, classical theory denies the premise of natural harmony. Instead, classical economists focus on conflict between the different classes and the division of output among them. Trouble and conflict, not beneficence and harmony, is the stuff of classical economics.

Francis Wayland

All three of the great post-Smith classicists, Malthus, Ricardo, and Mill, titled their major works *Principles of Political Economy* because they believed that society and social institutions were crucial for the setting of prices and the distribution of income. As *political economists*, they looked to reorder social policy and institutions to make the best of a cruel and stingy world. They consciously rejected any Panglossian optimism; and the feeling was reciprocated. The Panglossians had no need of *political* economy because to them the state has no useful function in a world of natural benevolence and harmony. Instead, to Malthus, Ricardo, and Mill, public action can improve a world where the private action of individuals leads to dismal outcomes of *subsistence wages*[19] and *stagnant steady-state economies*.[20] Political economists deny any dichotomy between "natural" individual action and "artificial" collective action. Instead, they focus on the *social* determinants of economic values including individual behavior and social institutions that shape the distribution of wealth, income, and conflict between social groups. Political economists draw on Smith's larger work to address the social determination of the level of national or regional income and its distribution among social groups and ask how a society's history and its institutions shaped production and distribution without regard for the motivation and actions of individuals. Because production and distribution are determined by a society's history, political economists expect different countries to have different distributions and different levels of output; they have no expectation that either will be optimized or maximized.

Classical economics and political economy as a discipline culminated in the work of Karl Marx (1818-1883) whose political work, as an advocate and theorist of a popular workers' revolution against capitalism, grew directly from his political economy. First, attention to the *social* roots of income distribution makes problems of poverty and inequality social rather than the product of individual and personal failures or achievements; the solution to poverty and inequality, therefore, must also be social, through political action rather than individual rehabilitation. Second, his economics led him to a precise identification of the source of inequality and popular poverty and a political response. Poverty and low wages, to Marx, are not due to some long-run population explosion, as feared by Malthus, Ricardo, and Mill. Instead, Marx argued that workers were poor because capitalism is designed *not* to increase welfare but rather to produce *surplus value* or *profits*[21] for the *capitalists*[22] who use a monopoly over the means of production to exploit workers.

Marx begins with Smithian value theory and the dilemma about the source of profit in a free market economy. There is no problem with wages; they are paid with the value produced by labor in making commodities. But if labor is responsible for the value of output, what is the source of profits? How can competitive firms pay profits out of the output produced by labor? Marx argued that capitalists profit from hiring workers because they hire workers for time rather than paying for their output. They pay for *labor power* or potential work, which they use to produce commodities with embodied labor that they sell for a labor value greater than the cost of the labor power they bought. The capital-

David Ricardo

ist's ability to profit from workers' labor power depends on their control over access to the means of production, the system of private property in the means of production, where workers must sell their labor time in exchange for wages. Note that Marx does not assume any crooked dealing, clever bargaining, or that anything sells at a price different from its value. On the contrary, workers are paid for the value of their labor time, the wage is the price of the worker's time and depends on the cost of subsistence, the cost of reproducing the workers. The capitalist buys the worker's time at its fair value, and then drives the workers to work hard so that they will embody their labor in commodities that the capitalist can sell at their fair market value. A successful capitalist is one who can drive his or her workers to put enough labor into commodities to cover their wage while leaving *surplus value* for the capitalist.

Labor protest against "wage slavery," New York City 1909.

Marx defined surplus value as the value of the labor provided by the workers over and above the value of the wages they are paid where the wage is generally just enough to insure the survival and reproduction of the labor force at its customary standard of living. This surplus, he argued, reflected the workings of capitalist class processes rather than the natural ebb and flow of demography and population; it could, therefore, be eliminated through social change. In addition to the employed wage-earning proletariat are others, other *proletarians*,[23] who are either unemployed or under-employed in home production or small family businesses. These comprise the *reserve army of the unemployed*[24] and they are available to be drawn into capitalist firms during periods of economic boom and expansion. During the course of any expansion, economic growth will drain the reserve army until capitalist competition begins to push wages above subsistence. Eventually, rising wages will begin to reduce the rate of surplus until capitalist investment slows and even stops. This turn from economic boom to bust will lead to a rise in the reserve army of the unemployed that will drive wages back down to subsistence, restoring the conditions for capitalist profitability and renewed accumulation.

By attributing economic distress, including poverty, low wages, inequality, and the business cycle, to social institutions rather than accidents or personal error, Marx the political economist discounted Panglossian ideas of natural benevolence. He directed attention away from the stingy nature blamed by earlier classical economists and towards oppressive society. Note that disagreements between Marx and earlier classicists like Ricardo do *not* reflect differences in their analytical framework. On the contrary, Marx reached different conclusions by pushing the analysis further and making it coherent. In the process, he made himself the greatest and most famous intellectual revolutionary of all time.

Marx challenged other Smithians because he used Smith's classical method to reach non-Panglossian conclusions. Instead of society organized to make the best of all possible worlds, Marx argued that society is organized to oppress the real producers, the workers, to hold down the great majority to benefit a few capitalists. This plus his brilliance made Karl Marx the last of the classicists. Today, economics is conventionally divided into three parts: *macroeconomics* and *microeconomics*, with a few, often associated with the political left, practicing *political economy* as a separate approach. The problem was that in practicing political economy, the classical economists opened the door to disturbing political implications. Even before Marx, their method led them to challenge the existing distribution of power because it favored the landed aristocracy over progressive capitalists and workers. Their arguments that market processes lead to the impoverishment of the masses of the population cry out for political action to regulate markets. Their argument that income reflects the social distribution of power and property rather than merit and work effort begs for conscious income redistribution. Then

Karl Marx

when Marx took the classical method to its logical conclusion, the time was ripe for a new economic method. Those who favored the current distribution of wealth and power needed an economic theory to rationalize what they had, and what they wanted to keep. Marx published the first volume of his masterwork, *Capital: A Critique of Political Economy* in 1867. Within a decade, a new approach had been developed to economics that rejected political economy to restore a vision of Panglossian beneficence through methodological individualism. This approach, modern *neoclassical microeconomics*,[25] was codified in the 1870s and 1880s in the works of the Austrian economist Carl Menger (1841-1921), the English economists William Stanley Jevons (1835-1882) and Alfred Marshall (1842-1922), the French economist Léon Walras (1834-1910), and the American John Bates Clark (1847-1938). Almost simultaneously, but independently, in the 1870s they all developed similar ideas that refounded economics. Abandoning the class analysis and political concerns of classical political economy, along with their disconcerting political implications, they brought economic analysis

back to the Panglossian dichotomy between virtuous individuals and evil collectives. In their analysis, they refounded economics on the basis of individual action coming from autonomous and independent individual preferences. To avoid the disconcerting politics of Smithian value theory, they abandoned any concept of objective value, substituting an approach where value is subjective, reflecting individual taste and preferences outside of any social influence. Economic value, in their approach, is determined by supply-and-demand for commodities, where both depend on individual choices, individual preferences for products and for work, subject to constraints of technology and the supply of productive inputs, land, labor, and capital, without regard for any social interaction. The economic process for neoclassicists would be the same for a Robinson Crusoe, alone on an island, as for a new immigrant in Los Angeles or New York City, the same in 1800 as in 2010.

May Day demonstration, Belfast, 2011

In the work of the neoclassicists of the 1870s and 1880s, economics came into its own as a system founded in methodological individualism, built on the enlightenment liberals' faith in a beneficent nature against public authority or collective action. The English economist Abba Lerner (1903-82) said that neoclassical economics has been so successful because it chose as its domain solved political problems. The central concern for the neoclassical microeconomists has been to explain relative prices, the distribution of income, and the mix of products produced in a society with a settled distribution of property and power. With power fixed, none of the variation in economic outcomes will be attributed to political action or changes in social institutions. Discounting any social influence on individuals, neoclassicists treat all economic activity as if it took place on Robinson Crusoe's island. They assume that individuals come to the economic system pure and virtuous: uninfluenced by others and without any influence on the behavior of others *except* through considerations of the price of buying and selling commodities. Assuming extreme individual autonomy, they ignore social interactions and build models solely in terms of individual wishes and unavoidable constraints coming from the existing technology and the mix of available inputs of land (including natural resources), labor, and capital.

This does not mean that neoclassical economics has no political program, only that their politics are hidden behind an apolitical facade. Developed as a response to Marxism, neoclassical economic theory consciously assumes a perfect Panglossian world with clear and accepted property rights and minimal public or community action against any other social arrangement; compared with perfection, any of these other arrangements is inherently worse. The entire neoclassical microeconomics can be seen as a defense of virtuous individuals against evil collectives. By explaining output and distribution in terms of individual motives, neoclassical microeconomists begin with the assumption that the level and distribution of output are *optimal*[26] given a society's resources and technology because, to put it simply, if individuals wanted something else, they would have changed their behavior to get it.

The American neoclassicist **John Bates Clark** sought an economic answer to Marxian socialism.

Dealing with a world of solved political problems, where there is no need for any changes in social policy beyond the elimination of any and all social regulations on individuals' market behavior, neoclassicists have come to focus on technique, the elegance of their modeling and the mathematical precision of their analysis, rather than any meaningful connection between their theory and the world around us. Nonetheless, there is some meaning in the system for those who would understand what economists often derisively call "the real world." By assuming that all behavior is meaningful, neoclassical economics has a deeply democratic orientation and a respect for the choices individuals make. At its best, neoclassical research involves an honest attempt to untangle the reasons behind individual behavior.[27] Nor should one discount the neoclassical political program merely because it is based on completely unrealistic premises; neoclassicists have been deeply committed to the defense of individuals against state and community oppression and to the promotion of individual self-expression.[28]

Building a theory of prices and income distribution up from individuals interacting through markets, neoclassical microeconomists ignore any discussion of the stuff of macroeconomics,[29] aggregate employment and economy-wide market outcomes. Nonetheless, neoclassical microeconomists needed a theory of the general level of employment and output; without it they could not make definitive statements about the outcome of individual market transactions. Without a theory of *general equilibrium*,[30] how can we know if there will be any *partial equilibrium* in a *particular market?* The French economist Marie-Esprit-Léon Walras (1834-1910) was to provide a formal solution to this problem by building a *general* economic model showing how demand and supply curves for each individual product can be brought together into aggregate equilibrium.

In his *Éléments d'économie politique pure*, or *Elements of Pure Political Econo-*

Marie-Esprit-Léon Walras was born in Évreux, Normandy, son of the economist Auguste Walras. To satisfy his parents, who wanted him to have a stable career, he enrolled in the Paris Ecole des mines in 1854. Uninterested in engineering, he neglected his studies and instead devoted himself to literature (he wrote two novels, *Francis Sauveur* and *La Lettre*) and to socialist politics. Only in 1858 did he abandon literature to become an economist.

After working as a journalist and in a private bank, he was called in 1870 to occupy a newly founded chair in political economy at the Academy (later the University) of Lausanne in Switzerland. At Lausanne, Walras called upon the aid of his mathematical colleagues to help him begin systematically to lay theoretical foundations for his equilibrium analysis. His own policy proposals aimed at a socialist reorganization of society through the nationalization of land and through the state ownership of such enterprises as could not operate under conditions of perfect competition. The underlying purpose of his general equilibrium model was to define the limits within which free enterprise could contribute to maximum social welfare. Needless to say, few have used his work for the purposes that he had intended.

BEHAVIORAL ECONOMICS:
AN ALTERNATIVE TO CONSERVATIVE
METHODOLOGICAL INDIVIDUALISM?

Orthodox neoclassical microeconomics assumes that individual behavior will lead to socially desirable outcomes under the assumptions that individuals are rational and society unproductive. Accepting methodological individualism but uncomfortable with the orthodox theory's conservative political implications, some progressive economists have questioned the orthodox theory's assumption of rationality to ground their economics in "more realistic" assumptions about human behavior. "Behavioral economics" studies the way individuals make decisions and shows that they often use inappropriate "rules of thumb," act impulsively, and on the basis of inadequate or even irrelevant information. Behaviorists have shown, for example, that people have a large "status quo bias," they tend to repeat past decisions; people often use "anchors" where they make decision on the basis of irrelevant information; and people are often both unreasonably optimistic and heavily discount future benefits and costs.

Among the economists associated with the behaviorist movement are Dan Ariely and Daniel Kahneman.

my (1874), Walras provided this general equilibrium theory by drawing on the work of Jean-Baptiste Say (1767-1832). In "Say's Law," Say had argued that there would always be a balance of supply and demand because individuals would produce only in order to consume. Similarly, Walras's "general equilibrium theory" argues that in the presence of efficient markets for all goods, aggregate demand will always equal aggregate supply and market exchanges will always lead to full employment of all resources where everyone who wants work at the prevailing wage will be employed.

Walras reaches this conclusion by assuming, as did Say, that individuals work and produce only in order to consume an equal amount. From this, he develops what is known as *Walras' Law of Markets:* that if there is excess demand, or short supply, in any particular market then there will also be a shortage, or excess, respectively, in another market. If producers work in order to consume, then the sum of excess demands and supplies over all the markets must equal zero regardless of whether all markets are in (general) equilibrium. In this case, if prices move freely, then these excesses and shortages will lead to equilibrating price changes that will eventually balance supply and demand for the entire economy; products in short supply will be bid up in price, reducing the amount demanded and increasing the quantity supplied, and the reverse will happen to products in excess supply. These price changes will continue until there is a balance of the quantity supplied and the quantity demanded at the market price in all markets. At "Walrasian equilibrium," there will be full employment: the amount of every good that is produced will be consumed, and everything that consumers want to buy will be produced. At these prices and quantities, every producer and consumer is as well-off as is possible given society's resources and technology and their own tastes or preferences.

From the beginning, many questioned whether "Walrasian equilibrium" can provide a useful description of the economy. For John Maynard Keynes (1883-1946), it was the experience of living through a prolonged recession in Britain, a recession that began even before the First World War and continued through the 1920s only to culminate in the worldwide Great Depression of the 1930s. This experience led an otherwise eminently respectable economist to reject his earlier enthusiasm for neoclassical microeconomics to argue that *macroeconomic* outcomes, or the aggregate level of employment and output in an economy, cannot be explained by individual preferences. Instead, Keynes came to argue that aggregate, macroeconomic behavior, was driven by the behavior of social groups and social conditions that cannot be reduced to individual motivations. In 1936, he published his *General Theory of Employment, Interest, and Money*, and the economics profession was transformed. Instead of grounding his macroeconomics on individual motivation, Keynes argued that social outcomes and collective behavior reflect group behavior and dynamics independent of any individual volition. By rejecting the idea that individual choices determine social outcomes, Keynes denied that there was necessarily any rational or efficient process behind aggregate behavior. Instead, macroeconomic outcomes, Keynes argues, are shaped by irrational processes as likely to lead to inadequate levels of investment, high unemployment, and an unfair distribution of income as to adequate investment, full employment and a fair distribution of income.

KEYNES AND ECONOMIC METHODOLOGY

Keynes fundamentally changed the politics of economic theory.[31] For Keynes and those who followed him, state intervention does not undercut individual choice and a beneficent natural order because personal choice contributes to social outcomes only through an opaque and often irrational group process that makes individual volition virtually irrelevant. If individual choice does not explain social or aggregate outcomes, then there is no reason to respect these outcomes. Indeed, it may be possible to reach better outcomes, higher levels of income or a more desirable distribution of income, if we substitute a *conscious social process*[32] for the an unconscious and irrational social process perpetuated to maintain the pretense, because it is nothing but a pretense, of individual volition.

By providing a coherent explanation for high unemployment between the wars and for the Great Depression of the 1930s, and the promise of a strategy to avoid similar disasters in the future, Keynes swept the field. Most economists in the United States and elsewhere quickly accepted his approach to macroeconomics. For a time from the early 1940s through the early 1970s, *macroeconomics* was the dominant approach in the American economics profession, focusing concern on such issues as the social determination of economic behavior and the aggregate level of employment. Openly rejecting Panglossian beneficence, the assumption that the natural state of affairs is good, and methodological individualism, where all explanations are reduced to the motivations of individuals, macroeconomists explored how the aggregate behavior of individuals would lead to perverse outcomes that none desired. A favorite, for example, was how when everyone at a parade route stands up to see better, there is no change in who sees things except that now people are standing up rather than comfortably sitting.

This simple insight about the importance of social analysis has been forgotten by economists entranced by the beautiful simplicity of methodological individualism and Walras' law. Raised in this tradition, even Keynes himself understated his fundamental critique, writing at the end of the *General Theory* that his "criticism of the accepted classical theory of economics has consisted not so much in finding

JOHN MAYNARD KEYNES

Time magazine named John Maynard Keynes one of the most important people of the 20th century. Born in Cambridge, England, in 1883, the year Karl Marx died, Keynes' father John Neville Keynes was a noted Cambridge economist; his mother, Florence Ada Keynes, was one of the first women to attend Cambridge University and later served as the city's mayor. A brilliant student, the young Keynes did not aspire to academic life; he wanted to run a railroad. After serving in the civil service, including a spell in India, Keynes returned to Cambridge where he taught for the rest of his life, edited the *Economic Journal*, and surrounded himself with artists and writers, including his wife, the Russian ballet dancer Lydia Lopokova.

Keynes' first brush with fame came after the First World War when his short book, *The Economic Consequences of the Peace*, criticized the Versailles treaty's provisions for German reparations. Keynes argued that the reparations would burden the post-war economy by requiring Germany to run large trade surpluses that would depress the economies of its trading partners, including the victorious allies. Even before he published his *General Theory*, Keynes used what was later called "aggregate demand" theory to criticize British economic policy. In 1925, he published *The Economic Consequences of Mr. Churchill*, arguing that Britain's return to the gold standard would lead to a disastrous world depression. While he attacked deflationary politics, neoclassical microeconomics in practice, it was only in the 1930s that Keynes began to reevaluate the fundamentals of economic theory in light of his revised practice. One critical inspiration came from the work of his student Richard Kahn, who in 1931 developed the concept of the "investment multiplier," where an increase in investment activity can create the savings needed to finance it by increasing aggregate income. This became a centerpiece of Keynes' General Theory because it separated individual volition, the desire by individuals to save or invest, from the determination of the volume of aggregate savings and investment.

Keynes returned to public service in the British Treasury during World War II where he drafted a plan for post-war reconstruction that included the Bretton Woods institutions, the World Bank and the International Monetary Fund.

Two ways that individual behavior does not lead to optimal social outcomes in Keynesian economics:

Irrational behavior in groups: Individuals behave differently because of group dynamics—a large group of individuals becomes a crowd, and even a mob.

The "fallacy of composition": the erroneous view that what is true of the part must be true of the whole. In fact, a behavior may have no general consequence if one person does it, while the outcome may be dramatically different if everyone does the same thing. For example, one person can get somewhere faster by passing other cars, even by weaving across lanes of traffic. If everyone drives like this, however, there will be car crashes and then everyone will reach their destination later.

logical flaws in its analysis as in pointing out that its tacit assumptions are seldom or never satisfied, with the result that it cannot solve the economic problems of the actual world." Economists, he promised, could return to their old assumptions and individualist methodology once "central controls establish an aggregate volume of output corresponding to full employment as nearly as is practicable" because then "the classical theory comes into its own again from this point onwards."

There has been a lively debate over these passing remarks of Keynes's, not only about whether they are correct, but over whether he really meant them. Rejecting his suggestion, some of his students, including the late-English economist Joan Robinson (1903-83) and her student John Eatwell (1945-), have argued that Keynes' logic implies that aggregating individual action will not lead to a social optimum in any economic area. These arguments have fallen largely on deaf ears. Rejecting the idea of society, many economists have sought new "micro foundations" for macroeconomics where aggregate behavior is explained in terms of individual motivations. By assuming Walrasian equilibrium, this quest has inevitably led back to Panglossian natural beneficence and to the (re-)discovery that social institutions or political action necessarily makes life worse. One may argue about whether this was the original intention of those who promoted this revival of neoclassical microeconomics, but the result has been to make economics less able to explain economic behavior at the same time that the profession has become more conservative politically. Rather than recommending active government policies to improve life, it has become a "neoliberal" discipline concerned with reducing the scope of government action to leave markets alone, to ease the transformation of money and wealth into market outcomes.

I deeply regret this transformation in the economics profession, and a major purpose in writing this work has been to develop micro-foundations for an alternative economics, closer to the vision of the classical economists, and to that of Keynes and others who saw economics as a social science. Most economists would verbally agree that economics begins with the division of labor, would recognize the importance and independence of society and social institutions, and would acknowledge the individuals are often irrational in their decision making. Nonetheless, most economists teach and write something else entirely, ignoring the division of labor and the importance of social life. While orthodox economists write and teach as if individuals produce for their own use, virtually all human labor is part of a social or detailed division of labor. Most production uses *intermediate goods* produced by others, and most output is shared with others or exchanged for goods and services produced by others. Some psychologists might explain this as the result of motivations intrinsic to individuals before they join in a society, and that can be fine for a discipline primarily concerned with individuals within a particular society. It is a very different problem for economists who are concerned with explaining economic behavior across societies and over time.

Orthodox microeconomists today are *methodological individualists* who treat economic actors as if they were Robinson Crusoe in the novel of that name by Daniel Defoe (1660-1731). Yet even Crusoe was not a real individualist. He had language, technology, and his own human capital because of the society into which he was born and raised; were he born alone on a desert island he would have died quickly rather than grow into a competent and talented adult.

The original publication of Daniel Defoe's Robinson Crusoe in London, 1719.

Economists need to move past Robinson Crusoe to view economic life as it is, a product of social institutions, and to view individuals as they are, shaped by society. Economics is a *social* science because it studies the way people work together to produce and to consume goods and services. There never has been, and never could be, an isolated human living outside of society and without human interaction. Humans need others to care for them when they are young; they need human companionship to survive; and they need the division of labor and the help of others to produce anything beyond a minimal subsistence. Production and exchange are always social activities involving different people who produce and exchange different goods.

SOCIAL LIFE AND THE ECONOMY

The classical economists who founded the discipline *never* forgot the importance of society or social life because they began their analysis with the division of labor and the advantages and troubles with coordinating work among different people. A source of great productivity gains and rising income over the centuries, the division of labor has been at the root of economic analysis since the 18th century. Over two centuries ago, François Quesnay (1694-1774) and Adam Smith (1723-90) showed how the detailed division of labor raises productivity. In *The Wealth of Nations* (1776), Smith argues that "the greatest improvement in the productive powers of labour ... seem to have been the effects of the division of labour." Using "an example from a very trifling manufacturer," the "trade of the pin-maker," Smith shows how the division of labor makes workers more productive in three ways. First, *specialization*[33] improves "the dexterity of the workman" who develops skills through practice. In addition, by allowing workers to concentrate on one task, specialization allows them to save time "commonly lost in passing from one sort of work to another." Finally, by reducing tasks to their component parts the detailed division of labor facilitates the application of simple machinery to tasks.

It is ironic that a discipline that traces its roots to Adam Smith should follow methodological individualism. Basing his vision of human nature on sympathy and his vision of the economy on the division of labor, Smith was a true social scientist. We should return to this part of Adam Smith's original vision; economics should begin with the *division of labor*, the way society shapes the division of labor, and the way people and society are shaped by their participation in the division of labor. And here we should remember that there are two distinct aspects to the division of labor, each associated with different types of coordination. First, there is the *detailed division of labor* where people work together, each producing a part of the final product, an *intermediate* good passed along to others for further work. In modern America and other capitalist economies throughout the world, the detailed division of labor has led to hierarchies in production where supervisors instruct different detail workers what to produce, how to make it, when to complete their tasks, and to whom they should pass their products. Although it is ubiquitous, the detailed division of labor attracts relatively little attention because the process is usually handled behind closed doors and within workplaces.

THE DIVISION OF LABOR: SOCIAL AND DETAILED

More attention has been paid to the *social division of labor*, where each individual produces a *final* product that is exchanged for those produced by others. The social division of labor provides the real content of most economic analysis because it involves exchange and market prices, the social relations between people. The social division of labor also provides a more attractive vision for economists and others than does the detailed division of labor with its hierarchy and command. Coordinated through markets, the social division of labor is the realm of equality and voluntary exchange: I make my purchases by exchanging equal value for what you give me. The abundance of

Charlie Chaplin illustrated the detailed division of labor in his movie "Modern Times" (1936). Chaplin's tramp struggles to survive as a worker in a modern industrial society. He works on a production line in a factory where his task is to tighten two bolts on a passing plate.

An 18th century pin (or nail) factory of the type described by Adam Smith in *The Wealth of Nations*.

products and choices provided by the social division of labor is one of the stronger arguments for market capitalism. We might add that the social division of labor may lead to invidious inter-personal comparisons and consumption for purposes of social status rather than for any intrinsic utility.[34]

Despite the efficiency gains from the detailed division of labor, throughout history many have resisted taking part in specialized production. There are certainly many jobs these days where the detailed division of labor has made work miserable. Workers at chicken slaughterhouses, for example, cut the necks of as many as 90 chickens a minute, or 5400 an hour, for 8 hours a day. Even without the health hazards from repetitive motion syndrome or the horrors of standing in bird blood and offal for hours at a time, few of us would choose or seek such work. Smith identified the underlying problem: people are a product of their experience, including their experience at work, and where these experiences are too limited they limit the growth and development of the person. Warning that the detailed division of labor risked making workers dull and stupid, Smith urged that society expand educational and other cultural opportunities for workers to counteract the effects of mind-numbing work.

Alas, few economists today read far enough into Smith's *The Wealth of Nations* to reach the discussion of the dangers of the detailed division of labor. Instead, most research and writing in economics these days comes out of a fascination with the advantages of exchange. It seeks to develop the benefits of the division of labor without heeding the distinction between the social and detailed division of labor or the possible drawbacks to the latter. Writing soon after Smith, the English economist David Ricardo (1772-1823) developed the principle of *comparative advantage*[35] to argue for allowing free trade between countries. In a conscious analogy to Smith's argument, Ricardo argued that even when one country is more efficient in the production of every good than are other countries, the international division of labor raises productivity for every country by allowing them to specialize in the products in which they have a *comparative advantage*, or those in which they are *relatively* more efficient, and then exchanging these for those where its producers are *relatively* inefficient. Even when countries are at very different absolute levels of efficiency, he showed how they both benefit from trade that allows them to specialize in the products they are relatively good at producing to exchange for others at a price cheaper than the cost to themselves of making them.

Later economists have shown how specialization can lead to further efficiency gains over time. Three American Pauls—Paul David, Paul Krugman, and

The "ugly ducklings" of the merchant marine, Liberty Ships were designed to be mass produced during World War II using interchangeable parts so that the United States could produce cargo ships faster than German submarines could sink them. The first of the 2710 that were launched, the SS Patrick Henry, was built in 70 days; two years later, the SS Robert E. Peary was built in less than 5 days. The use of prefabricated parts sped up the work, as did the detailed division of labor which allowed the use of workers with relatively little training, such as Eastine Cowner, a former waitress, at work on the Liberty ship SS George Washington Carver at the Kaiser shipyards, Richmond, California

Location for "Cast Away," starring Tom Hanks and his volleyball friend, "Wilson"

Paul Romer—have shown how specialization allows a region's producers to build larger facilities to capture *economies of scale*[36] in production, economies that would have been lost if they were only producing on a scale appropriate for a relatively small regional or national market. Regional specialization, such as we see in the Bombay film industry, in California's Silicon Valley, or New York City's Theater or Fashion District allows *economies of agglomeration*[37] among regional producers working in the same industry, because they can support specialized services, such as banks, law firms, advertising firms, and other specialist supplies to the industry. Industrial districts associated with specialized production for broad and international markets can also provide specialized training for workers, such as the film schools and acting classes available in New York City and Los Angeles. These districts become centers for *learning by doing*[38] for producers who share knowledge when they change firms, use the same suppliers, or when they meet to socialize and talk shop.

Per-capita income[39] in the United States today, the total output of goods and services exchanged through markets divided by the population, is nearly $50,000, ten times the level when Adam Smith lived.[40] Smith, Ricardo, and other economists have shown how the division of labor contributed to this dramatic increase. Their writings led to the development of economics as a social discipline studying the way people interact and the way institutions shape their cooperation. It is this social component that distinguishes economics from psychology, the study of individual motivation, or engineering, or the study of how people can best use nature. Production by individuals for their own consumption, such as the Tom Hanks character trapped on a depopulated island in *Cast Away*, involves a collision between humans and nature, where people seek to maximize production while minimizing their own labor. Tom Hanks, or Robinson Crusoe, faced a problem of an individual dealing with nature. Individual production raises technical problems properly addressed by engineers and the natural sciences; Tom Hanks would seek the best engineering solution to the problems he faced, catching fish or building a boat; and he needed psychological advice to deal with the problems he faced. But these issues are distinct from economics because they do not deal with the division of labor. Engineering and psychology are important but they cannot contribute to economics, the study of social relations among people who work together to produce.

Instead of *technical* issues from engineering and the natural sciences, the detailed and the social division of labor raise *social* issues involving cooperation between individuals in production and exchange. These include questions of coordination and distribution between different producers. Once production involves multiple people, then how do we coordinate the flow of goods, including both intermediate and final consumer goods? How do we decide how much of each to produce? And, considering the issue Smith raises, balancing higher productiv-

ADAM SMITH ON THE EFFECTS OF THE DETAILED DIVISION OF LABOR:

"In the progress of the division of labour, the employment of the far greater part of those who live by labour, that is, of the great body of the people, comes to be confined to a few very simple operations, frequently to one or two. But the understandings of the greater part of men are necessarily formed by their ordinary employments. The man whose whole life is spent in performing a few simple operations, of which the effects are perhaps always the same, or very nearly the same, has no occasion to exert his understanding or to exercise his invention in finding out expedients for removing difficulties which never occur. He naturally loses, therefore, the habit of such exertion, and generally becomes as stupid and ignorant as it is possible for a human creature to become. The torpor of his mind renders him not only incapable of relishing or bearing a part in any rational conversation, but of conceiving any generous, noble, or tender sentiment, and consequently of forming any just judgment concerning many even of the ordinary duties of private life. Of the great and extensive interests of his country he is altogether incapable of judging, and unless very particular pains have been taken to render him otherwise, he is equally incapable of defending his country in war. The uniformity of his stationary life naturally corrupts the courage of his mind . . . His dexterity at his own particular trade seems, in this manner, to be acquired at the expence of his intellectual, social, and martial virtues. But in every improved and civilized society this is the state into which the labouring poor, that is, the great body of the people, must necessarily fall, unless government takes some pains to prevent it."

FIGURE 2-1
PER CAPITA INCOME, UNITED STATES, 1790-2010

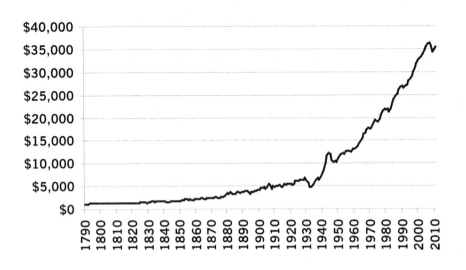

ity and the conditions of work for the workers, how do we choose an appropriate production technology? These questions are easily solved in a world of individuals where people consume what they produce; cast away on his island, Tom Hanks chooses for himself what to produce, when to consume it, and how to make it. All that changes with the division of labor when people produce goods different from those they consume as individuals.

Viewing economics as a social science raises issues distinct from those addressed by engineering, the natural sciences, or psychology. The division of labor requires socially established and widely accepted rules governing markets, establishing and protecting claims on products, establishing procedures for exchange, setting the terms of exchange between different people and their products, and formal procedures for choosing a technology. How are exchanges to be conducted? By command or by some type of voluntary exchange? How will we enforce contracts to ensure that producers supply the goods promised in a timely fashion and at the required quality? How is the rate of exchange between different goods to be determined? (How many fish will Tom Hanks give his new neighbor in exchange for a bottle of fresh water?) How will we govern the labor process: will workers work autonomously or under the command of supervisors? How, as a society, do we handle *inter-temporal production*—production that requires investment now to produce goods in the future? How will we support workers producing goods that require long gestation? Finally, how as a society will we care for those who are currently unproductive, including children too young to work, those who could be more productive if they received longer training, and those too old to work or unable to work due to disability?

The social institutions that manage the division of labor, laws, regulations, and bureaucracies, are the product of past political action and social conflict. To understand the division of labor, therefore, requires that scholars study history and understand the origins and operation of these institutions. Compared with the beauty of Leibniz's philosophy and the optimism of the Enlightenment, legal institutions, property law, and forms of bargaining may appear dull, even mundane. It is no surprise, therefore, that within the economics profession, the highest status goes to the theorists. This would be appropriate if the social sciences were a chess problem or a Rubik's Cube, challenging games that could be evaluated without regard for their relevance for understanding social life. Economics is different. Since it is a study of social life and social interactions, good economic analysis and useful theory must rest on a good understanding of economic institutions and the way they shape economic activity. Unless, like Leibniz, we are prepared to appeal to a beneficent deity, good theorists must be good empiricists.

An abundance of products is available for all consumers regardless of their own work. By exchanging the products of our labor for those produced by others, we can consume more because of the social division of labor.

DISCUSSION QUESTIONS

What is a "Panglossian" world-view? Is it wrong?

What is the "Labor Theory of Value" (LTV)? What determines the level of wages in the LTV? Where do profits come from?

Was Marx a follower of Adam Smith?

What is "neoclassical economics"? Is it a social science?

What is the division of labor? How is the social division of labor different from the detailed division of labor?

What are "industrial districts"? Why are workers and businesses more productive in some areas than others? Is this consistent with methodological individualism? With social science?

What is "learning-by-doing"? How do industrial districts and learning-by-doing suggest a role for the community in individual productivity?

ENDNOTES

[1] The institutions of higher learning and scholarship.

[2] Individualists believe that society can be explained by studying the motives of individuals.

[3] Communitarians believe that society exists separate from and prior to the individuals who compose it so scholars need to study society separately from the motives of individuals.

[4] Liberalism dates back to the ideas of individual liberty and the rights of individuals to autonomy in their bodies, ideas, and property.

[5] The Age of Enlightenment, broadly 1689-1789, was a period of secular philosophy and belief in the power of human reason.

[6] Theists believed in a divine spirit but questioned the idea that God intervened directly in human affairs. They were opposed to the Roman Catholic Church.

[7] Materialists question whether any nonmaterial things, such as Gods or ideas, can influence human behavior or society.

[8] Dr. Pangloss, a character in Voltaire's *Candide*, argues repeatedly that we live in the "best of all possible worlds and, therefore, all of Candide's suffering is for the best.

[9] By this I mean that even without belief in a divine being, economics maintains a faith that all is for the best in the best of all possible worlds.

[10] Adam Smith himself was a professor of moral philosophy, a field of study that encompassed history, political science, sociology, and economics to understand the best moral position for people and the best way to organize society.

[11] By conservative, I am suggesting the philosophic approach that urges caution in any program of social change for fear of disrupting a functioning society; Edmund Burke, *Burke's Reflections on the Revolution in France*, Macmillan's English Classics (London and New York: Macmillan and Co, 1890).

[12] The idea that God or some other divine force has arranged the world to promote human welfare.

[13] The labor theory of value, which dates back to John Locke before Smith, holds that relative prices depend on the labor required to produce different commodities. The labor theory of value also becomes a theory of social worth because it says that the distribution of income depends on the value of the labor supplied to the market; while the inherited wealth of aristocrats is illegitimate, coming from monopoly rather than work, those who acquired their wealth in their own lifetimes deserve it for their work and contribution to the general welfare.

[14]Smith and others would acknowledge that tools and machines would be used but these would add to the labor value embodied in the product according to their own labor content. For example, a tool that takes 10 hours to make and is used in catching 10 deer would add 1 hour to the value of each deer caught.

[15]Thomas Hodgskin, *Labour Defended Against the Claims of Capital; or, The Unproductiveness of Capital Proved with Reference to the Present Combinations Amongst Journeymen* (London: Hammersmith Bookshop, 1964); John Francis Bray, *Labour's Wrongs and Labour's Remedy; or, The Age of Might and the Age of Right*. D. Green, 1839, *Series of Reprints of Scarce Tracts in Economic and Political Science. No.6* ([London: The London School of Economics and Political Science, 1931); William Thompson, *An Inquiry into the Principles of the Distribution of Wealth Most Conducive to Human Happiness; Applied to the Newly Proposed System of Voluntary Equality of Wealth* (London: Printed for Longsman, Hurst, Ross, Orme, Brown and Green [etc.], 1824); *Production the Cause of Demand Being a Brief Analysis of a Work Entitled "The Social System, a Treatise on the Principle of Exchange," by John Gray: With a Short Illustration of the Principles of Equitable Labour Exchange* (Birmingham: Published under the superintendence of an Association for the Dissemination of the Knowledge of the Principles of Equitable Labour Exchange, 1832), http://libproxy.smith.edu:2048/login?url=http://galenet.galegroup.com/servlet/MOME?af=RN&ae=U104840410&srchtp=a&ste=14&q=Mlin_w_smithcol; Karl Marx, *Wage-labor and Capital* (Chicago: C. H. Kerr & company, 1935); Karl Marx, *Capital: A Critique of Political Economy* (London & Toronto: J. M. Dent & sons ltd, 1934); For the social context around the Ricardians, see E. P Thompson, *The Making of the English Working Class* (New York: Pantheon Books, 1964).

[16]Leave free to act and to pass; a slogan epitomizing the libertarian ideal of minimal government regulation of markets.

[17]Neoclassical theory treats all economic outcomes as the result of the interaction of free individuals through markets subject to the constraints of technology and the relative supply of the different productive factors: land, labor and capital.

[18]The tendency of the poor to become steadily poorer until starvation reduces their numbers sufficiently to allow an increase in wages at least to the subsistence level.

[19]Wages just high enough to allow workers to avoid starvation.

[20]An idea popular among classical economists like Ricardo that economic growth will eventually stop because all the benefits will accrue to a corrupt class of landowners.

[21]Surplus value is a Marxian concept that some of the value produced by labor is taken from workers as "surplus" over the workers' subsistence wage. This forms the basis of capitalist profit.

[22]Capitalists control access to the means of production or the machinery, tools, and other resources needed to produce things.

[23]Proletarians are workers who have no independent access to the means of production and therefore must sell their labor power, their time, to the capitalists in exchange for wages.

[24]Proletarians available and looking for wage work but without jobs.

[25]Microeconomics addresses individual behavior. Neoclassical economics is the economic theory which views economic activity as the result of individuals, their preferences, the available technology (or methods) of production, and the supply of factor inputs, including labor, land, and other raw materials.

[26]An optimal distribution is one where there is no possible reallocation or resources or products that can make someone better off without making someone else worse off.

[27]This is the logic behind some of the more popular writing in economics; see Steven D. Levitt, *Freakonomics: a Rogue Economist Explores the Hidden Side of Everything*, Revised and expanded edition (New York, NY: William Morrow, 2006); for different approaches, see Dan Ariely, *Predictably Irrational: The Hidden Forces That Shape Our Decisions*, 1st ed. (New York, NY: Harper, 2008); George A. Akerlof, Identity Economics: How Our Identities Shape Our Work, Wages, and Well-being (Princeton, NJ: Princeton University Press, 2010).

[28]See, for example, Milton Friedman, *Capitalism and Freedom* (Chicago: University of Chicago Press, 1962).

[29]Macroeconomics is the study of the behavior of the economy as a whole and addresses questions like the total output of the economy, the total amount of employment, and the general price level.

[30]General equilibrium is where all markets clear, that is where the price of goods in all markets is such that the amount produced just equals the amount consumed. Partial equilibrium is where markets are in equilibrium for a particular product.

[31]John Maynard Keynes, *The General Theory of Employment, Interest and Money* (London: Macmillan and Co., limited, 1936); John Maynard Keynes, *The Economic Consequences of Mr. Churchill* (London: L. and V. Woolf, 1925); John Maynard Keynes, *The Economic Consequences of the Peace* (London: Macmillan, 1919); John Maynard Keynes, *Essays in Persuasion* (London: Macmillan, 1933).

[32]By this we mean political decisions openly arrived at rather than leaving economic outcomes to a market process where no one in particular claims responsibility.

[33]Specialization is where an individual becomes more adept through practice performing a single task.

[34]The social division of labor became the basic source of institutionalist economics, see Richard T. Ely, *The Past and the Present of Political Economy* (Baltimore: N. Murray, publication agent, Johns-Hopkins University, 1884); Thorstein Veblen, *The Theory of the Leisure Class; an Economic Study of Institutions*, New ed. (New York: The Macmillan Company; [etc., etc.], 1912).

[35]Comparative advantage is found where different countries have different levels of productivity between different commodities leading to price differentials such that a country less efficient in every product is still able to furnish one product at a comparatively lower price in terms of the other product.

[36]In some industries, there are economies to scale because the use of large machinery or other facilities allows dramatic increases in efficiency.

[37]Economies of agglomeration are found where firms become more productive because they operate near other firms in the same industry.

[38]Learning by doing is where firms or workers become more efficient through practice over time.

[39]The average income in a country or region, computed by dividing the gross domestic product by the population.

[40]This is corrected for price changes as best one can, considering that so many products that we consume today were not available at any price in 1776.

CAPITALISM, SLAVERY, AND THE ECONOMY

ECONOMIC INSTITUTIONS AND THE DUALITY OF HUMAN NATURE

We are individuals, but we live our lives and interpret our experiences in ways fundamentally shaped by our communities and institutions established before us. Some of these institutions are manifested as physical structures: the rooms and buildings to which we go for work, school, and play, the roads on which we travel, even the outlets into which we plug our appliances. Others guide our behavior and consciousness. Belonging to a religious denomination, we pray to a particular deity in communion with fellow believers; belonging to a particular nationality, we adhere to certain laws, and we pledge our loyalty to uphold this nation and its values. Members of a community, we share language, forms of artistic expression, and accepted modes of behavior, including familial and gender roles.

Economics as a social science is distinguished from sciences of individual behavior and consciousness, such as some types of psychology or biology, by the idea that social institutions exist prior to individuals and have power over individuals' ideas and actions. The French sociologist Émile Durkheim (1857-1917) identified institutions as *social facts* that impose external constraint on individuals. Constraints can be physical, such as the location of buildings, roads or other social infrastructure that constrain the location of markets and production facilities. The most powerful social facts, however, are more fundamental because they are "psychic" or the nature of "common sense" within a community. Social facts for Durkheim are "ways of acting, thinking and feeling which possess the remarkable property of existing outside the consciousness of the individual." External to the individual, institutions imbue patterns of behavior and thinking "with a compelling and coercive power" so that "whether he wishes it or not" an individual must accept. Regardless of any intrinsic desires of our own, we confront the values and behavior norms of the group as external constraints on our behavior. Born into a social world, we experience our society, accepted ways of thinking and acting, as fixed institutions or social facts existing prior to ourselves and into which we are brought and educated. In Durkheim's words:

> When I perform my duties as a brother, a husband or a citizen and carry out the commitments I have entered into, I fulfill obligations which are defined in law and custom and which are external to myself and my actions. Even when they conform to my own sentiments and when I feel their reality within me, that reality does not cease to be objective, for it is not I who have prescribed these duties; I have received them through education. Moreover, how often does it happen that we are ignorant of the details of the obligations that we must assume, and that, to know them, we must consult the legal code and its authorized interpreters! Similarly the believer has discovered from birth, ready fashioned, the beliefs and practices of his religious life; if they existed before he did, it follows that they exist outside him. The system of signs that I employ to express my thoughts, the monetary system I use to pay my debts, the credit instruments I utilize in my commercial relationships, the practices I follow in my profession, etc., all function independently of the use I make of them. Considering in turn each member of society, the foregoing remarks can be repeated for each single one of them. Thus there are ways of acting, thinking and feeling which possess the remarkable property of existing outside the consciousness of the individual.

Social facts and social institutions are the framework for economic life. By facilitating or inhibiting different activities they shape the organization of the economy. Without common standards of meaning and of value, individuals could not interact or exchange goods and services. Institutions like language, law, standard weights and measures, and currency are necessary for exchange. It is institutions like property law, the police, and the judiciary that make the division of labor possible by allowing individuals to rest secure in the product of their work. There would be no exchange and no division of labor without social institutions to facilitate exchange and to protect transferred property. Moreover, without social institutions to compel support for the young and dependent, humanity would die out. Norms, values, and mores make life predictable, allowing individuals to anticipate and to plan their economic lives. Where these values include honesty and respect for the work and property of others, individuals can devote fewer resources to guarding their possessions, and more in investing to produce more in the future.

There are a wide variety of institutions shaping economic life. Some are familiar, like states, forms of corporate enterprise, and the rights of private property. These set ground rules for economic cooperation, including establishing rules for choosing the technology of production, for allocating the costs of production, and for the distribution of output. Other institutions are important economically but can be neglected by economists who mistakenly view them as outside the economy. For example, from our infancy through old age, we organize our material life within family units, groups of individuals united by common ancestor or common genetics, committed to provide support and nurturance to each other, especially to children and their direct care givers. Often living in the same household and interacting regularly, families share resources and allocate labor based on common concerns for the growth and development of the group and its individual members. By providing a "care economy," families are essential for the maintenance of many of those unable to earn income through standard market exchange, including children, many of the disabled, and the elderly.

Émile Durkheim (1858-1917) was a founder of the field of sociology. Born in Épinal, in the French Vosges, he was raised to be a rabbi like his father, but abandoned his religious studies to study philosophy in Paris. There he adopted the cause of the newly installed French Third Republic (1870-1940). In his scholarship, Durkheim sought to defend the secular basis of the Republic and to promote social reform. Teaching in Bordeaux, he was called to Paris during the Dreyfus Affair in 1902 to take up a chair at the Sorbonne.

Like businesses and governments, families set the framework for a division of labor and allocate resources among family members. Businesses, states, and families all go beyond simply providing an open framework for the division of labor. They are forms of governance, social facts that compel obedience. For this reason, there is absolutely no reason to assume that they are optimal in any way or guarantee that we will be in "the best of all possible worlds." Institutions are the way they are because they were established this way in the past, and they persist in a particular form until social movements arise to change them. Institutions have uses, they perform social functions, but, as Durkheim observed:

> To demonstrate the utility of a fact does not explain its origins, nor how it is what it is. The uses which it serves presume the specific properties characteristic of it, but do not create it. Our need for things cannot cause them to be of a particular nature; consequently, that need cannot produce them out of nothing … since each fact is a force which prevails over the force of the individual and possesses its own nature, to bring a fact into existence it cannot suffice to have merely the desire or the will to engender it. Prior forces must exist, capable of producing this firmly established force.

In all three arenas—businesses, states, and families—institutions have arisen which have been widely seen as imperfect. Within recent history, since 1800, we have ended particular forms of these institutions, abolishing slavery, replacing dictatorship with elected, representative government, and ending the system of legal patriarchy where men owned their wives and children. Still, many see oppression within existing institutions and continue to struggle for broader liberation. Struggling against monarchy and dictatorship, movements for liberty and equality have fought to bring democracy to the governance of states. Against the power of capitalist firms and managers, radical workers and socialists have campaigned to bring democracy to the workplace. Feminists and others have struggled to free the family from the oppression of patriarchs, to bring equality to the governance of family life. Each of these movements—for socialism, feminism, democracy, and equality—has in its own way struggled for the same goal: to ensure that all people are treated equally and have a voice in decisions shaping their lives. Social movements, like these, succeed by changing the social institutions that have maintained systems of oppression. This is because oppression is a social phenomenon, independent of the wishes of individuals. These movements matter because they create new institutions that reshape our lives, have lives of their own, and create a fairer, more egalitarian and democratic society.

SLAVERY AND THE BUILDING OF A MARKET ECONOMY

> This division of labour, from which so many advantages are derived, is not originally the effect of any human wisdom, which foresees and intends that general opulence to which it gives occasion. It is the necessary, though very slow and gradual, consequence of a certain propensity in human nature which has in view no such extensive utility; the propensity to truck, barter, and exchange one thing for another.
>
> —Adam Smith, *The Wealth of Nations*

While Adam Smith may be right that humans have an innate propensity to trade, I never trusted this argument. Resorting to human nature has always struck me as too easy. Yes, it simplifies his writing, but in resorting to psychology rather than social or historical analysis, he avoids the serious work of exploring how particular forms of exchange and the division of labor came to be in 18th century Britain. And his ease came at the price of abandoning any attempt to explain the dramatic change in the extent of trade over previous millennia. While there was trade throughout human history, the volume of interregional trade increased dramatically after the 15th century. There was, for example, an extensive interregional division of labor in the Roman Empire during its height and through late-classical times. This division declined during the period of civil war and foreign invasion after the 2nd century, and then collapsed with the fall of Rome and the rise of Islam along the southern Mediterranean and in Italy and Spain. It would be almost a millennium before the revival of trade in the late middle ages and early modern times would allow as extensive a division of labor in Europe as had existed in Roman times. Through the 12th century, the division of labor was relatively undeveloped throughout Europe. Trade and the division of labor revived thereafter, only to get set back again during the 15th century.

Under the Empire, the Roman economy had been organized around slave plantations producing staple crops for sale. The collapse of Roman power not only inhibited trade, it also undermined slavery by reducing the owners' ability to hold their slaves, while ending the Romans' ability to acquire new slaves through military conquest. Combined with the rise of a new social ideology, Christianity, this led to the collapse

The Rev. Dr. Martin Luther King Jr. (1929-1968) was a leader in the Civil Rights struggle in the United States who urged Americans to rise to the standard of social justice set in the words of the American constitution and Declaration of Independence. In August, 1963, he said: "In a sense we have come to our nation's capital to cash a check. When the architects of our republic wrote the magnificent words of the Constitution and the Declaration of Independence, they were signing a promissory note to which every American was to fall heir. This note was a promise that all men, yes, black men as well as white men, would be guaranteed the unalienable rights of life, liberty, and the pursuit of happiness."

TO BE SOLD & LET
BY PUBLIC AUCTION,
On MONDAY the 18th of MAY. 1829,
UNDER THE TREES.
FOR SALE,
THE THREE FOLLOWING
SLAVES,
VIZ.
HANNIBAL, about 30 Years old, an excellent House Servant, of Good Character.
WILLIAM, about 35 Years old, a Labourer.
NANCY, an excellent House Servant and Nurse.
The MEN belonging to "LECCUY" Estate, and the WOMAN to Mrs. D. SMIT

TO BE LET,
On the usual conditions of the Hirer finding them in Food, Clot in s. and Medical   ance,
THE FOLLOWING
MALE and FEMALE
SLAVES
ROBERT BAGLEY, about 20 Years old, a good House Servant.
WILLIAM BAGLEY, about 18 Years old, a Labourer.
JOHN ARMS, about 18 Years old.
JACK ANTONIA, about 40 Years old, a Labourer.
PHILIP, an excellent Fisherman.
HARRY, about 27 Years old, a good House Servant.
ELIZA, a Young Woman of good Character, used to House Work and the Nursery.
FLIZA, an Excellent Washerwoman.
FANNY, about 14 Years old, House Servant.
SARAH, about 14 Years old, House Servant.

Also for Sale, at Eleven o'Clock,
Fine Rice, Gram, Paddy, Books, Muslins, Needles, Pins, Ribbons, &c. &c.
AT ONE O'CLOCK, THAT CELEBRATED ENGLISH HORSE
BLUCHER,

The institution of slavery, the product of European military superiority over divided Africa, allowed an enormous extension of the division of labor in the Atlantic economy from the 16th through the 19th centuries.

of the old Roman economy of slaves and trade. A new economic order replaced it, built around independent, largely self-sufficient villages under the protection, and legal domination, of a feudal lord. In the villages, production was organized in open fields where the entire community worked the land in tandem. This system ensured that the village council, made up of the leading serfs, would regulate the production process regardless of the wishes of the feudal lords. Similarly, in urban areas, production was organized around self-governing guilds. Artisan masters controlled the production process and prices, training new craftsmen and thus controlling the supply of labor to the trade. This new *feudal*[1] order was distinguished by this combination of worker control over the production process *and* the restriction of the workers to a particular estate or occupation. Unlike under capitalism or slavery, the workers themselves controlled production; unlike under capitalism or socialism, the workers were also restricted to a particular occupation or location, their bodies under the control of the lords. Under feudalism, the workers controlled the production process, but they owed personal services to their lords to whom they were bound by a myriad of personal obligations. They had to pay fees to marry, had to offer their children to the lord's service, and could not leave the estate without permission.

TABLE 3-1
SLAVERY, FEUDALISM, CAPITALISM, SOCIALISM? WORKERS OR BOSSES CONTROL PRODUCTION OR PERSONS

		Control over persons	
		Bosses	Workers
Control over means of production	Bosses	Slavery	Capitalism
	Workers	Feudalism	Socialism

Beginning in the 15th century, Europe's early modern period saw a great expansion of the division of labor in two dimensions. First, there was a great increase in trade and the *social* division of labor both within Europe's newly emerging *nation states*[2] and extending to international trade. Within Britain, for example, different regions began to specialize in particular products. Textile producers in Lancashire, for example, began to eat cheese grown in Cheshire. This paralleled increasing international trade between regions and countries throughout Western Europe. British woolens found their way throughout northern France and the Low Countries and down to the Mediterranean. Perhaps most important, Europeans began to travel further afield outside of Europe. Especially important was the emerging international trade that brought pepper and other spices to Europe in exchange for precious metals and, occasionally, European slaves.

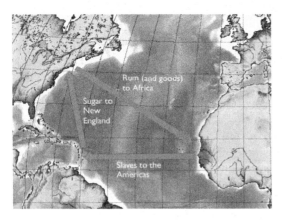

The African slave trade was one part of an emerging international trading system that brought alcohol, guns, and cloth to Africa, slaves to the Americas, and tropical products, like sugar, to Europe.

The spread of systems of authority and oppression in what European historians call the early modern period (15th-18th centuries) laid the foundations for a prosperous capitalist world economy of free trade and open markets. Both new forms of the social division of labor, intra-national trade and international trade, depend on new systems of political power and centralized force. Expensive to find and to map, long-distance trade routes required the deep pockets of rich and powerful monarchs to finance. Europe's emerging trade with Africa, Asia, and the Americas depended on state-sponsored navigational research, including the expeditions that carried the Portuguese around Africa to the Indian Ocean or that brought Columbus and his followers to the New World. The new nation-state institutions were just as important in establishing the intra-national division of labor. Within regions, force created nation states, breaking down local barriers to trade by imposing uniform legal systems, languages, and currencies. The consolidation of English rule over Scotland in the 18th century, for example, allowed London pubs to sell Scottish whiskey (Scotch), a product grown within the British customs and currency zone. Similarly, the French came to drink Champagne and Bordeaux after the French state consolidated its rule over these regions. And the failure of the French monarchy's drive to the Rhine left the Germans drinking Riesling grown in the Rhineland. These patterns were solidified when the establishment of the German Empire, in 1871, placed the Rhineland, and Germany's Riesling vineyards, in an area governed by German law to be sold within the ambit of Germany's system of national protective tariffs.

European states purposefully created the social division of labor, using their political and military power to force previously self-sufficient peoples to produce market commodities. Through the process of "primitive accumulation" within the British Isles, English, Irish, Scottish, and Welsh peasants were stripped of their own land and forced to work for others or to pay rents in cash. Where the boundaries of nation states ended, international trade was also promoted at the barrel of a gun, or a cannon's mouth. Spanish *conquistadores*' conquest of the Americas established a new trading system, bringing precious metals and the products of tropical agriculture to Europe. The most important part of this growing international commerce after the 15th century was the African slave trade and the trade in its products. Between 1500 and 1900, Europeans exchanged alcohol, textiles, guns and other goods for over 10 million African slaves.[3] Most of the slaves were brought to the Americas to grow staple crops, especially sugar but also coffee, tobacco, cotton, and rubber among others, on plantations run by Europeans on lands they had stolen from the native peoples, often with the help of African soldiers.[4]

The African slave trade depended on the overwhelming force wielded by Europeans, who had developed effective ways to use firearms, cannon, and other instruments of war in centuries of internecine warfare. Others, notably the Chinese, had developed gun powder and cannon before the Europeans; the Chinese had used these in war with the Mongols and others. The Europeans did more with gun powder because political decentralization led to continuing warfare, which gave the Europeans practice in using firearms and incentives to learn to use them more effectively. The Europeans were able to deploy overwhelming force in America and in Africa, and later in Asia, because they had failed to solve the political problem of making peace among warring states or creating a single dominant empire able to force peace on them.[5] Instead, what emerged from centuries of European warfare were nation states, mid-level empires, organized around maintaining and funding armies and navies with the world's most sophisticated weapons. The Europeans were able to conquer America and enslave Africa because they had developed more than the technology of weapons; they had the bureaucracy and means of finance to recruit, organize, and sustain powerful armies and navies. They were able to enslave the Africans because they had developed social systems to use gun powder and firearms effectively to overwhelm resistance to enslavement.

The Europeans' guns were doubly effective in enslaving Africans. The most important European goods provided in exchange for slaves were firearms, because with these the Europeans increased warfare and political instability in West Africa, creating states, such as Asante and Dahomey, who grew powerful and wealthy by enslaving other Africans. Other Africans states were completely destroyed, with their populations enslaved or absorbed by rivals. The effect on Africa was devastating, with millions killed or forcibly removed from their homes and towns and villages.

The slave trade helped to widen the division of labor. Within Britain, it allowed free workers to specialize producing goods for the trade, including textiles, guns, rum, glass, and iron products for sale in Africa, as well as boats and seafaring services. The trade also promoted specialization by forcing slaves to specialize in producing crops for the profit of their owners, including, most notably, sugar and rum but also cotton, ginger, rice, rubber, and indigo.[6] Within Africa, the slave trade promoted the social division of labor specializa-

Contrast this painting of a Roman slave market by Jean-Léon Gérôme with the African slaves in the 19th century engraving below. The Mediterranean slave trade was as extensive as the Atlantic slave trade but it involved a different population, mostly European women sold for domestic service. African slaves sold in the Atlantic slave trade, illustrated below, were used in the production of commodities for sale, especially sugar; men were favored because their greater physical strength made them more useful in the sugar fields.

tion with merchants providing provisions to the European ships and slave traders specializing in the provision of slaves.

There is no logical requirement that the growing *social division of labor*, specialization in domestic production and the rise of slavery and the sugar trade, should entail a second transformation of the European, especially British, division of labor: the growing use of the *detailed* division of labor based on the ex-

These Mandan girls are gathering berries for their own consumption and to feed their family and community. Their work fits with "Say's Law": they consume what they produce, and produce to consume.

ercise of command over workers. In medieval times, most workers were farmers or craftsmen who produced a finished product that they either consumed themselves or exchanged with others for something else that they would consume. Younger workers were either employed on their parents' farms or shops, or else as domestics or, in industry, as apprentices and journeymen learning all parts of a trade in order to become independent producers of final products. Aware, even without reading Smith, of the enervating effects of the detailed division of labor, workers throughout history have gone to great lengths and material sacrifices to avoid participating in the detailed division of labor in factories or other supervised work places. They understood well that remaining an independent producer, outside of a business where someone else could dictate technology and the form of the detailed division of labor, was their only way to ensure that they could control the pace of work and choose production technologies that suited them.

It was the chattel slaves transported from Africa who first experienced a new labor system where bosses told specialized workers which task to perform in the *detailed division of labor*. Kidnapped in Africa to work under their owner's whip in New World plantations, slaves lacked the political power, the social organization, and religious, legal, and traditional standing to avoid submission to the detailed division of labor.[7] Under their masters' guise, or, more often, under his overseer, they were compelled to labor hard and fast at whatever task they were assigned. Organized in gangs working on plantations with hundreds of slaves, the kidnapped Africans participated in a detailed division of labor specializing in tasks ranging from cutting sugar cane to building barrels, boiling sugar syrup, and caring for children.

THE POLITICS OF PROLETARIANIZATION

The use of Africans as slaves avoided political and religious problems that enslaving Europeans would have raised. It also had the paradoxical effect of establishing freedom as a prerogative of Europeans, establishing a type of democratic equality among Europeans in contrast with the status of their African slaves.[8] Appalled at the working conditions of the slaves, European freemen would fight the detailed division of labor and refuse to work "like slaves" or under the supervision of "slave drivers." Nonetheless, through the modern period, Britain, France, and the United States saw a new labor system emerging, *capitalism*,[9] where the slave specialist workers were to be joined in growing numbers by an almost new class of "wage laborers." Just as the creation of a class of slave workers depended on the successful use of force to separate Africans from the means of production, the creation of a class of *wage-earning proletarians*[10] depended on the use of force to separate journeymen craftsmen, feudal serfs, and peasants from the means of production in the tools of manufactured work and land. In Britain, this process took several centuries, starting after the 14th cen-

---

WHO WERE THE FIRST FACTORY WORKERS?

Those who had any alternative resisted working in factories. Unable to recruit free adult men, the early factories were filled with vulnerable dependents: women, children, orphans and prisoners. In England and elsewhere, capitalists benefited from a system of patriarchy where fathers and husbands commanded the labor of their sons, daughters, and wives to force them to work in factories in situations shunned by free adult men.

This association between early factory work and patriarchy has continued with each new industrial economy. New England capitalists relied on girls as young as 10 to staff their mills, including the famous "Lowell Girls" who moved from their fathers' home to supervised dormitories to provide docile labor. In Lowell, as later in the American South, in Japan, and recently in China, Korea, Malaysia and elsewhere, the girls' docility proved transient. Throughout the world, wage earning has given young women the independence to reject forced marriages, to stand up against their parents, and even to resist employers' oppression. When the company moved to reduce wages in 1834 and again in 1836, the girls struck. They ended their petition to their employer with a song:

> Oh! isn't it a pity, such a pretty girl as I
> Should be sent to the factory to pine away and die?
> Oh! I cannot be a slave, I will not be a slave,
> For I'm so fond of liberty,
> That I cannot be a slave.

Workers at a London match factory around 1879; note the predominance of young women.

tury, in a process called by the "Enclosure Movement" in agriculture and, later, the "Rise of the Factory System" in manufacturing.

The enclosure of common lands previously open to all and the rise of factories created a new class called *proletarians*. These were workers distinguished by their independence from the means of production. In this case, independence had a paradoxical or double nature. Unlike serfs under feudalism or chattel slaves, proletarians are independent in the sense that they are not bound to any particular production site or means of production; they are free to move or to quit if they are unhappy with their employment. They are also independent in the sense that they can be separated involuntarily, or fired, from an employment. Like slaves, proletarians have no rights to the means of production, no claim to access the tools and resources needed to produce goods or to make a claim on the products of labor. Their employer's property rights trump any claims they might make on either the means of production or the products of their own labor.

Without direct control over the tools and places of work, fear of starvation compelled the new class of proletarians to seek work for pay under the supervision of others, producing goods for others to sell, in exchange for simple wages for themselves. Like the African slaves working under drivers in the new American plantations, proletarians worked under supervision and were forced to accept such terms as were offered from fear of unemployment and complete impoverishment. With the creation of a class of dependent wage laborers, Britain, and soon other places in Western Europe and North America, experienced a social revolution. By the early 19th century, these areas had seen the creation of a *capitalist* class who controlled access to the means of production, and a *proletariat*, wage workers who gained access to the means of production only at the choice of the capitalist. Capitalism facilitated both the detailed and the social division of labor because it clearly separated the production from consumption decisions. Wage workers have no expectation of consuming what they produce because it becomes the

American railroads imported Chinese workers to build the transcontinental railroad; other capitalists used women because they lacked the vote and political rights. Whether in 18th century Britain, 19th century United States, or in China today, capitalists want docile workers who will obey orders without argument or question. This demand conflicts directly with the rise of democracy and equality. When citizen workers object to being commanded at work, capitalists seek to recruit workers from politically disadvantaged groups, such as children, women, immigrants, and racial and ethnic minorities.

PRODUCTION FOR USE AND SAY'S LAW

"You say, you only want money; I say, you want other commodities, and not money. For what, in point of fact, do you want the money? Is it not for the purchase of raw materials or stock for your trade, or victuals for your support? Wherefore, it is products that you want, and not money .... Money performs but a momentary function in this double exchange; and when the transaction is finally closed, it will always be found, that one kind of commodity has been exchanged for another .... It is worth while to remark, that a product is no sooner created, than it, from that instant, affords a market for other products to the full extent of its own value. When the producer has put the finishing hand to his product, he is most anxious to sell it immediately, lest its value should diminish in his hands. Nor is he less anxious to dispose of the money he may get for it; for the value of money is also perishable. But the only way of getting rid of money is in the purchase of some product or other. Thus, the mere circumstance of the creation of one product immediately opens a vent for other products."

property of their employer, and by employing others, capitalists can produce without regard for their own consumption. They produce for profit, surplus value, not for use. They pay their wage laborers to produce commodities for sale, to earn money to pay the workers.

THE EXPANSION OF CAPITAL

Producing commodities for profit, the new economies of capitalism and chattel slavery were a new form of economic organization, fundamentally different from the subsistence economies of feudal households and peasant agriculture, and necessarily expansive in a way that had never been seen before. Capitalism has also marked a break with the vision of economic activity held by classicists like Smith and Ricardo, and still held by most economists. For these economists, firms and households engage in economic activity—work, produce, and exchange—in order to consume; they produce goods and services for *use*,[11] either for their own consumption or to exchange for consumables produced by others. When Smith develops his value theory, for example, he considers the case of hunters exchanging deer or beaver according to what they caught themselves and what they want to eat. The Scottish economist John Ramsay McCulloch (1789-1864) expressed this view: "In exerting his productive powers, every man's object is either directly to consume the produce of his labour himself, or to exchange it for such commodities as he wishes to obtain from others." As expressed in "Say's Law," named after the French economist Jean-Baptiste Say (1767-1832), this view holds that all production is for purposes either of direct consumption or to be exchanged for things to be consumed.[12]

In their daily lives, people engage in production for use when they prepare lunch or dinner for themselves or for their family and friends, when they do their own laundry, or when they clean house. They also produce for use when they work for pay. One of my daughters, for example, worked reading scripts for an actress so that she could raise money to buy a smartphone, and her sister cleaned horse stalls to make money to finance a trip to Greece; both worked to produce equivalent *use values*, they worked to consume, exchanging commodities (their commodity time or *labor power*) for value equivalents as consumer goods.

Production for use may be a reasonable characterization of much household activity now and throughout human history. It certainly represents subsistence farmers, including most European peasants, feudal serfs, and even many artisans active at the time of Locke and Smith. Their subsistence economy did not preclude active participation in the social or even in the detailed division of labor. As Smith noted, subsistence hunters might exchange products to vary their diet, and workers might divide labor in order to raise their productivity and allow increased consumption without extra work. Smith and his followers assume that the purpose of work and production is the same for the pin factory workers as Robinson Crusoe, where production for use is necessarily limited to the consumption needs of the workers and their households. The choice of production technology would always be balanced between the interests of the producer as worker and consumer.

Writing at the very beginning of the capitalist era, and ignoring chattel slavery, Smith missed the dramatic change that command over the labor power of others would bring to the economic process. Smith analyzed market production as if it is all intended for consumption, either the consumption of what is produced or the consumption of products received in exchange for that production. He never considered the motivation of capitalists and slave-holders who need not consume their products or, indeed, need not consume *at all* because the purpose of their productive activity is to make profit and to dominate markets. Capitalists' and slave-owners' consumption is only loosely related to the size of their product. Instead, they produce to make profit by selling the commodities that their slaves and their workers produce. Using their powers of sympathy to put themselves in the place of others, they imagine the respect with

THE ANALYTICS OF CAPITALIST PRODUCTION

Production for use:
Workers produce a good which they consume.

Production for use with barter exchange:
Workers produce a commodity (C) which they exchange for another commodity (C') which they consume. C — C'

Production for use with money exchange:
Workers produce a commodity (C) which they sell for money (M) which they use to buy a commodity (C') which they consume. C — M — C'

Production for profit using wage labor:
Capitalist uses money (M) to hire labor power (C) which he uses to make a commodity (C') which he sells for more money (M').

M — C — C' — M'

Profit = M' - M.

Capitalist then reinvests profit into hiring more labor to produce more commodities leading to a dynamic expansion of capitalism.

which they are held because of their wealth. Rather than means to gain consumption goods, wealth becomes an end unto itself, putting the capitalist on an endless treadmill, seeking more and more profit in order to impress others endlessly.

While often benefitting from conflict, capitalists and slave-holders do not compete by waging war. Instead, their competition is for status and to preserve their independence against market rivals by maintaining and gaining *market share*,[13] production scale and efficiency, and the largest profit. Unlike consumption, which is naturally limited by human appetite and time, this drive for increased profit can continue without end. The slave-firm or capitalist enterprise will expand its production, will add more workers and produce more commodities, limited only by the extent of the market for *commodity product*[14] and for workers.

In their desire to impress, capitalists are just like everyone else in Smith's world, seeking respect in the eyes of their fellows. Unlike these other forms of competition, however, the capitalists' Sisyphean labor produces social benefits by expanding the means of production and raising output. The expanding profits and the growing efficiency of production driven by the profit motive provided the weapons and incentive to expand slavery and capitalist production. Much of the history of the last centuries has been the search by capitalists and slave-holders for new markets to sell their produce and to recruit more workers. This search spread chattel slavery and capitalism to new areas, along an *external dimension*, beginning with a few English and Dutch towns on the edge of the European world in the 15th century, until today where virtually all human societies are capitalist. Capitalism has also expanded on an *internal dimension* by integrating more productive activities into capitalist labor processes so that more of what we do is done through capitalist work processes and commodity markets. When paid child and elder care, laundry services, or restaurant meals replace care work previously done within families, capitalist markets expand and there is more scope for profit making.

Both processes, the external and internal expansion, will continue until the world is entirely oriented towards capitalist or slave profit making. Today, however, the world is *capitalist* with little remaining chattel slavery. So what happened to chattel slavery? The answer is that while both slavery and capitalism are rooted in the social division of labor and utilize an extensive detail division of labor, they rest on fundamentally opposing, and ultimately incompatible, visions of society. Like feudalism, slavery rests on a division of society between distinct social castes, owners and slave-workers, who belong to worthy and inferior castes, respectively. Consigned to a lowly status by virtue of race or other signifier, slaves work so their superiors can enjoy the refinements of culture and civilization. In a slave society, work is shameful because it is performed by slaves. It may be necessary, but work is socially repugnant, a mark of inferior status to be shunned by all who

EXAMPLE OF THE EXTERNAL EXTENSION OF CAPITALISM: GLOBALIZATION

Unable to sell their expanding production, capitalists seek new markets. American firms seek to open new markets and now sell their wares throughout the world, from Chicago to Beijing.

EXAMPLE OF THE INTERNAL EXTENSION OF CAPITALISM: WHO COOKS?

With more and more workers drawn into the capitalist labor process, less time and energy remain for traditional home production. One area where Americans have embraced the internal deepening of capitalism has been in food preparation. Nearly half of Americans food expenditures are now for prepared foods.

can avoid it. Those who work are to be despised for their involvement in such mundane activities.

Capitalism thus marked a step forward for human dignity. It was ultimately incompatible with both feudalism and slavery because the anonymity of capitalist markets upholds the value and merit of labor against those who would claim a right to live off of the work of others on the basis of their birth. Against the pretensions of landed aristocrats and other gentlemen, the urban bourgeoisie and their allies among rural farmers and gentry upheld a social theory that ennobled work and those who labor. Against the "divine right of kings" *and* the claims of aristocrats and slave-owners that they were entitled to their wealth and power by virtue of birth, rural and urban capitalists campaigned under the banner of the *labor theory of value*[15] to claim a larger share of society's wealth and social and political status. It is no accident that John Locke developed his analysis of the labor theory of value in the course of his defense of the rights of Parliament against the King in the era of the "Glorious Revolution" of 1689. Capitalism emerged as a revolutionary doctrine that denied all claims of natural superiority and inherited status. In this way, it has been part of the democratic movement that has swept the world, overturning both feudalism and slavery, in the past 250 years.

By reducing all labor power to a common level as a commodity, and valuing all according to their power over commodities, capitalism has been a great *egalitarian*[16] force. Developed against feudalism, the egalitarian ideology of the labor theory of value became a battering ram against other forms of oppression, including slavery and misogyny. With the first industrial factories in the United States, campaigns were launched in favor of property rights for women and against slavery. Bruce Laurie, Professor of History at the University of Massachusetts, has shown how Massachusetts proletarians and some industrial capitalists formed the Liberty Party, a precursor of the Free Soil Party and the Republican Party, to campaign against slavery and for equal rights for African Americans. Yale historian David Montgomery has shown how a coalition of proletarians and some capitalists was forged in the Civil War in defense of social equality, including rights for African Americans, women, and wage workers. Socialist and other anti-capitalist movements were to emerge and flourish in the same ideological milieu. In this way, capitalism became its own worst enemy.[17]

KARL MARX

No social theorist appreciated the power of capitalism as much as the system's great critic, Karl Marx. In the *Communist Manifesto*, which he wrote with Friedrich Engels, Marx shows how capitalism has "pitilessly torn asunder the motley feudal ties that bound man to his 'natural superiors,'" leaving nothing between them except "naked self-interest." By drowning "out the most heavenly ecstasies of religious fervor, of chivalrous enthusiasm, of philistine sentimentalism, in the icy water of egotistical calculation," capitalism liberated workers to pursue their own self-interest in promoting a democratic society. Viewing capitalism as a system of commodity exchange, Marx and many of his followers accept the claim by capitalism's defenders that capitalism itself treats all equally without regard for religion, race, or gender. Indeed, for Marxists, this claim has often been crucial to their politics. They favor a revolution against capitalism while seeing no particular need for action against other forms of exploitation, including racial, religious, or gender, because these, Marxists assert, will themselves be overcome when capitalism is overturned.

Disputes over the meaning and value of labor have shaken societies since the rise of slavery and capitalism. Eventually, such conflicts overturned feudalism, inaugurated democratic regimes throughout the world, and led to the virtual eradication of chattel slavery. This came hard, even requiring the bloodiest war in the history of the United States. Before the war, there was a fascinating ideological debate between slavery's defenders and those who favored capitalist labor relations. Slavery's defenders criticized capitalism for promoting conflict between labor and capital. "All great enterprises," George Fitzhugh (1806-1881) defender of American slavery wrote in 1854, "owe their success to association of capital and labor." Capitalism, Fitzhugh charges, begets "war in the bosom of society …. It arrays capital against labor." Capital's interest is to drive down wages, using competition to reduce wages to the level of subsistence or even below. "The capitalist cheapens their wages; they compete with and underbid each other, for employed they must be on any terms. This war of the rich with the poor and the poor with one another, is the morality which political economy inculcates."

Going further, Fitzhugh identifies a fundamental flaw within the logic of capitalist markets. Under slavery, he argues, the master has an interest in promoting families because in supporting child rearing, he is investing in his own property. Under capitalism, however, *no one* owns children and, therefore, no one has a financial stake in their care. Instead, work necessary for the reproduction and survival of society is performed by workers and their families *outside* of the normal circuit of capital. Because caring labor is done outside of the market economy and business does not profit from it, such work is discouraged. This, Fitzhugh argued, threatens the very viability of a capitalist society.

> MARX AND ENGELS ON THE EXPANSIVE POWER OF CAPITALISM
>
> The bourgeoisie … has been the first to show what man's activity can bring about. It has accomplished wonders far surpassing Egyptian pyramids, Roman aqueducts, and Gothic cathedrals; it has conducted expeditions that put in the shade all former exoduses of nations and crusades.
>
> The bourgeoisie cannot exist without constantly revolutionizing the instruments of production, and thereby the relations of production, and with them the whole relations of society …. Constant revolutionizing of production, uninterrupted disturbance of all social conditions, everlasting uncertainty and agitation distinguish the bourgeois epoch from all earlier ones.
>
> The need of a constantly expanding market for its products chases the bourgeoisie over the entire surface of the globe. It must nestle everywhere, settle everywhere, establish connections everywhere.
>
> Karl Marx and Friedrich Engels, *The Communist Manifesto*.

The dissociation of labor and disintegration of society, which liberty and free competition occasion, is especially injurious to the poorer class; for besides the labor necessary to support the family, the poor man is burdened with the care of finding a home, and procuring employment, and attending to all domestic wants and concerns. Slavery relieves our slaves of these cares altogether, and slavery is a form, and the very best form, of socialism. In fact, the ordinary wages of common labor are insufficient to keep up separate domestic establishments for each of the poor, and association or starvation is in many cases inevitable. In free society, as well in Europe as in America, this is the accepted theory, and various schemes have been resorted to, all without success, to cure the evil. The association of labor properly carried out under a common head or ruler, would render labor more efficient, relieve the laborer of many of the cares of household affairs, and protect and support him in sickness and old age, besides preventing the too great reduction of wages by redundancy of labor and free competition. Slavery attains all these results. What else will?

As well it should, Fitzhugh's politics, his unabashed defense of slavery, discredited his writings. Still, the first American to use the word "sociology," Fitzhugh had a real insight into capitalism and the problem of providing care labor in a capitalist market economy. More than Fitzhugh's politics may explain why this dilemma has been largely ignored by orthodox economics. Fitzhugh challenges the idea that a society can meet its needs through the market. Worse, he challenges the misogynist assumption that only work done through the market, only commodity production, creates value. Along with it, he challenges the assumption that capitalist economies distribute rewards according to the value of the labor expended.[18]

Had critics of capitalism pondered Fitzhugh's writings, rather than discounting him as an apologist for slavery, they would have found a critique of general interest. By exposing capitalist misogyny, Fitzhugh exposes a fundamental contradiction within capitalism, a contradiction that sits at the heart of a system that justifies an unequal distribution of wealth and power on the basis of the labor theory of value. Gender bias, he shows, contradicts the system's alleged respect for labor; more, it threatens the future of capitalist societies. Capitalism, Fitzhugh shows, can survive only by including a bit of socialism or slavery because market capitalism will not provide for the care of children and the reproduction of society.

Oddly enough, this advocate of slavery provides a basis for integrating socialism and feminism. Perhaps it is just as well that this defender of slavery has been forgotten, but it is unfortunate if his critique of capitalism is ignored. Critics have denounced capitalism as a system of exploiting labor through a monopoly over the means of production, but by neglecting the exploitation of family and caring labor performed outside of the capitalist market, they have missed the gender bias at the root of capitalism.

CAPITALISM AS A SOCIAL INSTITUTION

Exasperated with me, my father once told me that his business was "not an eleemosynary institution." After a quick trip to the dictionary, I appreciated his larger point: capitalists are not in business from love of their fellows or even interest in the products they sell. They are in it for the money. Capitalists produce *use values* only by accident; the purpose of capitalist production is profit, *surplus value*.

To understand capitalism as a so-

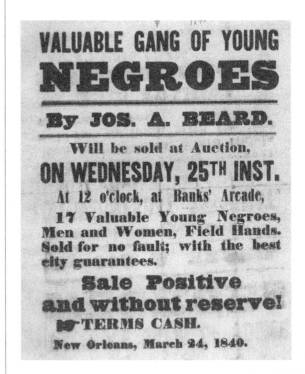

George Fitzhugh's insights about the slaveowners' interest in the survival and reproduction of their slaves may have had more theoretical than practical validity. Especially during the time of the African slave trade, when slaves were cheap and their produce valuable, owners often profited by overworking slaves and breaking up their families through sale. Slave auction notice from 1840.

cial institution, we must follow the money. Capitalists endeavor to make profit by hiring workers, having them produce commodities, and then selling the commodities for at least as much money as the workers were paid in wages. This process is a flow like the following:

$$M — C — C' — M'$$

Where M is the initial money, C represents labor hired; C′ is the commodity produced; and M′ is sales revenue. Profit = M′ - M.

Note that each step in this process involves challenges that could derail the process of profit-making (or accumulation). Individual capitalists try to manage these processes for themselves, but they extend beyond the scope of individual capitalists. For each, capitalists need social institutions to support their individual actions in pursuit of profit.

M — C: Hiring Labor Power

- Capitalists need institutions to raise children and to train them to be workers.
- When accumulation proceeds, they need institutions to recruit additional workers, either from outside the country or else by expanding the domestic labor force.
- Capitalists need institutions to restrain wage competition between them, so that rising wages do not squeeze profits.

C — C': The Labor Process

- Capitalists need institutions either to motivate workers to work hard or else to scare them into working hard.
- Institutions are needed to protect the capitalist's profit in the product of the workers' labor.

C' — M': Realization

- Capitalists need a large and elastic market for their commodity products.
- When accumulation proceeds, if the domestic market is too small to absorb the growing volume of commodity product, they need institutions to open new, foreign markets.
- They need institutions to restrain competition so that falling prices do not squeeze profits.

> ## SOCIAL STRUCTURES OF ACCUMULATION
>
> The theory of Social Structures of Accumulation (SSAs) was first suggested in 1978 by David Gordon as a framework to understand the economic crisis afflicting capitalist societies in the 1970s. Gordon suggested that an SSA is a set of integrated institutions necessary for capitalist accumulation, the key to understanding alternating periods of rapid and slow capitalist growth is in the successive creation, and construction anew, of SSAs

Capitalist profit-making and continued accumulation depends on establishing social institutions to provide labor, to limit wages, to maintain order and discipline in the workplace, to provide markets, to limit capitalist competition, and to guarantee capitalist control over access to their productive property. Without such institutions, profits are irregular and economies lurch from economic crisis to crisis; where a set of working institutions is in place, accumulation often proceeds at a steady pace. In the latter situations, we can say that a capitalist society has established a working *social structure of accumulation*.

Life is change; social structures evolve in ways that eventually undermine the continued accumulation process, leading to a crisis period of low profitability until a new set of working institutions is developed and the accumulation process is renewed. Some are heavy-handed institutions, such as those that directly limited wages in the early years of capitalism in Britain or the use of the United States Navy to force Japan to open its markets to American and European commodities. After the New Deal and World War II, a set of institutions was developed that exchanged labor peace for union recognition and steady wage growth. Under this *labor accord*, world capitalism experienced its fastest growth with steadily rising wages. This accord broke down, however, when rising wages and rising worker expectations led to a breakdown of labor peace. By the late 1970s, capitalists had abandoned the labor accord social structure of accumulation, eventually replacing it with a neoliberal social structure with higher unemployment, slower wage growth, and the use of international trade to discipline workers. (Since 2006, there is evidence that this neoliberal social structure may be breaking down. If so, then we may be entering a period where the nature of the next set of social institutions will be developed.)

Capitalism, of course, is not unique in requiring a set of social institutions for support. Like capitalism, chattel slavery was a social institution rooted in a distinct legal system. Africans became property in the Americas because the law said so. Slavery could not survive without legal protection, including the provision of judges and police to return slaves to their "owners." Both capitalism and chattel slavery rest on control by a few over the means of production needed for all.

Capitalism involves two types of institutions, one popularly associated with liberation, the other not. On one side, capitalists use commodity markets: capitalist

FIGURE 3-1

CHANGING CLASS STRUCTURE OF THE UNITED STATES LABOR FORCE, 1860-2007

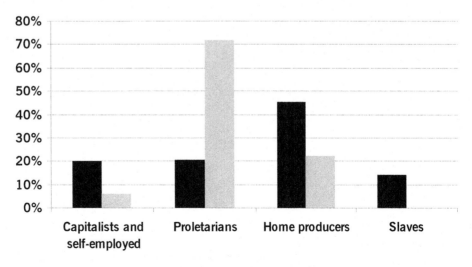

■ 1860   ▨ 2007

THESE LOAVES OF BREAD REPRESENT A DRAMATIC SOCIAL CHANGE

In the past, when done in the home, baking bread or canning vegetables exhausted women. Today, such work is usually done outside the household through a market-mediated division of labor that, on one side, has freed homemakers from much drudgery in exchange for greater work outside the home.

STUDYING CAPITALISM

Marxist economists are social scientists who study the economy from the perspective of distinct social systems, such as feudalism, slavery, capitalism. Marxists believe that each social system creates distinct economic processes including conflict between groups. A group of prominent Marxist economists were active at the University of Massachusetts, including (l.-r.) Richard Wolff, the late Stephen Resnick, and David Kotz.

businesses produce for sale in markets where consumers are free to choose, to buy or not. Over time, the use of commodity markets has increased, not only with the decline of slavery but with the increased substitution of market production for home production. For many who are now free to buy bread in a store and to wash clothes in a machine, marketization of home production has been liberating.

There is another side to capitalism: the capitalist monopoly over access to the means of production. Under chattel slavery, the slave owner has legal control over the very person of the worker. Capitalists do not own the workers, but law maintains capitalism by giving capitalists exclusive control over use of the means of production. *Production goods*,[19] including land, tools, ideas, and even genomes become capital only where laws give people or corporate groups the right to prevent others from using them. It is this exclusive control over the means of production that creates both profit and a phenomenon unique to capitalism, the combination of unemployed workers and idle means of production.

Capitalism thus relies on *monopoly power*,[20] the legal authority of the capitalist to *restrict access* to the means of production, and to restrict production. It may seem odd, therefore, that capitalist societies have been so remarkably productive. Indeed, capitalism's great productivity has been accidental because capitalists do not seek to create wealth or useful things. They seek *profit*: producing "use values" and meeting people's needs *is* only a happy accident. As we have seen in the fight over music downloads or software piracy, capitalists are perfectly ready to do the exact opposite of creating value. They restrict access to goods and even destroy valuable commodities in order to limit competition and inflate

FIGURE 3-2
AFTER-TAX CORPORATE PROFITS, PERCENT OF GDP

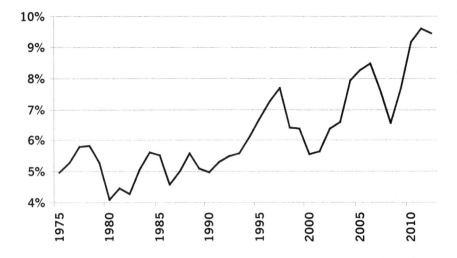

American capitalists have been successful at making profits. After falling for decades, the share of American income going to corporate profits began to rise steadily since the early 1980s. Despite the Great Recession, it has continued to rise to new heights since 2007.

Migrants from El Salvador harvesting strawberries in Salinas, California In the 1930s, this work was done by refugees from the Oklahoma dust bowl. Later, it was done by workers from the Philippines, then by Mexicans, now by Salvadorans.

prices and profits. Capitalism is not a system to create products, to create useful things, but to create *scarcity*, to *reduce* the availability of things and access to productive resources so that people will pay a premium to have them and workers must accept the capitalists' conditions to work.

Capitalism directly reduces productivity by restricting access to the means of production to create unemployment to drive down wages. It discourages hard work and innovation by separating the workers from their own product. Yet it has been an incredibly productive social system. Rather than a system *designed* to create wealth, capitalism is productive because the capitalists, like slave-owners under chattel slavery, have power over their workers and they use this power to drive the workers to work harder and to be more productive without regard to their own wishes. Wage earners must seek employment from capitalists or starve; capitalists use the leverage this gives them to drive the workers to produce more, and to create more profit.

Under feudalism, competition among elites was waged in tournaments and war, jousts and armed conflict. Under capitalism, elite competition is to increase profits by driving down the cost of production, expanding output, and increasing market share by developing new products. By comparison, capitalism is a benign, even a remarkably productive system. Capitalism is never at rest. Fear of their rivals drives individual capitalists to constantly reinvest their profits (M' - M in the equations above) by hiring more labor and searching out new markets for their produce. This competition drives an expansion of capitalism to new sources of labor, both *internal* by recruiting domestic workers into wage labor and *external*, by searching out workers from non-capitalist economies. Competition also drives capitalists to seek markets by replacing home production with the product of capitalist labor, selling factory bread to replace home baking, for example, or ready-to-wear clothing and commercial laundry services to replace home production, and professional day care to replace family care. Together, the abolition of slavery and the capitalist drive to expand production and commodity markets has increased the capitalist share of the U.S. economy from barely 20% when Adam Smith wrote, to 40% in 1860 and up to 80% today.

Over the centuries and throughout the world, capitalists have found that they can increase their profits by getting their workers to work harder and more productively. Capitalism has been associated with the greatest gains in productive efficiency ever seen because capitalism gives the capitalist exclusive control over any surplus. At the same time, the capitalist monopoly over access to the means of production creates "unemployment" and forces workers to accept work under the capitalist's supervision, at a higher level of intensity and under a more extended division of labor. Thus, the growth in labor productivity under capitalism is not accidental; it is a secondary result linked to the pursuit of capitalist profit. What is fundamental for capitalism is the extraction of profit through a monopoly over the means of production. This monopoly, like slavery, is secured by state action and allows capitalists to boost productivity by overriding the objections workers would have to their assigned work.

CAPITALISTS RESTRICT ACCESS

Courtesy of a company called "Flexplay®," Staples® sells DVDs for $4.99. The catch is that the DVD is coated with an acid finish so that it will decompose within 48 hours after it is opened. This is a physical manifestation of a larger policy of Digital Rights Management (DRM) by major entertainment and software producers. Supposedly intended to prevent digital piracy, the Electronic Frontier Foundation (EFF) finds that "DRM interferes with perfectly legal uses of digital media . . . now backed up by the Digital Millennium Copyright Act (DMCA). If you circumvent DRM locks or create the tools to do so, even to enable noninfringing fair uses, you might be on the receiving end of a lawsuit." The EFF concludes that "DMCA has been a disaster for innovation, free speech, fair use, and competition."

CURRENT CONTROVERSIES

WHAT HAPPENED TO WAGES?

HOW WAGES STAGNATED AND CAPITAL CAPTURED PRODUCTIVITY GAINS

From the dawn of American industrialization in the 19th century until the 1970s, wages generally rose with labor productivity, allowing working people to share in the gains produced by capitalist society. Since then, the United States has entered a new era, in which stagnant wages have allowed capitalists to capture a growing share of the fruits of rising productivity. The divergence between productivity and wages challenges orthodox economic theory, which expects employers to bid up the wages of more productive workers. What's more, the success American capitalists have had in monopolizing productivity gains undermines the social justification for capitalism: If working people no longer share the benefits of rising productivity then why should they continue to tolerate capitalist hierarchy?

Sources: *Historical Statistics of the United States Millennial Edition Online*; *Economic Report of the President 2014*; Edward Saez and Thomas Piketty, "Income Inequality in the United States, 1913-1998," *Quarterly Journal of Economics*, 118(1), 2003, 1-39; Bureau of Economic Analysis (bea.gov).

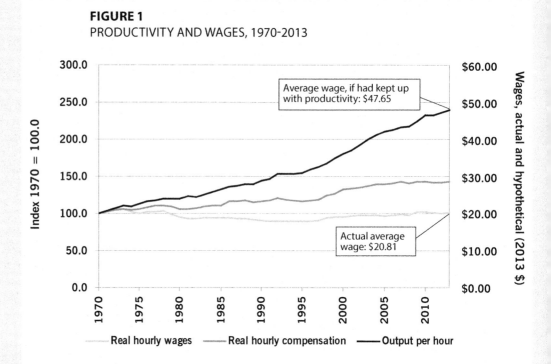

FIGURE 1
PRODUCTIVITY AND WAGES, 1970-2013

Wages have stagnated despite continued productivity growth. While productivity has increased dramatically, average hourly wages have barely kept up with inflation. Total hourly compensation (including not only wages but also the rising cost of employer-provided health insurance) has increased by just 0.8% a year, still much less than the 2.0% average annual increase in labor productivity. This rise in total compensation does not benefit most current workers, since it is mostly driven by the rising cost of health insurance and higher Social Security taxes to provide for an aging population. Had real wages kept pace with productivity, they would have risen from $19.97/hour in 1970 (in constant 2013 dollars) to $47.65/hour in 2013—more than double the actual average real wage of $20.81/hour in 2013.

FIGURE 2

PRODUCTIVITY AND PAY FOR THE HIGHEST-PAID EMPLOYEES, 1970-2012

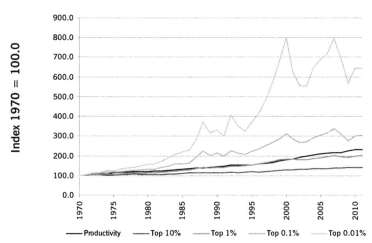

Pay has increased only for those at the very top. Pay has lagged behind productivity for all but the highest-paid employees. Even workers at the 99th percentile—those whose earnings are higher than 99% of workers—have fallen behind productivity growth. Only for employees in the top 0.5% of the pay scale has hourly pay increased as much as average productivity has. For the very highest-paid employees—the top 0.01%, just 13,000 people—pay has risen much faster than productivity. This group includes top corporate executives and other "super managers."

FIGURE 3

WAGES, NON-WAGE COMPENSATION, AND PROFITS, PERCENT OF GDP, 1970 AND 2012

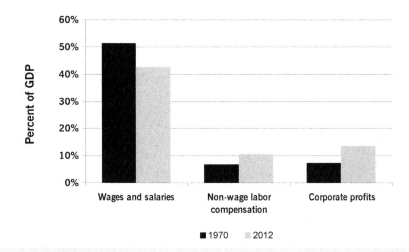

A growng share of income goes to profits, health insurance, and paying for retirement. When profits and the costs of health insurance and pensions (largely Social Security taxes but also private pensions) increase faster than productivity, it reduces the share of income available for workers' wages. Since 1970, the share of income going to wages has fallen by nearly a fifth, dropping by over 9 percentage points—from over half of GDP down to barely 42%; the share going to other forms of labor compensation has risen by almost 4 percentage points, from 7% to 11%; and the share going to corporate profits has risen by nearly 6 percentage points, from 7% to nearly 13%.

Capitalists profit by restricting access to competing products including:
(Left to right) generic drugs, hybrid corn seed, digital books, and copies of Prada shoes.

Profit and monopoly, not value and competition, define capitalism and are the source of profit. Consider, for example, the capitalist business of selling alcohol in restaurants and bars in Cambridge, Massachusetts, versus Paris, France. Selling drinks is a *very* profitable capitalist business in Cambridge because restrictions on the number of licenses, which are needed to sell alcohol in restaurants, have driven the price of a license up to over $400,000. By contrast, even though Parisian diners and drinkers will pay a premium for a good wine selection and a knowledgeable *sommelier* (or a staff waiter who specializes in wine), selling alcohol *per se* is less profitable in Paris. Drinking wine is a national, and tourist, pastime in the City of Light, but the business is less profitable in Paris than in puritanical Cambridge because a legal restrictions on the sale of alcohol forces Cantabrigians to pay a premium to drink. Paris restaurateurs can only profit by providing a distinctive and valuable service, such as good advice or a particularly interesting selection. It is the legal monopoly over the wine trade that makes a liquor license *capital*[21] in Cambridge. By contrast, because of the unlimited availability of wine licenses, in the Parisian retail wine trade there is no *capital* in rights to sell alcohol. Consequently it is the *sommelier* who captures profits because he (or, less often, she) produces value by making the restaurant attractive. (Similarly, in competitive restaurant markets such as New York City's Chinatown, it is the chef and landlord who receive most of the profits because they own the resources in scarce supply, location and quality cuisine.)

Because capitalists compete for *surplus* not for *use value*, any who focus on value rather than profit will be driven out of business by their more-ruthless competitors. As a system, capitalism depends on *restricting* output rather than increasing it: there is no profit in goods so widely available that they can be had at minimal cost. Consider the music industry where digital material can now be reproduced and distributed at virtually no cost. How have music companies responded? They have waged legal war to stop students and others from using the new technology to create more value by exchanging (and enjoying) music and video. It is restriction rather than production that links capitalism as a system of surplus creation with capitalism as a monopoly over access to the means of production.

Capitalists profit by limiting production by limiting access to their products and to the means of production. If everyone could produce freely, then capitalists would compete until competition drove prices down to the real cost of production, the workers' wages and the price of inputs, leaving nothing for profit. They create space for their profits by creating little monopolies that limit competition, carving out a role for themselves as intermediaries between consumers, productive workers, and the tools and other means of production. Under capitalism, the world has experienced vast increases in wealth and rising productivity. How ironic that this has been an accident, ancillary to the main purpose of capitalism: to use a monopoly over the means of production to restrict output and create profit.[22]

THE RECORD INDUSTRY ASSOCIATION OF AMERICA

The Record Industry Association of America represents capitalists in the music industry. Its campaign against internet file sharing and music downloads is intended to restrict access to entertainment products to protect capitalist profits. Others who profit by restricting access to products easily provided include the pharmaceutical industry (in its campaign against generic drugs), hybrid seed producers, sellers of brand-name clothing, and publishers who campaign to restrict the resale of textbooks.

DISCUSSION QUESTIONS

What are "social facts"?

What is "capitalism"? How does it differ from "feudalism"? How does it differ from "domestic slavery" and from "chattel slavery"? How is it similar to both?

How do capitalists make profits? In what sense do they exploit their workers? Does this make capitalist labor the same as slave labor?

Does capitalism lead to greater social efficiency and the production of desired commodities?

Is feudalism an expanding system? Is domestic slavery? Is chattel slavery? Is capitalism?

ENDNOTES

[1]Feudalism was a social system where a small elite, the landed aristocracy, provided military protection to the producers, serfs, in exchange for a share of the produce.

[2]Unlike multi-national empires or local fiefdoms, nation states gain legitimacy as representing the will of a distinct people, united by a common language, culture, and history. Much of this culture and history would have to be created, including a common language imposed through the nation state's bureaucracy and schooling system.

[3]While this is the number loaded on ships, even more were enslaved, with many dying on the voyage from their homes to the coast and on the slave ships.

[4]Most of the natives died of diseases brought by the Europeans and Africans; see Charles C. Mann, *1491: New Revelations of the Americas Before Columbus*, 2nd Vintage Books ed. (New York: Vintage, 2011); Charles C. Mann, *1493: Uncovering the New World Columbus Created*, 1st ed. (New York [N.Y.]: Alfred A. Knopf, 2011).

[5]The key to the European triumph may have been the division between the Catholic Church and secular authorities, such as the Holy Roman Emperor, which prevented either from developing a monopoly on force; see Douglass Cecil North, *The Rise of the Western World: A New Economic History* (Cambridge [Eng.]: University Press, 1973); Social Science Research Council, *The Formation of National States in Western Europe*, Studies in Political Development 8 (Princeton, N.J: Princeton University Press, 1975); Charles Tilly, *The Contentious French* (Cambridge, Mass: Belknap Press, 1986).

[6]Sugar was the major slave crop, the largest reason for the slave trade and, indeed, for European settlement in the New World. Cotton was widely produced only after the 1790s, late in the slave trade. Cotton was a major product of the southern United States, the destination of fewer than 6% of the slaves brought from Africa to the New World; see Robert William Fogel, *Without Consent Or Contract: The Rise and Fall of American Slavery* (W. W. Norton & Company, 1994); The argument that slavery led to the British industrial revolution is made better if the emphasis is on the rise of capitalism and the development of commodity production than by attempts to link slavery directly with factory production; see Eric Eustace Williams, *Capitalism & Slavery* (Chapel Hill: University of North Carolina Press, 1994); Sidney Wilfred Mintz, *From Plantations to Peasantries in the Caribbean*, Focus Caribbean (Washington, D.C: Latin American Program, Woodrow Wilson International Center for Scholars, 1984); Sidney Wilfred Mintz, *Sweetness and Power: The Place of Sugar in Modern History* (New York: Penguin Books, 1986).

[7]Note that the use of African slaves rather than Europeans avoided the problem that the enslavement of Europeans would have created a continuing war of all against all, especially in the context of continued political decentralization in Europe; see David Brion Davis, *Inhuman Bondage: The Rise and Fall of Slavery in the New World* (Oxford, England ; New York: Oxford University Press, 2006); David Brion Davis, *The Problem of Slavery in Western Culture* (New York: Oxford University Press, 1988); David Brion Davis, *The Problem of Slavery in the Age of Revolution, 1770-1823* (New York: Oxford Uni-

verstiy Press, 1999); the use of African slaves also facilitated the transfer of African agricultural products, such as yams and peanuts, to the New World; see Mann, 1493.

[8]Steven M Wise, *Though the Heavens May Fall: The Landmark Trial That Led to the End of Human Slavery* (Cambridge, Mass.: Da Capo Press, 2005); Sean Wilentz, *The Rise of American Democracy: Jefferson to Lincoln*, 1st ed. (New York: Norton, 2005); David R. Roediger, *The Wages of Whiteness: Race and the Making of the American Working Class*, Rev. ed., Haymarket Series (London. New York: Verso, 2007).

[9]Under capitalism, wage workers sell their time to capitalists in exchange for a fixed wage. The capitalists then try to profit by selling commodities that their workers produce under their supervision.

[10]Wage earning proletarians have no legal rights to the means of production and, therefore, have to sell their labor time to capitalists to gain their subsistence.

[11]Production for use is where people make things to consume. In contrast, production for surplus value, or for profit, is where they make things to accumulate wealth. Production for use is directed at consumption and limited by the ability to consume; production for profit and wealth is unlimited.

[12]Say's Law has also been important in the development of orthodox macroeconomics. Followers of Say's Law deny even the possibility of a "general glut" with involuntary unemployment, on the assumption that any production is equivalent to an increase in demand.

[13]Capitalists compete to sell more than their rivals. With increased sales, they can accumulate more profit, allowing more investment so that they can produce more efficiently on a larger scale, increasing their share of the market further and driving their competitors bankrupt.

[14]Commodities are products produced for sale rather than made for direct consumption by the workers themselves.

[15]The labor theory of value asserts that the value of products, the price at which they are exchanged, is set by the amount of labor needed to produce them. As propounded by Locke, Smith, and others, the theory went much further to assert that income and wealth should reflect the amount of labor that one puts into producing useful things, and that social worth should reflect labor rather than status at birth or inheritance.

[16]Egalitarians hold that all people, regardless of birth, are entitled to the same rights including an equal share in society's product and wealth.

[17]Bruce Laurie, *Beyond Garrison: Antislavery and Social Reform* (Cambridge: Cambridge University Press, 2005); David Montgomery, *Beyond Equality; Labor and the Radical Republicans, 1862-1872*, 1st ed. (New York: Knopf, 1967); Gerald Friedman, *State-Making and Labor Movements: France and the United States, 1876-1914* (Ithaca: Cornell University Press, 1998); Gerald Friedman, *Reigniting the Labor Movement: Restoring Means to Ends in a Democratic Labor Movement* (Abingdon, Oxon: Routledge, 2007).

[18]George Fitzhugh, *Sociology for the South; Or, The Failure of Free Society* (Richmond, Va: A. Morris, 1854); note that one of the most interesting evaluations of Fitzhugh's work, and the work of other slave apologists, is by a then-Marxist, see Eugene D. Genovese, *The World the Slaveholders Made: Two Essays in Interpretation* (Middletown, Conn. : Scranton, Pa: Wesleyan University Press ; Distributed by Harper & Row, 1988); also see Drew Gilpin Faust, ed., *The Ideology of Slavery: Proslavery Thought in the Antebellum South, 1830-1860*, Library of Southern Civilization (Baton Rouge: Louisiana State University Press, 1981).

[19]These are the means of production, machinery and other things needed to produce and market commodities. Without access to these, proletarians are forced to sell their time for wages working for capitalists.

[20]A monopoly exists where one business has the exclusive right to produce a particular product. Capitalists have a monopoly because as a group they have exclusive control over access to the means of production.

[21]An often misunderstood concept, capital is not stuff. It is not a pile of machinery or other products. Instead, capital is a social relation marked by some having a legal monopoly over means of production. Wine is capital in Cambridge because there are restrictions on its sale; it is only a beverage in Paris where every restaurant can sell it.

[22]For recent developments in American Marxism, see Stephen A. Resnick, *Knowledge and Class: A Marxian Critique of Political Economy* (Chicago: University of Chicago Press, 1987); David M. Kotz,

Terrence McDonough, and Michael Reich, eds., *Social Structures of Accumulation: The Political Economy of Growth and Crisis (Cambridge* ; New York: Cambridge University Press, 1994); for earlier American Marxism, see Paul M. Sweezy, *The Theory of Capitalist Development: Principles of Marxian Political Economy* (New York: Oxford University Press, 1942); Paul A. Baran, *Monopoly Capital: An Essay on the American Economic and Social Order*, 1st Modern reader paperback ed, Modern Reader Paperbacks PB-73 (New York: Monthly Review Press, 1968).

WHY ECONOMISTS DON'T STUDY INSTITUTIONS, BUT SHOULD

Just today, a stranger came to my door claiming he was here to unclog a bathroom drain. I let him into my house without verifying his identity, and not only did he repair the drain, he also took off his shoes so he wouldn't track mud on my floors. When he was done, I gave him a piece of paper that asked my bank to give him some money. He accepted it without a second glance. At no point did he attempt to take my possessions, and at no point did I attempt the same of him. . . .

Society runs on trust. We all need to trust that the random people we interact with will cooperate. Not trust completely, not trust blindly, but be reasonably sure (whatever that means) that our trust is well-founded and they will be trustworthy in return (whatever that means). This is vital. If the number of parasites gets too large, if too many people steal or too many people don't pay their taxes, society no longer works.

SOCIAL INSTITUTIONS AND TRANSACTIONS COSTS: THE NORMS AND VALUES OF A PRODUCTIVE SOCIETY

The general public is often suspicious of orthodox economics. An aroma, even a stink of selfishness rises from economic analysis that assumes universal selfishness, treating all of us as sociopathic egoists. Economists are widely seen to be uncaring for the needs of the poor, the disabled, and the environment, indifferent to all moral values. Their theories treat individuals as behaving purely from self-interest, without regard for community values or the needs of others. And their teachings have been shown to lead economics students to behave more selfishly, to give less to charity, than students in other disciplines.[1]

If studying the self-interested models of individual action used by economists can make you a worse person, the only justification of such study would be that it provides a better understanding of social life. But this is certainly not the case! Indeed, grounding their theory in individual motivations, most microeconomists have little or nothing to say about social institutions which they regard as secondary, even epiphenomena, to individual motivations and technology. But even the most committed methodological individualist must acknowledge a place for institutions because these are necessary to maintain a division of labor, which is limited by the cost of coordinating activities between different people.[2] Economists call these *transactions costs*, the costs of making and enforcing exchanges. Transactions costs include the costs of evaluating offers from others, negotiating bargains, ensuring compliance, and protecting property. Standing between potential buyers and sellers, they limit the division of labor through markets by raising the costs of exchange. If transactions costs are high enough, lowering the net returns that an exchange brings to buyers and sellers, they can prevent exchange. From this perspective, *firms*, or their equivalents, are created to limit transactions costs with set rules that limit internal debate and

There are over 3 million cashiers in the United States, as many as the number of elementary and middle school teachers.

Including other categories of workers involved in policing and negotiating transactions, the transactions cost sector employs over 46 million Americans, including accountants, cashiers, retail sales clerks, security guards, and sales agents,   Over a third of Americans are employed in the transactions cost sector, policing the market transactions of the other two-thirds.

JOHN STUART MILL ON SELFISH INDIVIDUALISM

As the idea is essentially repulsive of a society only held together by the relations and feelings arising out of pecuniary interests, so there is something naturally attractive in a form of society abounding in strong personal attachments and disinterested self-devotion.

RONALD COASE

Economic analysis of transactions costs begins with the English economist, Ronald Coase (1910-2013). In his 1937 article, "The Nature of the Firm," Coase argued that firms were established to limit transactions costs and the boundary of the firm, the point where the firm moved from producing intermediate products internally and buying them from the outside, reflects the balance of transactions costs saved by the firm and administrative costs incurred. This analysis contributed to Coase winning the Nobel Prize in Economics in 1991.

bargaining in order to facilitate the detailed division of labor. My economics department is one such "firm" where we coordinate service and teaching work without directly negotiating every decision. Other "firms" include my family, General Motors, IBM, and Toyota. All allow us to economize on transactions costs by agreeing in advance on a general division of labor and responsibility. The difference between my department and family on one side, and General Motors, IBM, and Toyota on the other, is that my department and family do not set out to *limit* production and quality by restricting access to the means of production. Instead, we try to coordinate production to demand, and to facilitate a "fair" distribution of the proceeds of our industry; but more on these differences later.

Beginning with methodological individualism, some economists have studied how institutions affect economic activity by raising or lowering transactions costs. There is good evidence that transactions costs vary across countries and regions. People will establish businesses to produce for sale only where they are reasonably confident that they will be able to negotiate exchanges and enjoy the product of the exchange. Fear of crime and excessive taxation has prevented potential capitalists and others from launching productive businesses throughout Africa, the former Soviet Union, and elsewhere. One entrepreneur showed me the paperwork required to open a hair-salon in the Ukraine: over 100 approvals, each of which required at least one bribe as well as government fees. Many others would give up long before the end of this process, leaving the Ukraine with one fewer productive business.

In *The Wealth of Nations*, Adam Smith suggested that the division of labor, "from which so many advantages are derived, is not originally the effect of any human wisdom …. It is the necessary, though very slow and gradual consequence of a certain propensity in human nature which has in view no such extensive utility; the propensity to truck, barter, and exchange one thing for another." Even if Smith is right, people are better able to *act* on this tendency if there are social institutions that restrain transactions costs. These institutions include some familiar ones: common language, systems of weights and measures, stable currency, financial systems to provide credit for transactions, means to transfer and save money, and police, judges, and a legal system that protect property rights and enforce contracts. Other institutions are less familiar in an economic analysis but are as important. In a *kleptocracy*,[4] such as the former Zaire, there is no recourse to public authority for protection of property or contract. Public redress, however, is cumbersome and time-consuming even where authorities are honest. Far better to live where people can trust others because our parents and our community have taught values of honest dealing and respect for others. Best of all is a society where individuals practice *generalized reciprocity*, performing generous acts for others as a matter of course, without expecting any immediate return but confident that in the future *someone* will return the favor.

Respect for others and generalized reciprocity allows us to economize on transactions costs because we trust that others will honor their commitments and respect our property. When people are honest, we can leave our property unguarded and trust others to respect contracts. When people help each other, we can economize on formal transactions and contracting. For example, general honesty and respect for the property of others allows me to leave my bicycle unattended when I run into the liquor store for a bottle of wine, or get money from the ATM; this saves time, and wear and tear on my bicycle lock. If I can trust others, I can make contracts with handshakes rather than hiring an expensive lawyer to draft a formal agreement. Generalized reciprocity also improves the standard of living. When people hold the elevator door for others, it allows more efficient utilization of our elevators by reducing wait-times. Holding the door for someone carrying a large load of groceries, even though I have no idea who that person is and I have no expectation that she will ever return the favor, allows people to shop without hiring someone to help carry their groceries. Similarly, by not stealing my neighbor's groceries when she unpacks her car, I allow her to shop without the expense of a private guard.

Believing in benevolent nature, Adam Smith said that human nature leads a person to care for others "and render their happiness necessary … though he derives nothing from it except the pleasure of seeing it."[5] *Social norms*[6] allow us to leave our newspapers and mail unattended, confident that our neighbors will not steal them. They support the community provision of snacks to Sunday school, the sharing of childcare responsibilities, and the provision of chaperones for school dances without cumbersome accounting systems. In respecting the property of others, and helping strangers, people follow common norms of behavior taught when they were young. These norms enhance social welfare because they allow us to trust each other even without negotiating and enforcing contracts.

If we trust each other, we avoid the expense of transactions costs and formal markets, conducting our exchanges informally without clear accounting for each side's contribution. Family members and neighbors often do this, maintaining relationships on a strictly *affective*[7] basis without formal accounting. Often, such accounting would undermine the relationship by suggesting that the relationship is an exchange subject to mistrust. *Not* specifying contributions leaves open the possibility that some will contribute dispropor-

---

"SELF-INTEREST PROPERLY UNDERSTOOD":
MORAL VIRTUE IN 19TH-C. AMERICA, FROM ALEXIS DE TOCQUEVILLE, *DEMOCRACY IN AMERICA*

Visiting America in the 1830s, de Tocqueville was struck by the readiness of Americans to help each other and to form groups for collective self-improvement. From this he concluded that a democratic and egalitarian society was possible provided that the population learned values of cooperation and mutual aid.

"They therefore do not deny that every man may follow his own interest, but they endeavor to prove that it is the interest of every man to be virtuous. …. [The Americans] are fond of explaining almost all the actions of their lives by the principle of self-interest rightly understood; they show with complacency how an enlightened regard for themselves constantly prompts them to assist one another and inclines them willingly to sacrifice a portion of their time and property to the welfare of the state …. The principle of self-interest rightly understood is not a lofty one, but it is clear and sure. It does not aim at mighty objects, but it attains without excessive exertion all those at which it aims. As it lies within the reach of all capacities, everyone can without difficulty learn and retain it. By its admirable conformity to human weaknesses it easily obtains great dominion; nor is that dominion precarious, since the principle checks one personal interest by another, and uses, to direct the passions, the very same instrument that excites them.

The principle of self-interest rightly understood produces no great acts of self-sacrifice, but it suggests daily small acts of self-denial. By itself it cannot suffice to make a man virtuous; but it disciplines a number of persons in habits of regularity, temperance, moderation, foresight, self- command; and if it does not lead men straight to virtue by the will, it gradually draws them in that direction by their habits. If the principle of interest rightly understood were to sway the whole moral world, extraordinary virtues would doubtless be more rare; but I think that gross depravity would then also be less common. The principle of interest rightly understood perhaps prevents men from rising far above the level of mankind, but a great number of other men, who were falling far below it, are caught and restrained by it. Observe some few individuals, they are lowered by it; survey mankind, they are raised."

WHEN ARE WE MORE PRONE TO HELP OTHERS?

Recognized as "one of the human rocks on which societies are built" (Mauss, 1954), one of the basic interactions that makes a bundle of individuals into a society, generalized reciprocity" or "self-interest properly understood" varies widely between countries and regions. Most common in families, kinship groups, and among the members of some religious communities, generalized reciprocity is also found in much larger groups. A famous economic theorist, Mancur Olson, suggested that it would be common only in small groups where we could expect some rather immediate return. There is evidence of this: workers in smaller offices, for example, are more likely to pay for bagels and donuts offered on an honor system. However, generalized reciprocity is also found in experimental situations, even among anonymous individuals. Following the model suggested by de Tocqueville in Democracy in America, individuals are more likely to offer assistance when they have experience of others helping them, when they have experience of participating in collective action, and when they are raised in communities that value honesty and collective help.

ARE PEOPLE SELFISH? SHOULD THEY BE?

Generalized reciprocity is gift giving without expectation of immediate return. The custom of giving birthday presents is one example, as is the practice of being courteous to strangers in public spaces. Such practices ease social life, reduce stress, and promote economic efficiency by facilitating collective action and lowering transactions costs. Found even in some very large communities, generalized reciprocity may be more common in smaller groups where it is reinforced by direct personal contact.

tionately and some activities will not be performed consistently. In many neighborhoods, for example, residents watch the street to make sure that children and property are safe. This important "eyes-on-the-street" work is performed without any formal scheduling and with no formal compensation, and it produces no property rights. Informal "neighborhood watch" is cheaper and more effective than formal policing, but requires that we trust that our fellow neighbors will all do their share of street watching. (This assumes, of course, that our neighbors are on our side!) Similar arrangements are often used by parents to arrange car pools and babysitting. It is possible to track everyone's contribution and provide for formal exchanges of babysitting and car pool work. This is sometimes done, but most parents avoid the administrative expense and impersonality of formal accounting to conduct their babysitting and car pooling on an ad-hoc basis, where decisions are often made on the spur of the moment about who will drive or watch the kids. (Informality allows some to cheat and perform less work than would be their fair share. But formal arrangements remove the sense of caring and personal commitment that parents value, especially in those involved with their children. Instead, parents rely on a sense of generalized reciprocity in their community of parents. They accept the danger that some will take advantage of the informal accounting.

THE ECONOMIC VALUE OF TRUST

Honesty, generalized reciprocity, and trust are economic assets to a community. By lowering transactions costs, they lower the cost of doing business and, thereby, encourage the division of labor. For example, if people are honest, businesses can dramatically lower transactions costs by operating on an honor system. Many farm stands are run this way. Rather than employ someone to sit around to guard the produce and collect payment, they leave the produce out with a jar for money trusting that customers will honestly pay for what they take. Paul Feldman, an MIT trained economist, delivers bagels and donuts to offices around Washington, D. C. leaves a cashbox of payment; he estimates that 89% of people pay and *no one steals the cashboxes*.[8] Honesty allows these businesses to operate more efficiently because they do not have to pay for security. Indeed, it is possible that these services would not be provided at all if people were not honest. The bagel man estimates that he would have to close his business if the payment rate fell below 80%. Many farm stands do not generate enough business to pay for security. If people were less honest, they too would have to close.

The American political theorist Robert Putnam calls generalized reciprocity the "touchstone of social capital," facilitating all social interactions. Generalized reciprocity is related to *reciprocal altruism*,[9] a form of altruism where one party performs generous acts towards another in expectation of some future return, but it occurs where individual help others without expectation of direct or immediate reward. As such, generalized reciprocity can be vulnerable to exploitation. If enough do exploit, it will break down, and social cooperation will cease except on an explicit, contractual basis with formal accounts and policing, a much less efficient system.

Rather than unbridled short-term selfishness, Alexis de Tocqueville argued that people could do better for themselves by deferring some immediate advantages in order to help society function more smoothly so that we can all be benefit from the gains that come from the social division of labor. Using modern language, de Tocqueville's "self-interest rightly understood" is a strategy pursued by rational, selfish individuals looking to make themselves better off by minimizing social transactions costs. If we resist temptation to take advantage of each other, if we look out for our neighbors and follow norms of honest behavior that make for a *trustful community*, we all gain because we can all avoid some of the expense of policing exchanges and property rights, and we all gain by extending the social division of labor. Without an honest society, transactions costs would prevent most exchanges, forcing us to wall ourselves into self-sufficient fortresses where we would have to produce everything we need for ourselves, fearful that others would steal our property and exploit any contract.

"Self-interest rightly understood" allows us to economize on transactions costs. This allows us to divide labor, relying on others to provide many of the goods and services that we want, including the gas to run our cars, discs for our computers, our newspaper and coffee from Amherst Coffee, and our pastrami on rye for lunch at Amherst's best deli, The Black Sheep. Even with low transactions costs, many resist using the market to coordinate the social division of labor. Critics complain that the market is "cold" and impersonal, and fear relying on the quality provided by self-interested vendors, but they are wrong to say that markets prevent people from considering the needs of others. We will be discussing many of the problems with markets throughout this work. Here we should note that even selfish motivations can lead to empathetic behavior. Participation in markets can encourage aspects of the trustful community and "self-interest rightly understood" because those who sell commodities need to empathize

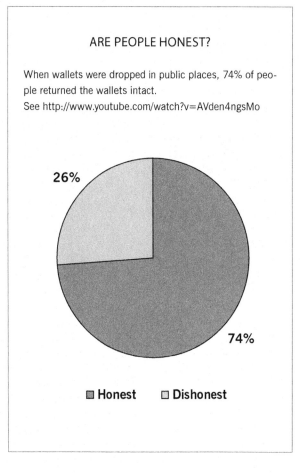

ARE PEOPLE HONEST?

When wallets were dropped in public places, 74% of people returned the wallets intact.
See http://www.youtube.com/watch?v=AVden4ngsMo

26%

74%

▣ Honest   ▢ Dishonest

TABLE 4-1
TRANSACTIONS COSTS

Cost	Example	Social Institutions that Lower Cost
Evaluating offers	Measuring the quantity of cheese; checking whether the money offered is legal or counterfeit.	Uniform standards for weights and measures; easy signifiers for legal currency; government regulations for product safety, quality, and honest labeling.
Negotiating bargain	Haggling over the price.	Common language; common standards for property rights and contracts; market publicity to share information about price and quality standards.
Insuring compliance	Making sure the money and cheese both exchange hands. Making sure that the goods and money exchanged are those evaluated earlier.	Easy access to public courts and police; common norms of honest behavior to make a *trustful community*.
Protecting property after exchange	Making sure you are not robbed of your cheese or money as soon as you turn the corner.	Effective police system; public involvement in protecting property rights; common norms of honest behavior to make a *trustful community*.

Jacoby Ellsbury, hero of the Boston Red Sox World Series victory in 2013 signed with the rival New York Yankees because they offered him more money and a longer contract. Should he have cared more for the people of New England and stayed with the Red Sox?

An honesty box at an English farmstand. This stand is too small to pay for a full-time attendant to guard the flowers and make sure that people pay for what they take. Without trust, the farmer could not operate his stand and might stop growing the flowers.

with potential consumers in order to sell to them. Far from ignoring the needs of others, successful businesses think all the time about their customers and try to anticipate their needs and wants because that is the best way to sell things to them. In a market system, buyers and sellers are rewarded for thinking about others because that is the way to get rich. Knowing that I might sell this book to others, for example, encourages me to improve it and make it more accessible.

Still, if the market encourages a certain type of empathy and even sociability, its concerns are entirely instrumental: we think of others only so that we can make profit by selling to them, not because we care about their welfare. Our market-based empathy and sociability are limited. They are directly proportional not to people's needs or worthiness but to their income. We care a great deal about the needs and wishes of the rich, even those who have done nothing worthy to gain their wealth, and nothing about those who are poor, whether from some social failure or simply due to bad luck, youth, or disability. We have no market-based interest in those who are too poor to buy our product or have otherwise removed themselves from our customer base. Worse, market sociability provides no incentive for honest dealing if we can profit more from cheating. The market relies on generalized reciprocity but, at the same time, if we are concerned only about the market and getting rich to participate in the market, we have very little motive to promote or build community.

IS LOVE EFFICIENT?

Market incentives reward us for tending to the interests of the rich, and for looking out for our selfish interests without regard for the well-being of our community and its values. The market obliges participants to think of others as instruments, means to their own ends rather than as citizens, members of a community, or human beings. This is why people mistrust the market for many of the things that really matter where we are particularly vulnerable to *sharp trading*.[10] Even when we rely on the market for our daily bread, music, and other necessities of life, we

INEQUALITY AND SOCIAL CAPITAL

The great increase in inequality over the past 30 years, especially in the United States, has led social scientists to look for connections among inequality, reliance on the market, and levels of trust and community involvement. They have generally found that people trust each other less and are less likely to participate in social groups where there is a wider disparity in income. One study found: "More inequality leads to less trust and less caring for people who are different … Where there is less trust, there are fewer acts of kindness toward others. … charitable donations and volunteering."

Source: Eric Uslander and Mitchell Brown, "Inequality, Trust, and Civic Engagement." Russell Sage Foundation (russellsage.org).

want doctors, lawyers, teachers, and even baseball players who care about us. We want them to act from caring feelings and concern for others rather than to be in it "only for the money." (Consider how Boston Red Sox fans felt when Wade Boggs, Johnny Damon, and now Jacoby Ellsbury left to play for the New York Yankees.) We depend on people to work for money to get us many of the goods and services that we want but can do without. Yet when we are most vulnerable and needy, we want to have people helping us because they care, because they like us and work for *affective motivations*,[11] acting for emotional and caring reasons rather than to make money off of our suffering or for other instrumental goals. Even the wealthy among us want to be valued for who they are, not for what they can pay.

Be careful who you trust or you may form relationships with vampires.

We value *affective motivations* because we want direct human connection with others. We want others to like us, and we value care that is given freely because it is given out of caring motivations. Even if we have the money, we would rather not rely on paid care labor and mercenary motivations because we know that mercenaries will betray us if the incentives change or someone else offers more money. This sentiment contributes to the common dislike of market systems but even more is involved here. Our relations with the natural world are relatively simple: we work and nature gives us something. But in social situations arising from the division of labor, in every social relationship, others have the power to hurt us because we benefit from our relationship. Power is inherent in any beneficial relationship because others can hurt us by ending the connection, denying us the benefit that we have from the relationship. (Power is not lessened because they, too, benefit from the connection and would lose by truncating it; knowing that they, too, lose may give us some satisfaction if they break-up with us but it gives us no guarantee that they won't accept this damage in order to damage us. I remember my older sister storming out of our house, slamming the door, and then screaming at our mother: "This hurts me more than it hurts you." But she accepted that pain in order to punish our mother.)

Human connections make us vulnerable. If we can trust others, and benefit from the trust that we share, then we are exposed if others violate this trust. That is why sensible people are careful to enter relationships with others, whether these are friends, lovers, or purveyors of needed services. (This is why parents worry about their children's romantic involvements.) Since we depend on our doctor, teacher, accountant, or lawyer, for example, they can hurt us, leaving us with no option except to sue them or to refuse to pay their bill, options that will do little to restore our health or good feeling. We want care-givers to value our interests even beyond the money they get from us, and we hope that they will be guided by other considerations than profit, whether professional pride or caring emotion. We rely on feelings to support our instrumental interests in maintaining friendly relations with us. Where we do not see such feelings, we hesitate to enter into market relationships.

There is a danger here because as a capitalist society we rely on both types of motivations, material incentives and affective or emotional connections. Usually we carefully separate these two: for example, we plan to marry for love and assume that the people we date are not having sex for money. We are a capitalist society, however, and sometimes we try to combine motivations. While many of us, for example, donate blood from a sense of responsibility to others, some get paid for their donations. Here we enter treacherous terrain. Affective motivation may wither if those who act from emotion begin to seek the material rewards provided to others. Will those who donate from affective motivations continue to give if others are being paid? Will you continue to help your elderly grandmother if you find out that she is paying an aide to help her when you are not available? Will your doctors continue to work long hours from a sense of responsibility and professional dedication if they learn that others use their position to maximize their income even at the expense of their patients' health? And if you suspect this, will you trust their recommendations? Where will you then turn?

TV medical interns are well-paid. We rely on real interns to staff our hospitals, working long hours for little money but a feeling of responsibility and commitment to others. What happens if they start insisting on material rewards commensurate with their work? Would you trust a doctor who is motivated by money?

She's not a doctor, but she played one on TV.

This is not Frances's pool.

Affective motivations can solve many of the problems we encounter in social action, at least until they are overwhelmed by material incentives. Consider my neighbor Frances and her swimming pool. Frances wanted a pool but could not afford the full cost herself. I, and other neighbors, wanted her to build one that we could use so that we would no longer need to drive and pay to use other pools. There are clear grounds for a mutually advantageous exchange where she would build a pool and then recoup her investment by renting it to me and her other neighbors. A little social division of labor would benefit us all!

How to execute this exchange? Unless we can overcome transactions costs, we will not be able to coordinate a flow of funds from the community to Frances to finance her swimming pool. We need mechanisms to expedite contracting, to overcome bargaining problems and to allocate risk. Frances could directly ask her neighbors to help pay for her pool, but why would anyone do so? If she promised to open the pool to all, then it would be a *public good*,[12] available to all whether they paid or not, and selfish individuals would have every incentive to encourage their neighbors to pay while they themselves had a good swim at no cost. On the other hand, to restrict access to those who paid, she would need to establish and, more important, to enforce *property rights*[13] in the pool. This would require that she track who has paid, monitor who uses the pool, compare the list of those who paid with that of those using the pool, and then exclude intruders either with her own use of force or with the help of the Amherst police. Note that by allowing *some* to use the pool, she has dramatically raised the cost of enforcement because now she needs a monitoring mechanism, perhaps with guards and print-outs, to distinguish between the paying customers and freeloaders. If she does this herself, then she will spend much of her summer guarding her pool. If she hires others to police the pool for her then she will be paying for guards, as well as paying for a bureaucracy to police the guards so that they don't let their friends in for free or sell access at a discount below what Frances charges. Enforcing property rights is cheaper if the town provides police; but, of course, then we need taxes to pay the police and we need a way to monitor and regulate the state apparatus and its potentially out-of-control police. More, what happens to the good feeling in our neighborhood when some have access to Frances's pool but others are turned away at gun point? Do the freeloaders then try to sneak in at night?

Raising money for the pool by enforcing property rights in access is expensive. It is also only a partial solution because many essential aspects of the pool remain unspecified. What happens if a neighbor's dog, or a child, wanders into Frances's yard and falls into the pool? Who is responsible for rescuing them? Who is liable for medical expenses? What about the pollution coming from her chlorinated pool? Does Frances have the property right to let chlorine gas dissipate into the neighborhood air? Does her right extend to dumping chlorinated water down the town's storm drains? What if she dumps the water in her own yard and it then makes its way to the public water supply? What about noisy pool parties; when must Frances quiet her raucous friends? After 9 PM? After midnight? Later? Should she put up a wall to protect the neighbors' tender eyes from the sight of people in skimpy bathing suits? What about skinny dipping? And who must pay for these adjustments: those who are offended by public nudity or those who would show skin?

Property rights must also be specified for Frances's neighbors. Before we will pay Frances for use of her pool we need some mechanism to enforce our claims; we need a clear statement of the pool time we can expect. What should we do, for example, if Frances reneges and decides to keep the pool to herself and her family? Before we contribute, we need a clear statement of our rights to the pool and what we can do to enforce them: when we can swim, what condition the pool will be in when we arrive and when we leave, and what constitutes fair use of the pool, such as whether we can eat in the pool area, wear suntan lotion into the water, and, most of all, bring our dog. The contract will need mechanisms for grievance adjustment, what do we do if there is a dispute between us and Frances, or between us and another rental party or an outsider. There must be mechanisms for enforcing the contract and resolving disputes about the contract's terms. But writing such contracts involves expenses well beyond those Frances anticipated when she asked us to come swimming. If she knew that she would need such a contract, she never would have asked us over; and she may not have built her pool.

Specifying property rights like this becomes even more expensive because of the ubiquitous problem of *asymmetric information*.[14] *We* know how much the pool is worth to *us*, our neighbors presumably know how much it is worth to them, and Frances knows how much it costs to build and maintain. We do not know how much the pool costs Frances, or what it is worth to her or to our other neighbors. Worse, we all know the extent of everyone's ignorance, giving us every incentive to mislead the others by understating, for example, the value of the pool to us, and for Frances to exaggerate how much it costs. Once bargaining begins, we would all try to trick each other into paying more for the pool and agreeing to let us pay less.

Again, the use of the market can lead to ill will among neighbors and generate more costs because we all pay specialists to improve our bargaining position. Hiring lawyers, surveyors, accountants and others to identify issues and to specify solutions in legal form is an expensive business. You know that you cannot trust used car dealers and that you should always have your own mechanic evaluate a car before you buy, but that mechanic is an expense added onto the cost of the used car. Society can make asymmetric information less expensive by encouraging honesty, and by clearly specifying rules and providing inexpensive means to contract, monitor, and enforce agreements. By providing standard legal forms, and police, judges and courts to enforce contracts, for example, society seeks to lower transactions costs. Dishonesty and the possibility of dishonesty raise transactions costs by leading all parties to check their contracts extra carefully. We are all much better off if we can trust each other because then we can dispense with some of the expensive legal formalities. That is one reason why people often like to do business with family members and friends.

Bargaining becomes an even larger problem when it involves an inherently risky activity, such as building a swimming pool. Because it is an expensive and long-lived asset, the pool involves inherent risks, gambles on the future. What if the pool breaks? Or what if it rains all summer and no one wants to swim? How do we allocate these risks? For example, if Frances charges her neighbors a fixed fee for the whole summer, then the neighbors bear the risk of rain, and they receive the pleasure of everyday use if the summer is hot and dry. If they pay each time they use the pool, then the enforcement costs are higher and Frances accepts more risk if it is cold and dreary and no one wants to swim. If we pay for the summer but the pump breaks, then more ill will is created because we will want Frances to have the pump fixed at once without regard to cost but she will want a less expensive, if more time-consuming, repair.

If we cannot solve the various bargaining problems, rather than take the chance of bearing all by herself the expense and risk, Frances may not build the pool. Similarly, if the costs of establishing and protecting property rights for Frances and her neighbors are too high, then she won't build the pool. Social institutions, such as the police and the courts, can encourage pool building by lowering the costs of making and enforcing contracts. (but not in this case because there is no contract/police involvement?) Common standards of honesty and reciprocity also encourage pool building because they lower the cost of bargaining and enforcement. Without these inexpensive means to establish, enforce, and exchange goods and services, there will be little social cooperation through market exchange.

Thinking about transactions costs, we can identify cases where gains from trade are realized, the social division of labor happens, because buyers and sellers work out ways to come together at relatively little expense. We can identify other cases where transactions costs remain so high that they prevent trade, and there is no exchange and no social division of labor. When I was young, for example, my sister and I traded parts of cherry pie. When she gave me her cherries in exchange for my crust, it was an exchange transaction that was easy to enforce from both sides. It was easily specified, simple to negotiate, and involved no significant risk that either party would cheat because it was completed quickly. Other transactions are more expensive to enforce, leading to great social waste. A local cooperative market (People's Market) spends great sums on its cash registers to process and enforce transactions. The result of collecting for each cup of coffee is that during prime times, the lines waiting to pay can be so long that the cost in time spent waiting exceeds the price of the commodities purchased. Rather than wait to pay, some even skip lunch or do without coffee. Others wait in line and show up late to class. At least they are fed and caffeinated.

IS THERE A POLITICS BEHIND METHODOLOGICAL INDIVIDUALISM?

How should we try to understand the economy? Where should we begin? Should we analyze economic outcomes in terms of individuals and their motivation or should we study them as the product of society and its history, of institutions separate from individuals? Is society the sum of the individuals within it, or is it something else, something independent? *Methodological individualism* looks at behavior in terms of the individuals within it, their individual drives, their interests, capacities, and their genetic dispositions. All behavior and all social outcomes are explained in terms of the wishes and drives of individuals. *Social sciences*, by contrast, study society as a product of its own history and politics. Methodological individualists begin with individual psychology and assume that social institutions are built up from individuals; social scientists begin with institutions by assuming that individual action is constrained by institutions, and individual psychology is the product of upbringing and participation in social life.

Individualism is celebrated within American society. Our founding myths celebrate great individuals (usually men) who accomplished great things by acting on their own initiative: Paul Revere riding to warn of the English, Davy Crockett opening the west, and Sam Houston freeing Texas from the Mexicans. We pride ourselves that we encourage individual diversity and respect individual choice. At times, we seem to interpret "pursuit of happiness" entirely in individual terms, as something that individuals do by themselves. This individualism carries over to American economics, where economic outcomes, wages, prices, and the mix of output are explained in terms of the wishes and talents of individual consumers and workers. This was not the approach of the discipline's founders. Adam Smith, David Ricardo, Karl Marx, and other *classical economists* studied the economy as a social system independent of the will of the individuals within it. Nor was it the approach of the first American economists, who pursued a social orientation. This was maintained in the United States by *institutional economists*,[15] including Henry Carey (1793-1879), Richard Ely (1854-1943), John R. Commons (1862-1945), Wesley Clair Mitchell (1874-1948), Thorstein Veblen (1857-1929), and by John Bates Clark's (see pp. 2, 16) own son and student, John Maurice Clark (1884-1963).

Beginning with the division of labor, classical economists and their institutionalist followers studied the economy as constituted by markets. Their studies included the cultural mores and norms, laws and state institutions that sustain markets, and the political conflicts over these mores, norms, and laws. In their view, *social institutions* direct economic activity and individual behavior without regard to the wishes or psychology of any single individual within society. The product of past political conflicts, including conflict between economic *classes* (groups of individuals who share the same property relationship to the means of production), these institutions shape the individuals so that they can functions within society.

Classical economics and its offshoot, institutional economics, are *social* sciences because they study the economy as the product of *social facts* that exist independently of individuals. As such they draw on the thinking of sociologists like Émile Durkheim. Because classical economics treats the production and distribution of wealth as determined by social institutions and political history, it did not provide a justification for any particular income distribution. Things are not inherently *fair*, and there is no assumption that we live in the "best of all possible worlds." Society is arranged only because of past politics and the political and military power of one or the other side. If the only justification for economic arrangements is that they are the product of past political conflict,

Robinson Crusoe had a community, with his man "Friday" and a larger community that built the boat that brought him to his island.

then they have no more legitimacy than the power of the ruling group can confer. If authority grew out of the barrel of a gun, then it can, legitimately, be changed when someone new holds new guns.

The rise of the socialist movement in the 1860s and 1870s, associated with classical economics through Marxism, made these political concerns particularly clear and heightened the politics of economic theory. Uncomfortable with the political implications of classical theory, *neoclassical economics* arose to provide a justification for the distribution of income and wealth that is independent of power and force. John Bates Clark (1847-1938), one of the first American neoclassicists and still one of the most famous, taught for many years at Smith College and then at Amherst College before settling at Columbia University in New York City. Clark was well aware of the political implications behind economic theory, behind the choice of an individualist or a social approach. He developed the modern neoclassical theory of income distribution as part of an explicitly anti-socialist political program, to defend capitalist social relations against Marxist and other radical challenges. In his classic paper "The Modern Appeal to Legal Forces in Economic Life," he called on economists to accept the socialists' challenge to address the basic question: "Is industry proceeding on a principle of fraud?" Challenging his colleagues, he warned that if the socialists' "theoretical point was completely established it is difficult to see how any good man could remain outside of the socialistic ranks."[16]

Clark answered the socialists with a theory of distribution where each worker and each unit of capital (whatever that is!) is paid its "marginal product," an amount equal to the change in output due to its presence in the production process. (His theory of *marginal productivity*[17] will be discussed more later.) Explicitly individualist, Clark begins his model by considering the economic problem of Robinson Crusoe, an isolated individual, living and working alone, who must decide how to allocate his labor between producing goods for immediate consumption and investing in "capital," or goods that will allow more consumption in

MARGINAL ANALYSIS

Marginal analysis has played a central role in economic theory since the late-19th century. By "marginal," economists mean a small addition or reduction in the quantity of a particular good.

At the beginning of the 19th century, David Ricardo showed how the rent of land, or other scarce input, would depend on productivity along the margin of cultivation, or the last unit of land brought into use. This idea was developed further by the American radical, Henry George.

Later economists, notably William Stanley Jevons and Francis Edgeworth, applied marginal analysis to consumption, showing the value consumers would place on a particular good reflected the utility they take from the good on the margin of consumption, or the marginal utility. John Bates Clark's great insight was to apply marginal analysis to production beyond land to show how the return to all factor inputs can depend on their marginal productivity, or the productivity of the last unit brought into production.

Ubiquitous in economic theory today, marginal analysis is fundamentally rooted in methodological individualism because it associates economic outcomes with discrete changes in individual inputs or consumer goods. Marginal analysis, therefore, is deliberately undertaken without regard for social context.

the future. Developed for an asocial individual, even a sociopath, without history and living outside any social interactions or social institutions, Clark's theory ignored the division of labor that was the basis for classical economics. By definition, his model describes production and distribution for a world without institutions or history.

It is this freedom from the division of labor and from social institutions and history that make Clark's model so powerful. Today, most economists are neoclassicists and orthodox economics in the United States is neoclassical. Following Clark, economists have abandoned the social science approach to ground their work in methodological individualism. There are some wonderful advantages to this approach. By ignoring social institutions, by grounding economics in what they assume to be *universal* motives of individuals, neoclassical economists have developed a theory that they claim can be applied universally, to different times and places. Neoclassical economists regularly apply their models to countries throughout the world, caring little and, often, knowing even less of any country's particular political situation, its history, or its social structure. Neoclassicists have been criticized for ignoring history and social institutions, but their theory is powerful and can be applied universally *because* these are irrelevant in their models. Clark's theory makes distribution the result of universal principles, forces independent of social arrangements, property rights, or politics. And, without force or power, there can be no exploitation. But Clark's theory only *appears* to be free of force or power because it is developed for an individual, isolated from any force or power. Because it is grounded in the actions of individuals, the neoclassical system suggests that we do live in the "best of all possible worlds": if economic outcomes are driven by the individual choices of rational people freely undertaken, then doesn't this conclusion seem obvious?

TABLE 4-2
ROOT ASSUMPTIONS AND EXOGENOUS FACTORS IN NEOCLASSICAL ECONOMICS

Factor	Source	Example
Individual preferences	God and genetics	Mexicans like spicy food because they have evolved to eat chili peppers.
Technology	Engineers and geniuses	The invention of the spinning jenny led to the industrial revolution and the rise of the factory.
Factor endowments	God and geography	Kenyans are better runners because they have long legs. India uses brooms to clean the streets because it has lots of people but little capital; the US uses trucks because we have more capital than people.

Instead of the inconvenient complications of social history and institutions, neoclassicists explain economic behavior in terms of only three *exogenous* factors, determined outside of the economic system: individuals' *preferences*[17] (determined at birth or by God), the available *technology*[18] associating output with inputs (determined by engineers), and the relative supply of three inputs, the different *factors of production*[19] (land, determined exogenously, as if by God; labor, determined by fertility and disease; capital, again exogenously determined and by past savings). These three factors determine all economic systems.

Note what neoclassicists omit from their list: social relations, laws, institutions, all the products of human history and past conflict. Neoclassicists can leave these out because rather than treating economic relations as being conducted between people, they treat them as *asocial*, as if they were between an *isolated person* and *things*—animals, coconuts, or other aspects of an uncooperative nature. Because Robinson Crusoe does as well as he can, subject to the constraints of a stingy nature, they assume that a society of Robinson Crusoes is also doing as well as possible, subject to that stingy nature. So long as they are voluntary, any interactions between individuals are then held to be good, increasing welfare, on the grounds that these individuals would not have agreed to them unless they were made better off. Any involuntary or compulsory social interactions are suspect. Neoclassicists

explain behavior on the basis of individual motivations, on the underlying assumption that all people seek to maximize their well-being without regard for others. They assume humans are rational maximizers, *homo economicus*,[20] seeking as much as they can for the least effort. Certainly, this is a type of behavior we might expect for individuals when dealing with inanimate nature; what other attitude would I take towards my vacuum cleaner? When dealing with problems like climbing stairs or hammering nails, it is reasonable to treat individuals as selfish and rational, maximizing their individual interests against material nature subject to the *constraints*[21] (or limits) set by the available technology and the available factors of production. Ignoring the need for rules to structure the division of labor and the impact of social norms on individual values, neoclassicists apply this same logic to all economic actions, treating all of social life as if it were nothing more than the work of a carpenter framing a house.

The neoclassical approach makes life easy for economists. There are no messy histories to be studied, no institutions to learn about. There is more than intellectual laziness here; there is also a politics. Grounding a theory in terms of individuals allows neoclassicists to treat market outcomes as presumptively good because they are the outcome of free individual choice. Social interventions, by contrast, are presumptively bad because they interfere with individual choice. This depends on neoclassicists turning their backs on Adam Smith's original insights that our sense of "sympathy" makes us social beings, and the division of labor makes us more productive as a community than we could be as individuals. Neoclassicists avoid these complications by assuming something that could never happen: an isolated individual without any society.[23] In this fantasy, Rob-

Kenyan runners at the Berlin Marathon, 2012

inson Crusoe produced canoes and hunted on his own because doing so advanced his individual interests. He did the best he could because he didn't want to waste his efforts, without regard for the welfare of the trees and stones he used. Crusoe lived without a society, unable to gain from the division of labor or by cooperating with others. Because neoclassicists ignore the gains from a division of labor that Robinson Crusoe could not join, they dismiss any benefits from society. By neoclassical assumption, communities add nothing to what individuals produce; all they do is to interfere. All social life can do is to redistribute what individuals produce.

ARE SOCIAL INSTITUTIONS ORGANIZED EFFICIENTLY?

The assumption that social institutions are efficient is hard to maintain when we consider that different societies have different institutions; not all of them can be efficient. For example, if metric is better, then why does the U.S. shun this more efficient system of weights and measures? Or if metric is worse, then why has it been adopted by all the world except the United States, Liberia, and Burma? If it is better to drive on the left, then why do countries in the Americas and on the European continent drive on the right? If it is better to drive on the right, then why do the British, India, Japan, and much of Africa still drive on the left? Is there any way to make an efficiency-based explanation of why most people use Windows-based PCs?

EFFICIENT MARKETS FOR SOCIAL INSTITUTIONS: OR WHY NEOCLASSICISTS IGNORE HISTORY, AND WHY THIS IS A MISTAKE

Most neoclassicists are not foolish. They recognize the benefits of the division of labor and appreciate that efficient social organization can raise productivity. But they insist that they can ignore history and institutions because they believe that rational individuals will always reshape these institutions to maximize output, thus negating any *independent*[24] role for history. Neoclassicists believe that social institutions have no independent economic impact because wherever they interfere with individuals' maximizing behavior they will be replaced by others that will better facilitate individuals in their welfare maximization. Once people identify *inefficient* institutions, bad laws or social mores that lower income and raise transactions costs, they will replace them with better, efficient, institutions. Social institutions thus have no independent standing. They are epiphenomena, secondary manifestations of underlying causes rooted in the drive of individuals to maximize their welfare, a drive constrained only by factor endowments and technology.

Neoclassicists assume that individuals will seek out opportunities for efficient exchange until production is allocated as efficiently as possible among producers and all possibilities for mutually beneficial exchange have been exhausted. Consider the alternative: were there opportunities for efficient exchange that were unexploited due to some institutional arrangement, then neoclassicists expect that individuals would reorganize the institutions to capture these opportunities for gain. Neoclassical economists use an old joke to illustrate this *efficient market hypothesis*,[25] or their concept of how rational behavior leads to social efficiency. Walking with an economics professor (supposedly the late George Stigler), an undergraduate bent for a $20 bill on the sidewalk, only to

Why Stay in North Dakota When You Can Move to Massachusetts?

St. Peter's Basilica. Is the Catholic Church "efficient"? Does it evolve directly with changes in the wishes of individuals? Or does it have a life of its own?

be held back by the professor who assured her that the bill is a mirage because if it were real someone else would have picked it up already.

Neoclassicists use this same logic to discount any independent impact of social institutions. Social institutions that inhibit efficient production and exchange are like $20 bills on the sidewalk: transforming them is "free money." For example, if there are poorly organized markets for donuts and large *price differentials*[26] between the same donuts in adjacent towns, then individuals would have an incentive to buy in the lower cost location to resell at higher prices elsewhere. By raising demand in the low-price area and increasing supply in the high-price location, this *arbitrage*[27] will reduce price differentials to the level of transportation costs. If some government or other social policy restricted buying and selling donuts, then the price differential, the reward to arbitrage, would give individuals an incentive to change these policies. In general, neoclassicists expect that if social institutions (such as government regulations or the allocation of property rights) inhibit productive actions or mutually advantageous exchanges, then the gains that could be made by changing these institutions will lead individuals to reform them until they no longer inhibit efficient economic production and exchange. At that point, the efficient social institutions will be those that best facilitate economic activity, as governed by the neoclassical trinity of preferences, technology, and factor endowment. Thus the efficient market hypothesis allows neoclassical economists to acknowledge and at the same time to dismiss social institutions.

Having thus dispensed with social institutions, the fundamentally conservative program of orthodox neoclassical theory becomes clear. If individuals know best what is good for them, then society can add nothing to the work of individuals except to get out of the way, and the best social policy places the fewest social restraints on individual maximization. Assuming that voluntary actions always make individuals better off, neoclassicists move to the not-necessarily-logical conclusion that a world of voluntary action will make everyone as well off as is possible given the constraints of technology, preferences, and factor endowments.

We will explore the neoclassical model in all its rigorous glory later. But we should note here how limited it is as a theory of social life. Perhaps my problem is that I *have* found $20 bills lying on the sidewalk and even at supermarket cash registers, and I believe that such bills are lying around throughout the world. To take one case in point, consider the returns to migration and let us question why everyone isn't living in Connecticut. Moving from Canada to the United States, for example, can increase one's annual income by over $3,000. (This is the difference in per capita income; the gap in earnings is higher.) This is a tidy sum but only a fraction of the really large gains to be made from migrating from a poor country to the U.S. Moving from Ireland to the United States doubles income; moving from Mexico raises income four-fold; and moving from Bangladesh to the U.S. raises income over 30-fold. International moves, of course, involve border crossings and immigration police.[28] But even within the United States, there are large gains to be made from even short moves. Among states in the United States, median family income is over 60% higher in Connecticut than in Mississippi, Louisiana, or Kentucky, and over 60% higher in Maryland than in adjacent West Virginia or in Alabama, South Carolina, or Tennessee. Why does anyone continue to live in poverty-stricken places when they can legally move? Do people forego over $9000 to remain in Idaho rather than moving to California because of the view? If so, then how to explain why so many remain poor in truly wretched locales rather than raise their incomes by moving to Minnesota, Oregon, or Massachusetts?

EXPLAINING THE EVOLUTION OF INSTITUTIONS

The persistence of large bills on the sidewalk contradicts the neoclassical assumption that we can ignore social institutions because they will always be organized and reorganized to capture any efficiency gains. This point is not incidental: the assumption that social institutions are epiphenomenonal is central to the view that individuals alone are productive and society is sterile. If institutions are seen to have an independent existence, then economists not only need to reject their methodological individualism, but rethink their political conservatism and opposition to social regulations that may be an improvement over existing *inefficient* social regulations. If society and social values have economic impacts, both productive and destructive, then these impacts should be included within the scope of economics, at least along with preferences, technology, and factor endowments. If institutions have an independent life—if they are *ontologically*[29] prior to preferences, technology, and factor endowments—then economists should study social institutions, their origins and impact. Rather than building a theory on assumptions of individual psychology, they should become social scientists and historians.

Institutionalists believe that we cannot explain individual behavior without regard to social pressures, the way existing social institutions create and constrain individuals, and the independent evolution of these institutions. In this approach, social institutions shape the underlying material of methodological individualism by constructing individuals' aspirations and preferences, by the development of technology, and accounting for the relative supplies of different productive inputs. Perhaps most important, institutions like property rights shape individual incentives.

Consider, for example, some simple observations we can all make here and now. Why do American men almost all have shorter hair than women? This is a question of obvious economic significance, especially if you own a hair styling business or sell hair products. In order to discount the role of social institutions like gender roles and the media, a neoclassical economist might say that women have longer hair because of individual preferences. Perhaps, there is a "long-hair" or a "short-hair" gene linked with the X or Y chromosome? Otherwise it may be hard to come up with an individualist explanation for gender hair lengths, but a neoclassicist must find one because, by assumption, there are no social influences prior to the individual.

TABLE 4-3
ROOT ASSUMPTIONS OF INSTITUTIONAL ECONOMICS VERSUS NEOCLASSICAL ORTHODOXY

Factor	Source	Economic Impact	Example
Individual Preferences	Acculturation, early upbringing, and supply of complements shaped by historical legacy.	Leads to demand for different products and willingness to supply labor.	People are taught to use Microsoft products in schools. If you use something else then it is harder to work with others. Therefore, Microsoft gets a higher price for its products.
Technology	Engineers develop technologies to solve economic problems posed by their employers within framework of existing technologies.	Leads to demand for different types of inputs.	Drug companies have invested much more in developing drugs to reduce waistline fat than in a vaccine for malaria. Workers in Africa are less productive because they are sick with malaria and U.S. and European businesses shun Africa to avoid malaria.
Factor Endowments	People and resources are discovered by businesses looking for inputs, and markets shaped by existing transportation and industrial systems.	Available labor supply and supply of raw materials affects prices.	Western railroads and mines looked to lower labor cost by recruiting workers from China. Chinese immigration has lowered the cost of Chinese restaurant meals.
Incentives	Legal system and property rights developed over time. Community values of honesty and mutual support.	Encourages or discourages creative work.	Capitalists have incentive to increase labor productivity because they are residual claimants on output. Producers have incentive to abuse natural assets unless they are charged for the use of air, water, etc.

Unimpressed with hair length? Consider another factor of great economic significance: we speak English but in Germany people speak German and in Japan people speak Japanese. Why? Is it because we each choose our language based on some individual assessment of the advantages to us as independent individuals? Or are there social pressures that have constrained us to speak English? This is a factor of great economic significance. Non-English speaking countries devote enormous resources to teaching their young people to speak their own language before then spending again to teach them English so that they can participate in world commerce and culture. Japanese businessmen pay large sums to American tourists (including visiting college students) to converse in vernacular American English; French or German travelers, by contrast, have few such opportunities. Because American English is understood throughout the world, American actors/actresses, musicians, movie moguls, software writers, even writers and academics, can all sell their products more cheaply and without translation. Of course this great economic boon is not due to *individual* choice; rather, it is a legacy of the British Empire, and the Anglo-American triumphs in the Napoleonic Wars, in World War I, in

THE ECONOMICS OF QWERTY

Even if individuals can be expected to act to achieve the best possible outcomes for themselves in a static sense, at any point in time, can we expect that individual action will lead to the optimal choice of technologies over time, in a dynamic sense? The persistence of the QWERTY keyboard seems to contradict any ideas of efficient institutions. Over a century ago, letters were arranged on typewriters, including the QWERTY keys along the top row, to slow typists because early, mechanical typewriter keyboards would jam if keys were pressed too quickly. Other arrangements of letters allow typists to go much faster, but have never replaced QWERTY which is favored by typists who have learned to use QWERTY boards in the past and producers who supply QWERTY boards for QWERTY-trained typists. The "network" efficiency of using QWERTY dominates the arrangement's inherent inefficiency. Once QWERTY became widely accepted, we have remained "locked in." Premature standardization on the wrong system left us with an inefficient typing keyboard, where decentralized decision making has kept us.

World War II, and in the Cold War. And before we get all smug about it, consider another legacy of our English heritage, our Imperial measurement system of inches, feet, yards and miles. Why would rational individuals ever choose to use that system rather than the relatively simple metric system?

And then there is the matter of high heels: would anyone choose this form of abuse *except* because of social influences? Would Robinson Crusoe have ever worn high heels?

Can there be a science of institutions? Can we explain the evolution of institutions as more than a process of random action, one thing after another? There are two general approaches to institutional economics: *random walk*[30] or *systematic exploitation*.[31] Paul David uses a "random walk" to explain the QWERTY arrangement of letters on the keyboard. No one in his story is trying to hurt anyone, and no one is trying to take advantage of anyone else. Instead, institutions, like QWERTY, develop to solve a particular problem. Each time they are efficient solutions to particular social or technical problems but, because they are rigid solutions to changing circumstances, society become locked into an inefficient set of institutions. We have the inefficient QWERTY keyboard arrangement on computers today because it was a way to slow typists using mechanical typewriters that before the early 20th century could not handle fast typing. Some may benefit from a particular inefficient institution, but this is secondary. The institution was developed as an efficient solution to a real problem, efficient at the time. It is an unfortunate accident, but an accident nonetheless, that a society is stuck with that old, now relatively bad, institution.

Would anyone choose to wear high heels alone on a desert island?

Others, ranging from the anti-government political right and the Marxist or radical left, have a different view of institutional development. In a "political economy" approach to institutionalism, institutions are created by people with power who then use them to exploit the rest of the community. Those on the libertarian right blame state officials, union leaders, and other leaders of social groups who use their group power to create unproductive institutions, such as minimum wage laws, to exploit others. Some have even propounded a general rule that all regulatory regimes will be "captured" by those they regulate and then used against the public.[32] Scholars on the Marxist left have a similar approach, but they blame capitalists instead of politicians and union leaders for creating exploitative institutions. Others—feminists, scholars of race or heterosexism—have different villains.

The "villain" approach has the advantage because recognizing the place of conscious social power in historical development provides a motive for historical change: the ongoing conflict between oppressors and the oppressed. Can corsets or high heels be explained in this way? Has women's fashion developed as a social institution to perpetuate male privilege? Do uncomfortable clothes leave women physically vulnerable to assault and therefore dependent on men for their safety? Long hair means that women spend hours every week on grooming, hours that men have available for other purposes, whether money making or watching SportsCenter. Why then do ambitious and talented young women continue to wear make-up and to keep their hair long? Or consider the often dangerous and definitely uncomfortable matter of high-heeled women's shoes. From the perspective of methodological individualism, the popularity of these dangerous shoes would be explained as reflecting women's individual interests in teetering and tottering; individualists might attribute this to a gene linked with X-chromosomes. Those who believe in historical accidents would argue that due to some past circumstance, women started wearing high heels, and it has since become a tradition, a gendered institution. Against both of these approaches are those who see history as an ongoing conflict between oppressors and the oppressed. They see high heels as a distinctively feminine article developed to im-

VARIETIES OF INSTITUTIONALISM

The first institutionalists were "Smithians": they argued that social institutions are economically significant because people are more productive when part of a community. The American Economic Association was founded in 1886 by **Richard Ely (1854-1943)**, a leading proponent of this type of institutionalism.

Popular through the mid-20th century, Smithian institutionalism lost favor after World War II. Dissatisfied with the narrow scope of orthodox neoclassical theory, some economists looked to found a new institutionalism with more general theoretical foundations. The economic historian and Nobel laureate Douglass North (1920-), for example, argues that social institutions are important because they determine transactions costs. Paul David sees institutions as historical accidents that, like the arrangement of letters on our keyboards, then shape the possibilities for further growth and technological progress. Mancur Olson (1932-1998) argues that institutions shape the ability of groups to exploit each other, a position that brings his views closer to those of Marxist economists like David Kotz, discussed below.

PROFESSOR R. T. ELY.

OPPORTUNITY COST

The concept of "opportunity costs" is central to neoclassical economics and to its politics. By opportunity costs, economists mean the next-best use of the resource, or the goods or services that would have been produced instead of what was produced. This is represented in the production possibilities frontier in the downward slope of the PPF. In well-behaved, perfectly competitive markets, the opportunity cost would equal the price of the output so consumers would be paying the real cost of what they consume, the products foregone to produce that commodity.

To be meaningful, opportunity costs require that all resources be utilized, or that we are producing along the PPF. Otherwise, if production used otherwise idle or badly used resources, the opportunity cost would be zero.

mobilize women and to make them dependent on men. In this approach, heels rise and fall according to the balance of power between patriarchy and the struggle for equal rights for women.

PRODUCTION POSSIBILITIES FRONTIERS AND EFFICIENCY

For neoclassical economists, the fundamental economic problem is the conflict between isolated human producers and stingy nature. Considered outside of society and the division of labor, production is a purely technical problem, a matter for engineers. Neoclassical economists visualize the world, and draw political implications by assuming that rational individuals use all available resources efficiently. Why, they ask, would an individual behave differently? Why leave resources idle? Why would anyone use them less than fully efficiently? Under this "full employment" assumption, the resources needed to produce anything new must come from those already employed productively. New production requires that something be given up. This concept of "opportunity costs" is expressed in the central tool in the neoclassical kit: the *production possibilities frontier*[33] (or PPF).

Production possibilities frontiers show the maximum output possible of one good as a function of the amount produced of the other good. A downward slope of these curves reflects a *trade-off* of one good for the other; the slope of this line reflects the opportunity cost of producing more of one or the other. Neoclassicists assume that these curves are downward sloping because output of either good can be increased only by reallocating resources, materials and labor time, away from the other good whose output then falls. By showing the maximum output possible of the different goods, the PPF shows the *trade-offs*[34] necessary to increase production of either one by reducing output of the other. Neoclassicists are fond of saying that there is no such thing as a free lunch; every increase in output comes at the price of reduced output for other goods. The real price of your lunch to the community is the goods that are not produced because productive resources are used to make your lunch. This is the *opportunity cost* of your lunch, the products or services that could have been provided had resources not been used for your lunch.

The *opportunity cost* concept comes from the downward slope of the PPF. Note that two assumptions have crept in here. First there is the technological assumption that products are *substitutes* in production, so more of one means less of the other. Second, there is the social assumption that people and economies are on the frontier. Otherwise, it is possible to increase production without foregoing output, by using otherwise idle resources.

With these assumptions, the concept of a trade-off, where something must be given up to increase production of something else, can be a useful one. There are certainly situations where output is maximized and all resources are fully and efficiently utilized. I am so busy revising this book that the only way that I could find time to write a book review that I had promised a journal would be by not revising a chapter. Or not making dinner. By assuming that societies are *always* on their PPF, neoclassical economists have used the PPF methodology to erect a dogma that nothing good could ever be done without giving up other good things. They assume that rational behavior through efficient market

Free lunch for sailors and students at the US Naval Postgraduate School Monterey, Calif. (Sept. 17, 2002) including the world's largest sandwich.

transactions will *always* ensure that society is at the PPF for the same reason that there are no $20 bills floating around. This assumption leads neoclassicists to see society as a *zero-sum game* where gains for one are matched by losses for others. This is the source of the famous saying: "there is no such thing as a free lunch." Anything benefitting one group in society must come at the expense of others.

A typical PPF is presented in Figure 4-1 showing different ways Jo and Jean can spend their evenings. They can sleep for nine hours, make love for nine hours, or do some combination in between. Points beyond the line are unattainable because there is no way to make more time. They cannot spend three hours making love *and* sleep for eight hours because they only have nine hours to use. The phrase "some combination in between" reflects the concept of a trade-off: an hour of sleep comes at the expense of an hour of sex, and sex comes at the expense of sleep. The (Newtonian) physics of the PPF are unassailable: there are only a certain fixed number of hours in a day for Jo and Jean to use. But it is the economics that are in question, because two assumptions have casually slipped into

Surveys find that happily married women sleep better. Is this because they have more sex?

the analysis. First, the interpretation of the PPF assumes that Jo and Jean use all their time efficiently so that there are no wasted hours to add to both sex and sleep time. And, second, the PPF itself assumes that sex and sleep are substitutes rather than complements.

The latter assumption is essential for the downward sloping PPF and the idea of trade-offs. The PPF in Figure 4-1 treats sex and sleep as substitutes, like the choice of whether to use cherries for pie or for preserves. But it is by no means obvious that sex and sleep are substitutes like those cherries. On the contrary, they may be *complements* and go together like apples and honey—the apple blossoms provide pollen for the bees to use in making honey, and the bees pollinate the apple blossoms so they produce apples. Good sleep may lead to better general physical conditioning and better sex, and good sex may leave people relaxed, leading to better sleep. Indeed, it may be the *lack* of sex that disturbs sleep, both because of frustration and from time spent cruising bars.

Relaxing the former assumption, that people are on their PPF, may also produce an apparent upward sloping PPF, not only for possible complements like sex and sleep but for all products. The assumption of efficiency is standard to neoclassical economists. Why, they would ask, would Jo and Jean waste time? If they enjoy sex and sleep, then why would they spend time doing other things, like quarreling and sulking? Should Jo and Jean find themselves at an inefficient point, for example by making love for one hour, sleeping for four, and fighting for four, then it is assumed that they would be rational enough to do the efficient thing, quit fighting and add to their sleeping or sex time.

Once again we are back to assuming that there are no $20 bills lying on the sidewalk because someone else should have already picked them up. *This* is the real economic assumption behind the PPF, not the physical limits of the 24-hour day. The key to the PPF and tradeoffs is the assumption that people and communities will always be on the PPF, never inside the line, because they should have already realized the easy

FIGURE 4-1
PRODUCTION POSSIBILITIES FRONTIER: SEX vs. SLEEP TRADE-OFF

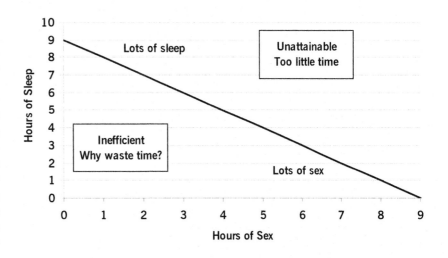

The Mercato Centrale, or old market, in Florence, Italy. It is customary to bargain before buying, usually settling on a price 50-67% what the seller initially offered. Tourists sometimes find it easier to bargain in anonymous situations like this than in dealing with car dealers and others back home.

gains of eliminating inefficiency and moving to the line. Once all the bills have been picked up and Jo and Jean have moved to the PPF, the only way to get more sleep, or more sex, is by giving up some of the other. But the real issue is whether they will be at the PPF.

I suspect that it is rare for anyone to be at the PPF and common for individuals and communities to be inside the PPF, in the realm of inefficiency. Why is this? Moving, in Figure 4-1, from the inefficient point to the frontier could allow more sex *and* more sleep, presumably allowing both Jo and Jean to get more of whatever they want. Why then would Jo and Jean miss these easy gains?

Of course, they may simply be ignorant. People make mistakes all the time that put them inside their PPF. Look at all the people who pay extra at the supermarket rather than use a Stop and Shop or Big Y card. From there, it is easy to imagine societies making mistakes. Without taking any particular political position, it is clear that either the United States or Canada is making a mistake about health care finance and the metric system; either the UK/Japan/China or the rest of the world are wrong about which side of the road to drive on; either the US or the Europeans are wrong about the most efficient electric voltage. Someone is inside the PPF.

Beyond mistakes, people are inside their PPF because social production requires cooperation and it is hard to get people, even lovers, to work together. Good sex requires communication between lovers in positions of intimacy and vulnerability. Jo and Jean may find it hard to talk about what they really want to do with their evenings, and communication problems, especially common with sex, can produce disagreements that lead to fighting about things rather than doing them. Tranactions costs, the costs of doing business using commodity markets, usually associated with establishing and enforcing property rights, may be especially important in discussions outside of markets where the parameters are less clear. We all know that communication can be particularly difficult among lovers and about delicate issues like sex. I won't ask how many of you have had serious discussions with a potential partner before having sex, but there may be a reason why high school health classes devote so much time to this matter.

Built into the PPF approach is the insidious and, once it is said, ridiculous assumption that people will work together, cooperatively, to achieve an efficient outcome. While reasonable for an individual, this is an absurd assumption where there are two or more people involved, and where changes in production technology or output mix also involve questions of status, respect, and the distribution of wages and profits. Unlike an individual, who would never forego moving to the PPF from the interior, there may be social situations where increases in efficiency will be missed because people are too busy posturing or bargaining to agree on how to divide the gain, or just too busy talking to listen to each other. Unless control rests with an unquestioned dictator, changes to move a group towards their PPF may be challenged by those whose share of output may drop with the change in practice. In these cases, political power can interfere with achieving social efficiency if those who may lose relatively can veto changes.

Even in social situations, neoclassicists view moving from the interior to the frontier as unproblematic where increases in output *can* be shared to leave everyone at least as well off as before the movement. A situation where output increases and everyone is at least as well off is called Pareto superior, after the conservative Italian sociologist Vilfredo Pareto (1848-1923). Neoclassicists focus on *Pareto-superior* changes because these allow them to avoid distributional concerns, since everyone is at least as well off as before and some are better off. While economists applaud changes that could leave everyone better off, one can easily imagine circumstances where people or groups would oppose Pareto-superior changes. Even if their total income rises, they may resent declines in their *relative income*,[36] or they may resist changes in hopes of getting a larger share of the benefits of the change. Or they may resist change out of spite or malice. Whatever the motive, one can-

Vilfredo Pareto

not assume in general that society would endorse all Pareto-superior changes. In any case, few situations are simply and clearly Pareto superior.[35] It is more common to have changes that will raise production (moving the economy closer to the PPF) but leave some worse off. Economists may favor these changes and might argue that so long as national income increases everyone *could* be made better off. But these arguments will rarely resonate with those who experience immediate losses and can only hope that the winners will be generous.

Would you leave this on the ground?

The problem with a theory that ignores power considerations is that power and control over resources affect economic behavior regardless of the wishes of economists. Of course, it was control over property rights in their slaves' humanity that allowed the British sugar planters to work their slaves extraordinarily hard (even to death) so that they could make huge profits from Caribbean sugar plantations. After emancipation, sugar production plummeted because the freemen walked away from these plantations and their deadly work routines. No deal was ever negotiated to restore production by sharing the gains from efficient sugar cultivation and harvesting.[37] Power—control over property rights in productive property—allowed British capitalists to increase productivity in their farms, textile mills, and other workplaces because they could compel workers to labor for them. Stephen Marglin and others have demonstrated that efficiency gains would not have happened except that capitalist power and control over the work process allowed them to ignore complaints from the workers involved.[38] For their part, those with power—the ability to shape economic outcomes without regard for the wishes of others—may resist income-increasing changes that threaten their income or reduce their hold on power. If we all came to agree that *socialism*[39] would raise society's income, would we really expect capitalists to endorse it?

Even people with similar interests often find it difficult to make Pareto-improving changes. Jo and Jean may fail to make the Pareto-superior changes that would move them towards the PPF line if they are unable to communicate their needs, or if each holds out for more of what they want even at the expense of sabotaging the negotiations. The potential for breakdown and inefficiency is much greater when the sides have different interests. Both Jo and Jean may dislike wasting four hours fighting, but Jo may want to use those hours for sleep while Jean wants them for sex. From a Pareto-efficiency perspective this is a relatively easy problem because gains can be split; eliminating the four hours of nightly fighting could give them the extra sleep Jo wants or the extra sex Jean wants, or some of each. But they will need to agree on the division of their social gains before they can stop fighting and both may be so committed to their side that they will be unable to reach any agreement to use those four hours more efficiently. It may be that both Jo and Jean would both see a compromise as representing a surrender of their personal autonomy, rather than an agreement that recognizes that their partner has different, conflicting, but legitimate wishes. People can get that way when they are in a vulnerable position where they desperately depend on the good will of others.

Of course there are possibilities for accommodation if both Jo and Jean are ready to compromise. But compromise *is* hard. It can be especially hard to compromise with friends and loved ones because we want them to show us that we can trust them to look out for our interests and needs. (Sometimes even without us telling them what these are.) Compromising requires that we recognize differences with people with whom we want to share values. For this reason it may be even harder than with someone with whom we have a short-term relationship, such as a rug merchant in the bazaar at Istanbul, even though (?) we have no reason to trust that person. Indeed, agreement may be harder between people in a long-term relationship because both may engage in strategic bargaining, holding out for more in order to establish that they are a tough bargainer. Once Jo and Jean are in a bargaining situation, they may both try to force the other to agree to their demands. Even if they lose this fight, by holding out they show that they are tough for future

FALLBACK POSITIONS AND BARGAINING POWER

Generally, economists assume that bargaining power in a relationship depends on one's fallback position, or the next best alternative open. Those with a better fallback position are assumed to be better able to hold out for more from any bargain.

Bargaining, however, also reflects one's emotional stake in the relationship. Those less involved, those readier to leave, are often able to dominate any negotiation with those who are more invested in the relationship without regard for their nominal fallback position.

disputes. Ironically, once they start bargaining and enter a market-type situation, they may lose any chance of reaching a Pareto-efficient compromise because they begin a game of "chicken" that will leave them both worse off. Thinking long term, they may prefer a bad outcome now if it reinforces their future bargaining position.

Once transactions costs, ignorance, distributional issues and bargaining become involved, there is no reason to expect that anyone or any society will be on the PPF. These problems can cause societies to leave many $20 bills on the street. We would not expect any society to be on the frontier because there are always groups trying to redistribute income even at the expense of reducing the total. Ironically, smaller groups may be particularly good at advancing their particular interests, even against the general good and the interests of much larger groups, because they are better able to mobilize their small constituencies against much larger groups that suffer from their actions.[40] We see this in government all the time. Subsidies paid to a handful of sugar farmers cost Americans billions. Why do we spend billions of dollars subsidizing small groups of wealthy men? Concentrated in three states (Florida, Louisiana, and Hawaii), sugar growers donate large sums to political candidates and parties. Against them, there is a much larger group of consumers who lose more than the growers gain. But they are dispersed and find it harder to mobilize to act on their interests. Their greater numbers can even be a handicap because many will wait for others to take action on their interests. Those who pay for the sugar subsidies suffer because while the benefits of the subsidy program are concentrated in a few hundred individuals, the larger aggregate losses are spread among a large number of people whose individual losses are too small to motivate action. There may be a general principle here. Even though there are very few of them, the wealthy, especially capitalists, are better at influencing government tax and spending policies than are the great mass of the working class, because it is easier to mobilize small groups of wealthy investors than to energize the larger population of workers and consumers.[41]

In general, capital is treated better than labor in society, even though there are many more workers than capitalists. The excessive power of capitalists, those who by law control access to the means of production, is clear when we consider the relative *fallback positions* of capitalists and wage workers. What do you do after you tell your partner to take his or her pajamas and go home? You are more likely to have your way in an argument with your partner if you have relatively good options if the relationship dissolves. The person who will be out on the street is in a relatively weak bargaining position because there will be a larger fall in his or her standard of living, if a bargain is not reached, than will be the case for the person who owns the apartment and has other suitors at the door. How well you can uphold your argument in a dispute depends in part on how much you will lose if there is no bargain and the relationship dissolves. Your bargaining power depends on your fallback position, or where you will be if bargaining breaks down. Between capital and labor, capital's fallback position is generally stronger because capitalists can survive longer without new income.

The legal environment has a large role to play in the balance of capital and labor. Policies of deregulation and free trade favor capital because they improve the fallback position of capitalists. Capital's relative power is enhanced by laws that allow it to relocate easily and those that allow it to ship products back to old markets from new production facilities. Capital's position is stronger and labor's weaker if there are many unemployed workers to replace currently employed workers. On the other hand, labor's bargaining position is strengthened where political institutions restrain capital mobility and trade, thus limiting capital's fallback position. Democratic governments with universal suffrage and civil liberties strengthen labor's fallback position by reducing unemployment and helping the unemployed and the poor. This gives workers a better fallback position if they lose a job or cannot find one. Note here that capital has a vested interest in weakening labor's fallback position by promoting higher rates of poverty and unemployment. In this way, they compel labor to make concessions from fear of loss of income. We will discuss this more later.

Generally, mobile groups have more power because, by definition, they have better options if bargaining fails than do less mobile interests. Within relationships, those less committed are better able to force their will on the others regarding dinner plans, movies, or whose relatives to visit for the holidays. Following the "principle of least interest," those who are least committed to a relationship can often dictate terms. It is often a sad fact that if you are ready to move on to another lover, then you may be more likely to get your way in choosing the evening's entertainment than if you are the one who is more committed to the relationship. In a similar way, capital can threaten to leave the state and the country more credibly than can labor because workers would have to leave family and friends behind to relocate. As a result, governments shift the burden of taxation from capital to labor and reorient spending priorities to appease mobile capital. In all these cases, distributional reallocation favors some over others, and it may, along the way, make everyone worse off.

MOVING THE PPF

Neoclassical microeconomists like to use the production possibilities frontier because it turns all economic questions into *trade-offs* between different goods or different interests. As we have seen, this approach collapses once we relax the assumption that groups are always on their PPF. The trade-off approach also makes the fallacious assumption that the PPF is fixed exogenously and does not move in response to social policy. The assumption that the PPF is fixed is based on the premise that the supply of productive factors is independent of the distribution of income, independent of what is produced, and that the technology of production is fixed. Both of these assumptions are questionable. Real factor supplies and technology depend on the way a community is organized. Different societies have wildly different rates of technological creativity, and factor supplies and technology are often both *endogenous* or depend on what has been produced in the past. Compare, for example, the rapid pace of economic growth under capitalism with the leaden growth rates in earlier feudal societies, or compare the technological dynamism of modern Japan with the sluggish economy of the Philippines, or the United States compared with Haiti. Clearly, a society's social institutions influence its growth rates and the position of its PPF. And look at the areas where technological progress has happened in each country: progress is most common in the industries where a country has put more resources. People and industries get better at doing what they have done.[42]

The PPF approach resembles a dictatorship where mechanical workers follow instructions from an overseer. Income increases only if there are more slaves or if the dictator figures out better instructions. By contrast, it is a fundamental premise of democratic societies that mutual respect and open communication can make us all better off by cultivating better ideas and motivating better work. One reason capitalist societies have been so much more dynamic and creative than feudal ones is that capitalism involves more people in planning the production process. All capitalists and wannabe capitalists have their eyes out for better ways to produce things and better products to make; the economic ideal of a democratic society would be to extend that creative energy to all citizens. Democratic societies progress by involving more of the population in finding better ways to do things, and democrats believe that if citizens get involved in formulating policies, the greater number of minds involved will find better solutions to problems. By showing respect for each citizen, involving people in public decisions encourages us all to treat each other better, reducing dishonesty and corruption and increasing productivity. A trustful community is constructed through public participation in decision making. This applies to workplaces as well. Within a business, for example, workers are more likely to work hard (increasing labor supply) and to work smart (improving technology), and less likely to steal, if they feel respected and if they expect a share of increased output and protection in their jobs. (We will discuss this more when we discuss *efficiency wages* later.)

Respect and open consultation can improve a community by facilitating cooperation and solving bargaining problems. Consider Jean and Jo. People who feel disrespected by others are unlikely to try to make life better for the other. On the other hand, when people find ways to talk, they may be able to have better sex that will enhance their sleep experience, thus achieving the equivalent of an increase in hours and a shift out in the PPF. The way people communicate and the way they treat each other can shift the PPF—out when the treatment is good, and in when people abuse each other.

Once we drop the assumptions that we are on a fixed PPF, then the whole idea of inherent trade-offs disappears and we can see how different institutions can shape people's values and lead to different economic outcomes. Social programs that make life better for some may be self-funding by increasing income for all; there may be free lunches out there.

APPENDIX: DRAWING PPFs

Imagine Robinson Crusoe on his desert island with five acres of usable soil. He could grow potatoes, or he could grow strawberries. Potatoes and strawberries are production substitutes. They both require the same inputs, land, labor, and water, and they contribute nothing to each other; producing more strawberries does nothing to make the potatoes grow better. The more land Crusoe devotes to potatoes, and the less to strawberries, the more potatoes he will grow but the fewer strawberries, and vice versa.

You can make a table with the quantity of potatoes and strawberries that Crusoe could grow as a function of the amount of land devoted to each crop. Assuming that each acre of will give 10 boxes of

TABLE 4-4
ROBINSON CRUSOE'S PRODUCTION POSSIBILITIES FRONTIER

Acres of potatoes	Potatoes (boxes)	Strawberries (bushels)	Acres of Strawberries
0	0	50	5
1	10	40	4
2	20	30	3
3	30	20	2
4	40	10	1
5	50	0	0

potatoes or 10 bushels of strawberries, the table would look like the following:

This table can be graphed as a production possibilities frontier.

Note that this shows the maximum production possible given his land and technology. It is impossible for Crusoe to produce at point B with more strawberries and potatoes than the line on the graph without getting more land or a better production process. It is possible for him to produce at point A, below the line, but that leaves the question: why would he choose to do so?

While it is not possible for Robinson Crusoe to produce at point B, he can reach that point if he can increase his acreage. This is what happens in Figure 4-3 where he has 100 acres instead of 50. With more land, he can produce more of both, more strawberries and more potatoes. There is still a trade-off, however: more of one comes at the cost of less of the other. And the trade-off ratio, the price of strawberries in terms of potatoes, remains the same: one bushel of strawberries is foregone for every bushel of potatoes grown, and vice versa.

Potatoes and strawberries are assumed to be production substitutes, competing for the same inputs and contributing nothing to the productivity of the other. That is why there is a trade-off between the output of each. This is not the case for many other products, products that are complements in production where producing more of one raises output of the other. Apple blossoms attract bees that produce honey, so growing more apple trees contributes to honey production. Hot water is used by Con Edison to make electricity. It also heats New York City apartment buildings so the more electricity is made, the more hot water for your grandmother's shower. Corn husks and other waste from growing corn for chips are then fed to cattle. In all of these cases of production complements, producing more of one thing can give you more of another. This would give an upward sloping PPF, like the following:

FIGURE 4-2
ROBINSON CRUSOE'S PRODUCTION POSSIBILITIES FRONTIER

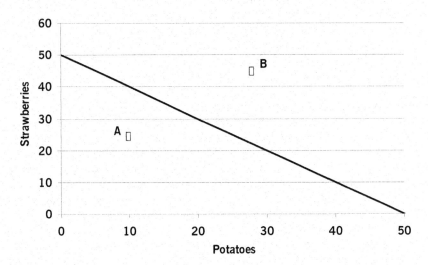

FIGURE 4-3
PPFs FOR POTATOES AND STRAWBERRIES WITH DIFFERING AMOUNTS OF LAND

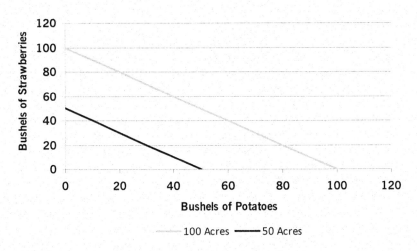

FIGURE 4-4
PRODUCTION POSSIBILITIES FRONTIER SLOPES UP FOR PRODUCTION COMPLEMENTS

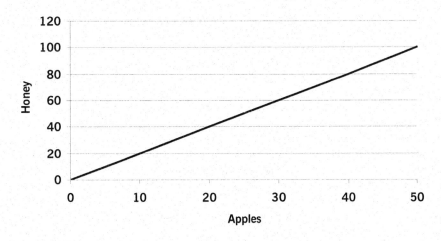

DISCUSSION QUESTIONS

What are "transactions costs"? How do they slow economic growth and lower efficiency?

What is "trust"? How does it lower transactions costs and promote economic efficiency?

What are the three root assumptions of neoclassical theory?

Do social institutions evolve to promote greater efficiency?

What is QWERTY? How does this story relate to the question of efficient social institutions?

What is the "Production possibilities frontier" (PPF)? How does it illustrate opportunity cost?

What moves the PPF? Are we always on it? What are the conditions for it to be downward sloping?

Are there free lunches?

ENDNOTES

[1]Steven D. Levitt, "An Economist Sells Bagels: A Case Study in Profit Maximization, Working Paper" (National Bureau of Economic Research, April 2006), http://www.nber.org/papers/w12152.

[2]Frank, Gilovich, and Regan (2008) report that economics students were less likely to donate money, more suspicious of others, and more likely to "defect" in a "Prisoner's Dilemma" game. They report evidence that the differences in cooperativeness are caused in part by training in economics with the gap in defection rates between economics majors and nonmajors widening as students take more courses in Economics.

[3]Humans are not the only species to engage in the division of labor. The leafcutter ants of Brazil also have an elaborate division of labor with four distinct kinds of workers: gardeners, defenders, foragers, and soldiers. With the ants, however, the division of labor is genetically determined, assuring each ant that they can rely on their fellows.

[4]A society governed by thieves.

[5]Adam Smith, *The Theory of Moral Sentiments; to Which Is Added, a Dissertation on the Origin of Languages*, New ed, Bohn's Standard Library (London, New York: G. Bell & Sons, 1892) I, I, 1.

[6]Standards and conventions governing social relations.

[7]Affective relations are maintained by emotional attachments and governed by norms rather than legal rules.

[8]Steven D. Levitt, "An Economist Sells Bagels: A Case Study in Profit Maximization," Working Paper (National Bureau of Economic Research, April 2006), http://www.nber.org/papers/w12152.

[9]An action that costs someone to the benefit of someone else, done in the hope that the person who benefits will reciprocate in the future, or that some third party will do so.

[10]Aggressive bargaining and financial maneuvering to capture every advantage possible in a market exchange.

[11]Where people act from feelings of emotional connection rather than for money.

[12]Public goods have two aspects: access cannot be restricted, they are nonexcludible; and the use by one person does not reduce the amount available for others, they are nondepletable.

[13]Property rights have many possible dimensions. In this case, she would need to establish and to enforce a property right for some of her neighbors to use the pool while continuing to exclude others.

[14]A situation where one party to a bargain has more information than do the other parties.

[15]Institutionalists dominated the American economics through the middle years of the 20th century. They were social scientists who believed that historical experience and social institutions influenced economic circumstances. Institutionalism declined precipitously in the 1950s and 1960s,

replaced by the neoclassical orthodoxy that dominates American economics today.

[16]John B. Clark, "The Modern Appeal to Legal Forces in Economic Life," *Publications of the American Economic Association* 10, no. 3 (March 1, 1895): 51–53; also see John B. Clark, "The Possibility of a Scientific Law of Wages," Publications of the American Economic Association 4, no. 1 (March 1, 1889): 39–69; John Bates Clark, *The Distribution of Wealth; a Theory of Wages, Interest and Profits* (New York, London: The Macmillan company; Macmillan & co., ltd, 1899).

[17]Marginal productivity is the extra output, productivity, that comes from adding one more unit of any particular input. The marginal productivity of labor, for example, is the extra output that comes when one more worker is hired.

[18]Preferences are people's relative valuation of different products or services.

[19]The technology refers to the ways businesses and people know to connect different levels of inputs with output.

[20]The factors of production include the supplies of land, labor, machinery, and other productive inputs.

[21]Literally, "economic man," a fictitious construct who always chooses the most efficient way to maximize his well-being without regard for relationships with other people.

[22]Constraints limit what people can produce and consume. These constraints depend on the available supply of factor inputs, the preferences held by others, and the technology of production.

[23]Obviously, no human could be born without parents. Beyond this, none could live to maturity without a community, and none could survive long without the companionship of others.

[24]The contrast is here between institutions playing an independent role, where they influence economic outcomes without regard for individual rationality, and a view where institutions are epiphenomena without independence, because rational individuals always organize and reorganize institutions to facilitate economic efficiency.

[25]This is the idea that competition and arbitrage will eliminate any opportunities for gain because rational actors will bid up the price of any asset priced below its value and will sell, driving down the price, of any overpriced asset.

[26]Price differentials refer to differences in the price of the same commodity in the same place.

[27]Arbitrage is the act of buying commodities at low prices and reselling them at a higher price in other markets. In this way, arbitrage pulls up prices in low markets and drives down inflated prices in expensive markets.

[28]And, millions of people do move across international borders, generally from poorer countries to richer ones.

[29]Ontology refers to the study of the nature/existence of things. The suggestion here is that institutions have origins independent of the will of individuals.

[30]With a random walk, institutions change in response to unpredictable and random events.

[31]If institutions are established to maintain the power of particular groups then their evolution may reflect changes in the political power of these different groups.

[32]Mancur Olson, *The Rise and Decline of Nations: Economic Growth, Stagflation, and Social Rigidities* (New Haven: Yale University Press, 1982); for a theoretical take on this issue, see James M. Buchanan and Gordon Tullock, *The Calculus of Consent: Logical Foundations of Constitutional Democracy*, The Selected Works of Gordon Tullock, v. 2 (Indianapolis: Liberty Fund, 2004); for historical, by a prominent leftist historian, see Gabriel Kolko, *Railroads and Regulation, 1877-1916* (Westport, Conn: Greenwood Press, 1976); Gabriel Kolko, *The Triumph of Conservatism; a Re-Interpretation of American History, 1900-1916* (New York: Free Press of Glencoe, 1963).

[33]A production possibilities frontier shows the maximum output possible for one good in a society as a function of the amount of another good. This frontier is downward sloping because resources are taken from the production of one good to increase output of any other and it is assumed that goods are not complements in production. If they are complements, then increasing output of one would raise production of the other.

[34]Tradeoffs are required when we need to reduce production of one good to free resources to increase output of another.

[35]A reallocation is Pareto-superior if it improves the position of someone without reducing the

welfare of anyone.

[36]Relative income refers to one person's income compared to another person's. Absolute income refers to one's income without regard for anyone else's.

[37]Seymour Drescher, *The Mighty Experiment: Free Labor vs. Slavery in British Emancipation* (New York: Oxford University Press, 2002); Seymour Drescher, *From Slavery to Freedom: Comparative Studies in the Rise and Fall of Atlantic Slavery* (New York: New York University Press, 1999).

[38]Stephen Marglin, "What Do Bosses Do? The Origins and Functions of Hierarchy in Capitalist Production.," *Review of Radical Political Economics* 6, no. 2 (n.d.): 60–112.

[39]Socialism is an economic organization where resources and power are allocated in a more egalitarian way.

[40]This is the public policy point made by Mancur Olson in *The Rise and Decline of Nations*.

[41]David Johnston, *Perfectly Legal: The Covert Campaign to Rig Our Tax System to Benefit the Super Rich—and Cheat Everybody Else* (New York: Portfolio, 2003); Jacob S. Hacker and Paul Pierson, *Winner-Take-All Politics: How Washington Made the Rich Richer—and Turned Its Back on the Middle Class* (New York: Simon & Schuster, 2010).

[42]This process, called learning by doing, will be discussed more later.

5

ECONOMICS, WELL-BEING, AND THE LIMITS OF MARKETS

Pastries and chocolates at Pierre Hermé (Paris). Near Saint-Sulpice in the 6th Arrondissement, this is the best pâtisserie in Paris.

"Money cannot buy happiness. But chocolate is something else entirely." — Rosa

PARADOXES OF WEALTH

We study the economy because we believe that income effects individuals' *utility*,[1] or their well-being. Of course, we all know that money cannot buy happiness, but we assume that it can increase peoples' happiness by allowing them to consume things that make them happier. It may be reasonable to assume that giving *individuals* more will make them happier. Robinson Crusoe would be happier if he had more things: more food, more warmth in winter, more lights at night, more clothes, maybe a car with a GPS system. From this many economists think it reasonable to assume that more things will make all of us happier. If a car and a CD player make us happy, then shouldn't we be ecstatic if we had two, three, or ten? Indeed, the wealthy are happier than the poor *within* countries: Americans with two cars are happier than those with one, but not as happy as those with three.

By this logic, contemporary Americans should be euphoric. Over the past two centuries, Americans have attained affluence never before imagined. Since 1790, *income per capita* has grown by nearly 1.7% per year to a level over 20 times that of 1820; in my lifetime, since 1955, per capita income has almost

FIGURE 5-1
HAPPINESS AND INCOME, UNITED STATES, 1972-2006

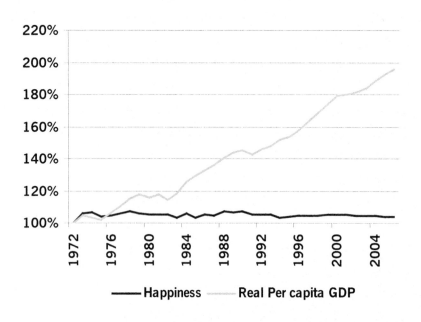

tripled. At the same time, leisure time has increased because the standard work week has fallen, more retire at younger ages, and young people begin their work lives at older ages. Americans in 2014 consume items previously unavailable, including cell phones, jet travel, high-definition television, Spotify, and Net-flix. Consider the luxuries that are now standard in American households of vir-tually all income levels: frozen ice cream, winter vegetables, fresh fruit year-round. Over 98% of Americans live in a house with a color television (63% have cable), 89% own a VCR, 92% own a car, and 62% own two or more cars. As late as 1970, fewer than 25% of households had frost-free refrigerators and only 34% had central heating and air condi-tioning; those proportions have grown to nearly 90% today. One measure of our prosperity is the low proportion of Americans' income spent on food. One hundred years ago, Americans spent nearly half their income on food with less than half available for clothing, housing, medical care, and leisure activities. Today, American spend less than 10% of their income on food; we have over 90% of our income available for other consumption goods.

Rising consumption levels have also been associated with measurable welfare improvements in the United States. Male life expectancy at age 10 (the *additional* number of years of life expected, after reaching age 10) has risen from around 50 years in the early 1800s to 72 years today. Girls do even bet-ter: a girl today can expect one day to extinguish 86 candles at a birthday party, 20 more than her 19th-century great-grandmother ever saw.[2] Most of us are better off in ways that seem universal and beyond question. Americans today are healthy until the very end of their long lives, we are several inches taller than our colonial ancestors, we retain more of our teeth into old age, more of us are literate, relatively few of us go to bed hungry, and few experience the death of a child.

If we work less, eat better, and consume more stuff, what is there not to like? Yet all this consump-tion has bought surprisingly little happiness, maybe even none at all. Evaluating survey evidence, over 40 years ago, economist Richard Easterlin found little or no association between happiness and per capita national income except in the poorest countries. Since then, much economic research on the "Easterlin Paradox" has confirmed his 1974 finding. Within the United States, for example, income has almost tripled since 1950 but the proportion of Americans who say they are "very happy" has fallen from 35% in 1957 to 32% in 1993; from 1972 to 2006, per capita income doubled without moving the average level of happiness (see Figure 5-1).[3] Yes, within countries, higher income people are happier; but, as Easterlin found, comparing *different* countries or comparing countries *over time*, higher income is associated with greater happiness only up to about $25,000 in income (in US dollars), a level reached by the United States over 40 years ago. Increases in income above that level have little or no impact on happiness subjectively perceived. Reviewing the evidence on happiness and income across different countries (see Figure 5-2), the British economist Richard Layard seconded Easterlin: "despite massive increases in purchasing power, people in the West are no happier than they were fifty years ago."[4]

It is easy to understand why more wealth would lead to greater happiness. Wealth buys freedom from hunger, clean water, sanitation, and childhood immunization that reduces the danger that your children will be sick or will die. Certainly, the *lack* of wealth will reduce happiness, by leaving you and your loved ones cold, hungry, and lacking in decent sanitation and dental care. Beyond these ba-sics, however, the relationship between material wealth and well-being is less clear. Indeed, beyond an income sufficient for basic nutrition and sanitation, there is little physical gain from additional income. Instead, as countries' income grows beyond about $6,000 per person, additional income is increasingly used to satisfy socially generated rather than intrinsic material needs. For example, countries with a per capita income of about $20,000, half that of the United States, have a life expectancy comparable to those of the level of the United States and Europe.[5] Beyond that level, there is little relation between income and life expectancy. Indeed, the World Health Organization reports that life expectancy is now lower in the United States (at 78) than in 30 other countries including some, like Greece, Ireland, and Italy, with *much* lower incomes. Some

FIGURE 5-2
LIFE SATISFACTION AND PER CAPITA INCOME, UNITED NATIONS

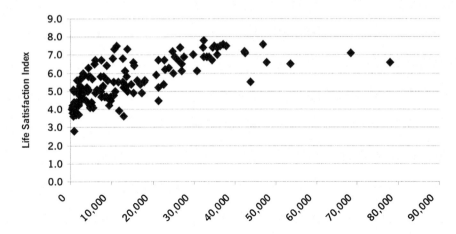

Americans do even worse. Life expectancy for African Americans is barely above the level of people in China, and it is less than in poorer countries like Costa Rica or in parts of India. In general, it appears that a per capita income of $6,000–10,000 is enough to assure intrinsic needs for food and shelter. Further increases in income give us goods that we want for various social reasons but do not need, and, it seems, do little to make us happier.

Economists who think about the economy and society as a collection of Robinson Crusoes, and the economy as involving relations of people to things, cannot understand the rising-income/stagnant-happiness paradox. They expect that higher incomes should lead to greater satisfaction. More consumption must make people happier because, at worst, people can simply choose not to consume, leaving them no worse off than before. The problem with this approach is that it ignores the way greater wealth affects our relationships with others.[6] Once we are beyond satisfying basic material needs, happiness becomes a matter of our relationships with other people, and material goods do not necessarily enhance these. On the contrary, more material goods may detract from our social life. Once we have enough food and warmth to satisfy our intrinsic physiological needs, affluence can bring costs due to pollution, crowding, and other externalities. And accumulating things may do nothing to address the real source of happiness, which comes from our social relations with others.

THE SOCIAL CREATION OF NEED

Once we have satisfied our basic material needs, the real sources of our happiness are our relationships with others. For 900 Texas women, none of the four activities that brought them the most happiness (sex, socializing, relaxing, and prayer) benefited from rising income (see Table 5-1). At least two of these highly-valued activities are necessarily social and need the in-

FIGURE 5-3
ABRAHAM MASLOW'S HIERARCHY OF NEEDS

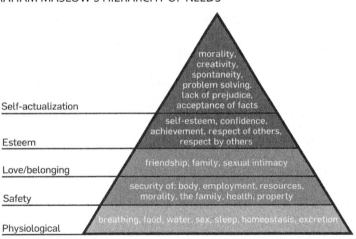

TABLE 5-1
HAPPINESS AND ACTIVITY, 900 TEXAS WOMEN

Activity	Average Happiness
Sex	4.7
Socializing	4.0
Relaxing	3.9
Prayer	3.8
Eating	3.8
Exercising	3.8
Watching TV	3.6
Shopping	3.2
Preparing food	3.2
Talking on the phone	3.1
Caring for children	3.0
Computer/internet	3.0
Housework	3.0
Working	2.7
Commuting	2.6

volvement of others; Robinson Crusoe could not have sex or socialize with another person. The paradox of wealth goes further: increasing income was associated with more time spent at one of the least popular activities, working, and on two associated unpopular activities, commuting and housework. Here lies the problem: while owning stuff can enhance our relationships, it can also detract by pulling us away from the social activities that are the true source of happiness. For every class of needs, wealth can enhance our life experience, or make it more difficult. The paradox of rising income/stagnant happiness arises because most of the ways income affects social relationships have negative as well as positive implications.

The problem with reasoning from individual preferences is that most of our needs in a modern, affluent society are socially generated. They are things that we need to belong to our community and to participate in modern life. While physiological needs are fixed, our social needs, including the ways that we meet our physiological needs, evolve to reflect the capacity of the society. Our standards of acceptable living conditions have changed to include indoor plumbing with regular showers, winter fruits and vegetables, and an extensive wardrobe. Growing wealth may satisfy these and our need for safety and security, but at a price. Our growing wealth of stuff demands our time and resources both to use the stuff, such as to listen to our iPod, and to maintain and protect it, including the time spent downloading software updates. This time and energy devoted to the things comes out of the time and energy we have for our human relationships.

WHAT DO WE NEED?

What are our "needs"? A physiological definition, in terms of proteins and vitamins, would clearly be inadequate because even subsistence depends on more than mere caloric balance. We are social beings who need social connections even to maintain our physical well-being. Neglected children in orphanages do not grow and even die without any shortage of calories or nutrition.

Properly understood, needs are a social product reflecting not only the physical and chemical requirements of survival but our need to live as members of a community. For American college students, this includes an iPod, cell phone, and a Facebook account because without these it is hard to remain connected with peers. Note that these requirements for connection will vary in different societies.

Needed for modern American life?

POSITIONAL GOODS

There is worse still. When we view happiness through the lens of our social relations, we see that much of the pleasure we get from wealth derives from the message our wealth sends to our family, friends, and neighbors. We may get intrinsic pleasure from many of our possessions, but for many, this pleasure is enhanced from knowing that our neighbors are envious of what we have. Sometimes, our greatest pleasure comes from having *more* than our neighbors, a feeling that enhances our self-esteem and our social status, albeit at their expense. Many of the things we buy are *positional goods*,[7] consumed less for their intrinsic pleasure than because they elevate our standing, our local rank or status in the eyes of our neighbors.

Experiments have consistently found that people choose a lower income that is greater than that of others rather than a higher income that is lower than that of others. A recent Swedish survey found 75% of survey participants would prefer a situation where they earned 6% less if their income would be higher than that of their neighbors rather than earn more money but less than their neighbors. Two-thirds of participants would prefer a cheaper car so long as it was more expensive than their neighbors. On the other hand, leisure does not appear to be positional. A majority of respondents would prefer more leisure time even if others would have still more leisure.

We can, of course, enjoy things both for their intrinsic pleasure and for the feeling of superiority we feel owning them. I am sure that it would be fun to drive a Lexus, for example, because of the material comfort and convenience. Heated leather seats would be nice on a morning with temperatures in single digits. This pleasure only compounds that joy that I would get from the message that my Lexus would send to my neighbors: that I am successful, valued by my customers and my employer, and worthy of envy. By contrast, riding my ancient bicycle is not only uncomfortable but involves a loss of status as well. It tells my neighbors that I cannot afford gas and parking for my ancient Dodge Caravan.

While comfort and convenience can increase for everyone when we become more productive and wealthier, status is a *zero-sum game*[8] where *aggregate happiness*,[9] the sum of the happiness felt by all the individuals, does not rise with higher incomes. On the contrary, the more people value material goods and evaluate status on the basis of owning goods, the more status becomes a zero-sum game with many losers for every single winner.[10] When

ADAM SMITH UNDERSTOOD THAT NEEDS ARE SOCIALLY GENERATED

"By necessaries I understand, not only the commodities which are indispensably necessary for the support of life, but whatever the custom of the country renders it indecent for creditable people, even of the lowest order, to be without. A linen shirt, for example, is, strictly speaking, not a necessary of life. The Greeks and Romans lived, I suppose, very comfortably, though they had no linen. But in the present times, through the greater part of Europe, a creditable day-labourer would be ashamed to appear in public without a linen shirt, the want of which would be supposed to denote that disgraceful degree of poverty, which, it is presumed, nobody can well fall into without extreme bad conduct. Custom, in the same manner, has rendered leather shoes a necessary of life in England. The poorest creditable person, of either sex, would be ashamed to appear in public without them. In Scotland, custom has rendered them a necessary of life to the lowest order of men; but not to the same order of women, who may, without any discredit, walk about barefooted. In France, they are necessaries neither to men nor to women; the lowest rank of both sexes appearing there publicly, without any discredit, sometimes in wooden shoes, and sometimes barefooted. Under necessaries, therefore, I comprehend, not only those things which nature, but those things which the established rules of decency have rendered necessary to the lowest rank of people."

TABLE 5-2
WEALTH, HAPPINESS, AND UNHAPPINESS: EXAMPLES USING MASLOW'S HIERARCHY OF NEEDS

Source of happiness	Example of promoting happiness	Example of detracting from happiness
Physiological needs	Satisfy hunger, thirst, and keep us cool in summer and warm in winter.	Rising expectations of what constitutes adequate food and shelter.
Safety	Can afford locks and security systems.	Have more stuff to guard, more things to worry about.
Forms connections, sense of belonging and love.	Facebook and social networking sites. Email and cell phones.	Time spend dealing with material goods, e.g. downloading software updates, instead of with people
Self-image, status, social recognition.	My neighbor's sit-down mower makes him feel successful.	Status becomes a zero-sum game: Your Lexus makes me feel like a failure with my Caravan
Self-realization	Better computers allow me to concentrate on my ideas rather than worry about formatting, spelling, or computation. I have money and can hire a nanny to free my time for writing.	Standards for formatting have risen, interfering with creativity. My nanny leaves her own children to care for mine

JOHN STUART MILL ON POSITIONAL GOODS:

"A great portion of the expenses of the higher and middle classes in most countries, and the greatest in this, is not incurred for the sake of the pleasure afforded by the things on which the money is spent, but from regard to opinion, and an idea that certain expenses are expected from them, as an appendage of station"

I acquire something of high status, any increase in *my* position is balanced by an equivalent loss in *my neighbor's* because he can no longer claim to be first. When you get a raise and buy a Lexus, you feel happy because of the added comfort and because of the increase it gives to your social standing. But your Lexus has now lowered *everyone else's* relative status. My Caravan was good enough until my neighbor got a BMW, and now your Lexus makes us both feel inadequate. In ancient times, even affluent suburban high school seniors walked, bicycled, or took the bus to school; no one had a car of their own to use. When the first seniors started driving to school, it marked an increase in their comfort level and a huge boost in their social status. Now, consider the position of those poor seniors who ride the school bus! They are *worse off* because other people's incomes have risen, because others are *better off.* But they are not alone. It is not enough to drive to school, to gain status you need to drive a *good* car. And when the norm becomes a Lexus, those who drive to school in Toyota Corollas, or in their mom's Caravans, lost status.

This is not to deny that a higher income, having a Lexus or a Rolls Royce, will make you happier; Robinson Crusoe would have really enjoyed the air conditioning, not to mention a good music player. (Of course, he would have had trouble maintaining it without access to spare parts and trained mechanics, not to mention the trouble driving without paved roads or gasoline.) He also would have missed the pleasure of demonstrating his success to his neighbors. Much of the pleasure of a higher income, and even a Lexus, is *social*, and comes from having more income than others. If *everyone's* income rises, if the *reference* or your *target income*[11] rises, then you benefit little from the increasing affluence. An international study of income and happiness over the last 40 years finds that "income matters a great deal" and is the main factor raising happiness over time in the United States. But, much of the happiness gain for Americans from income has been negated by rising income expectations due to our neighbor's growing income.

It is said that a man feels rich if he earns a dollar more than his sister's husband. If this one-to-one competition was all, then we could at least be assured that one person would be happy (because he earns more) to balance a person who is sad (and earns less). Alas, status is probably more nefarious and it is possible for everyone to feel worse because of the rising level of status competition. We can all suffer from living in a status-driven environment because even when you earn a dollar more than other people, you worry about being supplanted if they earn more still.[12] If you take your Rolls to school, you wonder what others will do next: a helicopter? When our sense of well-being and personal status is associated with our personal characteristics or even with the comfort we derive from consumption, then we are insu-

FIGURE 5-4
EFFECTS OF RISING INCOME ON HAPPINESS

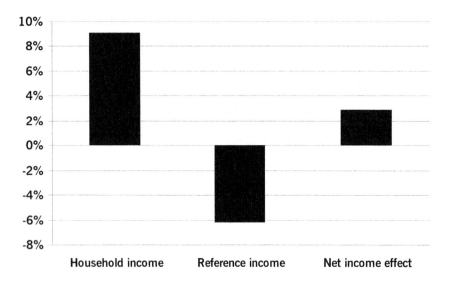

Note: This figure gives estimates of the determinants of changing levels of reported happiness for the United States, 1975-2002. By itself, for example, rising household income would have increased the average level of happiness by nearly 10% but, at the same time, our happiness fell by over 6% because increases in the income of neighbors made Americans feel poorer!

Source: Bartolini, Bilancini, Pugno, "Did the Decline in Social Capital Depress Americans' Happiness?" Working Paper 540, University of Siena, August 2008.

A Rolls Royce and a Schwinn: which would you take to school?

lated from loss from the actions of others. To the degree that our increasing income is being spent on buying positional and status goods, it can be associated with rising status anxiety for everyone and declining net *welfare*[13] even for those at the top.

To be sure, it does not have to be this way. Instead of a single hierarchy where everyone is ranked according to their consumption of a uniform type of product, we could have a community that appreciated the diversity that each brings by consuming distinct goods. We could disarm the arms race by rewarding individuality: valuing my bicycle because it is good exercise and good for the Earth, your Lexus because it is a sign of affluence and a style of comfort, and the Caravan driven by someone else because it is good for car pooling and carrying trees. By reducing status consumption, a community that rewards individuality makes consumption a matter of satisfying physical needs.

At least we can make more Lexus automobiles so that more people can enjoy a comfortable ride. Cars are *reproducible* goods; when society gets wealthier, more can be produced so that more people can enjoy them. But there are other positional goods that are *nonreproducible*,[14] such as houses on Nantucket or original Cézannes. The supply of some goods is fixed, including works of art, particular locations, documents with Napoleon's signature, or original manuscripts of Mozart's violin concertos. When incomes rise, more money can be spent on these goods because more affluent people will want the joy and status that comes from them. Because there is no increase in supply, the market price will rise to balance greater spending with fixed supply. All that happens when incomes rise is higher prices and more frustration and anger among people disappointed that despite their economic success and rising income they *still* cannot own an original impressionist or spend the summer at the beach. Rising productivity and increasing national income cannot produce more paintings by Van Gogh, more space on the Mount Mansfield ski trails, more beachfront homes on Nantucket Island, or more seats at Paris's finest restaurants. Rising incomes only feed more disappointment that we still cannot afford to hang a Picasso in our living room.

The problem of positional goods goes beyond luxury houses and unique art works. Growing affluence places a premium on *time* because that becomes the ultimate constraint on our ability to consume. A great privilege of the rich is that they can "buy" free time by avoiding time-wasting activities and queues that afflict the rest of us. These privileges are nonreproducible; only one person can be at the head of the line and only one car can have the best parking space. Worse, like some other nonreproducible goods, the demand for these time-saving privileges grows with affluence, both because people are wealthier and because physical congestion grows when peo-

---

THE LIMITS OF WEALTH: POSITIONAL GOODS AND ZERO-SUM GAMES

Goods that we enjoy because they give us recognition and status are often zero-sum games where any gains for one person are balanced by losses for others, whose relative status falls when mine rises. Worse, status can become a negative-sum game if many people suffer a loss in position when I move up.

THE LIMITS OF WEALTH: CARING FOR OUR STUFF

Owning things can become a time sink: requiring time for a range of activities from cleaning the house to picking up the dry cleaning or watching the computer go through a software update. Americans are much wealthier than in the past but report sleeping less and having less time for recreation and exercise. A 2002 survey found 68% of American adults get less than 8 hours of sleep per night; many report feeling drowsy during the day; and almost 75% of mothers in the labor force report that they do not feel rested and ready for a new week "on Sunday nights, after doing household chores and running errands on weekends,"

MEASURING WELL-BEING
GDP AND ITS ALTERNATIVES

Economist Simon Kuznets won the Nobel Prize for developing national economic output measures, including Gross Domestic Product (GDP). He was well aware, however, of GDP's shortcomings as a measure of well-being. Kuznets acknowledged that GDP ignores the distribution of income; fails to include some outputs, such as home production; counts some outputs of dubious value, such as military spending; and takes no account of some valuable inputs to well-being, such as leisure. Nor does GDP measure an economy's sustainability: the exploitation of natural resources is often counted as a positive, rather than as a negative (depletion of our finite resources).

In 1972, Yale economists William Nordhaus and James Tobin proposed a new Measure of Economic Welfare (MEW) as an alternative. It discounted spending on "wasteful" activities like the military, while attaching values to leisure, home production, and the "free" inputs of the environment. Perhaps they did not weigh these other factors strongly enough, as their measure ended up highly correlated with Net National Product (GDP minus depreciation). Nonetheless, their work did inspire later attempts to revise national income accounting, including the UN's Human Development Index (HDI), the Genuine Progress Indicator (GPI), and the Happy Planet Index (HPI).

The charts below show that while GDP is a weak measure of well-being, and only weakly correlated with direct measures, there is no single clear substitute. Three of the alternative measures that have been developed value diverse economic activities differently, so they have very different associations with GDP, and with each other.

FIGURE 1
PER CAPITA GDP AND SUBJECTIVE WELL-BEING, 151 COUNTRIES

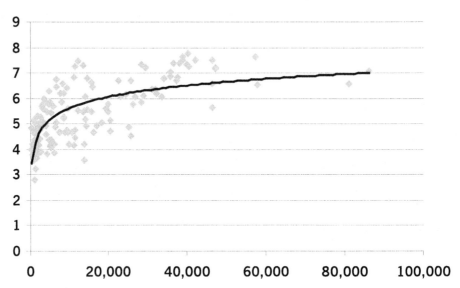

GDP is not a good proxy for "subjective well-being" (happiness). While surveys show that the rich are happier than the poor within countries, affluent countries (in terms of GDP) are not necessarily much happier than poorer countries. Nor do countries grow continually happier as they get richer. There is a dramatic increase in reported well-being with growing per capita GDP up to about $10,000—the level of Costa Rica—with little increase in happiness with per capita GDP growth beyond that point.

FIGURE 2

GENUINE PROGRESS INDICATOR AND PER CAPITA GDP, UNITED STATES, 1950-2004

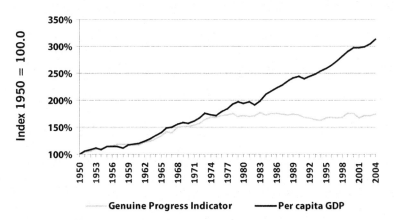

The Genuine Progress Indicator (GPI) closely paralleled GDP in the United States into the 1970s. Since then, however, the measures have diverged dramatically, with continued growth in the GDP leading to almost no increase in the GPI. Much of the discrepancy between these measures comes from the weight that the GPI puts on income distribution. The large increases in the incomes of the rich since 1975 have little weight in the GPI.

FIGURE 3

HUMAN DEVELOPMENT INDEX AND PER CAPITA GNI*, 187 COUNTRIES

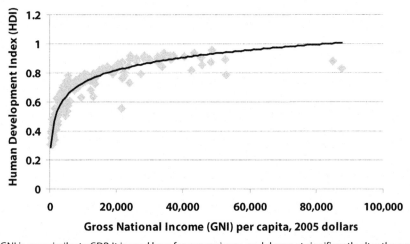

*GNI is very similar to GDP. It is used here for convenience, and does not significantly alter the graph.

The Human Development Index (HDI) includes direct measures of welfare, such as life expectancy and education, as well as per-capita income. Because HDI does not include any measure of environmental sustainability, and does include income, there is a strong (though not straight-line) association between the HDI and per-capita GDP. Like happiness, HDI increases quickly as GDP rises from a very low level, but much more slowly over higher ranges of GDP.

Sources: S. Abdallah, *et al.*, *The Happy Planet Index: 2012 Report.*, New Economics Foundation (London); United Nations Development Programme (UNDP), *Human Development Report 2013*; John Talberth, *et al.*, *The Genuine Progress Indicator 2006*, Redefining Progress.

DISAPPOINTED WITH THE WEAK ASSOCIATION BETWEEN ECONOMIC GROWTH AND WELFARE, SOME HAVE PROPOSED NEW MEASURES

Since the 1930s, governments have calculated the Gross Domestic Product (or GDP) as the sum of all market transactions in a country. Dividing this by the population gives per capita income, or the average value of market transactions per person. Increasing GDP has become a major goal of economic policy throughout the world.

GDP has provided a convenient measure of welfare because it includes commodities that people value. Others point out that GDP includes many economic "bads," such as military expenditures and expenditures repairing damages caused by crime or natural disasters. It also neglects many economic "goods," such as home production, the value of leisure, and love. And it ignores distribution, treating a dollar of output as the same regardless of who gets it.

Some have proposed new economic measures. The United Nations, for example, uses a Human Development Index as a weighted average of per capita income, life expectancy, and measures of education. France sponsored a new Commission on the Measurement of Economic Performance and Social Progress charged with examining "the limitations of GDP as a measure of economic performance and well-being." This commission, which included Nobel Laureates Kenneth Arrow, Joseph Stiglitz, Amartya Sen, as well as Nancy Folbre of the University of Massachusetts, suggested a variety of measures to improve the measurement of welfare including the use of other indicators in addition to GDP, empirical measures of health and education services, measurements of household and other nonmarket production, and adding information on income distribution.

So far, this debate has not addressed issues raised by the social context of consumption.

ple have more material goods. Consider, for example, an American suburban high school. In the 1960s and 1970s, the limited number of available parking spaces and drop-off sites was quite adequate because only the very wealthiest students drove to school and parents rarely dropped kids off. Most students, even seniors, took the bus. Affluence has changed this. With economic growth, more students can afford to drive to school, and more parents are pressured to drive their children or to give them cars so that they do not have to ride the bus with the under-classes. This reduces the welfare of parents. It also reduces the welfare of everyone attending school because of increased congestion. More, the value of a good parking space rises because we cannot decrease the number of parked cars or increase that of good parking spaces. Instead, we get more disappointment and frustration.

COMMUNITY

Here we have another reason for stagnant happiness among affluent nations: the more stuff we have, the more we crowd each other both physically and temporally. We live in an increasingly crowded world that filled with material possessions demanding our attention. Consider, for example, the position of the first student to drive to Amherst Regional High School: arising 5 minutes before the school day begins, she jumped in her car and drove along the quiet streets of downtown Amherst to park across from the entrance. Compare this with the experience of high school students today who climb into their cars to jockey through appalling traffic, competing with each other for limited parking and almost as limited space on the roads themselves. How much time do they save from having cars? Or, to put it another way, how much more benefit would they get if their peers did not have cars?

The point is that the pleasure we take from our consumption depends on what others are doing. In this respect, positional goods are one aspect of a general crisis of time in affluent economies where time-dependent services are becoming more and more expensive relative to material goods. Higher income often buys little happiness because of the *Baumol Effect*, named after the American economist William Baumol. Baumol observed that over time the relative costs of providing services has risen because services are

Iraqi men drinking tea while the world passes. Because of low labor productivity and wages, sitting around and socializing is a more accessible form of entertainment in poor than in rich countries.

bound to the one resource that does not increase with afflu-ence: time. Labeling this the *cost disease*[15] of the service sector, Baumol warns that services become steadily more expensive as a society grows wealthier because they are valued for pro-viding time, the ultimate nonreproducible good. In material handling industries, such as agriculture and manufacturing, technological progress and rising capital investments raise *labor productivity*,[16] allowing workers to process more materi-als in any time period. This is the source of income growth over time. When productivity rises in these industries, mate-rial goods become cheaper.

Services, by definition, cannot become more productive because the value of the service is the time devoted to per-forming it. Compared with goods, therefore, services become more expensive when society becomes wealthier. Nothing can be done about this problem because the rising cost of the services comes from improvements in productivity in other areas. It is not that services are produced badly but that it has been possible to make commodities faster but the only way to increase productivity in services is to reduce the time spent, and this is often the value of the service. It is a good thing to produce a car using half as much labor, but we complain when health care, live music, or teaching become more expensive, because cars are cheaper. Still, no one would feel happy to hear Chopin's Minute Waltz played in 30 seconds or substituting a five-minute appointment with the doctor for a fifteen-minute meeting.

The Baumol Effect holds in the United States, where over the last decades of the 20th century, the price of material commodities rose by under 3% a year but services rose twice as fast (see Figure 5-5. The Baumol effect has contributed to the crisis in the public sector in advanced capitalist economies such as the United States. Public services, including schooling and health care, are particularly time intensive and even providing the same amount of them has become increasingly expensive relative to material-intensive goods and services. When personal care, medical attention, and education become more ex-pensive, people naturally feel disappointed because they thought they could get more of them when

they became wealthier, only to find that they are still unable to afford them be-cause of rising prices. What, they may ask, is the value of working hard and earning a high income if the cost of the stuff (services) you buy goes up just as fast or faster? Sometimes, people learn to economize on labor-inten-sive activities. In poor coun-tries, men go to the barber for a luxurious shave; even affluent American men, however, shave themselves. The problem with some ac-tivities, especially social ones but also some private hobbies, like fishing, is that they require a lot of time just when Americans have more

WHY DOES SCHOOL COST SO MUCH?

The cost of educating young Americans has been rising twice as fast as prices in general. This has put strains on family budgets, and on the budgets of cities, towns, and states where taxes have to be increased to cover the rising costs of services. To some degree, ris-ing costs reflect improvements in quality. American schools provide more services to their students than they did 30 years ago, includ-ing, for example, more opportunities for women to participate in or-ganized sports, and they are much more open to the disabled. Rising costs for schooling as well as for other services, including medi-cal care, reflect the cost of hiring workers at salaries competitive with those paid in occupations experiencing productivity increases. Because there are no productivity increases in these service occupa-tions, relative prices must increase at the rate of productivity growth elsewhere to provide competitive wages.

FIGURE 5-5
RISING RELATIVE PRICES FOR SERVICES RELATIVE TO PHYSICAL COMMODITIES, UNITED STATES, 1999-2013

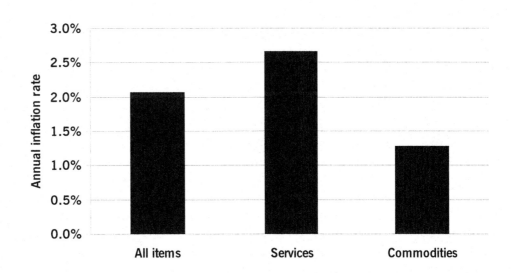

SUBSTITUTING THINGS FOR TIME?
OR, DOES AFFLUENCE NECESSARILY MAKE US UNHAPPY?

The cheaper goods become relative to our time, the stronger the temptation to economize on time by substituting things. We save time by using machinery, like a dishwasher, to clean, and a car to get us places faster than we can walk or bicycle. But there is no way to substitute for social time, time spent with friends and lovers, because the value of the interaction is measured by the time we put into it. If our happiness depends on our connections with others, therefore, then affluence can become a threat by pulling us away from relationships.

Are these women socializing with each other while one talks on the phone?

and more time-hogging material possessions. Instead of fishing, we use our time to download software updates, or to reprogram our clocks after a power outage, or to clean our ever-expanding houses.[17]

Residents of affluent economies buy more toys than those in poorer countries, including more video games, computers, stereos, and larger houses. But their doctors rarely make house calls, few can afford a leisurely dinner, and to not miss out on playing with their new material toys, people in affluent countries sleep less and have less sex. (They have less frequent sex and quicker sex. The average American, 18-55, who is involved in a serious relationship with another person reports spending only half an hour a week in sexual relations. This is the *average*: how sad to be those who spend less than the average time!) Some learn to multi-task. Sex while driving is a really bad idea but Americans have learned to listen to their new stereo while making love or cooking, and they regularly eat and talk on the phone while driving. (I read a letter to an advice columnist complaining that the person's partner answered the phone during sex to avoid missing out on a business deal.) Some residents of advanced capitalist economies say they envy those from poor countries for their calm lifestyle and the quality of their personal and community relations. They can at least imagine giving up some of their material goods if they could live in a society where everyone has less stuff but more time for other things. It is curious how societies become too rich to afford pleasures readily available to their poorer neighbors.

One of the most important time-intensive activities that we risk losing is our sense of community. Beginning with the common observation that Americans are less involved in politics, political scientist Robert Putnam showed in his pioneering study, *Bowling Alone: The Collapse and Revival of American Community*, that Americans are also less involved in a wide range of community and social activities.[18] As Americans have gained income, they have been watching more TV, buying more automobiles and other appliances, and living in larger houses further away from their neighbors. But they are now less likely to attend church or other public meetings, less likely to play bridge with neighbors, or to join a neighborhood association, less likely to have a friend over for dinner, and even less likely to eat dinner with their family.[19] Membership in civic organizations was once such a prominent part of American society that it was seen by Alexis de Tocqueville as the savior of American democracy. Now groups from the Freemasons to parent-teacher

FIGURE 5-6
DECLINING SOCIAL CAPITAL IN THE UNITED STATES, 1975-2002

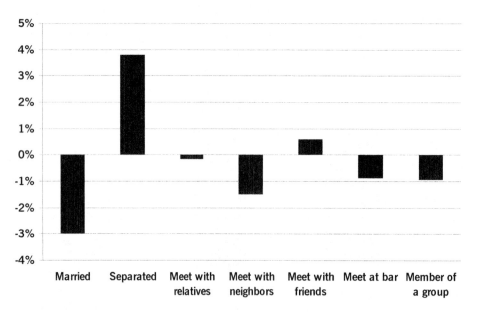

organizations in schools have suffered precipitous membership declines. Over 70% of Americans report performing no community volunteer work over the past year, and half of those who did volunteer did so for less than an hour a week.

With the decline in community participation, Americans have fewer social involvements. A recent study has confirmed that Americans' social networks have contracted, from three close friends in the mid-1980s down to two today. The proportion without *any* close friends has nearly tripled, from 10% to nearly 25%. The share with a close friend at work has fallen from 29% to 18%, a close friend in a group has fallen from 26% to 12%, and a friendly neighbor has dropped from 19% to 8%. Perhaps we have become too rich to have a social life, too busy with our possessions to have friends. Ironically, the happiness literature finds the strongest association with happiness is not with income but with community involvement and sociability—a casualty of our campaign to *buy* happiness.

Declining community participation reflects private choices to spend

FIGURE 5-7

EFFECTS OF CHANGING LEVELS OF SOCIABILITY ON REPORTED HAPPINESS, UNITED STATES, 1975-2002

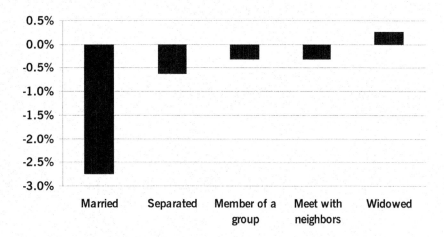

Note: This figure gives the effect on reported level of happiness of the changes in reported social involvements of Americans between 1975-2002. Declining levels of marriage, group membership, and time spent with neighbors were all associated with declining happiness, as was an increase in the proportion reporting they are separated from their spouse. On the other hand, a decline in the proportion widowed, because of falling death rates, was associated with an increase in happiness.

Source: Bartolini, Bilancini, Pugno, "Did the Decline in Social Capital Depress Americans' Happiness?" Working Paper 540, University of Siena, August 2008.

time with things rather than with people. But these private choices have public consequences that shape the choices available to others, because your decision not to participate in community and social groups can reduce the attraction such groups hold for others. Our social consumption is good for others—has *positive externalities*—by contributing to the creation of a broader and richer community life. Our consumption of material goods not only hurts others—has *negative externalities*—through producing pollution and congestion, but also by reducing our participation in community life. As we become wealthier and some of us remove ourselves from social activities, our community becomes impoverished, driving others out as well. For example, imagine a neighborhood where children play together after school. When some parents get more money they choose to buy private lessons or private toys (such as home video games) for their kids, removing them from the after-school community. This leaves fewer playmates remaining, leading other parents to withdraw their kids until there is no longer a large enough group for the playgroup, at which time everyone is forced either to buy activities or to go without. Of course, for most, the cost of paying for lessons and childcare is much more than the cost of community sociability, especially because these services are themselves becoming more expensive over time due to the Baumol Effect. Suddenly, the newly affluent members of what had been a well functioning community have to pay more to replace what they had been receiving for free outside their doors.

Declining sociability is a real cost of American affluence, because it undermines our society's *social capital*. In her classic 1961 book, *The Death and Life of Great American Cities*, Jane Jacobs (1916-2006) showed how safe and productive communities are built on the informal contacts made among neighbors with their local grocer, on the front stoop while watching their kids, at street fairs, and at neighborhood association meetings. "The sum of such casual, public contact at a local level," Jacobs argues, "is a feeling for the public identity of people, a web of public respect and trust, and a resource in time of personal and neighborhood need."[20] The loss of *neighborhood sociability*[21] is a serious public problem. Even at the declining rates of recent social involvement, volunteers in 2005 contributed nearly 9 *billion* hours to America's churches, food kitchens, schools, and sports programs, a contribution worth well over $100 billion dollars. Declining civic involvement puts this contribution at risk, forcing civic and religious programs to either close or to raise fees to replace lost volunteer contributions.

Putnam and others have shown that the decline in social capital has contributed to rising crime rates and inferior public schools. There are fewer crimes and more effective schools where neighbors know each other and are active in neighborhood associations and political groups. Declining social capital is also associated with costs to individuals. Distinguishing humans from other animals, Aristotle declared man unique because "he lives in a community." Wealth allows us to occupy ourselves with our things instead of with each other; but there is a price to lost sociability. People with few friends who live isolated from others are more subject to depression, are more likely to commit suicide, and are in poorer health than those with more social connections. Similarly, those living in states with less social capital have higher *mortality* and *morbidity*[22] rates than those in states with more social capital. I mentioned earlier a study of recent happiness trends in the United States and Europe. This study found that the negative happiness trend in the U.S. after controlling for income may be due to the association between social capital and happiness. People with more social involvements, including belonging to more groups, having more friends and stable marriages, are happier. The decline in these aspects of social capital accounts for the decline in American happiness. If social capital had remained at its 1975 level, our estimates suggest that happiness might have increased. Instead it decreased, because declining social capital more than negates any gains from rising income. In particular, the decline in marriage and marital stability alone accounts for nearly half of the decline in social capital, and nearly half of the decline in happiness.

CARING LABOR

What we know about public sociability and well-being gives us further insight into the limits of economic growth as a means to promote happiness. While it may be possible in some circumstances for markets to allocate some goods and services efficiently, their anonymous and impersonal nature prevents them from efficiently allocating labor to care for dependents and for others in need who, by virtue of their dependency and need, are unable to pay for care. Of course, some care labor is done for pay and through the market—including paid medical care, paid house cleaning, escorts, and babysitting. It is in the very nature of their condition that most dependents, including children, the disabled, and the sick, cannot pay for the care that they need and depend on some *third-party payment*.[23] When combined with the personal nature of the care services needed, this dependence on third-party payments makes it inherently difficult to operate efficient markets. Unable to pay for needed services, dependents can be denied needed care. Without control over the payment, they are doubly dependent because they lack *exit*, the ability to leave a market relationship. Without effective markets, they depend on the kindness of strangers, friends, and family.[24]

Subrata Ganguly, an Indian home maker, preparing Rotis for her family's dinner. This production is not included in calculations of India's GDP.

Even those who favor using GDP and per capita income as measures of national welfare admit that GDP misses much of the economy, including much of what really matters to people. Even today, almost a fifth of the labor force works full-time outside of market exchanges, as housewives or stay-at-home husbands, and studies of people's use of time find that about half of work hours are spent outside of the market economy. Every time your mother does your laundry or your father cooks you dinner, they increase your real income and welfare. Had you bought these services from a cleaning service or restaurant, it would enter into our measures of national GDP and welfare; because it was done within the household, however, it is ignored. Including transactions within businesses as well as within households, *most* production of goods and services is allocated outside of the market. Economists who concern themselves exclusively with commodity transactions miss the great volume of activity allocated by command or through other types of exchange, and as gifts, allocated by business decision, family, government, or by tradition.

Sometimes, this is a deliberate omission by economists who prefer market exchanges over other types of transactions. They have good reasons to favor market transactions. There is a presumption of efficiency, fairness, and democratic equity in market transactions that so attracts economists that they disdain other forms of economic interaction. Markets can be democratic. The anonymity of market exchange protects members from discrimination. Money is the same whether it comes from the wallet of an African-American or a European-American, and market exchanges reward companies and individuals who treat others fairly, i.e., solely on the basis of their wealth and productivity, while punishing those who try to underpay or overcharge members of particular social or ethnic groups. Because market exchanges are voluntary, economists assume that they

> ### THE COST OF CARING: THE MOTHERHOOD PENALTY
>
> Apart from the economic losses they suffer for being women, employed mothers earn 5% less for every child. For women under 35, the pay gap between mothers and non-mothers is greater than the gap between women and men. It appears that employers assume that mothers are less committed to their jobs, less dependable, and less authoritative, but warmer, more emotional, and more irrational than other women.
>
> Shelley Correll, a sociologist at Cornell, conducted an experiment to test for prejudice against mothers. She and her colleagues prepared identical resumes distinguished only by gender and parental status. Submitting these for various jobs, mothers were recommended for hiring consideration 47% of the time, significantly less than the 84% recommendation for women who were not mothers. Mothers were held to higher standards, with higher test scores required. They were recommended for significantly lower salaries.
>
> Prejudice against care givers is gender specific. Fathers were seen as more reliable and better workers than other men. They were more likely to be recommended for hiring and were offered a higher starting salary.

are welfare enhancing for both parties and occur only *because both parties to the transaction are made better off*; anyone who did not feel that the exchange improved their situation, presumably would not do it. Furthermore, market exchanges encourage productivity growth by rewarding entrepreneurs who produce products at a lower price, and encourage entrepreneurs to be sensitive to the needs of others, so they can sell things.

Markets can also enhance efficiency by communicating information from consumers to producers, even in situations where neither has any direct contact: if my products do not sell then I know that my prices are too high or quality too low. The opportunity for exit, plus the incentive markets give producers to pay attention to consumers, makes markets self-correcting. If the wrong products are produced, consumers will send a clear signal of this to producers by refusing to buy them, and producers will attend to this signal because to neglect their consumers would mean losing sales and profits.[25]

CARE LABOR AND THE EFFICIENCY OF THE MARKET

Behind the efficiency and equity of the market is the presumption that non-coerced exchanges must be fair to both parties because unhappy participants would protect their interests by leaving, exercising *exit*. But this option is unavailable to those who need "care," both because they are dependent on others to provide or pay for care, and because the nature of their *idiosyncratic*[26] transaction limits their op-

portunity to exit. Dependents depend on the good will and caring empathy of their caregivers because they cannot replace them through the market as you would a bad auto mechanic or supermarket. Consider, for example, the situation facing children: why do they tolerate abusive parents? Why not just divorce their parents, as Drew Barrymore tried to do in her 1984 movie, *Irreconcilable Differences*? (One may assume that the movie was inspired by Barrymore's own experiences described in her 1991 autobiography, *Little Girl Lost*. Drew won her lawsuit against her absent father, John Drew Barrymore, and her irresponsible mother, Jaid Mako Barrymore.)

Three circumstances prevent children from exiting bad parental relationships, and in gen-

NANCY FOLBRE

Emeritus professor of economics at the University of Massachusetts at Amherst, **Nancy Folbre**'s (b. 1952) work focuses on the interface between feminist theory and political economy, with a particular interest in caring labor. She has received a fellowship from the MacArthur Foundation and also served as co-chair of the MacArthur Research Network on the Family and the Economy.

FIGURE 5-8
POPULATION NEEDING CARE, 2001

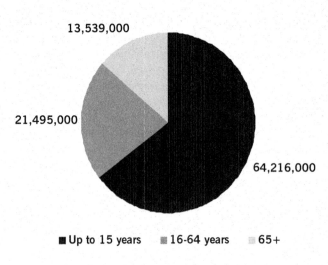

13,539,000

21,495,000

64,216,000

■ Up to 15 years   ■ 16-64 years   ■ 65+

eral prevent care markets from operating efficiently. Most needing care cannot work full time and, therefore, lack the resources to pay for their care. Whether they are children, disabled adults, or the infirm elderly, they depend on third parties, including parents, insurance companies, and government agencies, to subsidize the care they receive. Even well-intentioned third parties have an incentive to skimp on the quality of care, especially because it is very difficult to measure either the inputs or the outputs of care. In the case of children, this is compounded by legal restrictions that give parents control over their children's assets. Finally, care givers are in a particularly powerful position with respect to care recipients. Care is highly idiosyncratic; what people need is usually distinct—even unique—and its provision is intimately tied to the provider. Children need care, but the care they need must come from particular people because they need to know that these people care for them. (That is the root of the famous parental statement that they treat each sibling equally by treating them differently.) Perhaps you could get someone else to make your breakfast and wash your laundry; but would that replace your mother? When your ballet class or soccer team performed, would it be the same if your parents hired someone to watch you for them? Since you need *that* parent, they have disproportionate bargaining power.

With little opportunity to exit bad relationships, dependents cannot use market discipline to protect their interests. In practice, care has traditionally been relegated to the family, where it is part of the unpaid responsibility of women and mothers, a household division of labor where husbands

TABLE 5-3
WONDERS OF ANONYMOUS COMMODITY MARKETS

Advantage of Market	Example
Encourages hard work and creativity by rewarding businesses that produce what consumers want at a relatively low price.	Steve Jobs got rich by making the personal computer, the iPod, and by supporting Pixar Animation Studios.
Fair because involves exchange of equivalents.	I buy a cup of coffee at Rao's and pay for it a price that makes it worthwhile for Rao's to sell me the coffee and worthwhile for me to buy it.
Encourages empathy because producers must concern themselves with the wishes of their consumers.	Henion's Bakery makes challah every Friday because consumers have requested them.
Allows individual expression.	CVS sells *dozens* of different shades of lipstick. CVS is encouraged to provide this range of products because they can make money at it (reason 1 above).
Democratic, inhibits discrimination.	I don't know who made my car. But regardless of whether they were black, white, gay, straight, male or female, I pay the same price.
Gives opportunity to complain through exit.	Unhappy with service at the Indian restaurant next to the Black Sheep, I no longer go there. (This punishes their transactions and may also encourage them to provide better service.)

work in the market while wives provide care at home. This could be efficient if specialization is a good thing in care—a debatable point. It would be efficient if women systematically had a comparative advantage in care, if they had a "care gene." On the other hand, by relegating all females to the care economy and men to market work, this arrangement denies human diversity, and denies children and others the opportunity to receive care from husbands, sons, and fathers. It leaves women as well as dependents, vulnerable if the husband/father chooses to leave with his fungible market skills. Having children impoverishes some households, but the effect is much greater when there is only a mother present.

If teachers and other care givers could collect a fee each time someone benefits from their work, then they would have a market incentive to be productive. Absent that incentive, we must rely on their good will and sense of professional responsibility.

In all, about a third of the population of the United States, nearly 100 million people, need care at any one time (see Figure 5-8). Millions more, most of us, need care at *some* time during a year when we are temporarily sick or injured. Much of the care provided comes from family members, but over time more is done through the market. For example, children are taught at school rather than learning occupations at home, and paid childcare begins at younger ages. Nancy Folbre and Julie Nelson estimate that the share of the labor force employed in professional care occupations has risen from 4% in 1900 to over 19% today, with more care workers than workers in manufacturing and mining.

Because of ubiquitous *market failure*[27] in the care sector, it is likely that we are providing too little care, underpaying care givers, and the quality of care we provide is too low. Even if dependent children, the sick and disabled, and the elderly were the only ones victimized by the market failures in the care economy, then the problem would be significant. Market failure in the care sector has much worse implications because the care sector is responsible for maintaining the current population and for producing the next generation of citizens and workers. The economist Frank Knight noted almost a century ago that "individuals are born naked, destitute, helpless, ignorant, and untrained and must spend a third of their lives acquiring the prerequisites of a free contractual existence." This type of productive dependency describes not only children but all of us: we all need care at some points throughout their lives. Illness, injury, or other forms of distress render all adults temporarily unproductive at some time. Most adults, with proper care, are able to return to society as a productive worker and citizen.

TABLE 5-4

THE CARE ECONOMY: EMPLOYMENT AND PERCENTAGE FEMALE IN TEN LARGEST CARE OCCUPATIONS

Occupation	Employment (000s)	% female
Elementary and middle school teachers	2,701	82.2
Registered nurses	2,529	91.3
Nursing, psychiatric, and home health aides	1,906	88.9
Maids and housekeeping cleaners	1,423	90.3
Child care workers	1,401	94.2
Hairdressers, hairstylists, and cosmetologists	767	93.4
Other teachers and instructors	705	64.9
Personal and home care aides	703	87.3
Social workers	698	82.6
Preschool and kindergarten teachers	690	97.7
Total:	13,523	88

MARKET FAIILURE;
OR IS THE MARKET A FAILURE?

A "market failure" is a situation where a free market will not lead to an efficient allocation of resources. Market failures may include situations where the quantity producers supply at a given price does not equal the quantity consumers want. Other market failures may include situations where prices do not reflect the true social costs of production because of externalities, public goods, or monopolistic practices by business.

When economists speak of "market failures," they leave the implication that the standard situation would be market "success" where the socially optimal amount of output would be provided at the right price. This is different from a situation where the "market is a failure" because it is impossible to get the right allocation of resources through a process of individual choice through a free market. In the care economy, for example, it is impossible to have an efficient free-market allocation because children are incapable of paying for their care and efficiently choosing care providers through a market process.

WOMEN'S WORK?

Quality care, in raising children and restoring adults to health, produces external benefits enjoyed by all of us. But it impoverishes many care givers. On average, an American family with two children spends about 40% of its income directly on children, about $13,000 per child; this figure does not include additional spending by other relatives or the cost of the parents' time, which can be even greater than the direct expenditures.[28] This is because care givers depend on someone other than their dependents to pay for the services they provide. Regardless of whether we directly contributed, all of us benefit when children are brought up to be responsible, skilled adults who treat each other with courtesy and respect. Employers benefit when they can hire cooperative, productive and trustworthy workers. We all benefit from having law-abiding neighbors. Those in the care economy produce not only *human capital*[29] but *social capital*[30] that contributes to the well-being of us all. They cannot charge their dependents for this care: children and the disabled lack resources to pay, and also they themselves do not capture the external benefits of their good citizenship. Furthermore, it is impossible for parents, teachers, and nurses to charge a fee each time someone benefits from their good, caring work.

Lacking good financial incentives, care givers draw on other motives. Some are altruistic, imbued with a sense of responsibility and a desire to care for loved ones and for the needy in general. Many women are raised to do care labor. As girls, many are deputized as assistant mothers and put in charge of younger siblings. From such upbringing, many adults, both men and women, accept care as a feminine responsibility: real women *listen*, *sacrifice*, and give *emotional support*. This association with femininity drives men from caring occupations, including many who might be well suited for caring work. On the other hand, many women, including those poorly suited for it, are led to signal their proper gender identity to themselves and to prospective mates by choosing caring occupations. As a society, we may lose many good care givers by discouraging men, and we may force too many unwitting women into vocations to which they are ill suited.

Paradoxically, the provision of voluntary care labor and the crowding of women into caring work can drive away those interested in performing care labor but needing well-paid work. The market provision of caring labor is limited by competition with free services. Why pay for restaurant meals if the wife/mother will cook at home? Why hire a house cleaner when that is the wife/mother's responsibility to do for free? With the movement of women into the paid labor force, there has been a drift towards the market provision of care, but this market continues to be distorted by the over-supply of women for these feminine occupations, driving down the wage and, in effect, substituting the provision of care services through the market for their provision at home. Paid child care, psychotherapy, take-out meals, and nursing homes for the elderly are all paid care services directly replacing services previously provided by family members. This raises the worrisome possibility that the market provision of care will drive out non-market care even without providing an adequate substitute. Why, one may ask, should we expect wives, daughters, and mothers to provide free services for which others are being paid? If we continue to underfund care, then who will replace the family and friends who leave for paying work?

If women stopped caring for free, then at least we would reduce some of the glaring economic inequities afflicting American women. The care economy thus suffers from its strength. The willingness of many, mostly women, to devote themselves to helping the needy is necessary to provide an adequate level of care and to motivate care workers to do their work well. This willingness also leads to an over-supply of workers for care jobs, driving down wages even while pay for these jobs is held down by competition with free home services. In this way, women's traditional responsibility for the unpaid work of

TABLE 5-5
MARKET FAILURE IN THE CARE ECONOMY

Market failure	Reason
Too little care provided	Those who need care lack resources to pay for it and, therefore, depend on the kindness of others and on third-party payments. Those who benefit from externalities of quality care do not contribute.
Care givers are underpaid	They compete with free care provided by families. Care occupations are overcrowded by women.
Care quality is inadequate	High turnover in care occupations because care givers are underpaid. Third party payers have incentive to save money by providing low quality. Those who benefit from externalities of quality care do not contribute.

caring for dependents undermines their own financial well-being, making them more dependent on men and raising a risk of dire poverty if they do not marry or if they divorce. Because of the low pay and low status associated with much care work, there is high turnover in care jobs and little investment in training and motivation. Poorly paid, many care workers hold more than one job, sapping the energies they need for both. All of these lower the quality of care received by dependents, with consequences for the women providing care, for those needing care, and for all of society.[31]

DOES CARING UNDERMINE ECONOMIC GROWTH?

The care economy is one of several places where modern capitalist market economies rest on the values and activities of an older nonmarket society, even while chipping away at these to increase capitalist surplus. Within families, there is extensive production and redistribution process outside of the market. Goods and services flow from parent to parent, from adult children to elderly parents, between siblings, and, most of all, from parents to children: all outside of the market and all directed by emotion and other non-market processes. Without these feelings and the activities they generate, society would literally die out: children would not be born or survive to adulthood and the disabled and elderly would die. Capitalist society survives only becaue of the persistence of the noncapitalist care economy.

The noncapitalist economy persists and plays a crucial role beyond the family. All functioning societies use nonmarket rewards and punishments. We reward good citizenship with promises of mutual aid within communities—the exchange of favors—and by distributing honor and prestige, including medals, special hats, team jackets, and public respect. Sometimes we tip the violinist but we also reward a good concert performance with applause and shouts of "bravo." We celebrate our public figures, including artists, civil servants, and soldiers, with medals and praise. Even when we use market incentives, we often do so surreptitiously, almost to conceal that a market transaction has occurred. We put payment into envelopes or even pay in gift cards rather than cash or checks.

The continued use of nonmarket allocations raises a dilemma that the American economist Arthur Okun addresses in his 1975 book *Equality versus Efficiency: The Big Tradeoff*.[32] Beginning with the position that markets promote

FIGURE 5-9
EQUALITY VERSUS EFFICIENCY: OKUN'S VIEW

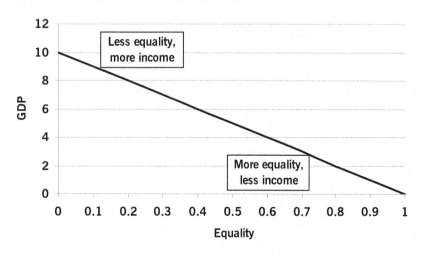

FEMINIST ECONOMICS

While associated with the work of contemporary economists like Nancy Folbre and Marianne Ferber (b. 1923), the ideas behind feminist economics go back to the late 18th century. An open supporter of the French Revolution, Mary Wollstonecraft (1759-1797) published *A Vindication of the Rights of Woman* (1789) to defend women as the equals of men and to insist on their equal right to education and to work freely. Against those who charged that women were frivolous because they wasted their time at home, Wollstonecraft insisted on the importance of the domestic work done by women.

These themes, the equality of women and the importance of both women's domestic work and of the right to earn an independent living, have formed the basis for feminist economics. Writing a century after Wollstonecraft, Charlotte Perkins Gilman (1860-1935) argued in *Women and Economics* (1898) that the exclusion of women from the market economy and an "excessive sex-distinction" makes women dependent upon men

for their livelihood. It is not only inequitable but it checks and perverts the "progress of the race."

Over the last 50 years, economists like Ferber and Folbre have developed these early feminist insights into a program for scholarly research exploring the economic importance of the domestic economy and the impact of gender segregation in the economy.

From left: Mary Wollstonecraft, Charlotte Perkins Gilman, Marianne Ferber.

economic efficiency, Okun then asks, why we do reduce our economic efficiency by limiting markets? Is this a big mistake or is there some rationale behind the apparent madness? If markets provide incentives for people to be productive, then restricting markets, using nonmarket mechanisms to allocate output, must undermine efficiency by reducing the weight of these incentives. Why, Okun asks, would we persist in using other modes of reward and distribution? Instead of nonmarket allocation, he argues that we should use the market more and, if we want to assist those who do badly in the market, redistribute afterwards when our higher level of efficiency would give us more to distribute.[33]

Thinking of trade-offs, Okun suggests that we can view society's output along the production-possibility frontier between equity and efficiency, as in Figure 5-10. Allocating only through the market, leaving market incentives intact, we would achieve the maximum possible output; every step away from market allocation, every step towards some greater level of equality, would reduce output. We would not choose to bury some of our income in deep holes in the ground. So why, Okun asks, do we limit the reach of the market at the expense of lowering our income?

We discuss Okun's arguments more later. In short, he presents three explanations for reducing the scope of the market. First, society hedges its bets: unsure about whether the market really is the best way to allocate production, we use other forms of rewards, like praise and medals, to encourage desirable behavior. A great deal of money went with Milton Friedman's Nobel Prize, but even without the money such awards are a powerful incentive to economists to work hard and to be productive. Second, we value citizens as people even if they are unproductive. Even unproductive citizens have rights, including the famous "life, liber-

FIGURE 5-10
EQUALITY VERSUS EFFICIENCY: ALTERNATIVE VIEW

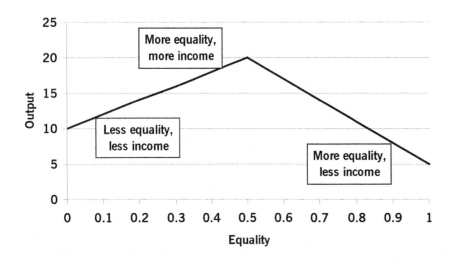

ty, and the pursuit of happiness." A certain measure of redistribution and egalitarianism is needed to ensure that all citizens have their rights protected in our democracy. Finally, he makes a *utilitarian* argument for redistribution, favoring redistribution from the rich to the poor on the grounds that the poor will value income more because they have less of it.

Okun's arguments may be reasonable, but our discussion of social capital and the care economy may suggest another argument for a more egalitarian distribution of income. Moving away from the market may *raise* income by correcting market failures in the provision of care and community that would otherwise lower income. Rather than Figure 5-10, the correct production possibilities frontier may be 5-11, where output rises with increases in equality because greater equality promotes community and allows for a more caring society that nurtures more productive people. Including *human capital* as a product of care labor, equality becomes more efficient when it encourages more care and more investment in people. Recognizing the limits of the market provision of care, it is possible for society to improve on the market, creating a better *and* more productive economy.

Born in New Jersey in 1928, Arthur Okun was a Professor of Economics at Yale when he was appointed to be senior economist on President Kennedy's Council of Economic Advisors, At the Council, Okun formulated "Okun's Law" relating unemployment to lost output. He was deeply involved in debates over anti-poverty programs during John F. Kennedy's New Frontier and Lyndon Johnson's Great Society. Okun favored high taxes on the rich and welfare programs for the poor to redistribute income but he warned in his 1975 Godkin Lecture at Harvard that such programs might reduce total output.

Okun (standing, left) with Pres. Lyndon Johnson

DISCUSSION QUESTIONS

Does more make people happier? Why would having more make us happier?

What is the relationship between people's income and happiness within a country? What is the relationship between a nation's per-capita income and its average level of happiness?

Give some of the ways increasing national income may increase happiness. Give some ways it may reduce happiness.

What does it mean for needs to be socially generated? What does this process mean for the relationship between national income and happiness?

What are "positional goods"?

What is the "Baumol effect"? How does it relate to the cost of education? Health care?

What are some characteristics of strong communities? How do they promote individual happiness?

What is "caring labor"? Who needs it? Who does it? Who pays for it?

What are some of the economic problems with caring labor? What is "third-party payment"? How does relying on third-party payment reduce the efficiency of caring labor markets? Who suffers from this market failure?

What is "human capital"? How is it produced? How could we produce more? How could a focus on market production and increasing personal income undermine the production of human capital?

ENDNOTES

[1]Utility refers to the amount of happiness enjoyed by a person.

[2]These are estimates by the Social Security Administration on June 10, 2014 at http://www.social-security.gov/cgi-bin/longevity.cgi

[3]Figure 5.1 is based on the General Social Survey, question 157. Taken all together, how would you say things are these days--would you say that you are very happy, pretty happy, or not too happy? The index of happiness is constructed by counting "very happy" as 3 points, "somewhat happy" as 2, and "not too happy" as 1 point. Per capita income is from the Bureau of Economic Analysis.

[4]Richard Easterlin, "Does Economic Growth Improve the Human Lot? Some Empirical Evidence.," in *Nations and Households in Economic Growth* (New York: Academic Press, 1974); Richard Layard, *Happiness: Lessons from a New Science* (New York: Penguin, 2006); criticisms are in Angus Deaton, *The Great Escape: Health, Wealth, and the Origins of Inequality*, 2013; Betsey, Wolfers, Justin Stevenson, "Economic Growth and Subjective Well-Being: Reassessing the Easterlin Paradox," *Brookings Papers on Economic Activity 2008* (2008): 1–87.

[5]Deaton, *The Great Escape*, 30.

[6]This is a point made in many works of literature; see, for example, John Steinbeck, *The Pearl* (New York: Viking Press, 1947); Robert Edwards Lane, *The Loss of Happiness in Market Democracies* (New Haven: Yale University Press, 2000); a more nuanced argument is made that the key issue is not income alone but how the income is distributed and what it is used for, in Benjamin Radcliff, *The Political Economy of Human Happiness: How Voters' Choices Determine the Quality of Life* (Cambridge: Cambridge University Press, 2013).

[7]Positional goods are those where relative quantity matters most, where the link between context and evaluation is strongest. Nonpositional goods, by contrast, are those where our pleasure is independent of the behavior and possessions of others.

[8]In a zero-sum game, total winnings are fixed so if anyone gains then someone else must necessarily have lost.

[9]Aggregate happiness is the sum of the happiness of everyone within the society. This is a problematic concept because we have no way of comparing the experience of happiness felt by each individual. (It is possible to observe brain activity with modern imaging technology but this science is still in its infancy.) As a community, furthermore, we may also sacrifice some amount of happiness to achieve other goals, such as social equity or to reward socially meritorious behavior.

[10]Like a military arms race, competition for status can have only one winner because only one competitor can come in first and have the most money, toys, or guns; see Robert H. Frank, *Luxury Fever: Why Money Fails to Satisfy in an Era of Excess* (New York, NY: Free Press, 1999); Robert H. Frank, *The Winner-Take-All Society: How More and More Americans Compete for Ever Fewer and Bigger Prizes, Encouraging Economic Waste, Income Inequality, and an Impoverished Cultural Life* (New York: Free Press, 1995); Juliet Schor, *The Overspent American: Why We Want What We Don't Need* (New York: HarperPerennial, 1999); Juliet Schor, *The Overworked American: The Unexpected Decline of Leisure* (New York, N.Y.: Basic Books, 1991).

[11]A reference or a target income is the standard by which you evaluate your own income. In a poor community, you may be satisfied with a low income. When your community's standards rise, this may pull up your reference or target income causing you to feel dissatisfied with an income that was perfectly satisfactory before.

[12]The greater stress of living in a competitive economy has been associated with worse health and shorter life expectancy; see Richard G Wilkinson, *The Spirit Level: Why Greater Equality Makes Societies Stronger* (New York: Bloomsbury Press, 2010); Ichirō Kawachi, *The Health of Nations: Why Inequality Is Harmful to Your Health* (New York: New Press, 2002); Steven H. Woolf and Laudan Aron, editors, Panel on Understanding Cross-National Health Differences Among High-Income Countries; Committee on Population; Division of Behavioral and Social Sciences and Education; National Research Council; Board on Population Health and Public Health Practice; Institute of Medicine, *U.S. Health in International Perspective: Shorter Lives, Poorer Health* (Washington, D.C.: The National Academies Press, 2013).

[13]By net welfare we mean the increase in well-being for some people from their increasing income and happiness, net of the welfare loss suffered by others who suffer a loss in status.

[14]The supply of reproducible goods can be increased without diminishing their value. We can make more Pez dispensers, for example, without reducing the usability of existing dispensers. By contrast, either we cannot make more nonreproducible goods—Van Gogh will never paint another picture—or we can increase the supply only by diminishing the value of existing goods, by putting more hotels on Miami Beach, for example.

[15]The Baumol Effect refers to the tendency of services to rise in price relative to goods when an economy becomes more productive because productivity increases are concentrated in goods production. This is because labor services are valued not for their output but for the amount of labor that goes into them and, therefore, cannot have productivity increases. This leads to the cost-disease in the service sector where the cost of providing services rises relative to the price of goods.

[16]Labor productivity is the ratio of output to the labor input, either the number of workers or the workers' time.

[17]Alternatively, we may spend our time working so that we can pay someone else to do these things.

[18]Robert D Putnam, *Bowling Alone: The Collapse and Revival of American Community* (New York: Simon & Schuster, 2000).

[19]Religious services have also grown shorter. You can observe this by standing outside churches in richer and poorer neighborhoods.

[20]Jane Jacobs, *The Death and Life of Great American Cities*, 1961.

[21]Casual friendly relationships with people in one's geographic community.

[22]The mortality rate is the death rate in a community, deaths divided by the population. The morbidity rate is the proportion in the population experiencing poor health or illness.

[23]This is where someone other than the party receiving the service pays for it. These "third parties" include parents, insurance companies, governments, and other charities.

[24]Albert O. Hirschman, *Exit, Voice, and Loyalty: Responses to Decline in Firms, Organizations, and States* (Cambridge, Mass: Harvard University Press, 2004).

[25]Albert O. Hirschman, *Rival Views of Market Society and Other Recent Essays*, 1st Harvard University Press pbk. ed (Cambridge, Mass: Harvard University Press, 1992); Albert O. Hirschman, *The Passions and the Interests: Political Arguments for Capitalism Before Its Triumph* (Princeton, N.J: Princeton University Press, 1977); Hirschman, Exit, Voice, and Loyalty.

[26]A relationship is idiosyncratic if one party needs special services for which the other is a unique supplier. For example, Drew Barrymore needed the idiosyncratic services of a "mother" and there was only one person in the world, Jaid Mako Barrymore, qualified to provide that service.

[27]Market failure describes a situation where the market outcome does not maximize welfare for society or even for the individuals involved. Failure can be due to the lack of markets, monopolies, or lack of information.

[28]Nancy Folbre, *Valuing Children: Rethinking the Economics of the Family*, The Family and Public Policy (Cambridge, Mass: Harvard University Press, 2008); Nancy Folbre, *Who Pays for the Kids?: Gender and the Structures of Constraint*, Economics as Social Theory (London ; New York: Routledge, 1994); Mark Lino, *Expenditures on Children by Families*, 2011 (Washington, D. C.: United States Department of Agriculture, Center for Nutrition Policy and Promotion, June 2012), http://www.cnpp.usda.gov/Publications/CRC/crc2011.pdf.

[29]Human capital is the ability of individuals to be productive because of their health and training.

[30]Social capital refers to the organization of the community allowing the efficient structuring of production, exchange, and the division of labor.

[31]Folbre, *Valuing Children*; Folbre, *Who Pays for the Kids?*; Nancy Folbre, *Greed, Lust & Gender: A History of Economic Ideas* (Oxford; New York: Oxford University Press, 2009), http://public.eblib.com/EBLPublic/PublicView.do?ptiID=472259; Nancy Folbre and Project Muse, *For Love and Money: Care Provision in the United States* (New York: Russell Sage Foundation, 2012), http://muse.jhu.edu/books/9781610447904/; Marianne A Ferber and Julie A. Nelson, *Beyond Economic Man: Feminist The-*

ory and Economics (Chicago: University of Chicago Press, 1993); Charlotte Perkins Gilman, *Human Work* (New York: McClure, Phillips, 1904); Charlotte Perkins Gilman, *Women and Economics: A Study of the Economic Relation Between Men and Women as a Factor in Social Evolution*, 9th ed (New York: Gordon Press, 1975); Mary Wollstonecraft and Carol Poston, *A Vindication of the Rights of Woman: An Authoritative Text, Backgrounds, Criticism* (New York: Norton, 1975).

[32]Arthur M Okun, Equality and Efficiency, the Big Tradeoff (Washington: Brookings Institution, 1975).

[33]This is also the perspective of other liberal economists, see Alan S. Blinder, *Hard Heads, Soft Hearts: Tough-Minded Economics for a Just Society* (Reading, Mass.: Addison-Wesley Pub. Co., 1987); Charles L Schultze, *The Public Use of Private Interest* (Washington, D.C.: Brookings Institution, 1977).

6

PUBLIC GOODS AND COLLECTIVE ACTION

PUBLIC AND PRIVATE GOODS

It may appear odd that economists focus on the least common of economic transactions: market exchanges involving isolated producers and consumers without any effect on others. Exchanges without spilloves, with no *external effects* where others benefit or suffer, are rare, virtually unknown. Almost everything we do has at least *some* effect on others. The effects may be relatively small, as unobtrusive as the leakage from your iPod earphones, or they may be large, such as when production of greenhouse gases warms the planet, drowning cities and entire countries. Acknowledging *externalities* does not require any particular action. We can choose to discount small or even large spillovers to leave individuals space to pursue their own individuality. In practice, there is always a balance, and how we feel may depend upon where we are. We may feel differently about externalities when we hold a loud party than when our neighbor holds one without inviting us. And with a loud band blaring music that we do *not* like. The real issue is not whether there are externalities, but how large they are, and how important we feel it is to respect people's private choices in this matter versus the cost of their actions to neighbors. Pretending there are no externalities does nothing to help us in finding this balance.

Externalities help to distinguish *public* from *private* goods. Pure private goods are both *excludable* and *depletable*. No one besides the owner can use private goods, and use by anyone depletes the good's value. Not only can others be kept out, excluded from use excluded from impact, but owners want to keep them out because any use depletes the good. Pure public goods differ on both dimensions. Access to pure public goods cannot be restricted, no one can be prevented from the impact of these goods, and the supply is not depleted by use.

> The concept of externalities was first developed by the English economist **Arthur Pigou (1877-1959)** in his book The Economics of Welfare (1932). Pigou identified externalities as costs imposed or benefits conferred on others through our private action. Since external costs and benefits are not considered in standard market transactions, Pigou argued that they called for government intervention. Taxes, dubbed Pigouvian taxes, on negative externalities would discourage activities like pollution that impinges on others. He also favored subsidies to encourage positive externalities, such as education.

The South Pacific island nation of Tuvalu with almost 10,000 people may be the first nation to disappear because of global warming. Barely a meter above sea level, the island has already initiated negotiations with New Zealand and Australia for resettlement if sea levels continue to rise.

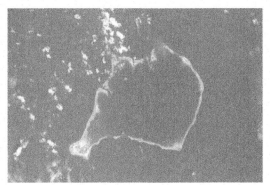

These are abstractions. There are few pure private goods because virtually everything we do affects others. Not all of these spillover effects are bad. There are positive as well as negative externalities, *public goods* and *public bads*. Of course, we hear more about the public bads because people complain more about them. You consume your lawnmower, for example, to cut your grass; I consume it when I breathe its pollution and listen to its noise on an otherwise delightful summer morning. But the public goods are also ubiquitous. Even if I am less likely to talk about it, I observe and appreciate your neatly tailored lawn and flower garden. While I appreciate the blossoms on your apple orchard and my flowers are pollinated by your bees, I am almost unconscious of the positive externality that I enjoy from you. Certainly, I am more likely to

While on-farm manure storage is organic, the smell bothers neighbors and it endangers water supplies if not properly contained.

complain about the negative externalities of your orchard, the pollution and noise produced by your harvest machinery and the trucks that carry your apples away. And I do not like getting stung by your bees. I may even complain of the privatization of land around your trees. Your property rights in the orchard harm me by restricting my ability to wander freely when I walk my dog.

By allowing people to ignore some of the costs of their actions by passing them on to others, externalities lead people to overproduce undesirable things. Positive externalities, public goods, work the same way: because people do not receive all the benefits of what they do, they do not produce enough good things. While we do not want people to dump their bads on others, we may want them to produce things that produce the public bads if in doing so they produce very large benefits. Organized correctly, everyone would pay for the negative externalities associated with their activities and be rewarded for the good they do. In this way, they would produce negative externalities only if the benefits were great enough to exceed the costs. This would discourage people from abusing the commons, polluting, making loud noises, and otherwise desecrating public space. Paying for positive externalities would also encourage people to do good things. You painted your house to protect the wood, I enjoy the nice paint job and wish that you would paint more often. If I paid you for the pleasure I get from seeing your house painted, then you would have more incentive to paint. We planted a wildflower meadow on the side of our property for our enjoyment. Others too have enjoyed looking at the flowers, and if they all paid then everyone would have more incentive to plant pretty flowers. (Some also take souvenirs, annoying us because it depletes our stock of flowers.) My decision to bicycle to work avoids negative externalities from pollution and traffic: should the University, and the town, pay bicyclists for each ride? Should it charge car and truck drivers? Should it charge me because my bicycling annoys some drivers? You buy an organic apple, which helps all of us by promoting production processes less harmful to the environment. Should we subsidize organic growers and tax the use of pesticides and inorganic fertilizers?

Sometimes I think that people wish that we could throw our hands up at the difficulty of managing externalities and simply hope that your negatives and positives will more or less balance my negatives and positives. Instead of trying to regulate or to price all the externalities and spillover effects to our decisions, we ignore them, and often it takes mammoth fish kills or toxins in our drinking water to rouse us to action. Behind this seeming indifference is a valid social policy, respect for individual choices and a desire to give the maximum space for individual creativity. You tolerate my eccentricities, I tolerate yours, and we have in the United States a community that is often both exasperating and exciting, full of creative people doing things that annoy others.

There are also reasonable economic motives behind our seeming indifference to externalities. Sometimes, the transactions costs of policing the externalities in our consumption and production decisions will exceed any efficiency gain. Regulating externalities, positive and

WHO SHOULD SAVE VENICE?

With global warming, the frequency and magnitude of ocean flooding has increased dramatically. The danger of flooding is, obviously, greatest in low-lying coastal cities like Venice and New Orleans. The Italian government has already begun a 3 bn. euro program to build dams to protect Venice from rising sea levels; it is likely that the final cost of any Venice rescue will go much higher. Who should pay? Is it the responsibility of the Venetians and the Italian government? How about those whose use of fossil fuels is causing the global warming tha

HOW SELFISH ARE WE?

Do you properly dispose of your trash or do you drop it in the street when no one is looking? Contradicting the assumptions of orthodox economic theory, the great majority of people hold onto their junk until they can put them in trash cans rather than simply (and conveniently) tossing it out the window. Even when no one is looking, most people go to some trouble to not litter. Why is this?

Adam Smith, in his *Theory of Moral Sentiments*, explained that "How selfish soever man may be supposed, there are evidently some principles in his nature, which interest him in the fortune of others, and render their happiness necessary to him, though he derives nothing from it, except the pleasure of seeing it." This power of "sympathy" makes us all social beings who seek the approval of others in order to share in their pleasures and avoid the thought of their recriminations. "Though it may be true," Smith concludes, "that every individual, in his own breast, naturally prefers himself to all mankind, yet he dares not look mankind in the face, and avow that he acts according to this principle."

Dog does not want to be stung by neighbor's bees

negative, involves the same problems of measurement, monitoring, and enforcement that market transactions do. That may be why we are more inclined to regulate larger and centralized processes where there is a larger payoff for the same regulatory effort. We are more likely, for example, to regulate pollution from giant smokestacks and large power plants than the pollution (noise and gaseous) from home lawn mowers and family powerboats. We want to encourage education and training because it promotes productivity and good citizenship, but while we subsidize education in schools, we do little for those seeking training in the crafts. Is this because activity in school can be monitored relatively easily while training in crafts is scattered among decentralized workplaces?

TAXING AND SUBSIDIZING GOODS WITH EXTERNALITIES

Recognizing the importance of transactions costs, economists often recommend that rather than directly monitoring and directing activities, governments regulate externalities through tax or subsidy programs, Pigouvian taxes and subsidies[1] that change the market price of the pollutant or positive spillover. For example, many economists have urged that the United States fight global warming by taxing carbon in fossil fuels. By raising the price of gasoline or electricity from coal-fired power plants, for example, this tax would discourage the burning of fossil fuels that put $CO2$ into the atmosphere, while leaving it to producers to find the most efficient way to make these reductions. We also encourage alternatives to burning fossil fuels, with subsidies to windmills and the installation of solar panels to generate electricity without producing carbon dioxide.[2] Similarly, rather than banning nicotine as a dangerous drug, the way we discourage cocaine or heroin use, economists recommend that we tax cigarettes so people who really need nicotine can still get it while the higher prices will provide a strong incentive to cut back.

Tobacco use is the leading cause of death in the United States. According to the Centers for Disease Control, it is responsible for over 440,000 deaths in 2013, including nearly 50,000 deaths among nonsmokers who suffered from exposure to second-hand smoke. As many as 300,000 children suffer respiratory damage.[3] While pushing to regulate tobacco, to restrict access, and to raise taxes while reducing subsidies, the campaign against tobacco has also demonstrated a different approach to address externalities by directly suing producers of tobacco products for damages. By vesting individuals with rights we allow them to demand compensation from others who produce nuisances or enjoy the fruits of their labor. By bringing suit against tobacco companies for health damages caused by their products, state governments and individuals have collected billions of dollars in restitution, raising the cost of tobacco products and discouraging their use.[4]

TABLE 6-1
PUBLIC AND PRIVATE GOODS

		Excludability	
		Yes	No
Depletability	Yes	[Pure private good]: my stock of Lake Champlain chocolate.	Breathing oxygen (and emitting carbon dioxide).
	No	Listening to concert in a *very* large stadium; viewing paintings at the Museum of Fine Arts.	[Pure public good]: light; justice; national defense; looking at our wildflower meadow.

United States Navy on patrol in the Persian Gulf, protecting the flow of petroleum so that we can continue to warm the planet.

Similar damage suits have been brought against gun manufacturers, car makers, the fast food industry, and others who produce products with significant negative externalities (public bads). Along with the cases of fossil fuels and ethanol, these reveal problems we have as a democratic society in taking account of externalities. While Pigouvian taxes are a sensible approach to restricting externalities, it has been difficult to enact a coherent Pigouvian program—sometimes we even tax and subsidize the same products. Democracies find it difficult to impose Pigouvian taxes on powerful industry groups and committed consumers. Consider petroleum, a major pollutant and the source of greenhouse gas emissions threatening the planet. The government provides huge subsidies to the oil industry, including military protection to tankers and oil fields, access to ports and terminal facilities, and direct cash payments to oil companies for research and development. Including subsidies to the petrochemical industry from the Defense Department and the Department of Energy, the real cost of producing a gallon of gasoline was, in a 1997 study in the *New York Times*, about $5 per gallon. (Since then, global warming and wars in Iraq and elsewhere have raised the real cost of gasoline to well over $7.) In addition, the external costs due to local pollution (smog), congestion, and accidents would, according to a 2007 article in the *Journal of Economic Literature* justify a gasoline tax of $2.10/gallon, ten times the current federal tax of 18 cents.

A large majority of economists favor raising gasoline taxes, including both liberals and conservatives, such as Greg Mankiw, chief economist in the former George W. Bush Administration and Henry Paulson, Bush's Treasury Secretary.5 But an alliance of automobile companies and oil interests with large fuel consumers has prevented any change in the tax since 1993, even in the face of rising prices in general that have eroded the value of the tax. Ethanol does not do much better. Studies at Cornell University and the Department of Agriculture estimate that the energy needed to produce corn-based ethanol, including the energy required to grow and process corn and then distill the ethanol, comes to between 83% and 170% of the energy produced by burning the ethanol. Furthermore, because subsidized ethanol is cheaper than the oil it replaces, ethanol use encourages *more* gasoline use by lowering the price at the gas pump. Using ethanol, therefore, results either in minimal reduction in our imported oil use or, more likely, increased consumption at a multi-billion dollar cost to the public! (This does not even take into account the environmental damage associated with corn production, including herbicide and pesticide use (greater than for any other U.S. crop), soil erosion and ground-water depletion.) Attempts to eliminate the ethanol subsidy have foundered, perhaps because Iowa, a large corn producer, is also a battleground state in national elections, and the first state to pick delegates to nominate presidential candidates.

Democracies find it difficult to impose costs on voters. They are better at granting subsidies, even though every subsidy is paid for by some other constituent and, therefore, implies costs. For this reason, we may say that democracies do a bad job of regulating external effects. This is a real problem because virtually all consumption blends into the public goods realm. A classroom lecture is almost a public good. We do not police admission and, given adequate seating, the presence of another (quiet) student has virtually no effect on your ability to listen and learn. Your ideas are also public goods. A funny joke at the professor's expense can be enjoyed by additional people without diminishing its

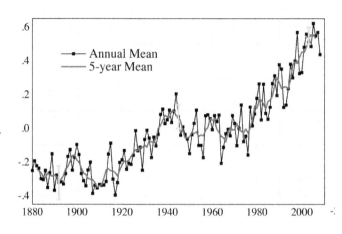

Rise in temperatures 1880-2006

humor (it is nondepletable) and its creator can exclude some from hearing it only at great expense (it is largely nonexcludable).

MARKETS AND EXTERNALITIES: CAN THEY BE MADE COMPATIBLE?

It is a truism that we produce and consume goods if the private benefit we receive exceeds the cost, but in any case, this would lead to the socially optimal level of production only for pure private goods. In cases without externalities (positive or negative), we might want people to produce and consume whenever their private benefit exceeds the cost. Otherwise the good is worth less than it costs to produce and lowers real welfare. Manufacturers will produce when the benefits received and paid for by private consumers exceed the cost of production and will stop production where costs exceed benefits.

This calculus fails for most products because virtually all have at least some public aspect, public benefits and public costs that are not considered by producers and consumers. For public/private goods, we might want an omniscient social planner to order production where the *sum of production benefits* exceeds the *sum of private costs*. Individuals who think (and may know) only of their own benefits and costs cannot make these calculations. I will only paint my walls well enough to protect the wood without regard for the pleasure others might get from a better paint job. Similarly, I will plant wildflowers only to the extent that I enjoy them without regard for the pleasure others would take in a larger meadow. I will tell jokes about Professor Friedman only to the extent that I enjoy them without considering the pleasure others would get from the humor.

Since producers do not respond to the negative and positive externalities suffered and enjoyed by the public, they will *overproduce* negative externalities and *underproduce*[6] public goods; I will make too many bad jokes and will not plant enough wildflowers. The underproduction problem extends to the market for all public goods because, by definition, producers stop producing goods where their return equals their cost; they do not take account of the free benefits others receive. The problem goes still further for pure public goods with nonexcludability. Without restrictions on access, producers have no way to charge for their goods and, therefore, no incentive to produce at all. If notes and information I publish on the web are available free to all, what financial incentive do I have to bother putting information up there? But if the *marginal cost*[7] of providing an additional unit of any nondepletable public good, such as my internet blog or the view of my wildflowers, is zero, more can be consumed without reducing the amount available for others. And we want people to produce much more of these public goods, produce until the *marginal benefit*, the *marginal utility*[8] to the last consumer, is zero. Alas, because they are nonexcludable, when the price that can be set is zero producers

---

THE TRAGEDY OF THE COMMONS

In 1968, the ecologist Garrett Hardin (1915-2003) argued that people will tend to overuse a common pasture. He presented this as an example of how unregulated externalities will lead to social and ecological disaster. In Hardin's words:

"As a rational being, each herdsman seeks to maximize his gain. Explicitly or implicitly, more or less consciously, he asks, "What is the utility *to me* of adding one more animal to my herd?" This utility has one negative and one positive component.

"1. The positive component is a function of the increment of one animal. Since the herdsman receives all the proceeds from the sale of the additional animal, the positive utility is nearly + 1.

"2. The negative component is a function of the additional overgrazing created by one more animal. Since, however, the effects of overgrazing are shared by all the herdsmen, the negative utility for any particular decision making herdsman is only a fraction of - 1.

"Adding together the component partial utilities, the rational herdsman concludes that the only sensible course for him to pursue is to add another animal to his herd. And another .... But this is the conclusion reached by each and every rational herdsman sharing a commons. Therein is the tragedy. Each man is locked into a system that compels him to increase his herd without limit -- in a world that is limited. Ruin is the destination toward which all men rush, each pursuing his own best interest in a society that believes in the freedom of the commons. Freedom in a commons brings ruin to all."

THINKING MARGINALLY

When economists use the word "marginal" as in terms like *marginal utility* or *marginal cost*, they mean the next, not "unimportant" or "secondary." Marginal utility, for example, refers to the pleasure (or *utility*) that one gets from *consuming one more unit* of something, and marginal cost refers to the cost of *producing one more unit* of a good.

PUBLIC AND PRIVATE GOODS

Our tree flowers are a public good since they can be seen from the street and they produce benefits for which we are not paid and which provide no incentive to us to plant more trees. Our Roman mosaic hangs in our hall. It is a private good: we have it because the pleasure we get exceeds the cost.

cannot sell them and they have no incentive to produce them. Producers have no incentive to make public goods beyond what they would want for their own consumption.

Of course, the underproduction problem for public goods is balanced by an overproduction problem for negative externalities (public bads). If I considered the benefits to others, I would produce more good public goods. Similarly, if I considered the losses borne by others, then I would produce fewer public bads. If my neighbor considered how much we dislike his power mower, he would never use it, at least not early Sunday morning. At the extreme, the problem of overproduction of negative externalities can lead to a "tragedy of the commons," where rational individuals will overuse public goods—e.g., by dumping pollution into public air and waterways—until they have been totally wasted. Because we have not put a price on many public commons, such as the life-sustaining capacity of our planet, we have no market incentive to conserve this capacity. We have no market incentive to reduce our greenhouse gas emissions, to conserve clean air, water, fish and wildlife, or to protect biodiversity. And we risk abusing these until they are exhausted and we are all worse off.

COLLECTIVE ACTION AND GAME THEORY

Going back many centuries, Anglo-Saxon common law has addressed externalities as "nuisances," acts or omissions that obstruct or cause inconvenience or damage to the general public. Before the 19th century, the presumption was that the nuisance was due to new activity and the maker of the nuisance, the entrepreneur, would have to compensate neighbors with established claims or stop their own activity. In the early 19th century, for example, builders of water-powered textile mills would have to compensate downstream water users for changes in water pressure due to their new dams, railroads would be cited as nuisances for noises that scared horses, and mill operators would have to pay compensation for smoke damage to neighbors' laundry.

By favoring existing claims over any entrepreneurial right to use property, to make noise or smoke, this interpretation of nuisance law was fundamentally conservative and discouraged innovation.[9] Nuisance law required entrepreneurs to buy out existing claims, raising the cost of investment in facilities that produced externalities and slowed polluting economic growth. While this was desirable to those concerned about clean air and water, others seeking to promote industrialization and faster growth sought changes in nuisance law to put the burden of compensation on those who favored retaining existing conditions. A series of court decisions in the first half of the 19th century fundamentally changed the nature of American nuisance law to favor entrepreneurs initiating new activities. While changes in environmental law in the late-20th century reversed some of this change, giving more weight to the rights of neighbors to a clean and quiet environment, the weight of American jurisprudence remains on the side of investors and innovators.[10]

Early 19th century changes in nuisance law forced aggrieved parties to turn to collective action rather than the courts to address problems of externalities and the production of public goods. They needed direct regulation, laws addressing noise and other forms of pollution. Without possibility of redress through the courts, public goods were seen to require public action where the choice was between Pigouvian taxes and subsidies or direct regulation by state authorities, setting limits on the production of negative public goods

Morton Horwitz is the author of *The Transformation of American Law.*

and require the production of positive public goods. Examples of the political provision of public goods would include the building of public roads and parks, funding of health and other scientific research, and public schools, as well as subsidies to ethanol and oil. Examples of regulations restricting the production of negative public goods include laws restricting pollution and limiting the public display of pornography, as well as taxes on cigarettes.

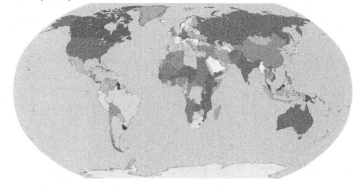

While China with its huge population produces the most greenhouse gasses, North America, Australia, South America, and Europe are still the largest polluters per capita.

The case for public action to address public goods and externalities does not rest only on the public nature of the outcome but also on the inherent difficulty in coordinating individual action to achieve a public purpose. This conclusion can be demonstrated with some simple axioms from a field of economic analysis called *game theory*.[11] Game theory is a branch of microeconomics because it involves individual action and choice. Unlike other branches of microeconomic theory, game theory involves conscious, strategic interactions among rational individuals. Scholars use game theory to explore how individuals will behave when they consciously consider their actions, including how others will react to their own actions. The analysis of interactions allows game theory to address questions of collective action and collective behavior, albeit usually under the assumption that each agent is independent, a Robinson Crusoe who happened to discover others like himself. Nonetheless, exploring human interactions gives game theory a dynamism lacking in other neoclassical analysis that only addresses individual behavior against inanimate nature. The back-and-forth of strategic action and reaction can cause surprising outcomes.

One of the most widely used "games," the "prisoner's dilemma" exposes problems associated with the provision of public goods and the control of negative externalities. The game begins with two thieves captured by police. The police have enough evidence to hold and to convict them for minor offenses but need corroboration to nail them for more serious crimes. Put in separate cells, each is offered a deal: rat on the other and walk free while the other takes the time for the more serious offense. Their options can be represented in a *payoff matrix* showing the outcomes for each depending on their own choice and the choice made by the other:

If both stick to their story, then the police will not have enough evidence to convict either for anything serious; both will get a slap on the wrist and serve parole. If one rats and talks to the police while the other sticks to the story, then the rat gets off but the other is slammed. Finally, if both rat, then they are both in jail. This last is comparable to the alternative facing Socrates and the Athenians at Delium, or the different countries of the world facing global warming today. If all act on their own selfish interest then all face the worst possible outcome.

SOCRATES AND THE PRISONER'S DILEMMA

The Athenian philosopher, **Socrates**, fought against the Boeotians in the Battle of Delium during the Peloponnesian War (424 BCE). This was a catastrophic Athenian defeat and in Plato's dialogue *Laches* Socrates recalls thinking: "If we win, my contribution will not be essential but I risk death or injury. If the Boeotians win, then my chances of death or injury are higher and my contribution immaterial." Following this line of thought, thinking of his own best interests, Socrates would save himself and flee. Of course, if all the Athenians thought like this, they would all flee, leading to a disastrous stampede. According to Alcibiades, in the *Symposium*, Socrates himself fought bravely and well, helping to save many Athenians from the disaster.

We can generalize this by giving utility values to the prisoner's dilemma matrix. If both cooperate and stick to their story, then they both receive parole. But if one rats and takes advantage, then he walks and the other, the sucker, is seriously screwed. Both, therefore, would rather rat on the other than cooperate. But when both cheat, then

TABLE 6-2

PRISONER'S DILEMMA PAYOFF MATRIX

Prisoner 1	Prisoner 2	
	Stick to story	**Rat**
Stick to story	1: Parole; 2: Parole	1: Long jail; 2: Walk
Rat	1: Walk; 2: Long jail	1: Jail; 2: Jail

they both get punished with serious jail time. Note that the best outcome for them both would be if they *both* stick to their story but that will not happen if they both choose the options that is best for themselves. Prisoner 1 does better cheating if the other cooperates, and he does better cheating if the other cheats. And, the same holds for prisoner 2.

Left to their own devices, both will cheat, leading to the worst outcome possible, the cheat-cheat box with returns P. Each chooses the best option for herself given that she cannot know what the other will do. For each, the best option is to talk, regardless of what the other does. This leads to a situation where both talk and, with sufficient evidence against them both, both will do time.

The essence of the prisoner's dilemma is that the best option for each individual leads to the worst of all consequences for all participants. In this, the prisoner's dilemma is a variant of the "tragedy of the commons" discussed by Hardin: individual maximization leads to the worst outcome for the entire community, including each individual. Social life is filled with these situations. Acting to advance our own individual interests, we discount the public good and disdain participation in collective action, leading to outcomes that are bad for everyone. Even when we all agree on some unquestionably desirable collective action, rational individuals will still undermine the process by trying to "free ride". As individuals, we will still try to do better for ourselves by letting others pay while we share the benefits. Unfortunately, when all individuals try to do better for themselves by waiting for others to bring about the collective action, the action never happens.

In Table 6-4, I give an example of the *free rider problem* emerging from the prisoner's dilemma. Where public goods are involved that everyone can consume regardless of their own contribution, people have no direct incentive to contribute to their production. Instead, once individuals conclude that their own contribution is irrelevant to the success or failure of the collective enterprise, their best course is to let others produce the public good—let others incur the costs—and then consume the fruits of their public labor. (Again, this is the problem that Socrates identified in the battle of Delium described in the *Laches*.) I might reason that if others contribute, the collective exercise will succeed without regard to whether I contributed (see Table 6-4, Cases I or III), and if others don't contribute, then it will fail even if I have contributed (Case II). Regardless of what others do, I am better off *not* contributing: Case III is better for me than Case I if others contribute, and Case IV is better for me than Case II if others do not contribute. Ideally, I'll enjoy the benefits of the contributions others make to a successful collective enterprise without contributing (Case III); at worst, I will have saved myself a contribution while still watching a celebration by the other side (Case IV).

TABLE 6-3

GENERAL FORM OF PRISONER'S DILEMMA PAYOFF MATRIX

Prisoner 1	Prisoner 2	
	Cooperate	**Cheat**
Cooperate	1: R = 3; 2: R = 3	1: S = 0; 2: T = 4
Cheat	1: T = 4; 2: S = 0	1: P = 1; 2: P = 1

Note: This table show the net returns received from participating in collective action where the individual's contribution has minimal impact on whether the action succeeds.

TABLE 6-4
FREE RIDING: PAYING $25 TO SUBSIDIZE SOLAR POWER, REDUCE GREENHOUSE GAS PRODUCTION
AND GLOBAL WARMING

Prisoner 1	Others	
	Contribute	**Cheat**
Contribute	Case I. Action succeeds; world is better off but I am out $25	Case II. Action fails; polar ice caps melt and world goes to hell and I'm out $25
Cheat	Case III. Action succeeds; world is better off and I still have my $25.	Case IV. Action fails; polar ice caps melt and world goes to hell but at least I still have my $25.

Note: This table show the net returns received from participating in collective action where the individual's contribution has minimal impact on whether the action succeeds.

The problem is that if we all try to free ride, there will be no public goods and we will all be worse off. We see the consequences of free riding all the time in the poor state of our communal affairs. Why pick up trash on the street, or why not throw trash on the side of the road? If others clean the streets then they will be clean without regard for what we do, and if others do not clean then the streets will be a mess regardless of what we do. Neighborhoods suffer problems with cars driving too fast, drug addicts dealing on the street, and other behavior. These problems all persist because too few take the initiative and 'stick their neck out' to fix things—most are waiting for someone else to do it.

TIT-FOR-TAT

There is something wrong with an analysis that concludes that collective action will not happen, because we know that collective action happens all the time. Working from methodological individualism, orthodox microeconomists find it almost impossible to explain the persistence of collective action. The best they have done has been the work of economist Mancur Olson, who argued that collective action will happen with very small groups or where the benefits are extraordinarily large.[12] Where the benefits of collective action are large enough, and the group receiving them small, even selfish individuals will find it pays to contribute regardless of the behavior of others. This would be the case, for example, if a small group all contributed to buying a lottery ticket. Each could anticipate that their share of the payout would exceed their cost of the ticket, so it would pay for them to buy the ticket even if no one else contributed. In these cases, the small size of the group also allows easy policing so that all can ensure that there are no free riders. Based on this analysis, many economists conclude that it is easier for small groups to mobilize resources for collective action because each member will receive a large share of the total payout if it succeeds and because it is easier to police against free riders in groups where everyone knows each other, rather than in larger, more anonymous communities. This analysis certainly explains some political behavior. It often happens that small groups dominate large groups in setting tax and trade policies, for example, or in setting water policy in the West, where a few farmers gain at the expense of large cities. This is also the case for the ethanol subsidy or policies restricting sugar imports, where a relatively small number of producers benefit at the expense of the larger community.[13]

By recognizing the significance of a group mechanism to police free riding, this analysis goes beyond group size. When there are repeated engagements, players may come to value a reputation for cooperation because this allows them to establish long-term cooperative relationships. You are more likely to behave well around people with whom you will be living than with strangers. The role of repeated engagements and reputation can be generalized through the most successful experimental approach to the prisoner's dilemma game, *tit-for-tat*. It turns out that in repeated games between competitors who get to know each other, there is a rational pro-social strategy: tit-for-tat, or cooperate on your first move and then repeat your opponent's previous move.

TIT-FOR-TAT WINS!

Against any other strategy, in a repeated game like in Table 6-3, tit-for-tat will accumulate the most points. In 200 rounds, tit-for-tat will score the highest both against itself and on average.

Strategy\other party	T-f-T	All D	Alt D
T-f-T	600	203	400
All D	199	200	100
Alt D	400	500	400
Average score	400	301	300

Note: T-f-T strategy: cooperate then do what the other party did in the last round.

All D: Always cheat.

Alt D: Alternate cheat and cooperate.

Early in the modern computer age, a group of economists, political scientists, and others interested in game theory ran a series of computer tournaments comparing the effectiveness of different strategies in the prisoner's dilemma in a very large number of trials.[14] In these competitions, tit-for-tat won, easily dominating other, more complicated strategies, not to mention other strategies that relied more on cheating and narrowly self-interested behavior. Comparing the dozens of competing strategies, tit-for-tat won because of four characteristics: niceness, retaliation, forgiveness, and clarity.

• **Niceness**: Tit-for-tat begins with cooperation and it continues to cooperate as long as the other party cooperates. It assumes cooperation, and will continue unless provoked.

• **Retaliation**: Tit-for-tat has zero tolerance of bad behavior. If the other party tries to cheat, tit-for-tat *immediately* punishes by cheating back.

• **Forgiveness**: Tit-for-tat bears no grudges. If the other party cheats, tit-for-tat retaliates, but once the other party returns to cooperation, tit-for-tat cooperates as if there had been no conflict.

• **Clarity**: Tit-for-tat's strategy is so very simple that it is easy for other parties to understand. And once they understand what tit-for-tat is doing, they will realize that their best strategy over the long run is to cooperate.

The analysis of tit-for-tat is revealing in other dimensions because tit-for-tat is not always the best strategy. In particular, its success depends on the number of engagements and the value put on time. In a one-round competition, for example, tit-for-tat and other "nice" strategies will lose to "mean" strategies that begin by cheating. If you will never again meet someone, then cheating can be a rational strategy because those you cheated will not have an opportunity to get revenge. Because the benefits of a tit-for-tat strategy increase over time, the rate at which people value future benefits compared with present pains is crucial. For people with a high *rate of discount*, who put a very low value on future benefits, the early gains from a "mean" strategy may overwhelm the later gains from "niceness." Tit-for-tat wins for people in settled relationships and stable communities who put a high value on the future. On the other hand, a lesson from this research is to be careful in one night stands, especially with people who put a low value on the future.

The literature on tit-for-tat is exciting because, from the perspective of methodological individualism, it explains why individuals might contribute to the public good. That said, I suspect that there is a great deal more collective action than can be explained by tit-

Winner of the 2009 Nobel Prize in Economics (with Oliver Williamson), **Elinor Ostrom (1933-2012)** did pioneering research showing that people are able to work together to manage common resources, whether in forests, fisheries, pastures, or irrigation systems. Her work contradicts the pessimistic assumptions of Garrett Hardin and others that self-interest will undermine the protection of public goods. Among her most famous works is *Governing the Commons: the Evolution of Institutions for Collective Action* (Cambridge, 1990).

for-tat, which would suggest that focusing on free riding and prisoner's dilemma problems might be the wrong way to explain the motives behind collective action and social cooperation. We observe collective action and the production of public goods all the time, not only in families and among neighbors in stable communities but among people who will never see each other again. Yes, people clean, cook, and do laundry for their families and are kind to their friends; but they are also polite to

Two examples of community social action. Volunteers clearing litter as part of an annual cleanup of the Mason Neck River in Virginia (left). The Nazi Nuremberg rally, 1938 (right).

strangers on the streets, hold doors for and behave considerately to people they will never see again, and anonymously return lost wallets to strangers who they have never met and never will meet. (Indeed, they often behave best towards strangers, including tourists and visiting students.)

It may be that people are so kind to strangers because they follow the biblical command, in Deuteronomy (10: 19), "Love ye therefore the stranger: for ye were strangers in the land of Egypt." Much of childrearing is spent teaching children to see themselves as members of communities, with responsibilities to contribute without regard to any personal payout. This collective action is less the result of the behavior of rational individuals than of people who comprehend themselves as belonging to a family and a community, from which they draw benefits and to which they owe obligations. Collective action is most common where there are strong community bonds; people feel pressured from their friends and neighbors to contribute. Cooperation and collective action also helps to create a sense of community. Cheering for your high-school basketball team, for example, forges school ties that last through lifetimes. After participating in the collective effervescence of school sports assemblies, as Durkheim called it, you would be more ready to work at your class car wash to raise money for your prom, a behavior that some economists might find utterly mystifying.

Durkheim may be right that collective action relies on a certain suspension of rational thought, a willingness to accept ones position as a member of a community and the responsibilities that go with that status. We need this community feeling to survive, but it can be abused terribly. Community spirit is wonderful when we need to clean debris off the side of a major road or to build hiking trails through conservation lands. But Hitler's Nuremberg rallies were also designed to build a sense of community and collective spirit. The same communal spirit that kept Germans from littering also led many to cooperate in "cleansing" their country of Jews and other undesirables. We might reasonably assume that a two-person free-market exchange with no externalities will be a "good thing," but there is no similar guarantee that collective action will be directed at the right objects.

To some extent, methodological individualists are right. In large groups, collective action requires coercion to prevent free riding by forcing all to contribute. Rational individuals will not voluntarily contribute enough to maintain public services even if they favor those services and favor everyone making the necessary contribution; that is why governments rely on taxes. However, once coercion is involved we enter a dangerous world where we must rely on political processes and voting rules to ensure that we make the right communal decisions. We need taxes to maintain civilization. But that does not mean that we have best met our community's needs with this particular set of taxes and spending policies. Because most collective action relies on some form of compulsion to overcome free riding, either through physical force or social pressure, it is necessarily vulnerable to abuse. Within families and communities, only personal feeling and good will ensure that the benefits (to your parents, siblings, neighbors) of the lawn work you did for your Dad will exceed the costs, or that the work your Mom did in the kitchen preparing dinner is worth the pleasure you and your family get from the meal. Like generalized reciprocity, community spirit and a commitment to collective action often relies on unspecified measures, matters of values and trust. Therefore it is

HOW DID UNIONS GROW?
THE CRUCIAL ROLE OF STRIKE WAVES

It has been so long since American unions have grown significantly that one might excuse those who have forgotten how growth happened. Scholars and union strategists these days speak of union growth as a process of trench warfare where members are recruited retail by organizing individual workplaces and new shops. But real union growth has been a completely different process with whole-sale growth coming in sudden, volcanic bursts where new groups of workers—even whole industries—suddenly join the labor movement, usually through massive strikes.

Over 50 years ago, the English historian Eric Hobsbawm observed that "the graph of the membership of virtually every trade-union movement ... looks like a series of sloping steps, or of broad valleys broken by sharp peaks ... very rarely is it a mere rising slope." He observes that most of the increase in British union membership before 1914, for example, came in three dramatic leaps, in 1871, 1889, and 1911. Leaps marked qualitative as well as quantitative changes in the labor movement, taking the labor movement "into new industries, new regions, new classes of the population." During these leaps, labor developed new institutions; new unions organized along new dimensions, often with new goals and new politics.

As with much that the late, great British historian wrote, Hobsbawm got this right: unions grow in leaps or not at all. Over a century of annual union membership statistics for 14 countries, most growth came in a few years when membership grew by nearly 50% a year compared with less than 2% in the other years (see Figure 1). These were years of great upheaval and political turmoil. Most important, they were years of major strikes.

Comparing the years with the greatest strike activity with other years, unions grow nearly six-times as fast in years of high strikes (see Figure 2). Since the beginning of the Labor Movement, workers have joined the working class through participation in mass strikes. General and theoretical rigor was first given to the study of mass strikes before World War I by a Polish-born, Jewish economist, Rosa Luxemburg. Disappointed with the German Social Democrat's policy of building an organization to win reforms, Luxemburg argued that the socialist revolution needed to be made through a continuing struggle that would not only win concessions but would build class consciousness. "[T]the great Socialist importance of the trade-union and political struggle," she argues, "consists in socializing the knowledge, the consciousness of the proletariat, in organizing it as a class."

For Luxemburg, participation in strike movements promotes organization by changing workers. Strikes are the collective effervescence of the labor movement exposing the fundamental conflict of in-

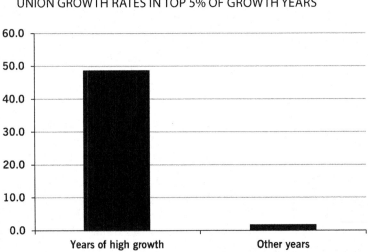

FIGURE 1
UNION GROWTH RATES IN TOP 5% OF GROWTH YEARS

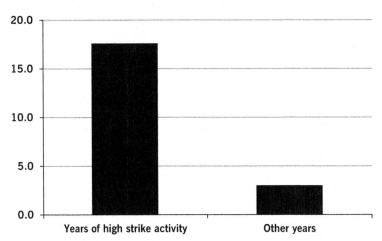

FIGURE 2
UNION GROWTH RATES IN TOP 5% OF STRIKE YEARS

terest between management and labor and teaching workers of their collective power. By demonstrating the workers' ability to manage for themselves, conducting a strike belies the essential claim for all systems of hierarchy: the idea that workers are incompetent and need to be managed. Through strikes, individual workers become part of a class, conscious of their power and confident in their abilities.

Labor activists focus on the way strikes and participation in militant action changes workers. Without discounting this effect, strikes are as important for shaping employers and state officials. It is a too-common mistake for activists and labor scholars to view the labor movement in terms of the workers alone. Unionization is not simply a choice made by workers because, in the class struggle, workers are the weaker party. Workers are a necessary but not sufficient condition for unionization; union growth happens when workers mobilize at a time when employers and state officials are ready to tolerate unions, often as the lesser evil when confronted by militant strikers. Strikes promote organization by transforming workers' consciousness but their larger effect may be to persuade employers and state officials to accept unions.

Thinking about employers and state officials gives a more nuanced view of why strike waves led to rapid growth, and why the effect of strikes on union growth may have declined over the course of the late 20th century. It should go without saying that employers resent unions and avoid recognizing them whenever they can. They accept unions reluctantly, only when they believe that the alternative, uncontrolled popular militancy, is even worse and they believe that unions can and will restrain unrest. They accept unions because they believe that the union leadership will behave "responsibly," channeling popular demands into avenues acceptable to capitalists, and will act with authority, maintaining control over the workers collective action through effective, even nondemocratic, union organizations.

In the United States, unions grew by promising management a solution to labor militancy, an alternative to revolution. But we cannot step in that river again; capitalists have moved on beyond needing labor unions to resolve labor unrest; and they no longer believe that unions can deliver on this promise. Instead, we have to come to grips with the dilemma that consumed Rosa Luxemburg: reform and revolution are not differences in degree but in kind, in essence. If our goal is to improve capitalism, we may give up on unions because it may suffice to work with the human relations departments of powerful corporations. But if we truly want to transform a society of hierarchy into a world of free people, then we need institutions and forms of struggle that will deny the legitimacy of managerial hierarchy and insist on equal rights to all and to all an equal voice.

Sources: Eric Hobsbawm, "Economic Fluctuations and Some Social Movements," in Hobsbawm (ed.), *Labouring Men: Studies in the History of Labour* (Basic Books, 1964); Eric Hobsbawm, *The Forward March of Labour Halted?* (Verso, 1981); Rosa Luxemburg, *Reform or Revolution, and Other Writings* (Dover Books, 2006); Aristide Zolberg, "Mom Madness," *Politics and Society* 2 (1972): 183–208.

vulnerable to poor communication, a curious reluctance to express one's wishes and needs, and the authority of charismatic individuals. These problems are inherent in collective action because there are no mechanisms to check abuse comparable to market exit. People can voice grievances but there is no guarantee that authorities will listen. In the end, we must rely on building values of mutual respect and strong institutions for democratic self-governance.

EXTERNALITIES AND PROPERTY RIGHTS

Subject to manipulation by the rich, the powerful, and those who belong to relatively small and well-organized groups, political processes are highly imperfect, with no guarantee that public regulation of externalities and public goods will result in a social optimum. Even if we get the right mix of policies, there remain major problems with state regulation. For one, coercive regulation undermines the sense of voluntary participation that make communities function well in the first place. Once the government *mandates* good behavior, some people will be good only when the police are around. For those who are not inclined to behave well, the threat to put them in jail unless they behave works only when they believe they will be caught; in other cases, the law gives no positive incentive. On the contrary, once regulations are promulgated, regulated groups see them as an attack on their personal standing, to be fought even at the expense of legal bills and lobbying expenses that may dwarf the cost of compliance. Governments must establish a bureaucracy and enforcement police against this, all at the public expense, and an expense magnified by the need to collect tax revenue to fund the enlarged bureaucracy. Wouldn't it be better if we could rely on everyone to contribute out of a sense of community concern and neighborly good will? Or leave it to individual action to directly regulate externalities?

Frustrated with regulation but aware that the free market does not necessarily address public goods and externalities, economists have looked for other ways to protect the public interest. Market-oriented economists have naturally looked to markets, and to opportunity costs. Using these concepts, Nobel-laureate economist Ronald Coase proposed an idea. The *Coase Theorem*[15] states that where transactions costs are minimal and property rights are clearly specified, where one side or the other has a clear legal right to impose or to reject the externalities produced by the other, externalities could be resolved efficiently through individual bargaining because any aggrieved could either demand compensation or offer to pay off the other party to cease.[16]

The basic logic is that there is a functional equivalence between someone paying you to remove the externality, because you have a right to produce it, and you paying someone else to tolerate the externality, because they have a legal right to protection from your production.

Consider, for example, a situation where a neighbor has an ugly tree that you would like to remove. You complain but your neighbor likes her tree. Now suppose that she has the legal right to keep it; then you would have to pay her to remove it. If it would cost her more to remove the tree than the cost of your discomfort, the maximum that you would pay her to remove it, then the tree will stay. You won't be willing to pay your neighbor enough to remove the tree, which is good because the benefit she gets from keeping the tree exceeds your loss. (This is Case 3 in Table 6-5). Alternatively, if you hate the tree enough to pay your neighbor more than it would cost her to remove the tree, then she will accept your offer and the tree will be removed. (This is Case 4 in Table

Officials of the Environmental Protection Agency inspect pesticides while a company manager watches. Founded in 1970, the EPA is charged with enforcing laws regulating pollution and other activity damaging the environment. Its activities are often criticized by the companies it regulates, and by economists who believe it would be more efficient to address externalities by encouraging side bargains between individuals and companies.

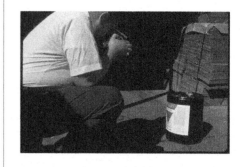

6-5). Again, this is as it should be because the cost to you of the tree is greater than the benefit to your neighbor. If you have a right to protection from her pernicious tree, then she can pay you to tolerate it if removal costs are higher than your discomfort (Case 1), or she can remove it if that is cheaper than paying you (Case 2). In all cases, the allocation of property rights will affect the distribution of income—you have more if you have property rights, less if your neighbor has the property right. But, the efficient outcome will be reached regardless of property rights. The tree will be removed if the costs of removal are less than the discomfort it causes and remains otherwise.

Coase's market-based solution to the problem of externalities is attractive because it has the appearance of avoiding government regulation. All that is needed is a clear statement of property rights and the externalities will be addressed efficiently through decentralized and voluntary deal making. Whoever has property rights in this situation, private exchange will insure that the tree is removed if the benefits in sunlight to you exceed removal costs to her. Otherwise, the tree will stay. Regardless of who has the property rights, if the rights are clearly specified, the tree's fate depends on whether you dislike it enough to cover the cost of removing it.

Rather than political processes of voting, drafting and fighting regulations, and enforcement, Coase's resolution appears to rely on voluntary transactions among individuals. With outcomes freely negotiated between the parties, we can assume that both are satisfied, even if they would prefer a different allocation of property rights. To those enamored of the Coase Theorem, there are problems only if property rights are not clearly specified because then the lawyers and judges get involved.

Coase won the Nobel Prize for this work and his work on transactions costs,[17] and his paper on "Social Cost" has been one of the most cited articles in all of economics. His work is widely read by policy makers, lawyers, and government officials, as well as by economists. But Coase's elegant system only *appears* to avoid the problem of externalities. It only holds where there are no real public goods, where the issue is posed between one individual and another, with only individuals, no community, hence no collective action problem. Once a community is involved, the problem of externalities reappears as a problem of mobilizing a group against an individual producer of external costs or benefits. As such, in a case with real public goods, Coase's bargaining solution falls to free riding.

Even with isolated individuals, Coase's solution is likely to fall to bargaining problems. Like other neoclassicists, Coase would treat social relationships as engineering problems, problems between people and things rather than as social problems between people and people. To reach an efficient reso-

The English economist **Ronald Coase (1910-2013)** is best known for two theorems relating to transactions costs and the extension of the free market. In his 1937 paper on the nature of the firm (1937), he argued that firms exist to minimize transactions costs in the detailed division of labor. In his 1960 paper, he developed the "Coase Theorem" arguing that economic actors can internalize externalities through negotiation and side payments, and that the result will be identical regardless of which party has rights of ownership over the cause of the externality. Where there are no transactions costs, the initial allocation of property rights affect the distribution of income, not the efficiency of resource allocation.

TABLE 6-5
COSTS AND BENEFITS FROM HYPOTHETICAL TREE REMOVAL

Property rights	Relative costs	
	Removal cost exceeds your gain	Removal cost less than your gain
You	Case 1: She pays you to tolerate tree.	Case 2: She pays to remove tree.
Neighbor	Case 3: Nothing happens; tree stays.	Case 4: You pay her to remove tree.

Note: This table suggests the outcome of the tree problem according to the relative costs of removing the tree, compared with how much you dislike the tree, and who has property rights in the air-space. This table is constructed assuming there are no transactions costs.

CAN COASE WORK? MAYBE, SOMETIMES.

Individual action can help to resolve disputes over externalities, but transactions costs and bargaining problems can prevent an efficient outcome. For example, consider the problem of loud parties. In my neighborhood, it is customary practice to invite neighbors to a loud party as a way of giving them some compensation for the noise and traffic. I appreciate this recognition that my neighbors' parties inconvenience me, though the party invitation is paltry compensation. I could call the police, but that would lead to an unpleasant conflict, lawyers, and further expense. Instead, I go to the party, have a drink, and leave with my earplugs.

lution, Coase must assume that both parties know the costs and benefits for the other so that they can reach an efficient bargain. But why would this be the case? Imagine a game of poker between two individuals, one producing an externality which the other seeks to stop. Instead of bargaining honestly, wouldn't each try to mislead the other to drive prices up or down? I might approach my neighbor about her tree, but I may not if I assume that we would not be able to reach a fair bargain. As long as my costs exceed hers, I can pay her to remove the tree, but asymmetric information, transactions costs, and bargaining all get in the way, because she has every incentive to drive up the cost to me by taking advantage of my arborphobia. My suspicion of her motives may lead me to reject even a favorable offer from her, just as her ignorance of my real feelings may lead her to try to drive an excessive bargain that will prevent any agreement. Moreover, because we are neighbors, we have many interactions where good will is important. I will think carefully before approaching my neighbor with what she may perceive as a criticism of her taste in trees, and she may accept an inefficient settlement in hopes of maintaining my good will for other issues, such as the car pool to my daughters' ballet class. Worse still, once bargaining begins, my neighbor may choose to increase her annoying behavior just to drive up what I will pay to get her to stop.

Of course, these bargaining problems between individuals pale compared to the collective problems facing a large group trying to negotiate the removal of true public goods and offensive externalities. Far from avoiding political issues, an attempt to resolve externalities following the Coase Theorem pushes political questions out of the regulated and duly constitutional realm of the state into the wholly deregulated and unorganized realm of private and neighborhood action. Consider, for example, the situation of the residents of East Boston facing airport noise coming from Logan Airport. Planes taking off from or landing at Logan Airport are directed as much as possible out to sea but they still produce loud noises over East Boston and other areas around the airport. If the residents had a legal right to peace and quiet, then the airport and its users would be forced to pay them to tolerate the noise. Instead, residents must seek redress from government regulation, against the political power of the commercial airline industry and air travelers. Or, they could pay Logan Airport to reduce noise. To do that, all they would have to do is to negotiate a price with Logan Airport and all its users, and then devise a mechanism to collect money from those who would benefit from the noise reduction, a process that makes established politics seem easy.

Far from removing the politics from externalities, Coase only shifts the political process away from the established arenas where there are rules protecting minorities and civil liberties, and where established bureaucracies and civil servants can manage regulations. Instead, the Coase Theorem would require that we recreate all of this political apparatus every time that we need to negotiate the regulation of externalities. The Coase Theorem may work in the same types of situations where tit-for-tat works to maintain good collective behavior. Elsewhere, however, there are large groups with important interests who need some more effective mechanism, for example, to protect endangered species, limit greenhouse gas emissions, and remove destructive dams. It is safe to say that some-

ENVIRONMENTAL JUSTICE

The rich can sometimes avoid pollution and other environmental externalities produced by their market activities. For example, if local water is polluted, they can buy clean bottled water; if a toxic dump locates in town, they can move away.

Professor James Boyce of the University of Massachusetts at Amherst has been one of the leaders in the emerging field of environmental justice, which explores the interplay of environmental degradation and economic inequality.

FIGURE 6-1
MELTING OF ARCTIC ICE SINCE 1979

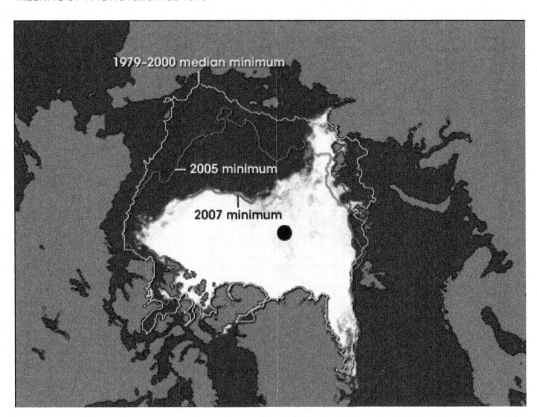

one has brought Coase's article to the attention of the leaders of Tuvalo, Venice, Bangladesh, West Bengal, and other places threatened by global warming and rising sea levels. In principle, large populations threatened by the greenhouse effect could pay a few auto companies a few billion dollars to produce cars that emit less carbon dioxide. Italian art-lovers alone might be willing to pay tens of billions of dollars to save Venice. Bargaining and collective action problems prevent effective action.

Who will protect this bear from global warming? Can she sue for her ice?

Coase has become an icon to reactionary legal scholars and economists for whom his analysis is a model of asocial economic reasoning and an argument against state regulation.[18] This reflects a shallow reading of his work. His bargaining process would provide a poor substitute for regulation. There is a larger issue here: Coase himself never intended his paper to be used against state regulation. He believed it demonstrated the power and importance of regulations establishing and enforcing property rights. His original goal was to demonstrate precisely how income distribution and wealth depend on the allocation of property rights, an allocation that reflects political history and past conflicts as well as the distribution of wealth and social power. What, he asks, prevents you from walking into your neighbor's yard and cutting down the offending woody plant? What except tradition and values? And a ready police force paid for with taxes working at the behest of those with power.

DISCUSSION QUESTIONS

What are "public goods"? How are they different from "private goods"?

What are "externalities"? Are they all negative? How do externalities reduce the efficiency of competitive markets? What are "Pigouvian taxes"? What are "Pigouvian subsidies"? Can tax-policy and subsidies correct the market failures that come from externalities?

Should we put a tax on carbon?

What is the "Tragedy of the Commons"? How does it come from externalities and public goods?

What changes in prices might stop global warming?

What is the "Prisoner's Dilemma"? How would it apply to Socrates at the battle of Delium?

What is "Tit-for-Tat"? How would it lead people to avoid the bad consequences of the Prisoner's Dilemma?

Why can small groups do better than larger groups at providing public goods?

What is the Coase Theorem? Would free exchange and side payments prevent all externalities? How would they prevent inefficient externalities? What is the difference between efficient and inefficient externalities?

Would Coasean exchange prevent all inefficient externalities? What conditions would be necessary for fully efficient outcomes? Would these efficient outcomes necessarily be just and fair?

ENDNOTES

[1] By raising the cost of goods with negative externalities, a tax would bring the price of the good more in line with the social impact. Similarly, by lowering the price, a subsidy would encourage consumption of goods with positive externalities. These are called "Pigouvian" because they were suggested by Arthur Pigou in his *Economics of Welfare*.

[2] We also subsidize nuclear power but that raises other externality issues.

[3] http://www.cdc.gov/chronicdisease/resources/publications/aag/osh.htm

[4] It tells us something about how profitable cigarette manufacture is that the industry has absorbed hundreds of billions of dollars in civil damages but remains active and profitable.

[5] Henry M. Paulson Jr, "Lessons for Climate Change in the 2008 Recession," *The New York Times*, June 21, 2014, http://www.nytimes.com/2014/06/22/opinion/sunday/lessons-for-climate-change-in-the-2008-recession.html.

[6] Because the price to consumers of a good with negative externalities is below the proper social cost of that good, people will buy too many; similarly, if a good with positive externalities is not subsidized, it will cost consumers too much and producers will make too little.

[7] This is the cost of making the next additional good.

[8] The marginal benefit or the marginal utility is the benefit from the last unit of the good.

[9] Morton J Horwitz, *The Transformation of American Law, 1780-1860* (Cambridge, Mass.: Harvard University Press, 1977); William J Novak, *The People's Welfare: Law and Regulation in Nineteenth-Century America* (Chapel Hill: University of North Carolina Press, 1996); Frank Bourgin, *The Great Challenge: The Myth of Laissez-Faire in the Early Republic* (New York: G. Braziller, 1989).

[10] William J. Novak, *The People's Welfare: Law and Regulation in Nineteenth-Century America, Studies in Legal History* (Chapel Hill: University of North Carolina Press, 1996); *Property Rights in*

American History: From the Colonial Era to the Present (New York: Garland Pub, 1997); James W. Ely, *The Guardian of Every Other Right: A Constitutional History of Property Rights*, Bicentennial Essays on the Bill of Rights (New York: Oxford University Press, 1992); Richard Allen Epstein, *Free Markets under Siege: Cartels, Politics, and Social Welfare*, Hoover Institution Press Publication, no. 536 (Stanford, Calif: Hoover Institution Press, 2005); University of Massachusetts at Amherst, *Natural Assets: Democratizing Environmental Ownership* (Washington, DC: Island Press, 2003); James K. Boyce, *The Political Economy of the Environment* (Cheltenham, U.K.; Northampton, Mass., USA: E. Elgar Pub, 2002); *The Sanctity of Property Rights in American History* (ScholarWorks@UMass Amherst), http://scholarworks.umass.edu/peri_workingpapers/30.

[11] Game theory is the branch of microeconomics that studies strategic interactions among individuals conscious of the strategy of others.

[12] Mancur Olson, *The Logic of Collective Action; Public Goods and the Theory of Groups*, Harvard Economic Studies, v. 124 (Cambridge, Mass: Harvard University Press, 1965).

[13] Mancur Olson, *The Rise and Decline of Nations: Economic Growth, Stagflation, and Social Rigidities* (New Haven: Yale University Press, 1982).

[14] Tit-for-tat is described in Robert M Axelrod, *The Evolution of Cooperation*, rev. ed (New York: Basic Books, 2006).

[15] The Coase Theorem states that in a situation with clearly specified property rights and without transactions costs, an efficient allocation of resources and externalities will be reached through free markets. By efficient, Coase meant that products will be produced where the marginal cost is less than the marginal benefit, and will not be produced where marginal costs exceed marginal benefits (where costs and benefits both include external costs and public goods).

[16] Ronald H Coase, "The Problem of Social Cost.(reprinted from 1960)," *Journal of Law and Economics* 56, no. 4 (2013): 837–77.

[17] R. H. Coase, "The Nature of the Firm," *Economica* 4, no. 16 (November 1, 1937): 386–405, doi:10.1111/j.1468-0335.1937.tb00002.x.

[18] On the rise of conservative legal thought in the United States and the influence of Coase, see Steven Michael Teles, *The Rise of the Conservative Legal Movement the Battle for Control of the Law* (Princeton, N.J.: Princeton University Press, 2008), http://site.ebrary.com/id/10312554.

7

MARGINAL UTILITY AND NEOCLASSICAL CONSUMER DEMAND THEORY

WHERE DO PREFERENCES COME FROM? AND WHY DO WE CARE?

Orthodox economists argue that free markets maximize people's welfare by assuming that competition will lead producers to produce what people want. To show that this maximizes the sum of individual welfare, they must argue that people know what they want independently of the wishes of business or the influence of society. When people bring their preferences to market transactions, then it is assumed that free exchange can only make them better off.

Thus, to reach this welfare conclusion, one must begin with the preferences of individuals and argue that these preferences are determined outside of the market economy, that they are *exogenous* with respect to whatever goes on in the marketplace.[1] This approach is vulnerable to challenges that preferences are *endogenous* to the market, and are shaped by participation in the market process.[2] This might be the case for several reasons. Preferences could be endogenous because they are socially constructed through the influence of social institutions such as businesses, which seek to increase profits with advertising and other measures to manipulate consumer preferences. Or they may be socially constructed by participation in the market. The experience of buying and selling commodities, and observing others doing the same, can change people's preferences. In either case, the welfare conclusion, supporting *laissez faire* on the grounds that free markets lead businesses to meet consumer needs, is not justified if these needs are themselves socially constructed.

There are things that people want because of intrinsic human needs: companionship, warmth, food, sex, healthy gums. Most of our economic activity, however, has little to do with such basic needs. Most of what we buy and sell is a matter of wants rather than needs, and these wants vary between communities and nations. Unlike physiological needs, wants are not dictated/decided/set by our physical nature but are socially determined, shaped by upbringing and experience. Different communities—with different market structures, child-rearing strategies, and politicalsocial systems—teach different values and preferences.

The social construction of wants is familiar beyond the world of Madison Avenue executives. Playground drug dealers who distribute free samples are constructing preferences through experience, as are parents who take their children to art museums, religious events, and Boston Red Sox games in hopes of teaching them to appreciate the finer things in life. Whether it is pushing drugs or trying to shape preferences by exposing children to positive experiences, adults try to manip-

FIGURE 7-1

CONSUMPTION PATTERNS: FRANCE, GERMANY, THE UK, AND THE U.S., C. 2004

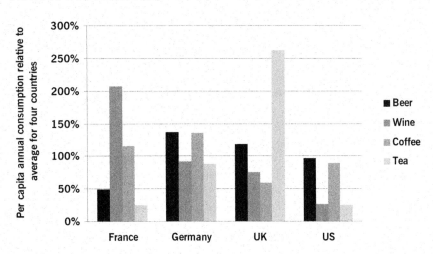

ulate the preferences of children so that they will buy the things we want them to buy. We may try to raise our children to want Monet posters, to go to church on Sunday, and to buy tickets to Fenway Park. No doubt we feel that these are good things to want. But other parents may disagree: they will teach their children to value Jackson Pollock, to attend synagogue on Saturdays, and to go to Yankee games.

Opium, wine, beer.

There can be dramatic differences in preferences even between neighboring countries. Compare Germany and France, for example, countries that border each other and have shared a customs union for over 50 years. The French drink relatively little beer but much wine, consuming over a liter of wine per person per week.[3] Germans, by contrast, drink much beer but little wine, consuming less than half as much wine as the French but nearly three times as much beer. Do these differences reflect physiological differences between the French and the Germans? If so, how to explain differences between Britain and the United States? In the United States, we drink nearly twice as much coffee per person as do the British, but we drink only one-tenth as much tea.

Far from being exogenous, determined by God or genetics, governments and businesses shape preferences through advertising, schools, and public policy. Wine, beer, coffee, tea: all of these reflect conscious state action. After defeat in the 1870-71 war with Germany, the French Third Republic campaigned to persuade the population of France that wine, especially Champagne, was the proper drink of the French people. As much as the histories of Michelet and Lavisse, or the sociology of Durkheim, wine and *haute cuisine* became part of the construction of the French republic where wine drinking was taught in elementary schools.[4] In Germany as well, drinking was a matter of national policy. While the 16th-century German theologian Martin Luther had pronounced that "beer is made by man, wine by God," later German leaders rejected wine as a French drink. Beer, on the other hand, was a true Teutonic beverage. After the defeat of France in the Franco-Prussian War and the formation of the German Empire in 1871, beer was promoted across the Rhine as the German beverage, not alcohol but food for citizens of the new, reunited German empire. Bavaria's beer purity law was made national, and subsidies were extended to beer festivals.

The most infamous case of the construction of preferences was the systematic campaign by the British to "persuade" the Chinese to consume opium. Through the early 19th century, there was a steady and growing flow of European specie (precious-metal currency) into China to pay for the products craved by European consumers, including silks, porcelain, and tea. Against this imbalance, the British settled on opium as a product that could balance their trade with China. Grown in British-ruled India, opium was banned in China except for medicinal use. After attempts to smuggle significant quantities of opium into China were quashed by Chinese authorities, the British invaded China, in 1839. Quickly overcoming the resistance of the ill-equipped and poorly trained Chinese imperial forces, the British imposed the Treaty of Nanking (August 29, 1842). Under this treaty, China ceded the island of Hong Kong to Great Britain, opened five "Treaty" ports (Canton, Amoy, Foochow, Shanghai, and Ningbo) to Western trade and residence, granted Great Britain most-favored nation status for trade, and paid nine million dollars in reparations to merchants whose opium had been destroyed. (The Manchu signatories accepted the principle of "extraterritoriality," where Western merchants were no longer accountable to China's laws.) No sooner had peace been negotiated than British merchants began to hawk opium. Thus the Royal Navy made opium a drug of choice in China for a century.[5]

COFFEE, DIMINISHING MARGINAL UTILITY, AND NEOCLASSICAL DEMAND THEORY

For Father's Day 2004, my children (and my wife) gave me an espresso maker. Every morning, I get up, make some coffee, and drink. The first cup is bliss: warm, tasty, caffeinated. The second cup is delightful. The third one is good; the fourth is OK and, while I still enjoy the flavor, the fifth makes me a little jittery. If I drink a sixth cup, I begin to quiver uncomfortably. I love coffee, but each cup is less desirable than the one before until, finally, I don't want more.

This illustrates a general law: the more you have of anything, the less valuable the next bit becomes. *Marginal utility*, the pleasure we get from consuming the next thing, diminishes. Robinson Crusoe really enjoyed his first coconut, but by the time he ate his hundredth, he was almost ready to starve rather than eat another one. In graduate school, I met someone who grew up in a village in the Canadian Maritimes where they harvested lobster. He ate lobster for breakfast, lunch, dinner. He swore to me that he would never eat another lobster.

From examples like these, neoclassical economists infer that the more you have, the less you will *pay* for the next unit, and they made this the central idea behind neoclassical *consumer demand*, or the theory of how individuals decide how much to buy.[6] A second computer is less valuable than the first, but more valuable than a third, which is worth more than the fourth. The more one has of normal goods, the less pleasure one gets from another and the less one is willing to pay for more. The principle here is of *diminishing marginal utility*: the pleasure you get from another bit of consumption declines with greater consumption.

Marginal utility is the pleasure one gets from consuming more. It declines because *satiation*[7] sets in when more is consumed. When you have more of something, you tire of consuming still more. One bowl of ice cream is wonderful, a second is OK, the third is getting to be much, and the fourth becomes a problem of disposal. (Maybe the dog will eat it.) Note right away that the degree of satiation, the marginal utility of any good, depends not only on the number of goods but on the availability of *complements*[8] to be consumed with it. You may feel better about getting more ice cream if you have a large freezer. And you may want more if you have hot fudge. Even at this point, at the very center of neoclassical value theory, there is a social dimension. After three weeks in Paris I may be a little tired of the city and ready to go home, but I might feel differently if my wife is with me, even if we lack the money to eat in fancy restaurants.

Scarlett Johansson's favorite food is buffalo chicken wings. Why does she eat anything else?

You can see right away that marginal utility theory fails in the original motivation of neoclassicists, which is to separate value theory from society. The driving idea of neoclassical theory is to put economics onto an asocial plane, safely removed from political choice. Confined to Robinson Crusoe's world, neoclassical analysis treats value as determined by relations between people and the things they consume rather than emerging from a theory of social, and political, behavior. Marginal utility is downward sloping because people tire or grow sated with any particular goods. Neoclassical economists use this insight into individual behavior to form a general theory of *demand*, the amount that will be purchased at any price by a group of individuals. When we move to a theory

Are two too many?

FIGURE 7-2
MARGINAL UTILITY FROM WINE

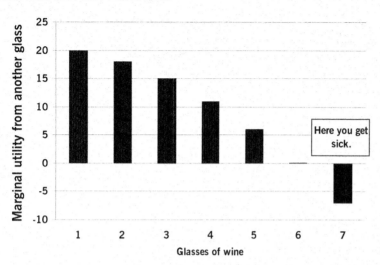

of demand, however, we consider consumption as not only an individual activity, involving you and your ice cream, but also a social one, where you consume your ice cream with your friends. Then demand depends on social concerns, like eating ice cream with friends after a school concert. The asocial individual's demand curve applies to individuals confronting the material world, consuming only because of the material pleasure coming from the goods consumed. In a human world, life is much more complicated.

Marginal utility almost always declines only for an individual consuming stuff by him or herself.[9] Yes, even beer or wine becomes less desirable after you have consumed more. You might gulp down the first drink, have the second at a moderate pace, and slowly savor the third. After some seven drinks, you may feel so sick that you cannot imagine ever drinking again; someone would have to pay you to have more (see Figure 7-2 and Table 7-1). This gives a downward sloping curve of marginal utility as a function of quantity, with marginal utility diminishing because of satiation. This graph becomes the *asocial individual's demand curve*[10] for alcoholic beverages, where we will consume more only at lower prices because our lower marginal utility then is balanced by the lower sacrifice required. At lower prices, additional drinks are worth the price, and when they become cheap enough, consumers can substitute alcohol for other goods, like pot. Because marginal utility is downward sloping, an individual will buy more of anything but only at a lower price—*demand is downward sloping*[11] because of satiation.

DEMAND CURVES SLOPE DOWN FOR INDIVIDUALS

How much wine to buy? Assume that the price of wine is fixed at $7 and the marginal utility schedule is that given in Table 7-1 and Figure 7-2.[12] The first glass costs $7 and gives $20 worth of marginal utility. For this glass, the *marginal surplus utility*, or the *consumer surplus*, the net pleasure after paying for the wine is $13 (or $20 - $7). From there, the surplus utility declines because diminishing marginal utility comes up against constant cost. The second glass gives $18 worth of marginal utility at the same $7 cost, netting a surplus of $11. The third gives $15 of marginal utility, for a marginal surplus of $8, and the fourth gives $11 worth, for a surplus of $4. Should you buy a fifth glass, at a price of $7, then you would regret it because the wine would give only $6 worth of

TABLE 7-1
DIMINISHING MARGINAL UTILITY AND CONSUMER SURPLUS FROM WINE DRINKING

Glass of wine	Marginal utility	Marginal surplus		
		P=6	P=15	P=18
1	20	14	5	2
2	18	12	3	0
3	15	9	0	-3
4	11	5	-4	-7
5	6	0	-9	-12
6	0	-6	-15	-18
7	-7	-13	-22	-25

marginal utility at a cost of $7. Marginal surplus utility would be negative, minus $1. That is why you should stop at four glasses: any more isn't worth it, any less and you miss some pleasure. (And you thought there was no limit.)

What happens when the price drops? At a price of $5, the first five glasses are worthwhile with a non-negative marginal surplus utility. If wine were free, you might drink yourself silly on six glasses, but you would stop there because the seventh would have *negative* marginal utility; someone would have to pay you to drink the seventh glass! From this, you can construct a *demand curve* for wine, or any product, where the quantity consumed increases as the price drops and decreases at higher prices. For an individual, this curve will be downward sloping and will resemble the marginal utility curve, because at each price one will buy until the point where the marginal utility equals the price (see Figure 7-3). At lower prices, marginal utility and price will balance at greater consumption: more must be consumed to drive the marginal utility down to the lower level. At higher prices, on the other hand, less is consumed to drive up marginal utility. The individual's demand for any product increases at lower prices because a lower price makes less desirable additional marginal consumption worthwhile. Satiation leads to diminishing marginal utility which leads to downward sloping demand curves.

FIGURE 7-3
DEMAND CURVE FOR WINE—SAME AS THE MARGINAL UTILITY CURVE

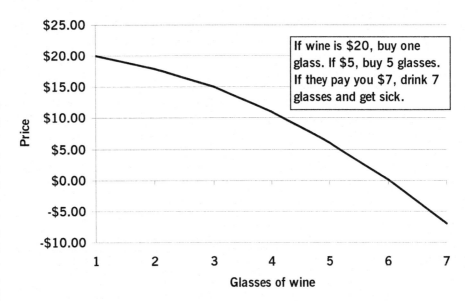

If wine is $20, buy one glass. If $5, buy 5 glasses. If they pay you $7, drink 7 glasses and get sick.

TABLE 7-2
COMPUTING AGGREGATE COMMUNITY DEMAND FROM INDIVIDUAL MARGINAL UTILITY, FOR COMMUNITY WITH 100 PEOPLE

Cones	MU	Price	Cones	Community Cones
1	$18.00	$18.00	1	100
2	$14.58	$14.58	2	200
3	$10.63	$10.63	3	300
4	$6.97	$6.97	4	400
5	$4.12	$4.12	5	500
6	$2.19	$2.19	6	600
7	$1.05	$1.05	7	700
8	$0.45	$0.45	8	800
9	$0.17	$0.17	9	900
10	$0.06	$0.06	10	1000

HISTORY OF MARGINAL UTILITY THEORY

The idea of marginal utility dates back at least to the Italian abbot and official, Fernando Galieni (1728-87). Ambassador from Naples to France, Galieni knew many of the French Physiocrats (a group of 18th century French Enlightenment thinkers who also influenced Adam Smith) and came to reject their approach, which ascribed all value to the product of the land. Galieni developed an alternative theory of value based on utility and scarcity.

Galieni's work received little notice. Instead, through Smith and Ricardo, classical economists argued that price reflected the cost of production, and ultimately depended on the labor embodied in a commodity. A small group of "Ricardian Socialists," notably William Thompson, John Gray, John Bray, and Thomas Hodgskin, used the classical Labor Theory of Value to argue that capitalist profit came from the exploitation of labor. When Karl Marx developed this approach, notably in Capital (1867), orthodox economists began to question classical value theory. Almost simultaneously, the English economist William Stanley Jevons (1871), Carl Menger in Vienna (1871), and Léon Walras in Switzerland (1874) developed a new value theory based on diminishing marginal utility, leading ultimately to modern neoclassical theory. Observing the near-simultaneous development of marginal utility analysis so soon after the publication of Capital, the American economist Wesley C. Mitchell observed: "No one can read the Austrian writers, whose general scheme was similar to Jevons's, without feeling that they are interested in developing the concert of the maximising of utility largely because they thought it answered Marx's socialistic critique of modern economic organisation."

It is ironic then that even before Marx, one of the Ricardian Socialists, William Thompson, had propounded a form of diminishing marginal utility theory to argue for socialism and an egalitarian distribution of income as the best way to maximize social utility.

CONSTRUCTING AGGREGATE COMMUNITY DEMAND CURVES FROM INDIVIDUAL DEMAND

Here we have a theory of individual behavior grounded in what appears to be reasonable psychological assumptions about individuals. For social scientists, however, this is nothing. We have no particular interest in understanding individual behavior or why a person drinks or buys any particular amount of wine. We want a theory of *social* behavior, a theory that will give us an *aggregate*[13] demand curve showing how much a community will buy at different prices. Neoclassicists take this step for granted. By assuming that the individual marginal utility and demand curves are independent of each, they conclude that the aggregate demand curve is the sum of the individuals' demand curves. They assume that the individual demand curve is a miniature version of the *aggregate* or *community demand curve*, and the amount the community will buy at any price equals the amount the individuals will all buy on their own at that price. This is a conclusion that they can reach only under drastic assumptions, dismissing everything that is social in community life.

To move from individual behavior to social demand curves, neoclassicists assume *identical*,[14] *independent*,[15] and *homothetic*[16] preferences. These assumptions are convenient and allow one to construct a demand curve that is the sum of all individuals' demand curves and is independent of changes in the distribution of income. Not all the assumptions are essential: assuming that demand curves are identical and homothetic is convenient but not at all essential to the theory. Indeed, there is no reason to believe that everyone's preferences are the same and, in particular, there is overwhelming evidence that people's preferences change when they become wealthier, violating the assumptions of identical and homo-

AN ESSENTIAL FASHION ACCESSORY: THE CORSET

Close-fitting undergarments, often reinforced by stays, corsets were worn to support and shape women's waistline, hips, and breasts. Victorian hour-glass fashions would contrast very wide skirts and large sleeves with a dramatically narrowed waist achieved with a tight corset. Tight corsets would constrict the stomach and lungs, causing many women to pass out from pain and lack of oxygen. Their use was restricted to women who could afford their cost, and also did not need to breathe deeply or to bend to work.

Is Your Figure Stylish?

You can see a difference between personal style and common fashion. Style is the air, the pose, the grace—the movement that is your own—through every change of fashion. Fashion is common to every woman who can pay for it. Only one corset helps the development of that individuality which is true style: La Grecque Corset. Not a hard mold for the figure. It helps the figure to mold itself.

DUQUESNE

THORSTEIN VEBLEN

The American economist **Thorstein Veblen (1857-1929)** first identified *conspicuous consumption* in his book, *The Theory of the Leisure Class* (1899). Veblen was born on a frontier farm in Wisconsin to parents who came to America in 1856. Land speculators drove his parents off their first land claim, and they had to sell half their land in their second farm to pay usurious interest rates. Hatred of tricksters, speculators, and lawyers ran deep in his family tradition.

Veblen briefly studied economics with the reform economist Richard Ely at Johns Hopkins, before moving to Cornell where he studied with the conservative economist J. Laurence Laughlin. Following Laughlin to the University of Chicago, Veblen alienated most students and many faculty with his idiosyncratic teaching and active love life. He also developed close intellectual relations with a chosen group of congenial colleagues. In *The Theory of the Leisure Class*, one can trace the influence of his Chicago friends, including Jacques Loeb, Franz Boas, and William Thomas.

Due to his idiosyncratic manner and open love-life, his habit of having public love affairs with students and with colleagues' wives, Veblen found it difficult to hold academic positions. Nonetheless, he was a prolific writer whose works consistently challenged the economic and political orthodoxy. He rejected the notion that economic "laws" are timeless generalizations. Economic behavior, he argued, has to be analyzed in a social context. Rather than derive economic laws from alleged utilitarian and hedonistic propensities, he argued that the categories of the classical economists could be applied only to special historical circumstances and in very restricted contexts.

Veblen was influenced by Marx and Marxist ideas. He saw a fundamental conflict in society between "pecuniary" and "industrial" work, between profit making and the production of use values. Workers seek to be productive, but capitalist businesses seek profit regardless of efficiency or use. The goal of businessmen is purely pecuniary, not to provide service but to achieve relative wealth to be spent in conspicuous consumption.

---

thetic preferences respectively. Abandoning these assumptions makes constructing aggregate demand curves more complicated. It does not, however, call into question whether it is possible to construct aggregate demand curves from individual *utility functions*.[17]

The assumption of *independence*, the idea that what we buy is independent of what others buy, is essential for constructing aggregate demand curves from individual preferences. It is also certainly wrong. We cannot assume independence because our preferences change with the consumption behavior of others. We influence each other in two distinct ways: by influencing tastes and preferences (changing perceptions) and by making different goods more or less desirable because they are consumed by others even if our perceptions have not changed. We will discuss this last assumption much more.

Assuming identical, homothetic, and independent preferences, neoclassical economists construct a community demand curve that is the sum of all the individual demand curves. Total demand at any price is the sum of the quantities consumed by each individual at that price or, under the assumptions of independence and identical preferences, the product of the amount demanded by one person and the number of people. The community demand curve is downward sloping—less is purchased at higher prices—because the individual demand curves, due to diminishing marginal utility and progressive satiation, are downward sloping. If, for illustration, we assume that everyone in a community of 100 people has the same preferences, then the quantity of wine demanded at any price would be 100 times the amount that any one individual would demand. If one person would buy three glasses at $15, then the community would demand 300 glasses. At a price of $6, if one person demands five glasses, then the community demand rises to 500 glasses. At lower prices, people will consume to a point of lower marginal utility.

DO AGGREGATE DEMAND CURVES REALLY SLOPE DOWN?

Deriving aggregate demand curves from individual utility, neoclassical economists assume that every person's preferences are independent. Here is methodological individualism applied to the social

SODA DEMAND CURVES ARE DOWNWARD SLOPING

A study in a Boston hospital's cafeteria found that raising prices for sugar-sweetened soft drinks reduced consumption much more than did an educational campaign on the health benefits of cutting back on soda. Dr. Jason Block of Brigham and Women's Hospital led the study in his hospital. Raising prices of a 20-ounce bottle of sweetened soda by 35 percent, from $1.30 to $1.75 reduced consumption by 26 percent, an elasticity of about 0.75. (Some customers switched to diet sodas whose sales rose by 20 percent.)

By contrast, when an educational campaign was substituted for the price increase, soda consumption returned to its old level until the price increase was reintroduced. Source: Boston Globe (June 21, 2010, G3).

TABLE 7-3
SOME SOCIAL EFFECTS ON CONSUMPTION

Source of social influence	Effect	Example
Veblen effects	Consumption to demonstrate status and wealth because a good is expensive.	Prada, Lexus
Stampedes	Individuals value a good more because others use it.	Trendy fashion attire (Iggy Azalea)
Price signals	Consumers infer product quality from the price.	Professional services
Network efficiencies	Production or consumption benefits from using the same products as others use.	Microsoft Word

sciences. Neoclassicists treat the motivations and behavior of individuals as the same whether they are Robinson Crusoe living alone on an isolated island or a person living in a community of dozens, thousands, or millions. Ask yourself: would Robinson Crusoe ever wear a tie if living alone? Would Roberta Crusoe ever wear high heels? How about a corset? Stating such questions suggests a problem, one raised at the beginning of this chapter when we discussed the social generation of "wants." Once we relax this extreme assumption of absolute independence, we can get aggregate demand curves that behave differently from the sum of individual demand curves because preferences are shaped by the community. Such an approach would use four concepts that are meaningful only in a community: *Veblen effects, stampedes, price signals*, and *network efficiencies*. Without questioning the assumption of diminishing marginal utility for individuals, all of these can lead to upward sloping aggregate demand curves for the community as a whole.

Fashion: For comfort? Or to be seen?

It is a truism that people buy things because they anticipate that they will enjoy consuming them. They buy paintings by Picasso or court-side seats at NBA games because they like looking at art and enjoy basketball. But this asocial view of consumption is like studying sex as dual masturbation. Very little consumption is private; most is in the public eye and is intended to communicate to others. Consumption signals not only our taste but our social status. Through our consumption, we identify ourselves as belonging to a particular social group, and we claim a position in the group's status ranking. Buying a Picasso, for example, signals to others, to your neighbors, friends, and rivals, that you are an art lover, have good taste and, perhaps even more important, that you are wealthy. Courtside seats tell your friends and neighbors that you are a loyal sports fan, a regular guy, *and* that you have money to burn. We claim a social identity and social status through our consumption; we are what we buy.

As statements of status, higher prices can make a good *more* desirable by signaling wealth and success. This *Veblen effect* creates the intriguing possibility that within a community one may value goods *because* they are expensive. People may like the feel of a Porsche or a BMW on the road, but they also value the way their neighbors and romantic interests admire them when they drive up in this expensive car. Would they enjoy the car as much if it cost $25,000 instead of $75,000? At the lower price they could also buy a Toyota for their daughter to take to college, but would that compensate for losing their neighbors' attention? More people might want the Porsche at $100,000 because, at that price, it not only drives well but impresses the neighbors. Price contributes to the pleasure people get from consumption. Part of what you buy is the fact that it is expensive.

High heels have been worn by women since the time of the Egyptian Pharaohs. While attacked as successors to foot binding and the tight-laced corset, perverse regulatory objects controlling women, heels have become a sign of success and comfortable sexuality for many professional women. Some women even have surgery to shorten toes or to inject padding into the balls of their feet to fit more comfortably into a pair of stilettos.

Thinking socially also suggests another way that demand curves may be upward sloping: *stampedes*. We consume to identify ourselves as belonging to a particular group. Observe what people wear to a college party. First of all, notice that no men are wearing skirts or dresses. (Unless you are partying at Hampshire College.) Is this because such attire is inherently inferior? Then why do women wear them? Or is it because wearing gender-inappropriate clothes would harm a guy's (or a girl's?) social standing? The need for socially appropriate attire may not change but the nature of that attire does. I once judged a cross-dressing fashion show sponsored by a center for Lesbian-Gay-Bisexual-Transgender students and *all* the men there wore dresses. Different circles have different stampedes. There are things we buy *because* other people, our peers and our social superiors, are also buying them. Few straight women wear work boots to class, cut their hair really short, or wear other male attire; to dress like that would be to identify with a different social group, confusing their friends and random strangers. A few years ago, the fad was for young men to wear baggy shorts and young women to wear low-rider jeans. These clothes were impractical and did not look comfortable, but people wore them because others were wearing them and they signaled that one was aware of fashion. Much of the value, the utility, of clothes comes from their popularity with particular groups. The utility we get from consumption depends on whether others value our choices. When more of our peers buy the same thing, the value goes up for us. Like the Veblen effect, fads or stampedes can give us an upward-sloping aggregate demand curve because our valuation of these goods increases when more is consumed by the community.

Buying because others are buying something can be a *fad* where we buy things in a stampede in imitation of others. There may, however, be rational aspects of fad buying. It may also reflect information that we might otherwise find difficult to acquire. How can we learn the value of a long-lived or one-of-a-kind commodity? How do we know, for example, if a bottle of wine is good? Or a car is built well enough to last 20 years and 250,000 miles? How do we know if an oncologist or a surgeon is good? We can hire wine tasters and car testers, but these are expensive, and are no more guaranteed than the good we hire them to test. Instead, many of us use the behavior of others and the price as signals of quality. We know a band is good because our

FIGURE 7-4

EFFECT OF NETWORKS ON DEMAND: WHEN MORE IS SOLD, CONSUMERS VALUE ADDITIONAL UNITS MORE HIGHLY

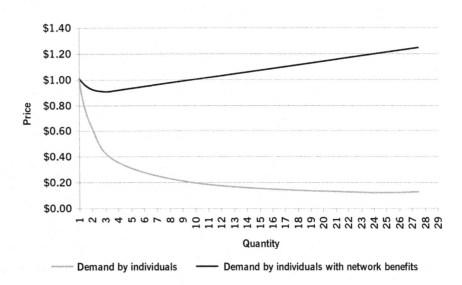

A ROSE BY ANY OTHER NAME MIGHT SMELL AS SWEET, BUT SLAP ON A HEFTY PRICE TAG, AND OUR OPINION OF IT MIGHT GO THROUGH THE ROOF.

Antonio Rangel, an associate professor of economics at Caltech, and his colleagues found that changes in the stated price of a sampled wine influenced not only how good volunteers thought it tasted, but the brain activity involved in our experience of pleasure. Rangel and his colleagues had twenty volunteers taste five wine samples that they identified by different prices. While the subjects tasted and evaluated the wines, their brains were scanned using functional magnetic resonance imaging, or fMRI.

Volunteers consistently reported that they liked the taste of the $90 bottle better than the $5 one, and the $45 bottle better than the $35 one. Scans of their brains confirmed their subjective reports: a region of the brain called the medial orbitofrontal cortex, or mOFC, showed higher activity when the subjects drank the wines they said were more pleasurable.

There was a catch, however, because the researchers had used the same wine in glasses labeled with different prices. When the subjects were told the wine cost $90 a bottle, they loved it; at $10 a bottle, not so much.

Source: http://media.caltech.edu/press_releases/13091

friends listen to it. (Or it is on a valued Spotify playlist.) Our neighbor's Porsche is a good car because she spent $75,000 to buy it. We know that the discount computer for sale at WalMart is junk because even WalMart cannot get a decent machine for $99. The oncologist is good because he charges *more* than anyone else. Prices convey information because we trust that someone has connected them with quality. To the extent that prices signal quality, then higher prices can lead to *upward sloping aggregate demand*[18] curves.

There may be other reasons than fashion why you want to follow the crowd and consume the same products that others buy. Smart businesses recognize this and appreciate the advantage that they can gain when increasing market share increases the value of their products. Consuming the same thing as others allows you to participate in a *network* where you can get complementary products and support. Consider the person who owns an Apple Macintosh: a wonderful machine with a relatively stable operating system that allows you to swap files conveniently with about 3% of the world's computers.[19] Don't bring your Mac to work in a business where you need to communicate easily with others who run Windows, and don't expect that you will be able to run your PowerPoint off the business projector without spending an extra 20 minutes wrestling with recalcitrant technology.

At least the Mac user is better off than someone who buys a cheap electrical appliance in Europe only to find that they must spend much more to adapt it to take North American current. Or, the person who, assuming that people must be high on the marginal utility curve for such tools, imports U.S. tools, using Imperial measurements of inches, etc., to Europe after noticing that few hardware stores there carry such tools. In all of these cases, goods are valued because others are buying them for good, rational reasons. They have added value *because* they are in greater demand by others; you will buy them only at very low prices *because* others do not use them. Because their products gain value when more people use them, businesses with products subject to network economies often find it profitable to give their stuff away until they reach a critical network scale.

SHIFTING DEMAND

Thus far we have been discussing *movements along the demand curve* where the amount people want to buy changes in response to changes in price. These are the movements most compatible with the orthodox neoclassical theory because they can be seen as grounding changes in behavior, changes in the amount people will buy, with individual preferences and diminishing marginal utility. Over long periods, movements along the curve are the less important factors in markets. Instead, behavioral change is dominated by *movements of the demand curve*[20] in

HOW MUCH DEMAND IS THERE FOR A EUROPEAN ELECTRIC PLUG IN THE U.S.?

Even at low prices? How about a set of Imperial tools in Europe? Or a car with left-side steering in England or Japan? In all of these cases, demand is greater because other people are using the same products and buyers can join a network where their products fit with those used by others.

The demand curve has shifted in for these.

response to changes in preferences, incomes, and the supply of complements and substitutes.

Movements *along* the demand curve come when the amount people buy changes in response to changes in price. Prices may change because of changes in *supply* and the cost of producing different quantities. There may be changes in the cost of inputs due, for example, to improvements in technology. Or there may be a reduction in price, an increase in supply at any price, because of a reduction in monopoly power. In all of these cases, consumers will change the amount they buy in response to price changes, responding passively to the active change in supply. We will consider these movements in more detail later.

Demand curves may also shift, because consumers are willing to pay a higher price for any quantity, or will buy more at any price. These movements of the demand curve can be caused by:

Changing preferences. Preferences change where people decide that they like a particular product more or less than they had before. For example, people may decide that they would like to see Rihanna or Beyoncé instead of Britney Spears, or Miley Cyrus and Lorde instead of Avril Lavigne. They will buy more tickets at any price, or would be willing to pay more for the same quantity of tickets, for the newly popular singers, and vice-versa.

Changing income. Changes in income lead people to buy more, or less, of a commodity. When you leave school and get a good job, you will buy more cheese at the same price; when you get laid off, you will buy less. You get rich, you buy more shoes at any price; you get poor, sell the shoes.

Mathematically, the income elasticity of demand is the percentage change in demand divided by the percentage change in income. If demand increases a lot with higher income, and demand increases by a higher percentage than the increase in income, then the income elasticity will be greater than 1.0 and the product is called *income-elastic*. Generally, we call highly income-elastic commodities *luxuries*, including fine wine, travel, and sports cars. There are other products where demand hardly changes with rising or falling income. If demand hardly increases with higher income, rising by a much lower percentage than the increase in income, then the income elasticity is less than 1.0 and the product is called *income-inelastic*. Commodities with a low income elasticity include *necessities* and relatively inexpensive ways to meet basic needs, including ramen, store-brand coffee, and bus tickets.

Complements. Your interest in buying things depends on how much it will cost to buy the things that go with

FIGURE 7-5
DEMAND CURVE SHIFTS OUT BECAUSE PREFERENCE FOR WINE INCREASES

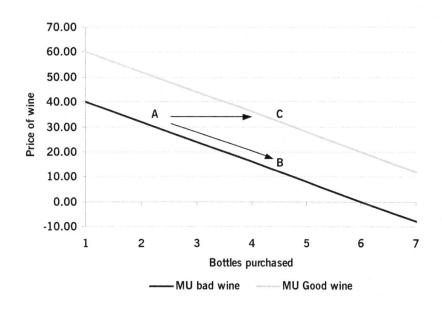

People will pay more for any amount of wine and will buy more at any price. Moving from A to B, more is bought because of lower prices and consumers will move down their MU curve; moving from A to C, more is bought because of better quality, and consumers' MU curve shifts out.

FIGURE 7-6
WHEN INCOME RISES, CONSUMERS WILL DEMAND MORE AT ANY PRICE

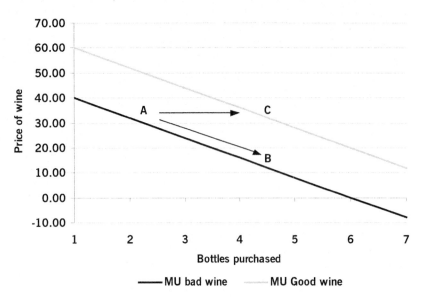

Note that demand is still downward sloping with respect to price: more will be bought at lower prices, moving from A to B. At the same price, more will be bought at higher income, moving from A to C. If the product is income elastic, the move from A to C will be large relative to the change in income; if it is income inelastic, then the movement from A to C will be small relative to the change in income.

that product. You don't just buy a dress, you also buy the matching shoes, hand bag, and necklace. If the shoes or the jewelry become more expensive, you may pass on the dress. When CD players became cheaper, people bought more CDs at any price: the demand for CDs rose because the cost of complements fell. If you want to encourage people to buy electric cars, then raise gas prices so gasoline vehicles become more expensive. And lower electricity prices.

Substitutes. Substitutes are goods you consume instead of something else. When substitutes become more expensive, then you are willing to pay more for a particular product at any price. The demand curve shifts out for a product when the price of substitutes rises. For example, if the price of gasoline rises because of a hurricane in the Gulf of Mexico, then people will be willing to pay more for bicycles and for bus fare. (Demand for high-calorie chocolate brownies, a complement for bicycling, may also rise because of the rising cost of gas.) On the other hand, if the price of substitutes falls, if improvements in technology make car travel really cheap, then people will buy fewer bus tickets (moving down the bus demand curve), fewer bicycles, and fewer chocolate brownies. The arrival of cassettes drove down the price of vinyl records and record players (what are those?). When CDs (and CD players) became cheaper, demand for cassette tapes and players fell. Now, with cheaper MP3 players and downloaded music, demand for CDs is falling.

ELASTICITY OF DEMAND:
MEASURING RESPONSIVENESS OF QUANTITY DEMANDED TO PRICES

The *elasticity of demand*, or E_d, is a measure of how much the quantity purchased of any particular good changes when its price changes. There are commodities where the quantity purchased changes little with price increases, such as cigarettes, gasoline, heroin, and home heating oil. For other products, the quantity purchased falls sharply with higher prices, including restaurant meals, pleasure boats, and theater tickets. Like the income elasticity of demand, the E_d is calculated as the percentage change in quantity consumed for any percentage change in price. We say that demand is *price elastic* if the percentage change in quantity exceeds the percentage change in price, or $E_d>1$. By contrast, demand is *price inelastic* if the percentage change in quantity is less than the percentage change in price, or $E_d<1$. Demand has *unitary elasticity*[21] if the percentage change in quantity is the same as the percentage change in price, or $E_d=1$. At the extreme, the elasticity of demand is 0 and there is a perfectly inelastic demand curve. In this case, there is no change in quantity purchased when prices change. This might be the case, for example, for chemotherapy drugs: no one who doesn't

---

THE ELASTICITY OF DEMAND IS GREATER THE MORE NARROWLY YOU DEFINE THE PRODUCT.

The elasticity of demand for nail polish as a whole may be low if people will pay more to keep painting their nails. But the elasticity of demand for a particular brand, such as "Finger Paints" or "Savvy" is much higher; if they raise their price then people could shift to Revlon or others without giving up their colored nails.

need them will take these up even at lower prices, while people who need the drugs will buy them even if they have to kill people and cook methamphetamine to pay for them.[22] By contrast, the elasticity of demand may be very high for frivolous commodities that people easily pick up or drop with small changes in price. These extremes are represented by straight-line demand curves. A perfectly inelastic demand curve will be a vertical line, a constant quantity will be purchased at all prices; a good with a perfectly elastic demand will have a horizontal demand curve at one price because any increase in price will lead to a drop to zero in quantity demanded.

Products are price elastic if a change in price has a big effect on demand. These include two types of products: frivolities that people can easily do without if they become more expensive, and things easily replaced by very similar products. Frivolities might include designer jeans, fancy collars for dogs, fancy perfumes and colognes. Demand may also be highly elastic for necessities if

FIGURE 7-7
DEMAND FOR WINE FALLS WHEN SUBSTITUTE (POT) IS MORE AVAILABLE (AFTER LEGALIZATION)

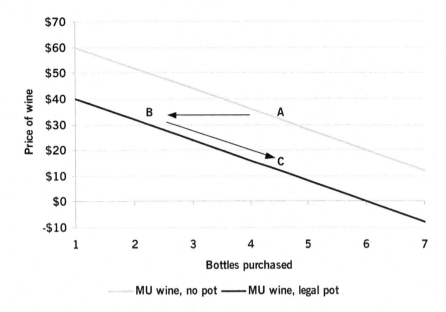

Note that demand is still downward sloping but less is demanded at any price. Movement from A to B because of falling prices; movement from A to C because of legalization of substitute

there are good substitutes. While the demand for food, for example, may be highly inelastic, the demand for any particular foodstuff is highly elastic because there are many substitute foods. We need food but if the price of peanut butter soars then we can easily shift to another fatty protein source, like cheese.

In general, the elasticity of demand for any particular product within a broad product category will be high because people can easily shift to a close substitute. The E_d for any particular nail polish, for example, is greater than for nail polish as a whole. For many women (and some men) nail polish is a necessity to be consumed even at higher prices. But the E_d for Revlon polish is still very high because there are many good nail polish substitutes: you can shift to another brand, or, you can stay home and never leave your room. The principle here is that the narrower we define the product, the higher the E_d, because narrower product definitions leave more room for substitution. The more broadly we define products, such as food, energy, or housing, the smaller the E_d.

ELASTICITY OF DEMAND VS. INCOME ELASTICITY

The *elasticity of demand* refers to the change in the quantity that people will buy with a change in price, reflecting movements *along* the demand curve.

The *income elasticity of demand* refers to the change in the quantity that people will buy at any price due to a change in their income. It reflects a *shift* in the demand curve: out if incomes rise, or in if incomes fall.

Inelastic demand means that the quantity consumed doesn't change much if price changes. This includes stuff people would have trouble doing without: housing, prescription drugs, food, gasoline, and heating oil, for example. Some college students would include beer in this group; others would include tobacco. Note that inelastic also means that demand changes little when prices fall. Very large price declines are needed to absorb even small increases in supply, and steep price increases follow even small shortfalls in supply. We have seen this in the world oil market several times.

Beowulf is very proud of his collar. We would buy him a collar even if the price rose. The elasticity of demand is low.

Economists and statisticians devote considerable effort to estimating the elasticity of demand for different products. These estimates are important for businesses setting prices for their products and public officials planning how to deal with shortfalls in supply. Really small firms producing products nearly identical to those sold by a large number of competitors, firms in highly competitive markets, face almost perfectly elastic demand curves because consumers can easily shift to their competitors if they raise prices. Such competitive firms have virtually no price discretion: if they raise prices even a little above their competitors' then they will lose all of their business. Most businesses, however, produce products distinguishable from others. They distinguish their products from their competitors with brand names, with distinctive packaging and marketing, and by claiming that their stuff is better than their competitors'. These normal firms have some discretion in prices with loyal consumers who will continue to buy even if prices rise. They face elastic demand curves that are less than infinite. If the elasticity of demand is low enough, they may even raise revenue when they raise prices.

Normal businesses want to know the elasticity of demand for their products, and they pay economists and statisticians good money to estimate the elasticity of demand. Inelastic demand is a mixed blessing. It means, on the one hand, that they lose very few customers when they raise prices, and they may be able to get away with raising prices. On the other hand, if demand is inelastic then they will have to lower prices a lot to sell more. If demand is highly elastic, then that limits their ability to raise prices, as any increase in price risks losing business to their competitors or to other products. On the other hand, even a small reduction in price may allow them to increase sales.

Governments are interested in estimates of the elasticity of demand for the same reasons as firms. Because consumers cannot easily stop consuming products in *inelastic* demand, changes in the supply of these products will cause dramatic price increases. For important products, like food, housing, or fuel, price increases coming after a shortfall in supply may cause significant unrest and will certainly redistribute income from consumers to producers. This is what happened with oil price increases in the 1970s, and it happens regularly in poorer countries when there are food shortages. Changes in the supply of products in highly elastic demand, by contrast, have relatively small effects on income distribution and provoke smaller public unrest because consumers move relatively easily to other products. Revenues from *excise taxes*[23]—money collected by taxes that raise prices on specific items like cigarettes, gasoline, or telephone calls—depend on the elasticity of demand. (Our policy of reducing the use of illicit drugs like cocaine and marijuana by reducing supply to drive up prices depends on the idea that higher prices will reduce consumption because demand is elastic with respect to price.) The most reliable tax, or the tax where we can expect a consistent flow of revenue because consumption falls less when the tax is imposed, is one placed on inelastic products. Taxes on energy or housing, for example, will raise the targeted revenue because they have little effect on behavior: people consume the same amount regardless of the tax. It is for this reason that European governments rely so heavily on gasoline taxes. They can plan for a certain revenue flow knowing that gasoline consumption will be little effected by the tax. On the other hand, taxes on commodities with a highly elastic demand, such as Styrofoam cups, might raise little revenue because consumers will change their behavior and stop buying the taxed product. Governments need to be careful before taxing highly elastic commodities because they may destroy an industry while collecting relatively little revenue. But, then again, that may be the goal.

CONSUMER SURPLUS MAKES LIFE WORTH LIVING

If people consume at the point where the marginal utility they get from a product just equals the price they pay, then they get no new pleasure from the last unit they consume. For example, if you pay $5 for a glass of wine that gives you $5 worth of pleasure, then the pleasure you receive equals the money you sacrificed. There is no net pleasure where the price paid equals the pleasure received.

If *everything* were consumed at the margin where marginal utility just equals the price, then life would be dreary. Everybody would get just enough pleasure from the things they consume to balance the cost of buying them. They would be exchanging pleasures—less from money, more from beer—with no additional pleasure. Fortunately, there is more to consumption than the margin. Since marginal utility is diminishing, every bottle of beer purchased *before* the final one—every *inframarginal*[24] beer—is worth more than that last one. Since the last beer is worth the price, and all beers cost the same amount, we may assume that every inframarginal beer, worth more than the marginal beer, is worth more than the price. Economists label the difference between the price paid and the value of inframarginal units the *consumer surplus.*[25] The sum of these individual consumer surpluses is the total net pleasure consumers get, net of the cost.

Consumer surplus, the difference between price and MU for inframarginal units, makes life worth living because it gives consumers more than they brought to the market. Instead of merely exchanging equal pleasures, giving up money for products of equal value, consumers can get more pleasure, more than they pay for from their inframarginal purchases. This also creates a realm for possible bargaining, because both producers and consumers receive benefits from the transaction that go beyond the price paid. They both will be willing to compromise on the price to maintain the transaction. Because of the surplus, consumers will continue to buy even if prices rise a little or quality declines. Hard bargaining, therefore, can change the price without changing the quantity bought or sold, leading to a redistribution of the surplus from one to the other.

This analysis suggests two additional lines of thought. First, the rule that maximizing consumer surplus also leads to consumption where the marginal utility equals the price. Every unit purchased before that level increases consumer surplus, while any bought beyond that level would lower consumer surplus. Second, consumer surplus analysis suggests an area for producer manipulation. There is a surplus generated by the consumption with diminishing marginal utility, but there is no logical necessity that the surplus go to the consumer. Businesses can "milk" the surplus by raising prices or squeezing quality. There is room for careful planning and manipulation by clever businesses employing, at very high salaries, smart young people who majored in economics in college and paid attention to the readings in their introductory microeconomics class. If producers can charge different prices for different consumers, for example, if they can *price along the demand curve*, then they can capture the consumer surplus for themselves. This would require that they charge different prices for different consumers, and it can only work if consumers cannot engage in arbitrage and resell products they purchased at these different prices. Producers of commodities and homogeneous material goods, such as computers, CDs, and books, find it difficult to do this because consumers who paid less can easily sell to those who are charged more. On the other hand, producers of services, such as doctors, airlines, and universities, regularly price along the demand curve and charge different prices to different con-

FIGURE 7-8

CONSUMER SURPLUS MAKES LIFE WORTH LIVING

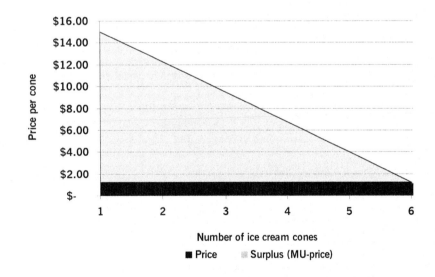

Note: This figure shows that at a fixed price for all the ice cream a consumer buys, she will receive a "surplus" of extra pleasure from the inframarginal cones because these are worth more to her than the marginal cone which is worth the price. The marginal utility from each cone is shown by the outer line of the surplus. Surplus (in gray) is the difference between the MU and the price (in black).

sumers who find it hard or impossible to resell their products. Doctors, for example, charge more if you have insurance than if you are uninsured, airlines charge business travelers more, and universities make financial aid awards, or price reductions, according to family income and readiness to pay. Universities, airlines, and hospitals have large paid staff working to manipulate prices to maximize profits from unwary consumers. All are employed to capture the consumer surplus for the producer.

Such a waste. The efforts made by companies to manipulate prices to milk the consumer surplus cost billions upon billions of dollars. And they lead to counter efforts by consumers to find lower prices in order to protect their surplus. All of this involves a redistribution of income—less for us, more for them—without creating any new value. It is one more price that we pay for our capitalist market economy. Think about this next time you try to figure out how to avoid some new airline charge or bargain with the university financial aid office.[26]

DISCUSSION QUESTIONS

What are "exogenous preferences"? What are "endogenous preferences"? Why does this distinction matter?

What is "marginal utility"? Why does it diminish?

If Scarlett Johansson likes Buffalo Chicken Wings, why does she eat anything else? How does this illustrate diminishing marginal utility? What happens when we have goods with increasing marginal utility?

With diminishing marginal utility, how do we decide how much to consume?

How do we use our marginal utility curve to determine our individual demand curve?

What is consumer surplus? How do you calculate it? What happens to our surplus when prices rise?

When they fall? When a good becomes more desirable?

How do neoclassicists estimate aggregate (or community) demand curves? What assumptions do they need about the relationship between different peoples' demand curves?

Are the demand curves for different individuals independent? What are "Veblen Effects"? What are "stampedes"? How do prices signal quality? What are "network effects"? How does each change the relationship between individual demand curves and aggregate demand curves?

How would changes in preferences and income move demand curves?

What are "consumption complements"? What are "consumption substitutes"? How do changes in the price of complements and substitutes change individual demand curves?

ENDNOTES

[1]Exogenous preferences are determined outside of the market, prior to market transactions.

[2]Endogenous preferences are determined through market processes. We cannot say, therefore, that the market leads businesses to meet consumer preferences if these preferences are themselves the product of market transactions.

[3]This is a dramatic reduction from a century ago when the French drank around twice as much wine.

[4]Kolleen M. Guy, *When Champagne Became French: Wine and the Making of a National Identity* (Baltimore: Johns Hopkins University Press, 2003).

[5]C. Cecil, Fairbank, John King, Teng, Ssu-yü, Fairbank, John K. Lingard, "Trade and Diplomacy on the China Coast: The Opening of the Treaty Ports, 1842-1854," *International Journal* 10, no. 2 (1955): 150; Peter Ward Fay, *The Opium War, 1840-1842: Barbarians in the Celestial Empire in the Early Part of the Nineteenth Century and the War by Which They Forced Her Gates Ajar* (Chapel Hill: University of North Carolina Press, 1975); on the failure of earlier British trade missions to China, see Alain Peyrefitte, *The Collision of Two Civilizations: The British Expedition to China in 1792-4* (London: Harvill, 1993).

[6]William Stanley Jevons, *The Theory of Political Economy* (London; New York: Macmillan, 1871), http://catalog.hathitrust.org/api/volumes/oclc/3598082.html; Léon Walras, *Elements of Pure Economics, Or, The Theory of Social Wealth* (London: Published for the American Economic Association and the Royal Economic Association and the Royal Economic Society by Allen and Unwin, 1954); John Bates Clark, *The Philosophy of Wealth; Economic Principles Newly Formulated* (New York: A.M. Kelley Publishers, 1967); ideas of diminishing marginal utility had been developed by British radicals before the neoclassicists, and used to justify programs of income redistribution, William Thompson, *An Inquiry into the Principles of the Distribution of Wealth Most Conducive to Human Happiness*, 1824 (New York: A.M. Kelley, Bookseller, 1963); Thomas Hodgskin, *Popular Political Economy* (New York: A.M. Kelley, 1966).

[7]Satiation is where the pleasure one gets is reduced because one has had enough.

[8]Complements are things consumed with other things to enhance their pleasure, such as hot fudge with ice cream.

[9]There are products for which marginal utility does not decline, addictive substances like cocaine, heroin, and, for many, alcohol. For these, there is the danger that individuals will come to devote more and more of their resources to consuming this one good until it drives out all others.

[10]A demand curve relates the quantity that will be bought to the price. An individual's demand curve tells the price for any quantity that the individual will buy; a social demand curve gives the price at which an entire community would buy any particular quantity.

[11]A downward sloping demand curve means that more will be purchased only at a lower price.

[12]I suspect that very few college students drink wine at $7 a glass!

[13]An aggregate demand curve would be the amount that the entire community would buy at any price. It would equal the sum of the individual demand curves only under the extreme assumptions given below. Lacking those assumptions, the aggregate demand curve must be formulated on some other basis than individual psychology.

[14]If everyone has identical utility functions, then the amount consumed by the community at any price equals the product of the amount that one person would consume times the number of people.

[15]Independence assumes that the pleasure everyone takes from all commodities is independent of what others consume.

[16]Homotheticity assumes that utility functions and demand curves are independent of income. This is equivalent to assuming that the percentage change in the amount consumed with a one-percent increase in income (the income elasticity of demand) for all products equals one.

[17]A utility function relates the pleasure one gets from any particular bundle of goods and services. Technically, marginal utility for any product is the derivative of the utility function with respect to that good.

[18]Demand curves are upward sloping if people buy more at higher prices.

[19]Even though she has MSWord on her Mac, my copyeditor still has trouble with the formatting of this manuscript!

[20]A movement of the demand curve means that more or less will be bought at any price.

[21]A product has unitary elasticity, the elasticity = 1, if a one-percent change in price causes a one-percent change in the quantity consumed.

[22]If you don't believe me, ask Walter White, high school chemistry teacher.

[23]Excise taxes are paid on particular products.

[24]Inframarginal goods are consumed before the last good purchased, or the marginal purchase.

[25]Consumer surplus is the difference between the marginal utility, the amount consumers would pay for each unit and the market price.

[26]Yes, bargaining happens all the time. If you have not tried to improve your financial aid offer, then do.

8

SUPPLY: MARKETS WITH MONOPOLIES AND OTHERS

MARGINAL PRODUCTIVITY: BACK TO ROBINSON CRUSOE

Working by himself on his lonely island, Robinson Crusoe could connect everything he produced with particular inputs of time and materials. The neoclassical theory of supply treats all production and supply as if we are all Robinson Crusoe, producing in isolation by combining his labor with machinery and raw materials, according to a particular production technology that perfectly relates his inputs to output. Isolated from any social, or human, context, the production problem for a neoclassical producer (often called the firm) is purely engineering. The neoclassical firm produces material output, things, by using material inputs, the *factors of production*, in combinations dictated by engineering blueprints, the available *technology of production*. The amount of output produced is always known given any technology and is specified by an equation called a *production function*. The more inputs, the more of any factor of production that is used, the more output is produced. The better the technology, the more output from any particular set of inputs. These two variables, the technology and the level of inputs, perfectly determine output that depends on these alone, so the only way to change the level of output is by changing the input levels or the technology. Adding more of any input results in more output, but increases come at a diminishing rate. The output gain from adding more of any input, the *marginal product*, declines as more of any input is added because additional inputs have less and less of the other inputs with which to work. Whether it is the *marginal product of labor*, the *marginal product of capital*, or the *marginal product of raw materials*, the increase in output from adding more of any input declines as more is added. As more of any input is added, there are *diminishing returns to the variable input*.

Diminishing returns are the central idea in the neoclassical theory of production and distribution. The marginal product of a variable input declines because when more of any particular input is added, other inputs become saturated with that input. Each additional worker on an apple harvest adds less to output because the low-hanging fruit is picked by the first workers and additional workers have to hunt higher and higher to get any apples. Or, consider a store. Additional sales clerks increase sales because customers receive better attention, the shelves are restocked faster, and the checkout lines are shorter. The first sales clerk is especially important: before she was hired, customers picked out their stuff themselves and left payment in a shoe box at the front of the store. The second sales clerk is almost as important because she guards the store while the first clerk is busy with customers. The third sales clerk is less important but she helps maintain the store by keeping shelves stocked and allows the first two to eat lunch. Each clerk adds to sales but each increases sales by less until, eventually, additional clerks add no more sales because there is nothing for the clerks to do. All the cash registers are staffed full time, the shelves are well stocked, there are enough eyes on the store that there is no

DIMINISHING RETURNS TO VAMPIRE SLAYING

Vampire slaying also faces downward sloping marginal productivity. Buffy, the first slayer, kills a lot of vampires. When a second slayer, Faith, arrives in the third season, she does not kill as many. A third would have found even fewer to kill. Adding more slayers leads to more dead vampires, but each slayer adds less to the kill because they exhaust the supply of weapons, run out of places to patrol, and prowling vampires to kill. This may be why there was only Buffy and Faith before the seventh season. (And the show really went down that year: another case of diminishing returns?)

TABLE 8-1

MARGINAL PRODUCTIVITY AND MARGINAL COST: MARIJUANA FARMING

Workers	Output (ounces)	Marginal Product of Labor (MPL)	Workers to get one more ounce	Marginal Cost to produce one more ounce at $10/worker
1	10	10	0.1	$1.00
2	19	9	0.11	$1.10
3	27	8	0.13	$1.30
4	34	7	0.14	$1.40
5	40	6	0.17	$1.70
6	45	5	0.2	$2.00
7	49	4	0.25	$2.50
8	52	3	0.33	$3.30
9	54	2	0.5	$5.00
10	55	1	1	$10.00

shoplifting, and any additional staff will get in the way of shoppers. At that point, the marginal product of labor is zero.

This is crucial: the marginal product of labor (or other inputs) declines because there is less with which additional inputs can work. The MPL does not decline because workers become less productive; if the workers had more to work with, their marginal productivity would not fall. This applies identically to labor and to every other input. Additional secretaries are less productive than earlier hires because they don't have computers, desks, phones, etc. Flipping this around, additional computers are less productive because there are not enough secretaries to use them. Workers on a pot farm have diminishing marginal productivity because there is no more weeding or watering to do; land and plants on the farm have diminishing marginal productivity because there are a limited number of workers to weed and water.

Note that a situation where individual inputs are increased serially is different from increasing *all* inputs together. If all increase together, then none are saturated and there is no reason for diminishing returns or declining marginal productivity. Instead of diminishing productivity, we have *economies of scale* where output should rise at least as fast as inputs. This is the situation in what economists call "the long run" or a period of time long enough that all inputs can be increased together. That is why, in the long run, marginal productivity is irrelevant in theory and the entire neoclassical value theory collapses. That is why, contrary to the neoclassical model, value depends on the cost of production at constant or rising productivity and constant or declining costs.

We can graph the marginal productivity of any input at any level of supply of other inputs (see Figure 8-1). The lines are downward sloping, reflecting diminishing returns to the variable input, and the MPL rises for every amount of labor if we add other inputs. Adding more of *complementary inputs* shifts the downward sloping marginal productivity line out. If there is more

FIGURE 8-1

MARGINAL PRODUCT OF LABOR, MARIIJUANA FARM WITH VARIABLE LAND

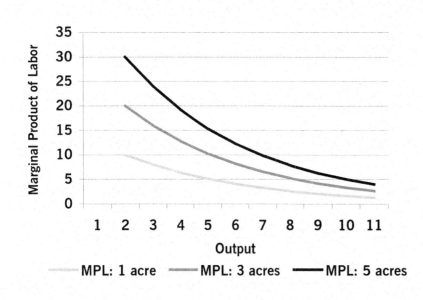

land with which to work, then pot farm workers can apply themselves more productively before they start to get in each other's way. Adding more computers, for another example, raises the marginal productivity of labor for the secretaries. Adding more store clerks shifts out the marginal productivity curve for cash registers, clothes racks, and store shelves, raising the marginal productivity of store capital.

Neoclassical production theory is founded in methodological individualism. Like Robinson Crusoe, it is *ahistorical*, assuming that production takes place outside of time and without regard to past experience or social context. This requires the premise that the technology of production is fixed outside of the production process, independent of experience and social context, and does not change with changes in the level of output or input. Like neoclassical consumption theory, *neoclassical production theory* is a theory of how *individuals* relate to *things* outside of any social or human context. Management has no role to play in production except for coordinating the supply of machinery, resources, and labor according to the blueprints of the production technology. (For a theory widely taught in business schools, this is an odd approach.)

There is a larger point here: neoclassical production theory ignores all the ways that experience shapes the development of technology, including *learning by doing* which is associated with *on-the-job training* and *endogenous technological progress*. Over time, many businesses become more productive because workers learn to do their jobs more efficiently and management discovers better ways to organize the production process. With no place for management, there is none for learning in the orthodox theory. In this view, technology is a black box that changes for reasons outside the purview of the economist. Orthodox theory expects that the same machinery and technology will allow firms to be equally productive in New York or Tokyo as in a small town in central Africa or southern Asia.

It is ironic that an approach founded on the idea that people act to maximize their income and welfare cannot explain the great investment that individuals and firms make in human resource management and in managers. Neoclassicists dismiss efforts by firms to increase productivity by improving morale or mobilizing their workers and building teams. This is inherent in an approach that views productivity as a result of applying individual workers and discrete amounts of capital to a set technology. By ignoring the social influences on productivity emphasized by Adam Smith, neoclassical production theory cannot explain such a common phenomenon as management. It cannot explain *industrial districts* or the tendency of firms to locate near others in their industry. Industrial districts (such as Hollywood, Wall Street, Silicon Valley, Route 128, or the City of London) can replace some of the functions of management. Banking is concentrated in New York City and movie making in Los Angeles because firms in these locations can employ skilled, specialized workers and buy needed inputs more easily than they can elsewhere. Through employment, purchasing, and social networks, firms in these locations, in industrial districts, are better able to keep up with developments in marketing and production technology.

Some communities are more productive, and good managers are able to organize workplaces to create productive communities. There are firms and localities that create productive communities where producers share skills and ideas. Marginal productivity is higher in these areas because of the collective experience of the entire community, experiences that raise workers' marginal productivity independently of the ratio of factor inputs or technology. While familiar to Adam Smith, these ideas have no place in the neoclassical production theory that studies production outside of any social context.

The marginal productivities of labor and capital are on a see-saw. Increases in the ratio of capital to labor, more cash registers per sales clerk, raise the marginal productivity of labor while lowering the marginal productivity of capital because there are fewer sales clerks per cash register. Similarly, raising the labor/capital ratio, adding clerks to the stock of cash registers, lowers the marginal productivity of labor while raising that of capital.

THE HORNDAL EFFECT

Productivity at a steel works at Horndal, Sweden, rose by about 2% a year for a decade without any change in machinery or technology and with little labor turnover. Similar effects have been found in airline productivity, shipbuilding, and cotton textiles production in New England. These productivity gains have been associated with "learning by doing," or improvements in work processes that come through small, incremental changes discovered through experience and practice. The concept owes much to the work of Harvey Leibenstein (1957) who observed large differences in productivity among firms and work places with apparently identical capital stocks and using the same technology.

FIGURE 8-2
MARGINAL COSTS FALL WITH HIGHER MARGINAL PRODUCTIVITY

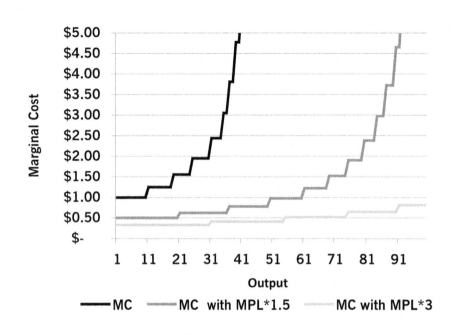

MARGINAL COST

In the neoclassical theory, additional output is produced by adding more *variable inputs*, usually labor or raw materials. In the short run , firms increase their output by adding to their variable inputs, which increases the ratio of variable inputs to fixed. Increasing the ratio of variable to fixed inputs lowers the marginal productivity of the variable inputs until common labor and raw materials have saturated the available supplies of capital and skilled labor, making additional variable inputs progressively less productive. Additions to output are achieved only by adding *ever more* of these variable inputs to the fixed inputs. Because the progressive saturation of fixed inputs requires ever-more variable inputs to achieve the same increase in output, the *marginal cost* of additional units of output rises. Each bit

MARGINAL COSTS RISE BECAUSE MARGINAL PRODUCTIVITY FALLS.

Marginal costs rise because additional output requires ever more of the variable input. This is another way of saying that the marginal productivity of the variable input falls as more and more is employed. If marginal productivity was flat or increased, marginal costs would fall and supply curves would be flat or downward sloping.

Marginal productivity falls because when more of a variable input is added, there are fewer complementary inputs with which to work. More workers are added but they find less land, fewer machines, and fewer resource inputs with which to work. But this is a *short-run* problem because in the long run, more of everything can be added. Also, this ignores any economies coming from greater scale or the greater utilization of the division of labor. If scale economies, or division of labor economies, are strong, then marginal productivity can increase.

The success of large factories and other production facilities suggests that marginal productivity does not necessarily fall with increasing scale, and marginal costs do not necessarily rise. This may be because of the greater use of the division of labor in larger facilities and the addition of complementary inputs, like robots.

of additional output comes at a progressively higher cost (see Table 8-1) because at any level of output, more inputs are needed to increase production (see Figures 8-2 and 8-3).

FIGURE 8-3

SUPPLY CURVE FOR AN INDIVIDUAL PERFECTLY COMPETITIVE POT FARMER

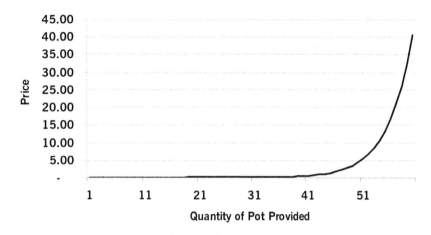

The *marginal cost* of producing additional output, the cost of each additional unit of output, rises because of diminishing returns to any single variable inputs. For any wage, marginal costs will rise with output because the more that is produced, the more inputs are needed to produce the next unit of output. Other factors will also drive up marginal costs. Marginal costs will rise if increases in demand for necessary inputs put pressure on the supply of variable inputs and drive up input prices. The steeper the supply curve of the inputs, the steeper the supply curve of the product, because more inputs are needed to increase output *and* their price is increasing. This is the case for elite baseball players, because it takes a long time to train one and the pool of available talent at the major league level is very thin. It is also the case for air travel. Costs rise because airlines experience declining marginal products for their labor and raw materials when they use older and smaller planes to fly more passengers. In addition, the marginal cost will rise because the costs of airplanes, fuel, and space in airports rise due to developing shortages and congestion.

Even without changes in the price of inputs, marginal costs rise because the marginal productivity of variable inputs falls when the variable inputs run out of complementary fixed inputs. This will only cause marginal costs to rise in the *short run*, because in the *long run* we can add enough complementary inputs, such as capital, machinery, skilled labor, and the like, to maintain constant or even rising marginal productivity. In the long run, marginal costs should be flat or declining if inputs are in elastic supply, because we can add more complementary inputs to maintain marginal productivity. There is no reason for marginal costs to increase if we increase all inputs. Logically, if we could double *all* inputs, for example, at worst we could maintain existing marginal productivity and marginal costs by duplicating existing production facilities. Marginal productivity may even increase and marginal costs fall because the extended division of labor leads to *increasing returns to scale.* In the long run, marginal productivity will fall, and marginal costs increase, only if there are some fixed inputs, such as location, management or idiosyncratic skills, that we cannot replicate.

Note also that neoclassical theory ignores the historical and social dimensions of production we discussed above. If learning happens through production or industrial districts increase productivity at individual firms (through their network or other economies), then productivity may rise with output. If productivity rises with output then that effect may swamp any losses in marginal productivity from increases in the ratio of variable to fixed inputs. And the marginal cost curves might be downward sloping, falling with increases in output due to learning and improvements in productivity that come from practice and experience. This certainly reflects the experience of many industries where productivity rises steeply with production experience. The positive association of productivity and experience can be used to justify protectionist measures and other supports to encourage the growth of *infant industries*, or new industries that may be relatively unproductive now but are capable of higher productivity as they develop.

Marijuana plant

SUPPLY CURVES AND PERFECT COMPETITION

While Paris grocers Hédiard and Ladurée sell many of the same products, they are not perfectly competitive. Each has a monopoly of its own name, reputation, location, and staff.

Or, perhaps, you would prefer to shop at Fauchon?

A firm's supply curve shows how much it will sell for any output price. Because they act as if their output will have no impact on market conditions and prices, perfectly competitive firms produce whenever they can profit from their marginal output (that is, until price equals marginal cost). Perfectly competitive firms are defined as acting as if they face a *horizontal* demand curve where they can sell any amount at the market price, cannot sell anything at a higher price, and could not sell more by lowering their price. Because they act as if their demand is horizontal, output is set by the intersection of the price with their upward sloping marginal cost curve. This curve is upward sloping because diminishing marginal productivity forces them to use ever more variable inputs to get increases in output. The marginal cost is increasing, so perfectly competitive firms will supply more at higher prices, and only at higher prices.

A perfectly competitive industry requires many small, independent producers, each producing a perfectly *homogeneous product*, indistinguishable by consumers, so that all change their output levels without having any influence on the market price. For perfect competition, each firm has to be a *price taker*, able to sell everything it produces at the market price but unable to sell *anything* at above the market price. A price taker is such a small share of the market that it has no impact on the market price, no matter how much it produces. This may be the situation for small vegetable growers at a farmer's market, a small coffee farmer selling beans in the world market, or for students offering to mow lawns during the summer. Note how strong the assumptions are here: to count as a perfectly competitive market, not only must there be no producer larger than a small part of the total market, but products must be indistinguishable so that they are all part of the same market. Companies, therefore, must be nameless.

For *perfectly competitive* industries, market supply at any price is the sum of the output of each individual firm at that price. As with individual demand curves in a neoclassical model, we assume that firms act independently, deliberately ignoring what others do under the *myopic* belief that they can change their output levels without having any effect on market prices. Each firm chooses its level of output in response to the price without regard for the behavior of others or how its actions affect the market. Therefore, total output is the sum of the output of all the independent firms. If there are "N" identical firms, then output at any price is N times the amount any one firm will produce at that price. Note how we remain in the world of methodological individualism, where the whole is the sum of the individuals within it.

Perfect competition? Not for coffee. Not for donuts. Not even for ice cream. We know all of these products: they have distinct tastes, locations, and reputations. (Locations in Seattle, Washington, Berlin, Germany, and Farmington, Connecticut.)

DO INTRODUCTORY TEXTBOOKS DWELL TOO MUCH ON PERFECT COMPETITION?

A recent article in the *Journal of Economic Education* questions why introductory economics textbooks devote so much space to perfect competition. While admitting that perfect competition is "rare;" almost unknown outside of a few agricultural products and raw materials, perfect competition is the center of economic modeling in most texts. This emphasis may reflect an ideological or an aesthetic choice.

It is hard to imagine a perfectly competitive industry. Even where there are many producers of a largely homogeneous product, as in agricultural markets or markets for raw materials, production is often coordinated and bundled by a few large suppliers. This, for example, is the case in North American grain markets where a few large companies, including Archer Daniels Midland and Cargill, buy from large numbers of independent, nearly perfectly competitive producers, and then operate as *oligopolists*, dividing the market among themselves.

MARGINAL REVENUE AND REAL MARKETS

Assuming perfect competition enormously simplifies the analysis of producer behavior because it allows us to treat markets as nothing more than an aggregation of identical individual firms. No additional analysis, research, or thought is needed. It also highlights the positive aspects of market capitalism because it separates market outcomes from market power. By assuming that firms have no market power and can influence neither prices nor consumer behavior, it establishes markets as spheres free of exploitation. Instead of being manipulated or exploited, it shows consumers ruling competitive markets where their preferences govern outcomes, subject only to impersonal technology and factor endowments. Neoclassicists do not deny that there are problems in the world, such as poverty and suffering, but they remove these problems from the political realm by attributing them all to failures of technology, preferences, or inadequate factor endowments.

The best in Paris?

This assumption of perfect competition is obviously inaccurate. It is hard to imagine *any* firms or markets that meet the conditions for perfect competition. Virtually no one produces products identical to those made by others. If they do at first, they immediately set out to distinguish their products from their rivals' by, at least, stamping their names on their output. Consider, for example, the New England village of Amherst, Massachusetts. Apart from home baking, bakeries in other towns, and bakers selling at the three weekly farmers' markets, this picturesque town has nine commercial bakeries: two Dunkin Donuts, an independent donut shop downtown, three other downtown bakeries, and three supermarket bakeries. Someone could try to present this as nearly-perfectly competitive market because there are so many places to buy bread, donuts, and cookies, and because each is a small part of a large, even obese, market. Instead, however, each bakery produces a distinct product with a unique taste, which is sold at a unique location by different people with unique histories of experiences with customers. Each bakery is a *brand*. The bakers at the downtown bakeries, for example, Henions, The Black Sheep, and Wheatberry, all make rich and tasty chocolate-chocolate chip cookies. But think of all the ways they are different! They are on different sides of town, Wheatberry down the hill, Black Sheep in town center, and Henions on the way to the university. Each specializes in a different type of baked good: The Black Sheep has the biggest apricot danish, Wheatberry the best bread, and Henion's the best birthday cakes.

Not all cafes have a view of Notre Dame, like Café le Flore en L'Ile.

Three Amherst bakeries, all selling different baked goods under different brand names.

Their workers are different, their cookies taste different, and the range of other products sold is different. The bakeries have different names. Customers have different experiences in each. They all are special, each in their own way.

Such differences make each bakery a little monopolist, the only one selling its particular product. This is the case for companies making seemingly similar products throughout the world. Visitors to Paris can shop at three of the world's best food stores without leaving Place de la Madeleine. You could buy lunch from Hédiard, Fauchon, or Ladurée; your best option might be to buy from all three to do a proper comparison. The best ice cream in France is made by a company on Ile St. Louis called Berthillon and in addition to Berthillon itself there are on the Ile at least half-a-dozen cafés and storefronts carrying Berthillon. But even selling an *identical* product, each outlet distinguishes itself by its name, its location, the view, and the sidewalk entertainment. One, Café le Flore en L'Ile, sells Berthillon to customers who sit at outdoor tables with a magnificent view of the choir and spire of Notre Dame de Paris; another, on Rue des Deux Pont, has tables inside and also sells good pizza; another, on Rue Saint Louis en l'Ile, only has take out (*à porter*) but is convenient for shopping; another café has a particularly friendly *garçon* who plays jazz drums and dreams of coming to America to play his music.

Consider the myriad forms of imperfect competition in these markets! Hédiard, Fauchon, and Ladurée are all monopolies with their own brand names and devoted clientele. Berthillon is also a *monopoly* because it is the only producer of Berthillon ice cream. From another perspective, each may be seen as a monopolistic competitor, the sole producer of a distinct products but still facing competition with other foods, other forms of ice cream, and other deserts. On Ile St. Louis, Berthillon can be seen as an *oligopolist*, one of a limited number of ice cream vendors, or it can again be seen as a monopolistic competitor, selling a particular ice cream eating experience, at a distinct location and café.

Seeing each company as producing a distinct product under a distinct brand name, thinking in terms of *product heterogeneity* rather than perfect competition, each company is a little monopolist. Each has some loyal customers who will stay with them even if they raise prices a lot, some who will leave if they raise prices *too much*, some who will leave if they raise prices at all, and some who will be attracted away from other little monopolists if they lower their prices enough. Consider, for example, what will happen if the Black Sheep raises cookie prices. If it were in a perfectly competitive mar-

---

FORMS OF IMPERFECT COMPETITION

Monopoly: one seller and no possibility of competition.
Monopolistic competition: many sellers of products that are all somewhat different.

Oligopoly: A few sellers of the same product, few enough that they can sometimes cooperate to set prices and restrict output.

ket then this would be suicidal, as all its customers would leave for a lower-cost supplier. But as a little monopolist, The Black Sheep can raise prices. It may lose some customers but will hold onto others who remain either out of loyalty, because they prefer Black Sheep cookies, because they like to have their cookies after a deli sandwich, or for some other idiosyncratic reasons. This is because the Black Sheep, like every business with a brand name, sells a distinct experience, different from the competition even when the physical product (the cookie or the ice cream) is similar. Different locations, *ancillary* products, appearances, wait-staff, histories—all these and more make each producer a little monopoly, the only one selling exactly what they sell. That is why some consumers will remain with The Black Sheep and will continue to buy their newly higher-priced cookies. Even at that higher price, they still prefer the

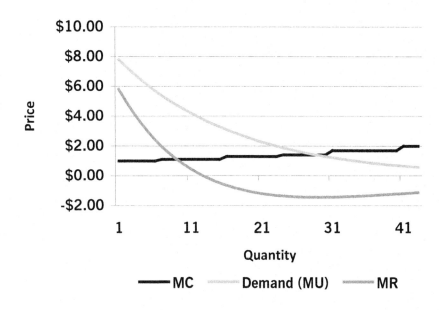

FIGURE 8-4
COMPARING MONOPOLY AND PERFECT COMPETITION

product they get from The Black Sheep over the next best alternative. Similarly, if The Black Sheep wants to increase sales, it can do so by lowering prices but the increase will be limited because some customers will remain at Henion's, Stop and Shop, Dunkin Donuts, etc.

This means that The Black Sheep faces a downward sloping demand curve: to sell more it must lower prices, drawing business away from rivals who produce competing products. From its demand curve, we can calculate a mar*ginal revenue* curve for the Black Sheep that gives us how much extra revenue is collected from each sale (see Table 8-3, p. 151). Calculating marginal revenue is straightforward. For each price, t*otal revenue* is the product of the amount sold and the price, the number of cookies

sold times the price. Marginal revenue is the change in total revenue, the difference between revenue from selling one amount at one price and that from selling a greater amount, one more unit, but by selling all units at a lower price. For the first sale, total revenue is the price times the number of cookies sold (or 1) and marginal revenue is the change from selling no cookies; marginal revenue for the first sale is the same as total revenue. For each sale after the very first, however, marginal revenue on an additional sale is less than the price because, to sell more, the Black Sheep must lower prices to those who would have been willing to pay more. To sell more, the Black Sheep has to lower prices to everyone. The new, lower price is paid not only by the new customers but also by the *inframarginal* customers who would have bought at the old, higher prices. People who were already buying Black

FIGURE 8-5
AMHERST COOKIE MARKET: THE BLACK SHEEP AS PERFECT COMPETITOR

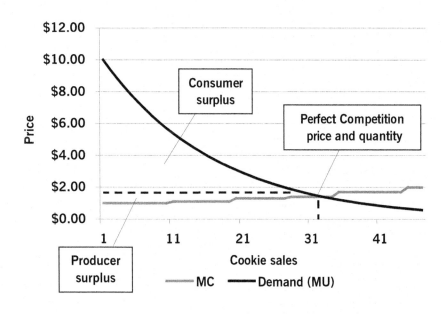

FIGURE 8-6
AMHERST COOKIE MARKET: THE BLACK SHEEP AS MONOPOLIST

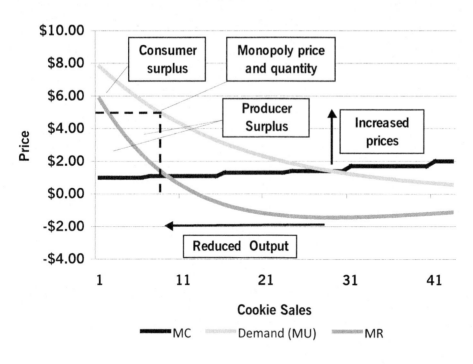

Sheep cookies are now able to get their cookies at a discount. The total discount is the difference between marginal revenue and the new revenue paid by new customers.

MONOPOLY

Perfectly competitive firms have flat marginal revenue curves because they are such a small part of a large market for homogeneous goods, and they can always sell more at the same price. This may be the case for a few firms, but many more, including most small businesses, are like the Black Sheep and face downward sloping demand and marginal revenue curves. Still, there may be some dumb, or *myopic*, firms who *act* like they are perfect competitors. They set prices and quantity to sell where their *marginal cost* (MC) equals the price (P). They do what economists recommend, and then wonder why they are losing money. Economists and consumers like this behavior because these firms will produce the optimal amount, producing until the *marginal utility*, or the additional pleasure, consumers get from one more unit of product just equals the marginal cost of that additional unit. The marginal utility (MU) is represented by the demand curve, where it equals the cost of the product, as represented by the marginal cost (MC) schedule. Thus marginal benefits just equal marginal costs to society, but at a point where the *marginal revenue* (MR) the firm receives is less than the marginal cost. Firms that produce where MU=MC risk bankruptcy. They will not be able to cover their fixed costs because their pricing behavior is based only on their marginal costs.

Economists applaud when firms behave like perfect competitors because it leads to the optimum level of output for society, even when it is not *profit-maximizing* for the firm. Smart entrepreneurs will remember from introductory economics that for firms offering differentiated products, the marginal revenue curve lies below the demand curve, and they will conclude that if they produce where MC equals price (or MC intersects the demand curve), they will be producing where marginal revenue (MR) is less than the MC. Having studied economics in college, they will reason further and conclude that because MR is less than MC, they should reduce output to raise prices (also raising MR) and move to a lower MC. They then move up the MR curve and down the MC curve until MR=MC, at which point their business will be selling at a price above MC. For the firm, this is a much better place and may even allow the business to cover its fixed costs. (Note that these are still being ignored by an analysis that focuses on MR

MONOPOLISTIC COMPETITION: TEXTBOOKS

No one likes the textbook industry. While students and faculty complain about the high cost of books, publishers insist that they make very little profit. The problem is that monopolistic competition inflates the cost of producing textbooks without giving publishers an incentive to produce better books. There are dozens of textbooks available for introductory courses in economics, and more are written every year with remarkably similar content. Publishers compete by spending on advertising, making slight changes in their products, and sending out a large staff of sales agents. (They also distribute large numbers of free copies to faculty.) While good practice for individual publishers, a strategy of marketing and product differentiation drives up costs for students without improving their educational experience. It also drives down profits. The costs of producing and marketing new editions every two years are so high that publishers lose money even when books sell for over $100.

and MC.) But this is less output than society would want because at that output level the marginal social returns (MU) exceed the marginal social cost (MC). Compared with the perfectly competitive industry, output is less and prices are higher. Smart, self-aware firms thus redistribute income away from consumers towards themselves. Smart capitalists are not in business for charity or to produce what people want. They are in it to make money and to do this they need to create scarcity.

Every firm wants to be a monopolist of some type. Some try to achieve this by finding ways to out-produce their competitors, producing better products more cheaply until they drive their competitors out of business. Others try to use advertising or other means to persuade the public that they have better products. The most effective may be those who can lure customers into their network so that the customer is forced to buy from them to maintain existing products (machinery, software, etc.).

Some of the most effective monopolies are formed through collusion among independent firms. While recognizing that firms have an incentive to cooperate with their rivals to form monopolies, most economists expect such arrangements to be short lived. They assume that successful collusion will self-destruct. By raising prices above the cost of production, collusion gives participants an incentive to cheat and produce more. This has been a chronic problem for collusive arrangements like OPEC (rganization of Petroleum Exporting Countries). Higher oil prices have repeatedly been driven down when member countries "cheated" and produced beyond their official quota to take advantage of high prices. Furthermore, success in raising prices above the cost of production encourages new entrants into the market. This too has been the OPEC experience where, for example, high prices in the 1970s led countries like Mexico and the United Kingdom to begin exporting oil. In a little more than a decade after OPEC dramatically raised oil prices in the early 1970s, its share of world oil production fell by almost half, from 55% in 1972 down to under 30% in 1985. Combined with cheating by OPEC members, rising production from non-members drove oil prices down by two-thirds in the same period.

Overcoming cheating and entry, OPEC has survived and continues to raise oil prices. One key to any monopoly's success is internal politics within the group forming a monopoly. OPEC remains powerful because there are only a few major oil exporters, a small enough group that they can sit together in a room to discuss their common interests. With 12 member states, OPEC includes almost half of the countries that export oil and it would take years for another country to join the export club. The coffee market, by contrast, is much harder to control, both because there are more participants (41 coffee exporting countries) and because additional countries could easily enter the coffee trade if it appeared lucrative.

Monopolies, like OPEC, benefit from *barriers to entry* that make it difficult or expensive to enter markets and compete. Increasing returns of scale, which allow large producers to undersell smaller competitors, are a major barrier to entry. This is the case with products requiring long lead times and large investments in R&D ("research and development") or in plant and equipment before production can begin. This is certainly the

DISNEY: A SUCCESSFUL MONOPOLISTIC COMPETITOR

In 1923, Walter and Roy Disney incorporated the Disney Brothers Cartoon Studio which soon became the Walt Disney Studio. Success with cartoon characters like Mickey Mouse, Donald Duck, and Snow White was soon followed by innovative use of television and the opening of the Disneyland theme park in Anaheim, California in 1953. The company has continually renewed its product line with new, youth- and teen-oriented products. Most recently, these have included one-time teen (and tween) stars Anne Hathaway, Lindsay Lohan, and Ashley Tisdale, as well as Vanessa Hudgens and Miley Cyrus.

The Airbus was decades in design and cost tens of billions of dollars. New microprocessors cost billions to design and require production facilities that can cost over a billion dollars. An oil rig like this can cost $1 billion and can require a decade of research and production before a single barrel of oil is sold. By contrast, a coffee grove can be up and running within 3 years—albeit only a low-quality coffee, not Costa Rican prime!—at a cost in millions. This difference in scale protects the monopoly position of the aerospace and oil industry while driving down prices for coffee and many other commodities.

Coffee plantation in Costa Rica, oil rig in the North Sea, Intel Dual Core2160 microprocessor, and Airbus 380 jet.

NOT ALL MONOPOLIES ARE SUCCESSFUL: U.S. STEEL

When founded in 1901, United States Steel was not only the world's largest company but, at $1.4 billion ($228 billion today), it was the largest company the world had ever known. Producing nearly 70% of the steel made in the United States and 30% of the world's steel, U.S. Steel maintained profits by keeping prices well above the cost of production, preventing its workers from forming unions, and resisting technological changes that would lower the value of its capital stock. Over time, however, these policies undermined its monopoly by attracting competitors who entered the steel industry to take advantage of high prices. These included both longstanding domestic rivals (e.g., Bethlehem Steel) and foreign. Eventually, new entrants using new and better technology drove U.S. Steel nearly to bankruptcy. Today, the company accounts for only 10% of steel produced in the United States and the company ranks 55th among United States corporations

case with new oil producers. It is also the case with the automobile industry, with computer chip manufacturing, with aerospace (where there are two viable companies, AirBus and Boeing), and with local cable television companies (though they now face competition from satellite dish providers). Some monopolies develop where network economies encourage consumers to buy from one producer, such as Microsoft. The monopolist may not produce more efficiently or sell for less, but its product is worth more than its competitors' to consumers who want the same product that other consumers use. By contrast, the coffee market is relatively easy to enter: all one needs is some land, seeds, and a little training. After that, Starbucks does the rest!

While presenting perfect competition as the norm, orthodox economics would treat monopoly as an extreme and unusual case. It is true that both perfect competition and monopoly are extreme cases, but the norm is much closer to the monopoly than to perfect competition. Some economists attribute monopoly power to brand-name loyalties. They imply that consumers are responsible for their own problems because they foolishly shop by brand. But brand loyalty can be a rational approach to product uncertainty and lack of information. Consumers prefer certain brands because experience gives them confidence in their quality. Consumers are attracted and loyal to Intel, IBM, and Toyota, for example, because they associate those brand names with quality and trust them to produce and stand behind a quality product. These examples highlight how monopoly can be common, even ubiquitous. Market power is not an unusual exception to the rule. Rather, it is the norm, the inevitable result of the consumers' search for the quality and the reliability that they associated with reputation.

Because they focus on relationships between people and things, neoclassical economists see monopoly as the result of external circumstances. They expect, therefore, that monopolies can be easily overturned because new entrants will be attracted to the industry by the lure of monopoly profits (as happened for United States Steel's monopoly). But focusing on engineering problems and production misses the real issue, which is the way entrepreneurs and firms are always creating monopoly power through conscious strategy and social action. The key to market power is not in the relationship between people and things, but rather the ability of firms to differentiate their product and narrow their market through conscious social action. Here we have the real issue: pure monopoly, where there is only one producer in the market in an invulnerable position, is as rare as perfect competition. Instead, virtually all companies are in broader markets where they face some competition for their products, because con-

NATURAL MONOPOLY

Some industries are seen to be natural monopolies because production requires such large fixed costs that other businesses will not enter. This is commonly seen in public utilities, such as water or cable television.

Without significant market competition, firms in these industries are expected to behave like monopolies, raising prices and restricting production and technological progress. To avoid these, governments regulate and in some cases manage firms in these industries as public utilities.

The theory of natural monopoly was first developed by the American economists Henry C. Adams and Richard Ely. It has been applied to industries with physical characteristics inhibiting entry and competition, including water or cable companies that need to lay pipe along streets or the high cost of building competing railway lines. Social conditions can also raise the cost of entry, including brand name loyalty, e.g. Disney, and strong network effects, e.g. Facebook or Microsoft Office.

sumers can shift to other producers and products, but they also have some market power due to location, brand name loyalty, or other factors. Smart entrepreneurs do not sit idly accepting whatever the market may give them. Instead, they are always trying to lock customers in by distinguishing their products, defining them as so special that they have some monopoly power.

How to do this? How to narrow the market for your product so that others are no longer seen to be viable substitutes? For some products, this is relatively easy because economies of scale establish a **natural monopoly** where there really are no comparable products available at a reasonable cost because one company can produce at a much lower marginal cost. (This is the case, for example, for local water, for long-distance commercial aviation, and for some information technology companies.) Even when competition is technically feasible, companies try to limit it so that they can raise prices and behave like a monopolist. There are a variety of strategies that they follow. While individually profitable, they are all socially wasteful because they expend resources without providing any value to the public. On the contrary, they reduce value by making it more difficult for consumers to evaluate products fairly.

MONOPOLY: OPEC'S MIXED SUCCESS IN A PRISONER'S DILEMMA

The Organization of Petroleum Exporting Countries (OPEC) was formed in 1960. Throughout its history, it has tried to use its leverage over the world oil market to raise prices by restricting production. Its power is limited because its 12 members face a prisoner's dilemma problem. Each gains when someone reduces production; but each gains more as an individual by cheating on quotas and increasing production to take advantage of higher prices. The result is that oil prices cycle between short supply/high prices and surplus/low prices.

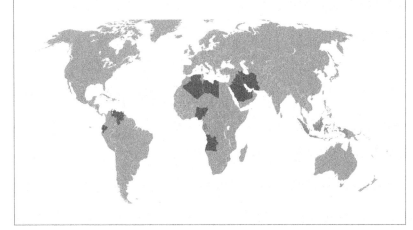

EVEN A MICKEY MOUSE MONOPOLY IS BAD, AND UNAVOIDABLE

Compared with perfect competition, monopolies produce less and charge higher prices to consumers. In this way, they redistribute income from consumers to themselves. They are wasteful too. Because they produce less than perfect competitors, they employ less labor, creating unemployment and lowering wages, and they engage in wasteful practices to distinguish their products from those produced by other firms.

This is a false comparison, however, because all firms have some degree of monopolistic power and all face some market competition. Perfectly competitive firms, furthermore, could never survive because they cannot cover their fixed costs. The choice, therefore, is not between perfect competition and monopoly but between different forms of monopoly, regulated or unregulated.

ADAM SMITH RECOGNIZED THAT PRODUCERS ALWAYS WANT TO FORM A MONOPOLY

"People of the same trade seldom meet together, even for merriment and diversion, but the conversation ends in a conspiracy against the public, or in some contrivance to raise prices. It is impossible indeed to prevent such meetings, by any law which either could be executed, or would be consistent with liberty and justice. But though the law cannot hinder people of the same trade from sometimes assembling together, it ought to do nothing to facilitate such assemblies; much less to render them necessary."

STRATEGIES TO REDUCE COMPETITION:

Advertising: Firms try to persuade consumers that their product is better, less expensive, and sexier than their rivals'.

Patents and copyright: They try to establish legal monopolies through extended patent and copyright protection.

Protection: Companies try to gain legal protection by restricting entry to their business by requiring expensive licensing procedures. They also try to limit foreign competition through tariffs and voluntary quotas.

Networks: Companies try to make it difficult for competitors to break into a field by integrating their product with a range of others. The Microsoft corporation pioneered the strategy of using interlocking technologies to extend its monopoly power in one area, operating systems, into other areas, such as word processing, internet browsers, and other applications. Boeing and Airbus both try to lock airlines into buying their services by making their products incompatible with their competitors'. Hewlett-Packard sells printers at a price that gives few profits because they expect to make money on their ink cartridges.

Lock-in and frequent-user programs: They provide wholesale and repeat business discounts to discourage consumers from changing products.

Market leverage to beget market power: They lean on retailers to force other products out of prime retail locations. Microsoft used this strategy when they required vendors to bundle other products with the Windows operating system. Soft drink companies do this by creating more products to grab store shelf space and pay stores for prime locations.

Product differentiation: Companies distinguish their product by quality, use, color, or simply by advertising.

RENTS, PROFITS AND PRODUCER SURPLUS UNDER MONOPOLY AND UNDER PERFECT COMPETITION

Monopolies raise profits by restricting output to raise prices. In this way, they redistribute some of the *consumer surplus* to the producer, with some surplus lost along the way. Even with this efficiency loss, the redistribution of income by a monopoly may not be so bad if we think the monopolist is more wor-

TABLE 8-2
STRATEGIES TO ESTABLISH MONOPOLIES

Strategy	Example
Advertising to persuade consumer that products are better, more reliable, and sexier.	T-Mobile ads with Catherine Zeta-Jones.
Legal strategies such as extended copyright and patent protection.	Disney's campaign for longer copyright on Mickey Mouse.
Protectionist measures.	Excess tariffs imposed on foreign steel; voluntary restrictions on Japanese cars.
Interlocking technology and networks.	Microsoft Office, printer-specific ink, cell-phone power cords.
Lock-in.	Airline frequent-flyer programs; software upgrade discounts.
Market leverage over retailers.	Tropicana issues variety of types of orange juice to hog supermarket space.
Product differentiation.	Dunkin Donuts advertises that its coffee is different and better than Starbucks'

thy of income than the consumer. Some have defended OPEC, for example, by suggesting that relatively poor member countries, such as Nigeria and Venezuela, need or deserve the money more than do affluent car drivers in North America, Europe, or Japan. (This argument may break down for extraordinarily affluent oil-producing countries like Saudi Arabia and the United Arab Emirates. And even in poor countries like Nigeria, there is no guarantee that the poor will benefit from oil revenues.) But even monopolies that do redistribute from the rich to the poor are inefficient Robin Hoods because they reduce the total welfare of society. In sum, by reducing output to raise prices, monopolies reduce the total surplus available to society. They reduce consumer surplus by more than they raise profits. The cost of monopoly power to consumers is the redistribution from consumers to monopolists plus a *deadweight burden* of the reduction in output below the optimal level.

Producer surplus, sometimes called *producer rent*, is the difference between the cost of production and the price. In the example in Table 8-3, the first cookies could be produced for no more than $0.45. If sold by a competitive firm for $1.50, this cookie would produce $1.05 in surplus for the producer. The third cookie, produced for $0.55, would likewise yield producer surplus of $0.95. Producer surplus drops with additional cookies because of rising marginal costs until the last cookie produced by a competitive firm at a marginal cost of $1.50 is sold at the same price. There is no producer surplus on that last cookie because it is sold at exactly the marginal cost of production.

The calculation of producer surplus is the same for monopolists. However, not only does the share going to consumers and producers change but the total falls because monopolists raise prices by producing less. Again, the producer surplus on each cookie sold is the difference between price and marginal cost. Compared with the perfectly competitive firm, there are two crucial differences. First, the monopolist produces less, producing only until marginal cost equals marginal revenue, which is less than the price. Both producer and consumer surplus are earned on fewer sales. (Some of the competitive producer surplus is lost on units that are no longer produced even though their marginal cost is below the marginal benefit—that is, marginal cost below the demand curve.) This loss from reduced output of consumer surplus (even where there is also a reduction in producer surplus) is called the *deadweight burden of monopoly*; compared with perfect

TABLE 8-3

HYPOTHETICAL AMHERST COOKIE MARKET: THE BLACK SHEEP AS MONOPOLIST OR PERFECT COMPETITOR

Price	Sales	TR	MR	MC	Producer surplus		Consumer surplus	
p	q	= p * q			PC	Mono.	PC	Mono.
$4.50	1.50	$6.75	$4.50	$0.45	$1.57	$4.20	$4.50	$1.88
$4.00	3.00	$12.00	$1.75	$0.55	$2.85	$8.10	$7.50	$2.25
$3.50	4.50	$15.75	$0.83	$0.67	$3.72	$11.59	$9.00	$1.13
$3.00	6.00	$18.00	$0.38	$0.82	$4.07	$7.28	$9.00	$0.36
$2.50	7.50	$18.75	$0.10	$1.00	$3.72		$7.50	
$2.00	9.00	$18.00	($0.08)	$1.23	$2.47		$4.50	
$1.50	10.50	$15.75	($0.21)	$1.50	$0.03		$0.00	
$1.00	12.00	$12.00	($0.31)	$1.83				
$0.50	13.50	$6.75	($0.39)	$2.23				
$0.00	15.00	$0.00	($0.45)	$2.72				
					$18.42	$31.17	$42.00	$5.61
					Sum PC:	$60.42	Sum Mono:	$36.78
					P=$1.50	P=$3.25	P=$1.50	P=$3.25
		Monopolist gain	$12.75	$12.75				
		Consumer loss	($36.39)	($36.39)				

MONOPOLISTIC COMPETITION AND JEANS: THE 4 F'S

You can buy a pair of department store jeans for under $20, or you can spend over $200 to buy "7 For All Mankind" jeans, like Jessica Alba. Jeans companies would rather sell in the $200 range than the $20, but to do so they have to clearly differentiate their product from the competition. This includes measures that improve the fit and comfort of their product, and others that do nothing except distinguish their product from others. Romney Evans, CEO of True-Jeans.com, explained to *USA Today* the four F's for raising the prestige of premium denim:

- Fit. The most prestigious jeans brands flatter different body types. Women often judge jeans based on how they look on their hips.
- Fabric. Superior fabric, finishing and stretch distinguish premium denim jeans from those that are mass produced.
- Finishing. Premium jeans undergo labor-intensive treatments, washes and finishing work to give them characteristics such as whiskering, fading, tearing and signature back-pocket stitching. Skilled craftsmen use belt sanders, sandblasters, hammers, metal brushes and pumice stones to create looks they hope give the jeans character and style.
- Fashion-forward. Premium designer jeans have high price points, which keeps distribution exclusive to luxury department and specialty stores frequented by those with high disposable income and, often, cutting-edge tastes. Premium denim brands often become popular fashion items when celebrities are photographed wearing them. Each jeans brand is identified by a distinctive signature back-pocket design that is often seen as a status symbol.

competition, we are all worse off due to the reduced output. Second, because less is produced, the monopoly price is higher than the competitive price and more producer surplus is earned on each sale. Selling at a price of $3.25 a cookie, the monopolist has a producer surplus of $2.80 on the first sales. Increased producer surplus directly corresponds to a reduction in consumer surplus: monopolists gain by capturing for themselves some of the consumer surplus. Note that because the monopolist produces where MR=MC instead of MC=Price, there is producer surplus earned on the last sale, but because the monopolist sets the price on the demand curve, there is no consumer surplus on this last sale.

Total producer surplus is the sum of the difference between marginal cost and the price of output. The total *social surplus* is the sum of the consumer and producer surplus. Without distinguishing between the income of producers and consumers, the social surplus is society's gain from production and exchange. It is the sum of the gap between the value of the goods to consumers and their cost to producers. The allocation of the social surplus between consumers and producers depends on the output price and the level of production. Monopolies reallocate surplus towards producers by lowering output and raising prices; they have a larger producer surplus and a smaller consumer surplus. If monopolies only reallocated, then our attitude towards them might depend on whether we like the monopolist more or less than we like the consumers. We might disapprove, for example, of a monopoly of rich Texas oilmen and be more sympathetic to a monopoly of struggling musicians. But monopolies don't just reallocate, they also shrink the total social surplus by producing only until MC=MR. This reduction in the sum of consumer and producer surplus is the deadweight loss of monopoly, the loss to society compared with perfect competition.

In the case of the Amherst cookie monopoly, for example, competitive firms would sell 10.5 cookies at a price of $1.50. The monopolist raises prices to $3.25 by selling only about 5.25 cookies. Lower output raises prices, reallocating consumer surplus to the monopolist as producer surplus. Compared with a competitive firm, the monopolist earns an *extra* surplus of $21.00 on 5.25 cookies at the expense of the consumer surplus. In addition, there is lost producer and consumer surplus on the cookies that are not produced by the monopolist, a loss of $8.25 for producers and a further loss of $16.50 for consumers. In total, consumers lose about $37 and producers have a net gain of $13. Adding together the monopolists' gain and the consumers' losses, the change in the total social surplus is a loss of about $25.

For both monopoly and perfect competitors, producer surplus will be greatest where there is a relatively *inelastic* supply because marginal cost increases sharply. This is because there will be a large difference between price and marginal cost where supply is inelastic and there can be a large producer surplus on the cost of producing inframarginal units. If the MC curve is nearly flat and there is little difference in the cost of producing the first and the last products sold, then there will be little surplus earned by competitive firms because they will be selling the product at the marginal cost of the last unit produced, which will be little different from the cost of the inframarginal units. On the other hand, if supply is inelastic because the marginal cost curve is steeply upward sloping, then the surplus will be large because the difference in cost between the marginal and the inframarginal units will be large.

There are a variety of products where there can be a large producer surplus earned because the product is produced with an inelastic supply curve. These would include some products where the short-run supply curve is highly inelastic because production requires a long lead time for planning and positioning equipment. Examples include petroleum and gasoline. The supply of petroleum can be increased easily in the long run by investing in oil exploration, introducing advanced extraction technologies, and building rigs, pipelines, loading facilities, tankers, and refineries. This infrastructure cannot be developed quickly and so the short-run supply is highly inelastic. Other products are in relatively inelastic supply even in the long run, such as urban real estate and major-league baseball players. Where supply is inelastic, there is an opportunity to gain very large producer surpluses. These super-profits are often the subject of considerable controversy, including demands for price controls or excess-profit taxes.

At the extreme, where products cannot be reproduced at all, price depends entirely on demand and large *rents* can be earned. This is the case for land: the higher price of land and housing in desirable locations translates into higher price and higher surpluses for owners. A fixed supply of houses in three towns, Amherst, Hadley, and Sunderland, will lead to different housing prices according to the different demands for housing. Where housing is in the greatest demand, Amherst, prices are highest and landowners receive the greatest surplus from their properties. They earn the highest rents and these rents are capitalized as higher prices for their property. Hadley landowners, by contrast, cannot charge as much for their housing and receive less surplus and lower rents; demand, prices, surplus and rents are lower still in Sunderland.

PRODUCER SURPLUS, FIXED COSTS, AND PROFITS

Be careful to distinguish between this view of producer surplus and the conventional concept of *profit*. Producer surplus is income minus the variable cost of producing products for the market. This does not take account of other expenses, costs that are fixed in the short run but must be incurred to operate the business. For example, it cost Lions Gate Entertainment less than $500,000 to put a copy of "Hunger Games: Catching Fire" in 1,000 theaters where it received half of a gross revenue of nearly $680 million after 5

Expensive to make and profitable.

Expensive to make and not profitable.

weeks. This is a huge producer surplus but in calculating profits you need to take account of the over $130 million Lions Gate invested in the movie—including $10 million to keep Jennifer Lawrence. (Before shedding tears for Lions Gate, consider the revenues from the other "Hunger" movies, plus spinoffs, DVD sales, and foreign rentals. Revenue sources other than ticket sales in United States theaters account for about 85% of Hollywood revenue.)

This type of upfront investment is found in other industries as well. Intel invested over $500 million in building its latest chip facility and $2 billion in research. With this investment, the company can produce chips for a few dollars that it sells for nearly $100. It uses its monopoly power to earn a large producer surplus on each transaction. But its rate of profit may still be very low because it has to cover the carrying costs of its large investment. The owners of New York apartment buildings may have very large producer surpluses because they have few operating costs on their buildings, but their rate of profit depends on the other, fixed costs they incurred in building the apartments.

Having explored monopoly and perfect competition, most economists favor perfect competition and conclude that we should adopt policies to favor competition and discourage monopoly. Perfect competition certainly has attractive features: lower prices and output at the social optimum. But however attractive it may be, perfect competition is so unusual that we might call it a social anomaly, even a fantasy no more realistic than Lions Gate's "Hunger Games" or New Line's "Hobbit." There are no perfectly competitive industries—none with homogeneous products, easy entry, and widespread consumer knowledge. Nor could we expect competition to persist even if there was a competitive industry. Competitive firms have every reason to try to form little monopolies through mergers, by discovering better production and distribution technologies, and by distinguishing their products from those of their rivals. If the producers do not do this, consumers will in effect create monopolies through their own search for usable information and the security of shopping for products that they recognize and share with their friends. Worse, if firms didn't establish monopolies then they would soon be driven out of business because they could not recover their fixed costs when pricing at marginal cost. It is reasonable to say that monopolies, or firms with at least some form of market power, are the *only* firms that can survive in a world of fixed costs.

WHAT DO BUSINESSES REALLY MAXIMIZE ANYWAY?

The orthodox model assumes that businesses try to maximize profits. With this assumption, neoclassical economists ignore any internal dynamics of the business firm, such as disputes between managers and shareholders over increasing scale or seeking immediate profits, or between managers over emphasizing alternative product lines or markets. By assuming profit maximization, the firm's strategy can be reduced to a set of simple choices driven by its technology, the relative costs of different factor inputs, and the demand and marginal revenue curves. Neoclassical economists then act as if they do not need to learn anything about the internal operation of the firm because they *assume* everything else follows from the firm seeking to maximize profits.

Again, it is very strange that this theory should be taught in business schools. There is a large literature about how to balance the interests of managers with those of shareholders, and courses are taught about how to calibrate compensation so that interests of managers are aligned with those of shareholders. As a theory, profit-maximization is clearly deficient outside of perfect competition, where there are no managerial decisions to be made anyway! It leaves unexplained *which* profits are to be maximized and the preferred time pattern of profits—every business must decide whether to maximize today's profits, or tomorrow's, or next week's. So it becomes a management decision: what is the preferred trade-off between profits now and profits in the future? A firm in a relatively strong market position, for example, could keep prices and profits low so as to maintain that position for a longer time and stretch out its period of monopolistic profits, transferring profits from today into the future. Or it could exploit its position now, raise prices so as to enjoy large profits now while inviting more competition and undermining its future position and profits. Profit maximization as such could provide a definitive rule for choosing between these strategies only if all participants shared the same discount rate and had the same rate of uncertainty. That is to say, profit maximization only provides a clear rule for a firm with a single manager-owner.

The relationship between owners and managers has been the subject of one of the most influential books in 20th century economics, *The Modern Corporation and Private Property*, by Adolf A. Berle and Gardiner C. Means. Writing at the depths of the Great Depression, Berle and Means were institutionalist economists who argued that the forms of property created by the modern corporation have fundamentally changed the way American business responds to economic conditions. Corporations, they argued, are controlled not by shareholders, a large group of anonymous stockholders with little knowledge of the business and less capacity to influence its decisions, but by their managers. Managers not only control the appointment and compensation of the corporate boards responsible for overseeing their performance, but control the flow of information from the business. Recent experiences with Enron, Tyco, WorldCom, Global Crossing, Lehman Brothers, and others shows how easy it can be for unscrupulous managers to conceal the real condition of their company in order to manipulate shareholders (see *asymmetric information*).

Instead of maximizing profits or shareholder value, Berle and Means argued, managers set policy to advance their own interests. The manager-controlled corporation could be run to maximize the managers' earnings, power, or some other measure of their welfare. Seeking to maximize their power in the world, managers may try to maximize firm size and the number of people under their command, increasing sales even when that involves extending production beyond the point where MR=MC. Fearing challenges to their authority and the disruptive effects of change, managers may also hesitate to invest in new technologies and new markets. A certain institutional inertia may set in where managers are concerned with maintaining the smooth operation of the existing business rather than seeking opportunities for profit and growth. Sometimes, managers seem to toy recklessly with their companies, confident that any losses will be suffered by shareholders while they will walk away with huge bonuses for successful investments. In other cases, instead of the profit-seeking and adventurous firm of neoclassical orthodoxy, managers are cautious, even lazy. Often, firms are run by managers selected according to the "Peter Principle" where people are promoted to their level of incompetence; so long as you do not make enemies or challenge those above you, you will be promoted. The cream rises until it sours.

Recent corporate scandals hidden by unscrupulous managers have brought down companies including Enron, WorldCom, and Lehman Brothers.
Enron's fancy new headquarters were still under construction when the company went bankrupt in 2001.

The idea of the managerial firm raises profound questions about the nature of private property in modern corporate America. Managerial hierarchy, the power that supervisors exercise over workers, has been justified on the grounds that owners should have control over their workplace. But if firms are run by their managers with, at best, loose regulation by owners, then what is the justification for hierarchical authority, for the authority that a group of usurpers has over workers? If there is no intrinsic justification for management autocracy in terms of property rights, then hierarchy becomes an instrumental matter, a question of whether it is the most efficient and constructive way to handle a large enterprise. Or would greater government regulation or worker autonomy be more appropriate? These are fundamental questions about the management of a capitalist enterprise within a democratic society: if democracy is right for the public sphere and for government, then should it also be applied to business?

SHIFTING SUPPLY CURVES?

As methodological individualists view the economy, the supply of products is an engineering problem between people and a stingy nature. Firms supply more at higher prices because the marginal cost of production rises with output, due to diminishing marginal productivity of any variable factor. Higher prices elicit more output by allowing producers to use more variable inputs (including workers and raw materials) to produce more *despite* diminishing marginal productivity. If output prices fall, then producers will discard some of their variable inputs, restricting themselves and moving back up their marginal productivity curve. By assuming perfect competition, neoclassical economists remove human volition from business managers, who are assumed to have no real power or choice in the market process. A matter of engineering, supply comes from the relationship between people and things, without social content.

In the neoclassical world, social intervention would involve attempts by monopolists and would-be monopolists to take advantage of the public by restricting output to raise prices. Since the time of Adam Smith, economists have devoted themselves to fighting monopoly and seeking to eliminate *static inefficiencies*, the output loss coming from monopolies and other restrictions on production. There is less merit to this approach than

Improvements in computer technology allow the use of supermarket barcode scanners, raising productivity, and so shifting the supply curve out, in the retail trade sector.

one might think because most of the increase in production over the last centuries has come from *dynamic efficiency*, increases in productivity, rather than from improvements in the allocation of existing resources. In a dynamic society like ours, movements *along* the supply curve from eliminating static inefficiencies are less important than the dynamic gains from *shifts* of the supply curve, where ever-more-efficient producers provide more output at all prices. Virtually all of enormous increase in income since the 18th century has come from technological progress that has shifted supply curves out, rather than by movements down the supply curve by eliminating static inefficiency.

Increasing supply works through the economy in three ways: by changing the costs of inputs, the productivity of inputs, and the readiness of competitive and monopolistic firms to sell. Higher prices for inputs, such as labor or raw materials, shift the supply curve up or in when producers demand higher prices to cover their higher input costs. Lower input prices, similarly, shift the supply curve down or out, with more supplied at any price. Improved production technology allows produces to supply more at any price, a shift down or out of the supply curve. Finally, static efficiency gains and inefficiencies spread through the economy when changes in price of inputs and intermediary products,

due to changes in the degree of market power, shift supply for other industries. If firms gain market power, through collusive arrangements, for example, or by successfully branding their product, the higher prices they charge shift the supply curve up or in for industries using their products.

The greatest economic changes have come from falling input prices due to rising productivity. Productivity, output per hour of labor, has risen over ten-fold in the last century, allowing producers to sell products at prices dramatically lower than in the 19th century. On average, productivity per hour worked has risen by nearly 2.3% per annum, allowing an increase in income and in leisure. Raw material prices have fallen dramatically because new countries first enter the world economy by selling food and mate-

FIGURE 8-7
COMPETITIVE SUPPLY CURVE WITH CHANGING INPUT COSTS OR PRODUCTIVTY

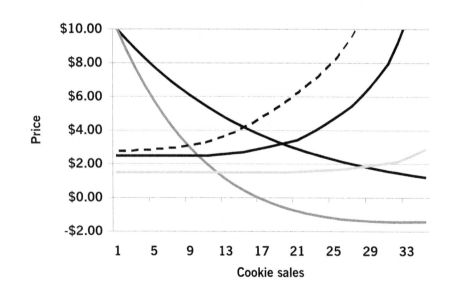

TABLE 8-4
FACTORS SHIFTING SUPPLY CURVE

Factor	Direction of change	Impact	Example
Input price	Higher wages	Less supplied at every price	Rising automobile prices
	Lower wages	More supplied at every price	Cheaper apparel
	More expensive raw materials	Less supplied at every price	Gasoline price shocks
	Cheaper raw materials	More supplied at every price	Milk
Productivity	Improved technology	More supplied at every price	Computers
Market power	Reduced monopoly power	More supplied at every price	Long distance telephone service
	Increased monopoly power	Less supplied at every price	Local cable television

rials. Since 1950, for example, food prices have risen at less than half the rate of all commodities and material prices have fallen almost by half over the last 50 years. Among crude commodities, only one has maintained its price relative to other goods (or services). Backed by an international cartel and large domestic companies with powerful political connections, petroleum prices have risen almost as fast as have other goods.

Rising output per hour worked has allowed an enormous increase in consumption and improvement in living standards. While productivity has grown significantly over the past 140 years in all of these countries, the pace of productivity growth has varied over time and between countries. Productivity growth accelerated sharply after World War II, rising on average from 1.7% for the 1870-1938 period to 4.3% in 1950-73, before dropping back down to 2.2% since. Not all countries shared equally in this remarkable acceleration of productivity growth. Productivity growth has lagged in the great Anglo-Saxon powers, the United Kingdom and the United States.

Rising productivity reflects individual genius less than the social conditions favoring economic growth. Without dismissing the contributions of Henry Ford (automobiles), the Wright brothers (aerospace), or Eli Whitney (cotton processing), there were many active in developing the same innovations at the same time, and all these great inventors drew on the ideas and inspiration of others. Great inventors always depend upon social circumstances for their success. Whitney developed his cotton gin while working as a tutor in the home of a Georgia planter named Catherine Greene, and her encouragement and financial support were crucial for his invention. His cotton gin, furthermore, was an important invention because of other social circumstances: the rapid development of the British textile industry and the availability of slave labor in the United States South to work at producing cotton. Ford and the Wright brothers also depended on the support and ideas of others. Their inventions were important because of developments in other industries that provided essential inputs (e.g., machine tools) and ways of utilizing their inventions.

Productivity growth also depends directly on social circumstances, including factors that help affluent countries grow fast. These factors help explain the variation in growth rates shown in Figure 8-8. Workers in affluent countries are more productive because they have more complementary inputs with which to work,

FIGURE 8-8
AVERAGE PRODUCTIVITY GROWTH, SIX ADVANCED ECONOMIES

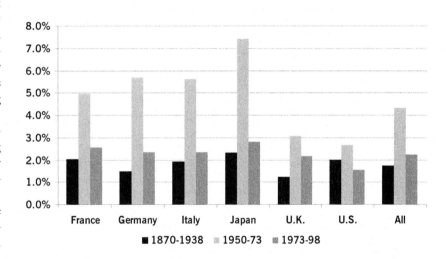

including more machinery and raw materials per worker. They also benefit from more education, which allows them to learn their work more quickly and also to communicate better with others, facilitating the division of labor. Along with education and training, affluent countries are able to invest in their workers' future productivity by providing children with good care, including good nutrition and health care. Healthier workers can work harder on the job and also come to work more regularly. As Adam Smith argued, the division of labor remains a great source of productivity growth but it does not happen spontaneously, and it depends on establishing common standards and a basis of social trust.

Productivity is a social phenomenon, a characteristic of productive societies. This is also the case in regions, such as California's film industry or Silicon Valley, Route 128 around Boston, and New York's fashion district. In these industrial districts, a concentration of producers in particular trades leads to higher productivity for all in a productive community. This is true of countries as well. Some are more productive because they are able to employ workers who are well educated, healthy, and ready and able to share ideas and to work productively as part of a team.

JOHN MAURICE CLARK (1884-1963).

The son of John Bates Clark, who supervised his PhD dissertation at Columbia, **John Maurice Clark** was a leading institutionalist economist. His most important book, *Studies in the Economics of Overhead Costs* (1923), demonstrated how perfect competition is both theoretically and practically unattainable. Clark went on to advise the Roosevelt Administration during the New Deal, and was a leading American liberal and defender of the welfare state.

DO LONG-RUN MARGINAL COSTS SLOPE UP?

The impact of rapid technological progress on supply curves has led some economists and other observers to question the orthodox approach with its upward-sloping supply curves and ask whether marginal cost curves may be flat or even downward sloping. A few years ago, when the Internet-based new economy was riding high, Alan Greenspan (then head of the United States Federal Reserve system) suggested that in the new world of information technology, supply curves may no longer be upward sloping because marginal costs do not increase with output. Companies that produce tangible materials have upward sloping marginal cost schedules because their material inputs and outputs require handling and space. Information, however, is a virtual product. Once created, often through an expensive process of research and development, information can be processed and disseminated at almost no cost.

Information-processing industries, such as television media, internet magazines, music distributors, or other entertainment disseminators, can add to their production almost without cost, simply by adding another name to a list or an address to a "cc:" line on an email. In our market system, this wonderful convenience has become a problem for musicians, record labels, and TV and movie companies: how can they maintain prices high enough to cover the fixed costs of creating a product when it can be disseminated at almost no marginal costs? Products that require enormous preliminary work and heavy fixed costs can be reproduced easily and inexpensively virtually without end. How are studios and musicians to recoup these large fixed costs if their products are distributed for marginal cost, i.e., for free?

These information-industries are particular cases of a general problem facing capitalist firms. In the long run, *marginal cost curves* do not slope up and businesses that price at marginal cost will go bankrupt. All industries require set-up costs and other fixed costs, expenditures on inputs that do not vary with the level of output. Automobile manufacturers spend billions on designing a car and building production facilities before they sell a single car; they hope to recoup these costs by selling a large volume of cars. An Air France flight from Boston to Paris is almost entirely set-up and fixed cost. The cost of the plane, the crew, landing and maintenance, and most of the fuel will be incurred regardless of the number of people on the flight. In this way, the airline industry resembles the neighborhood kid looking to make summer money by mowing lawns. Buying a lawn mower, this summer entrepreneur incurs costs that will be the same whether there is one lawn to mow or a dozen.

In all of these cases, more of the cost of production is in the initial set-up and relatively little is required to achieve marginal increases in output. Where *fixed costs* dwarf marginal costs, *average total costs*, or the total cost (fixed and variable) per unit of output, can decline with output but without ever reaching the level of marginal costs (see Figure 8-9). If prices are set at the level of marginal costs, they will be below, even well below, the level needed to cover the costs of production including fixed costs. If firms in these industries behave like perfect competitors, prices will be too low to cover the carrying costs of their fixed capital. They can linger for a little while by not replacing their capital, but they will soon head towards bankruptcy. Industries survive only if they have enough monopoly power to maintain prices above marginal cost. Perfect competition can survive only in those few, anomalous industries with minimal fixed costs. Elsewhere, not only is monopoly power ubiquitous in our economy, it is a necessity. Without at least some form of monopoly power, firms cannot maintain a large fixed plant, management, and research staff. Without monopoly, along with all the subsequent waste and income distortion, our capitalist economy would collapse. Perfect competition is not only an anomaly, it is an impossibility.

FIGURE 8-9
AVERAGE TOTAL COSTS EXCEED MARGINAL COSTS

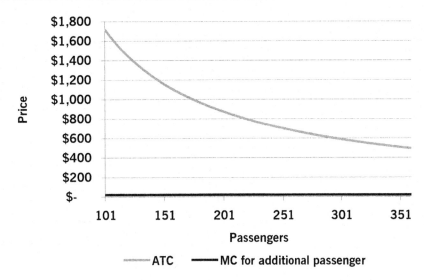

Fixed costs per flight are estimated to be $171,000 while marginal costs are assumed to be the cost of a meal, snack, glass of campagne, and the cost of cleaning a blanket and pillow.

APPENDIX: COMPARISON OF MONOPOLY AND PERFECT COMPETITION

Almost impossible in practice, perfect competition has been treated as the norm by orthodox economists. There are bad reasons for this, ideological and political motives and a desire to justify *laissez faire* policies. But perfect competition also provides a convenient foil against which we can compare other market forms.

We begin with the production process. A smart businessperson will calculate output as a function of the number of workers employed. This will give a spreadsheet that looks something like the first two columns in Table 8-5.

TABLE 8-5
DERIVATION OF MARGINAL COST FOR YOUR POT FARM

Workers	Output (ounces)	Marginal Product of Labor (MPL)	Workers to get one more ounce	Marginal cost at $10/worker
1	10	10	0.1	$1.00
2	19	9	0.11	$1.11
3	27	8	0.13	$1.25
4	34	7	0.14	$1.43
5	40	6	0.17	$1.67
6	45	5	0.2	$2.00
7	49	4	0.25	$2.50
8	52	3	0.33	$3.33
9	54	2	0.5	$5.00
10	55	1	1	$10.00

The marginal product of labor (MPL) can be calculated as the change in output when an additional worker is hired. The first worker increases output from 0 to 10 ounces; she has an MPL of 10. Output rises to 19 when two workers are hired; the second worker's MPL is 9.

For each level of output, you can calculate how much labor is needed to produce one more unit. Each of the first ten ounces requires 1/10 of a worker, the next nine each require 1/9, and the next eight each require 1/8 of a worker. If workers are paid $10, then the cost of each unit of output can be calculated as the product of the wage and the amount of labor needed. Note that the MC is upward sloping because the MPL is downward sloping.

In a perfectly competitive market, producers will produce up to the point where the price equals MC. The price that individuals will pay is indicated by the marginal utility (MU) for each additional ounce. The MU is downward sloping because of satiation. The value of MU, the amount that people will pay for each additional ounce, is shown in Table 8-6.

Perfectly competitive firms will produce where MU=MC. This would be about 33 ounces and a price of $1.40. We can graph demand and supply to show this market equilibrium.

Note that at this equilibrium, surplus is maximized with most going to consumers. If more were produced, at point B for example, the cost (MC) would exceed the benefit (MU), lowering surplus. If less were produced, at point C, the cost of the marginal unit (MC) would be less than the benefits (MU) and some surplus would be lost.

Also, note that producers at perfect competition are operating at a long-term loss. This is because they are pricing without regard to their long-run costs, including the cost of replacing their fixed capi-

TABLE 8-6
POT MARKET: MC, MU, AND MR

Q	MC	Demand (MU)	TR	MR	Average total costs	Fixed costs	Total costs	Profit at MC pricing
1	$1.00	$10.00	$10.00	$10.00	$41.00	$40.00	$41.00	($31.00)
2	$1.00	$9.40	$18.80	$8.80	$21.00	$40.00	$42.00	($23.20)
3	$1.00	$8.84	$26.51	$7.71	$14.33	$40.00	$43.00	($16.49)
4	$1.00	$8.31	$33.22	$6.72	$11.00	$40.00	$44.00	($10.78)
5	$1.00	$7.81	$39.04	$5.81	$9.00	$40.00	$45.00	($5.96)
6	$1.00	$7.34	$44.03	$5.00	$7.67	$40.00	$46.00	($1.97)
7	$1.00	$6.90	$48.29	$4.26	$6.71	$40.00	$47.00	$1.29
8	$1.00	$6.48	$51.88	$3.59	$6.00	$40.00	$48.00	$3.88
9	$1.00	$6.10	$54.86	$2.98	$5.44	$40.00	$49.00	$5.86
10	$1.00	$5.73	$57.30	$2.44	$5.00	$40.00	$50.00	$7.30
11	$1.10	$5.39	$59.25	$1.95	$4.65	$40.00	$51.10	$8.15
12	$1.10	$5.06	$60.76	$1.51	$4.35	$40.00	$52.20	$8.56
13	$1.10	$4.76	$61.87	$1.11	$4.10	$40.00	$53.30	$8.57
14	$1.10	$4.47	$62.63	$0.76	$3.89	$40.00	$54.40	$8.23
15	$1.10	$4.21	$63.08	$0.45	$3.70	$40.00	$55.50	$7.58
16	$1.10	$3.95	$63.25	$0.17	$3.54	$40.00	$56.60	$6.65
17	$1.10	$3.72	$63.17	($0.08)	$3.39	$40.00	$57.70	$5.47
18	$1.10	$3.49	$62.87	($0.30)	$3.27	$40.00	$58.80	$4.07
19	$1.10	$3.28	$62.38	($0.49)	$3.15	$40.00	$59.90	$2.48
20	$1.30	$3.09	$61.72	($0.66)	$3.06	$40.00	$61.20	$0.52
21	$1.30	$2.90	$60.92	($0.80)	$2.98	$40.00	$62.50	($1.58)
22	$1.30	$2.73	$59.99	($0.93)	$2.90	$40.00	$63.80	($3.81)
23	$1.30	$2.56	$58.96	($1.04)	$2.83	$40.00	$65.10	($6.14)
24	$1.30	$2.41	$57.83	($1.13)	$2.77	$40.00	$66.40	($8.57)
25	$1.30	$2.27	$56.63	($1.20)	$2.71	$40.00	$67.70	($11.07)
26	$1.30	$2.13	$55.36	($1.27)	$2.65	$40.00	$69.00	($13.64)
27	$1.30	$2.00	$54.04	($1.32)	$2.60	$40.00	$70.30	($16.26)
28	$1.40	$1.88	$52.68	($1.36)	$2.56	$40.00	$71.70	($19.02)
29	$1.40	$1.77	$51.28	($1.39)	$2.52	$40.00	$73.10	($21.82)
30	$1.40	$1.66	$49.87	($1.41)	$2.48	$40.00	$74.50	($24.63)
31	$1.40	$1.56	$48.44	($1.43)	$2.45	$40.00	$75.90	($27.46)
32	$1.40	$1.47	$47.00	($1.44)	$2.42	$40.00	$77.30	($30.30)
33	$1.40	$1.38	$45.56	($1.44)	$2.38	$40.00	$78.70	($33.14)
34	$1.40	$1.30	$44.13	($1.44)	$2.36	$40.00	$80.10	($35.97)
35	$1.70	$1.22	$42.70	($1.43)	$2.34	$40.00	$81.80	($39.10)

tal. Because average total costs include fixed costs, as well as the variable costs that count towards MC, perfectly competitive firms with fixed costs will usually be producing below ATC (average total cost). Firms may feel that they are doing well, making a profit on each additional sale. But, at the end of the year when they take account of their fixed as well as variable costs, these competitive firms will find that they have suffered a loss and are heading towards bankruptcy.

Aware that they are losing money on the margin by driving prices down below ATC, the smarter competitive firms will recognize that they are not in a perfectly competitive market. They will hire an economist—or at least someone who took introductory microeconomics!—who will calculate the marginal revenue curve (MR). Marginal revenue is the change in total revenue from one more sale, and the MR curve shows the actual change in revenue when they sell more along a downward sloping demand curve. Total revenue is the quantity produced times the price at which it can be sold, or the MU. The change in this is the MR in Table 8-10. Smart producers will calculate MR and then reduce production by not producing where MC>MR. Lower output will allow them to raise prices. In this way, they turn a loss into a profit.

At lower output, the monopoly reduces total surplus. By raising prices, it also transfers some surplus from consumers to producers.

DISCUSSION QUESTIONS

What is the economic "short-run"? What is the economic "long-run"?

What is "marginal productivity"?

Why would the marginal productivity of a variable input fall with increases in that input?

What would shift the marginal productivity curve in? What would shift it out? What would prevent marginal productivity from declining at all?

What is "marginal cost"? Why would marginal cost rise for increases in output? How does rising marginal cost relate to diminishing marginal productivity?

Would marginal cost rise in the long run?

Imagine that you are a naïve producer and that you believe that your output has no impact on prices. How will you decide how much to produce?

What is "marginal revenue"? What is the relationship between the marginal revenue curve and the demand curve facing a producer?

What is a monopolist? How does the monopolists production and pricing decisions differ from those of the perfect competitor? What happens to the amount produced when an industry is monopolized? What happens to prices?

How do firms establish monopolies? Name some things they do to maintain their monopoly? Are all monopolies successful?

What is "producer surplus"?

What happens to consumer surplus and to producer surplus when an industry is monopolized? Distinguish between the sources of change in surplus, between changes due to changes in price and changes due to changes in quantity produced.

What are "fixed costs"? What are "average total costs"? What is the relationship between average total costs and marginal costs for an industry with large fixed costs?

How does a perfect competitor take account of fixed costs when setting prices? What happens to a perfectly competitive firm with very large fixed costs if it continues to behave as a perfect competitor?

What happens to supply curves when input prices (e.g. wages) rise or fall? What happens to supply curves when there are improvements in technology?

ENDNOTES

[1] Factors of production, including land, labor, machinery, are inputs into the production process.

[2] The technology of production is a set of plans relating inputs to output.

[3] The marginal product is the change in output when a single unit of input is added.

[4] Diminishing returns to the variable input occur because the marginal product of any single input declines as more is added.

[5] The neoclassical theory of distribution was developed by John Bates Clark in response to socialist attacks on capitalism in the later 19th century; see John B. Clark, "The Possibility of a Scientific Law of Wages," *Publications of the American Economic Association* 4, no. 1 (March 1, 1889): 39–69; John Bates Clark, *The Distribution of Wealth; a Theory of Wages, Interest and Profits* (New York, London: The Macmillan company; Macmillan & co., ltd, 1899).

[6] Where all inputs increase together, the worst we could do would be to replicate the existing production process, in which case output would rise only as fast as inputs. Changes made possible by scale and a greater division of labor would allow output to rise faster than inputs.

[7] The long run, is a time period long enough that all factors of production can be altered and there are no fixed costs

[8] Joan Robinson and John Eatwell, *An Introduction to Modern Economics* (Maidenhead: McGraw-Hill, 1973); Maurice Dobb, *Theories of Value and Distribution since Adam Smith; Ideology and Economic Theory* (Cambridge [Eng.: University Press, 1973); a different view is in George J. Stigler, *Production and Distribution Theories, the Formative Period* (New York: Macmillan, 1941).

[9] Complementary inputs are inputs used in conjunction with an input, increasing its marginal productivity.

[10] The theory that demand depends on individual's downward sloping marginal utility curves.

[11] The theory, presented here, that production and the supply of goods depends on diminishing marginal productivity.

[12] Learning by doing is where workers and firms become more productive when they produce more because they become more skillful and discover ways to improve their technology.

[13] On-the-job training is where workers become more skillful and learn to perform their tasks better through practice and by direct supervision at work. Through practice, workers learn to produce up to the standards of the available technology. This is different from learning-by-doing which involves the development of new technologies through practice.

[14] Often associated with learning by doing, endogenous technological progress happens when firms and workers discover new and better technologies through practice.

[15] Harvey Leibenstein posed this challenge to orthodox economics nearly 50 years ago; see Harvey Leibenstein, "Allocative Efficiency vs. 'X-Efficiency,'" *The American Economic Review* 56, no. 3 (1966): 392; a criticism of the approach from a leading neoclassicist is in George J. Stigler, "The Xistence of X-Efficiency," *The American Economic Review* 66, no. 1 (March 1, 1976): 213–16.

[16] Variable inputs can be added to the production process to increase output in the short run. Fixed inputs can be added only over the long run. The difference between the long and short run depends on how long it takes to added inputs.

[17] We define the short run as the time period where firms do not have enough time to add significantly to their stock of other fixed inputs, such as machinery, skilled labor, and managers.

[18]Increasing returns of scale are found where increasing all inputs leads to an increase in productivity, either due to greater specialization and the division of labor or because more efficient machinery can be used at a larger scale.

[19]See the discussion of the Horndal effect in early American textile manufacturing in Paul A David, *Technical Choice Innovation and Economic Growth: Essays on American and British Experience in the Nineteenth Century* (London: Cambridge University Press, 1975); the case for infant industries in the United States was made at the beginning of our history by Alexander Hamilton, see United States, Miscellaneous Pamphlet Collection (Library of Congress), and Israel Thorndike Pamphlet Collection (Library of Congress), Alexander Hamilton's *Report on the Subject of Manufactures*, ed. Alexander Hamilton and Mathew Carey, 6th ed (Philadelphia: Printed by W. Brown, 1827).

[20]Perfect homogeneous products are indistinguishable from each other.

[21]Price takers have no impact on the market price. They can increase their output without causing prices to fall, and they can reduce their production without causing any increase in the market price.

[22]Myopic business managers fail to see that they have an effect on prices when they increase or reduce output.

[23]Oligopolists are a small number of companies who can influence the price of output by manipulating their production.

[24]That is to say, a shortage of raw materials, capital, or skilled labor.

[25]Soap, for example, was first sold in anonymous solid blocks where a store-keeper would cut off a slab for sale. Producers soon learned, however, that they could charge more by packaging their own brands in fancy paper with names. Soap manufacturers then pioneered the development of advertising intended to distinguish their own brand. One legacy is the name given to a particular type of TV drama, the "soap opera." Geoffrey Jones, *Beauty Imagined: A History of the Global Beauty Industry* (Oxford: Oxford University Press, 2010); Juliann Sivulka, *Soap, Sex, and Cigarettes: A Cultural History of American Advertising*, 2 edition (Australia; Boston, MA: Cengage Learning, 2011).

[26]The response would also be muted if Henion's and Wheatbury also raised their cookie prices in response to what The Black Sheep did.

[27]Both The Black Sheep and Henion's sell other products, like coffee and soup, ancillary (or secondary) to their main business of pushing chocolate cookies.

[28]These would include firms who mistakenly believe that their production has no effect on the market price.

[29]The cost of producing one more unit of output.

[30]From the perspective of society, the optimal output is where the marginal cost of producing one more unit just equals the marginal utility or extra pleasure gained from that production.

[31]Marginal revenue is the change in revenue from producing and selling one more unit of output.

[32]Profit maximizing firms produce the amount of output that gives them the most profit, where marginal revenue equals marginal cost.

[33]Formed in 1960, OPEC was founded to maintain oil revenues to producing countries. While not always able to prevent reductions in oil prices, it successfully raised world oil prices repeatedly in the 1970s.

[34]Oil is the only commodity whose price has not fallen relative to other commodities over the last 50 years.

[35]One OPEC member, Saudi Arabia, is able to enforce OPEC policy by reducing production to maintain prices and by raising production quickly to punish members who cheat on their quotas.

[36]This makes it hard for companies to regain a market position after they have lost consumer confidence – this is a problem facing GM today.

[37]The excess of consumer utility over the price of the product, calculated as the sum of the difference between marginal utility and price for inframarginal purchases.

[38]The deadweight burden of a monopoly is the loss in total social welfare when monopolies reduce output where the marginal cost is less than the marginal utility.

[39]The elasticity of supply refers to the change in output with an increase in price. If supply is inelastic, output rises slowly with higher prices.

[40]Rents are the surplus profits coming through the ownership of a fixed and nonreproducible asset.

[41]Just to be clear, AMC's "The Walking Dead" is totally realistic.

[42]This literature has been shaped by the work of Michael Jensen, see Michael C. Jensen and Kevin J. Murphy, "Performance Pay and Top-Management Incentives," *Journal of Political Economy* 98, no. 2 (April 1, 1990): 225–64; Michael Jensen and William Meckling, "Theory of the Firm: Managerial Behavior, Agency Costs and Ownership Structure," *Journal of Financial Economics* 3 (1976): 305–60; for another view, see Herbert A Simon, *Models of Bounded Rationality* (Cambridge, Mass.: MIT Press, 1982).

[43]Adolf A. Berle, *The Modern Corporation and Private Property* (New Brunswick, N.J., U.S.A: Transaction Publishers, 1991) Berle, the youngest graduate in the history of Harvard Law School, was a professor of law at Columbia. Both Berle and Means were active in the Roosevelt Administration. .

[44]Laurence F Peter and Raymond Hull, *The Peter Principle* (Taiwan: [publisher not identified], 1969).

[45]The long-run marginal cost curve shows the cost of producing one more unit of output where all factors of production can be adjusted.

[46]This would not be the case where MC exceeds ATC because firms are producing high up their MC curves. In these cases, however, we would expect firms to enter the field to take advantage of the relatively high costs by producing at a smaller scale and underselling existing firms.

MARKETS AND EQUILIBRIUM

FINDING PEACE?

When demand curves slope down and supply curves slope up, there will usually be a point where they meet (see Figure 9-1).[1] Under conditions of perfect competition, the intersection is the *market equilibrium*. At this equilibrium, the price is such that the amount consumers want to buy just equals the amount producers want to sell. Price and quantity supplied are such that everyone is content. They are not necessarily happy; they might wish that they had more money, a pet mongoose, or a nicer cat. But the price is such that no one wants to change their behavior, no producer wishes to sell more and no consumer would buy less. At the equilibrium price, supply equals demand and does so through the spontaneous, unplanned actions of individuals, without any social planning, bureaucracy, or command. Without any conscious planning, the spontaneous actions of individual producers will satisfy consumers' demand without shortages or surpluses. No producer's inventory is growing, no consumers wait in line, and no one would change their behavior. People may regret that they cannot do better, or they may wish that things were cheaper and they could consume more. They may wish they were more talented and better looking. But, given their income and the costs of production, this is as good as it gets. At this price and output, everyone is doing as well for themselves as they can. The market has found peace.

Economists are drawn to market equilibrium because, under the assumptions of perfect competition, producers and consumers will reach this equilibrium on their own through a process of trial and

FIGURE 9-1
ADJUSTMENT IN DEMAND AND SUPPLY RESTORES EQUILIBRIUM PRICE

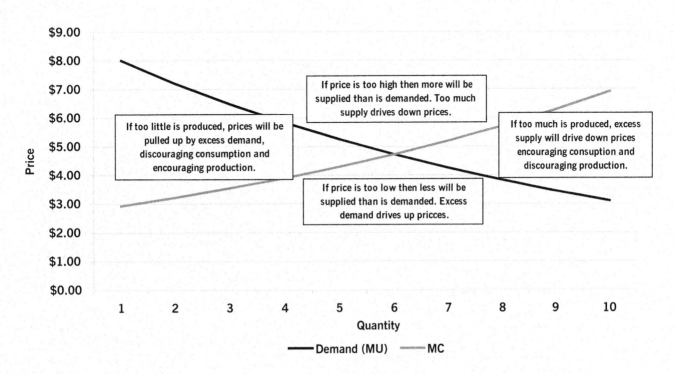

FIGURE 9-2

MARKET EQUILIBRIUM: PRICE IS SUCH THAT SUPPLY EQUALS DEMAND

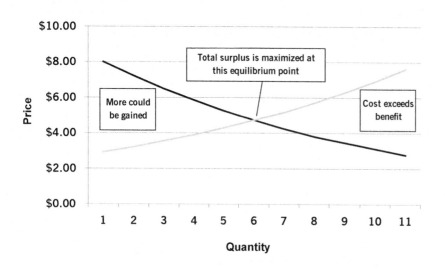

Note: At this price level, the amount that producers choose to supply just equals the amount consumers want to buy. No one wishes to change his or her behavior.

error, a process that the French economist Léon Walras called *tâtonnement*. In this process, producers will experiment with different prices. When the price is above the equilibrium, they will find that consumer demand drops off so much that they accumulate surplus inventories that lead them to reduce production and to lower prices. The process of inventory accumulation and price reduction will continue until the equilibrium is reached. Similarly, if prices are below the equilibrium, there will be such strong consumer demand that producers will experience shortages, leading them to raise prices and increase production. Again, the process will continue until the price rises to the equilibrium level, at which point production will just equal demand.

There is more to the equilibrium than this. The market equilibrium point under perfect competition attracts economists because it can be a social optimum where the spontaneous actions of individuals lead to

behavior that maximizes social welfare.[2] At the equilibrium, producers' marginal cost, the cost to society of providing the last good, just equals the consumers' marginal utility, or the social benefit of this good. We would not want more to be supplied because at the very next unit, the marginal cost exceeds the marginal benefit (or utility). Nor would we want less to be produced, because at lower output, the marginal benefit (or utility) exceeds the marginal cost. Note that this social optimum maximizes the

sum of producer and consumer surplus. Production beyond this level would reduce the total surplus because the line of marginal costs (the supply curve) would exceed the line of marginal benefits (the demand curve). Production below this level would pass up opportunities to enlarge total surplus by producing where marginal benefits exceed marginal costs.

The perfectly competitive market equilibrium also has *dynamic* qualities, adjusting market prices and quantities to changes in production and consumer preferences. Left to manage on their own in a perfectly competitive market, Walras argued that producers and consumers will spontaneously adjust quantities purchased and supplied to maintain equilibrium. There will be no need for a large government bureaucracy to collect and process information and formulate new policy directives because if changes in demand or supply conditions ever disturb the market equilibrium, consumers and producers will adjust their behavior to restore it. If, for example, a product becomes more desirable, then the shift out in the demand curve will lead producers to raise prices, leading them to hire more variable inputs to supply more of the newly

Ticket scalper at football game, 2005, offering tickets at $150, triple face value. Teams often price tickets at low prices to allow regular people to attend. While they resent scalpers, consumers sometimes appreciate the service they provide by having tickets available at the last minute.

more desired product. Lower demand will lead to lower prices and a reduction in supply. Similarly, if there is a technological change that lowers the product costs, the supply curve will shift out, lowering prices to consumers who will then consume more of that good.

Thinking of markets from the perspective of perfect competition and equilibrium leads economists to be suspicious of any measures that set prices without regard to demand and supply. Fearing surpluses or shortages, for example, they are suspicious of minimum wages or rent controls. Fixing prices is an intrusion on market equilibrium comparable to monopoly pricing and, like a monopoly, restrictions on this market will benefit some, but only at the cost of lowering social efficiency. To deal with the rising costs of some commodity, for example, a government might impose price controls and set a price below the market equilibrium. Unhappy with high prices, consumers might applaud this policy because they think they will save money. At the lower price, though, production will

FIGURE 9-3

DISTORTIONS FROM PRICE CONTROLS: PERFECT COMPETITION VERSUS GOVERNMENT PRICE SETTING

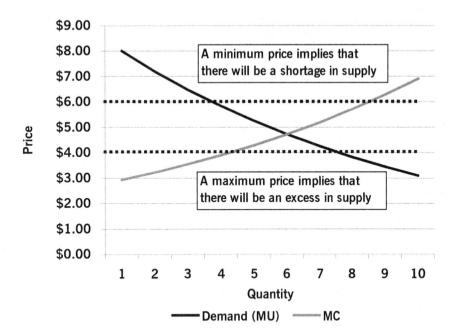

Note: This figure shows the market impact of government programs setting prices above or below the market outcome. With "maximum" prices, or price controls, the government sets prices below the market level and consumers want to buy more than the amount supplied. With "minimum," prices are set above the market level and consumers want to buy less than the amount supplied.

fall, even while consumers try to buy more. As a result, there will soon be a shortage when the amount demanded exceeds what producers are now ready to supply. Those who want to buy at the low price will be forced to form queues or they will get the product through nonmarket means, such as personal acquaintances or side payments to distributors or scalpers. Rock concert promoters sometimes set prices below market equilibrium as a form of advertising, hoping to create long lines to buy tickets, but low ticket prices also create opportunities for scalpers to pocket the difference between the market and controlled price. This also happens with urban rent controls. Those lucky enough to get a rent-controlled apartment reap a windfall by renting a valuable commodity at a low price. Their gain is balanced by the losses suffered by those who wait in vain and by owners forced to sell at a discount. You may favor rent control because you think the beneficiaries are more worthy than the losers. But there is a cost to moving away from the market system: an additional allocation mechanism is added on top of the existing price system.

Minimum prices have a similar effect, leading to excess production and accumulation of inventory. States and the federal government set a minimum wage for workers. Critics charge that the minimum wage reduces employment, raising some workers' earnings at the expense of others who become unemployed. Minimum prices can also lead to excess production and the accumulation of inventory. Without someone to buy the surplus, producers would lower prices below the minimum. To avoid this, minimum price programs

GETTING AROUND THE LAW

Over time, producers adjust to fixed prices by altering their product quality and payment terms. Under price controls during World War II, for example, producers reduced the quality of clothes, reducing the number of threads per inch, to match the lower price they could charge. In the New York City housing market, rent controls limit rents to a level below what renters would pay for the apartments. Those with knowledge of available apartments, including building supers and others, charge for their information, taking some of the difference between the fixed rent and the amount that renters would be willing to pay. For their part, because the apartments are worth more than they can charge in rent, landlords know that they can save money on maintenance.

TABLE 9-1
PROBLEMS WITH PERFECTLY COMPETITIVE MARKET EQUILIBRIUM

Problem	Impact
Market may not equilibrate: demand curve may slope up because of Veblen effects, stampedes, price signals, or network economies.	There may be no price at which supply would equal demand, or the market price may be set too low.
Market may not equilibrate: supply curve may slope down.	There may be no price at which supply would equal demand, or the market price may be set too low and too little will be produced.
The equilibrium price may be wrong because the market does not price externalities.	The market price will be too low and too much will be produced and consumed if the market neglects external costs, such as pollution and dishonesty.
Market does not price home production.	Producers are discouraged from home production, including caring for children, and are encouraged to perform less valuable market work.
Market does not price public goods.	Market does not adequately encourage the production of goods with positive externalities because these are not priced, including production of public art, community building, training, and network effects.
The market outcome depends on the distribution of income.	Demand depends on who has income as well as consumer preferences. Those born rich or those who stole have more say in production than others.

are joined with programs to buy surpluses. This has been the case of agricultural price supports in the United States where the federal government buys surplus foodstuffs, which it then distributes throughout the third world and to American food banks and schools. Under the federal government's old milk subsidy program, for example, the government paid producers a price above what consumers would pay for the milk and bought any surplus. This led to the accumulation of a large cheese inventory in subterranean caves in Minnesota. Some of you ate this cheese in the federal school lunch program. Again, depending on how expensive it is to store or dispose of the surplus, and how worthy we consider the producers who benefit (along with the recipients of the surplus) versus the consumers and taxpayers who lose, we may favor or oppose price minimums rather than the market equilibrium.

Price controls and subsidies may be inefficient when compared with perfect competition's market equilibrium, but this is an unreasonable standard. Perfect competitive market equilibrium is the social science equivalent of the Holy Grail, and is about as hard to find, or to believe. Perfect competitive equilibrium depends on well-behaved supply and demand curves that are never found in the world. Recall that market demand curves may slope up because of Veblen effects, stampedes, and information problems, and supply curves may slope down because of economies of scale, network economies,

WHY PRICE CONTROLS?

Maximum prices are sometimes set on products with very low elasticity of demand, such as rents, gasoline, or food. As with minimum wage laws, price controls are most commonly imposed on goods with highly inelastic supply and demand, where even small disruptions in supply will bring large swings in price and incomes. This was the case of gasoline and heating oil during the 1973 Arab Oil Embargo, the New York City housing market during and after World War II, and the supply of low-wage and unskilled labor. Even small changes in market demand or supply may lead to large swings in prices and incomes.

and other externalities. Even if the demand curve is downward slop- ing and marginal cost curves are upward sloping, the market probably won't have a neat, optimal equilibrium because monopoly power will keep production below, and prices above, the socially optimal level. Or else the supply curve may be nearly inelastic so that there will be wild swings in price for any change in consumer preferences.

The economic case against government price setting is remark- ably fragile. Even if the market equilibrium is optimal within the market, it will be the social optimum only under truly extraordinary circumstances. To produce a social optimum, all the external costs and benefits of the exchange need to be included in the formulation of the market price, including the costs of pollution and the use of natural assets. Public goods need to be priced according to the value that the whole public receives from the good, including those who do not buy the good themselves. The market price will be too low un- less it includes public benefits, including the benefits of developing new information, and worker and managerial training. It should also include the allocation of the costs of child rearing and other care ex- penses. And it must take account of the need to maintain society's *so- cial capital*, honest standards of behavior and concern for each other. Failure to incorporate these costs and benefits in determining the market price and market equilibrium may lead to a *partial equilib- rium* for an incomplete market where society may be worse off than with no equilibrium at all.

The market equilibrium also depends on the distribution of in- come. Any equilibrium is optimal only if we believe the distribution of income is fair. If income is distributed fairly, so that all of us bring to the market an income commensurate with our social worth, then the market outcome may be fair. But if income has been distributed according to other criteria, such as birth, race, gender, or political power, then the market distribution will reflect those criteria rather than social worth.

MINIMUM WAGES AND EMPLOYMENT

The first minimum wage in the United States was set in Massachusetts under a law enacted in 1912. Since then, a large economic literature has been produced seeking to measure the employment effect of minimum wage laws. Economists Alan Krueger, David Card, and Arin Dube have evaluated this effect by comparing employment changes in adjacent states and counties with different minimum wage rates and in the same county at the time of a rise in the minimum wage. In general, studies have found virtually no effect of minimum wages on employment, suggesting that the demand curve for low-wage labor is virtually inelastic, at least within the range of most minimum wage laws. If so, increases in the minimum wage redistribute income from employers and consumers to low wage workers without producing unemployment.

Minimum Wage Effects Across State Borders: Estimates Using Contiguous Counties

Source: Dube, Lester, and Reich 2010

CAN CONSUMERS FIND MARKET EQUILIBRIUM? AND SHOULD THEY?

Almost a century ago, the American economist Wesley Clair Mitchell made an empirical observation that consumers regularly make mistakes. "Important as the art of spending is, we have developed less skill in its practice than in the practice of making money." He continues:

> Common sense forbids us to waste dollars earned by irksome efforts; and yet we are notoriously extravagant. Ignorance of qualities, uncertainty of taste, lack of accounting, carelessness about prices—faults which would ruin a merchant—prevail in our housekeeping. Many of us scarcely know what becomes of our money; though well-schooled citizens of a Money Economy ought to plan for their outgoes no less carefully than for their incomes.[3]

People regularly spend their money in ways that they regret. They buy the wrong items, they pay too much, they miss opportunities to consume things that they would prefer. It is easy to understand why people make these mis- takes: not only do they lack the information needed to make many decisions but they lack the training, the technical apparatus to process this informa- tion to make the best choices, and they lack the time, or else value their time more highly than the expected benefit of devoting more time to choosing the right product. The problem of consumer error is magnified for decisions

Wesley Clair Mitchell (1874-1948) was the lead- ing American institutionalist economist of the first half of the 20th century. Founder of the National Bureau of Economic Research and architect of our current system of national income accounts and business cycle research, Mitchell rejected *a prio- ri* reasoning and insisted that economists should study economic facts to understand behavior.

CALCULATING THE PRESENT VALUE OF FUTURE RETURNS

Present value is the sum that invested today will give some amount in a year at the current interest rate:

$PV_t*(1+r) = S_{t+1}$ where PV_t is the present value in year t of the sum S_{t+1} from year t+1, and r is the rate of interest.

From this:

$PV = S_{t+1}/(1+r)$.

with implications for the future. Economists have a simple method to calculate the present value of future benefits and costs. If some future benefit is known, then its present value is discounted by the rate of interest between now and then; so $100 next year might be worth $95 today at an interest rate of 5%. Careful investors would use a greater discount factor if there were uncertainty about future returns. Instead of a known future benefit, they would make their best guess, which would be discounted by the rate of interest *and* some factor for risk. The greater the rate of interest, and the greater the uncertainty, the less investors would value any expected future returns.

It is simply impossible to know the future and even the most careful projections are regularly proven wrong. Between July 2000 and July 2002, the economists at the Congressional Budget Office, for example, changed their estimate of the Federal government's Fiscal Year 2002 surplus from +$405 billion to -$157 billion, a swing of nearly $600 billion. If, with all the resources and training at their disposal, they could not do better in projecting just two years into the future, then how can we expect regular people to do better in their investment and savings decisions? As John Maynard Keynes observed, "our basis of knowledge for estimating the yield ten years hence of a railway, a copper mine, a textile factory, the goodwill of a patent medicine, an Atlantic liner, a building in the City of London amounts to little and sometimes to nothing."

Mitchell and Keynes make arguments that are a standing rebuke to neoclassicists defending the free market. If people make mistakes, then there is no reason to believe that a free market will allocate resources to maximize well-being. Within the last decade, there has been increasing attention to this issue of the ability of individuals to make rational choices and how they choose in the face of complicated information. The field of "behavioral economics" has become one of the most exciting areas of economics, recognized with the Nobel Prize in Economic Science awarded in 2002 to Daniel Kahneman and Vernon Smith. Using experiments where people are presented with various types of choices in a laboratory-like setting, behavioral economists like Kahneman and Smith have found that individuals rarely behave "rationally."[4] They do not consistently act to maximize their own welfare. Instead, they apply cultural values that inhibit their selfish actions and economize on information with "rules of thumb." Highly paid Wall Street advisers do little better. Unable to know the future, they also rely on rules of thumb and go along with the views of others who, they hope, know better. While these rules often work out, they also led many of the world's leading banks to overvalue bad loans and discount the possibility of a general financial and economic meltdown—which became a reality in 2007 and 2008. Here again group culture is crucial because it led individual investors to accept the valuations and decisions of each other.[5]

The problem of consumer choice goes beyond the cost of finding and processing information. Experimental work has found that consumers not only lack information but also shun it because it is difficult to process. Consumers find it unpleasant to make decisions because every choice involves giving up al-

JAM, JAM, AND LESS JAM?

Columbia Business School professor **Sheena Iyengar** set up a tasting booth with a variety of exotic gourmet jams in a grocery store. Sometimes she displayed 6 different jams, sometimes 24. While conventional wisdom might say that consumers with more choices will be more likely to find what they want and buy, Iyengar found the opposite. While 30% of those who stopped at the 6 jam display bought jam, only 3% of those who stopped at the 24 jam display did so.

Sheena Iyengar   **Jars of jam at Ladurée in Paris. All are wonderful.**

THEORY OF SECOND BEST

Orthodox neoclassical theory concludes that perfect competition will lead to the best allocation of resources possible subject to the constraints of available technology and resources. From this, the orthodox have concluded that the optimal policy is always to promote free markets in every industry possible.

This policy recommendation was challenged 50 years ago by the Canadian economist Richard Lipsey (1928-1980) and the Australian Kelvin Lancaster (1924-1999). Lipsey and Lancaster showed that if there is a market failure in two industries then correcting the failure in only one may lead the economy further away from optimality. Instead, the "second best" position may require abandoning perfect competition in all industries.

---

ternatives. To avoid rejecting alternatives, consumers actively avoid making choices, even to the point of walking away from desirable choices. Experiments show how more choice can actually reduce happiness. For example, a widely cited study by Columbia University Business School's Sheena Iyengar found that when asked to choose among thirty different varieties of jam, consumers almost always regret their decisions, believing they failed to make the optimal choice. But when choosing among only five jams, most seemed satisfied, even when choosing the same jam they had chosen from the original thirty.[6] In another study, she found that the more options people had in a retirement program, the more likely they were not to participate at all: 75% of employees participated in retirement plans with only two options for investing, compared with only 60% in firms with 60 or more options.

Rather than *maximizing* by investigating and researching, people try to avoid making decisions under uncertainty by using shorthand decision rules that allow them to *satisfice*, or settle for something that is "good enough" even if the better may be just around the corner.[7] While systematic and consistent mistakes may allow businesses and governments to anticipate individual behavior well enough to design policy, they undermine the case for free markets. If people and businesses do not act "rationally" in all cases, then it is wrong to assume that free markets are the best way to reach a second-best allocation.[8] Instead, society may do better by abandoning markets, or abandoning them in some areas.

Facing the difficulty of making judgments under uncertainty and without perfect information, people rely on rules of thumb and other shortcuts. Behavioral economists have identified four of the most common of these:

Status-quo or familiarity bias: There are two aspects of this. First, people are reluctant to change even if they are unhappy with the status quo. This is the truth behind the common phrase, "better the devil you know than the devil you don't know." In practice, people tend to stay with familiar products or in familiar market positions even when it would be "rational" to change. (This is related to another shorthand rule: loss-aversion or putting a higher value on a possible loss than a larger possible gain.)

Anchoring: People base decisions on known "anchors" or familiar positions, even when these are irrelevant. For example, uncertain as to how much to bid on a bottle of wine, people with a higher social security number bid more after they were instructed to write down their numbers. We anchor ourselves to familiar prices. This leaves us vulnerable to manipulation, for example, by producers who post high prices that they then discount, giving the illusion that their products are available at a bargain.

Optimism or over-confidence: People often think that they are above average, their successes are the result of their unusual genius and they are not subject to the troubles awaiting others.

Extrapolation: We overvalue recent experience and assume that the future will be like the recent past, only more so. The fallacy here is that we undervalue the experience of the more distant past, and we especially undervalue the dangers of low-probability events that we have not recently experienced.

BEHAVIORAL ECONOMICS AND THE FINANCIAL CRISIS OF 2007+

Recent work by economists George Akerlof and Robert Shiller argues that changing thought patterns and irrational decisionmaking rules caused the housing and financial bubble that crashed in 2007-8. "[O]ur changing confidence, temptations, envy, resentment, and illusions … were the reason why people paid small fortunes for houses in cornfields; why others financed those purchases; why the Dow Jones average peaked above 14,0000 and a little more than a year later fell below 7,500."

Note that arguments like these exonerate capitalism from crises. Rather than the result of any inherent tendency within capitalism, or the system of production for profit rather than for use, Akerlof and Schiller ascribe the crisis to mistakes made by individuals, and the failure of individuals to maximize their welfare properly.

Simple rules help people make uncomfortable decisions and act in the face of uncertainty and a lack of information. They also leave people vulnerable to manipulation by others. Knowing of people's optimism and extrapolation, brokers and others can sell long-lived assets at inflated prices during business-cycle upswings, and can buy these back at overly deflated prices during the downswing. Aware how people anchor their judgments, sellers can offer a variety of goods at inflated prices to pull up what people will pay for their final purchase. Because of status-quo bias, people will often over-pay to remain in their existing position, undervaluing possible changes.

WHAT MIGHT MOVE THE EQUILIBRIUM POINT?

To the degree that the market equilibrium reflects supply and demand, analysis of changes in the market price and output can tell us about changes in underlying preferences and costs, which move demand or supply curves. Even while acknowledging that the market is much more complicated than this supply and demand analysis, it can be a useful exercise to use the theory because it allows us to explain changes in market outcomes, quantity sold and price levels as due to changes in demand or supply.

The dominant factor moving the equilibrium is summarized in Table 9-2 and Figure 9-4. The equilibrium is moved by changes in demand or supply and the way the equilibrium shifts can be related to these underlying changes. From the type of change, in price and quantity, we can infer whether the strongest change was in demand or supply.

There are only four possibilities, and each is listed in Table 9-2 and in Figures 9-5 through 9-8. Whether market prices go up or down, or the quantity sold rises or falls, changes in the market equilibrium can be interpreted as the result of shifts in the supply curve or demand curve. For example, if we observe more people buying computers and the price falling, then the supply curve must have shifted out by more than the demand changed, and some of those extra computer sales must have been to people who would not have been willing to buy computers at the old, higher price. On the other hand, resource shortages or rising wages can shift the supply curve up so that the market equilibrium will move up along the demand curve. In those cases, raising prices will lead some to stop buying products, and the quantity sold falls with rising prices.

Shifts in the demand curve are also reflected in changing prices and quantities. If quantity sold rises and prices went up, then the demand curve must have shifted out so that greater prices elicited an increased supply. This might be the case with the student housing market every September in a college town like Amherst, Massachusetts, when the students return to school. Prices may also fall even when quantity sold falls, when people lose interest in products, find substitutes, or the cost of complements rises. This would be the case for older model computers and for CD players in a world of iPods and smart phones.

In the *real world*,[9] both supply and demand curves move because more than one thing happens at once. Nor can we casually assume that markets are ever in a neat and

FIGURE 9-4

SHIFTING SUPPLY AND DEMAND: USING EQUILIBRIUM ANALYSIS

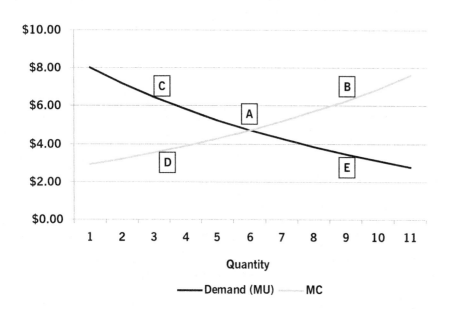

Note: This figure shows the market change coming from changes in supply and demand. A drop in demand, for example from point A to point D, will shift the demand curve down, lowering price and quantity. Increasing demand, to point B, will do the opposite. An increase in supply, to point E, will shift the supply curve out, raising quantity and lowering prices. A reduction in supply, to point C, will shift the supply curve up, raising prices and reducing quantity.

TABLE 9-2

MOVING EQUILIBRIUM: SUPPLY AND DEMAND CHANGES AND THEIR EFFECTS ON PRICE AND QUANTITY SUPPLIED

Price	Quantity	
	Down	**Up**
Down	Demand down; e.g. tickets to Britney Spears concerts. (Moving from point A to point D in Figure 9-4; see also Figure 9-8.)	Supply up; computers. (Moving from point A to point E in Figure 9-4; see also Figure 9-6.)
Up	Supply down; e.g. gasoline prices after Hurricane Katrina damaged oil facilities in the Gulf of Mexico. (Moving from point A to point C in Figure 9-4; see also Figure 9-7.)	Demand up; health care. (Moving from point A to point B in Figure 9-4.; see also Figure 9-5)

FIGURE 9-5

SUPPLY AND MORE DEMAND: PRICES AND QUANTITY CONSUMED RISE FOR HEALTH CARE

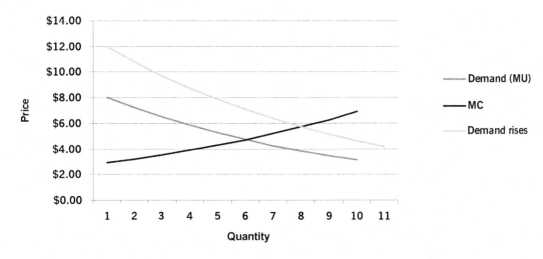

FIGURE 9-6

SUPPLY ABUNDANT: PRICES FALL AND MORE COMPUTERS ARE SOLD BECAUSE COST OF PRODUCTION FALLS

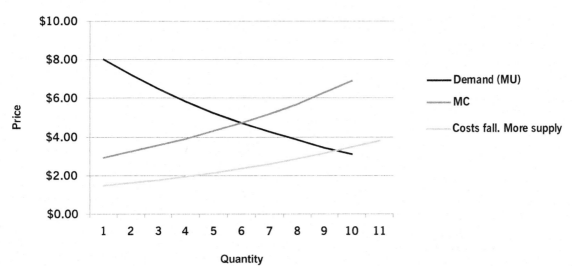

clean, peaceful equilibrium. Some of the change in price and quantity may reflect a movement towards equilibrium rather than a change in the position of the equilibrium. That said, using supply and demand analysis does give us a way to guess at whether, on balance, supply or demand has moved the most. In that way, it disciplines our speculation about the *net impact*[10] of changes in costs and preferences.

FIGURE 9-7
SUPPLY SHORTAGE: PRICES RISE AND QUANTITY SOLD FALLS
BECAUSE HURRICANE KATRINA DAMAGED OIL REFINERIES

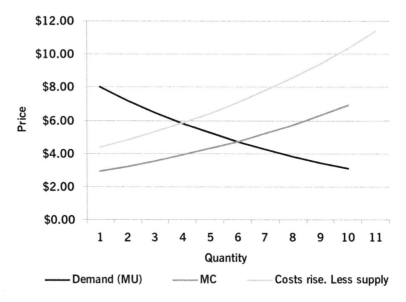

FIGURE 9-8
DEMAND FALLS: PRICE AND QUANTITY SOLD FALLS FOR CDs

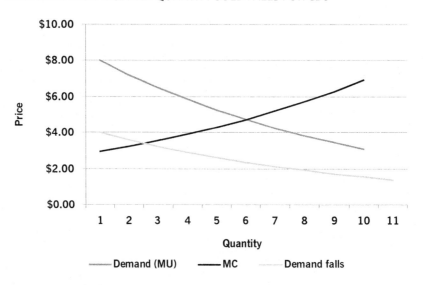

DISCUSSION QUESTIONS

What is "market equilibrium"? How might individual behavior lead perfect competitors to a market equilibrium price and quantity produced?

What is desirable about the market equilibrium in a perfectly competitive industry?

How would regulations setting minimum and maximum prices change the market equilibrium? How would each change producer and consumer behavior?

Why are there "ticket scalpers" at some sporting events and concerts but not at others?

Do consumers optimize? Do they buy the goods they want the most at the best price? If they do not, does this mean that they are irrational? Or are they optimizing something else?

What are "rules of thumb" and why do people use them in making decisions?

What is "anchoring"?

What would move demand curves?

What would move supply curves?

What happens to quantity sold and price when demand changes? What happens when the supply curve changes? How can you use changes in quantity sold and prices to infer that markets responded to changes in preferences or to changes in costs?

ENDNOTES

[1] The exception would be for products where the minimum MC is above the highest MU in which case there will be no production or sales. This would be the case for products that are too expensive to provide, such as vacation trips to the Moon or Mars.

[2] This led some socialists to favor the use of the market to allocate under socialism. These socialist planners would follow two simple rules: "lower production and prices when there is inventory" and "raise production and prices with shortages." Oskar Lange, Benjamin E Lippincott, and F. M Taylor, *On the Economic Theory of Socialism* (Minneapolis, Minn.: University of Minnesota Press, 1938); others have criticized the continued use of the market because it promotes individualism and inequality, see Michael Albert and Robin Hahnel, *Looking Forward: Participatory Economics for the Twenty First Century* (Boston, MA: South End Press, 1991); Robin Hahnel, "The Case Against Markets.," *Journal of Economic Issues* (Association for Evolutionary Economics) 41, no. 4 (2007).

[3] Wesley C Mitchell, "The Backward Art of Spending Money," The American Economic Review 2, no. 2 (1912): 269.

[4] Daniel Kahneman, Ed Diener, and Norbert Schwarz, eds., *Well-Being: The Foundations of Hedonic Psychology* (New York: Russell Sage Foundation, 1999); Vernon L Smith, *Rationality in Economics: Constructivist and Ecological Forms* (Cambridge; New York: Cambridge University Press, 2008); Dan Ariely, *Predictably Irrational: The Hidden Forces That Shape Our Decisions*, 1st ed (New York, NY: Harper, 2008); Richard H. Thaler, *Nudge: Improving Decisions about Health, Wealth, and Happiness* (New Haven: Yale University Press, 2008); Kent Greenfield, *The Myth of Choice: Personal Responsibility in a World of Limits* (New Haven; London: Yale University Press, 2011); Sheena Iyengar, *The Art of Choosing* (New York: Twelve, 2010); Sigal R Ben-Porath, *Tough Choices Structured Paternalism and the Landscape of Choice* (Princeton, N.J.: Princeton University Press, 2010), http://public.eblib.com/EBL-Public/PublicView.do?ptiID=617259.

[5]George A Akerlof and Robert J. Shiller, *Animal Spirits: How Human Psychology Drives the Economy, and Why It Matters for Global Capitalism* (Princeton: Princeton University Press, 2009); Robert J. Shiller, *Irrational Exuberance* (Princeton, NJ: Princeton University Press, 2000).

[6]Malcolm Gladwell, *Blink: The Power of Thinking without Thinking* (New York: Little, Brown and Co., 2005).

[7]To satisfice is to settle for an outcome that is "good enough" rather than seeking to maximize or achieve the best possible outcome. The term was introduced by Nobel Prize winner Herbert A. Simon, *Models of Man: Social and Rational; Mathematical Essays on Rational Human Behavior in a Social Setting* (New York: Wiley, 1957).

[8]R. G Lipsey and Kelvin Lancaster, "The General Theory of Second Best," *The Review of Economic Studies* 24, no. 1 (1956): 11–32; Kenneth J, Debreu, Gerard Arrow, "Existence of an Equilibrium for a Competitive Economy," *Econometrica* (pre-1986) 22, no. 3 (1954): 265.

[9]As contrasted with the world economists describe in their textbooks!

[10]If more than one thing changes, then changes in price and quantity will reflect the net impact of them both.

10

CITIZENSHIP, RIGHTS, AND DOLLARS

Such is the double standard of capitalist democracy, professing and pursuing an egalitarian political and social system and simultaneously generating gaping disparities in economic well-being. This mixture of equality and inequality sometimes smacks of inconsistency and even insincerity. Yet I believe that, in many cases, the institutional arrangements represent uneasy compromises rather than fundamental inconsistencies. —Arthur Okun[1]

HOUSING THE RICH AND OTHERS

With unemployment soaring in the summer of 2009 and millions facing foreclosure and loss of their homes, the hotel heiress Paris Hilton invested $350,000 of her fortune of over $100 million in a two story house. For her dogs. A Pepto-Bismol-colored replica of Paris's own Beverly Hills home, the backyard doghouse provides two floors of luxury living. Complete with abundant closet space. And central air.

To be sure, by the standards of America's rich these days, Paris's dogs are roughing it. In 2006, *Vanity Fair*'s Nina Munk described the residences of America's new financial elite in an article, "Greenwich's Outrageous Fortunes." Compared with the 2,405 square feet of the average new American home, hedge fund managers' homes in Greenwich, Conn., average 15,000 square feet, about the size of a typical industrial warehouse, and many included pool houses of over 3,000 square feet. Steven Cohen, of SAC Capital, paid $14.8 million for his Greenwich home, which he then filled with his art collection, including van Gogh's "Peasant Woman Against a Background of Wheat" (priced at $100 million), Gauguin's "Bathers" ($50 million), a Jackson Pollock drip painting (also $50 million), and Andy Warhol's "Superman" ($75 million).[2] Apparently unhappy with his purchase, Cohen spent millions renovating and expanding it, adding a massage room, exercise, and media rooms, a full-size indoor basketball court, an enclosed swimming pool, a hairdressing salon, and a 6,734-square-foot ice-skating rink. The rink, of course, needs a Zamboni, which Cohen houses in a 720-square-foot shingle cottage. Munk quotes a visitor to the estate who assured her, "You'd be happy to live in the Zamboni house." So too, I imagine, would some of the over 650,000 Americans sleeping in shelters or under highway overpasses, or the 6,000,000 "doubled up," living with family or friends for economic reasons.

By the time it was finished, Cohen's house had swelled to 32,000 square feet, the size of the Taj Mahal. Even at Taj prices, cost matters little to a man with a net worth of $8 billion and an income in 2010 of over $1 billion. Cohen's payday is impressive but by no means unique among America's hedge fund managers. In 2005, 25 hedge fund managers averaged $363 million, for a cumulative payday three times as much as New York City's 8,000 public school teachers.

THE UNEQUAL DISTRIBUTION OF INCOME

Some are rich, some are poor, and many are in between. Over the past two centuries, many scholars and observers have expected that in democratic societies, income differentials would narrow. Political theorists like Aristotle and Madison expected that the spread of democracy would allow the great numbers of poor to use state power to enact redistributive tax and welfare programs to narrow the gap between rich and poor. For a time, this seemed to be happening. Observing countries with different levels of income and over time, in 1955 the American economist Simon Kuznets (1901-79) even proposed what has become known as the *Kuznets Curve*,[3] where income gaps narrow as countries become

FIGURE 10-1
INCOME SHARE OF RICHEST 1%, 1913-2010

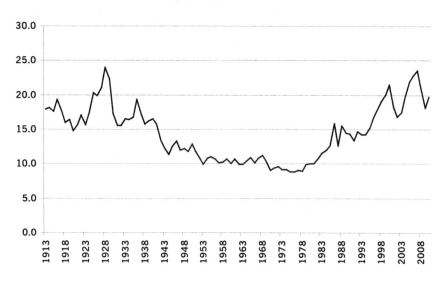

wealthier.[4] Indeed, through the first decades after World War II, economists observed a narrowing of income and wealth differentials throughout the advanced economies of Europe and North America.[5]

In the United States, the Great Depression and World War II brought on a great compression of income differentials.[6] Property income for the rich fell sharply during the Great Depression and the New Deal, and stronger unions pushed up income for the poor and for the working class. During World War II, government and tax policies squeezed the rich while favoring workers. These trends continued after World War II, when Americans in all income groups experienced rising income, but there was a steady tilt benefitting the poor, gradually narrowing the gap between the poorest and wealthiest (see Figures 10-1 and 10-2). Throughout the post-war decades, incomes rose more for the poor and the middle than for the rich, so that by the early 1970s, America had a substantially more equal distribution of income than ever before in its history.

By the 1970s, so great was the narrowing in income differentials that many conservatives and even some liberals were warning that narrow differentials were undermining incentives to work hard and to invest. Such concerns contributed to a remarkable political turnabout. The tide turned dramatically around 1979-80 with the election of the Conservative Margaret Thatcher as prime minister of the United Kingdom and the Republican Ronald Reagan as president of the United States. Thatcher and Reagan inaugurated a new economic policy of free trade, open capital markets, and tax cuts for the rich, and they opposed labor unions and government regulation of business. With the new politics came a dramatic change in economic fortunes. Before the 1970s, income in the poorest American households increased faster than for richer households (see Figure 10-2). Since then, income for the poorest Americans and for the middle class has barely grown while the rich have monopolized almost all of America's income gains.

FIGURE 10-2
INCOME GROWTH BY INCOME LEVEL, 1947-2010, CONSTANT DOLLARS

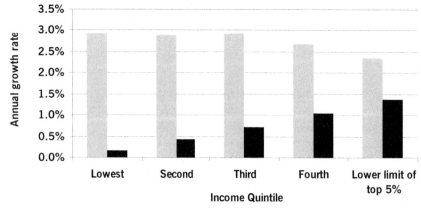

Rising inequality has created a chasm between wealthy and average Americans. In 1979, the wealthiest 1% had an average income of $337,100, 22 times that of the poorest 20%. This gap is dwarfed by the gulf that now divides rich and poor Americans. In 2006, with an average after-tax income in constant dollars of $1,200,300, the wealthiest 1% of Americans had an average income *73 times* that of the poorest 20%, whose average income of $16,500 had barely changed in 27 years (see Figure 10-3). The share of total income received by the wealthiest Americans has soared since 1980. In 2006, over half of total income went to the wealthiest 20%, including 19% going to the richest 1%. Put another way, the wealthiest 1% receive as much income as the bottom half of the American population; the richest three million have as much income as 150 million poor and middle-class Americans.

Furthermore, income distribution is *fractal*: zoom in and we find that inequality is as great among the rich and the super-rich as it is for the whole population. Incomes at the top eclipse even those of the rich. While the richest 1% of Americans (3,000,000 people) have nearly 20% of national income, nearly half of that goes to the richest 1/10 of 1% (or 300,000), and half of that goes to the richest 1/100 of 1% (or 30,000), who

FIGURE 10-3

AFTER-TAX INCOME BY INCOME GROUP, 1979 AND 2006, CONSTANT DOLLARS

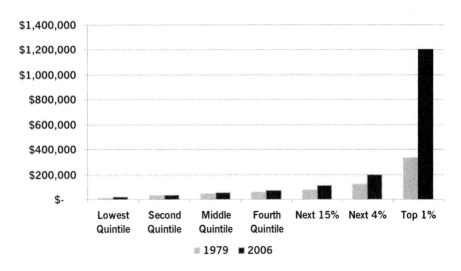

have incomes *131 times* those received by others in the top 1%. The richest 1/100 of 1% have nearly 5% of national income—as much as the poorest 20% of Americans (or 60,000,000 people). With an average income of $24,000,000, their incomes are over *1400 times* those received by the poorest 20% of Americans.

WHY HAVE THE RICH GAINED?

The rich have increased their share of national income because their incomes have grown dramatically faster than those of the rest of the population. The richest 1% has received no less than 85% of the total growth in income since 1979. The richest 5% (15,000,000 people) have received over 93% of the total income growth, leaving only 7% for the other 285,000,000 Americans. With rising income at the top, it takes more and more to make it there. Since 1983, *Forbes* magazine has compiled a list of the 400 richest Americans. As recently as 1995, one could make it into the list with as little as $310 million in wealth. Each year since then, however, the mini-

mum requirement for the list has risen by almost $100 million. In 2006, it required an even $1 billion, and in 2008, a minimum of $1.3 billion. In 1992, the wealthiest 400 tax returns averaged $47 million and had 0.52% of total income; by 2007, they averaged five times as much, $233 million, and had more than tripled their share of total income to 1.59%. The richest 400 tax returns went from 1,441 times the income of the rest of the population to 5,666 times.[8]

The richest gained on the rest of us because income from property, dividends, rents, profits, and capital gains has grown faster than wages.[9] Wage and salary income rose only slightly faster for the richest Americans than for others, increasing at an annual rate of 4.0% per annum for the richest 400, compared with an annual increase of 3.4% for all Americans.[10] By contrast, nominal nonwage income rose by 14.9% per annum for the richest 400.[11] Because of rising non-wage income,

FIGURE 10-4

SHARE OF GROWTH IN AFTER-TAX INCOME, 1979-2006

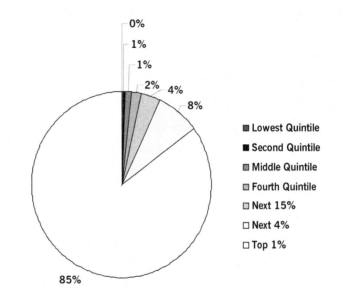

FIGURE 10-5
WAGE AND SALARY SHARE OF GDP

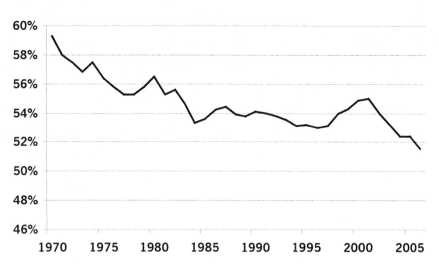

by 2005, wages and salaries, account-ed for less than 10% of income for the richest 400 Americans, compared to about 70% of income for all Americans. The rich and super-rich have benefited from a dramatic shift in income from labor to property. Slow wage growth has meant that national income has shifted towards higher corporate profits. Not only does this shift income towards those who own corporations and other businesses, in the form of higher profits and dividends, but it has also raised the value of businesses, producing capital gains income for their owners.

The shift in national income from labor to capital has produced a dramatic tax cut for the richest Americans. In the early 1990s, the richest Americans paid significantly more in taxes than did others, including much higher income taxes. This is no longer the case. Reductions in income tax rates, especially on unearned income, and the shift in sources of income for the rich, have reduced their payroll tax liability. Since the mid-1990s, dramatic tax cuts have lowered federal income and payroll taxes paid by the super-rich from over 30% of their incomes down to less than 17%. By contrast, the average federal tax burden for all Americans, including income and payroll levies, has hovered around 23%, (see Figure 10-6).[12]

HOW DO YOU BECOME A RICH AMERICAN?

Studies by the "capitalist tool," *Forbes* magazine, provide some insight into the nature of America's rich. Every year, *Forbes* compiles a list of the 400 wealthiest Americans and the 100 wealthiest families. Some quarrel with the names on the list, and those left off, but these are certainly very, very rich people with incomes at least 5,000 times that of the median American family in 1995 and is now at least 20,000 times as great. Using data for the years 1995-97, the activist group United for a Fair Economy collected characteristics of the 488 individuals and 114 families who appeared on the list at least once in those three years (see Figure 10-7). The 250 separate families represented, including those of people listed as individuals, included some 1200 people in total. Compared with the average American whose net worth was well under $100,000 in those years, the people in the *Forbes* 400 are in a different world. The average wealth of a member of the *Forbes* 400 1995-97 was $1,431,000,000. The minimum wealth needed to make the list rose sharply in these three years. In 1995,

FIGURE 10-6
AVERAGE FEDERAL TAX RATE, TOP 400 RETURNS AND ALL RETURNS, 1992-2007, INCOME AND PAYROLL TAXES

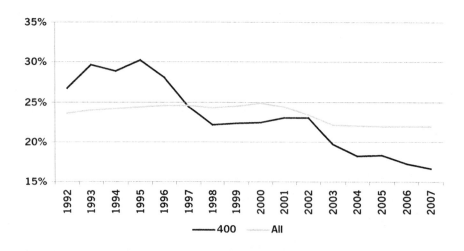

THE GENETIC LOTTERY

Where you are born has more to do with your future income than any decision you make. There are several dimensions to this:

- Are you born in a rich country, like the U.S., or a poor one?
- Are you born, and do you remain, healthy? Or are you born with chronic disease or suffer a debilitating accident?
- Are your parents able to care for you?
- Are your parents wealthy?
- Do you remain lucky?

two individuals, Oprah Winfrey of Chicago, Ill., and Leon Levy, a New York investor, were able to squeak in with only $340 million. By 1997, however, both of these had moved up in the world, to a more respectable $550 million. That year, it took $470 million for a Florida movie theater developer, Abraham Gosman, to crack the list. In the late 1990s, these 400 individuals averaged over a billion dollars in net worth, with a total of over $500 billion in 1995 rising to $628 billion in 1997.

The rich continued to accumulate wealth over the next decade. In 2008, it took $1.3 billion to crack the *Forbes* list and the average wealth of the 400 people on the list was over $3.9 billion. The total wealth of the *Forbes* 400 in 2008 was *$1.6 trillion*, double the $624 billion held by the richest 400 in 1997. Over the 13 years 1995-2008, the wealth held by the richest 400 Americans increased at an annual rate of nearly 11% a year, triple the rate of growth in the economy as a whole, and the ratio of their wealth to total gross domestic product rose from 5% in 1995 to over 11% in 2008. With $1.6 trillion, these 400 individuals own 3.2% of the total net wealth in the United States, 25,000 times their share of the population.

At the top, there are familiar names. The Walton Family (WalMart) is represented by six separate individuals with a total worth of about $100 billion in 2008. Candy is represented by three heirs to the Mars fortune, each worth $12 billion. Levi's has clearly lost its cachet, along with all of its production workers in the United States. In 1997, the family fortune was still good for nearly $8 billion spread among seven presumably jeans-wearing members of the Haas family; none made the 2008 list. No longer tied to Levi's, the Gap had five representatives of its own, worth a total of $4.7 billion in 1997; only one remained in 2008, Robert Fisher with $1.5 billion. Reebok too has fallen on hard times. The entrepreneurial Paul Fireman fell off the list between 1997 and 2008, even while Nike's Philip Knight soared from an already comfortable $5.4 billion in 1997 to $10.5 billion in 2008. Off the list in 1995, Donald Trump returned in 1997 with $1.4 billion and stayed on with $3 billion in 2008—how much from TV royalties I cannot say. Entertainment treated Stephen Allen Spielberg well, with $3.1 billion.

His friend George Lucas has fared even better with $4 billion in 2008, double his 1997 wealth; apparently "Attack of the Clones" did better at the box office than among the critics. Representing old money, David Rockefeller remains on the list with nearly $3 billion. New money is represented by, among others, New York's Michael Bloomberg. The media mogul and former Mayor of New York City was worth only a billion in 1995 but moved up to $1.3 billion in 1997 and came in as number 9 in 2008 with $20 billion. Microsoft's Paul Allen was worth $17 billion in 1997 but slipped to $16 billion in 2008, just barely ahead of

FIGURE 10-7

WEALTH OF FORBES 400, TOTALS FOR FORBES 400 MEMBERS BY CLASS BACKGROUND, BILLIONS OF DOLLARS, 1997

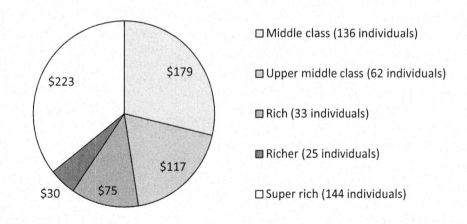

- ☐ Middle class (136 individuals)
- ▨ Upper middle class (62 individuals)
- ▨ Rich (33 individuals)
- ▨ Richer (25 individuals)
- ☐ Super rich (144 individuals)

HOW TO GET RICH

Few great fortunes are "earned" even with the highest wages and salaries. More are the product of capital gains through the ownership of assets, such as companies, real estate, mineral resources, or particular talents or patents that become dramatically more valuable.

Of course, the best way to become rich is to inherit a fortune.

The Beverly Hillbillies discovered oil on their farm; Gisele became rich by owning unique assets and having the good fortune to connect with the right modeling agency and support staff; Hal Steinbrenner's father owned a unique asset that appreciated in value (the New York Yankees).

Google's Sergey Brin and Larry Page at $15.9 and $15.8 billion. Other familiar names top the list: Bill Gates at $57 billion in 2008 (up from a mere $39.8 billion in 1997), Michael Dell at $17.3 billion, and Warren Buffet at $50 billion. Paris Hilton does not make the list, but her dad comes in at 179th place with $2.5 billion, more than enough to pay her bail.

The *Forbes* list provides evidence of class mobility and of the advantages of privilege. Almost no one on the list comes from a poor family and only a handful ever worked at manual labor or in lower-level jobs. Fewer than 20% of American adults are college graduates but virtually all of the *Forbes* 400 have at least a BA degree, and nearly 25% of the *Forbes* 400 went to Ivy League schools, compared with 0.3% of the population as a whole. A refugee from the Nazi Holocaust, George Soros is almost unique on the list as one who rose from nothing to great wealth. (Even he benefitted from the social capital of living in London.) Still, almost half of the members of the *Forbes* list come from less than super-rich backgrounds. In these families, bills were paid, food bought with money from regular paychecks, and children attending college looked for summer work and scholarships to help pay their way. Steve Jobs, for example, was off the list in 1995, but Apple's recovery put him back by 1996 at #362 with $470 million. He rose to #256 with $710 million in 1997 and, powered by the iPod and by Pixar, his wealth rose to $5.7 billion by 2008. Coming from an affluent, but by no means rich, middle-class background, Jobs benefitted from a good public school education and had family help with college expenses and in starting his business. William Henry Gates III also did well. He had an affluent father, a patent attorney, who was able to support his son's interest in computers from a young age and send him to good schools, including Harvard College. Dad was also able to help connect Bill III with others able to support his business aspirations. It was Dad who had the prescience to urge his son to license MS-DOS to IBM rather than to sell the program.

Obviously, very few make it into the upper stratosphere of the *Forbes* 400, but some have a better chance than others. Native-born white men from rich backgrounds dominate the list. Nearly 90% of the people on the list, 361 of 400, are men, and 96%, 385 of 400, are of European descent. (Another 12 are Asian, and three are of African descent, including one Egyptian, one Kenyan, and Oprah.) Of the 39 women on the list, all but one, Oprah Winfrey, either inherited their fortunes or received them from their husbands.

INEQUALITY, INHERITANCE, AND POLICY

Not only at the top but throughout the income distribution, much of American inequality is due to inheritance, in all forms, rather than to personal effort. This distinguishes the United States from other capitalist economies. Overall, parental income is a far better predictor of whether someone will be rich or poor in America than in Canada or much of Europe, and a better predictor than many measures of intrinsic ability, intelligence, or commitment to work hard. In America, about half of the income disparities in one generation are carried on in the next, while in Canada and the Nordic countries that proportion is only about a fifth. Affluence is transmitted directly by passing money and businesses down to the next generation. Affluent parents also can better prepare their children for adult economic success by sending them to better schools and giving them private opportunities to learn and to develop skills.[13] They give their children personal advantages, better health care, better *educational opportunities*,[14] and training in the *behavior norms*[15] expected of the economic elite. They introduce their children to people and institutions connected to the economic elite. Gates, Jobs, Spielberg, and most of the other entrepreneurs on the *Forbes* list came from families with incomes well above the median for Americans. They did well in the *genetic lottery*,[16] albeit not nearly as

FIGURE 10-8

INCOME RELATIVE TO U.S. MEDIAN, AFFLUENT (TOP 10%) AND POOR (BOTTOM 10%) FOR SELECTED CAPITALIST COUNTRIES

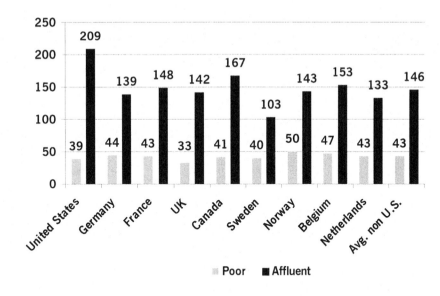

well as the other half, the wealthier half, of this elite group who inherited vast sums of money. This includes the Waltons, all of whom inherited their money, the Rockefellers, the Fords, and the Mars, Koch, Getty, Hearst, Hass, and Bass families. Over a third of the wealth on the list was inherited. This helps to explain the almost total absence of non-whites, of Hispanics, or of Asian-Americans from the list. In 1997, for example, only one non-white was on the list, Oprah. Only two other African-Americans, Bill Cosby and James Johnson (of BET), have made the list in recent years. A long history of slavery, discrimination, and grinding poverty has prevented most African-Americans from accumulating large fortunes to pass along to their children or even the comfortable affluence to support their children's business aspirations.

Inherited wealth raises a general quandary for those who see great wealth as a reward for productive labor. One can argue, as does Arthur Okun, that we need inequality to provide incentives for people to work hard and productively. Perhaps it was the promise of wealth that led Paul Fireman to make running shoes or George Lucas to invent R2D2. But this provides little justification for disparities due to inheritance or other forms of blind luck. Does society benefit from the $2 billion bestowed as an inheritance on Ray Lee Hunt? Perhaps the prospect of passing wealth on to one's children motivated Sam Walton to work hard, and we need to allow great wealth and inheritances if we want to have future Wal-Marts. But can anyone really say that John D. Rockefeller built Standard Oil because he wanted to leave a fortune to his great grandchildren over a century later?

The effect of income inequality in promoting economic growth is a crucial issue for economic policy. Today, the United States stands

FIGURE 10-9

COLLEGE ADMISSION RATES BY PARENTAL INCOME AND SAT SCORES

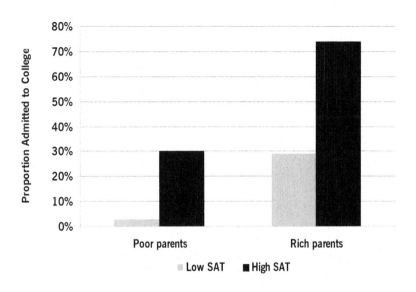

out among capitalist democracies for the range of income differentials coming from our reliance on market incentives to encourage productive work (see figure 10-8). The income range between rich and poor is dramatically wider in the United States than in other advanced capitalist economies. Not only are our rich richer, but our poor are dramatically poorer than the poor in other countries. While Americans in the top 10% of the income distribution enjoy incomes 50% higher than their German counterparts, those in the *bottom decile*,[17] the poorest 10%, have an average income 12% lower than their German counterparts. The range between the richest and the poorest 10% is 5.4:1 in the United States, much higher than the 3.5:1 average for the other affluent economies.

IT MATTERS IF YOU ARE RICH OR POOR

Rising inequality affects people's lives, their ability to maintain good health and productivity, and their capacity to invest in their children's human capital and future productivity. The greater poverty of America's poor is apparent in their poor health and short stature compared with lower-income people in Europe or Japan. At age 45, compared with being middle class, being poor takes six years off the life of a white man, seven years off the life of a black man, although less than three years off the life of a white woman. (Poor black women lose almost four years.) The poor are several times more likely to suffer poor health than the rich, and they are three times more likely to have an activity limitation because of their health. Cancer and other killing diseases afflict the poor at several times the rate of the rich. Some of these ailments are directly related to low income. The poor and the uninsured are four times more likely to postpone seeing a doctor or receiving care because of the cost, they are three times more likely to fail to fill a prescription, and they are five times more likely to not have a regular doctor and, therefore, are more likely to receive substandard care.

Over a lifetime, relative poverty reduces life expectancy by over a decade. For those who live to 55, men in the top 10% of the income distribution have a life expectancy of 35, and can expect to see their 90th birthday; the poorest 10% can only expect 24 more years.[18] At least life expectancy is increasing for the poorest American men. This is not the case for women, however. As is the case with men, richer women have a longer life expectancy at age 55 than do poorer women, a gap of over nine years. But unlike poorer men, poorer women now have a shorter life expectancy than did their counterparts 20 years ago. Despite all the improvements in medical technology that have helped to raise life expectancy for other Americans, and for people throughout the world, life expectancy has fallen by two years for the poorest women, and by smaller amounts for the poorer 40% of American women. Like canaries in the coal mine who would warn of toxic gas by dropping dead, these poorer women may be warning us of the dangers of rising inequality and continued wage stagnation and cutbacks in social services.

Just as there are disadvantages to poverty, there are privileges to wealth that go beyond simply having more stuff. The children of the affluent generally receive better educational opportunities, either at relatively well-funded public schools or at private schools. These allow them to do better on the standardized tests required for admission to better colleges. Even without good test scores, the children of the affluent are more likely to graduate from college than are students with very good test scores but from poor families. Being rich, or at least in the top quintile (20%) of the income distribution, counts for more in college than does performing well on tests.

FIGURE 10-10
LIFE EXPECTANCY AT AGE 55, MEN BORN IN 1920 AND 1940, BY INCOME

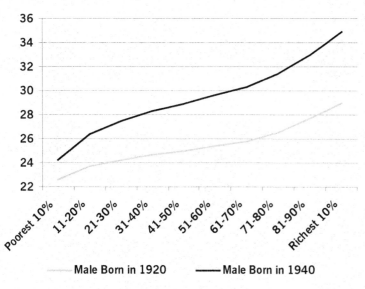

EARNINGS DISPARITIES AND EDUCATION

The advantage children of affluent families have in attending college is particularly important because wages rise with education. As the economy continues to shift away from manual labor occupations, and new technologies are developed that require specialized training, education is more important than ever in gaining good jobs with high wages. Since the mid-1970s, increases in the return to education explain some of the rise in inequality.[19]

The gap between the wages paid to high school graduates and those with a college degree has widened significantly since the 1970s. College graduates now earn over 70% more than those with only a high school diploma, and those with advanced degrees now earn over twice as much as high school graduates (see Figure 10-12). While this explains some of the rise in inequality in the 1970s through the 1990s, education explains little of the increase since then, as wage differentials by education have changed little since the 1990s (see Figure 10-13). Instead, much of the rise in wage dispersion is within education groups, especially for the most educated, where a few "winners" earn dramatically higher wages than the rest.

Compared with being a high school graduate, having *any* type of college degree is a great advantage—college is an excellent investment even if one has to borrow to pay tuition.[20] To be sure, the gains are greater for some students. While economics majors top the list with an average wage of $43/hour, $1.50/hour more than electrical engineers, those majoring in the caring disciplines ("women's work") do not do as well. Education majors earn $21.17, social work majors earn $23.19, and psychology majors earn $24.61.[21]

While rising differentials by education level contribute to rising inequality, most of the increase in inequality, and the greater gains for the super-rich, are not due to these. Rather, they come in the widening differentiation of earnings within groups, and in the rising returns to capital. Even for college graduates, there has been little growth since the early 1990s in income at the median. Instead, most of the widening income differentials with earnings have come from growing income disparities within occupations for workers with similar education and schooling. *Income dispersion*[22] has increased and the share of income going to the highest paid has grown within virtually every occupation. Since the early 1970s, for example, the *real median earnings*[23] of dentists have barely changed, but the number earning over $120,000 has increased by 78%. But great gains at the top have been balanced by an increase in the share of dentists earning

FIGURE 10-11

LIFE EXPECTANCY AT AGE 55, WOMEN BORN IN 1920 AND 1940, BY INCOME

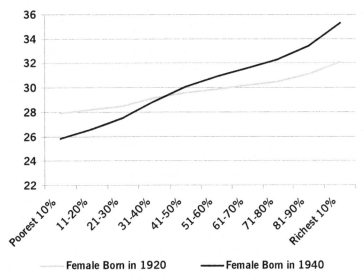

FIGURE 10-12

RETURNS TO SCHOOLING: EARNINGS RELATIVE TO HIGH-SCHOOL GRADUATES

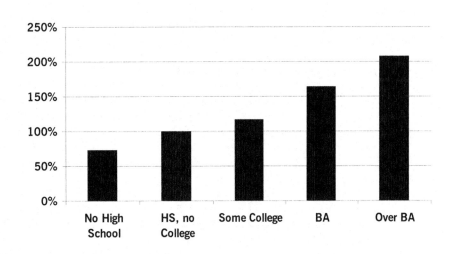

FIGURE 10-13

AVERAGE EARNINGS BY EDUCATION LEVEL, 1991 AND 2012

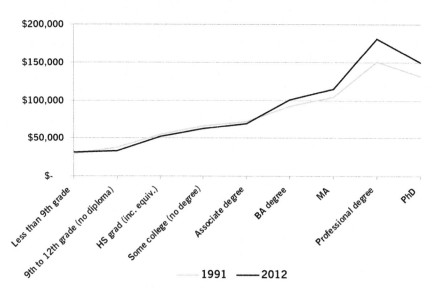

1991 ——2012

less than $60,000. In their book *The Winner-Take-All Society*, economists Robert Frank and Philip Cook characterize this as "runaway incomes at the top." This has happened for lawyers, doctors, entertainers, college professors, CEOs, and basketball, football, and baseball players. In all of these occupations, incomes have shot up for a small group within the occupation even while there has been little change in the average income for the occupation, and the number with very low incomes has increased. Among college graduates, those with the highest incomes have increased their earnings dramatically faster than have others, increasing the gap between their earnings and those of low-wage college graduates.[24]

THE POLITICS OF INEQUALITY

Beyond the effect of education and technological change, income dispersion reflects the growing power of capital, both in higher returns to capital and greater rewards for corporate managers. The greatest income gains have been at the very top. In 1970, the CEOs of 100 large public companies earned 39 times as much as the average production worker under them. By 1995, these CEOs had raised their relative pay to 343 times average worker's pay.[25] (This compares with 21 and 16 times in German and Japanese companies respectively.) But this was not enough. From 1992 to 2005, the median CEO saw pay rise by 186%, or by 8.1% a year, four times the rate of inflation. This dramatic run up in CEO pay raised their relative earnings to over 700 times the average pay in 2005, when CEO pay consumed 10% of corporate profits, double the ratio of the mid-1990s. In only one other country, Switzerland, does the average CEO make over half the average for the United States. Even *Fortune* magazine (in its April 2003 edition) has criticized bloated CEO pay, putting a well-dressed pig on the cover of an issue with the lead story on CEO compensation.

Rising CEO pay is reflected down the corporate ladder with higher compensation for others in top management: senior VPs, CFOs, and the like. These increases do not make their way down to the shop floor, however. While CEO pay more than doubled between 1992 and 2005, the median worker's wage rose by just 7%. CEO pay has not been rising because of changes in the education requirements of their work or changes in managerial technology. On the contrary, productivity appears to have no effect on the relative earnings of CEOs and the workers under them. Sharply rising worker productivity did not boost worker pay, and extensive research has shown that rising CEO pay does not reflect businesses performance.[26] The difference between CEOs and the rest of us may be that they get to appoint the people who set their salaries.

The political determination of CEO pay points to a larger point: rising income differentials reflect social and political factors, a breakdown in the institutions that narrowed income differentials in the decades before 1970. Rising salaries for CEOs and other managers, and the shift in income towards property owners, are two ways in which power and control over the institutions of the economy are changing the distribution of income and wealth.

While this scene on New York's Upper West Side, of a homeless man helped by neighbors, is common in America these days, there were few homeless in the late-1960s and early 1970s. Rising wages and expanded social programs allowed most poor people to get off the streets and into homes in the early 1970s. Greater economic equality reduced begging and nearly eliminated homelessness.

Since the late 1970s, there have been dramatic changes in government policy and a weakening of the social institutions that had previously maintained wages. In particular, there have been sharp declines in unionization, reduced government protections for the incomes of low-wage workers, growing international competition for workers, and a shift in the burden of taxation from capital to labor.

DECLINING UNIONIZATION

In the 1930s, the United States government made a conscious political decision to support labor union organization under the auspices of the National Labor Relations Act, in hopes that stronger unions would promote economic democracy and maintain wages. Since the enactment of the 1947 Taft-Hartley Act, however, national policy has favored capital against labor, contributing to a steady erosion of union membership. Union members made up a third of workers in the early 1950s; now they comprise less than 10% of private-sector workers. While unions continue to raise wages for their members and, to a lesser extent, for nonmembers, their impact on wage levels is reduced because they cover fewer workers, and the effect of unions on wages falls with the declining proportion that is organized.[27] Falling union membership also contributes to rising inequality because it removes a factor restraining corporate pay and dividends. Weaker unions are less able to restrain (or to shame) CEOs and other managers from pushing up their own salaries.[28]

Declining labor-union membership has had the greatest effect on the wages of blue-collar workers because unions have traditionally been strongest among workers in relatively low-wage occupations and had the largest effect on their wages. Indeed, union decline among blue-collar workers and union growth among public-sector workers like teachers and nurses has transformed the union movement so that union membership is now greater among the college educated. At 21%, the unionization rate among professional workers is higher than the 18% rate for production workers. When unions united low-wage workers to raise wages, they reduced wage differentials between blue-collar and white-collar workers. Declining union membership over the last 25 years, especially among those with relatively little education and low wages, has widened inequality and reduced wages for low-wage workers. It accounts for over half of the relative decline in blue-collar wages and a quarter of the decline in wages for high school graduates.

MINIMUM WAGES AND INCOME SUPPORT

Unions have declined because the Federal government has abandoned its commitment to the right of workers to form institutions for collective action.[29] This has been one piece in a broader attack on American wages. Government policy has lowered wages by exposing workers to increasing competition, both with foreign workers and with others at home, by removing government regulations over wages and competition and by weakening unions. In another age, in 1937, Congress enacted the Fair Labor Stan-

> **EXPLAINING RISING INEQUALITY**
>
> Rising inequality has been one of the hottest topics in economic research over the last 20 years. Explanations have fallen in two areas: market and institutional explanations. Market-based explanations include "skill-biased technological change," which would increase the relative demand for educated workers, driving up their relative pay, and the increasing globalization of both labor and product markets, which increases competition for low-skilled workers and the demand for skilled workers.
>
> Institutional explanations include the decline in unions and changes in government policy, such as the decline in welfare programs, a lower real value of the minimum wage, and reduction in progressive taxation.

FIGURE 10-14
DECLINING UNION DENSITY, UNITED STATES, 1973-2012

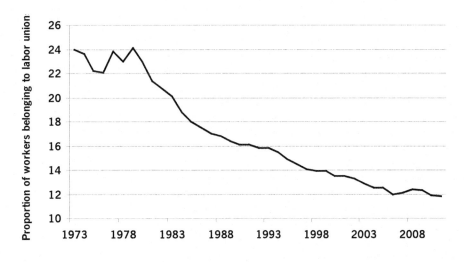

FIGURE 10-15
DECLINING REAL VALUE OF MINIMUM WAGE (1985 DOLLARS)

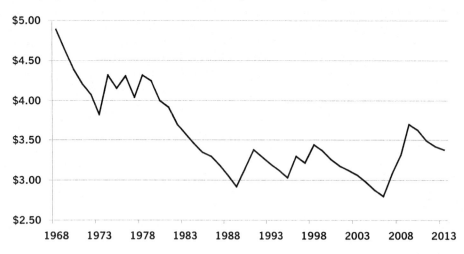

dards Act to establish a minimum wage, raising the wages of common workers. Always opposed by employers, especially in low-wage industries and regions (Southern manufacturing, for example), the wage rate has been set in *nominal* terms that regularly lose value during periods of rising prices. To maintain the *real* value of the minimum wage, Congress has periodically amended the law to raise the nominal value to catch up with inflation. Opposition from business and conservative politicians, including President Reagan and both Presidents Bush, prevented the enactment of such "catch-up"

legislation. It passed only once under President Clinton in 1996, and then again in 2007. As a result, the national minimum wage has lost real value since the late 1970s, down to only half its 1978 value by the early 2000s.[30] Because nearly 10 million workers are paid the minimum wage, 9% of the total labor force, and another 9.6 million are paid just above it, the declining value of the legal minimum wage has directly lowered real wages for nearly one fifth of American workers. Lower wages for these workers has directly contributed to wider income inequality. One might almost say that these low-wage workers have been paying the bill for rising CEO compensation.

Other changes in social policy have also increased inequality. Since the early 1980s, many government income support programs for the non-elderly population have been reduced or eliminated, ostensibly to encourage more people to work for pay. The social security program of Aid to Families with Dependent Children was replaced in 1996 by a much more limited Transitional Aid to Needy Families. Access to unemployment insurance has been made more difficult, and in most states, general relief has been eliminated. As a result, the impact of social welfare programs on income inequality has been reduced by half.

FREE TRADE

Since the early 1970s, the United States has made political decisions to open its economy to foreign products. We have negotiated a series of trade deals, including the North America Free Trade Area (NAFTA), and restrictions on foreign imports, including the Multi-Fiber Agreement restraining imports of textiles and apparel, have been allowed to lapse. Free trade has been promoted as a way to limit monopoly power and to stimulate technological progress and creativity among American businesses. It has also favored some industries, American exporters, at the expense of indus-

FIGURE 10-16
REDUCTION IN INCOME INEQUALITY DUE TO SOCIAL WELFARE PROGRAMS, HOUSEHOLDS WITH CHILDREN

"A RIGHT NOT A PRIVILEGE"

The demand for universal access to health care, without regard to income or wealth, is founded in the democratic assertion that all are equal in their rights and that society should be organized to provide equal opportunity to all. Seen in this perspective, this demand is similar to earlier democratic demands for universal education.

Massachusetts established public schools in 1635, with the founding of the Boston Latin School. In 1642, the Massachusetts Bay Colony passed the first law in the New World requiring that children be taught to read and write. In 1647, the Colony required that all towns provide  public schools, but this law was not strictly enforced for nearly 200 years. Appointed the Commonwealth's first Secretary of Education in 1837, Horace Mann (1796-1859) campaigned for universal schooling. Democracy, Mann argued, required an educated population, and equality of opportunity is too important to leave to the market, where some gain much more money than others. His work led, in 1852, to the enactment of a Massachusetts law that all children are required to attend school.

Equal educational opportunity remains an elusive target today with enormous disparities in the quality of education offered students in different towns with different levels of wealth.

Horace Mann, abolitionist, democrat, and champion of universal educational opportunity.

tries where the United States does not have a comparative advantage. Since then, imports have doubled as a share of consumption, and there have been significant improvements in some American products, notably automobiles.

The effect of education on earnings may have been enhanced by expanded free trade. Certainly, by providing more opportunities for footloose capitalists to seek higher returns, trade has increased profits, shifting income towards the rich. While growing capital mobility and international trade force American manual workers to compete with the lowest-paid workers from throughout the world, the workers that Robert Reich[31] labels *symbolic analysts*, educated workers dealing in concepts and language, are able to sell their products throughout the world.[32] Most of the industries that have flourished by exporting employ relatively large numbers of educated workers. (These include providers of business services, information and bio-technology, and entertainment.) This reflects the position of the United States as a country relatively abundant in educated labor. Our leading exporters include companies that rely on skilled and professional labor, creative businesses, such as Apple, Boeing, CitiGroup, Disney, Google, Microsoft, and Pfizer. The success these companies have in export markets leads them to recruit more educated workers, raising their pay. At the same time, the United States has become a large importer of the products made by labor-intensive manufacturing using less-educated workers. This has reduced employment and wages in textiles, apparel, and automobile parts, and for workers making cheap plastic toys.[33]

Expanded foreign trade, therefore, has increased demand for skilled workers and reduced demand for the unskilled. Some workers have been relatively insulated from these changes because they perform service labor that must be performed on site in the United States. Even these workers face growing competition from foreign workers within the United States. The United States has admitted over 16 million immigrants since 1980, raising the foreign-born share of the population to over 11% for the first time since 1930. Over one third of immigrants have not completed high school, compared with 9% of native-born workers. Both immigrants and imports compete especially with low-wage workers. Both rising imports and immigration have both driven down wages for some low-wage workers.

CITIZENSHIP AND THE MARKET

In a capitalist society, income and wealth are distributed unequally, but in a democracy, all citizens have equal *rights*. Regardless of income, all Americans have certain "unalienable rights" guaranteed by the U.S. Constitution, including a right to privacy (including the right to use contraception), the right to speak freely, to practice religion, and to have legal representation in criminal investigations and trials. These rights cannot be alienated, sold or taken away, without due process of law. We each have the right to cast one and only one vote in elections. Regardless of wealth, we are each supposed to have an equal say in choosing our leaders and in setting government policy. The Constitution of the Commonwealth of Massachusetts goes even further, as do other state constitutions. It guarantees all residents, regardless of income, the freedom to worship "God in the manner and season most agreeable to the dictates of his own conscience; or for his religious profession or sentiments" (Article 2). All are protected in their property: "no part of the property of any individual can, with justice, be taken from him, or applied to public uses, without his own consent, or that of the representative body of the people" (Article 10). All have the right to seek recourse in the courts for injuries inflicted by others: "Every subject of the commonwealth ought to find a certain remedy, by having recourse to the laws, for all injuries or wrongs which he may receive in his person, property, or character. He ought to obtain right and justice freely, and without being obliged to purchase it; completely, and without any denial; promptly, and without delay; conformably to the laws" (Article 11). Within my hometown of Amherst, Massachusetts, all have an equal right to walk on the sidewalks and the Town Common, all have an equal right to police and fire protection in their homes, and all have a right to loiter in front of pizza parlors (as long as they stay out of the street and are not a menace to others).

Rights are special. They are different from other things that we may have or use. Rights are distributed equally to all residents or citizens, and they cannot be alienated or sold. You don't have rights because of something you did; as the late Mr. Rogers would say, you have rights merely for being you. In the Declaration of Independence, Jefferson said that we have rights because we are endowed with them by our creator. Perhaps we could say that we have rights because we are endowed with them by the creators of our nation, Washington, Madison, Adams, Jefferson, Lincoln, and others. Or, perhaps we could say that we have rights because that is what we are as a country. Elsewhere, people form countries because they are a nation, people who speak the same language and share a culture. Germany, for example, is the country of Germans and France is the country of the French. The United States is different because one can be an American without speaking any particular language, eating any particular cuisine, or practicing a state religion. What makes us a nation is a shared commitment to egalitarian and liberal values, to a belief in equal rights, in the value of each individual, and our faith in the concept of self-government by equal citizens.

Like an alarm bell calling people to arms, the establishment of the United States inaugurated an era of democratic revolution that continues to spread the idea of equal rights throughout the world. With America came the broader idea of social democracy, a regime where, without regard for income, everyone has equal rights before the law, an equal voice in the organization of society, an equal opportunity to participate in collective government, and an opportunity for individual self-expression.[34] This makes American democracy fundamentally different from a market economy. The marketplace allocates dollars because you produced something or sold something that you owned; it allows you to buy the privilege to drive a Lexus or to eat in a fancy restaurant. In a democracy, you do not have privileges, you have rights because you are a citizen, and you have them without regard for what you own or sell. In a democracy, you have equal rights with your neighbor, no more and no less, and there is no way that you can use your money to get more. In the marketplace, dollars are a reward for being productive. Through the market, you get good

DEMOCRACY AGAINST FEUDALISM

On August 26, 1789, the French National Assembly voted a "Declaration of the Rights of Man and the Citizen" beginning with the assertion: "Men are born and remain free and equal in rights. Social distinctions may be founded only upon the general good." Drafted by the Maquis de Lafayette with the help of the American ambassador, Thomas Jefferson, the French revolutionaries proclaimed a democratic vision that citizens have equal rights, including the right to participate as equals in the setting of public policy. They proclaimed citizenship and equality for all without regard to birth or property.

A French revolutionary poster proclaiming, "All mortals are equal. It is not by birth, it is only by virtue that they are distinguished."

things in life as an incentive to be productive, to work hard, and to work smart. In a democracy, you have rights because the purpose of a democratic state and society is to give everyone equal rights that allow all of us, in Jefferson's words, "life, liberty, and the pursuit of happiness."

This contradiction between market and democracy creates a continuing tension in liberal democracies like the United States. We have both citizenship rights and the market. What explains our granting equal rights in some areas alongside our readiness to accept large differences in life opportunities in others? If everyone has a right to life, does this mean that we should provide universal access to health care? If we think everyone should have an equal opportunity to practice their religion, then should we give everyone enough money that they can pay for a church and Sunday school? If we have an equal right to speak freely and to petition the state, then should everyone have access to a printing press? If we believe in equality in government decisions that affect us, then why not an equal voice in other decisions with public consequences, including investment decisions by companies?

Arthur Okun, a prominent liberal economist, addresses these questions in his book, *Equality versus Efficiency: The Big Trade-off*.[35] One of the more widely cited works in economics of the last fifty years, this book spelled out the rationale for the great conservative reversal of economic policy in the United States since the late 1970s. In a nutshell, he argues that "[t]he contrasts among American families in living standards and in material wealth reflect a system of rewards and penalties that is intended to encourage effort and channel it into socially productive activity. To the extent that the system succeeds, it generates an efficient economy." Unequal living standards are the price we pay to maintain a productive economy because, Okun argues, there is trade-off between distribution as a matter of rights and efficiency. To Okun, the more we give as matters of right, the more we undermine the incentives needed to drive people to work efficiently. On the other hand, the more we allocate through the market, the more we undermine our values of equality and democracy.

As a market-oriented economist primarily addressing others like him, Okun begins by asking why we bother with "rights." Why not distribute everything through the market? Citizenship rights, he argues, reflect a fundamental *humanism*, a belief that all of us are equal and, in some basic sense, deserving without regard to our success in the marketplace. Note that in the Declaration of Independence, Jefferson wrote, "We hold these truths to be self-evident, that all men are created equal, that they are endowed by their Creator with certain unalienable Rights, that among these are Life, Liberty and the pursuit of Happiness." He did not say "life, liberty, and property," as did the 17th-century English philosopher John Locke (1632-1704). Instead, in this fundamental statement of the American creed, Jefferson put equality and the right to pursue one's individuality above property and the market distribution of income.[36] This is the logic behind slogans like "health care should be a right, not a privilege." People with this bumper sticker are saying that the American right to "life, liberty, and the pursuit of happiness" should include the material support needed to achieve these. To protect the right to life and the opportunity to pursue happiness, there should be universal access to health care and a universal minimum income. Most of us would accept Jefferson's argument that there are some things that we should all receive equally, and some things that no American should have to do without. But few of us argue that *everything* should be distributed equally. Most political debates are about where to draw the line between these extremes.

Unwilling to rely on moral arguments about the intrinsic sanctity of rights, Okun finds utilitarian grounds for promoting rights. He argues that the sum of individual well-being in an economy is higher with a more equal distribution of income. If we believe in *diminishing marginal utility*, then extra money given to the rich is of less value to them than it would be if given to the poor, because the rich are already *saturated* with wealth and possessions. Precious to the

REVERSE ROBIN HOOD: UPWARD REDISTRIBUTION

Many government programs redistribute income up the economic ladder, giving more to the wealthy and upper middle class. Among these are programs supporting public higher education, used mostly by upper-income families, subsidies to home ownership, and subsidies to air travel. Most of the benefits of government health programs, including the subsidy offered by employer-provided health insurance, go to high-income individuals and families. Subsidies to banking and mining interests, and to producers of sugar, rice, and other crops, go almost exclusively to the wealthiest Americans, as do subsidies to ethanol producers, the merchant marine, and other industries. While these programs are often defended for other reasons, their affluent supporters are well aware of who receives the benefits.

Opposition to subsidies going to the rich is an area that unites some on the libertarian right with those on the egalitarian left.

The American philosopher **John Rawls (1921-2002)** was arguably the most important political philosopher of the 20th century. His book A Theory of Justice revitalized the social-contract tradition, using it to articulate and defend a detailed vision of egalitarian liberalism.

poor who lack most things, additional money means more to them than to those who have a lot already. In the utilitarian approach, associated with the English philosophy Jeremy Bentham, any transfer from richer to poorer will raise total happiness, until there is a complete equality of income. If adopted, the classic utilitarian goals of maximizing the sum of individual welfare and the "greatest good of the greatest number" would require taking from the rich and giving to the poor until all have equal incomes.[37]

Utilitarianism has been criticized for assuming that we can compare the happiness of different people, and create a social utility measure by adding individual utility. The Italian sociologist Vilfredo Pareto, in particular, rejected the utilitarian case for egalitarianism on these grounds.[38] The late Harvard University philosopher John Rawls developed an alternative defense of egalitarianism on utilitarian grounds without interpersonal utility comparisons.[39] Because of diminishing marginal utility, Rawls argues, people are *risk-averse*; we fear bad things more than we relish the prospect of an equally good thing. This is why we buy insurance, giving up some money now for the prospect of protection against bad things in the future. Rawls argues that an egalitarian distribution of income is a form of social insurance. If we imagine ourselves behind a *veil of ignorance*, where we don't know whether we will be rich or poor, then we would want an egalitarian distribution of income with minimal differentials between rich and poor because this will protect us from the bad outcomes, albeit at the risk of losing some of the good. If you don't know, for example, whether you will be blind or clear-sighted, Rawls would argue that you will want a society with good provision to help the blind, even if it lowers income for the clear-sighted.

Rawls has one giant exception to his egalitarian principle. Under his *Difference Principle*, Rawls argues that individuals behind the veil of ignorance would agree to some level of inequality so long as this divergence from strict egalitarianism would make the least advantaged materially better off than they would be under strict equality. Okun was clearly influenced by Rawls and his Difference Principle. While arguing that it is sometimes efficient to allocate according to rights and other non-market criteria, the heart of *Equality and Efficiency* is an argument that any redistribution of income away from the market allocation will lower total output. Taxing the rich to give to the poor discourages the rich from working harder by lowering the returns to their work, and it discourages the poor from working harder because they can get without work. Furthermore, the process requires a bureaucracy that adds nothing to total output, because all it does is supervise redistribution. A well-ordered society committed to utilitarian principles will, nonetheless, allow considerable inequality and will limit redistribution in order to maintain incentives for productive work.

Okun is concerned about a loss of incentives for hard work due to the burden of redistributive taxation and the opportunities to receive social welfare benefits. The market encourages work, by rewarding those who work hard and well with more income. This means, of course, that those who work less or are less productive have lower incomes. He fears that the extension of citizenship rights undermines these incentives by raising the post-fisc (after govern-

WHAT WOULD YOU WANT FROM BEHIND THE VEIL OF IGNORANCE?

If people choose a distribution of income between the healthy and the sick, the fortunate and the unlucky, then they will make their choices knowing how these choices will affect them. Rawls proposed an alternative vision where people would pretend that they are ignorant of how they will fare. Making decisions from behind this veil of ignorance, Rawls suggests, people would act risk averse and choose a distribution of income that would protect themselves, and everyone, from bad outcomes

ment taxes and benefits) income of the unproductive and low-ering it for the productive. He fears that many will ask, why work hard if much of what you might earn is taken in taxes? And why not remain out of the market, sleep late or bake bread at home, if government welfare and other payments will give you an adequate income without market work?

To illustrate his argument, Okun suggests that income redistribution is conducted in a leaky bucket. When soci-ety takes 'water' from the rich to bring to the poor, some is lost along the way. Leaks due to reduced work effort reflect the impact of substitution effects on labor supply. At higher wages, people work harder because they are willing to toler-ate less pleasant work to get more consumption goods, and because they substitute market work for home production and leisure. Lower take-home pay, because of higher taxes for redistribution programs, reduces incentives for the rich to take less pleasant work, to accept the disutility of working harder, and gives them less reason to substitute market work for home production.

Redistributive programs can also reduce labor effort by the poor. Giving them income even though they don't work creates an *income effect* where people work less because they are wealthier. As incomes rise, either through work or through government grant, people have greater incentive to seek out leisure or to engage in home production, both because leisure time is more de-sirable, as with higher income there are more things to do with one's leisure, and because work is less desirable, as the marginal utility of money falls with higher income. Program design can also discour-age work. If people lose benefits when they begin earning, then there can be a strong *substitution effect*, reducing labor supply by the poor.

There are also immediate "leaks" caused by the administrative burden of redistribution, the bu-reaucratic costs in any government program. Some of the revenue raised in taxes has to be used to collect the taxes. The United States government is very efficient compared to most, but the Treasury still spends over $10 billion administering and enforcing the tax laws, or 0.6% of the amount col-lected in taxes. Each income tax return, for example, costs $10 to process, down substantially from $50 in the early 1990s, and the compliance costs are much greater on the other side, where taxpayers spend their own time or money collecting information and filing returns. There are also bureaucratic costs on the spending side of government programs. It costs resources for a redistributive state to help the poor. Government officials must decide who should receive help, who is worthy, and who should receive services in lieu of, or in addition to, cash assistance. The Social Security Administration em-ploys 65,000 workers to administer the old age, survivors, and disability programs, or 1.4 bureaucrats for every 1,000 ben-eficiaries. Without dismissing the work they do, these bureau-crats are not productive. They are no longer available to make things we want or to provide useful services for others, such as building cars, harvesting crops, or cutting hair. The welfare system is even more expensive to administer because of all the checks built into it to prevent people from receiving benefits to which they are not entitled. Programs like the Federal and State Child Support Enforcement Program spends over 25% of its budget on administration. High administrative expenses are by no means unique to government services—some pri-vate health insurance plans cost over 20% to administer.[40] In addition to these administrative costs, government programs create the possibility of fraud and, therefore, an incentive for

---

EXAMPLES OF REDISTRIBUTIVE PROGRAMS

- Progressive income taxes require the rich to pay a higher share of their income.
- Earned Income Tax Credit subsidizes market wages for low-income households.
- Medicaid, Medicare, SCHIP, health insurance subsidies under the Affordable Care Act, Hospital Free-Care Pools provide access to health care for low-income people and the elderly regardless of income.
- Public schools admit all regardless of income.
- Police and fire departments provide security for all regard-less of income.
- WIC (Women, Infants, and Children) provide nutrition and health counseling to mothers and children.
- Food Stamps offer subsidized food for lower income peo-ple.
- Section 8 housing provides subsidized housing for lower-income Americans.

LEAKY BUCKETS

Okun suggests that society can only redistribute income from rich to poor in a "leaky bucket." Some of whatever is taken from the rich, he argues, never reaches the poor because it goes to administra-tive expense, or is lost in reduced output and productivity. Politics, Okun argues, revolves around different preferences for redistribu-tion vs. efficiency. Economic conservatives oppose redistributive programs unless redistribution can be done with minimal "leaks": say, no more than five cents on the dollar. Liberals, by contrast, value equality so highly that they might accept losses as high as eighty cents on the dollar.

individuals to engage in fraud. Businesses and individuals spend billions devising strategies for tax avoidance and to collect benefits licitly or illicitly. Classes in law school, accounting programs, and business schools are essentially devoted to teaching how to scam the government.

LEAKY BUCKETS AND OTHER FABLES

Okun recognizes that marketization can trample on the rights of citizens and lay waste to our national creed that all should be entitled to "unalienable rights" regardless of income. However, he also fears that redistributive policies will make us worse off by reducing national income. He sees a tradeoff between equality and efficiency, and to provide a convenient way to measure the value we put on rights, he imagines the following thought experiment. Suppose government can redistribute income from rich to poor but it can only do so in a *leaky bucket*, where some of what it tries to redistribute is lost en route. How much leakage will we accept? Some extreme conservatives and market fundamentalists might oppose redistribution even if there is 0% leakage, while extreme egalitarians might favor redistribution even if there is 100% leakage and the poor get nothing from lowering the income of the rich. Most of us, Okun believes, are in between. We would like to narrow income differentials but fear the loss in total income. Okun himself said he would accept a lot of leakage, even 60%. The debate over economic policy, Okun argues, is really a debate about the amount of tolerable leakage: conservatives would accept very little; liberals would accept more.

Okun's argument suggests a continuum along which countries can be arrayed according to the value they put on equality and the extent to which they equalize incomes. He expects that those with more egalitarian economic policies will have slower growth rates and, eventually, lower income; those who accept more inequality now will be rewarded with higher growth and, in the future, with higher incomes. Given this clear hypothesis, it is curious that Okun devotes so little of his book to empirical analysis, to what he calls "inspecting the leakages," or identifying just how much is lost through government tax and welfare programs, and how much equality lowers efficiency. Since Okun published *Equality and Efficiency*, his work has sparked a cottage industry of research that has provided very little support for Okun's hypothesis. On the contrary, both between countries with different levels of equality, between regions within countries, and within the same countries over time, there is no evidence that more equality, more rights, reduces efficiency. On the contrary, greater equality is associated with greater efficiency and more rapid growth rates.[41]

The evidence suggests that Okun is wrong. Or, at least, there is no evidence that he is right. A large literature in empirical growth economics has concluded that either there is no link between economic growth and inequality or that economic equality is associated with somewhat *higher* rates of economic growth. Among OECD members, states within the United States, and for a large group of countries, scholars have found no evidence of a negative relationship between growth and equality. On the contrary, there is evidence that growth rates are positively associated with equality. Some countries with relatively egalitarian income distributions have grown very quickly, including Taiwan and Norway, as well as South Korea, and Singapore. All of these have grown much faster than the United States and the United Kingdom, where income is less equally distributed.

This pattern of faster growth in places with less inequality also holds within the United States. States with a highly unequal income distribution and few welfare or social programs, including Alabama, Mississippi, and Louisiana, have relatively slow growth despite active support from the Federal government. By contrast, the American economy has been powered by innovations and economic dynamism in states with more egalitarian income distributions and state policies, including Connecticut, Massachusetts, and Oregon. Nor is there evidence that the widening income gaps since the 1970s have led to accelerated eco-

---

INCOME AND SUBSTITUTION EFFECTS IN OKUN'S LEAKY BUCKETS

Okun relies on two principles of labor economics to argue that redistribution will reduce efficiency by reducing work effort.

- Substitution effect: people work more when wages rise because the price of leisure, the income foregone by not working, is higher.
- Income effect: people work less at higher incomes because the marginal utility of leisure rises with income, while the marginal utility of income falls.

Okun argues that redistribution reduces work effort for the rich through the substitution effect, and for the poor through the income effect. He ignores the income effect on the rich; higher taxes would encourage greater work effort by reducing their income. Redistribution programs could also be designed to enhance the substitution effect for the poor. This is what the Earned Income Tax Credit does by providing a wage subsidy for low-income households.

While government programs always require some administrative support, the bureaucratic cost of public programs is often less than would be required to operate a private sector counterpart. The large scale of government programs allows economies of size, and universal coverage simplifies checking eligibility. The traditional Medicare program, for example, has an administrative overhead of under 2%, barely one tenth that of most private health insurance plans.

The early days of the Social Security Administration

nomic growth. If Okun were right, then we should have had a burst of productivity growth since we have reduced welfare and cut back on progressive taxation. Instead, growth has slowed while inequality has widened. On the other side, land reform and income redistribution to the poor have been associated with faster economic growth in one-time Third World countries, like Taiwan, South Korea, and Japan, that have since industrialized.

Direct studies of Okun's "leakages" also suggest that he is wrong about the magnitude of the economic loss from egalitarian policies. Many of the leakages he emphasizes are relatively small. The labor supply effects emphasized by Okun are certainly very small, and may even go the other way, working against his argument. While the *substitution effects*[42] are very small, virtually nil for adult men, there may be a significant income effect where higher-income people may work harder to make up what they lose in higher taxes. Work is a relatively undesirable activity (which is why people are paid to do it), so people will work more when higher taxes make them poorer. Higher taxes may encourage more work, not less, by making people poorer. When *income effects*[43] balance the substitution effect, the net effect on work efforts may be small.

The lack of a *strong negative labor supply effect*[44] contradicts Okun's claims. On the other side, there is considerable direct evidence that income redistribution towards the poor raises productivity by enhancing human capital accumulation and promoting better health and education, especially among the young. Children and their parents are among the poorest people within market economies because children can never pay their parents for their caring services. Income redistribution favors children, and by allowing parents to invest more money in their care and in their education, it allows for a healthier, better educated, and more prosperous future. Child poverty rates are much lower in countries that conduct more active redistribution programs. In Sweden, for example, the government spends 18% of GDP on social welfare, and only 3% of children live in poverty. By contrast, in the United States, the government spends 3% of GDP on social welfare,

FIGURE 10-17
THE POLITICS OF OKUN'S LEAKY BUCKET:
HOW MUCH LEAKAGE WILL YOU ACCEPT TO RAISE INCOME OF THE POOR

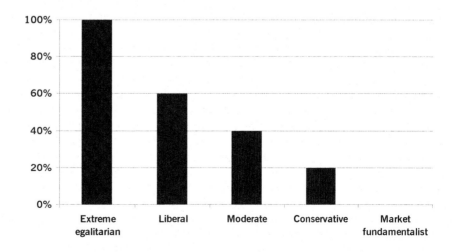

Heroes like this New York City firefighter on September 13, 2001, do not sacrifice for their neighbors from a rational calculation of the personal interests. Would he do less if his after-tax pay were 10% lower? Or more if he had a raise of 10%?

and over 20% of children live in poverty. More egalitarian societies have healthier and better educated children, leading to longer and more productive work lives. Mortality rates, for example, are significantly lower in American states with less inequality, such as Wisconsin and Vermont, than in Louisiana, Mississippi, and other states where there are larger income differentials. Desirable in themselves, lower morbidity and mortality rates are also economically productive because healthier workers are more productive and have longer working lives.

Caring for children and educating the young are humanitarian acts that cannot be rewarded through normal markets because children have no resources to pay for their own care. The market discourages caring for families, cooperating, and being a good neighbor. Welfare states promote growth by supporting productive activities like these. Welfare programs support investments in human capital and lower the costs parents pay for providing their children with health care, nutrition, and education. Welfare states can also discourage unproductive activities that the market would otherwise reward well. A market economy encourages activities besides productive work, including bribery, polluting, forming monopolies, and unproductive litigation. In these cases, the market rewards do not go to the productive but to those able to drag down their rivals even at the expense of social welfare. To the degree that people devote themselves to earning money, they may work hard and well, as Okun hopes, or they may cheat and steal. Those who remain outside the market may, as Okun suggests, be wasting time in selfish consumption and sleeping late. Or they may be helping at their neighborhood school, cleaning the vacant yard next door, and helping their elderly in-law get to the doctor.

This suggests a broader problem with market economics. Like other neoclassical economists, Okun sees a world of scarcity where people must be coerced to work productively and where productive work is rewarded by gaining greater command over nature. But in focusing on the engineering of nature and the costs of *slacking*,[45] Okun neglects the social costs of using the market, including both transactions costs and the damage market incentives do to group cohesion. Social cohesion, caring, and cooperation are essential for modern societies. It is through them that we develop the human capital that allows teamwork, and thus the efficiency gains from dividing labor among individuals with complementary skills and knowledge. Cooperation within teams can be undermined by the use of the market if individuals seek to take advantage of their own private knowledge and attempt to exploit monopolies over particular skills. If those who have willingly contributed out of friendship or community spirit start working only for themselves, then we risk entering the world of prisoners' dilemmas and collective action problems. Friendship and commitment to the community may appear as scatterbrained and frivolous motivations when others are being paid to exploit their position within the group, but these motivations are crucial for efficient team production. By promoting selfish thinking, market incentives also encourage crime and contribute to the great waste that is the American criminal justice system.

The decline of cooperation becomes a social problem when there are important services that are hard or even impossible to buy. Volunteer work, such as that done by parents and community members in local government and neighborhood schools, is hard to replace, due to both the large volume of volunteer services performed and the specialized knowledge and skills neighbors bring to solving local problems. If the goal is to make money, then people try to restrict access to their knowledge and skill to drive up the price they can receive. Here we see why work done outside the market can be more efficient: it draws on information that is willingly shared by volunteers, all interested in solving community problems cooperatively.

Consider a situation that has become too common in recent years: soldiers in a foxhole when the order comes down to get up and attack. Why would anyone leave relative safety to follow orders? Is it because they signed a contract? What about the medics who crawl across the battlefield under fire to rescue the wounded? Do they do it for money? Why don't they use their monopoly position to auction off the blood plasma and antibiotics they carry?

What market incentives led the New York City firefighters who ran into the burning World Trade Center on September 11, 2001? We call them heroes because we cannot buy the kind of commitment we expect from soldiers, firefighters, police officers, or from our doctors, teachers, clergymen, and others. And if we try to buy it then we will cheapen what they do, alienating those whose work is properly seen as a service and a sacrifice. When it really matters, we do not rely on money to motivate people. We reward doctors, soldiers, fire fighters, baseball players, parents, teachers, and others with respect, medals, even adulation, and not only money. Market economies survive because people don't work just for money. If we treat them as if they do, then it endangers their work incentive by devaluing their commitment, threatening the very survival of our economy, even our species.

By promoting cooperation and human capital development, government policies—the recognition of rights and redistribution—can promote economic efficiency and growth. These policies can correct market failures stemming from the market's incapacity to value home production, community service, and public goods. This can make the Okun equality-efficiency line *upward* sloping, more equality leading to more efficiency, if not infinitely, at least for a time.

DISCUSSION QUESTIONS

What happened to the distribution of income and wealth in the United States through the first 75 years of the 20th century (1900-75)? What has happened to these distributions since? How does this relate to the Kuznets Curve?

How have the rich gained on the rest of us? What has happened to the distribution of income between wages and profits?

Discuss some of the ways people get rich.

Discuss some of the advantages of being rich; what can the rich do that the rest cannot?

What has happened to the distribution of income among the bottom 99%? Whose incomes have been rising? Whose have not?

How has social policy contributed to rising inequality? Discuss some of the policies during the New Deal (the 1930s and 1940s) that contributed to reducing inequality, and some of the policies since the 1970s that have exacerbated inequality.

What is "utilitarianism"? Why do utilitarians favor an egalitarian distribution of income? Under what circumstances would utilitarians, such as John Rawls or Arthur Okun, favor inequality?

What is Okun's "leaky bucket" experiment? Where would you put yourself along the leaky-bucket continuum? (How much leakage would you accept to transfer $100 from the rich to the poor?)

What are "income effects" and "substitution effects" on labor supply?

How does Okun's hypothesis that equality undermines efficiency depend on a particular view of labor supply effects? What would happen to his hypothesis if the rich had strong income effects but the poor had strong substitution effects?

ENDNOTES

[1]Arthur M Okun, *Equality and Efficiency, the Big Tradeoff* (Washington: Brookings Institution, 1975), 1.

[2]Cohen could pay for some of the art with the proceeds from selling his 9,000 square foot New York City apartment on E. 58th Street, which he offered for $98 million (http://www.businessinsider.com/most-expensive-homes-for-sale-in-nyc-2014-6?op=1). That is only the third most expensive apartment in New York. First place goes to investor Vincent Viola's on E. 69th Street, which was priced at $114 million. This is up from only $20 million when he bought it in 2005, an annual increase of over 19%.

[3]Kuznets proposed this after observing the narrowing of income differentials in the mid-20th century. In retrospect, it is likely that rather than reflecting economic trends, the narrowing of income inequality in the mid-20th century reflected political changes, especially the turmoil around the Great Depression, the challenge of Soviet Communism, and World War II.

[4]Simon Kuznets, "Economic Growth and Income Inequality," *The American Economic Review* 45, no. 1 (1955): 1.

[5]Thomas Piketty, *Capital in the Twenty-First Century*, 2014.

[6]Claudia, Margo, Robert A Goldin, "The Great Compression: The Wage Structure in the United States at Mid- Century," *The Quarterly Journal of Economics* 107, no. 1 (1992): 1–34.

[7]A fractal figure is one where each part has the same structure as the whole. In this case, income is as unequally distributed within the top 10% or the top 1% as it is for the entire population:

[8]Internal Revenue Service, *The 400 Individual Income Tax Returns Reporting the Highest Adjusted Gross Incomes Each Year, 1992-2007*, 2012, http://www.irs.gov/pub/irs-soi/07intop400.pdf Table 1.

[9]This is, of course, the argument in Piketty, *Capital in the Twenty-First Century*.

[10]Much of this increase is due to inflation. In real terms, after taking account of rising prices, average wage and salary income rose by 1.4% and 0.8% respectively.

[11]Nonwage income rose by 6.7% per annum for other Americans.

[12]State and local taxes tend to be regressive, taking a larger share of income from lower than from higher incomes. After taking account of them, the richest Americans are now paying an even smaller share of their income in taxes.

[13]Samuel Bowles, Herbert Gintis, and Melissa Osborne Groves, eds., *Unequal Chances: Family Background and Economic Success* (New York; Princeton, N.J.: Russell Sage Foundation; Princeton University Press, 2005).

[14]These include attending schools with better teachers, more personalized instruction, and access to tutoring and other services as needed.

[15]These include manners of dress, speech, and deportment at social events.

[16]The "genetic lottery" not only includes one's personal genome and the way it influences health and appearance, but also the family into which one is born including their ability to help. It also includes one's ethnic background, color, and gender because these influence discrimination and economic success. And it includes the neighborhood into which one is born, because access to successful peers is associated with economic success and access to environmental toxins is associated with illness and economic failure.

[17]The *bottom decile* refers to the poorest 10% of people; those in the top decile are the wealthiest 10%.

[18]Barry P. Bosworth and Kathleen Burke, "Differential Mortality and Retirement Benefits in The Health And Retirement Study," The Brookings Institution, accessed April 21, 2014, http://www.brookings.edu/research/papers/2014/04/differential-mortality-retirement-benefits-bosworth.

[19]Goldin and Katz, *The Race between Education and Technology*; Robert B. Reich, *The Work of Nations: Preparing Ourselves for 21st Century Capitalism*, 1st Vintage Books ed (New York: Vintage Books, 1992); Thomas Lemieux, "Postsecondary Education and Increasing Wage Inequality," *The American Economic Review* 96, no. 2 (May 1, 2006): 195–99; Nicole M Fortin and Thomas Lemieux, "Institutional Changes and Rising Wage Inequality: Is There a Linkage?" *Journal of Economic Perspectives* 11, no. 2 (May 1997): 75–96, doi:10.1257/jep.11.2.75.

[20]Christopher Avery and Sarah Turner, "Student Loans: Do College Students Borrow Too Much—Or Not Enough?" *The Journal of Economic Perspectives* 26, no. 1 (January 1, 2012): 165–92 Figure 3.

[21]Joseph G. Altonji, Erica Blom, and Costas Meghir, "Heterogeneity in Human Capital Investments: High School Curriculum, College Major, and Careers," Working Paper (National Bureau of Economic Research, April 2012), http://www.nber.org/papers/w17985.

[22]This refers to the difference in income between the wealthiest and others. See Thomas Lemieux, "Increasing Residual Wage Inequality: Composition Effects, Noisy Data, or Rising Demand for Skill?," *The American Economic Review* 96, no. 3 (June 1, 2006): 461–98; Lemieux, "Postsecondary Education and Increasing Wage Inequality."

[23]Real income refers to dollar income adjusted for changes in the price of goods. Median earnings are the earnings of people at the middle of the income distribution where there are as many people earning more as earning less.

[24]Robert H Frank and Philip J Cook, *The Winner-Take-All Society: How More and More Americans Compete for Ever Fewer and Bigger Prizes, Encouraging Economic Waste, Income Inequality, and an Impoverished Cultural Life* (New York: Free Press, 1995).

[25]This is from data in Piketty and Saez spreadsheets from http://eml.berkeley.edu/~saez/.

[26]Michael J. Cooper, Huseyin Gulen, and P. Raghavendra Rau, Performance for Pay? The Relation Between CEO Incentive Compensation and Future Stock Price Performance, SSRN Scholarly Paper (Rochester, NY: Social Science Research Network, January 30, 2013), http://papers.ssrn.com/abstract=1572085; Philippe Jacquart and J. Scott Armstrong, "The Ombudsman: Are Top Executives Paid Enough? An Evidence-Based Review," *Interfaces* 43, no. 6 (December 1, 2013): 580–89, doi:10.1287/inte.2013.0705; Armstrong and Jacquart estimate that American CEOs are now paid ten-times what is needed to recruit and motivate the best corporate managers, J. Scott Armstrong Philippe Jacquart, "Business School Experts: High CEO Pay Hurts American Companies, Stockholders," Text. Article, FoxNews.com, (April 15, 2014), http://www.foxnews.com/opinion/2014/04/15/business-school-experts-high-ceo-pay-hurts-american-companies/.

[27]Richard B Freeman, *What Do Unions Do?* (New York: Basic Books, 1984).

[28]Rafael Gomez and Konstantinos Tzioumis, What Do Unions Do to Executive Compensation?, CEP Discussion Paper (Centre for Economic Performance, LSE, 2006), http://ideas.repec.org/p/cep/cepdps/dp0720.html; Qianqian Huang, et al., "The Effect of Labor Unions on CEO Compensation, "SSRN Scholarly Paper (Rochester, NY: Social Science Research Network, March 1, 2014), http://papers.ssrn.com/abstract=1571811.

[29]Freeman, What Do Unions Do?; William Gould, "Does the National Labor Board Work for Labor?" *WorkingUSA* 4, no. 4 (2001): 34–48; William B. Gould and IV, "The NLRB at Age 70: Some Reflections on the Clinton Board and the Bush II aftermath (National Labor Relations Board)(Forum: At 70, Should the National Labor Relations Act Be Retired?)," *Berkeley Journal of Employment and Labor Law* 26, no. 2 (2005): 309–18.

[30]A growing number of states and some localities have since enacted minimum wages at levels above the Federal rate. A good source is http://www.ncsl.org/research/labor-and-employment/state-minimum-wage-chart.aspx

[31]Economist and former Secretary of Labor under President Clinton.

[32]Reich, *The Work of Nations*.

[33]Timothy J. Minchin, *Empty Mills: The Fight against Imports and the Decline of the U.S. Textile Industry* (Lanham: Rowman & Littlefield Publishers, 2013).

[34]A classic expression of the meaning of rights and democracy in America and elsewhere is by an English scholar, T. H Marshall, *Citizenship and Social Class, and Other Essays* (Cambridge [Eng.: University Press, 1950); for a native American advocate of egalitarian democracy, see J. David Greenstone, *The Lincoln Persuasion: Remaking American Liberalism, Princeton Studies in American Politics* (Princeton, N.J: Princeton University Press, 1993); Garry Wills, *Lincoln at Gettysburg: The Words That Remade America* (New York: Simon & Schuster, 1992).

[35]Okun, *Equality and Efficiency, the Big Tradeoff*.

[36]This instrumental view of property, as a means to higher ends, has shaped American law since the early 19th century; see "The Sanctity of Property Rights in American History" (ScholarWorks@UMass Amherst), http://scholarworks.umass.edu/peri_workingpapers/30; Morton J Horwitz, *The Transformation of American Law, 1780-1860* (Cambridge, Mass.: Harvard University Press, 1977).

[37]Jeremy Bentham and Laurence J. Lafleur, *An Introduction to the Principles of Morals and Legislation* (New York: Hafner Pub. Co., 1948); John Stuart Mill, *Utilitarianism* (Raleigh, N.C.: Alex Catalogue), http://search.ebscohost.com/login.aspx?direct=true&scope=site&db=nlebk&db=nlabk&AN=1085956.

[38]Vilfredo Pareto, *Manual of Political Economy* (New York: A.M. Kelley, 1971); he developed an alternative approach where allocations are efficient if it is impossible to reallocate without hurting someone. Under this criterion, an allocation is efficient if one person has everything.

[39]John Rawls, *A Theory of Justice* (Cambridge, MA: Belknap Press of Harvard University Press, 1971).

[40]Under the Patient Protection and Affordable Care Act, administrative overhead is capped at 15% for large and 20% for small health insurance plans. In the first two years of the law, hundreds of plans had to pay refunds because their overhead expense exceeded the law's maximums.

[41]"IMF: Reducing Inequality With Transfers Increases Growth," *Demos*, accessed March 30, 2014, http://www.demos.org/blog/2/27/14/imf-reducing-inequality-transfers-increases-growth; Samuel Bowles and Herbert Gintis, "Productivity-Enhancing Egalitarian Policies," *International Labour Review* 134, no. 4/5 (1995).

[42]*Substitution effects* occur when people work less when tax increases lower wages because they substitute leisure and home production for the suddenly less remunerative paid work.

[43]*Income effects* occur when taxes lower people's income so they decide to seek more market work to compensate for their relative poverty.

[44]*A strong negative labor supply effect* of government programs would be where government welfare spending is associated with lower income growth and lower labor force participation rates.

[45]*Slacking* occurs when people respond to government welfare programs by working less, relying on the government and avoiding market work because of higher taxes.

11

LABOR MARKETS

THE DEMAND FOR LABOR: LABOR'S MARGINAL PRODUCT?

The neoclassical theory of income distribution begins with the *marginal product of labor* (MPL), the change in output when an additional worker is employed to fixed resources and capital inputs. The MPL declines because of the saturation of the fixed inputs. Because they have less stuff to work with or things to do, additional workers are less productive than their inframarginal predecessors. This means that the additional benefit that employers get from hiring workers falls when more workers are hired, since each additional worker produces less stuff.

Less stuff produced means less value for the employer from hiring additional workers. The revenue produced by adding one more worker, the value of their productivity, is the *marginal revenue product of labor* (or MRPL). At a fixed output price, the MRPL is the price times the marginal product of labor, or MRPL = P *MPL. Because the MPL is downward sloping the MRPL is also downward sloping, falling as more workers are hired. (If output prices fall with more output, as may be the case with a monopolist or a monopolistic competitor, then the MRPL will slope down even more sharply.)

Rational employers will hire workers where their productivity covers their wage; that is, where the MRP is greater or equal to the wage. In the examples given in Figures 11-1 to 11-3 and Table 11-1, the MPL and MRPL fall when additional workers are hired. For ex-

FIGURE 11-1
OUTPUT RISES WHEN MORE WORKERS ARE HIRED, BUT AT A DIMINISHING RATE

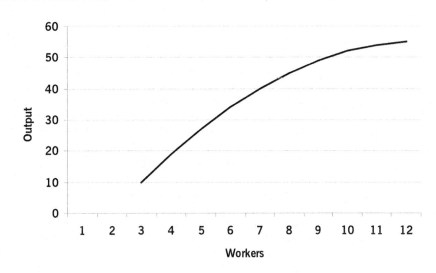

FIGURE 11-2
MARGINAL PRODUCT FOR PRODUCTION IN FIGURE 11-1

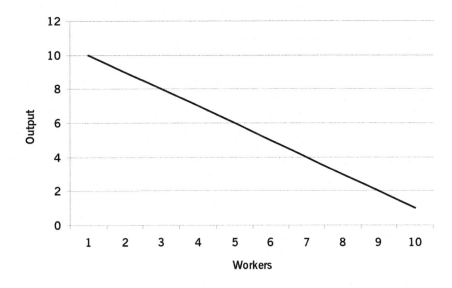

FIGURE 11-3
MARGINAL REVENUE PRODUCT, PRICE OF OUTPUT = $3 FOR MP IN FIGURE 11-2

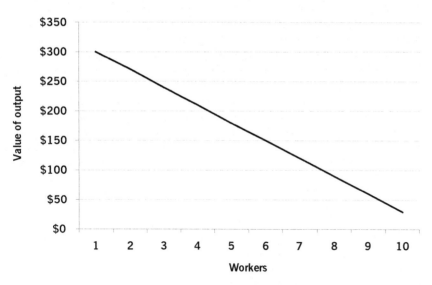

ample, at a price of $30 and a wage of $180, five workers will be hired (Table 11-1). If productivity increases or the price rises, it will pay employers to hire more workers (the MRPL curve shifts up). Fewer will be hired at lower productivity or output prices (the MRPL curve shifts down). For example, if the price stays the same, but productivity rises, the employers will hire seven workers. If productivity stays the same, but demand for the product falls and the price declines to $20, it will pay to hire only two workers (Table 11-1). At lower wages, more will be hired, and fewer will be hired at higher wages (see Figure 11-4).

Resting on the idea of diminishing marginal productivity, this approach depends on the same restrictive assumptions of the larger theory. It separates individual productivity from the efforts of others, neglecting the efficiency gains that Adam Smith identified as coming from the division of labor, and ignoring any role for management in promoting greater work efforts and building morale. It is timeless, neglecting the productivity gains that come from learning through experience. It is also time-limited because the marginal productivity of variable factors *only* declines when there is a fixed factor of production. Added to these problems, as a theory of aggregate demand for labor, the marginal productivity approach assumes Say's Law. In a Keynesian or a Marxian macroeconomics, the demand for labor is determined by the de-

TABLE 11-1
MARGINAL PRODUCTIVITY AND MARGINAL REVENUE PRODUCT

Workers	Total Output	Marginal Product	Regular Productivity		
			MRPL (P=$15)	MRPL (P=$20)	MRPL (P=$30)
0			MPL*15	MPL*20	MPL*30
1	10	10	$150	$200	$300
2	**19**	**9**	**$135**	**$180**	**$270**
3	27	8	$120	$160	$240
4	34	7	$105	$140	$210
5	**40**	**6**	**$90**	**$120**	**$180**
6	45	5	$75	$100	$150
7	49	4	$60	$80	$120
8	52	3	$45	$60	$90
9	54	2	$30	$40	$60
10	55	1	$15	$20	$30
11	55	0	$0	$0	$0

TABLE 11-2
MARGINAL PRODUCTIVITY AND MARGINAL REVENUE PRODUCT, HIGH PRODUCTIVITY

Workers	Higher Productivity				
	Total Output	Mar-ginal Product	MRPL (P=$15)	MRPL (P=$20)	MRPL (P=$30)
0			MPL*15	MPL*20	MPL*30
1	15	15	$225	$300	$450
2	28.5	13.5	$203	$270	$405
3	40.5	12	$180	$240	$360
4	51	10.5	$158	$210	$315
5	60	9	$135	$180	$270
6	67.5	7.5	$113	$150	$225
7	**73.5**	**6**	**$90**	**$120**	**$180**
8	78	4.5	$68	$90	$135
9	81	3	$45	$60	$90
10	82.5	1.5	$23	$30	$45
11	82.5	0	$0	$0	$0

TABLE 11-3
MARGINAL PRODUCTIVITY AND MARGINAL REVENUE PRODUCT, LOW PRODUCTIVITY

Workers	Lower Productivity				
	Output	Mar-ginal Product	MRPL (P=$15)	MRPL (P=$20)	MRPL (P=$30)
0			MPL*15	MPL*20	MPL*30
1	7	7	$105	$140	$210
2	13	6	$90	$120	$180
3	18	5	$75	$100	$150
4	22	4	$60	$80	$120
5	25	3	$45	$60	$90
6	27	2	$30	$40	$60
7	28	1	$15	$20	$30
8	28	0	$0	$0	$0
9	27	-1	($15)	($20)	($30)
10	25	-2	($30)	($40)	($60)
11	22	-3	($45)	($60)	($90)

FIGURE 11-4
LABOR DEMAND (MRPL) WITH DIFFERENT LEVELS OF PRODUCTIVITY

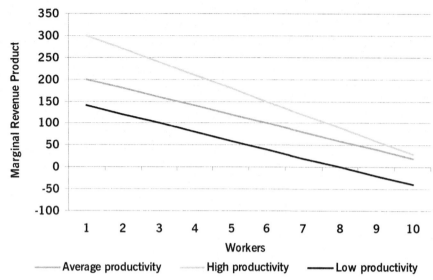

FIGURE 11-5
MORE WORKERS WILL BE HIRED AT ANY WAGE IF THE PRICE OF OUTPUT RISES

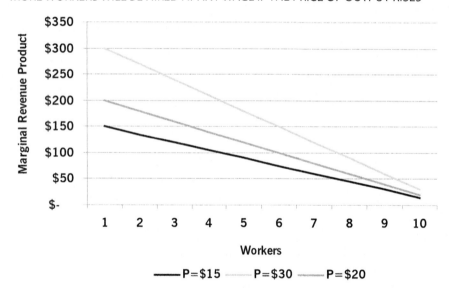

mand for products rather than by the productivity of individual workers.

The marginal productivity approach ties wages and employment levels to the contribution individual workers make to society through their productivity. There are two parts to this. First, the demand for labor is a derived demand that comes from the demand for the workers' products. Employment increases and wages rise when products become more desired and consumers are willing to pay more. Second, the demand for labor increases with productivity, rising when the worker produces more, and demand is higher for more productive workers. Demand will be stronger for more skilled and productive workers who have education and training, and for workers who are willing and able to work hard, because these workers will have a higher marginal productivity. Increases in the availability of complementary consumer goods raise the demand for labor. Cheaper gas, for example, raises the demand for auto workers. Similarly, increases in the supply of other productive factors, such as machinery and raw materials, raise wages and employment by making workers more productive and, therefore, more valuable to employers.

THE SUPPLY OF WAGE LABOR

When government agencies report on the supply of labor or the size of the labor force, they are not counting all productive workers. Instead, they count *labor* as *market work*[1] paid for with wages in a particular social relationship. In this, the government neglects much productive work. Cleaning you own house, caring for your own kids or those of your siblings, or even for your neighbors' kids as a favor—all this is not considered labor because it is not *market labor*. Only paid market work is counted as labor by the government. The government does not even consider paid work as labor if it is not mediated through the market. When they were young, we gave my children an "allowance" and expected that they would help manage the house by washing dishes, walking the dog, and doing laundry and some housecleaning. This is not *labor* according to the government because they cannot quit, be fired, or replaced; there is no market for their labor. One can say that by receiving a share of his spouse's pay, a stay-at-home spouse is "paid" an implicit wage for caring for the kids and the house. But this too doesn't count as labor, because "quitting" or "being fired" involves changing personal relationships beyond what happens when one changes a job.

MEASUREING THE LABOR FORCE

Every month, the Bureau of Labor Statistics (BLS) measures the labor force. The labor force includes civilians living outside institutions, sixteen years old and over. Excluded are persons under sixteen years of age, all persons confined to institutions such as nursing homes and prisons, and persons on active duty in the Armed Forces. The labor force includes the employed and the unemployed. The remainder—those without a job and not looking for one—are counted as "not in the labor force." These include full-time students, the retired, and those whose family responsibilities keep them out of the labor force. The labor force is measured using a monthly survey, the Current Population Survey of about 50,000 households. This survey is the source for the official count of the labor force and of the unemployment rate.

The official approach to the labor force is useful because it characterizes a particular part of the whole economy: the production and exchange of commodities through the use of wage labor. While this is a measure of the *capitalist* economy, it should not be confused with the entire production of useful things, as it leaves out home production and community work. Because this undercount of the economy was greater in earlier years (not only for the United States but for all market economies) when commodity production was less developed, the official definition of the labor force leads to an exaggerated measure of economic growth over time. It counts the transfer of production from nonmarket to market venues as growth in output.[2] Worse, because women do a disproportionate share of this unmeasured work, while men predominate in commodity production, the official definition of the labor force creates a gender bias. Perhaps it is not an accident that the official definition discounts the work of women, while exaggerating that of men.

What the government counts as the *labor force* is, therefore, the number of people with market jobs or actively looking for market employment. It is *not* a measure of the number of people engaged in productive activity. There are two ways, therefore, that higher pay can lead to an increase in "labor supply." The labor force can increase with higher wages if people decide to forgo leisure to work. Or, the labor force can increase when wages rise if people decide to substitute money and stuff bought with it for home production. At higher wages people may decide to forgo leisure, thinking that more money will allow them to increase their well-being more through buying things: higher wages, more market work, less fishing, and more eating in fish restaurants. They may also decide to provide more market labor because a higher income will allow them to replace home-produced goods and services, like home-baked bread and childcare, with those provided through the market. Both of these motives contribute to the *substitution effect* that associates higher pay with more labor. For example, if workers value their home production at $15/hour because that is how much they value their own childcare, meal preparation, and TV time, then they would refuse all job offers below this *reservation wage* because their home time is worth that much. Poorly paid workers then might prefer to stay home. But the labor supply and *labor force participation rate*[3] will increase as wages rise because rising wages will exceed more and more workers' *reservation wages*.[4]

LABOR SUPPLY:
SUBSTITUTION AND INCOME EFFECTS FOR MEN AND WOMEN

Over a very long time, market labor supply has been falling for men, with longer adolescence, earlier retirement, and fewer hours worked per year. This suggests that the income effect is stronger than the substitution effect for men. Women's labor force participation responds differently. Over time, more women work in the market and they work longer hours, suggesting that the substitution effect is greater than the income effect for women. The difference between men and women may reflect the greater involvement of women than men in nonmarket production where it becomes possible to substitute market work for nonmarket work when wages rise.

FIGURE 11-6

LABOR SUPPLY CURVES ARE BACKWARD-BENDING

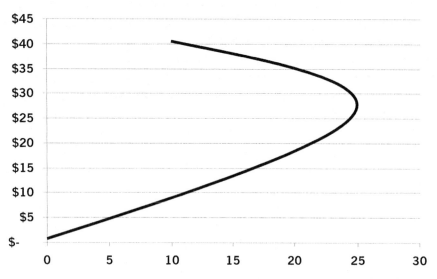

There is every reason to expect the supply of labor to the wage-labor market will increase as wages rise from low levels because more workers will find they can meet their needs better by working outside the home and buying products than making them themselves at home. At some higher income level, however, less labor will be offered because workers find that they would rather use their relatively scarce time to play with their more abundant toys. Eventually, people become so rich that they will choose not to do market work even at very high wages. This is called the *income effect*, where people decide that rather than work more, they will use higher wages and greater income to stay home to enjoy their money. (The income effect can be clearly observed when workers receive grants of money from parents or spouses or by winning the lottery.) The substitution effect dominates at low income levels, where low wages are below the reservation wage, while the income effect dominates at high wages where rich people withdraw from paid labor. Putting these two together gives a labor supply curve that is "backward bending," with labor supply less for both low and high wages.

The location and shape of the labor supply curve depend on factors shaping the reservation wage and the strength of the income effect. Less labor will be supplied at any wage if home production becomes more valuable, raising workers' reservation wage. This may be the case, for example, for parents of young children, for those who care for dependent elders, or for owners of large houses needing much cleaning. It will also be the case for those without access to commodity markets providing substitutes for home production, such as restaurants and laundry services. Higher nonwage income also lowers labor supply because higher incomes allow workers to buy more stuff to enhance their leisure. Lottery winners often leave the labor market, as do children with large inheritances and the spouses of high earners.

Cultural mores influence labor supply and people's willingness to substitute market commodities for home production. Many men shun cooking, cleaning, and child care as "woman's work," and try to obtain these services through the market by buying them, even if they have to pay for them by working themselves for relatively low wages. Others use their market pay to support a stay-at-home spouse. For men, this cultural norm lowers their reservation wage and increases labor supply. Recently, in the United States, there has been a decline in labor force participation for adult men. This may reflect increasing willingness by American men to perform these household services directly rather than buy them.[5] Nonetheless, the great majority of adult men have accepted a social role as breadwinners and providers, earning money to buy commodities, and supporting their families through wage work rather than the direct production of goods and services in the household.

American women have been more flexible, ready to produce or to buy home services. For this reason, there has been more elasticity in their labor supply. At low wage levels, many will remain at home, producing goods and services at home rather than buying them. When wages rise, however, women substitute store-bought products for their own home production, working for pay and using their money to buy commodities rather than producing them. At low wages, moms stay home and cook and care for their children. When wages go up, they feed their families take-out meals and buy daycare for their children. At the highest income levels, there are many women with a high earning capacity on their own but who are married to higher-income men. Many of these women reduce their market work to concentrate on raising children, supporting their husbands' careers.

IMPORTING WORKERS: IMMIGRATION AND LABOR SUPPLY

Immigration has also made the aggregate labor supply more elastic in the United States because immigration flows respond closely to wage and employment levels in the United States. Since the 19th century, immigration has been highly procyclical (definition?). Because immigrants come to the United States to earn money by working, more come when the economy is expanding and jobs are abundant, and fewer come during recessions when jobs are scarce. This tendency is magnified by the work of labor recruiters, including both businesses, transportation companies, and local recruiters. These are all more active in recruiting immigrants during business expansions when companies need workers. When employment drops, many immigrants leave the United States to return to their homelands and spend money earned in America. Because more immigrants come to the United States when employment rebounds and wages rise, the aggregate labor supply curve is more elastic than it would be without immigrants.

COMPENSATING DIFFERENTIALS

Not all jobs are the same. Some, like mine, a college professor, involve minimal physical hazard, can be done in comfortable offices, and have opportunities for pleasant self-expression. Honestly, I would do my work for free. Other jobs involve unsafe working conditions and bad smells. Given the same wage, everyone would choose my job rather than work cleaning septic systems or disposing of toxic nerve gas. Bad jobs that involve unsafe conditions or unpleasant work will, presumably, have higher reservation wages and less labor supply at any wage while good jobs with pleasant working conditions will have lower reservation wages and greater labor supply at any wage. When workers shun bad jobs and move to good ones, they shift the labor supply curve in for bad jobs, driving up wages (see Figure 11-7), while shifting it out and lowering wages for good jobs. Adam Smith identified these effects; the higher wages workers earn for dangerous and unpleasant jobs and those requiring training are now called *compensating differentials*. Smith identified five principal circumstances contributing to wage differentials. Two are most important for us: "the agreeableness or disagreeableness of the employments themselves" and "the easiness and cheapness, or the difficulty and expence [sic] of learning them."

We would expect to observe compensating differentials in a variety of occupations where the work is particularly unpleasant. The military, for example, provides hazardous duty pay for soldiers in combat zones, and many employers provide premium pay for night work and for work on weekends and holidays. In general, workers in occupations with high mortality rates, including policemen, fire fighters, and workers on oil rigs, are paid more for their jobs. Overall, around 2000, annual wages rose by about $5,000 for every 0.1% increase in the occupation's mortality rate. (This suggests that workers are valuing their lives at about $5,000,000. This is twice what the federal "Special Master"[6]

> ### ADAM SMITH ON "COMPENSATING DIFFERENTIALS"
>
> "The five following are the principal circumstances which, so far as I have been able to observe, make up for a small pecuniary gain in some employments, and counter-balance a great one in others: first, the agreeableness or disagreeableness of the employments themselves; secondly, the easiness and cheapness, or the difficulty and expense of learning them; thirdly, the constancy or inconstancy of employment in them; fourthly, the small or great trust which must be reposed in those who exercise them; and fifthly, the probability or improbability of success in them."

FIGURE 11-7

REDUCED LABOR SUPPLY FOR DANGEROUS TRADES LEADS TO COMPENSATING DIFFERENTIALS

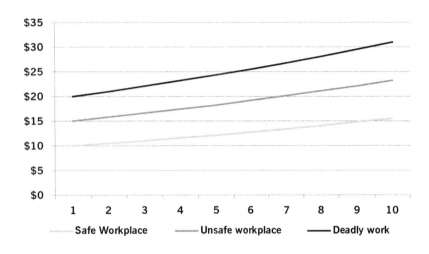

ECONOMIC ESTIMATES OF THE VALUE OF LIFE

Economists have estimated the value people put on reducing the risk of death from both consumer decisions about buying safer or less-safe products, and from the compensating differentials paid workers on more dangerous jobs. In present dollars, the estimates of the value of life cluster in the range from $3 million to $9 million. In practice, this means that to reduce the risk of dying in an automobile by 1 in 10,000, people will pay between $300 and $900. Similarly, people will accept a more dangerous job, e.g. one that increases the risk of dying in a year by 1 in 10,000, if they are paid $300 to $900 more. These estimates are of more than academic interest because they have been incorporated into government planning and in making decisions about how much to invest in greater safety, e.g. on highways, or in approving regulations to increase worker or consumer-product safety.

Sources: W. Kip Viscusi, *Fatal Tradeoffs: Public and Private Responsibilities for Risk*; and "Misuses and Proper Uses of Hedonic Values of Life in Legal Contexts."

awarded as compensation to families who lost a member in the terrorist attacks of September 11, 2001.)[7]

It is less clear whether Adam Smith is right that workers receive compensation for their time and expense of schooling. Some like being in school and an education is something that many value regardless of its economic rewards. It is true that educated workers and those who have had more training are paid more. Maybe it is a compensating differential for the time spent in training. A high school diploma is worth a 27% increase in wages over those earned by workers who did not finish high school, and the premium on a college degree is even higher. Compared with high school graduates, college graduates earn about 64% more. Continued schooling beyond college is also associated with higher earnings to compensate for the onerous burdens of graduate school. Of course, there may be other explanations for the education wage premium. After all, attending school might be viewed as pleasant consumption compared with work, and employers may be paying more for educated workers if education makes workers more productive or if it is seen as evidence of a productive character.

Contrary to Smith, there are few obvious wage compensations for taking difficult jobs. Unpleasant job characteristics, including lack of autonomy on the job, dirty working conditions, and non-fatal accident and disability rates, are rarely associated with higher wages. On the contrary, most "bad" jobs are also poorly paid. Workers who take these jobs may have few alternatives. Poor education, racial and ethnic discrimination, and poor employment histories may prevent them from getting better jobs. Low wages for bad jobs may also reflect ignorance. There is evidence for ignorance because quit rates are much higher in firms with high accident rates. It may be that workers take unsafe jobs unaware of their true nature and then quit when they learn more about them. It must be that bad jobs pay enough that they can attract new workers, but apparently not enough to hold workers after they discover how unsafe the job actually is. And, because these unsafe firms do not have to pay a wage premium to attract workers, they have little incentive to improve working conditions. On the contrary: these employers often view the high turnover, low morale, and low productivity as sufficient justification to keep wages low and not improve working conditions.[8]

The low pay in bad jobs may reverse the neoclassical direction of causality. Rather than low productivity leading to low wages, low wages in these jobs may be the cause of low productivity. Low productivity in these jobs may reflect the poor working conditions that lead to low worker morale and high turnover. Instead of productivity determining wages and working conditions, wages and conditions may determine productivity.

TRENDS IN LABOR SUPPLY: CHILDREN AND THE ELDERLY

Market labor supply depends on both the age and gender composition of the population and the readiness to supply market labor by people in any age and gender group. Over time, the rise in market labor supply in the United States has come from an increase in the readiness to supply labor more than a change in the population.

The population mix has changed both in ways that have increased labor supply and reduced it. On one side, because of improving health, rising life expectancy, and a decline in fertility that has lowered the number of younger Americans, more of the population is elderly: less than 4% of the population was over 60 years of age in 1850 compared with nearly 20% today. For the 19th century, an increase in the elderly population had little effect on the relative size of the labor force because the proportion with jobs fell little with age.[9] Private pensions and Social Security were established in part to help younger workers to find jobs by encouraging older workers to retire. They succeeded in this and the proportion of older Americans working fell dramatically into the 1990s, when fewer than 20% of America's elderly were working. Since then, however, the proportion of elderly Americans with jobs has risen, along with the elderly share of the population. Better health and a decline in the share of jobs requiring physical strength have contributed to the increase in labor force participation among the elderly. There have also been legal changes, the end of mandatory retirement and the Americans with Disability Act (1990), which requires that companies make reasonable accommodation to the needs of workers with disabilities.[10]

Balancing the rising numbers of the elderly, there are fewer and fewer children to support. In 1850, over 40% of the population was under fifteen years of age. The share of children is half that today. The elderly and the young are often added together to make a national "dependency ratio," or the share of the population who might be expected to depend on support from the rest. This ratio fell sharply over time, increasing the proportion of the population available to work, falling from 46% in the mid-19th century to 38% in 1990. For the twentieth century, the share of dependent children (under fifteen) in the population fell faster than the increase in the population who are dependent elderly (over age sixty). While the dependency ratio will probably increase over the next two decades, because of the rising elderly population, it will remain well below its 19th-century levels. Rapid immigration will help to hold down the dependency ratio. Because most immigrants come here to earn money, they are disproportionately of working ages. While helping to provide a good retirement for America's elderly, they will pay for schools and will help to care for her children.

Actor Harrison Ford at a recent Cannes film festival. Born in 1942, Ford continues to act and to make movies. He is scheduled to reprise his role as Han Solo in the forthcoming Star Wars movies, and he is rumored to be planning a new Indiana Jones—all after he turned 70.

TRENDS IN LABOR SUPPLY: MOTHERS

As with the demographics, there have been countervailing trends in the labor-force participation rate within different population groups. Among adult Americans, despite longer periods of schooling at the beginning of life and earlier retirement at the end, more have been working outside of the home. This is entirely due to rising participation by women in the paid labor force. Until 1950, most white American married-couple households were of a standard pattern with an employed husband and a stay-at-home wife/mother involved in home production. While a high proportion of African-American women worked outside the home, even after marriage, and many single white women worked outside the home, the great majority of adult women were white, married women who left the labor force upon marriage.[11]

Among white Americans, the intrafamily division of labor meant that men worked for pay and wives worked at home sharing in their husbands' earnings. This reflected a strong social convention that married women should stay home caring for husband and children. Failure to adhere to this convention, working in public, was a sign of marital distress or else of the husband's failure to earn enough to support his family honorably. Or else it was a sign of loose morals on the woman's part. Indeed, into the 1970s, the convention was supported by active public policy. Many companies, including many governments and public schools, maintained formal "marriage bars" where women received their layoff notice at their bridal shower.[12] Married women continued to earn money but they did it quietly through home-based activities such as running a boarding house or daycare, or home production, such as sewing dresses, raising vegetables, or assisting their husband's farm or home business. The gender division of labor was reflected in the choice of marriage partners. Women sought husbands able to support a family and a stay-at-home wife, while men sought younger partners

MARRIAGE BARS

The low labor force participation rate for married women reflected more than the free choice of individual wives and their husbands. Many businesses and public services, including public schools, would fire women when they got married and would not hire married women. These bars remained in effect in much of the United States well into the 1950s and beyond. Some were only struck down after the passage of the 1964 Civil Rights Act.

FIGURE 11-8
LABOR FORCE PARTICIPATION RATES, ADULTS, BY GENDER, 1890 TO 2012

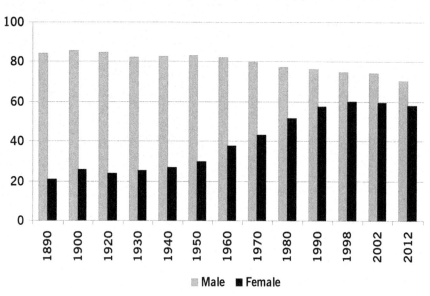

with more remaining childbearing years and more likely to be financially dependent. At the beginning of the 20th century, the average age at first marriage was four years higher for men (26) than for women (22). While the age at first marriage fell through the first half of the 20th century, the differential changed little. Men continued to marry younger women with less education.

Change began in the 1950s when the proportion of adult women working outside the home rose from under 30% to nearly 40% and the male labor force participation rate dropped to 82%. From there, the labor force participation rate for adult women has continued to increase, to almost 60% today, even while the proportion of adult men in the labor force has fall-en, to barely 70%. Changing labor force participation has paralleled a decline in marriage. Reversing long trends, since the 1970s, people are marrying later, and more are never marrying at all. After falling to 24 for men and 20 for women in the 1950s, the median age at first marriage has risen sharply, to 28 for men and 26 for women. The proportion of married couples in the United States has also been declining since the 1970s, until barely 60% of men and women ages 25-44 are living with a spouse.

Those who continue to get married are forming a different type of union than in the past. Marriage has been changing and increasingly is an alliance of *likes* rather than of *complements*. With the changing job market, it is increasingly common for both husbands and wives to work outside the home, and it is increasingly common for them to be working in similar occupations. In this sense, husbands and wives may be becoming substitutes, people who do the same things, rather than complements, or people who contribute different work in a family economy built around a division of labor. Instead of seeking economic complementarities through marriage, people buy those services through the market and look to get different types of support, emotional and cognitive, from a spouse. Since we are buying cooking, cleaning, and even child-rearing services in the market economy rather than getting them from a marriage partner, we look to a spouse for understanding and affection. We have symmetrical rather than differential marriages: people increasingly want a marriage partner who can understand us rather than one who will fill gaps in our own resume. More people now marry spouses similar in age and education (see Figure 11-9). Among college-educated men, the groom had more education than his bride in 60% of the marriages in 1970, and bride and groom had equal levels of education in 35% of the marriages. These ratios were nearly reversed in 2000 when bride and groom had equal levels of education in 57% of marriages and the groom was more educated in only 32% of marriages. Rather than

FIGURE 11-9
NARROWING EDUCATION DIFFERENCES, BRIDES AND GROOMS, 1970-2000

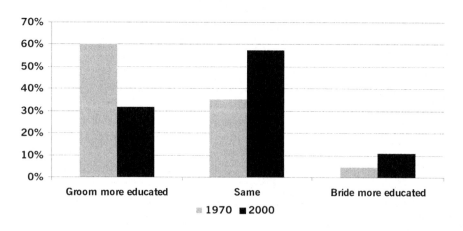

marrying to maximize household income through an alliance with a complementary producer, people marry for the companionship that comes from being with someone with similar goals and facing similar challenges. And if we cannot find that companionship, we do not marry.

TRENDS IN LABOR SUPPLY: HOURS WORKED

For much of the last century, the number of hours worked per worker has declined steadily. From an average of ten-hour work days for six-day weeks in the late 19th century, the work week fell steadily for the early 20th century. It began with a half day off on Saturdays after 1900 and then the spread of the eight-hour day after World War I. The work week fell to 40 hours in five eight-hour days during the Great Depression of the 1930s. It was made national policy by the New Deal's 1938 Fair Labor Practices Act, which mandated overtime pay for more than 40 work hours per week. In 1950, workers in the United States worked fewer hours than their counterparts in other advanced economies and, as late as 1979, they worked about the same hours as the average for other countries (see Table 11-4).

WHY SHORTER WORKWEEKS? WHY DID THE MOVEMENT STOP?

Historically employers and employees often agreed on very long workweeks because the economy was not very productive (by today's standards) and people had to work long hours to earn enough money to feed, clothe, and house their families. Economic progress and rising productivity have contributed to the long-term decline in the length of the workweek by allowing workers to "buy" more leisure time; the number of hours worked falls with national per capita income except in the United States where the work year is about 150 hours longer than would be expected on the basis of national income per capita (see Table 11-4). Shorter workweeks were also the result of collective action by organized labor which campaigned to reduce competition for work by reducing the workweek. Shorter workdays were among the first goals of organized labor. The first national general strikes, May Day 1886 in the United States and May Day 1890 in Europe, were called to demand an eight-hour workday. Throughout the world, pressure from unions and strikes combined with government regulation led to dramatic reductions in the workweek around the World Wars and during the Great Depression. The continued strength of organized labor and socialist political movements probably contributes to the strength of shorter hours movements outside the United States; labor's weakness in the United States since the 1970s may explain the stagnation in the workweek here.

Since the beginning of the labor and socialist movements, one of the primary goals has been to reduce the workweek. In 1863, for example, Ira Steward, a Boston machinist known as the father of the eight-hour day, proposed a resolution to the convention of the National Union of Machinists and Blacksmiths saying "From East to West, from North to South, the most important change to us as working men … is a permanent reduction to eight of the hours exacted for each day's work." The campaign for shorter workdays was meant to improve living standards by providing more leisure and family time. It was also intended to raise wages by reducing labor supply.

This steady reduction in work hours slowed after the 1930s and ended completely in the 1970s. Since 1990, it has reversed and Americans have become relative workaholics compared with people in other advanced economies, where work hours have continued to decline. European workers now regularly work fewer than 35 hours per week, in addition to enjoying 35 or more vacation and holiday days per year. By contrast, the American work week has drifted up since the 1970s, reversing a century of decline (see Table 11-4). From 1870-1979, on average the number of hours worked in a year fell by over 1100 hours, or by nearly four minutes per day. Each year, for over a century. Since then, while the work year has continued to fall elsewhere, there has been little change in the American work year. According to the most recent data from the Organization for Economic Cooperation and Development (the OECD), workers in the United States in 2012 worked fewer hours than did their counterparts in some relatively poor countries, fewer than workers in Mexico, Poland, or Russia, for example, but more than workers in most affluent countries.

Red beach on Santorini in the Mediterranean (technically the Aegean), crowded with Europeans who are not working.

TABLE 11-4

ANNUAL HOURS WORKED, THE UNITED STATES AND OTHER ADVANCED CAPITALIST ECONOMIES, 1870-2000

Country	1870	1950	1979	2004	Per capita income (PCY) 2004	1870-1979	1979-2004	PCY/Hours 2004
Australia	2945	1838	1904	1816	$31,231	-9.6	-3.5	$17.20
Canada	2964	1967	1832	1751	$31,395	-10.4	-3.2	$17.93
Finland	2945	1926	1837	1736	$30,594	-10.2	-4.0	$17.62
France	2945	1926	1806	1520	$29,554	-10.4	-11.4	$19.44
Germany	2941	2316	1969	1443	$28,605	-8.9	-21.0	$19.82
Italy	2886	1997	1722	1585	$27,699	-10.7	-5.5	$17.48
Japan	2945	2166	2126	1789	$29,664	-7.5	-13.5	$16.58
New Zealand	n/a	n/a	n/a	1826	$24,498	n/a	n/a	$13.42
Norway	2945	2101	1514	1363	$38,765	-13.1	-6.0	$28.44
Spain	n/a	n/a	2022	1799	$25,582	n/a	-8.9	$14.22
Sweden	2945	1951	1513	1585	$30,361	-13.1	2.9	$19.16
Switzerland	2984	2144	n/a	1556	$33,678	n/a	n/a	$21.64
UK	2984	1958	1815	1669	$31,436	-10.7	-5.8	$18.84
United States	2964	1867	1845	1824	$39,732	-10.3	-0.8	$21.78
Average	**2949**	**2013**	**1825**	**1662**	**30914**	**-10.4**	**-6.8**	**$18.83**

Source: Maddison, *Dynamic Forces*, 270-71; *State of Working America*, 2002/3, 425; *OECD Factbook*, 2006.

Note: The last two columns give the annual change in hours worked over the period. Note that the reduction in annual hours worked in the United States 1870-1979 is around the average for all countries, but Sweden was the only country besides the United States that had an increase in hours worked 1979-2000, although to a level over 250 hours less than the United States

The average work year in the United States is now eighty hours more than the work year in Canada, 136 hours more than in the United Kingdom, 311 hours more than in France, and 393 more than in Germany. Workers in the United States work 409 hour per year more than do workers in the Netherlands, the equivalent of ten weeks of lost vacation time.[13]

MARKET SUPPLY AND DEMAND FOR LABOR WHERE MRP AND SUPPLY CURVES INTERSECT: A HAPPY TALE, WOULD THAT IT WERE TRUE

In the neoclassical model, wages and employment are set at the intersection of the sum of the marginal revenue product curves for all producers, the market labor demand curve, and the sum of the individual labor supply curves, the market labor supply curve. Unemployment results when wages are raised above this equilibrium and the unemployed compete for jobs, driving down wages. Similarly, if wages are below the equilibrium, employers will try to hire more workers and will bid up the wage. In Figure 11-10, market competition will set wages at $75 with six workers hired.

Market competition will protect workers as a group from exploitation and will ensure that each is paid his or her marginal revenue product, the output of the last worker hired.[14] Any attempt by employers to maintain wages below the equilibrium will be defeated by competition among capitalists to attract labor. This competition will protect workers from exploitation by bidding the wages of underpaid workers up to their fair value, their marginal revenue product. Workers facing discrimination because of their race, religion, or gender will not be paid less than their contribution to output because they can sell their services to another employer until they are paid their marginal revenue product. Competition will also protect employers. Since no one can force an employer to pay more than that worker's marginal revenue product, to keep their jobs individual workers will be forced to settle for a fair wage equal to their productivity. Similarly, attempts by unions or even governments to keep wages above the equilibrium will lead to unemployment which will eventually drive down wages.

In the orthodox neoclassical model, the only way to raise wages and to increase employment is to make workers more productive or their product more desirable, persuading consumers to buy more at any price. Wages will rise if workers become more productive through training, or the addition of more machinery or resources. They will also rise if their product becomes more desirable. Wages will fall if there is an increase in labor supply, either because reservation wages fell, there was a decline in wealth, or a population increase drives more people into the labor market.

FIGURE 11-10
LABOR SUPPLY AND DEMAND, NEOCLASSICAL

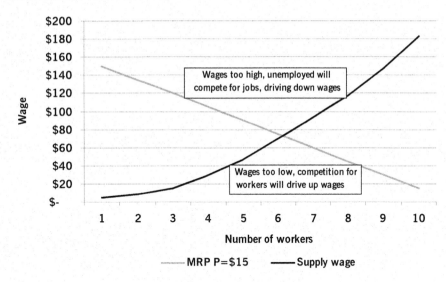

From this perspective, if labor markets are left alone, without government, union, or other collective regulation, they will help to maximize society's welfare by precisely balancing workers' readiness to work with their productivity. Market competition will also ensure that wages are fair for the harshness of the work. Competition will ensure that workers are compensated for investments they make in their own training and for harsh working conditions, because these will shift up the labor supply schedule, raising wages. If consumers want to have products that require dangerous working conditions, like off-shore oil or underground coal, they will have to pay enough to compensate the workers involved. As well as compensating the workers involved, this discourages consumers from buying products that require such working conditions, and it encourages employers to ameliorate them.

IMMIGRATION AND THE LABOR SUPPLY TO THE UNITED STATES

Since Columbus, the Americas have been a place of destination for Europeans and others. With abundant land stolen from the native peoples, the United States needed more people to produce wealth. For centuries, a large majority of the new workers were brought here as indentured servants or slaves. Throughout our history, however, millions more have come to the United States seeking refuge from hunger, discrimination, and oppression. Whether voluntary, coerced, or some combination of the two, immigrant workers have not only peopled America; they built it.

Immigration has always been a controversial political issue as some native-born resent the arrival of new Americans speaking different languages, practicing different religions, and with different customs. In recent years, there has been more controversy, especially because immigration has increased and immigrants comprise a rising share of the labor force and population. This marks a return to older patterns and earlier times when immigrants were a larger share of the population (see Figure 11-11). Immigrant labor performed many of the essential, and hardest, tasks in American economic development. Africans cultivated the tobacco and cotton that financed the American republic; Irish immigrants, fleeing famine in their home country, built the canals and western railroads of the 19th century; Chinese immigrants built the western railroads and gold mines. With relatively little social life, often without family, immigrants were ideal workers. Ready to work hard to gain money, they would put in long hours and accept risky work. Without family connections and with little claim on public or political support, they were also relatively easy to exploit. This was most clearly the case with African slaves but it applied to others

FIGURE 11-11
IMMIGRANTS SHARE OF POPULATION, ANNUAL IMMIGRATION PER 1,000

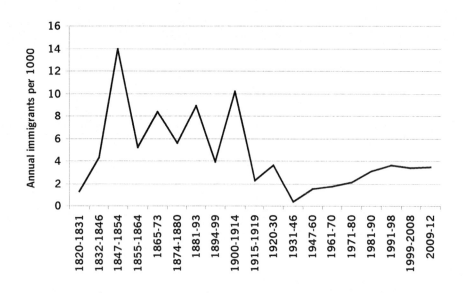

with little bargaining leverage, whether Chinese indentures, the desperate Irish, or Mexicans today fleeing the collapse of their agricultural economy.

Immigrants have come to the United States from all over the world. Migration patterns have changed over time to reflect how the margin of capitalist development moved east and south from its origins in England, northern France, and the Netherlands to Germany, southern and eastern Europe, and now Asia and Latin America. The first massive wage of immigrants were Africans and indentured English brought to the Americas by the Dutch, English, and French to work in the sugar plantations, mostly of the Caribbean, and to grow tobacco and the other staple crops of the American South. The Africans were transported by Europeans who had established military supremacy through the use of guns and powerful warships. Indentured servants included as many as 70% of the white migrants to the English colonies in the early colonial era. Some were looking to advance themselves. Many, however, came from rapidly changing agricultural and industrial districts of East Anglia where farmers had been dispossessed of direct claims on the land and were forced to seek their own and their children's fortunes elsewhere.

In general, labor has been the least mobile productive input. This is because workers are embedded in communities, with families, friends, and social lives attached to particular places and societies. Migration is an unusual thing and, where it is not compelled as in the case of the African slaves, it usually requires a major economic or social disruption before people will pick up and leave. Historically, the spread of capitalist relations has been such a disruption because it has torn apart traditional bonds that have connected neighbors with each other, farmers and serfs with their landlords, and workers with the means of production. Immigration levels have jumped in areas where capitalist relations spread. In the 1840s, for example, migration to the United States jumped not only from Ireland, with the potato famine, but also from Germany, where feudal ties were supplanted by capitalist relations after the French Revolution's spread across the Rhine. By loosening the ties binding workers to the land and to their lords, the spread of capitalist property relations led more workers to seek refuge and opportunity in the Americas. Following economic change, immigration moved south and east in Europe, from England to Germany to Poland, Italy, Greece, and Russia.[15] Rather than a phenomenon of the poorest agricultural and domestic

FIGURE 11-12
CHANGING SOURCES OF IMMIGRATION, THE UNITED STATES

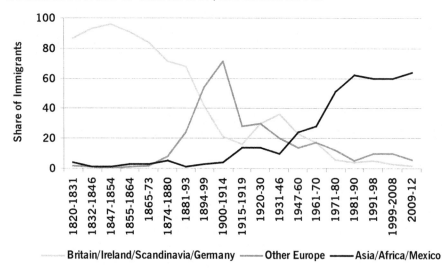

workers, it was more common among middling workers and in countries beginning to experience economic growth.

Immigration was facilitated in the later 19th century by the expansion of international trade in several ways. First, merchant ships bringing heavy and bulky produce from America to Europe had empty space on their return trip for immigrants. Second, grain and meat brought from the United States and the other European settlements (e.g., Argentina, Australia) drove down European agricultural prices, forcing farmers to seek better opportunities elsewhere and reducing the demand for agricultural workers. American agricultural exports also led to new government policies that pushed migrants out of European countries. International trade undermined the economic position of established elites, aristocratic landowners, and governments, who responded with xenophobic and repressive policies that drove minority groups to flee to America. This was the case, for example, in Russia, where the Czar sought to divert attention from economic distress by campaigning against minority groups. This led to anti-Jewish pogroms, driving Jews from Russia and Poland to America.

Like other forms of international trade, labor migration depends on the state of international relations. Migration falls during major wars, such as World War I, when countries prevent citizens from leaving to maintain their labor force and manpower for their armed forces. In the United States, fear of foreign sedition and the spread of *Bolshevism*[16] contributed to the enactment of restrictive legislation in 1921 and 1924 limiting immigration, especially from southern and eastern Europe. The average annual number of migrants entering the United States in the 1920s was less than half the average of the years before World War I.

Immigration would revive with the liberalization of laws after 1965 and the expansion of international trade. But the locus

HAS SERGEY BRIN LOWERED WAGES? HOW ABOUT VINOD KHOSLA?

Co-founder and technology president of Google, Sergey Brin was born in Russia and came to the United States when he was six. With Larry Page, he founded Google, one of the most successful companies in the world. He is one of over a dozen immigrants in the top management of Google. Migrant engineering and other talent helps provide jobs for millions of American workers.

Vinod Khosla father was in the Indian Army. He came to the United States in his early 20s to do his Masters (in Biomedical Engineering) at Carnegie Mellon University. He then earned an MBA at Stanford in 1980. Shortly after, in 1982, he founded Sun Microsystems.

Sergey Brin (left) and Vinod Khosla (right).

of migration changed again, moving with the frontier of capitalist expansion to the south and east. In the 1990s, when more people came to the United States than in any previous decade, only 5% of the migrants came from the British Isles and northwest Europe, and only 10% came from southern and eastern Europe. The rest, a flow equal to the annual migrant flow in any previous decade in American history, came from Asia, Africa, Mexico, and the rest of Latin America.

Migration changes American culture. In the 19th century, German immigrants brought lager beer to America, Russian Jews brought bagels, and Africans brought music. Recent immigrant groups have brought sushi, nachos, and saag paneer. Salsa now outsells ketchup in American stores, and cricket has gained new popularity, especially among the growing population of Americans of south Asian descent. Soccer stadiums are now filled, the result of decades of youth soccer but also of migration from football-loving countries in Latin America and Asia. Maybe, someday, one of these youth soccer players will lead a U.S. team to a World Cup victory.

Immigration has given the United States violinist Ashot Tigranyan and actress Selena Gomez.[17] While Tigranyan has helped to promote chamber music as one of the country's premier violinists, Gomez, one of Disney's teen starlets, has used her talent and international appeal to advance the American TV and movie industry. Both also increase the supply of musicians and actresses and may, therefore, drive down wages. Both effects are important in understanding the economics of immigration.

Because most immigrants come here to make money by working, and the population of immigrants is highly concentrated in working ages, immigration shifts out the supply of labor. Immigrants are also particularly responsive to economic conditions. Immigration declines when there are few

FIGURE 11-13
LABOR SUPPLY AND DEMAND WITH IMMIGRATION:
IMMIGRANTS ARE LABOR SUBSTITUTES

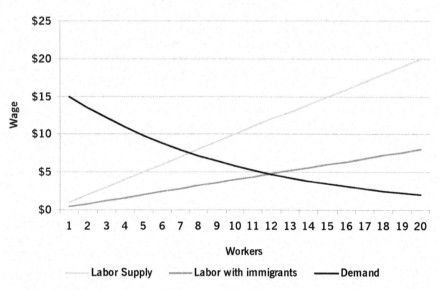

FIGURE 11-14
LABOR SUPPLY AND DEMAND WITH IMMIGRATION: IMMIGRANTS ARE LABOR
COMPLEMENTS

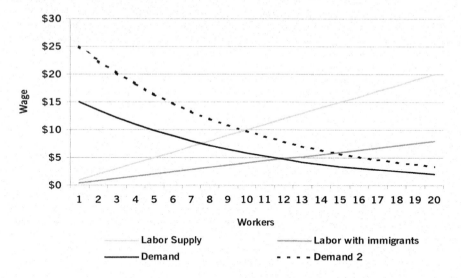

jobs and falling wages, and increases sharply when conditions are better. In this way, immigration makes the labor supply more elastic with respect to wages. In Figure 11-13, I present a traditional view of the effect of immigration on wages. Immigrants come looking for work and shift the labor supply curve out, driving down wages by increasing the number of workers at any wage.

But there is another view, presented in Figure 11-14. Here, immigrants increase both the supply and the demand for labor, raising wages even while increasing supply. This is the case where immigrant workers provide *complements* for native-born (or other immigrant) workers. Immigrant talent includes not only the engineers and doctors who staff so many American high tech and life sciences businesses, but also the marketing and design talent needed to make American businesses competitive in a world economy. Immigrants provide specialized engineering or artistic talent, but they also provide common labor that is also needed to make the United States economy flourish, including such tasks as harvesting crops, maintaining golf courses, cleaning restaurant dishes, and maintaining offices. These tasks could be performed by workers born in the United States, as is implied in Figure 11-13, but when they are performed by immigrants they increase the demand for other American workers with complementary jobs, as is suggested in Figure 11-14.

The evidence shows that in recent times the complementarity between native-born and immigrant workers has been more important than any substitution, and immigration has increased wages for native-born workers modestly (by about $4/week) even while lowering wages somewhat for the foreign born. This probably understates the positive effect of immigration on native-born Americans because immigration increases the quality and range of consumer products available.

DISCUSSION QUESTIONS

What is the "Marginal Product of Labor" (MPL)? What is the "Marginal Product of Capital" (MPK)?

Why are these downward sloping? Are they always downward sloping?

What might shift out the MPL and make labor more productive? What might shift out the MPK and make capital more productive?

What is the "Marginal Revenue Product of Labor" (MRPL)? Why is it downward sloping?

What happens to the MRPL if labor becomes more productive?

What are "income effects" and "substitution effects" on labor supply?

What do people do when they are not working for pay? How might differences in gender roles at home contribute to differences in the labor supply, the substitution and income effects, of men and women?

Why might the labor supply curve be backward bending? Do you think that labor supply increases indefinitely with higher wages for anyone?

What are "compensating differentials"? Name five conditions producing compensating differentials according to Adam Smith?

If workers are paid compensating differentials, do you believe that there should be government safety regulations at work? Could these be justified even if workers are paid more for hazardous work? (Are there externalities when workers are injured on the job?)

Do you believe that workers are paid full compensation for hazardous work? What circumstances might prevent them from being paid compensating differentials?

What has happened to the labor supply of different demographic groups: children, mothers, senior citizens. How has social policy shaped labor supply?

How have the sources of immigrants changed over the past 300 years?

What leads people to come to the United States?

Do immigrants lower wages? Can they? Must they?

ENDNOTES

[1]The alternative to viewing labor as market work is to view it as anything that people do that is useful for themselves or others.

[2]This point was noted by earlier economists, see Richard T. Ely, *An Introduction to Political Economy* (New York, Cincinnati: Hunt & Eaton; Cranston & Stowe, 1892); a study that attempts to correct for the bias is Nancy, Wagman, Barnet Folbre, "Counting Housework: New Estimates of Real Product in the United States, 1800-1860," *Journal of Economic History* 53, no. 2 (1993).

[3]The labor force participation rate as defined by the government is the share of the population with jobs or looking for a paid job.

[4]The reservation wage is the minimum wage people demand before they will take market work.

[5]While men are performing more of the childcare and other nonmarket work, it is still unusual for men to leave the labor force to care for their family. Only about 1% of married-couple households have a stay-at-home dad whose primary responsibility is caring for the household and its children. By contrast, about 30% of these households have a stay-at-home mother; Richard Morin, "Study: More Men on the 'Daddy Track,'" Pew Research Center, accessed June 18, 2014, http://www.pewresearch. org/fact-tank/2013/09/17/more-men-on-the-daddy-track/.

[6]After the attacks on September 11, 2001, the Federal government established a Victim's Compensation Fund to help those who lost family members. Attorney Kenneth Feinberg was appointed the Special Master to administer the fund. For his experiences, see Kenneth R. Feinberg, *What Is Life Worth? The Unprecedented Effort to Compensate the Victims of 9/11* (New York: Public Affairs, 2005).

[7]W. Kip Viscusi, *The Value of Life: Estimates with Risks by Occupation and Industry* (Harvard Law School: Harvard: John M. Olin Center for Law, Economics, and Business, May 2003), http://www. law.harvard.edu/programs/olin_center/papers/pdf/422.pdf; W. Kip Viscusi, *Fatal Tradeoffs: Public and Private Responsibilities for Risk* (New York: Oxford University Press, 1992).

[8]Further evidence of the effect of ignorance is that unionized firms are much safer and also pay higher compensating differentials. It appears that the union provides memory for workers, maintaining knowledge of accidents.

[9]The proportion of elderly Americans in the labor force is overstated somewhat for the earlier period because it is based on census records that do not record whether someone is currently working but only whether they have an "occupation." It is likely that at least some older Americans continued to report an occupation even though they did not have, and were not looking for, work. Alicia H, Sass, Steven A, Hutchens, Robert, Manchester, Joyce Munnell, "The Labor Supply of Older American Men/Comments on 'The Labor Supply of Older American Men' by Alicia H. Munnell and Steven A. Sass," Federal Reserve Bank of Boston. Conference Series, no. 52 (2007): 83–157,366,368–70; Roger L Ransom and Richard Sutch, "The Labor of Older Americans: Retirement of Men On and Off the Job, 1870-1937," *The Journal of Economic History* 46, no. 1 (1986): 1–30; Susan B, Sutch, Richard Carter, "Myth of the Industrial Scrap Heap: A Revisionist View of Turn-of-the-Century American Retirement," *The Journal of Economic History* 56, no. 1 (1996): 5; John C Henretta, "UNIFORMITY AND DIVERSITY: Life Course Institutionalization and Late-Life Work Exit," *The Sociological Quarterly* 33, no. 2 (1992): 265–79.

[10]The elderly work less because of both physical infirmity and the income effect of retirement pensions, including social security. Because of improving health among the elderly, more of them are working. While only 17% of men over age 65 had jobs in 1995, and 9% of women, the proportion with jobs in 2009 was 22% for men and 13% for women. A majority of the elderly workers are part time, but nearly half of men and one third of women are working full time. Anne Shattuck, *Older Americans Working More, Retiring Less*, Issue Brief (Carsey Institute, Summer 2010), http://www.carseyinstitute. unh.edu/publications/IB_Shattuck_Older_Workers.pdf.

[11]Claudia Dale Goldin, *Understanding the Gender Gap: An Economic History of American Women* (New York: Oxford University Press, 1990); Francine D. Blau and Marianne A. Ferber, *The Economics of Women, Men, and Work* (Englewood Cliffs, N.J.: Prentice-Hall, 1986); Claudia Dale Goldin and National Bureau of Economic Research, *Marriage Bars: Discrimination against Married Women Workers, 1920s to 1950s* (Cambridge, MA (1050 Massachusetts Avenue, Cambridge, Mass. 02138): National Bureau of Economic Research, 1988).

[12]In some cases, married women were allowed to hold jobs until they became pregnant. This was the case in most public school districts through the 1960s. The requirement that pregnant women resign their teaching positions was challenged in court but was overturned only in 1978 when the Pregnancy Discrimination Act was enacted to amend Title VII of the 1964 Civil Rights Act, extending the prohibition against gender-based discrimination to include pregnancy. Restrictions on the employment of pregnant women continue to be the subject of litigation into the 21st century.

[13]Data for work hours in all OECD members at http://stats.oecd.org/Index.aspx?DataSetCode=ANHRS

[14]This is John Bates Clark's answer to the question of whether capitalism is built on fraud; John Bates Clark, *The Distribution of Wealth; a Theory of Wages, Interest and Profits* (New York, London: The Macmillan company; Macmillan & Co., Ltd., 1899).

[15]Later in the 20th century, immigration to the United States would come from Asian and Latin American countries experiencing disruptive economic growth and change.

[16]Led by Lenin, the Bolsheviks were the faction of the Russian Socialist movement that staged the Revolution in 1917 that established the Union of Soviet Socialist Republics (USSR).

[17]The Armenian-born Mr. Tigranyan came here from Russia in 1989. Ms. Gomez was born in the United States. Her father came to the United States from Guadalajara, Jalisco, Mexico, and her mother is of Italian descent.

12

REAL LABOR MARKETS IN ACTION

EFFICIENCY WAGES AND PRODUCTIVITY

The neoclassical theory of the labor market separates demand and supply by assuming that workers have a determined output that is independent of their wage. This output is the maximum amount that the employer would pay, and, in a competitive environment, it is also the minimum amount that the worker would accept. In this orthodox approach, productivity and wages are separable for individuals and for the group. A worker's productivity depends on that worker's characteristics, as well as the technology used and the available machinery and resources, but is not affected by their wages nor by the community, the workplace organization, except the factor ratios and technology. Engineering productivity drives wages. No compa-

The Ford Model T

ny would pay workers more than the value of their product and, if a company tried to hire workers for less, others would swoop in to get that worker at a bargain rate. The policy implication is clear: if workers want higher wages or more employment they need to become more productive either by improving their training or by providing their employer with better technology or more machinery. Similarly, if workers lack work, it is because they are not productive enough to earn the prevailing wage. Again, the orthodox solution is either to lower wages or to raise productivity by improved training or investment in better technology and machinery. The politics are clear: conservative solutions to labor market distress involve lower wages, or encouraging investment in new machinery and better technology, while liberal solutions are to encourage investments in worker training.

Not only does this analysis discount any role for management, it is contrary to the way labor markets operate. Companies do not buy a determined output when they hire workers; they hire *potential output* when they buy time from their workers. Companies employ workers for a set time during which they try to get them to produce output. They may hire workers with clear expectations for how much they will produce, but how much they get is not determined in the market where they hire labor time, but through a labor process within the company. Rather than being defined when workers are hired, output is determined by a pro-

FIGURE 12-1

LABOR MARKETS, ORTHODOX APPROACH WHERE PRODUCTIVITY DETERMINES WAGES

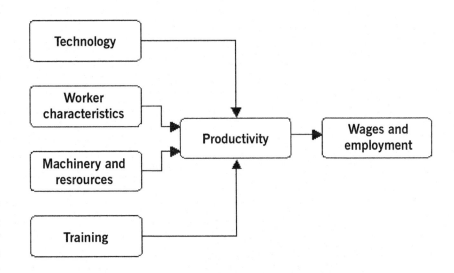

cess of conflict and accommodation at work. And that is where management gets involved, encouraging, prodding, supervising, and, if necessary, terminating workers to get them to work harder and to produce more output during any time period. For their part, workers seek longer breaks, hang out at the water cooler, and check Facebook at work. They hope to squeeze out time for themselves while also lowering the boss' expectations. The conflict between workers and managers over the workload creates a role for management, for human relations departments, and for line supervisors. Wages are one tool employers have to encourage productivity. It is odd to ignore it.

Work making Ford's Model T was both difficult and monotonous. But after the announcement of the $5/day, the company had no trouble attracting or keeping workers.

THE FORD STORY

In December 1913, Henry Ford had a problem. Business was booming. His Model Ts were selling as fast as he could make them and his assembly line was a wonder of the world, producing a car every 24 seconds. Things were not going so well in his factory, however. Not only was there rising worker discontent and campaigns for union organization, but productivity was stagnant despite his company's technological wonders. The problem was that Ford had invented a model of organizational efficiency that ignored a main factor: his human employees. His workers hated their jobs and their resistance threatened Ford's ability to maintain production and profitability. In 1913, the annual turnover rate at his new Highland Park facility was 370%. (That is, 370 workers were hired that year for every hundred positions at the plant.) Job tenure averaged under four months. Every time a worker came late, failed to show up for work, or quit, it disrupted production, forcing Ford to maintain a staff of redundant fill-in workers and a large staff of recruiters and trainers. And too many of his workers were new hires with little experience at their work. High quit rates also undermined efforts to maintain work discipline—workers disliked the jobs so much that they were almost indifferent to being fired. Absenteeism averaged over 10% a day, but it was hard to penalize workers for on-the-job drinking and sloppy work because they were so ready to

quit. There was enough unemployment in the Detroit area that Ford had no trouble attracting new workers, and his daily wage of about $2.50 was competitive. The problem was to get these workers to show up and work after they were hired, and before they quit.

To deal with rampant and disruptive absenteeism and quitting, Ford tried a novel approach. Starting in January 1914, he offered to double unskilled wages to $5 a day, provided that workers remained employed for at least six months and maintained good status with the company's new "sociology" department, which would visit their homes to check for "good morals," including cleanliness, use of English, and abstention from drink and gambling. Despite the intrusiveness of this policy, workers were excited by the opportunity to earn high wages. Between March 1913 and March 1914, the quit rate fell by 87%, absenteeism dropped by 75%, and discharges fell by 90%. Drinking and gambling also declined sharply.[1]

Ford's $5/day has been identified as an example of *efficiency wages*,[2] where the level of productivity depends on the wage rate rather than wages being determined by productivity. As such, efficiency wage theory offers an alternative to the neoclassical vision of the labor market. Instead of treating workers according to some pre-existing level of productivity and disciplining them to prevent slothfulness, efficiency wage theory suggests that workers who are paid well for their productivity will rise to the occasion and be more productive. It is part of a larger vision of social life that says that people are products of their treatment and we get back from others how we treat them. Respect begets respect.

Instead of hiring workers like machines with a set value, a company that pays efficiency wages sets wages for workers within the company at a higher rate than would be paid outside, a rate enough higher that it makes the job worth keeping. This requires a certain discipline because efficiency wage companies pay their workers more than would be required to replace the company's workforce. But because the pay is higher, it becomes justified, and earned, by workers who become more productive than their possible replacements because they want to keep their jobs. One piece of the efficiency wage puzzle is that companies that pay more can pick and choose the best workers. Efficiency wages allowed Ford to sort his workers, selecting only the best. The rest is that the higher wages make workers more productive. By paying his workers more than they could make elsewhere, Henry Ford made them more productive because they wanted to keep their good jobs. And they wanted to protect the company that was paying them well.

By linking high wages with *job tenure*[3] and good behavior, Ford and other high-wage companies, such as Boeing, Google, Harley-Davidson, IBM, NUCOR, Trek, UPS, and others, have separated their *internal labor markets*[4] from the outside market. Advancement within an efficiency wage company is along an established *job ladder*. These companies maintain entry-level jobs comparable to those at other companies but, more importantly, they have good jobs higher up the ladder. These are jobs that workers want because on these jobs anyone could become more productive and earn more. Desired by many, these good jobs were rationed. Promotions in the internal labor market are rewards to the most productive workers within the company. Because access to better jobs depends on performing well at the lower-level jobs, even these lower-level jobs become desirable. The possibility of moving up a job ladder encourages workers to take lower level jobs and to work hard.

HOW EFFICIENCY WAGES RAISE PRODUCTIVITY

Efficiency wages and internal labor markets are productive because they give workers wage and career incentives to be efficient. There are several mechanisms through which efficiency wages can determine productivity:

Higher wages reduce quits. About 3% of American workers quit their jobs every month. Quits are expensive. In addition to the costs of recruiting and training replacements, companies have to pay to fill their jobs while awaiting the arrival of a new trained worker. This requires companies to maintain a staff of redundant workers ready to fill in to replace quits. Otherwise the company has to accept lost output. But as Henry Ford discovered, paying higher wages discourages quits by raising workers' wages above the level they could earn at another employer. The workers then earn their higher wage because the company saves by lowering the quit rate.

Higher wages promote higher morale. Machines work as well, or as badly, as they

If workers are not paid a living wage, how do they live? They overwork, neglect their families, and are subsidized by the rest of us.

In 1999, the city council in Cambridge, Mass.., voted that all employers in Cambridge should pay a "living wage" of at least $11.11/hour so that workers could live decently and raise a family in Cambridge. Even after the Harvard Living Wage Campaign, many Harvard workers were paid less than a living wage. They survive by taking time away from family responsibilities, by working additional jobs, and by living far away so they spend hours commuting. The community also bears the burden of low wages by providing subsidies to low-wage families through the Earned Income Tax Credit, food stamps, Medicaid, health-insurance subsidies, and by providing emergency health care for workers whose wages do not allow them to see a doctor regularly.

HIGH- AND LOW-ROAD COMPANIES

Costco Wholesale pays its workers $17 an hour on average, nearly double the $10 an hour paid by its competitor, Wal-Mart's Sam's Club. Costco also provides 85% of its employees with health insurance, compared with less than half of the workers at Sam's Club. High wages and benefits do not come from the pockets of Costco's shareholders. Instead, high-wage Costco outperforms Wal-Mart on the stock market and sells at a higher price-earnings ratio. Costco employees respond to their higher wages and benefits by working harder, quitting less frequently, and developing more efficient work practices, including operating with much less supervision. Costco's largely self-managing workers generate slightly more sales than Sam's with 38% fewer employees.

Costco is representative of a small but important group of high-involvement American companies whose workers' high productivity more than justifies the high pay and good benefits they receive. Studies regularly find that participation in profit sharing and in organizational decision making is associated with greater well-being among workers, and higher productivity.

FIGURE 12-2
HOW EFFICIENCY WAGES RAISE PRODUCTIVITY

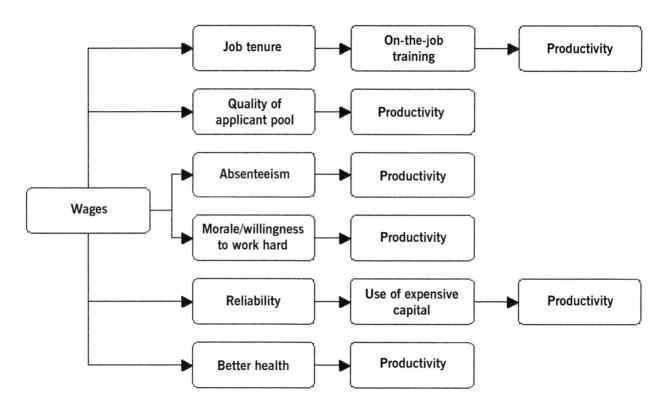

can, regardless of how they feel. (Because they don't feel, of course!) Humans are different. As mentioned earlier, it is one of the premises of democratic theory that respect will be met by respect. Workers who feel respected and valued will meet that respect and value by providing better work. Higher wages encourage workers to work efficiently and to identify problems and opportunities at work because they want to return quality work for quality pay.

Higher wages allow better training and the use of better equipment. Companies are more interested in training workers if they are confident that the workers will stick around, because the companies anticipate a longer period during which they can recoup their investment in training. They are also readier to invest in equipment if they believe their workers will treat the equipment well. Workers will also try harder to develop their skills so that they can hold onto these good jobs. Henry Ford's workers cut back on the drink to keep their $5 /day jobs. Since baseball player salaries began rising sharply in the 1970s, players have been working harder to stay in shape and to hone their skills so that they can remain active for longer. In low income countries, higher wages allow workers to eat better and to receive medical attention, and healthier workers are then more productive. Even in affluent countries, higher wages can promote efficiency by allowing workers to buy services that make them more productive, such as higher quality daycare or transportation to work.

Higher wages attract better workers. High-wage companies choose their workers from a superior applicant pool, which economizes on supervision and training costs. The high earnings of workers at Google allow the company to recruit from the best trained and most creative workers.

High wages keep workers healthy. Higher wages and benefits allow workers to take care of themselves and their families so that they can concentrate and be productive at work. Even minor illnesses can substantially reduce efficiency; productivity can drop by 50% when a worker has the flu. The National Federation of Independent Business (NFIB) advises small businesses to encourage sick workers to stay home, so they don't make other workers sick. "Sniffles," the NFIB warns, "can have trickle-down effects on [small businesses'] bottom lines."[5]

Efficiency wage theory explains some of the anomalies found in wage studies. Most empirical work on wages finds that much of the variation in wages among individuals cannot be explained by individual productivity. Instead, some companies pay higher wages than do others and there are high-wage industries where all workers are paid more than in other industries. Secretaries at GM, for example, earn more than secretaries at some local apparel company. Wages in different occupations often have more in common with other wages in their company and industry than they do with wages in the same occupation in other companies. Moving along *wage contours*, wages in different occupations in the same company or industry move together even though they are almost uncorrelated with wages elsewhere.[6]

Efficiency wages are paid to workers at so-called *high-road* companies where all of the company's workers are paid well and are expected to work hard and productively. As a society, we want to encourage this type of wage setting. At high-road companies, high wages verify a strong reciprocal commitment from both workers and employers to maintain their relationship. This commitment encourages workers to work hard to support the company, and employers to invest in training their workers and in providing them the tools and machinery they need to be efficient. Commitment, hard work, training, and investment all lead to the high productivity that justifies the high wages earned. By contrast, companies that pursue a *low-road* strategy match low wages to low productivity, investing little in their often mobile workers and providing them with minimal tools to do their jobs well.

Efficiency wage theory also helps to explain why wages are *sticky*, or fall slowly even in the face of high unemployment. This is true for jobs in many of America's largest employers, and is the norm in Europe and Japan. Oil prices, wheat prices, steel, and even automobile prices fall when there is excess supply. Within high-road companies with internal labor markets, however, wages are largely unaffected by levels of unemployment. They rise little when unemployment is low and do not fall when unemployment is high. Isolated from outside labor markets because of their internal promotion strategy and job ladders, high-road companies do not compete much with other companies in hiring workers on public labor markets. High-road employers maintain wages when unemployment rises rather than risk undermining their relationship with their workers, endangering morale, job commitment, and productivity. These employers also hesitate to raise wages at any particular job because to do so risks upsetting the pattern of wages in different occupations along the ladder.

EFFICIENCY WAGES IN PUBLIC POLICY

Efficiency wages raise productivity by encouraging workers and giving them reason to feel good about their employment. High wages also give employers power over their workers by making them want to keep their jobs. In high-road companies, productivity depends on the job and the social relationship between workers and their employer rather than the individual worker's characteristics. For this reason, workers cannot expect to earn their high-road efficiency wage if they leave the company. The benefit to workers of employment at a high-road company is the high wage. The cost is that they become *inframarginal*, no longer able to change jobs at will and without cost. Because leaving their jobs would cause a significant wage cut, efficiency wages and internal labor markets give employers power over workers. The threat of discharge gives employers a weapon to use to force workers to work harder.[7]

NOT EVERYONE GOT HIGHER WAGES AT FORD

Henry Ford

Historian Stephen Meyer has said that the $5 day was meant to "fit the immigrant worker into the mold of the ideal American." "We want to make men in this factory as well as automobiles," Henry Ford said. Ford believed, as sociological-department head S.S. Marquis said: that "nothing tends to lower a man's efficiency more than wrong family relations." The $5/day was linked explicitly to worker behaviors. It was a reward for long job tenure without any absence or lateness, and good evaluations from supervisors. The higher pay also depended on workers "living high." Ford's "sociological department" sent 150 investigators into workers' homes looking for evidence of "thrift, cleanliness, sobriety, family values, and good morals in general." Excessive drinking, gambling, buying on credit, a dirty home, and an unwholesome diet were all grounds for probation; if a worker failed to clean up in six months, not only did he not earn his $5 a day, he was fired.

Efficiency wages encourage hard and productive work by raising workers' wages above what they could earn at an alternative employment or by being unemployed. By raising wages, good jobs create a *cost of job loss*[8] or the difference between the worker's wage and her *fallback position*,[9] or her income at her next best alternative. Costly job loss gives employers power over their workers, because individual workers are afraid of opposing their employers and losing their jobs. The cost of job loss depends on both the alternative employments for the worker, and the condition of the unemployed. Companies can raise the cost of job loss by raising wages but they get the same effect when workers' alternatives get worse, either because there is more unemployment so workers would expect to remain jobless for longer, because alternative wages fall, or there is less social support

Trade unionists at the 1963 March on Washington for Civil Rights. Best remembered for Martin Luther King's "I have a dream" speech, the march was largely funded by unions, notably the United Auto Workers led by Walter Ruether, second from the right in the front row.

to maintain income when unemployed. That is why employers are generally against social insurance, and concerned when government policy drives down the unemployment rate. Even with low unemployment and generous social welfare spending and support for the unemployed, employers can maintain leverage over their workers and keep them working hard because they value their jobs, but they maintain this leverage by paying higher wages. Employers can achieve the same efficiency level, the same power over their workers, at lower wages if they can raise the unemployment rate, lower competitive wages, or reduce unemployment insurance and other support to workers between jobs.

Given any level of unemployment and public support, higher wages will raise the cost of job loss and encourage workers to commit more to their job and work harder. Efficiency increases with wages or when the workers' fallback position gets worse, either because the likelihood of getting another job falls, likely earnings on an alternative job are lower, or there is less financial support for the unemployed, either from public sources (e.g. unemployment insurance, food stamps, or welfare) or from family and community aid. The stronger the workers' fallback position, the higher the wage that employers must pay to maintain the same leverage, to maintain the same cost of job loss for their workers. For any level of welfare, higher wages will elicit more work effort and higher efficiency, but higher welfare is associated with lower levels of efficiency at any level of wages. At higher levels of public support for the unemployed, for example, or at lower unemployment rates, where workers can get another job easily, employers will need to pay higher wages to establish the same incentives for workers. Where unemployment is high, however, and welfare and public support for the unemployed are low, employers do not need to pay as much to keep their workers working hard. Workers will keep their noses to the grindstone, working hard to hold on to even bad jobs.

As a society, we want employers to pay high wages because this encourages greater productivity and a more even distribution of income between capital and labor. The efficiency wage impact of public policy towards the poor and unemployed suggests that higher public support programs will require higher wages to reach the same level of efficiency. The policy implications for capi-

FIGURE 12-3

EFFECT OF UNIONS ON LABOR MARKETS, ORTHODOX VIEW WITH WAGE TECHNOLOGICALLY DETERMINED

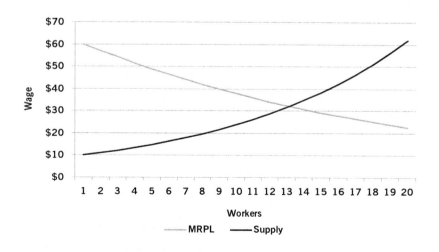

talists are clear. Public welfare spending and lower unemployment will hurt productivity unless capitalists pay higher wages. We can certainly understand why capitalists oppose public welfare and favor relatively high unemployment rates: less public support and more unemployment allow them to maintain productive efficiency without raising wages.

Efficiency wage theory provides a motive for public industrial policy that favors some companies over others because as a society we want workers to be productive and, therefore, we want higher wages. Total output increases when high-road companies expand because their efficiency wage policies raise workers' productivity above the level of other companies. For this reason, output falls when high-road companies shrink. Society has an interest in advancing these companies compared with their market-oriented, low-wage/low-efficiency rivals. From an orthodox perspective, assuming labor markets operate efficiently as described in Chapter 11 above, policies like import restraints and credit steering should be shunned for distorting the allocation of labor, lowering output and efficiency. From a perspective of efficiency wages, however, they may be economically efficient. By protecting high-road companies from low-wage competition, they might raise productivity and redistribute income towards working people.

EFFICIENCY WAGES: UNIONS, EFFICIENCY, DEMOCRACY

Many neoclassical economists are suspicious of labor unions because they see them as labor monopolies designed to raise wages for their members at the expense of the rest of the community. By forcing employers to pay higher wages to their members, they reduce employment in the unionized sector and lower output there below the socially desired amount. Furthermore, the unemployed forced out of the unionized sector flood the market in the nonunion sector, driving down wages and producing a socially wasteful surplus output there. While some may favor unions because they believe that most union members have relatively low income and deserve higher wages, they are seen in the orthodox view as a monopoly that produces inefficiency by distorting production.

As always with the orthodox view of labor markets, this interpretation views the economy as a set of asocial individuals relating to things in the world but not to each other. Unions do more than restrict labor market competition: they provide a means to enforce efficiency wage bargains and protect the inframarginal workers created by efficiency wage policies.

FIGURE 12-4
EFFECT OF UNIONS ON LABOR MARKET OUTCOMES

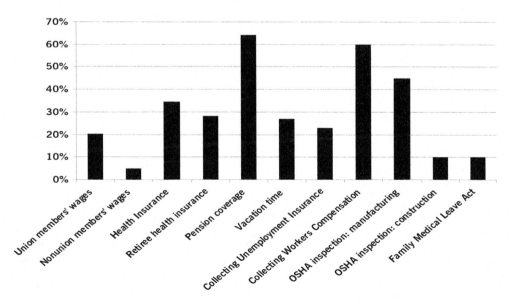

The Solidarity movement began as a protest by workers in the Gdansk shipyards; it ended by bringing down Communism in Poland and throughout Eastern Europe and the USSR.

Solidarity demonstrators in Poland against Communist oppression.

UNIONS AND DEMOCRACY: BOSSES AND A DEMOCRATIC WORKPLACE?

The labor movement has its origins in the democratic struggle to raise the social standing of workers and to give all citizens an equal voice in social decisions. The great French socialist Jean Jaurès expressed the movement's democratic aspirations:

> In the shop, the workers do not deliberate, they obey. In Parliament, they only deliberate through the intermediary of a few distant representatives. In unions and in cooperatives, workers deliberate by themselves; they pronounce directly on precise questions …. Thus the idea of direct government of the people by the people, which was inscribed in the republican and democratic constitutions of 1793, takes form in the economic organization of the proletariat.

As democratic institutions, unions give an equal say to all their members in formulating their demands. Involving workers in decision making can be desirable in itself since it provides experience in self-governance and promotes mutual respect. Democratic governance also changes conditions of employment by giving an equal voice to workers who would otherwise have little influence on market conditions because they are unlikely to leave their jobs. Otherwise, markets are driven by the possibility of *exit*,[10] participants influence market outcomes along the margin by threatening to leave. This might work well if everyone is in the same position with respect to exit. Otherwise, however, those ready to leave have disproportionate influence. The development of efficiency wage policies with stable employment, longer job tenure, and internal labor markets meant that a growing part of the workforce cannot leave their jobs without forsaking a large investment in their employment. No longer able to credibly threaten to exit, these workers are forced to accept whatever conditions of work their employer imposes. Concerned to recruit new and to retain old employees, companies will be attentive to the wishes of *marginal workers*, mobile workers ready to change jobs, and will neglect *inframarginal workers*[11] who are unlikely to change jobs in any case. Responding to marginal workers, companies will adjust their compensation package and personnel policies to favor younger, unattached workers at the expense of those who have been with the company longer. They will, for example, favor cash pay over insurance benefits because younger, unattached, mobile workers are less interested in pensions and health insurance benefits.

Unions represent these *inframarginal workers* who, because of their po-

WHAT DO UNIONS DO?

In 1986, economists Richard Freeman and James Medoff published a now-classic study, *What do Unions Do?* This book was based on the insight that unions reorder markets from a focus on the "marginal" worker, who tends to be young and unattached, to the "inframarginal worker" who is older, with more job tenure, and more likely to have a family. While sharing an interest in higher wages, marginal and inframarginal workers have different interests on issues like seniority and benefits. Without a union, companies will tilt their compensation package toward wages to attract marginal workers. Unions move compensation towards health and pension benefits and protect seniority rights to favor their inframarginal members.

sition on a job ladder, their age, or their family status, are reluctant to leave jobs. In the marketplace, they have no leverage because they are unprepared to exit. But in the union, these workers have a vote equal to any other worker. Unions provide all workers with *voice*[12] as an alternative to exit, which is especially important for these inframarginal workers with their lost exit option. From this we would expect unions to tilt the compensation package and the labor bargain towards the interests of inframarginal workers, workers who have greater seniority and longer job tenure, are more likely to have a family, and are older and more interested in insurance and pensions.

Policies favoring marginal over inframarginal workers are a natural response to market pressures. But they can be inefficient, by neglecting the interests of many workers, and thus can undercut morale and undermine long-term productivity. Worse, by responding only to exits and quits, companies encourage socially wasteful turnover that undermines worker training and cooperation. Representing inframarginal workers, unions can improve on the market outcome by providing a way for inframarginal workers to speak to management, to exercise voice rather than exit, and by forcing management to attend to the workers' needs at the risk of a strike or other collective job action.

> ## LIBERAL, CONSERVATIVE, AND RADICAL LABOR ECONOMICS
>
> Conservatives like Thomas Sowell and George Bush agree with liberals like Robert Reich and Barack Obama that the only way to raise wages and employment for the poor is to make them more productive. They differ in how to achieve this. Liberals would raise productivity by giving workers more access to education and early childhood health care and nutrition; conservatives believe the poor need better values and their employers need more physical capital to raise their employees' marginal product.
>
> Radical economists, such as Robert Pollin of the University of Massachusetts, differ from their liberal or conservative counterparts because they argue that wages determine productivity rather than the other way around. The way to raise productivity for the poor is to raise their wages either through direct government fiat (higher minimum wages) or by helping workers to build strong labor unions.
>
>
>
> Pollin (left), Reich (center), Sowell (right)

Union contracts contain provisions reflecting the union tilt towards democracy and voice. Virtually all contracts, for example, provide for grievance procedures, giving workers recourse with complaints. These procedures compel employers to hear grievances, often providing a mechanism for a third-party adjudication. By contrast, virtually no nonunion workplaces have independent grievance procedures with the option of independent arbitration. Virtually all union contracts, furthermore, protect workers with grievances, such as with provisions for seniority promotion and *standard rate*[13] wage programs that limit management's discretion to punish workers. Such protections allow workers to speak more freely and to criticize management, both to bring important information to the attention of managers and to speak about their own needs as workers and as citizens.

By promoting communication between inframarginal workers and management, unions can promote efficiency, which is 5-15% higher in union workplaces than in nonunion establishments.[14] By passing accurate information up the management ladder, better morale and enhanced communication can help management manage better. As with efficiency wages in general, unions dramatically reduce quits. Quit rates are as much as 80% lower for union members compared with nonunion workers. Lower quits help companies economize on turnover costs. They also dramatically reduce training costs, leading to higher productivity. Unlike efficiency wages, however, unions lower quits and raise productivity without imposing a wage burden on business. Unions achieve the benefits of efficiency wages independent of any effect on wages by promoting democratic values and giving voice to workers.

Despite the positive effect of unions on productivity, most employers oppose unions. In the United States they have fought unionization with

> ## THE EFFECT OF UNIONS ON PRODUCTIVITY
>
> A recent review of 73 studies on unions and productivity finds that within US manufacturing, union members are about 10% more productive. Higher productivity for union members reflects a greater investment in training and in machinery by employers concerned to minimize their more expensive labor input. In addition, unions dramatically reduce turnover and absenteeism, saving employers expensive retraining and the need to hire expensive substitutes.

CURRENT CONTROVERSIES

U.S. UNION DECLINE
IN COMPARATIVE PERSPECTIVE

Union membership in the United States has been declining, as a percentage of the labor force, almost continuously since the end of the Korean War. The sharpest decline came after the mid-1970s, with the rise of neoliberal "free trade" policies and restrictive macroeconomic policies putting low inflation ahead of full employment. U.S. unions have tried to stem their membership decline by increased spending on organizing and political action to bring changes in labor law. So far, however, neither has yielded significant gains and unions have hesitated to promote massive strike and protest movements like those that led to rapid growth in the 1930s.

FIGURE 1
UNION MEMBERS, PERCENTAGE OF EMPLOYED WORKERS, U.S., 1930-2003

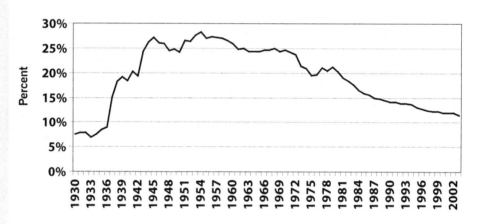

FIGURE 2
PERCENT DECLINE FROM PEAK UNIONIZATION RATE, SELECTED COUNTRIES

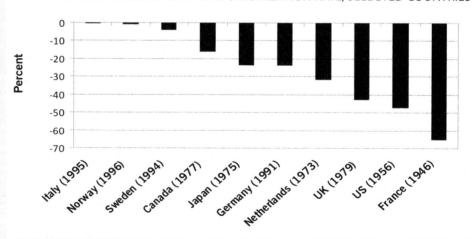

The graphs below show two comparisons. The first, between the unionization rates in private and public employment within the United States, suggests that union decline is due to conditions specific to private-sector employment, such as the weakening legal protection for union activities. The second, comparing the unionization rate in the United States to the average in other advanced capitalist economies, suggests a larger problem, one not specific to the American private sector but extending further, to all of the capitalist world.

FIGURE 3
UNION DENSITY, PRIVATE AND PUBLIC SECTORS, UNITED STATES

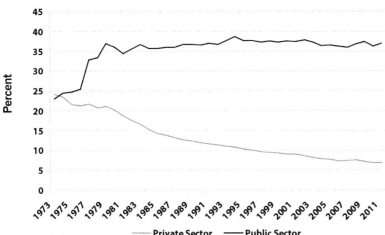

Private Sector · Public Sector

Declining union density in the United States is restricted to the private sector. Public sector unions grew rapidly in the 1960s and 1970s—just before private-sector unions went into their steepest decline—and have maintained their share of the public sector labor force since. Public sector workers now account for a majority of U.S. union members.

FIGURE 4
U.S. UNIONIZATION RATE, PERCENTAGE OF AVERAGE FOR 18 OTHER OECD COUNTRIES

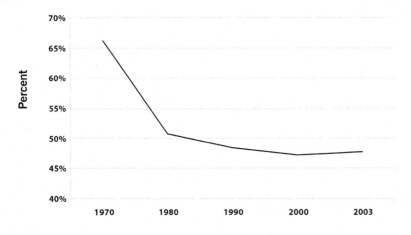

The U.S. unionization rate is lower than the average for rich capitalist (OECD) countries. Between 1970 and 1980, the U.S. rate fell relative to other countries', suggesting that conditions peculiar to the United States, including extraordinary employer resistance and a hostile legal environment, accounted for much of the U.S. union decline. Since 1990, however, U.S. unions have lost membership at about the same rate as those in other countries, suggesting that union decline in this period is due to conditions common to most advanced capitalist economies—especially the widespread adoption of neoliberal policies.

Sources: Gerald Mayer, Union Membership Trends in the United States, CRS Report for Congress, August 31, 2004, Table A1, Union Membership in the United States, 1930-2003 ; Gerald Friedman, "Is Labor Dead?" International Labor and Working Class History, Vol. 75, Issue 1, Table One: The Decline of the Labor Movemen

weapons ranging from anti-union law firms, legal injunctions against union organizing, private meetings with workers to discourage them from supporting a union drive, and the use of military-surplus airplanes and poison gas on strikers.[15] Nonunion firms also pay their workers significantly more if there are unions in the industry or region in order to discourage them from supporting a union drive. Employers fight unions because they often lower profitability, raising wages by at least as much as they raise productivity. But in virtually all cases, in the United States and abroad, unionized firms are profitable and earn solid dividends for their owners. The extreme hostility of managers and owners towards unions reflects their determination to remain in control of their business. Managers fight unions because they do not want to share power with workers. America's capitalists fight unions the way autocrats have fought democratic movements since Spartacus led a slave rebellion and the Gracci brothers campaigned for land reform during the Roman Republic.[16]

From a democratic perspective, unions improve society by creating a space for worker participation in the management of their businesses. This is precisely why they are opposed by employers who would run their businesses as totalitarian autocracies. From a narrow economic perspective, unions improve the functioning of the economy by redistributing income towards working people and by improving the mix of compensation by favoring otherwise-neglected inframarginal workers. But their most important role is to limit management's authority and to impose efficiency wages on management, forcing companies to do the right thing and raise efficiency by treating workers right. Employers fiercely resist any narrowing of management prerogatives almost without regard to any financial concern; they fight government or community regulation as much as they fight unions.[17] While American labor law, dating back to 1935, provides a mechanism for workers to choose whether or not to belong to a labor union without interference from their employer, a recent study found that virtually all private-sector employers interfere with their employees' choice. Over 60% meet individually with workers to dissuade them from supporting a union, 57% threaten to close the worksite if the workers choose a union, half threaten to cut wages, and one third fire union activists. All of these actions are illegal, but American labor law contains no criminal sanctions. And the enforcement body, the National Labor Relations Board, has a backlog of cases stretching back over a year.

ECONOMIC DEMOCRACY: CAPITALISM, UNIONS, AND WORKER SELF-MANAGEMENT

By giving workers a collective voice in management, unions balance the inherently undemocratic nature of capitalism. In the public realm, in the area of government and democratic politics, we believe that everyone is entitled to respect and equal rights. Everyone has a constitutionally guaranteed right to a voice and an equal vote in the management of public institutions, and public institutions draw their legitimacy in their respect for our individual rights, our liberty, and our right to pursue happiness.

Except where a union contract specifically limits the authority of managers, capitalist businesses are islands of autocracy within our democratic polity. At work, workers do not have the right to express their opinions, they do not have a voice in choosing their leaders or setting business policy, and they are not entitled to respect. They do not have the right to dress as they please or to speak on the job with their coworkers. They do not even have a guaranteed right to use restrooms. As one 19th century American activist said:

> The principles of Co-operation are more in harmony with the principles of our form of government than our present social system. Our social system in many things is at variance with our political institutions. The relation of Employer & Employed is not the normal condition of Freemen. Superiority & Inferiority is implied in the relation. . . . Co-operation supersedes this relation and places men just where the Declaration of Independence was designed to place them--equal--& with equal rights to liberty & the pursuit of happiness.

PRINCIPLES FOR WORKER COOPERATIVES

"A co-operative is an autonomous association of persons united voluntarily to meet their common economic, social, and cultural needs and aspirations through a jointly-owned and democratically-controlled enterprise .... Co-operatives are based on the values of self-help, self-responsibility, democracy, equality, equity and solidarity. In the tradition of their founders, co-operative members believe in the ethical values of honesty, openness, social responsibility and caring for others."

See the International Cooperative Alliance, http://www.ica.coop/coop/principles.html

Since the beginning of the capitalist era, workers have resisted capitalist autocracy by forming labor unions and by trying to develop a direct alternative to capitalist management. They have organized alternative forms of business organization, including consumer and worker cooperatives, democratically managed enterprises extending into the workplace democratic values of equal voice and one person, one vote.

There has been a paradox in the cooperative movement. On the one side, cooperatives have been shown to be more productive than capitalist businesses both in theoretical analysis and in practice.[18] On the other side, despite some striking successes, cooperation has never taken hold and remains a marginal social force. So here we have a case of a superior social institution, a superior social technology, left on the sidelines. It is as if a $100 bill was sitting on the sidewalk and no one bent down to pick it up.

Co-op Italia, Italy's largest retailer

The head of a federation of worker cooperatives in Italy's Emilia-Romagna region, north of Rome, explains the advantage cooperatives have over capitalist firms: "The gift of the cooperative is to create a sense of collective entrepreneurship. Membership requires thinking about the business. Workers are more committed than in private firms."[19] Cooperatives work better than capitalist businesses because they mobilize the energies and talents of the workers without relying on expensive and inefficient managerial hierarchy. Even more than in a workplace with a strong union, worker cooperatives gain from a workforce that is motivated to be productive both because they have rights to the product and because they want to protect their good jobs. Cooperation also eliminates the drive to conceal information from management. On the contrary, worker-managers join responsibility (the power to make decisions) with information (full knowledge of workers and production). And all these gains come from an organizational structure that economizes on managerial overhead.

The benefits of democratic cooperation are seen even in work places that are not run as cooperatives, including unionized establishments and some of the relatively nonhierarchical organizations common in the high tech sector.[20] The record for cooperatives themselves has been impressive. Productivity, output per worker and output per unit of input, is significantly higher in cooperative workplaces, and the greatest gains are in those with more worker participation and control. Some cooperatives have been spectacularly successful. In Spain, for example, the Mondragón enterprises employ nearly 100,000 workers, with employment increasing nearly 8% and capital investment rising by 10% a year for the last two decades. Mondragón is responsible for nearly 20% of industrial output in the Basque region of Spain, helping to make the Basque province one of Europe's wealthiest. Mondragón also contributes to the Basque region's particularly equitable distribution of income.

Cooperatives are even more important in the Emilia-Romagna region of Italy. Unlike the massive Mondragón Corporation, most co-ops in Emilia-Romagna are small, artisanal operations. Many were established during strikes or lock-outs when craftsmen pooled their assets, and a few were established by benevolent management. The co-op movement also extends to the service sector and includes 8,000 individual coops producing everything from ceramics to fashion to specialty cheese in many small establishments. They include one of Italy's largest ceramics producers, one of Europe's most successful scale producers, Italy's largest retailer, Coop/Coop Italia, and employee-owned CIR Foods, the country's third largest food service provider. The cooperatives are united in a commitment to return 3% of profits to a national fund for cooperative development and to provide mutual aid in finance, marketing, research and technical expertise.[21]

Professor Stefano Zamagni, at the University of Bologna in Emilia-Romagna, explains that in the cooperatives, "labor is an occasion for self-realization, not a mere factor of

Mondragón Corporation in Spain, one of Europe's largest industrial enterprises.

production." Every cooperative is a local, living democracy. This has been the guiding principle for nearly 300 cooperative Israeli settlements with a total population of 120,000. Collectively governed with shared work and income, the Israeli Kibbutzim are among Israel's most efficient businesses and also have produced a disproportionate share of the country's political, military, and intellectual elite. More than any other institution, the cooperatives represent and foster the democratic and egalitarian spirit of Israel with all the economic and social benefits this brings.

Workers at a kibbutz

There has been a long tradition of cooperation in the United States as well, going back to 19th-century cooperative settlements such as the Shakers, New Harmony, and the Oneida Community.[22] Cooperatives operate in a variety of settings, including machine tool manufacture (Isthmus Engineering of Wisconsin), baked goods (Portland's Nature's Bakery), and copying and printing services (Collective Copies of Western Massachusetts). With higher productivity and greater worker satisfaction, it is reasonable to ask why cooperation has not supplanted capitalism? Perhaps the answer may be that the entrepreneurial energies needed to form and maintain a cooperative can, if applied to an individual's business, lead to great personal wealth. Would Henry Ford or Steve Jobs have committed their energies to a coop?

POWER IN LABOR MARKETS?
EARNINGS DIFFERENTIALS BY GENDER AND RACE

The orthodox neoclassical theory relies on competition among employers to prevent any from exploiting workers by paying them less than their marginal product. There is no power in labor markets because workers can quit if they are not paid as well as their productivity merits, and competition will ensure that some employer will always hire workers who are suited for any job.

It is hard to reconcile this approach with experience. Within the United States, there are systematic differences in the average earnings and career prospects for male and female workers and for workers from different races. White men earn more than nonwhites and women. The differences are large and remain after controlling for levels of education, job market experience, and residence.

College-educated black men and white women earn barely as much as white male high school graduates. Gender and racial wage differences are magnified over a lifetime because of shorter workweeks, greater unemployment, and lower levels of market labor force participation for women and minorities. Among women, only highly educated Asian women earn as much over their lifetimes as do Asian men. At the same education level, only Asian men earn as much as white men. African-American men earn about 20% less over their lifetimes than do white men of the same level of education, and African-American women earn another 15% less than do African-American men.

Earnings differentials by race and gender are for the most part

FIGURE 12-5
EARNINGS BY EDUCATION AND GENDER

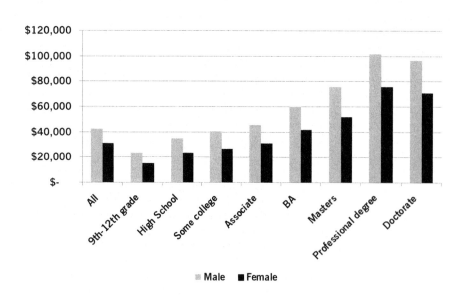

FIGURE 12-6
LIFETIME EARNINGS BY EDUCATION, GENDER, RACE

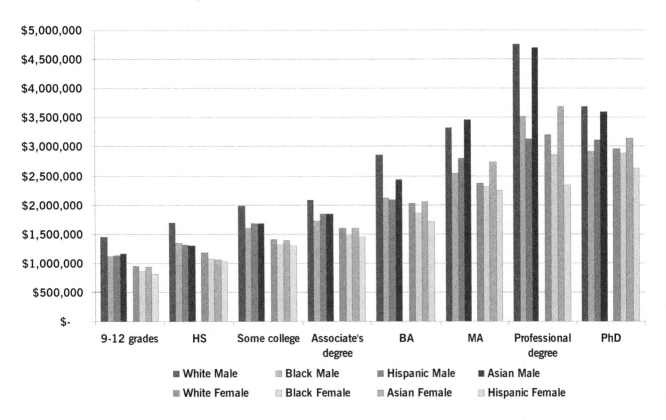

■ White Male   ▨ Black Male   ▨ Hispanic Male   ■ Asian Male
▨ White Female   ▨ Black Female   ▨ Asian Female   ▨ Hispanic Female

within education levels. Rather than due to a higher level of training for whites and for men, they reflect the greater access that white men in particular and men in general have to good jobs. Surveys have found that employers look to hire nonwhites and women for different types of jobs than those for which they recruit white males. Employers openly admit that they prefer to hire women for jobs where they use clerical skills and interact with the public, and they prefer to hire blacks for jobs requiring manual labor but utilizing few interpersonal or cognitive skills. For good, high-paying jobs using skills and intelligence, they prefer to hire white men. Because of these attitudes, companies continue to lose employment discrimination suits, including a recent settlement for $176 million by Texaco to black employees after taped conversations were revealed where executives expressed blatantly racist attitudes towards black workers. Recent studies have found that black workers with darker complexions have dramatically less success in job interviews than do workers with lighter complexions but identical job resumes. In experi-

FIGURE 12-7
FEMALE SHARE OF SELECTED OCCUPATIONS

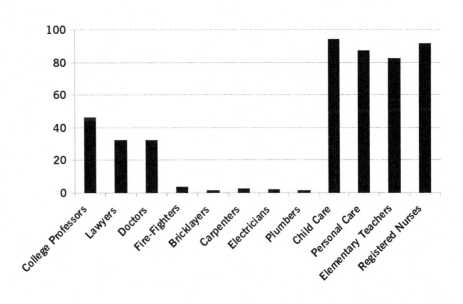

mental studies, when well-groomed black and white college graduates, posing as high-school graduates, were sent to apply for entry-level jobs with nearly identical qualifications, the whites had more success despite reporting criminal records on their applications than did the blacks who reported no criminal records.

Women also have faced great discrimination in employment, not only from employers but also from broader social attitudes. There are broad occupation classes with very few women, including the construction trades. Other occupations have virtually no men, including most of the caring occupations. A few occupations have both women and men, including law, medicine, and college teaching. Even there, however, there are considerable differences in the share of women within sub-disciplines. For example, women are more likely to be general practitioners than surgeons, or professors of French or English than of physics or chemistry.

WHY NEOCLASSICAL ECONOMISTS DO NOT BELIEVE IN DISCRIMINATION: THE JACKIE ROBINSON STORY

Neoclassical economists find it hard to explain these earnings and hiring differences because they expect that competition will erode differentials that don't reflect productivity, that are not "fair." Orthodox economists see labor market discrimination through the lens of the Jackie Robinson experience. Before Robinson, the owners of Major League Baseball (MLB) teams agreed that none would hire African-American players. By preventing talented African-Americans from playing MLB, this agreement held down their wages. By reducing competition, it also inflated the earnings of European-American players. When Branch Rickey of the Brooklyn Dodgers broke this agreement, he gave the Dodgers a competitive advantage because they could hire relatively inexpensive but talented African-Americans to replace less talented, higher priced European-Americans.

Rickey explained that he recruited African-American players for moral reasons; "I cannot face my God much longer," he said, "knowing that His black creatures are held separate and distinct from His white creatures in the game that has given me all that I can call my own." Operating in liberal Brooklyn, New York, he might have anticipated drawing more fans with an integrated team.[23] In addition, his Dodgers gained a great competitive advantage by breaking the color line. African-American talent helped the Dodgers to win the National League pennant in seven of the next ten years after hiring Robinson in 1947. In the years when the Dodgers did not win the pennant, they lost to teams like the New York Giants and the Milwaukee Braves, with prominent African-American stars like Willie Mays and Hank Aaron. By contrast, teams that were slow to hire African-Americans faced a competitive decline. For example, after winning the American League pennant in 1946, the Boston Red Sox, the last American League team to hire African-Americans, went 21 years without another pennant. This experience taught Major League Baseball (MLB) that one price of discrimination is loss of competitive edge. Having learned a lesson, MLB was quick in the 1970s to hire Dominican talent, and now actively recruits Asian players.

The Jackie Robinson experience shows that competition can quickly erode discrimination. The owners of MLB teams may have disliked African-Americans as much in 1956

THE REWARD FOR BREAKING THE COLOR LINE

Before Jackie Robinson, the Brooklyn Dodgers had three World Series appearances, losing in 1916, 1920, and 1941. After integrating baseball with Robinson in 1947, they won six National League championships in the next 10 years, and the World Series in 1955.

Jackie Robinson

UNDER A RACIST OWNER, THE RED SOX WERE THE LAST MAJOR LEAGUE TEAM TO BE INTEGRATED

After winning the American League pennant in 1946, the Red Sox went 21 years before another championship. They passed over Robinson, Willie Mays, and others. This certainly cost them World Series appearances. And maybe a win or two.

Competition and embarrassment finally forced the Red Sox to recruit the best players, regardless of race. But even in the 1980s and 1990s, the Red Sox had fewer black players than other teams. The "curse" is really the "curse of the racist Yawkey Group".

as in 1946, but by 1956 they were all looking to recruit African-American players because they needed their talents to compete with other teams that were hiring African-Americans. But this may be a special case. Competition could work in this case because even without access to the major leagues, African American could train as baseball players, both in colleges and in the professional Negro Leagues. Thanks to this access to training, there was in 1947, a pool of talented black players ready to play MLB. Compare this experience, however, with the situation facing women who would like to be plumbers and those who would like to be lawyers. Plumbers do well, earning over twice as much as bank tellers. Few jobs pay this well without a college degree. Why then are there so many women working as bank tellers, where over 90% of workers are female, and so few woman plumbers? And why don't contractors and others look to recruit female plumbers at a discount the way Branch Rickey hired Jackie Robinson?

GENDER, SCHOOLING, DISCRIMINATION

The difference between Jackie Robinson and would-be women plumbers is the existence of the alternate training route for Jackie Robinson, something that wannabe women plumbers do not have. Robinson learned to play baseball in local sandlots, in college, in the army, and in the Negro Leagues where he and other African-American players were able to develop and hone their skills to a professional edge. There is nothing comparable for would-be female crafts workers. Instead, training as a plumber (or electrician, carpenter, or auto mechanic) is largely provided by other plumbers (electricians, etc.). As we will soon see, practitioners can have a vested interest in discriminating against women and others in order to drive up their own wages by restricting the supply of labor to their trade. Control over training allows them to prevent market competition from undermining discrimination.

Expanded access to training explains many of the strides that women and others have made in overcoming discrimination. Under the terms of the 1964 Civil Rights Act, colleges and universities are forbidden from discriminating against students on the basis of gender or race. Free to compete on their academic ability, women have flocked to college and to the professions requiring a college or post-college ac-

FIGURE 12-8

COLLEGE ENROLLMENT BY GENDER: THE RISE OF THE COLLEGE-EDUCATED WOMAN

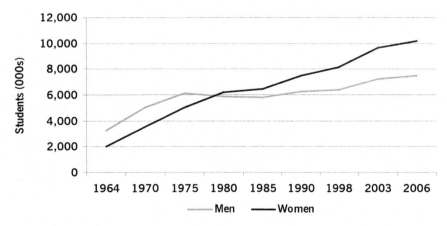

FIGURE 12-9
PROPORTION POST-BA DEGREES GOING TO WOMEN, BY FIELD, 1964-1998

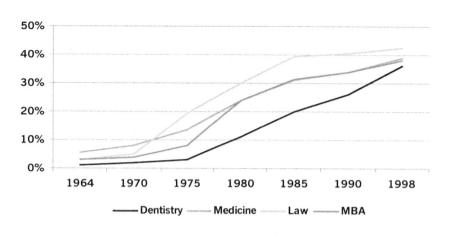

Dentistry — Medicine — Law — MBA

ademic degree. The share of women high-school graduates attending college has soared, from 38% in the 1960s to nearly 70% today. Only 38% of students were female in the mid-1960s, and an even smaller share of graduates. Women now comprise nearly 58% of college students and earn 58% of BA and professional degrees.

Growing enrollment of women in colleges and universities has led to a dramatic increase in the number of women in the professions and in top positions in business management. One key difference between plumbing or carpentry and law or medicine is that universities, forced by elected politicians to obey the 1964 Civil Rights Act and provide equal opportunities to women, control access to these latter occupations. Note that the difference has not been in the law itself. Courts have repeatedly ordered plumbers, electricians, and other tradesmen to train women, but male tradesmen have been able to evade these orders, and systematic harassment has successfully driven most women out of their apprenticeship and other training programs.[24] Only 1.9% of electricians, 1.8% of plumbers, and 0.7% of automobile mechanics are female, scarcely more than in 1960. By contrast, the proportion of female doctors has risen from 10% in 1970 to 32% today, and 33% of lawyers are female compared with 5% in 1970. These changes directly reflect decisions made in universities and colleges to comply with the 1964 law.

CROWDING

Despite the impact of the 1964 law and expanded access to college, most women and African-Americans are still employed in a subset of occupations. Nearly 68% of women workers in 1970 would have had to change their jobs to give women the same occupational distribution as men had. This *index of occupational segregation*[25] fell to 59% in 1980, 52% in 1990, and less than 50% today, as more women have moved into previously male managerial and professional occupations.

In many trades where training is still controlled by the workers themselves, tradesmen have been almost as successful in excluding racial minorities as they have been in excluding women. Today, only 5.9% of electricians, 8.9% of plumbers, and 5.0% of auto mechanics are African-American. Tradesmen resist training women or minorities in their trades in order to raise their own wages by reducing labor supply to their trade. By preventing women or members of minority groups from receiving training in their craft, electricians, plumbers, and others reduce labor supply and raise their own wages. At the same time, by pushing would-be female and minority plumb-

   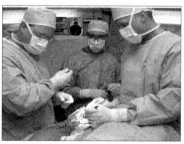

Left to right: Female nurse, male plumber, female elementary school teachers, male surgeons.

ers and electricians out of their craft, they increase the supply of labor to occupations open to women, such as bank tellers, nurses, school teachers, etc. Crowding, the same process that raises the wage to male tradesmen, thus lowers wages in "open" occupations.

The same process that raises the cost of goods produced by male tradesmen lowers the cost of goods produced in "open" occupations. Crowding redistributes wage income from blacks and women to white men, and from consumers of goods produced by white men to those who consume goods produced by blacks and women. It does this at considerable social cost. By reducing labor supply to privileged occupations, labor market crowding also reduces the product supply in these industries, reducing supply and raising prices to con-

FIGURE 12-10
LABOR MARKET FOR PLUMBERS, MEN AND WOMEN

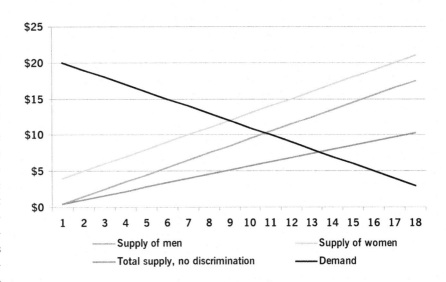

sumers. All consumers pay for white male privilege by paying more for plumbing, electrical work, and other services done by white men, and by having to make do with a smaller supply. All plumbing consumers would benefit from more female plumbers, and women workers would gain from having more choices. But most women are excluded from plumbing because male plumbers protect their own wages by refusing to train them.

Crowding has winners as well as losers. By increasing labor and product supply in traditionally feminine and minority occupations, crowding lowers prices for services where women and minorities have been employed, including nursing, child care, and teaching. Furthermore, by reducing occupational choice and lowering wages, crowding discourages women from working outside the home, encouraging home production and other nonmarket activities. Crowding thus reduces the social damage from the failure of the market to provide for caring labor. If parents followed market incentives, they would neglect children to focus on paid market work. By lowering the return to market work, crowding of women reduces their incentive to neglect their children. On the other hand, by raising wages

to men, crowding discourages them from caring for their children, reducing caring labor by men and making care a feminine preserve.

Raising pay for men and lowering it for women creates gender differences in the labor market that encourage a sexual division of labor within households. This division then reinforces labor market discrimination. By limiting their market opportunities, discrimination encourages women to specialize in family and home work, and then, in effect, to sell these services to male husbands. Labor market discrimination and the financial edge that it gives men thus encourages heterosexual marriage, rewarding women for attracting a male mate and making it easier for men to attract women. Women who expect

FIGURE 12-11
LABOR MARKET FOR CHILDCARE, NO DISCRIMINATION

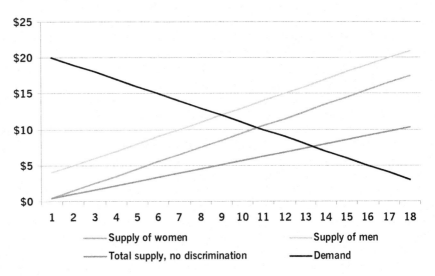

FIGURE 12-12
LABOR MARKET FOR PLUMBERS, WITH DISCRIMINATION

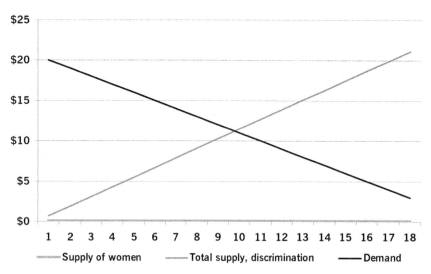

Supply of women — Total supply, discrimination — Demand

that they will devote most of their adult work time to home production will train for this work, studying child behavior and cooking, for example, rather than preparing for market work. By contrast, men train for market work because they expect to hire home production by marrying a woman and need a good income to attract such a mate. For their part, employers economize on thinking and on the costs of job search by looking only for men in jobs that require training and long-term commitments and hiring only women for jobs where seniority is less important because there is less on-the-job training. Of course, by shunning women for jobs rewarding longer tenure, they discourage women from training for them and they encourage women to look to their husbands for financial support. Anticipating the role that their daughters will play in the economy of their family, parents and neighbors encourage girls to develop home production skills, by babysitting and helping Mom to cook dinner, while encouraging boys to prepare themselves for careers. They will see it as their proper responsibility to prepare children for their future roles even if it means discouraging boys from playing with dolls or girls from planning for careers outside the home. Communal institutions will reinforce these expectations. Legislation, such as the benefit scales for Social Security and the tax code encourage husband-wife households with a "primary breadwinner" supporting a "dependent" spouse at home.[26] Even our infrastructure is set up to reinforce gendered work: baby changing tables, for example, are traditionally placed in women's restrooms, forcing fathers to change their baby's diapers over the sink in dirty men's rooms.

Diminished crowding in traditionally female occupations has raised wages for the women who remain there. This has also allowed more women to avoid traditional feminine roles in their family life as well as at work. Like other social divisions of labor, the intrafamily division of labor could be constructive for both sides, but it comes at a cost in efficiency and equity. Some women delight at the opportunity to support their husbands in their careers, while taking great pride in maintaining a smooth-running household and contributing to their community through volunteer service. Problems are inevitable, however, when a particular social arrangement is imposed without regard for individuals. There have

---

SOCIAL EXPECTATIONS AND GENDER ROLES

Expectations about the economic role to be played by adult women and men are reinforced by traditional gendered behavior. Straight women, for example, are encouraged to wear feminine clothes, including heels and skirts, poorly suited for jobs like plumbing or auto repair.

University of Massachusetts economist **Lee Badgett** confirms the significance of heterosexual gender roles. She has found that gay men earn less than straight men, but lesbians earn more than straight women. Gay men suffer economically because they tend to crowd into women's occupations while lesbians earn more than other women because they are willing to take men's occupations even when that makes them less attractive to heterosexual men.

FIGURE 12-13
DISCRIMINATION AGAINST WOMEN PLUMBERS PUSHES WOMEN INTO CHILD
CARE, LOWERING WAGES AND PRICES

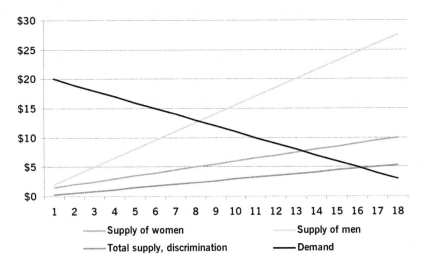

been women who would have preferred to concentrate on market work but found it difficult to find men willing to be house husbands or companies willing to hire them on equal standing with men. And men who would prefer to stay home but found it difficult to find high-income women, or tolerance from their communities. Not to mention those who would rather remain single, or live with someone of their own sex.

DISCUSSION QUESTIONS

What determines wage levels in the neoclassical model?

How did Henry Ford increase his workers' productivity?

What is the difference between "high road" and "low road" companies? How can some companies survive in competitive markets while paying higher wages?

What is "efficiency wage theory"?

How does efficiency wage theory justify industrial policy to favor some companies over others?

How do orthodox economists view unions? What is the effect of union wage increases in the orthodox model? What is the effect in efficiency-wage models?

Why do unions have more effect on benefits than on wages?

What is the effect of unions on worker productivity?

What is the relationship between capitalism and democracy? How do unions modify this relationship?

Who was Jackie Robinson? How did he change American baseball? Why does this experience lead many economists to assume that labor market discrimination will disappear on its own in competitive markets?

Discuss wage differentials by gender and race. Are they due to differences in education?

What is "labor market crowding"?

If some occupations are closed to women and some are open, what is the effect of crowding on wages for workers in open occupations? What happens to wages for men in closed occupations? What would happen to these men's wages if all occupations were opened?

How do some men maintain higher wages without attracting more women to their occupations? Why have other occupations, e.g. medicine and college teaching, been opened to women?

ENDNOTES

[1]Daniel M. G. Raff, "Wage Determination Theory and the Five-Dollar Day at Ford.," Journal of Economic History 48, no. 2 (1988); Stephen Meyer, *The Five Dollar Day: Labor Management and Social Control in the Ford Motor Company, 1908-1921*, SUNY Series in American Social History (Albany: State University of New York Press, 1981).

[2]Efficiency wage theory says that wages determine productivity rather than the other way around.

[3]Job tenure is the length of time workers stay with a particular job.

[4]In companies with internal labor markets, workers are promoted to better jobs from among those who are already employed. Workers in these companies move up along *job ladders* from entry-level jobs to better jobs.

[5]"Don't Let the Flu Disrupt Your Business | NFIB," National Federation of Independent Business, accessed July 2, 2014, http://www.nfib.com/article/dont-let-the-flu-disrupt-your-business-61883/.

[6]Alan B Krueger and Lawrence H Summers, "Efficiency Wages and the Inter-Industry Wage Structure.," *Econometrica* 56, no. 2 (1988); Lawrence H Summers, "Relative Wages, Efficiency Wages,

and Keynesian Unemployment," *The American Economic Review* 78, no. 2 (1988): 383–88; Peter B Doeringer et al., *Internal Labor Markets and Manpower Analysis* (Lexington, Mass.: Heath, 1971).

[7]Richard B Freeman, "The Exit-Voice Tradeoff in the Labor Market: Unionism, Job Tenure, Quits, and Separations," *The Quarterly Journal of Economics* 94, no. 4 (1980): 643–73.

[8]The cost of job loss is the value a worker would put on his or her current job because it measures the difference between earnings with the current job and the next best alternative.

[9]Fallback position is the position one takes if bargaining breaks down and an agreement cannot be reached. In the case of employment, it is one's next best job.

[10]Exit is when a worker quits a job or a consumer stops buying a particular product.

[11]Inframarginal workers are workers who are committed to a job, perhaps because of pension or benefit rights, and will remain on that job even if wages fall slightly. This is in contrast with marginal workers who are right at the top of the labor supply curve and will leave a job at any fall in wages.

[12]Voice and exit are alternative strategies for workers unhappy with their employment and for consumers unhappy with a product. Disgruntled employees exercise voice by complaining to the company management, explaining their unhappiness with company policies. Unlike exit, voice gives companies information directly about why workers or consumers are unhappy. This is discussed more in Albert Hirschman, *Exit, Voice, and Loyalty* (1970).

[13]Companies paying a "standard rate" pay the same wage to all workers with similar characteristics, such as all in the same occupation with the same seniority and training. The alternative is to give managers and supervisors the discretion to pay different rates to workers according to the managers' preferences.

[14]Charles, Medoff, James Brown, "Trade Unions in the Production Process," *Journal of Political Economy* 86, no. 3 (1978): 355–78; Richard B Freeman, What Do Unions Do? (New York: Basic Books, 1984); Christos, Laroche, Patrice Doucouliagos, "What Do Unions Do to Productivity? A Meta-Analysis," *IREL Industrial Relations: A Journal of Economy and Society* 42, no. 4 (2003): 650–91; C Doucouliagos and P Laroche, "The Impact of U.S. Unions on Productivity: A Bootstrap Meta-Analysis," *Proceedings of the ... Annual Meeting.*, no. Edit 56 (2004): 195.

[15]David Corbin, *The West Virginia Mine Wars: An Anthology* (Appalachian Editions, 1990).

[16]Robert Justin Goldstein, *Political Repression in Modern America from 1870 to the Present* (Cambridge, Mass: Schenkman Pub. Co, 1978); Gerald Friedman, *Reigniting the Labor Movement: Restoring Means to Ends in a Democratic Labor Movement* (Abingdon, Oxon: Routledge, 2007); Gerald Friedman, *State-Making and Labor Movements: France and the United States, 1876-1914* (Ithaca: Cornell University Press, 1998); Robin Archer, *Why Is There No Labor Party in the United States?*, Princeton Studies in American Politics (Princeton: Princeton University Press, 2007); Robert H. Zieger, *American Workers, American Unions: The Twentieth and Early Twenty-First Centuries*, Fourth edition, The American Moment (Baltimore: Johns Hopkins University Press, 2014).

[17]Jacob S Hacker and Paul Pierson, *Winner-Take-All Politics: How Washington Made the Rich Richer-and Turned Its Back on the Middle Class* (New York: Simon & Schuster, 2010).

[18]Douglas Kruse, Richard B Freeman, and Joseph R Blasi, eds., *Shared Capitalism at Work: Employee Ownership, Profit and Gain Sharing, and Broad-Based Stock Options* (Chicago; London: The University of Chicago Press, 2010); Joseph R Blasi, Richard B Freeman, and Douglas Kruse, *The Citizen's Share: Putting Ownership Back into Democracy*, 2013; Gregory K Dow, *Governing the Firm Workers' Control in Theory and Practice* (Cambridge; New York: Cambridge University Press, 2003), http://search.ebscohost.com/login.aspx?direct=true&scope=site&db=nlebk&db=nlabk&AN=120723

[19]Stefano Bolognesi, president of Cooperativa Ceramiche d'Imola; quoted in http://www.community-wealth.org/_pdfs/articles-publications/outside-us/article-logue.pdf

[20]Dan Senor and Council on Foreign Relations, *Start-up Nation: The Story of Israel's Economic Miracle*, 1st ed (New York: Twelve, 2009).

[21]Membership owned, they are governed by a membership-elected board that serves a three-year term. An annual membership meeting reviews the financial report and next year's budget. Most cooperatives also have quarterly or monthly membership meetings, and some have small group meetings to review the financial report and budget before the membership meeting.

[22]Originally a religious commune, the Oneida Community became one of the country's most successful manufacturers of silverware.

[23]My father and other New York Yankee fans have told me that for one year they rooted for the Dodgers.

[24]Apprenticeship is a traditional system of learning while earning where workers are employed for several years during which they work under the supervision of established tradesmen who teach them the craft. Today, it is utilized chiefly in the skilled crafts like plumbing. Because the established skilled workers control the training process, they regulate admission to the craft.

[25]The index of occupational segregation gives the share of women who would have to change jobs to make the occupational distribution of women the same as that of men.

[26]Alice Kessler-Harris, *In Pursuit of Equity: Women, Men, and the Quest for Economic Citizenship in 20th Century America* (Oxford; New York: Oxford University Press, 2001); Mary Virginia Lee Badgett, *Money, Myths, and Change: The Economic Lives of Lesbians and Gay Men* (Chicago: University of Chicago Press, 2001).

13

TIME, RISK, AND UNCERTAINTY

JAM TOMORROW, OR JAM TODAY?

It is easy to sympathize with Alice (in Wonderland). "It's jam every OTHER day; to-day isn't any OTHER day, you know" says the Queen. It is hard enough to choose among the often bewildering range of jams sold; how to choose between jam now and jam tomorrow? Comparing different products is hard enough but when considered over time and different possible states of the world, the range of choices we make explodes exponentially.

Somehow we make decisions. We decide to leave the good wine till tomorrow, the better wine till next year, and drink the cheap stuff today because it will not improve with age. We borrow to pay for college, go to the doctor today for that pain in our leg, and we gamble that the cats will not do something awful on our couch if we put off cleaning the kitty litter. In each case, we choose either to receive pleasure or pain today or to defer it to the future, balancing the pleasures of jam today and the possible pleasures of jam tomorrow.

Economists have a measure for balancing present and future pains and pleasures. The *expected present value*[1] of an act or asset is *our guess* as to the value of the act *discounted*[2] by an interest rate that equilibrates present and future pleasures. The interest rate is positive because we prefer pleasure today to pleasure tomorrow for two reasons. First, we have a positive rate of time preference because there is a risk that we will not live to the future or that the jam may somehow disappear. Second, we have a liquidity preference and prefer to have things now just in case we need quick access. If we have a ravenous appetite and desperately need a sandwich of peanut butter and jam, we do not want to wait and do not want to go running around looking to buy jam.

The expected present value equation gives us, for any interest rate, the amount that we would be willing to pay now for something in the future, or the amount that we would insist on receiving in the future for some amount now. In financial markets, for example, we discount money next year according to an interest rate r such that we would be indifferent between having $100 now and having $100*(1+r) next year, because we could put the $100 in the bank and receive $100*(1+r) next year. Next year's money, $M_{t+1} = (1+r)*PV_t$ where PV_t is this year's money, or the present value of next year's money M_{t+1}, if the discount rate is r. Where EPV_t is the discounted value of an expected sum (EM) in one year at an interest rate r, the equation for present value would be:

(13.1) $EPV_t = EM_{t+1}/(1+r)$

Note that this involves two calculations: the formation of expectations and the discounting of expectations to form present values. The first involves a measure of risk and uncertainty; the second is a question of *liquidity*[3] or the preference to have things in hand rather than out in the world somewhere. How much is a lottery ticket worth if it is the lucky ticket with the (randomly) chosen number? Even if you know that it is the winning ticket and will pay $100 tomorrow, a situation with no uncertainty, then you would still prefer cash to the ticket because it is more liquid, can more easily be turned into something else that you want. Add uncertainty and risk to

A lottery ticket from Massachusetts in 1758. Proceeds from the lottery were to be used to finance an invasion of French Canada. The lottery was to raise money for the war because consumers paid more than the expected value for the tickets, either from patriotism or from the excitement of participating in the gamble. Paradoxically, many of the same people who buy lottery tickets also buy insurance.

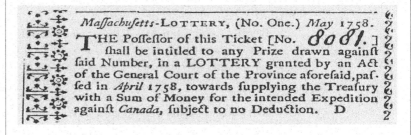

Massachusetts-LOTTERY, (No. One.) May 1758.
THE Possessor of this Ticket [No. 8081.] shall be intitled to any Prize drawn against said Number, in a LOTTERY granted by an Act of the General Court of the Province aforesaid, passed in *April* 1758, towards supplying the Treasury with a Sum of Money for the intended Expedition against *Canada*, subject to no Deduction.   D

On his 100th birthday, England's Abe Coleman might have been reluctant to save his cake for the future. By contrast, these young Iranians would risk police abuse to improve their country in the future because they expect to live for many more years.

this if there are other tickets for the lottery. Then you have to discount the value of the ticket still further, for the danger that it will not pay off and for the unpleasantness of the risk.

LIQUIDITY AND THE INTEREST RATE ON FUTURE CASH

Once the expected value of the gamble is established, it still needs to be put in present value terms so that money (or other costs and benefits) at different times and different liquidity may be compared. There are several ways to think about present values. The present value formula is a financial tool, a way to price assets which will give a return in the future. Given some interest rate and a guaranteed sum of money (M), the present value is how much you would be willing to pay for M to be delivered after some interval of time (the difference between t and t+1). Given some interest rate r and a guaranteed payout of M, PV is how much you would pay, how much you would lend someone who promises to give you M in the future, how much would you pay for a bond or a certificate of deposit with a payout in the future. This is really a question about how much would you discount the future payout for being illiquid now.

If we know for certain that we will receive the promised payment in the future, then we will still prefer to have it now, jam today rather than jam tomorrow, because we like having access to our stuff. This is the liquidity preference for things that are more easily turned into other things. High discount rates say that we want to hold onto our cash liquidity and will sacrifice that for future benefits unless these future benefits are very large. If your personal liquidity preference rate is high, you will lend money only with a very large payout and may even engage in activities that might seem self-destructive in order to have liquidity now. You won't fix your roof, for example, because you do not want to lock your wealth into the roof. You want it available to buy something else, even though not fixing the roof now will cost more in the future. You burn your candle at both ends and don't worry about tomorrow. Even where you are perfectly confident that a bond will pay off as promised, you may refuse to buy it without a high interest rate because you want to hold onto cash, an asset that is easier to use to buy other things. If you insist on a very high interest rate, that says that you really want to be free to buy things now and will charge others a lot to have the freedom to buy different things that you get with cash. Better cash in hand than a relatively illiquid promise of cash tomorrow. You may be perfectly confident, for example, that a shopping mall will be very profitable, but you will not invest in building it unless you are offered a very high interest rate because you would rather keep your wealth liquid so that you can have it to pay tuition. It is hard to pay tuition with shares of a shopping mall because colleges and universities want ready cash to pay *their* bills.

RISK, UNCERTAINTY, AND THE RISK-RETURN FRONTIER

There is another way to look at the present value formula: it is society's interest rate, a measure of the future's importance. How much money would you demand next year to sacrifice $100 today? You can use equation 13.2 to calculate your implicit interest rate from this question. If you would insist on at least $200, an interest rate of 100% or more, then you are extremely present-oriented and the interest rate that you would demand before you would save anything for the future would be very

Notoriously present-oriented, rock star **Sid Vicious** did not live to see his 22nd birthday.

high. Alternatively, if you would accept very little to give up $100 now, if you were very future-oriented, then your interest rate would be low.

(13.2) $(1+r) = M_{t+1} / PV_t$

Beyond liquidity preference, your discount rate reflects your assessment of the risk that an investment will fail. Some value the future less or more because they have different expectations that they will live to see it and that an investment in it will pay off for them. If you do not expect to live to tomorrow, then you want your cash now so you can enjoy it. What value is even a very high future return if you will not live to see it? We might expect r would be higher for those who do not anticipate seeing the future either because of age or poor health. We might expect, for this reason, that young people might be more concerned about the environment and about global warming; they might care more about a future that they would see.[4] And your children and later descendants may have a different rate of time preference. They may wish that you valued the future more.

If health and life expectancy provide one simple explanation of variation in discount rates, they also provide a clue about a larger condition: the impact of risk and uncertainty. In practice, we are always making decisions based on expected values and *probability*[5] rather than with certainty. We all know that we will die, for example, but few of us know when. The date of our death is a matter of *uncertainty*[6] and *risk*.[7] We make wagers or gambles on the probability that we will die. These bets are called "life insurance," where we put up relatively small amounts against much larger bets by the insurance company. So long as we stay alive, we lose the bet and our wager. When we die, we win and they have to pay off. Similarly, we make

Milton Friedman called **Irving Fisher (1867-1947)** the greatest American economist. He was a pioneer in monetary economics, utility theory, and theories of behavior under risk and uncertainty.

bets on card games, lottery tickets, horses and other sporting events based on our expectation of the probability of success. We value each bet according to that probability and the return if successful.

Knowing the risk of disappointment, we can discount any future returns by the probability that an enterprise will fail. If we have a fair coin that pays $100 for every time it comes up heads and $0 for every time it is tails, then we would expect an average return of $100*0.5+ $0*0.5 = $50. This is the highest amount that we would pay for the coin flip. To be sure, we might have a run of good luck, with repeated heads, or bad, with repeated tails. But if we flipped the coin a large number of times, then we would find that our returns would drift towards this average.

In truth, we know nothing with certainty about the future. Even a coin flip or a throw of the dice involves uncertainty because we do not know for certain if the coin or die is fair. Every financial decision we make involves larger gambles than this about the future. Some gambles have high probabilities, like whether the world will survive the night or our deposit in a national bank will be safe. Other gambles

Playing with fair dice, we know the probability of any particular outcome. Real life is way more complicated and often much less certain. It often involves more risk as well.

have lower probability, about whether our roommate will pay us back for lending him money or our team will beat the point spread in a game. All of these gambles involve two elements: known risk and unknown uncertainty. We don't know whether we will really need a new roof or if the old one will last through another year; we don't know if our old car will die or turn over the odometer again; we don't know whether we will have a job next year or if we will really enjoy the high return that we expect on a particular investment. We don't even know if the world will be there in which we can enjoy the fruits of our investments. Life is filled with uncertainty and risk. and we know less about much of it than we do of the odds on a game of dice or cards.

To decide on any course of action with known risk, we can make estimates like this of the expected value of the returns, estimates that are really just guesses about the joint likelihood of different events, and the likelihood of what it would be worth to us if it did. At best, these guesses reflect both risk and uncertainty, both things we do not know but believe that we can make informed guesses about, and things that are truly unknowable.[8] This was the seminal contribution of the American economist Irving Fisher in his 1892 Ph.D. dissertation at Yale, *Mathematical Investigations in the Theory of Value and Prices*. (The American economist Paul Samuelson called this "the greatest" economics dissertation ever written.)

Fisher's insight was to incorporate uncertainty into the long-established calculation of present values, showing that the discount factor applied to time is not only a measure of li-

U.S. Air Force **Lt. Gen. Douglas M. Fraser**, deputy commander, U.S. Pacific Command, performs the ceremonial coin toss before the National Football League's 2009 Pro Bowl game at Aloha Stadium, Hawaii, Feb. 8, 2009.

quidity but also a discount for the risk and uncertainty of an event occurring. Our discount formula, therefore, needs to include both the rate of time and liquidity preference and the probability leading to an expected value, and a measure of our uncertainty. Fisher shows, for example, that the difference between an investment in *bonds*[9] and in *stocks*[10] is not absolute but a matter of degree. Neither provides a perfect guarantee of payment, both investments would suffer significant loss if the company failed. For both, the likelihood of payment depends on the state of the company and the world. While bonds have a higher likelihood, a higher probability, of payment, Fisher argues that this is balanced against the stock having a higher probability of actually making a larger payment. In a competitive financial market, the greater risk means that the stock equity must pay out a higher regular return to balance the higher probability that it will default completely and pay nothing.

Describing what has come to be called *efficient capital market theory*, Fisher shows that in the absence of monopoly power or transactions costs, the prices of future assets, assets that will pay off differently in different states of the world, will be priced to reflect the probability of each state and the value of the payoff in that state such that, after taking account of the price of liquidity, an investor cannot make money on average by choosing any investment over any other. In an efficient capital market, you will be able to buy an asset that will pay off a certain sum in a particular contingency, a particular state of the world, and that asset will be priced to reflect the probability of that state and the market's current discount rate.[11] Arbitrage by financial institutions will have brought the price of each asset in line with its probable return such that you cannot earn higher returns any more than you would expect to make money by rolling dice or choosing cards from a fair deck.

From Fisher has come all of orthodox financial economics, along with the century-old campaign to de-

FIGURE 13-1

RISK-RETURN FRONTIER. VALUE OF BET WITH $100 RETURN. EFFECT OF DIFFERENT PROBABILITIES AND DIFFERENT ATTITUDES TOWARDS RISK AND UNCERTAINTY

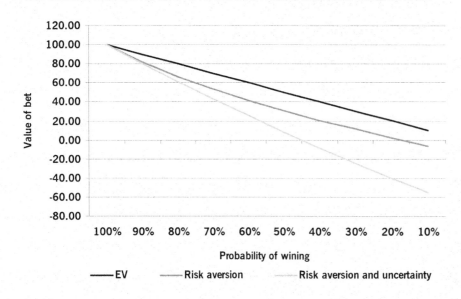

regulate financial markets on the grounds that regulation reduces economic welfare by preventing people from engaging in desired risky activities and arbitrage. Fisher replaced the concept of present value, appropriate for guaranteed outcomes with perfect certainty, with *expected value*.[12] Instead of equation 13.1, Fisher calculates expected value as the weighted average of the value of outcomes in the different possible states of the world where the weights are the probabilities of the different states. In equation 13.3, for example, the expected value of an investment with two possible outcomes is the value of the outcome in the first case (V1) times the probability that this would happen, plus the value in the second case (V2) times the probability that this will happen.[13]

(13.3) $EV_t = \alpha V1_{t+1}/(1+r) + (1-\alpha)V2_{t+1}/(1+r)$

EV_t is the expected value in time t of a certain sum (V1) in one year if the interest rate is r and the probability assigned to this is α and V2 is the value of the outcome otherwise (at probability $1-\alpha$).

If the probabilities are accurate, then the expected value would be the average value of this investment done over a very large number of cases. Consider, for example, a coin-toss game where nothing is paid if the coin lands tails but $100 is paid if it lands heads. Assuming a fair coin, the probability of each outcome is 0.5 and the expected value is:

Expected value = 0.5 * $0 + 0.5 * $100 = $50

If you conduct this coin flip a very large number of times, you would earn an average of $50. With a large number of trials, you could pay as much as $50 for each coin flip at a profit.

After taking account of liquidity, Fisher argues that it is uncertainty that explains any variation in return for different assets because people value more certain returns over those subject to more uncertainty and risk. The coin-toss game is worth $50 a flip. The value rises with the return to a win (say from $100 to $200) and with the probability of this return. Here we have three variables: the value of the asset, the return on the asset, and the probability that the return will be realized. With known risk, the value rises with probability of success. Higher returns will raise the value of the asset. At a constant return, lower probability of success will lower the value of the asset. And, at a constant value of the asset, a higher probability of success is balanced by lower returns.

This is the source of one of the most fundamental concepts in the economics of financial markets: the *risk-return curve*.[14] Investors will pay less for assets with greater likelihood of failure and will insist on higher returns before buying an asset with more uncertainty, giving an upward sloping risk-return frontier (see Figure 13-1).

At the far left of the line on Figure 13-1 is the risk-free rate of return. From there, investors will discount assets with greater risk, agreeing to buy them only at a discount that allows for a higher rate of return when they pay off, in order to allow for the losses suffered when the investment fails. This risk-return profile assumes perfect knowledge of the future and assumes that investors are *risk neutral* and indifferent between a guarantee of $50 and a 50% chance of $100 or $0. This would be the case, however, only in the case of constant marginal utility, so that the first $50 and the next $50 are of equal value. In the case of diminishing marginal utility, however, the first $50, the amount lost in the case of failure, is worth more than the next $50, the money gained in the case of success. In this case, *risk aversion* due to diminishing marginal utility will lead investors to insist on a premium before making a risky bet, creating a risk-return profile like figure 13-2.

The risk-neutral investor is indifferent between investments at different levels of risk. All investments will have the same expected value with discounts (or *risk premia*[15]) just large enough to cover the losses when the asset (predictably) fails. The risk-averse investor, by contrast, will insist on a risk premium, a higher value on the expected return, to compensate for the lesser value of high returns compared with what is lost at higher marginal utility. This premium is enhanced by *liquidity preference* and *uncertainty*. While liquidity preference discourages any fixed investment, true uncertainty, where outcomes are not

An act granting a royal charter to a maritime insurance company. Such companies assume the risk that a ship will sink by selling policies that will guarantee payment to their holders regardless of the outcome of the voyage. If the ship sinks or if the ship returns, the policy holder will receive the same amount. But the company loses if the ship sinks and pockets all the money if the ship returns safely.

only unknown but unknowable, leads investors to discount further any projected returns. The *risk-averse*[16] especially will insist on a larger premium on risk and uncertainty. They will buy uncertain risky assets only at lower prices and higher rates of return, or with a higher expected value even in cases where the risk is predictable.[17]

EFFICIENT CAPITAL MARKETS

Because risk-averse investors will price risky assets at below their expected value, we would expect that in cases of knowable and predictable risk, the risk-neutral will buy riskier assets from the risk averse, earning returns somewhat above the risk-free rate in exchange for assuming the extra risk. This is an efficient process in the sense that no one is worse off and some are better off: the risk-averse can shed risk, the risk-neutral can earn more, and companies can raise capital at a somewhat lower cost by dealing with risk-neutral rather than risk-averse investors. This is an argument for deregulating financial markets and encouraging the development of new financial instruments ranging from mutual funds to credit default swaps. By sharing and shedding risk, such instruments allow the risk-averse to transfer risk to the risk-neutral.

If everyone acts according to their own subjective beliefs about the likelihood of different outcomes, their own sense of risk aversion, and their own discount rate, then most will not pay as much for financial assets as their expected value. This allows optimists, those with low liquidity preference, and those with low rates of risk aversion to profit by buying riskier gambles from pessimists with higher preferences for liquidity and higher rates of risk aversion. In effect, they offer a form of insurance to other investors. By taking these assets off the hands of risk-averse and liquidity-loving investors, risk-neutral financial intermediaries allow them to dispose of undesirable assets and to gain liquidity. The financial intermediaries are able to profit on average because they are buying these assets at less than their expected value. If there are enough confident and optimistic market actors without risk aversion, then prices will be bid up close to a valuation where investments sell at their expected value. The pessimistic and those with high risk aversion or liquidity preference will sell at lower rates of return, in effect paying a premium to the risk-neutral for the equivalent of an insurance policy.

Financial institutions profit from a type of arbitrage when they buy risky bets at a price less than the objective expected value but higher than these bets are worth to individuals with risk aversion or uncertainty. In some long run, these institutions will profit, but there can be a sustained period of bad luck, a run of bad coin flips, that can challenge their liquidity. So long as financial institutions have enough liquidity, enough capital, to ride out these bad periods, they can provide a useful public service. By providing an array of investment vehicles, such as in a company selling mutual funds, they can provide investors with a variety of risk-return opportunities, matching investor's liquidity preference and risk aversion to different types of assets and different mixes of investments.

If there are enough competing risk-neutral financial institutions, then competition among them should drive up the price of financial assets to their expected value. At that point, there can be no profit from reallocat-

> **Frank Knight (1885-1972)** taught economics at the University of Chicago from 1927-1955. The author of many important works on capital theory, externalities, and social policy, he is best known for his first book, Risk, Uncertainty, and Profit (1921) where he demonstrates that profits will be earned in a perfectly competitive environment as a reward to assuming uncertain risks.

FIGURE 13-2

RATE OF RETURN ON FINANCIAL ASSETS, RISK AND LIQUIDITY PREMIA, 1928-2013

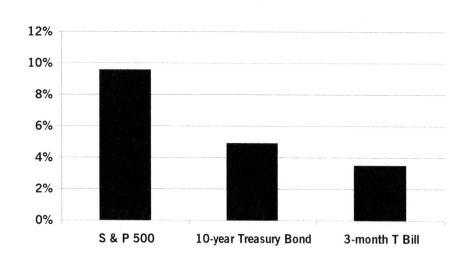

ing a portfolio, none from owning one asset or another. In *efficient financial markets*, market prices reflect all the available information. With adequate information, there will be just enough return to risk to compensate for expected failures, and just enough additional return to uncertainty to cover the commonly held expectation of risk for those assets.

If the risk-reward line has a higher slope than the actual risk, this may reflect consistently imperfect information. It may also be due to a failure of market arbitrage to equilibrate returns to different assets. If there are consistently higher returns to owning certain assets rather than others, it may be a sign of the *inefficiency* of financial markets: either market participants are consistently wrong in their evaluation of risk, or some participants are able to manipulate market prices. The risk-return framework can be thus used to explain differences in the rate of return to different assets, to explain the variation in returns across different assets with different risks, and to allocate returns between compensation for risk and uncertainty, and to market imperfections.

Economist Frank Knight went further and used this framework to explain the persistent return to corporate ownership, the relatively high profit/wage rate where passive owners can earn much more than active workers. Rather than a return to exploitation, he labeled profit a reward to investors for taking risks with their money.[18] For financial economists, the persistence of financial profit is one aspect of a larger phenomenon: the high equity premium, or the higher rate of return on equity investment (or stocks on the New York Stock Exchange), compared to safer investments in bonds, due to equity investment's greater risk. People will buy such assets only at a lower price and higher return to compensate for the risk that the company will fail. Over the past 85 years, this premium has averaged 4.6% per annum over safe investments in government bonds. At this rate, the relative wealth of equity-holders would double every fifteen years. If all of this excess return was due to risk aversion, it suggests an enormous price paid for safety, and it does not explain why competition among risk-neutral investors did not bid down this premium.

INEFFICIENT FINANCIAL MARKETS?

Financial economists have made a cottage industry out of studies measuring the equity premium. For individuals, the equity premium reflects the rational allocation of investments across different assets with risk-averse individuals shunning riskier assets unless they have a higher expected value. This cannot, however, explain the premium in competitive markets. In efficient-market theory, risk-neutral investors should bid up the price, and bid down the returns, on equity investments whenever their expected return is above the expected return on safer assets. Similarly, whenever the expected value of returns on safer assets is below that of equity and other unsafe investments, risk-neutral investors should sell safer assets, driving down their price and driving up returns until the expected value of the returns equals that of safer assets. Because risk-neutral investors are indifferent to predictable and calculable risk, as against true uncertainty, *arbitrage*[19] should bid away the equity risk premium.

It may be that the relative number of risk-averse investors is so large that

The American economist **George Akerlof (b. 1940)** won the Nobel Prize in 2001 for his studies of the impact of information asymmetry on markets. In his classic paper on used car markets, he shows that because a car's quality is in part unobservable except with experience, buyers will not believe a seller's claim that a car is of above average quality and will not pay what those cars are worth. This will prevent owners of good, well-maintained cars from selling them, while encouraging owners of bad cars ("lemons") to try to dump their cars. When consumers realize that the used car market is being flooded with lemons while good cars are withdrawn, they will lower their estimate of the quality of any particular car, driving down the price and leading to a further erosion of quality until the only cars available are lemons and the only buyers are those desperate for a ride and aware that they are buying a lemon. In this way, asymmetric information produces a result similar to that of "Gresham's Law" of money: the bad drives out the good, eventually destroying the market.

they swamp the risk-neutral and drive up risk premia; the risk-neutral may be so outnumbered that even over very long periods of time they cannot arbitrage away the equity premium. This is extremely implausible, since there are large risk neutral corporate entities, including bond-holding firms and investment banks that are able to drive markets. And, furthermore, the large equity premium suggests that risk-neutral investors will become relatively richer and a growing share of the market over time. In the long run, the equity premium should be narrowing.

Nor is it sufficient explanation to say that the equity premium reflects true uncertainty where all investors, risk-neutral and risk-averse, demand a risk premium. How much true uncertainty can there be after over eighty years on the New York Stock Exchange? How long should we give investors to figure out that it is a good idea to buy equity assets because their rate of return is consistently double that of government bonds? And if the equity premium reflects true uncertainty, shouldn't it be falling over time with the accumulation of information and better models of corporate profitability? If not, why do investors pay so much for advice and information? And, in any case, is there really enough uncertainty to explain an equity premium of almost 5%?

I suspect that explanations of the equity risk premium rooted in efficient market models are wrong because the fundamental premise, that financial markets are efficient and that arbitrage will eliminate price differentials, is wrong. Instead, I would suggest that the large equity premium measures the extent to which financial markets deviate from the expectations of efficient market theory. Financial market inefficiency may be caused by monopolistic control over particular sites, or it may reflect asymmetric information. Or it may be that this inefficiency is endemic to the nature of the financial markets themselves.

SOURCES OF IMPERFECT FINANCIAL MARKETS: MONOPOLIES, ASYMMETRIC INFORMATION, AND HERDS

The persistent equity premium comes from monopolistic restrictions on financial markets, both from legal restrictions on the buying and selling of financial assets and from the concentration of information about the real value and management of assets. One cannot buy and sell corporate equity at will. Not only are there complicated government regulations on markets but there are huge network effects so that market participants, both buyers and sellers, prefer to sell in large markets. (Larger markets are more efficient because of economies to scale in administering them and because they are less vulnerable to manipulation by a few actors, making them less volatile.) Because people prefer to invest in some markets over others, those who control access to those preferred markets are able to extract economic rents from their privileged position. To preserve these rents, incumbents, those who already have the right to buy and sell in these markets, restrict access. The right to buy and sell in the New York Stock Exchange (NYSE), for example, is highly prized because it gives one access to the New York financial market. A "seat" on the NYSE, with the right to buy and sell there, has sold for as much as $4 million (in 2005). The high price on these seats suggests that the NYSE raises the price of existing equity by restricting the ability of new entrants to enter the market. It also suggests one source of the equity premium, the restriction that formal markets, like the NYSE, place on financial transactions.[20]

Compared with even 20 years ago, there are many more large financial markets and many more ways for investors to exchange securities than in the past. But there is no evidence that the profits of financial market firms or the equity premium has been reduced by active competition among financial firms. The growth in the number of financial markets may only have kept pace with the growing volume of trading in these exchanges. It may also suggest that monopoly power in the institutions of financial markets

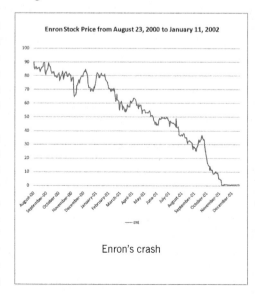

Enron's crash

The "curb market" at Broad Street in lower Manhattan, later became the American Stock Exchange. In this picture from 1902, the New York Stock Exchange building under construction can be seen in the background.

has relatively little impact on financial profits, or, at least, the monopoly access to equity markets contributes relatively little to these profits. If so, these particular monopolistic practices might be the least of the sources of financial market imperfections.

A more important source of financial market profits, and inefficiency, may be the presence of *asymmetric information*,[21] where one side to the financial market knows significantly more about the property being sold than the other. By itself, asymmetric information does not necessarily prevent a market from functioning efficiently and generating happy surpluses. On the contrary, we often buy products and services from vendors who know more than we do. There are large markets in professional services. We hire doctors, lawyers, engineers, financial advisers, and others *because* they know things that we do not know and cannot verify. We hire them for their specialized knowledge, their access to asymmetric information.[22]

If consumers distrust professionals, then market transactions will not happen. The Nobel Prize-winning economist George Akerlof described the working of one market with asymmetric information without trust in a classic article, "The Market for 'Lemons,'" where he showed that these markets can easily degenerate so that no trading will happen.[23] Trade happens in markets with asymmetric information because consumers are led to believe that the seller is providing honest information about the quality of the product or service. Sometimes, government regulations are imposed to assure quality, as happens with milk dating and drug safety. In other cases, consumers may be reassured because the seller relies on repeat business and consumers expect that the seller will fear antagonizing consumers. Sometimes, consumers are reassured because sellers (like physicians) have been trained in a professional tradition committed to honest service and belong to a professional association that vouches for its members' conduct. Other consumers shop around and choose vendors based on a "gut feeling" about the seller or on recommendations from friends or members of a community.

These last are particularly vulnerable because people regularly use the behavior of others as a marker of quality. Assuming that others know better about the real quality of assets, these consumers move in herds, investing where others are investing, buying in rising markets and selling on the downside. This can be a good strategy for a time. If you buy on a rising market then you may make profits, on paper at least, if the market keeps rising. Danger comes, however, if you hold too long and then sell on the decline.

As an alternative to herd behavior, government regulators and private associations have been most important in regulating financial markets, and their

Charles Ponzi (1882-1949), courtesy of United States Department of Justice.

In 1919, Italian-born **Charles Ponzi** noticed that currency upheaval had made U.S. postage cheaper in Italy than in the United States. He launched a Boston company promising to double investors' money within 90 days. While other costs prevented him from profiting from the planned arbitrage, Ponzi was able to pay off investors from the rapidly growing number of new investors. Soon people throughout New England and the United States were pouring money into his company, giving him the cash to pay high return to investors while withdrawing huge sums for himself. In February 1920, Ponzi pocketed $5,000 (about $54,000 in 2011 dollars), $30,000 ($324,000) in March, and in May, $420,000 ($4.6 million). When critics began to question his accounting, Ponzi's scheme quickly unraveled. Ponzi served five years in prison on federal and state charges. After his release, he moved to Florida where he opened a real-estate business promising 200% returns from the sale of swampland. Convicted of fraud, he was deported to Italy where he tried more frauds and eventually fled to Brazil, where he died indigent in 1949.

Alan Greenspan (b. 1926). As chairman of the United States Federal Reserve System from 1986-2007, **Alan Greenspan** was a leading advocate of deregulation of financial markets. After the crash of 2007-8, he admitted in congressional testimony that he had not anticipated such a serious crisis. "Those of us who have looked to the self-interest of lending institutions to protect shareholder's equity -- myself especially—are in a state of shocked disbelief."

failure led to enormous fraud since 1980 with devastating effects on the American and world economy. As a social experiment, this period illustrates the enormous profits that can be made from asymmetric information, especially where consumers believe that market regulators and professional standards are still being maintained.

Without effective regulation, consumers have been exploited by insiders with asymmetric information. Consider, for example, one of the most successful companies of the 1990s: Enron. An oil and gas servicing company, Enron moved into financial services and market management during the internet boom of the 1990s. For a time, its stock price soared and the company boasted that its management included "the smartest guys in the room," drawn from the best and brightest from Harvard Business School and other prestigious institutions. Whatever else it did, their intelligence and arrogance disarmed critics. When Jeffrey Skilling, Enron's president, suggested in 2000 that the company's money-losing broadband network business alone was worth $29 billion, investors believed him and his PowerPoint slide. (*The New York Times* called the slide "nifty.") Believers were rewarded when Enron's shares rose by more than 50% in 2000, tripling in barely two years. While some were skeptical of management's claims that Enron had become an Internet company, even most skeptics were loath to be left behind when there was so much money to be made. Most openly acknowledged that they did not understand Enron's new lines of business and, so long as everyone was making money, why quibble over a few murky details?

The same combination of greed and awe explained the behavior of many of Bernard Madoff's clients, who were happy to make so much money without questioning too deeply how he accomplished his financial legerdemain. The former head of the NASDAQ stock exchange, Madoff was one of the country's leading financial advisors with a reputation for brilliance. Investors competed for the "privilege" of having him manage their money. And a lucrative privilege it was! One investor, Jeffry Picower, received profits on his Madoff investments of over $7 billion between 1989 and 2009, with some accounts reporting annual returns of as much as 950%. The only problem is that there never was any real investment: Madoff left the money in an account at Chase Bank, forged transaction records and paid dividends out of money paid in by new investors. Suspicious of his remarkable success, some legitimate businesses, including many hedge funds, refused to deal with him. Others, notably Chase Bank, ignored any concerns to join the party. Chase eventually had to return over a billion dollars in profits and fees earned from Madoff's Ponzi scheme.[24]

Of course, it all collapsed. Madoff was undone when the stock market crash of 2007-9 led many of his investors to try to withdraw their money just when there was too little coming in to pay them off; Ponzi schemes do not run in reverse. Enron too was undone by illusory promises of huge gains. For a time it was protected by its accountants, happy to turn a blind eye so they could continue pocketing huge fees. And it was protected by regulators who were at best understaffed and, at worst, may have been swayed by the company's large campaign donations.[25] In 2001, its executives and their complicit accountants and regulators could no longer cover-up the company's mounting losses. When Enron filed for bankruptcy protection, it stranded many of the company's vendors and workers, who were left with nothing in retirement accounts that they had filled with high-flying Enron stock.

Bernard Madoff, mugshot

I WILL BE GONE, YOU WILL BE GONE

The Enron and Madoff cases illustrate how easily financial markets can degenerate. Using privileged information, company managers can drive up stock prices to enrich themselves and their friends at the expense of outsiders. Knowing that there is privileged information out there, investors choose to follow the lead of insiders. There is a market correction for mendacity: dishonest schemes eventually fail and the company, and those who trusted its lying managers, suffer. But this correction can take years to operate, and it is too uncertain and too slow to dissuade either managers or investors. Investors are lured by the huge returns being made and quiet any doubts by remembering how much smarter the company managers are and how much more they know. As for the managers themselves, they can profit from the eventual market correction if they sell their own stock short and, in any case, their profits from the scheme can easily dwarf what they lose from the crash, including the value of their reputations.

How much are reputations worth? In financial markets the answer may be not much. Mendacious managers can obfuscate their crimes; one great advantage of having asymmetric information is the greater ease of a cover-up! Even caught, they can usually leave the industry with their profits, often returning by hiding behind a new corporate name or position. (This is what Charles Ponzi did several times.) There may be long-term effects of dishonesty, but much of the burden is borne by the company, not by individuals.[26] Often, the burden is not even on the company because government regulators and other financial market authorities choose to intervene, bailing out irresponsible banks and other institutions. They feel that it is better to reward a few companies for bad behavior than to punish the entire economy for their crimes.[27]

It is disheartening when mendacity and lying are rewarded. Worse, such behavior threatens the functioning of financial markets. Without protection to balance the power that asymmetric information gives sellers, financial markets will collapse like the used car markets described by Akerlof—potential buyers will devalue all financial products. If consumers assume that sellers are mendacious, then honest sellers cannot profit by their honesty and will be driven from the market, unable to compete with the mendacious.[28] This will cause a general market collapse when even the mendacious cannot sell their products to consumers, who become convinced that all financiers are thieves and liars.

To survive, financial markets require third-party regulation to assure potential buyers of product quality. Without enforced government regulations to establish standards of accounting and reporting, investors will avoid anonymous equity markets and will only invest where they have direct knowledge and reason to trust the persons involved. Seen in this way, financial market regulations are not interference with markets but are necessary for the very existence of financial markets. Passed after the stock market bubble of the 1920s, and the collapse of 1929-33, the Securities and Exchange Act of 1933 allowed the great stock market recovery of the 1930s and the expansion of the post-World War II years. Deregulation since 1982 has allowed insiders to exploit asymmetric information at the expense of others. Their enormous profits from deceit, helped to bring on a series of escalating financial and economic crises, from the Savings and Loan Debacle of the late 1980s to the Internet bubble of the late 1990s and, finally, the great crash of 2007-8. In 2010, Congress passed a new regulatory bill, the Dodd-Frank Wall Street Reform and Consumer Protection Act, to close some of these loopholes. We will see whether this reform is as effective as that of 1933.

FINANCIAL MARKET SUCCESS: MANIPULATION, BILLIANCE, AND EMOTIONAL INTELLIGENCE

Sir Isaac Newton was one of the most brilliant scientists, mathematicians, and human beings in history. One of the inventors of classical mechanics and calculus, he built the first practical observatory, developed a theory of color, and invented the cat door. He used his new theory of gravity to solve some of the oldest problems in human thought and to calculate the movement of planetary

Lehman Brothers sign for auction after the company's bankruptcy in September 2008.

FROM TULIPS TO MORTGAGE-BACKED SECURITIES
FINANCIAL MARKETS AND THE MADNESS OF CROWDS

Thirty years ago, economist Charles Kindleberger published a little book, *Manias, Panics, and Crashes* (New York, 1978), describing the normal tendency of capitalist financial markets to fluctuate between speculative excess (or "irrational exuberance" in the words of a recent central banker) and panic. Kindleberger describes about 40 of these panics over the nearly 260 years from 1720–1975, or one every seven years. Following Kindleberger's arithmetic, we were due for a panic because it had been seven years since the high-tech bubble burst and the stock market panic of 2000–1. And the panic came, bringing in its wake a tsunami of economic woe, liquidity shortages, canceled investments, rising unemployment, and economic distress.

Of course, more than mechanics and arithmetic are involved in the current financial panic. But there is a sense of inevitability about the manias and panics of capitalist financial markets, a sense described by writers from Karl Marx to John Maynard Keynes, Hyman Minsky, John Kenneth Galbraith, and Robert Shiller. The problem is that financial markets trade in unknown and unknowable future returns. Lacking real information, they are inevitably driven by the madness of crowds.

Unlike tangible commodities whose price should reflect its real value and real cost of production, financial assets are not priced according to any real returns, nor even according to some expected return, but rather according to expectations of what others will pay in the future, or, even worse, expectations of future expectations that others will have of assets' future return. From Dutch tulips in 1637 and the South Sea Bubble of 1720 (see p. 264), to Florida real estate in the 1920s or mortgage-backed securities today, it is always the same story of financial markets floating like a

FIGURE 1
STANDARD & POOR'S 500 INDEX OF STOCK PRICES, 1986-2015

Source: Standard & Poor's 500, historical data accesssed at Chicago Board Options Exchange (cboe.com).

Stock prices rose over the period 1986-2014 but at a very irregular pace with major booms in the late 1990s and before 2008 followed by sharp falls where prices fell by as much as 50%.

CHAPTER 13: TIME, RISK, AND UNCERTAINTY | 263

FIGURE 2

CASE-SHILLER INDEX OF U.S. RESIDENTIAL HOUSING PRICES, 2000-2010

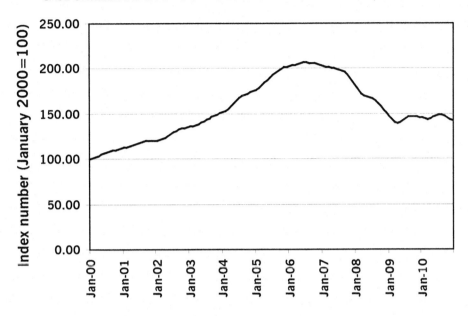

Source: Standard & Poor's, S&P/Case-Shiller Home Price Indices (standardandpoors.com).

Home prices more than doubled 2000-6 before falling by almost a third. This decline wiped out the equity that many Americans had in their homes, contributing to the Great Recession of 2008.

manic-depressive from euphoria to panic to bust. When unregulated, this process is made still worse by market manipulation, and simple fraud. Speculative markets like these can make some rich, and can even be exciting to watch, like a good game of poker; but this is a dangerous and irresponsible way to manage an economy.

There was a time when governments understood. Learning from past financial disasters, the United States established rules to limit the scope of financial euphoria and panic by strictly segregating different types of banks, by limiting financial speculation, and by requiring clear accounting of financial transactions. While they were regulated, financial markets contributed to the best period of growth in American history, the "glorious thirty" after World War II. To be sure, restrictions on speculative behavior and strict regulations made this a boring time to be a banker, and they limited earnings in the financial services sector. But, limited to a secondary role, finance served a greater good by providing liquidity for a long period of steady and relatively egalitarian economic growth.

Of course, over time we forgot why we had regulated financial markets, memory loss helped along by the combined efforts of free-market economists and self-interested bankers and others on Wall Street. To promote "competition," we lowered the barriers between different types of financial institutions, widening the scope of financial markets. We moved activities such as home mortgage lending onto national markets and allowed a rash of bank mergers to create huge financial institutions too large to be allowed to fail, but never too large to operate irresponsibly. Despite the growing scope and centralization of financial activity, the government accepted arguments that we could trust financial firms to self-regulate because it was in their interest to maintain credible accounting.

So we reap the whirlwind with a market collapse building to Great Depression levels. Once again, we learn history's lesson from direct experience: capitalist financial markets cannot be trusted. It is time to either reregulate or move beyond.

Tulipmania in Holland in the mid 1630s. Speculators drove the price of tulip bulbs up to the equivalent of over $250,000 before prices crashed. While many lost money, fortunes were made by those who profited from the run-up and sold before the crash.

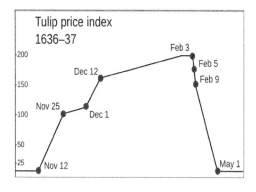

spheres. Yet, dealing with the London stock exchange, he himself whined: "I can calculate the movement of the stars, but NOT the madness of men."

Newton had a grievance with the London stock market. After a lifetime of hard work, he had accumulated a sizeable sum of about £7,000 (about $20 million), which he had invested in shares of the South Sea Company. Careful, he sold his stock, pocketing substantial profits. But, soon tempted by rising prices (the Company's stock price had doubled in his absence), Newton bought back in, just in time to lose everything.

If Sir Isaac Newton can go so wrong about stock prices, why should we be surprised if lesser men and women fail?

The problem with using the stock market as a measure or to direct economic activity is that profits and the value of stocks do not depend on what, if anything, the company produces or any profits it makes, nor on what the company will do in the future. Instead, the stock price depends on what other people *think* the company will do in the future or, worse still, what they think others will be thinking. Successful investing depends on choosing stocks that others will want, presumably because they will come to believe that, in the future, others will come to value these stocks. John Maynard Keynes, who was himself a very successful investor, compared successful investing to choosing which pretty face will be chosen by others, out of an array of photos, given the same instructions. The goal is not to choose the most attractive model but rather to choose the one that other people will choose as the most attractive. "It is not a case of choosing those [faces] that, to the best of one's judgment, are really the prettiest, nor even those that average opinion genuinely thinks the prettiest. We have reached the third degree where we devote our intelligences to anticipating what average opinion expects the average opinion to be. And there are some, I believe, who practice the fourth, fifth and higher degrees."

There were successful investors who made money from Dutch Tulips, from the South Sea Company, on Ponzi's scheme, from Bernard Madoff, and from Enron. They profited from these by anticipating the rise and selling out before the crash. Similarly, there are investors who lost money on important and successful companies like Apple or General Electric. Some financial analysts will say that you can always profit if you hold a portfolio of good companies and are ready to wait. Keynes may have better advice: "the market can remain irrational longer than you can remain solvent."

The important thing, if you want to make money, is not to be efficient, not to steer your investments towards good and well-managed companies, but to stay ahead of the market sense of what will be a good and well-managed company. Or, more correctly, you want to stay ahead of the market sense of what others will come to think of as a good and well-managed company. Because stock prices do not depend on "fundamentals" or any estimates of "the real value" of stocks, successful investors need to focus on the mood of others in the market. When moods alternate between waves of wild optimism and pessimism, stock prices cycle through what the late Charles Kindleberger called "manias, panics, and crashes." Stock prices move along a knife edge, always vulnerable to a panic collapse or a manic run up. Stock markets, therefore, are the most volatile economic indicator, fluctuating much more than real economic measures like gross domestic product or corporate profits.

For investors, there are warnings here, warnings about the dangers of manipulation and of the risks of being caught behind the curve of public opinion and forced to sell in a collapsing market. Success or failure in the market depends less on ability to read companies than on ability to read stock traders: are they manic or panicked? Even worse, success depends less on ability to read at all than on the sheer luck of being in the market at the right time, showing up with a tulip bulb in 1636 rather than 1638, or buying into Madoff in 1980 rather than 2008.

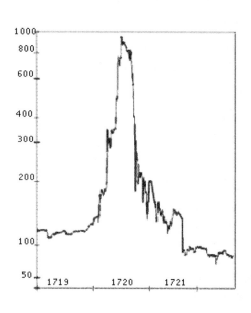

Price of shares of the British South Sea Company, 1720.

There are also implications for society and for the distribution of income. If emotional acumen and luck are so much more important than the ability to choose good investments, then should investors be rewarded so well? Are they performing an important social function for which they should be well rewarded? We leave to financial markets the important social functions of directing investment across businesses and industries, deciding where we will go as an economy. If stock prices are driven by irrational exuberance and mob panics, then do we want these crucial decisions to be made in financial markets?

Finally, if financial markets are inherently unstable, no more stable than the cumulative animal spirits of those involved, then can we trust them with the provision of old-age security and care for people's savings? And, if they are driven by such irrational exuberance, can we trust them with the management of our macroeconomies?

In early 2000, America Online purchased Time Warner for $182 b in stock and debt. This acquisition was made possible by the enormously inflated value of AOL stock. In 2009, AOL-Time Warner spun off its AOL division for about $3 b.

DISCUSSION QUESTIONS

What is the "present value" of a future return? How is it calculated?

What is the "expected present value"? How is it calculated?

What is the "discount rate" of future returns? What determines an individual's discount rate?

What is "liquidity preference"?

What is the difference between "risk" and "uncertainty"? How do individuals price an asset subject to risk? How do they price assets subject to uncertainty?

What is the "risk-return" frontier? What is its slope?

What is "risk aversion"? How does it relate to marginal utility? What happens to the slope of the risk-return frontier with increasing risk aversion? What happens to the slope with uncertainty? How does risk aversion change the slope of the risk-return frontier with uncertainty?

The great English economist **John Maynard Keynes (1883-1946)** was also the very successful bursar of Kings College, Cambridge University. During his tenure in this position, from 1927-45, he earned average annual returns on the college's investments of over 12%, during a time when the UK stock market fell by 15%. Notwithstanding his own success, Keynes warned against the belief that financial markets reflect real economic circumstances. In particular, he urged a much larger role for governments in allocating investment. "Speculators may do no harm as bubbles on a steady stream of enterprise. But the position is serious when enterprise becomes the bubble on a whirlpool of speculation. When the capital development of a country becomes a by-product of the activities of a casino, the job is likely to be ill-done."

In a fair market with full information shared by all, how can risk-neutral investors profit from the risk-aversion of others?

What is insurance? Why do people buy insurance policies? What type of people buy? Who sells insurance? How do they make profits?

Why have stock equities had higher returns than long-term Treasury bonds? Why have Treasury bonds had higher returns than short-term Treasury notes?

What does Akerloff mean by saying that used cars are a "lemon market"? What would you think if someone offers to sell you a used car? Would you pay full price? Would you sell a used car that you knew was in pristine condition?

What is "asymmetric information"? How does it undermine markets for used cars? How did it allow the managers and owners of Enron and other companies to make extraordinary profits? How does asymmetric information discourage investors in stock equity.

ENDNOTES

[1]This is the value of a future benefit or cost discounted to today. It is how much we would pay today for something (or to avoid something) in the future.

[2]The discount rate is the rate that equilibrates present and future values in the present value calculation. A high discount rate means future benefits are not worth as much (compared to if the discount rate were low); a low interest rate means that future benefits are worth relatively more today (compared to if the interest rate were high).

[3]Liquidity refers to the extent to which an asset can easily be converted into something else. For this purpose, cash is the ultimate liquid asset while a promise of "jam tomorrow" might be relatively illiquid.

[4]There is evidence of this. The proportion in a recent Gallup Poll who believed that "immediate" and "drastic" action was needed to protect the environment falls from 41% of those under age 65 to 27% of those over age 65. See: http://www.gallup.com/poll/26971/Environmental-Concern-Holds-Firm-During-Past-Year.aspx

[5]The probability of an event is an individual's belief about the likelihood that something will happen. Estimates of the probability of events range from 0 (completely impossible) to 1 (absolutely certain).

[6]The state of not knowing and not being able to know whether something will happen.

[7]A state of uncertainty, where there is unknown information about whether something bad or good will happen.

[8]I say "at best" because, as we will discuss, these guesses are often subject to malicious intervention by interested parties who seek to manipulate our judgments of both the risk and the uncertainty.

[9]A financial instrument issued by a government or business paying a fixed amount at a certain time.

[10]A financial instrument representing a share of the equity in a business paying a variable amount in dividends according to the performance of the company and management's decision whether to issue dividends or to retain earnings for further investment in the enterprise.

[11]A good description of Fisher's contribution and the theory of efficient capital markets is in Justin Fox, *The Myth of the Rational Market: A History of Risk, Reward, and Delusion on Wall Street*, 1st ed (New York: Harper Business, 2009); for empirical critiques, see Robert J. Shiller, *Irrational Exuberance*, 2nd ed (Princeton, N.J: Princeton University Press, 2005); John Cassidy, "Rational Irrationality: Postscript: Paul Samuelson: The New Yorker," *New Yorker*, December 14, 2009, http://www.newyorker.com/online/blogs/johncassidy/2009/12/postscript-paul-samuelson.html; Dan Ariely, *Predictably Irrational: The Hidden Forces That Shape Our Decisions*, 1st ed (New York, NY: Harper, 2008).

[12]Expected value is the average value of a project or activity if it could be repeated an infinite number of times. It is subjective and depends on the probabilities individuals assign to each outcome.

[13]Because these are the only two possible outcomes, the probabilities must sum to 100% and each is 100% minus the other.

[14]At a higher risk that an asset will lose value or return little, investors will buy the asset only at a lower price because of the expected value.

[15]The risk premium is the excess over the risk-free return that an investment is expected to earn. In a competitive equilibrium with risk-neutral investors, an asset's risk premium, the compensation investors receive for tolerating extra risk, will just equal the net expected losses on the investment so that all investments will have equal expected values.

[16]Someone is risk-averse who prefers a certain outcome to one of equal probabilistic expected value. In the case of a coin-toss where heads pays nothing and tails pays $2, a risk-neutral person will price this toss at $1, its expected value. The risk-averse person, however, will not buy it at $1 because they prefer the certainty of the $1 in hand to the gamble with a 50% risk of nothing (and a 50% risk of $2). The risk-averse investor would only buy uncertain investments like the coin flip at a lower price (that is, with a higher rate of return) and they will insist on an ever higher rate of return for more risky investments.

[17]Presumably they will insist on an even higher risk premium in cases of true uncertainty.

[18]One might question whether the risk taken by investors is greater than the risk that workers have:

they lose their jobs and livelihood if a company fails, while investors only lose money.

[19]The practice of buying in one market with low prices to resell in another market where prices are higher.

[20]Stock exchanges, like the NYSE, have been exempted from anti-trust laws on the grounds that they are regulated through the Securities laws (by the Securities and Exchange Commission) and that further competition might "lower the service and threaten the responsibility of members" (Congressional debate quoted in *Gordon v. New York Stock Exchange* 422 U.S. 659 (1975).

[21]A situation where one party to a transaction has access to significant information denied the other side.

[22]There is also a market in second opinions, including physicians, home and car inspectors, and others who are paid to verify the advice of others. In the case of financial markets, the analogous group would be accountants and financial analysts who are hired to verify company financial reports.

[23]George A. Akerlof, "The Market for 'Lemons': Quality Uncertainty and the Market Mechanism," *The Quarterly Journal of Economics* 84, no. 3 (August 1970): 488, doi:10.2307/1879431; John Cassidy, *How Markets Fail: The Logic of Economic Calamities* (New York: Farrar, Straus and Giroux, 2009); Shiller, Irrational Exuberance.

[24]Named after Charles Ponzi, a financial entrepreneur in Boston after World War I, a Ponzi scheme or *pyramid scheme* is an investment where old investors are paid not by the returns from productive investment but out of money paid by new investors. To be successful, the scheme's liabilities must grow exponentially: the first investor is paid from the investments made by the next two who are paid by the next four, etc.

[25]Enron's accounting firm, Arthur Anderson, went bankrupt shortly after its complicity in the firm's activities was exposed. Enron's CEO, Kenneth Lay, was the largest individual donor to the George W. Bush presidential campaign in 2000.

[26]Jail time is a more frightening prospect. Two top executives from Enron (Kenneth Lay and Jeffrey Skilling) served time. It is likely that Bernard Madoff will spend the rest of his life in jail. There also is the prospect of explaining one's behavior to family and friends.

[27]This was certainly the attitude of many of the actors in the recent financial crisis; see Timothy F Geithner, *Stress Test: Reflections on Financial Crises*, 2014; Henry M Paulson, *On the Brink: Inside the Race to Stop the Collapse of the Global Financial System* (New York: Business Plus, 2010); for a broader view of what happened and options, see United States and Financial Crisis Inquiry Commission, *The Financial Crisis Inquiry Report: Final Report of the National Commission on the Causes of the Financial and Economic Crisis in the United States* (Washington, DC: Financial Crisis Inquiry Commission : For sale by the Supt. of Docs., U.S. G.P.O., 2011).

[28]This is the market collapse described by Akerlof, where good products are withdrawn from the market because buyers assume that all products are bad, leaving only bad and worse products for sale. This process confirms consumer suspicions and sets off a new downward spiral where consumers assume that the remaining products are worse, leading sellers to withdraw more products until nothing of any value remains in the market.

[29]Charles Poor Kindleberger, *Manias, Panics and Crashes a History of Financial Crises*, 5th ed (Hoboken, N.J: John Wiley & Sons, 2005).

14

WELFARE STATES

GOVERNMENT KEEPS GROWING

Orthodox neoclassical economists assume that market exchange encourages efficient production of goods and services by rewarding hard work and creative thought and the optimal allocation of resources. They conclude that, since the market allocation is perfect, government can only make things worse. Encouraging resurgent support for free markets over the last thirty years, neoclassical economics has moved from an academic discipline to become a political program for business leaders and conservative politicians. Self-proclaimed tough-minded, practical politicians insist that, to foster economic growth and efficiency, we must do without established social programs and regulatory protection. *Market fundamentalists*,[1] most of whom are comfortably well-off, argue that we can no longer afford public goods, high wages, or to support those outside the wage labor force, such as mothers, children, and the disabled. Instead, to provide adequate incentives to the affluent, they urge us to make the "hard choices," to cut taxes on the rich and politically powerful while removing social benefits from the poor and friendless.

Market fundamentalists would roll back welfare-state policies that have been developed over the past hundred years in advanced capitalist economies in the United States, Europe, and elsewhere. Despite many successes, however, the campaign against government has done little beyond slowing, or in a few cases halting, the *growth* in government. Throughout the advanced capitalist world, stretching from Europe through North America to East Asia, government is still large, directly accounting for well over 25% of economic activity in almost every country and indirectly influencing much more through regulations, ranging from minimum wage laws to food safety rules to measures restricting monopolistic practices. Social spend-

SOURCES OF DEMAND FOR GOVERNMENT

Market failures and public goods:
- Providing structure for market activity, including language, law, police.
- Collective action and public goods, including environment, culture, and human capital.
- Correcting limits of market distribution of income for young and care givers.

Social insurance:
- Helping when bad things happen, including disability and illness.
- Market is bad at providing this type of insurance due to profits from "lemon dropping" and "cherry picking."

Political imperative to grow:
- Politicians and bureaucrats seek to expand the resources at their command.

Left to right: New York's Central Park; Social Security supporter; Tammany Hall.

Infrastructure includes more than physical roads and bridges. It also includes the laws, language, and standards that facilitate transactions. These, too, are most efficiently provided by some authority who assures uniformity and the integrity of the measures.

Transportation infrastructure from Wellington, New Zealand. No individual could capture enough of the benefits of these investments to justify producing this infrastructure privately.

ing now encompasses an average of over 20% of national income in most advanced economies, nearly 30% in Sweden, Denmark, and France, but less than 15% in the United States.

Notwithstanding the efforts by libertarian economists and market fundamentalists to roll it back, government does not and will not go away. Instead, government has become deeply embedded in the economies of all advanced capitalist countries. We might not be surprised to see new social insurance programs under liberals like President Barack Obama, but it was under President George W. Bush that we had the enactment of a prescription drug benefit and a law establishing a national commitment to elementary education. And it was under Bush that we had the massive government bail-out of the banks and the financial sector, with the virtual nationalization of the losses of the largest banks, mortgage brokers, and insurance companies.

THE PUBLIC SECTOR: WHAT IT IS AND WHAT IT DOES

The rising tide of government programs and spending reflects a demand for government services that is two parts real and one part bogus. The real demands reflect the need to correct for market failures, including the provision of public goods, public infrastructure including transportation, public safety, and the provision of public goods of education, market protection, and social standards. In addition, government has a role in providing *social insurance*,[2] public insurance for misfortunes either uninsurable by private means or where the profit motive would undermine the insurance function. The third reason for government expansion is the one that I would label "bogus," because it provides a justification without any general legitimacy: All public programs rely on political action and government agents to carry through public policy. By empowering individuals—politicians and bureaucrats—public programs establish a political class with an interest in the expansion of government without regard for the interest of the general public.[3]

CORRECTING MARKET FAILURES BY PROVIDING PUBLIC GOODS

Much government spending and regulation falls into a broad category of the provision of public goods, including national defense, infrastructure, and social programs to promote human capital development by subsidizing the otherwise under-rewarded work of caregivers. *Public goods* include some that benefit all, including the production of public art and the regulation of buildings, the establishment of parks, and programs to protect the environment. While public goods are vital for the development and growth of the market economy, for-profit companies are unlikely to provide these goods. Due to free-riders and other problems, they cannot charge for goods made available to all. The provision of public goods includes programs that support the market economy by reducing transactions costs and the cost of securing property rights. These include not only the construction of roads and bridges and subsidies for basic scientific research, but also the provi-

FIGURE 14-1

U.S. SPENDING ON PUBLIC GOODS, FEDERAL + STATE + LOCAL IN $BILLIONS, 2012

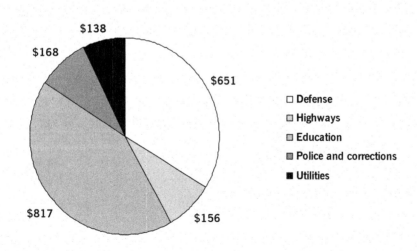

- □ Defense
- □ Highways
- ▨ Education
- ▨ Police and corrections
- ■ Utilities

sion of police and courts to enforce property rights, and programs to maintain common language and systems of weights, measures, and accounting. Such programs benefit all because they facilitate the social division of labor. Some may benefit more than others. The key is that it is difficult or expensive to charge anyone for the benefits.

In the United States, governments spend almost $2 trillion on public goods, over 12% of gross domestic product.[4] This includes spending on national defense and police. It includes spending on public infrastructure, including utilities and highways. And it includes almost $1 trillion spent on education, on training the next generation to make them more productive and better socialized. Even this understates the magnitude of government-directed spending because it does not include spending on public goods that is *directed* by government regulation but is not administered by government. These regulations range from requirements that people mow their suburban lawns to environmental regulations on power plants.

The provision of public goods benefits everyone by helping the market economy function smoothly. Social and physical infrastructure helps those who participate in the market economy by lowering transactions costs. All living things, including people, benefit from public goods like environmental protection, and everyone who expects to live beyond today benefits from programs to support care work since these promote human capital development. Because these programs have wide benefits, some market fundamentalists argue that they should be able to support themselves outside of government and taxes. This neglects, however, the meaning of *public*: because all benefit, no self-interested individual will voluntarily pay for public goods. Without government and compulsion, self-regarding individuals will try to free ride on the provision of public goods by others. Of course, some will contribute, just as some voluntarily contribute to the provision of public goods today. Without compulsion, in the form of taxation, there would be fewer public goods, and our market system and division of labor would be starved, as would our children. Insofar as there would be any public goods, their provision would be paid for by those good people who care about others, while those who care only about themselves would benefit from their good works.

> ### THE UNITED STATES WELFARE STATE
>
> Our welfare state involves programs to help the poor, the unemployed, children, the disabled, and the elderly poor. It also helps affluent homeowners, those who have good health insurance through work, and the affluent elderly. In addition to nearly $3 trillion in direct spending by federal, state, and local governments, nearly $600 billion goes through the tax code for expenditures made in the areas of education, health, income support, and housing.

Correcting Market Failures with Social Insurance

Other government programs redistribute from some to others. At the extreme, there can be simple extortion, government as a gangster enterprise such as the kleptocracies of Zaire under Mobutu Sese Seko or Haiti under the Duvaliers. The United States has sometimes resembled these; the William Tweed ring and Tammany Hall ran New York City as a criminal enterprise for a few years around 1870. But the great majority of redistributive spending in advanced capitalist democracies involves a different motivation. It is the provision of *social insurance* against the misfortunes of life.

Social insurance provides income when bad things happen: when

FIGURE 14-2
U.S. SOCIAL INSURANCE, SPENDING, FEDERAL + STATE + LOCAL, $BILLIONS, 2012

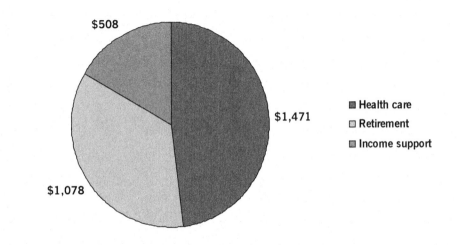

CURRENT CONTROVERSIES

UNIVERSAL HEALTH CARE
CAN WE AFFORD ANYTHING LESS?

America's broken health-care system suffers from what appear to be two separate problems. From the right, a chorus warns of the dangers of rising costs; we on the left focus on the growing number of people going without health care because they lack adequate insurance. This division of labor allows the right to dismiss attempts to extend coverage while crying crocodile tears for the 40 million uninsured. But the division between problem of cost and the problem of coverage is misguided. It is founded on the assumption, common among neoclassical economists, that the current market system is efficient. Instead, however, the current system is inherently inefficient; it is the very source of the rising cost pressures. In fact, the only way we can control health-care costs and avoid fiscal and economic catastrophe is to establish a single-payer system with universal coverage.

If health insurance were like other commodities, like shoes or bow ties, then reducing access might lower costs by reducing demands on suppliers for time and materials. But health care is different because so much of the cost of providing it is in the administration of the payment system rather than in the actual work of doctors, nurses, and other providers, and because coordination and cooperation among different providers is essential for effective and efficient health care. It is not cost pressures on providers that are driving up health-care costs; instead, costs are rising because of what economists call transaction costs, the rising cost of administering and coordinating a system that is designed to reduce access.

Source: Centers for Medicare and Medicaid Services, National Health Expenditures (cms.gov); Congressional Budget Office (cbo.gov); Centers for Medicare and Medicaid Statistics (cms.gov); Gerald Friedman, "Funding HR 676: The Expanded and Improved Medicare for All Act: How we can afford a national single-payer health plan," Physicians for a National Health Program (pnhp.org); Cathy Schoen, et al., "Access, Affordability, and Insurance Complexity" Health Affairs, Nov. 18, 2013; Kaiser Family Foundation (kff.org); CNN.com, "Obamacare: Enrollment numbers and Medicaid expansion."

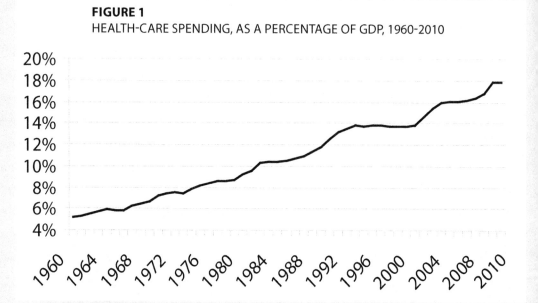

FIGURE 1
HEALTH-CARE SPENDING, AS A PERCENTAGE OF GDP, 1960-2010

Health-care costs have risen much faster than income in the United States over the last 50 years, rising from 5% of Gross Domestic Product in 1960 to nearly 18% today. Some of the increase in costs in the United States, as with other countries, is associated with improvements in care and longevity. Costs have risen much faster in the United States, however, because of the growing administrative burden of our private health-insurance system.

FIGURE 2
SOURCES OF SAVINGS, SINGLE-PAYER HEALTH PLAN

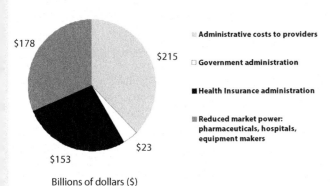

$178

$215

$153

$23

■ Administrative costs to providers

□ Government administration

■ Health Insurance administration

■ Reduced market power: pharmaceuticals, hospitals, equipment makers

Billions of dollars ($)

A single-payer system would produce huge administrative savings by simplifying billing and by redistributing the monopoly profits currently enjoyed by pharmaceutical makers and other companies. The savings would allow us to correct some of the problems within the current health-care system, extending coverage to all of those currently uninsured and improving coverage for those with inadequate insurance.

Under the Affordable Care Act (ACA), or "Obamacare," expansion of Medicaid and mandates for individuals to buy subsidized private insurance will expand health insurance to an additional 30 million people. Millions of others, however, will remain uninsured. Some are not covered by the act (including undocumented immigrants); others will be excused from the requirement to have insurance because of cost; and others will not comply.

FIGURE 3
PROJECTED EFFECTS OF ACA ON UNINSURED, 2013-2023

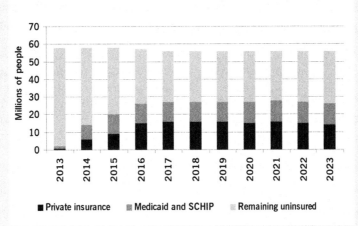

Millions of people

■ Private insurance   ■ Medicaid and SCHIP   ■ Remaining uninsured

FIGURE 4
PROJECTED HEALTH CARE SPENDING, PERCENTAGE OF GDP, ACA VS. SINGLE PAYER, 2006-2022

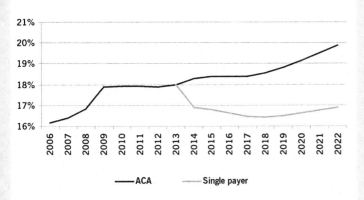

——ACA   ——Single payer

The ACA does not establish a sustainable health-care finance system in the United States. Under the ACA, health care spending will continue to increase significantly faster than the economy as a whole and the share of the economy going towards health care will rise in the next decade to nearly 20%. By controlling administrative costs and drug prices, a single-payer system can hold health-care spending to less than 17% of the GDP.

This man probably did not ask to be blind. Among those who maintain full-time employment, being blind reduces income by about 50%. Fewer than half of those with severe disabilities work full time. For those without full-time work, the cost of the disability is even higher.

we are young but our parents lose income and become poor, when we are sick, and when we are older and retire from work. In 2012, we spent over $3 trillion on social insurance activities, nearly 20% of national income. Almost half of this is for health care for the sick. Over a trillion is for retirement pensions and support for those with permanent disability. And half a trillion is for income support for the nonelderly including the unemployed, supplemental nutrition for mothers, children, and the poor, and housing assistance.

The largest part of housing assistance is in the federal tax code, where homeowners are able to deduct the interest on their mortgages from their taxable income. Because there is no comparable deduction for renters, this is a program that excludes most lower-income Americans. And because the deduction is worth more for owners of more expensive homes (with larger mortgages) and for higher-income tax payers (facing a higher marginal tax rate), this housing subsidy goes primarily to affluent households. Other social spending also goes disproportionately to the affluent. The federal government uses the tax code to subsidize employer-provided health insurance. This subsidy, worth about $200 billion, goes more towards the affluent, who are more likely to have health insurance. Social Security retirement benefits are more useful to the affluent both because benefit levels are linked to earnings and because the affluent live longer. Medicare, health insurance for the elderly, is provided for virtually all older Americans but the affluent also gain the most from it. They use more health care and, because they live longer, they have more time to draw benefits.

Some criticize America's social spending because so many of the benefits go to the affluent. While correct, this criticism misunderstands the nature of America's social programs. The point of most of our social spending is not to redistribute income to the poor. Instead, social security and other programs are *social insurance* intended to protect people from the bad things that can happen. For many of these, we buy insurance privately. My family has insurance, for example, to protect us if our car is struck by a drunk driver, our home is robbed or damaged in a storm, or if my bicycle is stolen. By buying insurance, we accept premium payments that lower our income in exchange for a commitment from the insurance company to compensate us if something goes wrong. With insurance, we guarantee a lower income most of the time in exchange for avoiding a substantial blow to our income if something bad happens.

LEMONS, MORAL HAZARD, ADVERSE SELECTION, AND THE FAILURE OF PRIVATE INSURANCE

Insurance makes us happier because the premium dollars are worth less to us than what we would lose if bad things happened and we were uninsured. This comes from diminishing marginal utility: the premium payments come from further along our utility frontier and therefore are worth less to us than what we would lose. The utility gains from insurance are shown in Figure 14-3. The upper line shows our utility as a function of income and the lower line shows the *expected value*[5] of our utility as an average of the utility we would have if we had "really good luck" and what we would have if "bad things happened" with substantially less income. Diminishing marginal utility makes the expected value less than the actual utility. We benefit less from really good luck than we lose from bad luck and, as a result, we will sacrifice our chance for really good things if we are assured of not having the really bad things.

We can use Figure 14-3 to estimate the benefit from insurance and the highest premium that a rational person would pay to be insured. Without insurance, we would calculate our well-being along the line of expected value. Imagine that you have a 50% chance of having an income of $212,000 and a 50% chance of having an income of $5,000. In expected value terms, you would anticipate (along the Utility of Expected Income line) an income of $108,500 (point A) with a utility of about 10.25, This is much less than the utility associated with a certain income of that amount (point C); it is same utility level, in fact, that you would receive from a guaranteed income of less than $30,000 (point B). You are willing to settle for $30,000 guaranteed income in both states rather than have a 50% chance of $212,000 and of $5000, and you will give up $80,000 in premiums every year to be assured this.

Insurance is sold privately against a wide variety of ills: death, robbery, house fires, plane crashes, kidnapping, divorce, ship sinking, and loss of athletic ability. But these are only a few of the ailments to which flesh is heir. People suffer illnesses and disabilities, they lose their jobs. Even more, they are born with disadvantages, with lower earning capacity or to parents unable to support them or to give them a good start in a capitalist economy. There should be no surprise if people seek insurance against these income risks as they do against other life risks.

The difference between privately insured risks and others has less to do with the nature of the loss than with the motive for buying or selling insurance. Insurance can become a "lemons market" dominated by *moral hazard*,[6] where people buy insurance because they know they are more likely to need it than the average. They may have asymmetric information about their true risks, or they may even take measures to increase their risk in order to scam the insurer.

To avoid moral hazard, insurers engage in a variety of administratively expensive and socially wasteful practices to police their clients. They police claims with investigators. They try to discourage claim-filing by requiring more cost sharing associated with their policies, by raising deductibles and copayments, for example. And companies engage in *adverse selection*,[7] where they sell insurance only to people who they are confident will not need insurance. This practice is called *cherry picking* or *lemon dropping*,[8] selecting customers who will not need the insurance and discouraging those who they anticipate will. These practices are profitable because most people do not file insurance claims in any given year.[9] About 70% of the reimbursements by health insurers go to only 10% of the group. Find those people and get them to drop their policies, and insurers can enormously increase their profits.

Much of the expense of market-based insurance goes to this process of concealment and discovery. Among health insurance companies in the United States, as much as 30% of expenditures are for company administration. Companies hire investigators to check applicants for evidence of fraud, applying for insurance against risks where the applicant knows that they already have the condition in question, and for moral hazard, where their behavior changes because they are insured. These company policies quickly shade into *cherry picking*, where companies review medical and other records to identify low-risk applicants, and *lemon dropping*, where they seek to rid themselves of people who will be filing claims for benefits. The process of screening and reviewing applicants is itself expensive and wasteful. The expense is compounded by the extra administrative expenses borne by applicants and others, such as doctors and care-givers. Nonetheless, these expenses can maximize profits for insurers if they can reconfigure their risk pool and drive away people who will file claims.[10]

By narrowing the risk pool, these policies lead insurers to undermine the insurance function. Without screening, cherry picking, and lemon dropping, however, private companies risk bankruptcy, a threat that may even prevent a private market from functioning at all. Consider the behavior of a well-meaning insurance company, one that does not screen. This com-

FIGURE 14-3

EXPECTED VALUE OF GAMBLE IS LESS THAN THE VALUE OF A GUARANTEED INCOME OF MUCH LESS

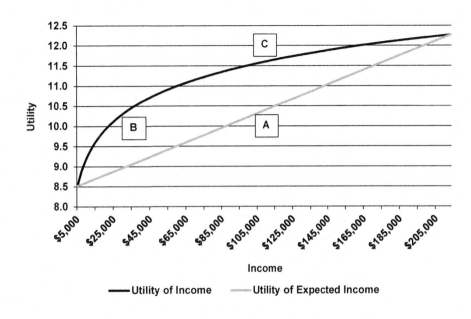

TABLE 14-1
EXAMPLES OF RISKS AND INSURANCE

Risk	Type of Insurance	Private or public?	Moral hazard and adverse selection?	Policy response
Death	Life insurance	Largely private	Suicide; fraudulent death claims	Suicide cancels policy. Death claims investigated by police
House fire	Homeowners insurance	Largely private	Arson	Arson cancels policy. Claims investigated by policy
Car accident	Car insurance	Private	Reckless driving	Police investigate accident
Theft	Homeowners insurance; car insurance; private guards. Also police and criminal justice system	Private and public	Leaving doors unlocked; fraudulent reporting of loss; buying insurance in known high crime areas	Cost sharing on losses (deductibles, insurance maximums). Police investigate thefts; legal penalties for false reporting. Rate setting by neighborhoods
Illness	Health insurance; Medicare for elderly; Medicaid for poor.	Private and public	Purchase of insurance when already ill; excessive use of medical system; overcharging for services	Cost sharing (deductibles, copays); claims investigators review charges
Permanent disability from work	Disability insurance; Social Security disability	Some private and mostly public.	Purchase of insurance when already disabled or when employed in known hazardous occupations; fraud	Medical examination before qualifying for insurance; rate setting by occupation. For public plan, universal coverage prevents adverse selection. Claim reviews.
Permanent disability at birth	Welfare; Social Security disability.	Public	Fraud	Claim reviews.
Unemployment	Unemployment Insurance	Public	Reject work to remain on unemployment insurance	Claimants required to show evidence of looking for work and must accept offered jobs
Low income	Welfare; Supplemental Nutrition Assistance	Public	Reject work to remain on welfare	Low benefits to encourage work; work requirements and claim reviews
Longevity	Social security retirement; Medicare; Medicaid.	Public	Fraud: lie about age	Claim reviews

Birth and luck? Some people are born to billionaire parents. Others are orphans in third-world countries.

pany will be subject to moral hazard among its clients who will use their idiosyncratic knowledge, their asymmetric information about their true risks, to buy policies when they anticipate that they are at a higher risk. This will drive up the insurer's premiums, leading those at a lower risk to drop their coverage, forcing higher premiums until the only customers for this well-meaning insurer will be those who know with perfect certainty that they will be filing claims.

ADVERSE SELECTION AND SOCIAL INSURANCE

While all insurance products can face adverse selection, the problem is greatest for risks subject to asymmetric information, or where there is more risk that the insured will submit fraudulent claims or engage in reckless practices increasing their risk. Insurers' response to the adverse-selection problem can be so severe that the private insurance market will break down completely. In some cases, social insurance can fill the gap with universal coverage financed through taxes as a substitute for private insurance.

In Table 14-1, I present the moral hazard risk for a variety of risks the types of insurance, and a brief description of the predominant insurance market. Sorted by the degree to which the markets face problems of adverse selection and moral hazard, the table is meant to demonstrate the way that social insurance has filled the policy space created by the failure of private insurance.

For some risks, such as death, private insurance works well because it is very difficult to commit fraud and moral hazard is a poor option. It is hard to fake one's death, and very risky to commit suicide to collect life insurance benefits for one's family. Similarly, it is relatively easy to avoid moral hazard for theft or automobile accidents. Private markets work less well, however, for risks that are more subject to individual characteristics and choice, risks like low income or poor health. In these cases, social insurance has two great advantages over private insurers. Universal state policies can avoid adverse selection because they are universal, and with government resources, state insurance investigators have access to better information and coercive authority to prevent fraud.[11]

Seen as a way to resolve problems of adverse selection and moral hazard, public programs of income redistribution fulfill a desire for insurance against risks of life, including disability, unemployment, and illness, as well as problems of low income that come from being born to the wrong parents.[12] At the extreme, social insurance and welfare programs can completely separate one's current income from the market. *Decommodifying*[13] education, health, nutrition, and housing, such programs can cancel the disad-

FIGURE 14-4

GOVERNMENT SOCIAL WELFARE SPENDING OF GDP, UNITED STATES AND OTHER AFFLUENT COUNTRIES, 2006

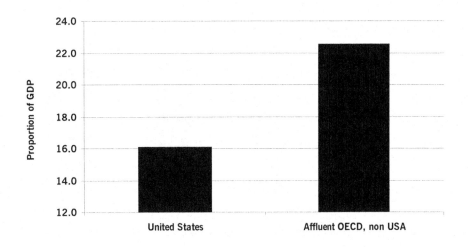

vantages, and some of the advantages, of birth.[14] These are distinguished from state infrastructure programs because they interfere with the market economy, even contradicting the distribution of income and products it provides. Government insurance programs are at least potentially decommodifying because they allocate resources according to a non-market logic, the logic of rights discussed by Arthur Okun. All residents of a certain age, for example, are entitled to an education, in some countries all are entitled to health care, and all people with some disabilities are entitled to income support. Reflecting the logic of democratic citizenship, universal and decommodifying benefits are the logical outcome of a now-centuries old campaign for the extension of equal rights to all. They reflect the famous socialist slogan: "From each according to their ability, to each according to their needs."

By separating income from market earnings, and reducing the value of market earnings by taxation, these programs interfere with the market. The lower *post-fisc*[15] income received by the lucky and affluent reflects an insurance premium paid for the income security provided to the unlucky. These programs help the disabled, the sick, and the less lucky, but to the lucky they may seem like a crass redistribution of income from earners to those who do not earn it.

AMERICAN EXCEPTIONALISM?

Since the 19th century, Marxists and some other social scientists expected socialist movements and working-class organizations to grow with capitalism until they would overturn capitalism. They expected to find the strongest socialist movements in the countries with the most advanced capitalism. This approach led to a vigorous debate over why the United States, with the most advanced capitalist economy, has had the weakest socialist movement. Some, such as the German sociologist Werner Sombart (1863-1941) and the American Seymour Martin Lipset (1922-2006), argued that the United States experience shows that socialism does not naturally emerge from capitalism because workers do not normally favor socialism if capitalists provide high wages and opportunities for advancement. Others have attributed the weakness of American socialism to the repression of radical alternatives and the political power of capitalists in the United States.

AMERICAN EXCEPTIONALISM

Compared with other affluent economies, the United States is exceptional in the small size and market-reinforcing (rather than decommodifying) orientation of government social insurance.[16] Compared with European nations and Canada, the United States spends less on social insurance, does less to reduce income inequality, and directs more of its social spending towards the affluent than do other countries. The United States also has by far the highest poverty rates, especially among children, and government does less to reduce poverty in the United States than it does in other affluent countries.

The relatively small size of the United States government and its reluctance about taxing and redistributing income has contributed to a lively scholarly debate under the name of "American exceptionalism." Two approaches shape this discussion: those who argue that Americans do not want a larger government regulating capitalism and providing more social insurance, and

FIGURE 14-5
PROPORTION FAVORING GOVERNMENT SPENDING PROGRAMS

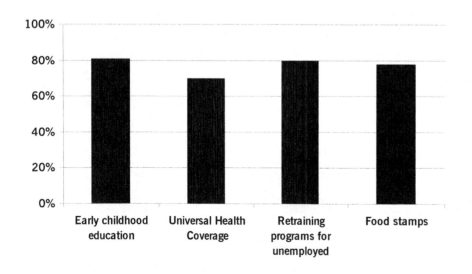

those who argue that American excep-tionalism reflects the greater political power of American capitalists and the repression of other alternatives.

The argument that Americans are hostile to social insurance and govern-ment regulation is often made by point-ing to America's democratic state. (If Americans wanted such programs, they would vote for them.) Beyond this, how-ever, the direct evidence is that Ameri-cans support an active government in about the same proportions as do resi-dents of other affluent countries with much larger welfare states. Overwhelm-ing majorities support social programs, including solid majorities of Republican voters as well as Democrats.[17]

While confirming that Ameri-cans favor a more egalitarian distri-

FIGURE 14-6

IDEAL, ESTIMATED, AND ACTUAL DISTRIBUTION OF INCOME, UNITED STATES, 2010

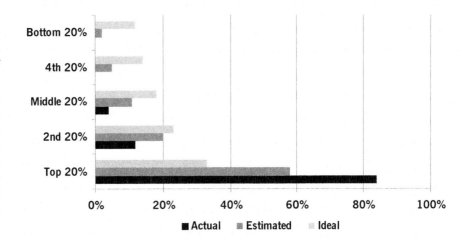

bution of income and would support active government action to achieve it, other polling data on Americans' attitudes may provide clues about the reasons for the weakness of the American welfare state.[18] When questioned about the actual and the desired distribution of wealth, sizable majorities of Americans of all income levels favor a more egalitarian distribution than that which they believe exists. The proportion of wealth that they believe should go to the top 20% (or top "quintile"), for example, ranges from 30% for those earning under $50,000 to 33% for those earning $50-100,000 and 38% for those earning over $100,000.[19]

What is striking in the survey evidence is not only that Americans favor a more egalitarian distribution of wealth but that they are so mistaken about the actual distribution. Americans be-lieve that it would be better if the richest quintile had only a third of the nation's wealth rather than 58% that they estimate that the richest 20% actually hold. But the richest actually have over 80% of the nation's wealth, while the bottom half hold so little that their shares do not even register (see Figure 14-6).

One could blame the victims and complain that the American public is happily ignorant and allows itself to be fed a thin intellectual diet by media mo-nopolies. It is a little hard to understand, however, how Americans became so much more ignorant than Canadians or Europeans, or how their ignorance has increased so dramatically in the last 30 years with the rise of conservative poli-tics and the redistribution of income towards the rich. Instead of focusing on the failure of individual Americans to keep track of changing income distribution, we should focus on the failure of social institutions to empower these individuals, and the way American institutions constrain the possibilities for social change.

Compared with other industrialized countries, the United States is also notable for the small size of its organized labor movement and the absence of a significant socialist political movement.[20] Elsewhere, strong labor and socialist movements have financed and organized campaigns for social insur-ance and other welfare programs. They have funded research programs and brought information about the distribution of wealth and power to the gen-eral public, providing a counter to capitalist organizations, especially large media companies.[21] There is no shortage of alternative thought and research in the United States. What is missing and will continue to be missing with the long-standing, growing weakness of the American labor movement is a vehicle to bring this research to the general public.

Martin Luther King and the United Auto Workers' union president Walter Reuther at the March on Washington, August 1963. The UAW paid for the signs and the busses for the rally, and Reuther arranged for King and others to meet with President Kennedy afterwards.

THE ATTACK ON THE WELFARE STATE

Welfare protections rose sharply after World War II and again in the decade after 1968. Beginning with the election of Margaret Thatcher as prime minister of the United Kingdom in 1979 and Ronald Reagan as president of the United States in 1980, opponents of welfare-state spending have mobilized intellectually and have checked most further state welfare initiatives. While the rightist attack has largely failed to roll back past welfare initiatives, it continues today in attacks on "entitlement" spending and demands to balance government budgets.

Friedrich Von Hayek (left), Margaret Thatcher and Ronald Reagan (right): the intellectual and political leaders of the attacks on the welfare state.

In the past, labor movements have done more than transform popular attitudes: they have mobilized popular sentiment and turned it into political action to promote social reform. In the campaign for the 1964 Civil Rights Act, for example, labor unions like the United Auto Workers (UAW) not only provided analysis and arguments, but organized their members and others to communicate with their members of Congress and the Senate. The epic march on Washington in August 1963 was largely financed by the UAW, and the UAW and other labor union lobbyists were instrumental in pushing the 1964 Act through Congress.[22]

Labor's role in enacting social reform in the United States has been especially crucial because the institutions of American government have been deliberately designed to make it difficult for the central government to act. Focused on the dangers of political centralization and tyranny, the authors of the American constitution established multiple veto points. Every law has to be approved by two houses of Congress, signed by the President, and found consistent with the constitution by the Supreme Court.[23] The election of two senators from each state, regardless of the state's population, furthermore, gives extra voice to the owners of large blocks of western land against city dwellers.

The institutional bias against social reform is magnified by an electoral system that pushes political actors towards the ideological middle. Almost without exception, Americans vote in single-member constituencies with first-past-the-post election, where the winner is the candidate who gets the most votes. This limits the importance of minor parties, whose only impact on the final outcome is to reduce the vote for the candidate the minor party's supporters find less objectionable, increasing the probability that the "greater of two evils" will win. This produces a dynamic where voters interested in influencing the final outcome abandon minor parties for one of the two likely to win, undermining any chance for the minor party candidate to win, leading minor-party support to hemorrhage until only a handful of hard-core supporters remain. The inevitable result of this electoral regime is a two-party system truncated ideologically by the need to capture centrist votes.[24]

Add to this dynamic the power of American regionalism. Regional loyalties suppress class divisions in the electorate. Throughout the country, the poor vote differently from the rich; they were more likely to vote for Barack Obama, for example.[25] Almost as important, however, is the regional effect within any income group. Compare, for example, a large northern state, New York, and a major southern state, North Carolina. Less-affluent voters in both voted for Obama, the liberal Democrat. In North Carolina, however, not only is the Obama vote less at every income level but the effect of low income is compressed. Poor southerners are more likely to vote for Obama than their more affluent neighbors but the gap is much less than in New York; they vote more like their affluent neighbors than do poor northerners. Being southern not only makes voters conservative but it makes them more alike regardless of income.

The South, as artists from William Faulkner to Lynyrd Skynrd have noted, is a different place. United by a distinct accent, cuisine, manners, music, and a history of rebellion, defeat, and occupation, southern whites are particularly focused on being southern rather than being members of a class or an economic group. Since slavery days, white southern members of Congress have with few exceptions devoted themselves to preserving, first, the South's "peculiar institution" of slavery, and then segregation and white supremacy. Some have favored progressive economic policies, not least because, as a poor region, the South would benefit more from these than would more affluent regions. Nonetheless, concerns about maintaining white rule restrained southern support for social insurance programs, and support was always contingent on these programs being designed to not interfere with southern institutions.[26] The southern bloc in Congress judged every reform measure first on the criterion of whether it would enhance or undermine white power. Any social insurance or decommodifying program open to nonwhites as well as whites was therefore suspect, and few have been enacted.[27]

Recognizing the strength of these institutional and political barriers to social reform makes even more impressive the achievements of the New Deal and Great Society era, from 1933 to 1974. Through remarkable political talent, and with the support of popular movements and the institutions of the labor movement, the United States built a welfare state that enhanced opportunity and security, and reduced inequality. By challenging capitalist power, however, the New Deal coalition provoked its nemesis, a resurgent capitalist class mobilized against what one spokesman in 1971 saw as an "assault on the enterprise system . . . broadly based and consistently pursued. . . . gaining momentum and converts."[28] American political economy since the 1970s has been dominated by the success of this capitalist counteroffensive.

LOCKE ON PROPERTY

The English philosopher **John Locke (1632-1704)** appears to base his defense of property in the rights of free workers to control their own labor. "Though the earth and all inferior creatures be common to all men," Locke writes, "yet ... [t]he labor of his body and the work of his hands, we may say, are properly his. Whatsoever then he removes out of the state that nature has provided and left it in, he has mixed his labor with, and joined to it something that is his own, and thereby makes it his property." He adds, "[f]or this labor being the unquestionable property of the laborer, no man but he can have a right to what is once joined to it ...." He then makes a critical exception: "at least where there is *enough and as good left in common for others*" (emphasis added). Locke thus limits the right of property to ensure that everyone in society have "enough and as good" for themselves.

DEBATING STATES AND POLITICS

Some would favor or attack state social spending for purely selfish reasons. Their political position depends on whether they expect to gain more from state spending or anticipate paying more in taxes. Those who expect to do well in the marketplace, to have a high pre-fisc income (before taxes and government spending), might oppose welfare spending. Those who expect to need government services because of disabilities, low earning capacity, or because they will be working at home and caring for children, might be expected to follow their personal self-interest to favor welfare spending.

Apart from personal interest, we might look for principled positions favoring or opposing social insurance programs for universal reasons that would hold even if we did not know whether we ourselves would benefit. The intellectual attack on social welfare comes in two parts: one ideological and one pragmatic. Some are against any form of government, viewing taxes as a form of involuntary servitude where the state compels individuals to transfer resources they have earned themselves. This view, of course, is grounded in an extreme individualism where people, Robinson Crusoe-like, produce income entirely through their own efforts only to have some taken from them by the government. Once stated, it may be obvious that this is an unsound approach to production. The 17th-century English philosopher John Locke, who is sometimes associated with this view of individual property, restricted it to "the state that nature has provided" and dismisses it for a developed community with the division of labor. By working together, we are all much more productive. When the contribution of others makes us more productive, what remains of an individual right to property based on our own output? Our earnings are a social product made possible by our participation in a social network that is developed and maintained by the efforts of others, including the government. Americans north of the Rio Grande are much more productive than are workers in Mexico because they work in the United States, because they live in a productive society with a well-functioning division of labor. It may be better to limit taxes and government spending. But government taxes are a payment to the community of some of what the community has given us.

Others oppose welfare programs for pragmatic reasons, arguing that they undermine other social goals such as the promotion of economic growth and productivity. Many of these claims go back to Arthur Okun's book, *Equality versus Efficiency*.[29] While some economists still repeat Okun's argument that citizenship rights undermine work incentives and reduce efficiency, any negative trade-offs must

JOHN KENNETH GALBRAITH

The Canadian-born economist **John Kenneth Galbraith (1908-2006)** is sometimes considered the last American institutionalist, as well as one of the first Keynesians. Moving to Washington to work in Roosevelt Administration as a New Dealer soon after receiving his Ph.D. from Berkeley in 1934, he was director of price controls during World War II. In 1948, he began teaching at Harvard, leaving there only occasionally to serve in Washington or, during the Kennedy Administration, as ambassador to India. Throughout his career, Galbraith argued that markets have less influence on economic outcomes than do institutions, including government, big business, and organized labor. He condemned the focus on individualism and consumerism, arguing that an "Affluent Society" needs a stronger public sector.

The young Galbraith

be quite small, seeing as there is no empirical evidence that social spending and an egalitarian income distribution are associated with lower productivity or slower rates of economic growth. Instead, much social welfare spending, including early childhood education and public health programs, are market-supporting infrastructure activities just as much as road building is. Welfare spending like this may provoke protests from libertarians and those who resent taxes, but it pays for itself by raising productivity and economic output. Even where they distract from market output, social insurance programs can promote productivity by promoting human capital development, by reducing stress and crime, and by promoting social cohesion.

THE DIVISION OF LABOR, JUSTICE, AND A GOOD SOCIETY

Over a century ago, Émile Durkheim put social justice at the center of a society's production process by arguing that the division of labor depends on cooperation that can only come from mutual care, shared morality, and a common sense of justice.[30] Social insurance is not flim-flam or a secondary luxury. It is essential for a functioning economy: without a sense of responsibility for each other, we risk degenerating into a war of all against all that would undermine the division of labor and grind down our highly complex and integrated economy. Social insurance is the lubricant that keeps our economy moving.

How to promote justice? The strongest case against social welfare may be a different pragmatic argument, that while government intervention may be good in theory, it will in practice degenerate and become a vehicle for the self-advancement of a few. This is built from a general critique of the political process which argues that these processes will be captured by small self-interested groups who will use the state to exploit the rest. Mancur Olson demonstrated in his work *The Logic of Collective Action* that small groups can dominate large groups because they can more easily overcome the free-rider problem to organize to advance their common interests.[31] Especially when allied with entrenched bureaucrats, relatively small groups, such as the Iowa ethanol lobby, Florida and Louisiana sugar producers, and Texas oil producers, can use state power to exploit the general public. In recent years, no group has been as effective in manipulating the political process as have the relatively small numbers of rich and super-rich.

While one may want to respond to the exploitative power of small groups by demolishing government, this is impossible in a world where the social division of labor requires that we work together constantly and need broad social institutions to sustain our work. Instead, concerns about the power of small groups allied with entrenched bureaucrats should lead us to strengthen our democratic practices so that the larger groups can organize more effectively. Where small groups exploit the rest from behind closed doors and far from democratic processes, we need a more open democracy.

The intellectual critique of welfare states raises real problems and real challenges, but none of these call for us to abandon the democratic public sector. All these problems would be worse without popular government and elections. If we are to be governed by a small elite, would we rather they be self-appointed or would we want at least the chance to vote them out? If government has problems motivating its workers and assessing the value of its product, then would we be better off with private businesses or with elected officials?

The real problem facing the public sector is not the limits of effective government but the problem of fostering and maintaining democracy in a busy world filled with private pleasures and other

Robert Kennedy speaking for civil rights

distractions. Effective democracy depends on an active and informed public, on skills and knowledge of effective political action. Citizens need to know how to interpret arguments, how to organize meetings and committees. Just as important, democracy depends on values: a willingness to listen to others, a commitment to work together for the common good, and a sense of mutual self-respect. Self-government does not come naturally in a market economy based on individual self-interest. Instead, it is built on knowledge and skills developed *against* values fostered by individuals participating in commodity markets. As Alexis de Tocqueville argued at the dawn of American democracy, self-government needs skills and values fostered through public participation. "One may think," he wrote in *Democracy in America*, "of political associations as great free schools to which all citizens come to be taught the general theory of association."

From de Tocqueville we can derive both hope and warning of the future of America's great experiment in popular democracy. Many of the political associations that fostered and supported American democracy have withered in recent decades: labor unions, parent-teacher associations, town meetings. Were this all, we would have reason to be concerned. But Americans are constantly developing new forms of association, ranging from social networking over the web to low-power radio stations and student activist groups. Democracy has always been in the streets, and its future remains there.

The need for democracy has never been greater. Opposition to social expenditures among American capitalists reflects their real economic interest, an interest that they would advance at the expense of us all. They would raise profits by reducing social protections, lowering taxes, and driving down wages. This is short-sighted of them. In the long run, even the business community has interests that transcend the individual business owner's interest in lower wages. All Americans have an interest in a healthy, educated population and a healthy environment, and all, citizens and businesses alike, have an interest in a community where people have a sense of commitment to each other. The United States was founded on the simple ideal that by empowering common people we would enrich us all. Better education, health, and social relations are all social products that give us a better, more productive, and happier community. Products of economic democracy, these are worth having, and worth fighting for.

Democracy is based in the idea that everyone can make a contribution, that when we all work together we can make a better world, and that participation in public life is itself ennobling. These truths are denied by orthodox economists, who see nothing beyond the isolated individual, and by those who profit from our silence and our divisions. Denying the social good, orthodox economics teaches lessons that enrich the few at the expense of the rest of us. It preaches the futility of our collective life, saying that there is nothing to be done about the problems we face as a community because we already live in the best of all possible worlds. Denying that we construct our economy and our society, it treats economic relations as occurring between some impossibly omniscient rational being and inanimate nature—leading, of course, to naturally efficient economic outcomes. Dismissing human interaction in this way, orthodox economics eliminates the very idea that people have power over others, or that there are any grounds for human conflict. They dismiss any possibility that people can improve their lot through collective action.

Billionaires **David Koch**, (left), brother Charles Koch (not pictured), and **Sheldon Adelson** (right) on their economic self-interest in fighting programs to redistribute wealth or to regulate capitalists. Together they spent $562 million to defeat Barack Obama in 2012. While unsuccessful, their spending ensures that elected officials will remember them. Does their spending also ensure that these officials do not remember the rest of us?

People with power use orthodox economics to tell you what you cannot do. Against this we can only offer the hope that by acting together, we can make life better for all. This hope is what America has always been about, and, as Barack Obama once said, "in the unlikely story that is America, there has never been anything false about hope." Denying that some have power over others does not liberate the oppressed. If we want to make the world better, we must work and struggle together. Struggle freed the slaves, gave Americans Social Security, ended British rule in India, Ireland, and Israel, won a measure of equality between men and women, between gays and straights, and brought down the Berlin Wall. When they tell you the world cannot change, that your struggles cannot succeed, that things cannot be better, remember the most revolutionary words: "Yes we can."

Decades before Nelson Mandela was freed and South African apartheid collapsed, an American Senator inspired a country. Invited to address a student group in Pretoria, Senator Robert Kennedy abandoned his official program and his government escorts. A former Attorney General of the United States and brother of a slain president, he put his prestige and status at the service of the world's most oppressed people. Walking the streets of South Africa's black neighborhoods, as he would walk through the slums of America, he inspired hope, the possibilities of change, and the "moral imperative of the now." His words there speak to us today as much as they did to South Africans in 1966:

> Few will have the greatness to bend history itself, but each of us can work to change a small portion of events, and in the total of all those acts will be written the history of this generation .... Each time a man stands up for an ideal, or acts to improve the lot of others, or strikes out against injustice, he sends forth a tiny ripple of hope, and crossing each other from a million different centers of energy and daring those ripples build a current which can sweep down the mightiest walls of oppression and resistance.

DISCUSSION QUESTIONS

What is "market failure"? Give examples.

What is "infrastructure"? Is it all physical?

Can government spending be economically efficient? How does the public sector support economic growth?

Why do people buy insurance? What is the economic benefit of insurance?

What is "social insurance"? How do we pay for this insurance? Who receives benefits?

What is "moral hazard"? What is "adverse selection"? How do these come from asymmetric information?

Would people freely buy social insurance to guarantee their income? Would they buy insurance if they were behind a "veil of ignorance" where they did not know their condition and income? Who would buy? Who would not? Would a private company be able to profit from selling income insurance?

How does asymmetric information affect the ability of private insurers to profit from selling insurance? How does it change the policies of private insurers? How does it add to the administrative burden of insurance?

What is "American Exceptionalism"?

Give some reasons why the United States has a smaller welfare state and provides less social insurance than do other countries. Does American Exceptionalism necessarily reflect the views of Americans? Discuss ways that American political institutions have inhibited the development of social welfare programs.

Discuss the utilitarian arguments for and against government redistribution and the views of John Rawls and Arthur Okun.

Discuss the moral argument against government redistribution and the views of John Locke.

Discuss the moral argument for government redistribution and the views of Émile Durkheim.

ENDNOTES

[1]Market fundamentalists believe that individuals acting through free markets will produce the optimal distribution of goods and services and maximize productivity. Virtually any government intervention or social program will make things worse.

[2]Social insurance is where government provides insurance when bad things happen, insurance funded through general taxation.

[3]Those on the political left have been quick to identify the Pentagon and defense contractors as a source of demand for expanded military spending without regard for any real national security interest. For their part, the political right has been quick to blame social service providers for the demand to expand social spending. Both sides recognize the interest that the political class may have in expanding government. Among the conservatives, see Gordon Tullock and Locke Institute, Public Goods, Redistribution and Rent Seeking (Cheltenham, UK; Northampton, MA, USA: E. Elgar Pub., 2005); James M. Buchanan and Gordon Tullock, The Calculus of Consent: Logical Foundations of Constitutional Democracy, The Selected Works of Gordon Tullock, v. 2 (Indianapolis: Liberty Fund, 2004); Kevin Phillips, The Emerging Republican Majority (New Rochelle, N.Y.: Arlington House, 1969).

[4]Theodore R. Marmor, Social Insurance: America's Neglected Heritage and Contested Future, Public Affairs and Policy Administration Series (Thousand Oaks, California: SAGE/CQ Press, 2014).

[5]Expected value is calculated as the weighted average of the high and low value of utility where the weights are the probability of each outcome. If there were a 50% chance of a good outcome worth 100 and a bad outcome worth 0, then the expected value would be $0.5*100 + 0.5 * 0 = 50$.

[6]A situation where someone buys insurance in bad faith either because they know that they already have suffered the risk, such as buying insurance on a car that has already been stolen, or because they plan to increase their risk to profit from the insurance, such as by leaving the car unlocked with the keys in the ignition for anyone to steal.

[7]Adverse selection by the buyer of insurance is an aspect of moral hazard where people buy insurance expecting that they will need it. Companies engage in adverse selection by only selling to people who they expect will not need it.

[8]Cherry picking is where an insurer sells only to people who it anticipates will not the policy; lemon dropping is where it discourages people likely to need insurance from buying.

[9]This is why people buy insurance, for those unexpected and rare events.

[10]One insurer in Wisconsin had an ingenious strategy to cherry pick and lemon drop. They offered to sell insurance to anyone who came to their office. Because it was a 5th floor walk-up, that automatically screened out the disabled and those with heart or lung issues.

[11]David A Moss, Socializing Security: Progressive-Era Economists and the Origins of American Social Policy (Cambridge, Mass.: Harvard University Press, 1996); David A Moss, When All Else Fails: Government as the Ultimate Risk Manager (Cambridge, Mass.: Harvard University Press, 2002).

[12]While it is obviously impossible to buy insurance against the risk of being born to bad parents, or born with a significant disability, these are some of the most important risks against which we would have wanted to be insured; John Rawls, A Theory of Justice (Cambridge, MA: Belknap Press of Harvard University Press, 1971).

[13]Decommodifying programs remove some goods and services from the market process so that they are not distributed as commodities. In the United States, these include the right to vote, to practice religion, to have a lawyer and jury trial, and to attend elementary and secondary school.

[14]The idea of decommodifying welfare programs comes from Gøsta Esping-Andersen, The Three Worlds of Welfare Capitalism (Princeton, N.J: Princeton University Press, 1990); he builds, of course, on the concept of social citizenship in T. H Marshall, Citizenship and Social Class, and Other Essays. (Cambridge [Eng.: University Press, 1950).

[15]Post-fisc refers to income after taking account of taxes and government programs.

[16]Esping-Andersen, The Three Worlds of Welfare Capitalism; Jonas Pontusson, Inequality and Prosperity: Social Europe vs. Liberal America (Ithaca, N.Y.: Cornell University Press, 2005).

[17]Lawrence R Jacobs and Benjamin Page, Class War?: What Americans Really Think About Economic Inequality (Chicago: University of Chicago Press, 2009) also see the comparative results of the World Values Survey at http://www.worldvaluessurvey.org/wvs.jsp.

[18]Dan Ariely, "Americans Want to Live in a Much More Equal Country (They Just Don't Realize It)," The Atlantic, August 2, 2012, http://www.theatlantic.com/business/archive/2012/08/americans-want-to-live-in-a-much-more-equal-country-they-just-dont-realize-it/260639/; Michael Norton and Dan Ariely, "Building a Better America -- One Wealth Quintile at a Time," Perspectives on Psychological Science 6, no. 1 (2011): 9–12.

[19]Norton and Ariely, "Building a Better America -- One Wealth Quintile at a Time."

[20]Walter Korpi, The Democratic Class Struggle (London; Boston: Routledge & K. Paul, 1983); John D Stephens, The Transition from Capitalism to Socialism (London: Macmillan, 1979); Gerald Friedman, State-Making and Labor Movements: France and the United States, 1876-1914 (Ithaca: Cornell University Press, 1998).

[21]Gøsta Esping-Andersen, Politics against Markets: The Social Democratic Road to Power (Princeton, N.J.: Princeton University Press, 1985).

[22]Clay Risen, The Bill of the Century: The Epic Battle for the Civil Rights Act, 2014.

[23]Gerald Friedman, "Les États-providence américains: valeurs et politique dans la fabrique du système redistributif des États-Unis," Cycnos: Les Études Anglophones 30 (January 2014): 3–22.

[24]Gerald Friedman, "Success and Failure in Third-Party Politics: The Knights of Labor and the Union Labor Coalition in Massachusetts, 1884-1888," International Labor and Working-Class History 62, no. 1 (2002): 164–88.

[25]See the exit poll results in http://elections.nytimes.com/2012/results/president/exit-polls

[26]Sean Farhang and Ira Katznelson, "The Southern Imposition: Congress and Labor in the New Deal and Fair Deal," Studies in American Political Development 19, no. 01 (2005): 1–30, doi:10.1017/S0898588X05000015; Ira Katznelson, Fear Itself: The New Deal and the Origins of Our Time, 2013; Gerald Friedman, "The Political Economy of Early Southern Unionism: Race, Politics, and Labor in the South, 1880-1953," The Journal of Economic History 60, no. 2 (2000): 384–413.

[27]Michael K Brown, Race, Money, and the American Welfare State (Ithaca: Cornell University Press, 1999); Jill S Quadagno, The Color of Welfare: How Racism Undermined the War on Poverty (New York: Oxford University Press, 1994); Katznelson, Fear Itself.

[28]Powell was chief counsel to the Chamber of Commerce. Shortly after writing this memo, he was appointed to the Supreme Court where he served for almost 20 years and was the architect of the legal principle now called "corporate personhood." Lewis Powell, "The Powell Memo (also Known as the Powell Manifesto)," Reclaim Democracy!, accessed June 27, 2014, http://reclaimdemocracy.org/powell_memo_lewis/; other studies of the political revival of American capitalism include Jacob S Hacker and Paul Pierson, Off Center: The Republican Revolution and the Erosion of American Democracy (New Haven: Yale University Press, 2005); Jacob S Hacker and Paul Pierson, Winner-Take-All Politics: How Washington Made the Rich Richer-and Turned Its Back on the Middle Class (New York: Simon & Schuster, 2010); Jefferson Cowie, Stayin' Alive: The 1970s and the Last Days of the Working Class (New York: New Press, 2010); Robert B Reich, Beyond Outrage: What Has Gone Wrong with Our Economy and Our Democracy, and How to Fix It (New York: Vintage Books, 2012).

[29]Arthur M Okun, Equality and Efficiency, the Big Tradeoff (Washington: Brookings Institution, 1975); "IMF: Reducing Inequality With Transfers Increases Growth," Demos, accessed March 30, 2014, http://www.demos.org/blog/2/27/14/imf-reducing-inequality-transfers-increases-growth.

[30]Émile Durkheim, The Division of Labor in Society (New York: Free Press of Glenoe, 1964).

[31]Mancur Olson, The Logic of Collective Action; Public Goods and the Theory of Groups, Harvard Economic Studies, v. 124 (Cambridge, Mass: Harvard University Press, 1965); Mancur Olson, The Rise and Decline of Nations: Economic Growth, Stagflation, and Social Rigidities (New Haven: Yale University Press, 1982).

GLOSSARY

Academy
The college and university sector of the economy and independent intellectuals.

Accumulation
The increase in "capital" when profits are made. This leads employers to hire more labor power in order to increase their production of commodities to make more profits.

Adverse selection
Where a buyer or a seller has asymmetric information, information unavailable to the other, it can use that information to buy products, such as insurance, at terms more favorable than the other party would have offered if it had access to all the information available.

Affective motivation
A situation where behavior is motivated by emotional attachments rather than self interest.

African slave trade
Over 10 million Africans were captured and transported over the Atlantic to the Americas between 1500 and 1900. Most were employed as slaves in the production of sugar for export to Europe.

Age of Enlightenment
In the 17th and 18th centuries, many European thinkers sought to understand the natural world and humanity's place in it solely on the basis of reason, without explicit reference to religious beliefs. The period was called the "Age of Reason" by the multi-national revolutionary Thomas Paine and held at its heart a conflict between religion and intellectual life that led to a challenge to all forms of established authority.

Aggregate or community demand curve
The relationship between quantity demanded and price for the community as a whole. In the orthodox, neoclassical model this is the horizontal sum of individual demand curves.

Aggregate welfare
The sum of the happiness, or utility, of everyone in the community. Any such calculation has been challenged on the idea that it is improper to compare the happiness of different individuals. It is also necessary to derive weights to use in adding different individual's welfare.

Ahistorical
An approach where behavior is independent of past experience.

Altruism
Behavior to promote the welfare of others even at the expense of one's own well-being.

American Exceptionalism
Marxists and others expected that economic development would lead to the creation of a proletariat class who would overturn capitalism. This expectation was not met in the United States which, by the early 20th century, had the world's most advanced capitalist economy but only a relatively weak socialist movement. Some attributed this to special American circumstances, such as large-scale immigration, or to the political power of American capitalists and state and employer repression of American unions and socialists. Others argue that the American experience contradicts the Marxist model and that socialism is not a natural result of capitalist growth.

Anchoring
A common tendency to rely heavily on one piece of information or experience in formulating expectations.

Arbitrage
A policy of buying in markets with low prices to resell where prices are higher.

Asymmetric information
A situation where one party to a transaction has significant and relevant information not available to the other.

Average total costs
The ratio of total costs (including fixed and variable) costs to total output.

Bargaining
Negotiation between buyers and sellers where both might benefit from cooperation

Baumol Effect
The tendency of prices to rise for services because productivity cannot increase as quickly for these as for materials-handling industries.

Behavioral economics
A field of economics that studies economic behavior by applying concepts and tests from individual psychology.

Behavioral norms
Expected modes of behavior for members of a community.

Bond
A financial instrument issued by a government or business paying a fixed amount at a certain time.

Brand
A product name that has come to be associated with a level of quality and value.

Capital
For neoclassicists, this is the stock of plant, equipment, and other productive assets. For Marxists, this is the social relation between capitalists who own the means of production (productive assets needed for production) and the workers who must work for the capitalist to have access to these resources.

Capital gains
The increase in price on goods because expected rents have increased or because interest rates have

fallen, increasing the value of capitalized rents.

Capitalism
An economic system where a small group, the capitalists, own the means of production and hire the time of workers to produce commodities for sale at a profit.

Capitalist expansion
When capitalists make profits they reinvest them into expanding their capital. They hire more work time to produce more commodities. This leads capitalists to look for more workers to employ and more markets to sell commodities.

Capitalists
A class of people who own the means of production and hire the time of workers (proletarians) to produce commodities.

Capitalized rents
The discounted current value of rents earned through ownership of an asset. This is the amount that one would pay for the asset at current interest rates.

Caring labor
Labor performed to care for individuals, especially those who need personal care, such as children and the disabled elderly.

Chattel slavery
An economic system where workers are owned by the slave owner, who also owns the means of production. The slaves are used to produce commodities.

Class
A group of people in the same relationship with the means of production.

Classical economists
Economists following Adam Smith and David Ricardo who believed that the labor embodied in commodities determined relative prices.

Coase Theorem
A suggestion attributed to Ronald Coase that parties to an externality will be able to resolve the externality efficiently so long as property rights are clearly specified. The allocation of property rights will determine which party, the producer or the victim of the externality, will pay the other and will determine thereby the distribution of income. But an efficient outcome will be reached regardless of who has property rights.

Coercion
Circumstances where one party to a bargaining relationship is able to impose his will on the other because the costs of dissolving the relationship are much higher for one party than for the other.

Collective action
Action by a group of people to advance their common interests.

Commodity production
Production of goods for sale in markets.

Communitarian
Social thought emphasizing the importance of the community in the formation of individuals and the

functioning of social life.

Comparative advantage
Where one can produce a good at a relatively low price because less of other goods must be sacrificed even if all goods are produced relatively inefficiently by this person or country.

Compensating differentials
Higher wages paid in a particular industry or occupation to compensate workers for the relative disutility of working there.

Conscious social process
Social processes where community are made through a social process rather than through as a byproduct of individual decision making.

Conspicuous consumption
Consumption where the chief concern is to appear in a certain way to others.

Consumer surplus
The difference between the value to the consumer of the goods consumed and the price.

Consumption complements
Two goods are complements if an increase in the quantity of one consumed increases the quantity demanded of the other.

Cost of job loss
The difference between the worker's wage and her income at her next-best alternative.

Countervailing power
The ability in bargaining of one monopolist to limit the power of another monopolist.

Crowding
An excess of supply in one market because of discrimination in other markets.

Deadweight burden
The cost of reduced output because of monopolistic behavior or government policies that lower the returns to market activity.

Decommodifying
Public policies that reward citizens regardless of whether they work through the market.

Demand curve
A line relating the amount that people buy with the price that they will pay for that quantity.

Demand is downward sloping
Higher prices are associated with a reduction in the quantity that consumers will buy; they buy more at lower prices.

Democracy
A social system where all citizens are accorded equal rights and have an equal voice in formulating public policy.

Depletability
A good or service where consumption reduces the amount available for others.

Detailed division of labor
A division of production where different workers produce components rather than final products.

Difference principle
A concept associated with John Rawls, that inequality is acceptable if opportunities are open to all and differences benefit the worst off members of society.

Diminishing returns to the variable input
The amount produced by adding additional units of variable inputs declines with additional inputs.

Dismal science
The Scottish historian Thomas Carlyle called economics "the dismal science" because economists sought to understand human society as a set of atomized individuals.

Dividends
Profits distributed by corporations among all owners of stock equity.

Division of labor
An approach where a complex task is broken down to a series of simple components to be completed separately. Adam Smith argued that this was the source of productivity increases.

Domestic slavery
A social system where people are owned by masters who use them in completing household tasks and domestic service. Unlike chattel slaves, or proletarians, domestic slaves are not used in the production of commodities.

Dynamic
An approach where behavior depends on past experience.

Dynamic efficiency or inefficiency
Economic outcomes that promote or retard economic growth and technological progress in the future.

Economic democracy
The application to economic relations of democratic principles of equal rights and the right to participate in social decision making.

Economies of agglomeration
Increases in productivity that come from a regional concentration of similar industries.

Economies of scale
Output increases faster than inputs.

Efficiency
Circumstances where output is maximized for the available inputs.

Efficiency wage line
A line showing the efficiency for any level of wages.

Efficiency wages
The hypothesis that output will increase with higher wages because workers will be more efficient.

Efficient market hypothesis

The hypothesis that market exchange will lead to the most efficient possible output and allocation of products.

Efficient financial markets

The hypothesis that financial markets use all available information to price assets at their expected value. Note that this requires the presence of highly-liquid and risk-neutral investors.

Egalitarian

A distribution where everyone gets what they deserve.

Elasticity of demand

The percentage change in demand for any percentage change in price.

Elasticity of supply

The percentage change in amount supplied for any percentage change in price.

Endogenous

Where economic factors are themselves the outcome of economic relations.

Endogenous technological progress

A theory where technological progress depends on the level and distribution of output.

Entry-level wages

Wages paid in an internal labor market to workers hired for entry-level jobs.

Environmental justice

A movement to treat environmental externalities as infringements on the civil rights of people victimized.

Epiphenomena

Secondary manifestations of underlying causes

Equilibrium

An economic circumstance where production and prices are such that actors have no reason to change their behavior.

Equity

An economic distribution that is fair, either because people receive what we think is right given their circumstances or people receive back from the economic process what they contribute.

Exchange

A social process where people give resources or products to each other and receive something back.

Excludability

A good or service where it is relatively easy to exclude some from consumption.

Exit

Leaving a market exchange.

Exogenous

Where economic factors are independent of economic relations.

Exogenous technological progress
Where technological progress occurs without regard for economic relations.

Expected value
The valuation that one would place on unknown events in the future. It might depend on the present value that we would put on future outcomes, and our estimate of the likelihood of uncertain events.

Exploitation
Economic outcomes where one side receives goods or services from the other without providing equivalent in exchange.

Externalities
An activity that causes benefits or damages to others not directly involved. Positive externalities produce benefits to others; negative externalities harm others.

Extrapolation
A projection for the future assuming that the future will be like the present with changes according to current trends.

Factor endowment
The supplies of land, labor, and capital available for an economy.

Factors of production
Inputs used to produce outputs, including land, labor, machinery.

Fads
A situation where many people want to consume something because other people are consuming it. The good's popularity, then, is independent of its own attributes but due to its popularity.

Fair
A distribution of income is said to be "fair" if it reflects prevailing moral values. In the United States, many feel a fair distribution reflects people's effort or their productivity.

Fallback position
The best situation people could have if bargaining broke down and they were unable to negotiate a contract.

Feminism
In economic analysis, the idea that the work done by women, including care labor performed outside the market, is of value.

Feudalism
An economic system where one group, the landlords, own the workers but the workers themselves are attached to the means of production and control the production process where they produce subsistence goods instead of commodities.

Firm
An established enterprise with rules governing internal transactions to facilitate the detailed division of labor.

Fixed costs
Cost of inputs whose quantity does not change with output.

Fixed inputs
Productive inputs that cannot be changed easily or quickly.

Fordism
A term coined by the Italian Marxist Antonio Gramsci to describe an economic regime joining mass production technology with mass consumption, where workers are motivated by high wages and their high wages allow the consumption of the mass products they produce.

Free capital mobility
The removal of barriers to the international movement of capital and investment.

Free riding
Enjoying public goods without contributing to their production.

Free trade
The removal of barriers to the international movement of products and commodities.

Gains from trade
The productivity gains that come from the social division of labor.

Game theory
Game theory is the study of the way strategic interactions among economic agents produce outcomes with respect to the preferences (or utilities) of those agents, where the outcomes in question might have been intended by none of the agents.

GDP (Gross Domestic Product)
Total output of goods and services exchanged through commodity markets. Alternatives have been proposed which would value nonmarket activity, such as home production including home care work, and would devalue some activities, such as pollution and military spending.

General equilibrium
A situation where there is equilibrium in all markets, where prices are such that that no one has incentive to change their behavior. This is sometimes called "Walrasian equilibrium." Neoclassical economists try to associate this with "Pareto equilibrium" where it is not possible to redistribute output to make anyone better off without making someone worse off.

General glut
A situation where an economy is producing a surplus of all commodities. Walrasian economists assume that this is not possible because they assume that people only produce in order to consume. In a barter economy, therefore, supply will be equilibrated with demand because individuals will reduce their production if they are not consuming an equivalent amount. The same mechanism will operate in a monetized economy where the price of goods in short supply will fall to lower production and lure increased consumption while the reverse happens for goods in short supply.

Generalized reciprocity
Social behavior where people act generously towards others from a general sense that others will reciprocate eventually.

Genetic lottery
An allusion to the good or bad fortune people have in their birth, both in their genetic constitution and in their family and social situation. Much of the difference between rich and poor reflects how well or poorly people fared at birth.

Globalization
The expansion of world trade and capital mobility increasing the international flow of commodities, including labor power, and competition on product and input markets.

Heterogeneous products
Products to meet similar needs but with different attributes.

Hierarchy
An organization where there is a chain of command where some have authority over others.

High-road
Company strategy to compete by providing higher quality products with a work force that is highly productive because it is well-trained and well-paid.

Home workers
Workers who produce at home for consumption by themselves, their families, and friends without market exchange.

Homo economicus
A person who maximizes his or her expected well-being in a purely self-interested way given the constraints he or she faces without regard for the well-being of others.

Homogeneous products
Indistinguishable products that are produced by different companies.

Homothetic preferences
The assumption that the marginal utility curves do not change shape with increasing income so that the quantity consumed at any price by two people of a certain income is the same as the quantity consumed by one person with twice as much income.

Horndal effect
Productivity gains through learning by doing with no new investment or planned change in technology. Named after a Swedish steel mill where output per worker increased steadily for 15 years, with no additional investment.

Human capital
Workers' skills and training that increase their productivity and cannot be separated from the workers themselves.

Humanism
Social philosophy that measures the value of all things according to their effects on people.

Identical preferences
The assumption that all individuals receive the same utility from consuming goods.

Idiosyncratic exchange
An exchange that involves a good or service that cannot be secured from another supplier.

Immiseration
The idea that economic growth will lead to the progressive impoverishment of the workers because of population growth or some other cause.

Income
Goods and services available for consumption gained during some period of time.

Income dispersion
A measure of the differences in income among people in a population.

Income effect
The tendency of people to change the amount they consume of a good when their income changes.

Income elasticity of demand
Change in the amount demanded at any price with an increase in income. An income elastic good, one with an income elasticity greater than 1.0, is one that becomes more demanded when people become rich; an income inelastic good, with an income elasticity less than 1.0, is one that people use relatively less of as they get richer.

Increasing returns to scale
A production process where output rises faster than the rate of increase in all inputs. (Decreasing returns are experienced where output rises less than inputs; constant returns have output rising at the same pace as inputs.)

Independent preferences
The assumption that each person's pleasure from consumption is independent of the amount that others consume.

Index of occupational segregation
A measure of the degree to which members of different groups have different jobs.

Individual's demand curve
The amount an individual will buy at different prices.

Industrial districts
Regions where different industries cluster because productivity is higher for companies near other companies producing the same goods.

Infant industry
A new industry where productivity may increase substantially if it has the opportunity to grow.

Inframarginal
Consumers or suppliers within the market margin who would continue to buy (or sell) even if prices rose (or fell).

Inframarginal workers
Workers who will remain in a job even if earnings decline or working conditions worsen somewhat.

Infrastructure: physical
Public goods, physical structures, that raise the productivity of production processes or facilitate exchange.

Infrastructure: social
Public goods, cultural norms and social institutions, that raise the productivity of production processes or facilitate exchange.

Institutionalism
Economic analysis that denies the universalist pretensions of much orthodox economic theory to argue that all economic "laws" are contingent on historical experience and social institutions.

Institutions
Social arrangements that act as constraints on individual behavior.

Insurance
An exchange where individuals pay a certain fixed amount, the "premium," in exchange for a commitment for compensation in certain specified contingencies.

Intermediate products
Produced inputs into production.

Internal labor markets
Where a company recruits workers for higher-level positions from among those in lower-level jobs.

International Division of Labor
The social division of labor with production in different countries.

Invisible hand
The idea that in trying to maximize their own well-being, individuals will be led by their own self-interest to produce a social optimum; led, as if by an invisible hand.

Job ladder
An arrangement of jobs within a company where workers progress from one to another in a fixed order.

Job tenure
Length of time on a particular job.

Jobs
A social relation where workers exchange their readiness to work, their time, for a wage.

Keynesian economics
Economic theories developed by the English economist John Maynard Keynes and his followers where aggregate demand has no natural relationship to aggregate supply because production is driven by different motivates than consumption.

Kleptocracy
A country run by thieves.

Kuznets curve
An empirical relationship where income inequality rises during early economic growth and then declines.

Labor
Productive work.

Labor force
Members of the population engaged in productive work. In the definition used by the United State Bureau of Labor Statistics, this includes only those with market work or looking for market work.

Labor force participation rate
The share of the population with jobs or looking for jobs. Note that this is not the same as the share working because it does not include home workers.

Labor theory of value
Economic theory (going back to Adam Smith and David Ricardo) that the price of goods reflects the labor used to produce them.

Laissez faire
Economic theory that says individuals should be allowed to act without government or other regulation to maximize their personal well-being.

Leaky bucket
The idea, from Arthur Okun, that society can redistribute income from rich to poor only at the expense of lowering productivity.

Learning by doing
Where producers become more efficient with practice.

Liquidity
The ability to convert assets quickly and at little or no cost into cash or another asset.

Long-run
A time period long enough that all factors of production can be altered and there are no fixed costs.

Long-run average total costs
Average costs fall in the long-run if there are increasing returns to scale.

Long-run marginal cost curves
The marginal cost in the long run where all factors of production are variable.

Low road
Company strategy to compete by providing products at a low price by paying low wages to poorly trained and often short-tenure workers.

Luck
Circumstances that raise or lower one's income or productivity through no action of one's own.

Macroeconomics
The field of economics concerned with the aggregate level of production and employment.

Managerial firm
Business firms run by their managers in their own interest without regard for the interests of their share holders.

Marginal analysis
Analysis that focuses on the impact of behavior on the margin, or the last unit of action.

Marginal cost
The variable cost of producing one more unit of output.

Marginal product
Output from adding one more unit of inputs.

Marginal product of capital
Output from adding one more unit of machinery and capital goods.

Marginal product of labor
Output from adding one more unit of labor.

Marginal product of raw materials
Output from adding one more unit of raw materials.

Marginal revenue
Revenue from selling one more unit of product.

Marginal revenue product
Revenue from selling output from adding one more unit of inputs.

Marginal surplus utility
The difference between the marginal utility from one more unit of consumption and the price of that consumption.

Marginal utility
The pleasure that comes from one more unit of consumption.

Marginal workers
Workers who are ready to change jobs if there is any reduction in their earnings or if working conditions get worse.

Market death spiral
A market collapse brought on when buyers evaluate products based on average characteristics, leading higher quality vendors to withdraw, lowering average quality and buyers' evaluations until there are no exchanges.

Market equilibrium
Market price and quantity where neither buyers nor sellers want to change the amount they buy or bring to market.

Market failure
A situation where there are buyers or sellers who at the prevailing price want a different quantity than is available on the market. This is distinguished from a failure of markets where markets do not exist for goods or services.

Market fundamentalists
Analysts who advocate policies of free markets and laissez faire.

Market imperfection
Where free markets provide inadequate incentive to produce desired goods, or do not discourage the production of undesirables.

Market power
Where one side to the market is able to force the other side to accept a market price and quantity away from the competitive market equilibrium, thus redistributing some of the surplus.

Market reinforcing
Public policies that reward work through the market by subsidizing market earnings.

Market share
The share of sales of a particular product going to one or a few companies.

Market transactions
An exchange of commodities.

Market work
Productive work that involves the production and exchange of commodities. In contrast with home production that involves the production of goods and services for direct consumption.

Marketization
The use of the market to allocate goods and services previously allocated within families or communities.

Markets
Social institutions where commodities are exchanged.

Marriage bars
Laws and mores forbidding the employment of married women.

Married Women's Property Acts
19th century legislation granting married women control over property they brought to the marriage or acquired while married.

Materialists
Philosophical position that all life reflects material things and there is no spiritual or ideal realm.

Means of production
Tools and other resources used in the process of production.

Methodological individualism
An approach that explains social outcomes in terms of individuals and their motivations.

Microeconomics
The field of economics concerned with the level and distribution of production by individuals and firms.

Microfoundations
The individual motivations behind macroeconomic activity.

Mobile groups
Individuals able to leave market transactions.

Monopolistic competition
Competition between firms each having a monopoly in a particular product.

Monopoly
A single producer of a distinct product or service.

Monopsony
A single seller of a distinct productive input.

Moral hazard
A situation where an insured party is more likely to take risks because the costs of failure will be borne by another.

Mores
Values and norms of behavior.

Motherhood penalty
The economic burden borne by mothers due the cost of time taken off from work, including the cost of lost promotions.

Movements along the demand curve
Where consumers change the quantity they want to buy in response to changing prices due to changing costs.

Movements of the demand curve
Where consumers change the quantity they want to buy at any given price. (This may be because of changes in preferences, income, or the supply and price of complementary goods.)

Nation state
Political organization where the country is organized along lines of a single culture and language.

Natural assets
Goods available from nature, including clean air and water.

Natural benevolence
The idea that that God or some other divine force has arranged the world to promote human welfare.

Natural monopoly
A market where there are such great economies to scale that there can only be one efficient producer.

Needs
Things that people want for intrinsic physical or psychological reasons.

Neoclassical economics
A branch of economics that explains economic outcomes in terms of individual motivations with fixed preferences, technology, and the supply of productive factors.

Neoclassical Say's Law
Supply equals demand because prices adjust. The prices of products in excess supply falls while the prices of those in short supply rises until supply and demand is equilibrated for all products.

Network efficiencies
Production or consumption benefits from using the same products as others use.

Nominal wages
Wages in unit of currency.

Nonmarket work
Productive work that is coordinated outside of the market.

Nonreproducible goods.
Goods in fixed supply either because they are unique spatial locations, or are the product of a

particular person.

Objets d'art
Material objects of particular beauty.

Oligopoly
A market where there is more than one but a only a few producers.

On-the-job training
Training and human-capital accumulation that happens through work.

Opportunity cost
The value of the next best alternative (the fallback position) that must be given up because of a decision.

Organization of Economic Cooperation and Development
An association of leading industrialized countries.

Overproduction problem for negative externalities
The tendency of producers to produce goods without regard for negative spillover effects because they do not pay for these.

Panglossian
The view that everything is for the best in the best of all possible worlds, even if it appears otherwise.
Pareto efficient outcome
A distribution where no reallocation is possible without hurting someone.

Partial equilibrium
A market equilibrium in one market without regard for whether other markets are in equilibrium.

Patriarchy
Legal regime where adult men have complete legal authority over the labor of their wives and children.

Per capita income
Total income divided by the population.

Perfect competition
An industry with many producers of homogeneous products and perfect knowledge by buyers and sellers so that no producer or consumer has market power.

Pigouvian taxes
Taxes or subsidies provided to internalize the costs or benefits of externalities.

Political economy
The field of economics concerned with the social determination of income and distribution; it asks how society's history and institutions shape production without concern for individual motivation.

Political regulation
Regulation of output or prices by state bodies.

Ponzi scheme
Where investors are paid not by the returns from productive investment but out of money paid in by

new investors.

Positional goods
Goods valued because they establish one's status relative to others.

Poverty
An income too low to allow one to participate in standard economic life.

Power
The ability to force others to accept a market price and quantity away from the equilibrium, thus redistributing some of the surplus.

Preferences
The valuation one puts on different goods, services, and activities.

Pre-fisc/post-fisc income distribution
Income distribution before and after the impact of government taxes and spending programs.

Present value
The value of future costs or benefits discounted to be the equivalent value today.

Price along the demand curve
The ability to charge different prices to different consumers according to their willingness and ability to pay.

Price controls
State regulations setting prices.

Price elastic
A market where consumers will make substantial changes in the quantity they buy if prices change.

Price inelastic
A market where consumers will not make substantial changes in the quantity they buy if prices change.

Price signals
A market where consumers infer product quality from the price.

Price taker
A producer or consumer who must accept the market price and act accordingly.

Prisoner's dilemma
A situation where the independent actions of two individuals lead to an outcome that is undesirable for both.

Private goods
Depletable goods or services where owners can exclude others.

Producer surplus
The difference between the cost of products to the producer and the price paid by consumers.

Production complements
Two goods are complements if an increase in the production of one increases the productivity of the other.

Production for profit
Production of commodities to make profit regardless of any intent by the producer to consume.

Production for use
Production for immediate consumption or else with intent to exchange to gain another product for consumption.

Production function
An expression of a determinate relationship between inputs and outputs

Production possibilities frontier
Different combinations of various goods that can be produced given available resources and technology.

Productivity
The amount produced per unit of input. Often means "labor productivity" or output divided by the labor input. "Total factor productivity" refers to output divided by some weighted measure of all inputs.

Profit
Revenues minus costs, including both variable and fixed costs.

Profit maximizing firm
A firm whose goal is to maximize profits, either in the current period or over some longer period. Other objectives may be to increase the firm size, its market share, or its productivity.

Proletariat
Wage workers employed in jobs.

Property
The right to exclusive use of a good or resource.

Public bad
Bad things (such as negative externalities and spillovers), without easy excludability, received by parties not involved in a market transaction.

Public good
Goods without easy excludability, over which there are no property rights.

Pyramid scheme
A financial scheme where participants profit solely by recruiting new participants into the program. These often promise extraordinary returns for doing nothing other than handing over your money and getting others to do the same. See Ponzi scheme.

QWERTY
Letters on one row of the standard keyboard. Because keyboards were arranged to slow down typists, the persistence of this arrangement has been taken as an example of the potential inefficiency of path-dependent technologies where once adopted technologies are hard to change.

Real median earnings
The real wages of the average worker, where half earn more and half less, adjusted for inflation.

Real wages
Wages adjusted for inflation to show their real purchasing power.

Reciprocal altruism
Actions that cost someone to the benefit of others done in the expectation, or the hope, that someone else in a similar manner towards the first person at a later time.

Reciprocity
Where people exchange goods or services outside of formal markets often without direct measure of the equality of the exchange.

Redistribution
The transfer of value by government or other compulsion.

Reference income
A target that people want to earn. It can vary by community.

Relative income
Income compared to other people.

Rents
Profits earned beyond the normal rate of return because of property rights in a scarce, nonreproducible asset.

Reproducible goods
Goods where more can be produced; in contrast with nonreproducible goods.

Reservation wage
The minimum wage that a person would accept before taking a job.

Reserve army of the unemployed
Workers available for work but unemployed. They are available for capitalist expansion and their presence keeps wages from rising.

Rights
Privileges and protections for individuals regardless of behavior or wealth.

Rising cost of time
Increasing productivity in the production of material goods raises the value of time, the material goods lost when time is spent on other things including the provision of labor services and the production of time-intensive services, like sex.

Risk
The possibility that an asset or activity will have lower returns than expected.

Risk-averse
A preference for a guaranteed outcome over a gamble of equal expected value.

Risk neutral
Indifference between a guaranteed outcome and a gamble of equal expected value. Characteristic of market actors with very long time horizons or such large portfolios that they can conduct repeated trials and survive a long string of unlikely events.

Risk-return curve
A curve relating the market returns demanded to the degree of risk or uncertainty for different investments.

Rules
Laws and social norms constraining behavior.

Satiation
The tendency to want additional units of any good or service less the more you have already consumed. This explains diminishing marginal utility.

Satisficing
Behavior directed to do reasonably well rather than trying to maximize or optimize outcomes. An approach often adopted in the face of uncertainty.

Saturated
The tendency of marginal products to decline when the ratio of an input to other inputs increases.

Say's Law
The economic principle that supply creates its own demand because there is no production except with intent to consume.

Secular theology
A social theory that assumes natural beneficence even without the presence of a divine being.

Services
Labor performed for someone without exchange of any material .

Sharp trading
Aggressive bargaining and financial maneuvering to capture every advantage possible in a market exchange.

Shifts in demand
Changes in the amount that people will buy at any price. This may happen because of changes in preferences, income, the prices of substitutes or complements, or in the extent of the market.

Shifts in supply
Changes in the amount that producers will supply at any price. This may happen because of changes in the cost of inputs, in technology, or a reduction in monopoly power in the market.

Short run
The period of time during which it is not possible to change fixed factors of production.

Slacking
When workers on a job do not work hard during the time that they have sold to their employer.

Smaller groups
A group of individuals small enough that they can work together to produce public goods.

Social capital
A society's infrastructure, values, and social relations that support economic activity.

Social division of labor
Exchange economy where different individuals or groups specialize in particular products that they then exchange for those produced by others.

Social facts
External structures, including physical structures, laws, and social expectations, that guide individuals, rewarding some behaviors, punishing others, and, when most effective, rendering some inconceivable.

Social institutions
A particular type of social fact where there are formal rules governing behavior.

Social insurance
The provision of insurance funded through taxes or other compulsory contributions in order to compensate individuals for income loss due to macroeconomic events, or due to illness, disability, or accidents of birth.

Social ontology (see institutionalism)
The idea that social facts exist independently of human volition and shape social outcomes and individual behavior.

Social optimum (see Pareto efficient outcome)
An allocation of goods and services where people cannot be made better off given society's preferences, resources, and technology.

Social science
The study of social outcomes in terms of social facts.

Social Structures of Accumulation
An approach that sees the economy as shaped by social structures designed to facilitate capitalist accumulation. When these structures are effectively challenged by working-class unrest or foreign conflict, they are transformed, eventually, into a new social structure to facilitate a new era of capitalist development.

Social surplus
The sum of producer and consumer surplus.

Socialism
The organization of production and distribution through conscious social action rather than through markets.

Specialization
A system of production where individuals concentrate on performing one part of the production process (in the detailed division of labor) or produce one set of goods (social division of labor).

Spirit of craftsmanship
The desire to do good work.

Stagnant steady-state economics
The expectation that economic growth will lead to a distribution of income that will inhibit and eventually stop the growth process.

Stampedes
Situations where individuals follow a fad.

Sticky wages
Tendency of firms with internal labor markets to adjust wages slowly.

Stock
Partial ownership in a collective enterprise entitling the owner to a share of the profits.

Strategic interactions
Market or other interactions where actors are conscious of the impact that their actions can have on others.

Subsistence wage
The lowest possible wage needed to maintain the size of the working population.

Substitutes
Goods that can be used (or consumed) instead of others if prices change.

Substitution effect
Tendency to reduce consumption of a good whose price has increased and substitute another good.

Sui generis
A situation constituting a class alone, unique unto itself and unlike any other, not subject to an explanation common to other situations.

Sum of private benefits
The sum of the utilities all consumers get from a public good, including those who pay for it and those who do not.

Sum of production costs
The sum of the costs incurred in producing a good, including all costs, those paid by the producer and spillover or externality costs borne by others.

Supply
The quantity of a good provided to the market.

Supply curve
A graph giving the amount supplied at any price.

Surplus value
The value of output beyond what is needed to pay for the workers' time and replace means of production used up in the production process.

Symbolic analysts
Workers whose tasks depend on creativity and the manipulation of symbols and concepts.

Talent
Individual ability.

Technology of production
Blueprints specifying how inputs are to be combined to produce outputs and the precise quantity of output coming from any set of inputs.

Theists
Those who believe in some divine being who may or may not be active in human affairs.

Third-party payment
Where goods or services are paid for by someone other than the recipient, such as an insurance company, government agency, or generous benefactor.

Tit-for-tat
Game theory where one responds to an opponent's action with that opponent's previous action. This encourages opponents to cooperate and can lead to cooperative behavior in a multi-turn prisoner's dilemma situation.

Total revenue
Price times quantity sold; P x Q.

Trade-offs
Goods or services forsaken when some other goods or services are consumed; related to opportunity cost.

Tragedy of the commons
Collective situation where individual action undermines the welfare of the community.

Transactions costs
Cost of using the market, includes costs of identifying and enforcing property rights and the cost of identifying customers or suppliers and contracting with them.

Trustful community
A community where members agree to be honest in expectation that others will also behave in the same way.

Uncertainty
The possibility that returns will vary in ways that cannot be predicted so that risks cannot be accurately discounted.

Underproduction problem for positive externalities
Tendency of market economy to underproduce public goods where producers cannot charge consumers for all the benefits received because of nonexcludability.

Use value
The value consumers get from a commodity.

Utilitarian
Social theory that values activities according to the pleasures received by consumers.

Utility
Individual happiness and welfare.

Value theory
Theory of the value of goods and services underlying relative prices.

Variable inputs
Inputs that can be changed in the short run.

Veblen effects
Consumption of goods intended to demonstrate social status to others.

Veil of ignorance
A hypothetical situation associated with the work of John Rawls (Theory of Justice) where people would choose a distribution of income ignorant of where they would be on the distribution.

Voice
Complaints about poor quality service, an alternative to exit.

Wage contours
Tendency of wages in different occupations to move together regardless of individual circumstances.

Walras' Law
The assumption that an economy will be at "full employment" because there cannot be a general surplus of production or supply. If there is a surplus in any commodity, its price will fall, leading to a reduction in supply and an increase in the quantity consumed. On the other hand, a surplus in one product implies excess demand for another, leading to price increases and reduced consumption there.

Walrasian equilibrium
A set of prices such that there is equilibrium in all markets.

Wants
Commodity that people will buy without any intrinsic need.

Welfare
Two meanings: (1) well-being; (2) social programs providing financial assistance to needy people.

Welfare state
A set of government programs providing social insurance to individuals.

Zero-sum game
A situation where gains to any one party in transaction come from losses to the other, so that total gains are fixed.

THE EVOLUTION OF ECONOMIC IDEAS

PHILOSOPHIC ANTECEDENTS

Aristotle
Greek philosopher (384-322 BCE) who viewed people as social beings distinguished from other animals because they lived in communities.

Thomas Hobbes
English philosopher (1588-1679) who wrote during the social disorders of the English Civil War of the 1640s. Hobbes warned that people were selfish egoists. In his masterwork, *Leviathan* (1651), he warned that outside of society, people are selfish egoists whose lives would be "solitary, poor, nasty, brutish, and short," a "war of everyman against everyman." When people formed society, they handed all authority over to a sovereign, a "Leviathan," exchanging obedience for protection.

John Locke
English philosopher (1632-1704) whose work was influenced by the much more tranquil "Glorious Revolution" of 1689 where Parliament peacefully replaced the English king. In *Two Treatises of Civil Government* (1690), he bases the right to private property on the labor people put into developing the property. Individuals form society, he argues, to protect their rights and their property.

Voltaire
French philosopher (1694-1778) critical of France's absolute monarchy and its alliance with the Roman Catholic church. Leery of any absolute system, he argued for an absolute right to free thought and speech, and was quick to search out the material interest behind any political policy or idea system.

CLASSICAL

Adam Smith
Scottish economist (1723-90) who developed a theory of economic behavior based on the division of labor and the Labor Theory of Value.

François Quesnay
French economist (1694-1774) who theorized about the social division of labor.

Jean-Baptiste Say
French economist (1767-1832) famous for enunciating "Say's Law" that total demand in an economy cannot exceed or fall below total supply in that economy because a "product is no sooner created, than

it, from that instant, affords a market for other products to the full extent of its own value."

David Ricardo
Early 19th century English economist (1772-1823) famous for his theory of comparative advantage explaining the benefits of trade.

Thomas Robert Malthus
English parson (1766-1834) who argued in his 1798 pamphlet "Essay on the Principle of Population" that population growth will exceed the growth of means of subsistence unless limited by "positive checks" (such as starvation) or "preventive checks" (such as postponement of marriage). His hypothesis has been interpreted to say that attempts to ameliorate the condition of the lower classes by increasing their incomes or improving agricultural productivity would be fruitless because they would only lead to population growth.

Jeremy Bentham
English barrister and gentleman (1748-1832), founder of philosophic doctrine of "utilitarianism" where laws should be evaluated according to the single ethical principle of "utility" or whether they increased the general happiness of the population.

James Mill
Scottish journalist and writer (1773-1836) famous for popularizing the laissez faire doctrines associated with David Ricardo and the utilitarian philosophy of Jeremy Bentham.

John Ramsay McCulloch
Scottish journalist (1789-1864) who wrote the first popular economics textbook, *Principles of Political Economy* (1825). A faithful follower of David Ricardo and advocate of laissez faire economic policies, McCulloch is also famous for developing the "wages fund" theory where the wage rate is determined by the ratio of the population to a pre-existing fund available for paying wages.

John Stuart Mill
English economist (1806-73) whose 1848 text, *The Principles of Political Economy* was the ultimate statement of the classical school.

Karl Marx
German philosopher (1818-83) who developed the Labor Theory of Value into a theory of exploitation and class conflict. His writings, often in collaboration with his friend Friedrich Engels, inspired socialist and communist revolutionary movements down to the present day.

BREAKUP OF THE CLASSICAL TRADITION

EARLY NEOCLASSICAL

W. Stanley Jevons
English logician, philosopher, and economist (1835-82) whose *Theory of Political Economy* (1871) helped launch the Marginalist Revolution that gave birth to Neoclassical economics.

John Bates Clark
American economist (1847-1938) who first established the neoclassical theory of income distribution.

Alfred Marshall
English economist (1842-1924) best known for popularizing neoclassical theory with his textbook *Principles of Economics* (1890).

Carl Menger
Austrian economist (1840-1921) who developed a value theory built from diminishing marginal utility.

Vilfredo Pareto
Italian economist (1848-1923) who contributed to the development of neoclassical general equilibrium theory. Deeply suspicious of government, he argued against state policies except those that benefitted all, or at least did not hurt anyone.

Léon Walras
French engineer and economist (1834-1910) was, with Jevons and Menger, one of the leaders of the marginalist revolution and neoclassical theory. His 1874 classic, *Elements of Pure Economics*, established the field of general equilibrium, or the mathematical analysis of the way individual activities can lead to equilibrium in all markets.

Arthur Cecil Pigou
English economist (1877-1959), Pigou was a founder of neoclassical welfare economics and is responsible for both the distinction between private and social marginal products and costs, and the idea that governments can correct market failures through taxes and subsidies that change private prices to reflect social costs and returns.

Lionel Robbins
English economist (1898-1984) who argued in his 1932 "Essay on the Nature and Significance of Economic Science" that economics was "the science which studies human behavior as a relationship between scarce means which have alternative uses." He defended the use of a priori theory against empirical and institutional economics.

Friedrich von Hayek
Austrian economist (1889-1992) most famous as a critique of socialism. In addition to his well-known 1944 work, *Road to Serfdom*, a polemical defense of *laissez-faire*, he argued in other articles that socialist economies would be inherently inefficient because they would lose the invaluable information about preferences and costs that is provided by market prices.

LATER NEOCLASSICAL

Irving Fisher
Called the most important American economist, Fisher (1867-1947) pioneered utility theory in monetary economics. In particular, he developed the concepts of expected value and theories of behavior under conditions of risk and uncertainty.

Frank Knight
A founder of the modern Chicago school of neoclassical economics, Knight (1927-1955) is best known for his first book, *Risk, Uncertainty, and Profit* (1921) where he argued that economic profits will be earned in a perfectly competitive environment as a reward for uncertain risks.

Paul Samuelson
Perhaps the most important 20th century American neoclassicist, Samuelson (1915-2009) established modern neoclassical economics as a series of problems of individual constrained optimization.

John Hicks
One of the most important 20th century English neoclassicists (1904-1989), his 1932 book, *Theory of Wages*, established modern marginal productivity theory, and his 1939 *Value and Capital* established the groundwork for modern neoclassical general equilibrium theory.

Kenneth Arrow

American mathematician and economist (1921-) who developed neoclassical general equilibrium theory and the "Arrow Impossibility Theorem": under reasonable axioms on individual preference, no voting system can be devised that will maximize social welfare except if there is a "dictator" whose preferences dominate everybody else's.

Milton Friedman

American neoclassical economist (1912-2006) best known as advocate of "Monetarism" against Keynesian macroeconomics, as an advocate of pure neoclassical price theory, and an opponent of government economic regulation.

George Stigler

American neoclassical economist (1911-91) contributed significantly to the revival of neoclassical price theory in the United States after 1950 and pioneered in the field of the economics of information. In a series of studies of industrial structure and behavior, Stigler also questioned the value of government regulation.

Gary Becker

American neoclassical economist (1930-) has pioneered the extension of neoclassical analysis to a wide range of human behavior and interaction, including nonmarket behavior.

Fritz Machlup

Austrian economist (1902-83) who taught in the United States after the rise of European Fascism, Machlup defended neoclassical theory from empirical criticisms.

William Baumol

American economist (1922-) who argued that firms in apparently monopolized industries may not actually have market power so long as they face the threat of entry or "contestability." Baumol also argued that the relative prices of services will rise in the course of economic growth because productivity cannot grow in service industries the way it does in materials handling industries.

Arthur Okun

American economist (1928-80) best known as macroeconomist and advocate of active counter-cyclical government policy. A liberal, he argued in his 1975 book *Equality Versus Efficiency* that economic inequality is necessary to promote economic growth and efficiency.

MARXIST

Karl Kautsky

German (1854-1938) socialist, journalist, and leader of the Social Democratic Party. Friedrich Engels's intellectual executor, Kautsky edited Marx's *Theories of Surplus Value* (1905-10) and was a staunch defender of orthodox Marxism during the period of the Socialist Second International.

Eduard Bernstein

German socialist, journalist, and leader of the Social Democratic Party, Bernstein (1850-1932) was the main instigator of the "revisionist" movement in the Socialist Second International. In *Evolutionary Socialism: A Criticism and Affirmation* (1899), he urged socialists to abandon Marxism as a predictive science and instead defend socialism as an ethical goal.

Rosa Luxemburg

Polish socialist and economist (1870-1919), Luxemburg was a critic of both the orthodox Marxism of Kautsky and Bernstein's revisionism. Writing after the abortive Russian Revolution of 1905, she argued that spontaneous action by the workers is more important to making a socialist revolution than is organization. In her treatise, *The Accumulation of Capital* (1913), she argued that continued accumulation of capital is impossible in a closed state because capitalist society cannot absorb all the surplus value it produces. She concluded that imperialism is central to capitalism because breakdown is avoided only by accessing non-capitalist societies.

Rudolf Hilferding

Austrian and German socialist and economist (1877-1941?) contributed to debate over whether capitalism was stabilizing and introduced the notion of finance capital in his 1910 *Finance Capital*. Minister of Finance in two socialist administrations in Germany in the 1920s, Hilferding fled to France to escape the Nazis and was handed over to them by the Vichy regime in 1941. His exact fate is unknown.

Lenin

Russian journalist and socialist (1870-1924) who rejected the orthodox Marxism of the Second International and the writings of Karl Kautsky. Lenin argued that imperialism was an inevitable stage in capitalist development because it was necessary to export capital to maintain profitability. The super-profits made through imperialism then allow the imperialist countries to pay off a part of the working class and its leadership to avoid revolution. Socialist revolution, therefore, must begin in the capitalist periphery and must be led by intellectuals who will bring socialist consciousness to the workers. Lenin led a faction of the Russian Social Democratic Party in its seizure of power in the Communist revolution of 1917.

Oskar Lange

Polish socialist and economist (1904-65) who rejected the Marxian labor theory of value for the Neo-classical theory of marginal utility and price. His 1938 work, *On the Economic Theory of Socialism*, argued that a state-run economy could be organized efficiently, even more efficiently than a capitalist economy, if government planners used the price signals as if in a perfect market economy and instructed state industry managers to respond to state-determined prices and minimize costs by producing where marginal cost equals price. He taught at the University of Chicago before returning to Poland after World War II where he worked for the country's Communist government.

Paul Sweezy

American economist (1910-2004) most famous for his analysis of monopolistic competition in the 1930s and for updating Marxian economic thought in his 1942 work, *Theory of Capitalist Development*, which reintroduced Marxian thought to modern economic analysis of prices (Marx's "Transformation Problem") and the theory of crisis. Denied academic employment because of his radical politics, Sweezy was editor of *Monthly Review* for over 50 years.

Ernest Mandel

Belgian Marxist economist (1923-95) who developed theory of long-waves of capitalist expansion.

INSTITUTIONALIST

Friedrich List

German economist (1789-1846) who taught in the United States. A forerunner of the German Historical School, he is best known for his *The National System of Political Economy* (1841), which attacks free-trade doctrines.

Henry Carey

American journalist (1793-1879) best known as advocate of protection to limit international specialization because he believed that the development of a diverse set of industries and agriculture would lead to greater economic efficiency and social welfare by encouraging the social division of labor.

Richard Ely

American economist (1854-1943), founder of the American Economic Association (in 1885) to promote historical method, institutional studies, and social reform.

Max Weber

German sociologist (1864-1920) who argued that economic outcomes are shaped by cultural values.

Émile Durkheim

French sociologist (1858-1917) whose 1893 *The Division of Labor in Society* argues that social harmony will not arise from individual self-interest and free contract. Instead, social cohesion and "organic solidarity" come from justice and respect for individualism.

Gustav Schmoller

German economist (1838-1917) and leader of the German Historical School. Rejecting attempts to establish universal economic laws, Schmoller sought to develop economic analysis particular to each place and time. In 1872, he formed the Verein für Sozialpolitik ("Society for Social Policy") to promote moderate social reform. While the Verein was condemned by socialists as pro-capitalist, liberals deplored it for favoring state intervention and labelled Schmoller and the Historicists as Kathedersozialisten (or "Socialists of the Chair"). The Verein was a model for the American Economic Association.

John R. Commons

American labor economist (1862-1945) who studied collective action to show the importance of institutions in understanding economic life. Building on Richard Ely's work, he developed labor economics and the study of labor history as academic disciplines and contributed to fact-finding and drafting legislation on a wide range of social issues that made Wisconsin a laboratory for progressive innovations in the early 20th century. He is perhaps best known for his students, many of whom played prominent roles in the New Deal of the 1930s and the development of Social Security and other social welfare programs in the United States.

Beatrice Potter Webb

English economist (1858-1943) best known for her studies of social welfare and support for social democracy and the British Labour Party. Born into a wealthy English family, Webb was largely self taught. At 25, she became active in the Charity Organization Society, work that eventually led her to prepare a study of the Cooperative Movement. In this, she formed a working relationship, and marriage, with Sidney Webb. Together, they helped to found the London School of Economics and wrote widely on economic policy and the nature of modern capitalism. Among their most famous works are *The History of Trade Unionism* (1894) and *Industrial Democracy* (1897).

John Maurice Clark

American economist (1884-1963) best known for his work showing the significance of fixed costs (which he called "overhead costs") and imperfect competition. By demonstrating that firms that sell at the marginal cost of production will lose money, John Maurice Clark demonstrated the fallacy of assuming perfectly competitive markets.

Thorstein Veblen

American philosopher and economist (1857-1929) best known for his critique of orthodox theory and his argument for a broader conception of economic behavior in society. In his 1899 book *The Theory of the Leisure Class*, he argued that consumer behavior is a social phenomenon where individual utility depends on individuals' position in a community. In his *Theory of Business Enterprise* (1904) he argued that. under capitalism, because of the role of finance capital, business firms risked being dominated by pecuniary concerns rather than production. This argument was amplified in *The Instincts of Workman-*

ship and the State of the Industrial Arts (1914), where he argued that workers seek accomplishment in their work through creative and productive labor.

Wesley Clair Mitchell
American economist (1874-1948) is best known for his pioneering empirical studies of the business cycle, which led to the formation of the National Bureau of Economic Research (1919), his 1913 book, *Business Cycles*, and (with Arthur Burns) *Measuring Business Cycles*. Mitchell's business-cycle work was one part of a larger project to show how economic activity cannot be understood using universal laws because each period's behavior depends on past behavior and the institutions formed in the past.

Rexford Guy Tugwell
American economist (1891-1979) argued that economics has no universal laws because economic behavior depends on time, place and history. He argued that the modern American economy is dominated by large institutions whose behavior is largely separate from competitive pressures. In 1932, he became a member of the Brain Trust that advised Franklin D. Roosevelt and served in the Roosevelt administration as undersecretary of agriculture and architect of New Deal economic reforms.

Karl Polanyi
Born in Vienna (1886-1964), the Hungarian historian and economist is best known for his 1944 book *The Great Transformation*, where he argues that capitalism is a historical anomaly because under capitalism culture is defined by economic relations. He shows how capitalism rejects non-market rules of reciprocity, redistribution, and communal obligation that have been central to other social formations.

John Dunlop
American labor economist (1914-2003) argued that wages are set to preserve regular differentials between workers in different occupations along "wage contours." Active in government, including service as Secretary of Labor, he sought to control inflation by using government leverage to restrain wage increases among pattern setters, or unions and occupations whose wage increases are widely imitated.

Mollie Orshansky
American labor economist (1915-2006), Orshansky was born in New York City, the third of six children born to impoverished Jewish immigrants. After attending public schools and Hunter College (of the City University of New York), she did graduate work at American University. Orshansky worked at the Children's Bureau, the Agriculture Department, and the Social Security Administration. Her primary responsibility was to estimate the cost of providing minimum nutrition. From this work, she suggested in 1963 a dollar figure for the income level below which people would not be able to sustain even a minimum standard of living. This has been used as the "poverty line" by the United States government. She summarized her findings in two books: *Counting the Poor: Another Look at the Poverty Profile* (1965) and *Who's Who Among the Poor: A Demographic View of Poverty* (1965). Throughout her work, Orshansky sought to promote government policy that would improve the lives of the poor. She said in 1999: "Poor people are everywhere; yet they are invisible. I wanted them to be seen clearly by those who make decisions about their lives."

John Kenneth Galbraith
Canadian-born American economist (1908-2006) developed the institutional analysis to show the need for active government policy. In his classic 1958 book *The Affluent Society*, he argued that free-market policies would systematically lead to the underproduction of public goods. Rejecting orthodox neoclassical theories of the perfectly competitive firm, he argued in *The New Industrial State* (1967) that firms were oligopolistic institutions largely autonomous from market pressures or even their owners, and increasingly similar in both the United States and the Soviet Unions.

David Gordon
American economist (1944-96) who argued in his 1984 book (with Richard Edwards and Michael

Reich) *Segmented Work, Divided Workers* that societies develop institutions, including political systems, ideologies, and systems of industrial and labor management, in order to support the accumulation of wealth by the ruling elite. Conflict between the elite and the working classes can lead to a breakdown in this "Social Structure of Accumulation" and the development of a new one.

Elinor Ostrom

Born in Los Angeles, Ostrom (1933-2012) was a political economist studying how institutions—conceptualized as sets of rules—affect the incentives of individuals interacting in repetitive and structured situations. Her focus has been on the use and regulation of common pool resources, including forests and water supplies. These are resources important for entire communities but, because they are not easily incorporated into systems of private property, it is important for communities to develop rules or systems for their regulation. A professor of political science, Ostrom was awarded the Nobel Prize in Economics in 2009.

James Boyce

American economist (1951-) at the University of Massachusetts, Amherst, where he directs the program on development, peacebuilding, and the environment at the Political Economy Research Institute. His work focuses on strategies for combining poverty reduction with environmental protection, and on the relationship between economic policies and issues of war and peace.

NEO-INSTITUTIONALIST NEOCLASSICAL

George Akerlof

American economist (b. 1940) best known for his work showing how information asymmetries can lead to dysfunctional markets. Akerlof was awarded the Nobel Prize in Economics in 2001 with Michael Spence and Joseph Stiglitz..

Ronald Coase

English economist (b. 1910) best known for two articles. In his 1937 article "The Nature of the Firm," Coase developed the concept of "transactions costs" to explain the organization of firms. In his 1960 article "The Problem of Social Cost," Coase argued, contrary to Pigou, that taxes or subsidies are not necessary to internalize externalities because negotiations between parties will lead to an efficient outcome where there are no transactions costs.

Albert Hirschman

German-born American economist (b. 1915) argued in *The Strategy of Economic Development* (1958) for policies that would promote economic growth by raising the returns to innovation. Later, in *Exit, Voice and Loyalty: Responses to Decline in Firms, Organizations and States* (1970), he argued against relying on consumer sovereignty as exercised through markets; instead, because of market rents, political processes and "voice" are often necessary to achieve efficiency.

Douglass North

American economist (1920-) and economic historian who argues that institutions are created to reduce transactions costs but then remain in place to shape future economic behavior.

Paul David

American economist (1935-) and economic historian best known for his argument that economic outcomes are "path dependent," so behavior in any period is shaped by past behavior.

KEYNESIAN

John Maynard Keynes
English economist (1883-1946) and social reformer. Professor of Economics at Cambridge, Keynes was a prominent critic of the Treaty of Versailles ending World War I. Through the 1920s, he was critical of British government policy for failing to address adequately the country's growing unemployment problem. In 1936, he published his *General Theory of Employment, Interest, and Money* to establish formal, theoretical grounds for rejecting orthodox neoclassical theory and Walrasian general equilibrium.

Joan Robinson
English economist (1903-1983). A student at Cambridge and then Lecturer there, Robinson wrote a pioneering treatise on imperfect competition in 1933, *The Economics of Imperfect Competition*. A leading participant in Keynes' seminar, his "Circus," in the 1930s, she was an early exponent of his ideas. Building on Keynesian models, she developed a general critique of neoclassical economics in her 1956 work, *The Accumulation of Capital*. She devoted much of the rest of her life to defending Keynesian economics and using his insights to undermined neoclassical theory.

Gerald Epstein
American economist (1951-), at the University of Massachusetts, Amherst, where he is the co-director of the Political Economy Research Institute. His work has focused on promoting stability in financial markets through government regulation and restrictions on international financial flows.

Robert Pollin
American economist (1950-), at the University of Massachusetts, Amherst, where he directs the Political Economy Research Institute. His work has focused on promoting full employment and programs to provide living wages.

FEMINIST

Charlotte Perkins Gilman
American economist and writer (1860-1935) born to a prosperous family in Hartford, Conn. When she was a young child, her father abandoned the family leaving them impoverished and dependent on the charity of relatives. After training as an artist (at the Rhode Island School of Design), she worked as a greeting card designer, married a fellow artist, and had one child. Leaving her husband after a bout of post-partum depression, she moved to California and became active in the radical Nationalist movement and lectured widely on the ideas of Edward Bellamy. In addition to her fiction and poetry, she is best known as an international defender of the rights of women and her 1898 work *Women and Economics*. Challenging those who argue that male supremacy and patriarchy have a biological basis, she argued that they are social constructs. Gilman believed economic independence is the only thing that could really bring freedom for women, and make them equal to men.

Margaret Reid
A Canadian-born economist (1896-1991) who received a Ph.D. from the University of Chicago in 1931. Her solid empirical analysis of the economics of households has served as the foundation of many important theoretical advances in economics, including studies of household production and the use of time. Her 1934 book *The Economics of Household Production* pioneered the measurement of the value of nonmarket home production. In 1980, she was named a Distinguished Fellow of the American Economics Association, the first woman so honored.

Marianne Ferber
Often seen as the founding mother of feminist economics, Marianne Ferber was born in Czechoslova-

kia in 1923. Fleeing Europe, her family moved to Canada and she received a Ph.D. in economics from the University of Chicago in 1954. In 1948, she moved with her husband, economist Robert Ferber, to the University of Illinois where she was hired on a semester-by-semester basis before finally being promoted to assistant professor in 1971. (She became a full professor in 1979.) In addition to *The Economics of Women, Men, and Work* (with Francine Blau), Ferber is best known as editor of the collection *Beyond Economic Man: Feminist Theory and Economics*.

Nancy Folbre

American economist (1952-) and professor at the University of Massachusetts at Amherst who specializes in the economics of caring labor, or work that involves connecting with other people and meeting their personal needs. Because much of this work is performed within families and outside the market, this research has led Folbre to propose expanding the concept of the Gross Domestic Product and redefining how we envision the economy as more than a collection of markets.

Marilyn Waring

Born in 1952 in New Zealand, where she served in Parliament 1974-84, Waring is best known for her 1988 classic *Counting for Nothing*, later republished under the title *If Women Counted*. This work reinterprets the modern economy, shows the importance of unpaid labor, usually performed by women, and criticizes the work of mainstream economists who ignore women's work.

BIBLIOGRAPHY

Akerlof, George A. *Animal Spirits: How Human Psychology Drives the Economy, and Why It Matters for Global Capitalism*. Princeton: Princeton University Press, 2009.

———. *Identity Economics: How Our Identities Shape Our Work, Wages, and Well-Being*. Princeton: Princeton University Press, 2010.

———. "The Market for 'Lemons': Quality Uncertainty and the Market Mechanism." *The Quarterly Journal of Economics* 84, no. 3 (August 1970): 488. doi:10.2307/1879431.

Albert, Michael, and Robin Hahnel. *Looking Forward: Participatory Economics for the Twenty First Century*. Boston, MA: South End Press, 1991.

Altonji, Joseph G., Erica Blom, and Costas Meghir. "Heterogeneity in Human Capital Investments: High School Curriculum, College Major, and Careers." Working Paper. National Bureau of Economic Research, April 2012. http://www.nber.org/papers/w17985.

Archer, Robin. *Why Is There No Labor Party in the United States?* Princeton Studies in American Politics. Princeton: Princeton University Press, 2007.

Ariely, Dan. "Americans Want to Live in a Much More Equal Country (They Just Don't Realize It)." *The Atlantic*, August 2, 2012. http://www.theatlantic.com/business/archive/2012/08/americans-want-to-live-in-a-much-more-equal-country-they-just-dont-realize-it/260639/.

———. *Predictably Irrational: The Hidden Forces That Shape Our Decisions*. 1st ed. New York, NY: Harper, 2008.

Arrow, Kenneth J, Debreu, Gerard. "Existence of an Equilibrium for a Competitive Economy." *Econometrica* (pre-1986) 22, no. 3 (1954): 265.

Avery, Christopher, and Sarah Turner. "Student Loans: Do College Students Borrow Too Much—Or Not Enough?" *The Journal of Economic Perspectives* 26, no. 1 (January 1, 2012): 165–92.

Axelrod, Robert M. *The Evolution of Cooperation*. Rev. ed. New York: Basic Books, 2006.

Badgett, Mary Virginia Lee. *Money, Myths, and Change: The Economic Lives of Lesbians and Gay Men*. Worlds of Desire. Chicago: University of Chicago Press, 2001.

Baran, Paul A. *Monopoly Capital: An Essay on the American Economic and Social Order*. 1st Modern reader paperback ed. Modern Reader Paperbacks PB-73. New York: Monthly Review Press, 1968.

Ben-Porath, Sigal R. *Tough Choices Structured Paternalism and the Landscape of Choice*. Princeton, N.J.: Princeton University Press, 2010. http://public.eblib.com/EBLPublic/PublicView. do?ptiID=617259.

Bentham, Jeremy, and Laurence J Lafleur. *An Introduction to the Principles of Morals and Legislation.* New York: Hafner Pub. Co., 1948.

Berle, Adolf A. *The Modern Corporation and Private Property.* New Brunswick, N.J., U.S.A: Transaction Publishers, 1991.

Blasi, Joseph R, Richard B Freeman, and Douglas Kruse. *The Citizen's Share: Putting Ownership Back into Democracy,* 2013.

Blau, Francine D, and Marianne A Ferber. *The Economics of Women, Men, and Work.* Englewood Cliffs, N.J.: Prentice-Hall, 1986.

Blinder, Alan S. *Hard Heads, Soft Hearts: Tough-Minded Economics for a Just Society.* Reading, Mass.: Addison-Wesley Pub. Co., 1987.

Bordo, Michael D, Claudia Dale Goldin, and Eugene Nelson White. *The Defining Moment: The Great Depression and the American Economy in the Twentieth Century.* Chicago: University of Chicago Press, 1998.

Bosworth, Barry P., and Kathleen Burke. "Differential Mortality and Retirement Benefits in The Health And Retirement Study." The Brookings Institution. Accessed April 21, 2014. http://www.brookings.edu/research/papers/2014/04/differential-mortality-retirement-benefits-bosworth.

Bourgin, Frank. *The Great Challenge: The Myth of Laissez-Faire in the Early Republic.* New York: G. Braziller, 1989.

Bowles, Samuel, Gintis, Herbert. "Productivity-Enhancing Egalitarian Policies." *International Labour Review* 134, no. 4/5 (1995).

Bowles, Samuel, Herbert Gintis, and Melissa Osborne Groves, eds. *Unequal Chances: Family Background and Economic Success.* New York; Princeton, N.J.: Russell Sage Foundation ; Princeton University Press, 2005.

Boyce, James K. *The Political Economy of the Environment.* Cheltenham, U.K.; Northampton, Mass., USA: E. Elgar Pub, 2002.

Boyce, James K., and Barry Shelley. University of Massachusetts at Amherst. *Natural Assets: Democratizing Environmental Ownership.* Washington, DC: Island Press, 2003.

Bray, John Francis. *Labour's Wrongs and Labour's Remedy; Or, The Age of Might and the Age of Right.* D. Green, 1839. Series of Reprints of Scarce Tracts in Economic and Political Science. no.6. [London: The London School of Economics and Political Science, 1931.

Brown, Charles, Medoff, James. "Trade Unions in the Production Process." *Journal of Political Economy* 86, no. 3 (1978): 355–78.

Brown, Michael K. *Race, Money, and the American Welfare State.* Ithaca: Cornell University Press, 1999.

Buchanan, James M., and Gordon Tullock. *The Calculus of Consent: Logical Foundations of Constitu-*

tional Democracy. The Selected Works of Gordon Tullock, v. 2. Indianapolis: Liberty Fund, 2004.

Burke, Edmund. *Burke's Reflections on the Revolution in France*. Macmillan's English Classics. London and New York: Macmillan and Co, 1890.

Carter, Susan B, Sutch, Richard. "Myth of the Industrial Scrap Heap: A Revisionist View of Turn-of-the-Century American Retirement." *The Journal of Economic History*. 56, no. 1 (1996): 5.

Cassidy, John. *How Markets Fail: The Logic of Economic Calamities*. New York: Farrar, Straus and Giroux, 2009.

———. "Rational Irrationality: Postscript: Paul Samuelson : The New Yorker." *New Yorker*, December 14, 2009. http://www.newyorker.com/online/blogs/johncassidy/2009/12/postscript-paul-samuelson.html.

Clark, John B. "The Modern Appeal to Legal Forces in Economic Life." *Publications of the American Economic Association* 10, no. 3 (March 1, 1895): 51–53.

———. "The Possibility of a Scientific Law of Wages." *Publications of the American Economic Association* 4, no. 1 (March 1, 1889): 39–69.

Clark, John Bates. *Social Justice without Socialism. Barbara Weinstock Lectures on the Morals of Trade*. Boston, New York: Houghton Mifflin company, 1914.

———. *The Control of Trusts. Rewritten and enl. ed. Reprints of Economic Classics*. New York: A. M. Kelley, 1971.

———. *The Distribution of Wealth; a Theory of Wages, Interest and Profits*. New York, London: The Macmillan company; Macmillan & co., ltd, 1899.

———. *The Philosophy of Wealth; Economic Principles Newly Formulated*. New York: A.M. Kelley Publishers, 1967.

———. *The Problem of Monopoly; a Study of a Grave Danger and of the Natural Mode of Averting It*. Columbia University Lectures. [Hewitt Foundation]. New York, London: The Columbia University Press, The Macmillan Company, agents; Macmillan & Co., Ltd, 1904.

Clark, John Maurice. *Social Control of Business*. Chicago, Ill: The University of Chicago Press, 1926.

Coase, R. H. "The Nature of the Firm." *Economica* 4, no. 16 (November 1, 1937): 386–405. doi:10.1111/j.1468-0335.1937.tb00002.x.

Coase, Ronald H. "The Problem of Social Cost"(reprinted from 1960). *Journal of Law and Economics* 56, no. 4 (2013): 837–77.

Cooper, Michael J., Huseyin Gulen, and P. Raghavendra Rau. *Performance for Pay? The Relation Between CEO Incentive Compensation and Future Stock Price Performance*. SSRN Scholarly Paper. Rochester, NY: Social Science Research Network, January 30, 2013. http://papers.ssrn.com/abstract=1572085.

Corbin, David. *The West Virginia Mine Wars: An Anthology*. Appalachian Editions, 1990.

Cowie, Jefferson. *Stayin' Alive: The 1970s and the Last Days of the Working Class*. New York: New Press,

2010.

David, Paul A. *Technical Choice Innovation and Economic Growth: Essays on American and British Experience in the Nineteenth Century.* London: Cambridge University Press, 1975.

Davis, David Brion. *Inhuman Bondage: The Rise and Fall of Slavery in the New World.* Oxford, England ; New York: Oxford University Press, 2006.

———. *The Problem of Slavery in the Age of Revolution, 1770-1823.* New York: Oxford Universtiy Press, 1999.

———. *The Problem of Slavery in Western Culture.* New York: Oxford University Press, 1988.

Deaton, Angus. *The Great Escape: Health, Wealth, and the Origins of Inequality,* 2013.

Dobb, Maurice. *Theories of Value and Distribution since Adam Smith; Ideology and Economic Theory,.* Cambridge [Eng.: University Press, 1973.

Doeringer, Peter B, Michael J. Piore, United States, Department of Labor, and Manpower Administration. *Internal Labor Markets and Manpower Analysis.* Lexington, Mass.: Heath, 1971.

"Don't Let the Flu Disrupt Your Business | NFIB." National Federation of Independent Business. Accessed July 2, 2014. http://www.nfib.com/article/dont-let-the-flu-disrupt-your-business-61883/.

Doucouliagos, Christos, and Patrice Laroche. "The Impact of U.S. Unions on Productivity: A Bootstrap Meta-Analysis." *Proceedings of the ... Annual Meeting.*, no. Edit 56 (2004): 195.

———. "What Do Unions Do to Productivity? A Meta-Analysis." *IREL Industrial Relations: A Journal of Economy and Society* 42, no. 4 (2003): 650–91.

Dow, Gregory K. *Governing the Firm: Workers' Control in Theory and Practice.* Cambridge; New York: Cambridge University Press, 2003. http://search.ebscohost.com/login.aspx?direct=true&scope=site&db=nlebk&db=nlabk&AN=120723.

Drescher, Seymour. *From Slavery to Freedom: Comparative Studies in the Rise and Fall of Atlantic Slavery.* New York: New York University Press, 1999.

———. *The Mighty Experiment: Free Labor vs. Slavery in British Emancipation.* New York: Oxford University Press, 2002.

Durkheim, Émile. *The Rules of Sociological Method.* 8th ed. Chicago, Ill: The University of Chicago press, 1938.

———. *The Division of Labor in Society.* New York: Free Press of Glencoe, 1964.

Easterlin, Richard. "Does Economic Growth Improve the Human Lot? Some Empirical Evidence." In *Nations and Households in Economic Growth*, A. New York: Academic Press, 1974.

Ely, James W. *The Guardian of Every Other Right: A Constitutional History of Property Rights.* Bicentennial Essays on the Bill of Rights. New York: Oxford University Press, 1992.

Ely, Richard T. *An Introduction to Political Economy.* New York, Cincinnati: Hunt & Eaton; Cranston & Stowe, 1892.

————. Monopolies and Trusts. *Big Business*. New York: Arno Press, 1973.

————. *The Past and the Present of Political Economy*. Baltimore: N. Murray, publication agent, Johns-Hopkins university, 1884.

Epstein, Richard Allen. *Free Markets under Siege: Cartels, Politics, and Social Welfare*. Hoover Institution Press Publication, no. 536. Stanford, Calif: Hoover Institution Press, 2005.

Esping-Andersen, Gøsta. *Politics against Markets: The Social Democratic Road to Power*. Princeton, N.J.: Princeton University Press, 1985.

————. *The Three Worlds of Welfare Capitalism*. Princeton, N.J: Princeton University Press, 1990.

Farhang, Sean, and Ira Katznelson. "The Southern Imposition: Congress and Labor in the New Deal and Fair Deal." *Studies in American Political Development* 19, no. 01 (2005): 1–30. doi:10.1017/S0898588X05000015.

Faust, Drew Gilpin, ed. *The Ideology of Slavery: Proslavery Thought in the Antebellum South, 1830-1860*. Library of Southern Civilization. Baton Rouge: Louisiana State University Press, 1981.

Fay, Peter Ward. *The Opium War, 1840-1842: Barbarians in the Celestial Empire in the Early Part of the Nineteenth Century and the War by Which They Forced Her Gates Ajar*. Chapel Hill: University of North Carolina Press, 1975.

Feinberg, Kenneth R. *What Is Life Worth?: The Unprecedented Effort to Compensate the Victims of 9/11*. New York: Public Affairs, 2005.

Ferber, Marianne A, and Nelson. *Beyond Economic Man: Feminist Theory and Economics*. Chicago: University of Chicago Press, 1993.

Fitzhugh, George. *Sociology for the South; Or, The Failure of Free Society*. Richmond, Va: A. Morris, 1854.

Fogel, Robert William. *Without Consent Or Contract: The Rise and Fall of American Slavery*. W. W. Norton & Company, 1994.

Folbre, Nancy. *Greed, Lust & Gender a History of Economic Ideas. Oxford*; New York: Oxford University Press, 2009. http://public.eblib.com/EBLPublic/PublicView.do?ptiID=472259.

————. *Valuing Children: Rethinking the Economics of the Family*. The Family and Public Policy. Cambridge, Mass: Harvard University Press, 2008.

————. *Who Pays for the Kids?: Gender and the Structures of Constraint*. Economics as Social Theory. London ; New York: Routledge, 1994.

Folbre, Nancy, and Project Muse. *For Love and Money Care Provision in the United States*. New York: Russell Sage Foundation, 2012. http://muse.jhu.edu/books/9781610447904/.

Folbre, Nancy, Wagman, Barnet. "Counting Housework: New Estimates of Real Product in the United States, 1800-1860." *Journal of Economic History* 53, no. 2 (1993).

Fortin, Nicole M, and Thomas Lemieux. "Institutional Changes and Rising Wage Inequality: Is There a Linkage?" *Journal of Economic Perspectives* 11, no. 2 (May 1997): 75–96. doi:10.1257/jep.11.2.75.

Fox, Justin. *The Myth of the Rational Market: A History of Risk, Reward, and Delusion on Wall Street*. 1st ed. New York: Harper Business, 2009.

Frank, Robert H, and Philip J Cook. *The Winner-Take-All Society: How More and More Americans Compete for Ever Fewer and Bigger Prizes, Encouraging Economic Waste, Income Inequality, and an Impoverished Cultural Life*. New York: Free Press, 1995.

Frank, Robert H. *Luxury Fever: Why Money Fails to Satisfy in an Era of Excess*. New York, NY: Free Press, 1999.

———. *The Winner-Take-All Society: How More and More Americans Compete for Ever Fewer and Bigger Prizes, Encouraging Economic Waste, Income Inequality, and an Impoverished Cultural Life*. New York: Free Press, 1995.

Freeman, Richard B. "The Exit-Voice Tradeoff in the Labor Market: Unionism, Job Tenure, Quits, and Separations." *The Quarterly Journal of Economics* 94, no. 4 (1980): 643–73.

———. *What Do Unions Do?* New York: Basic Books, 1984.

Friedman, Gerald. "Les États-Providence Américains : Valeurs et Politique Dans La Fabrique Du Système Redistributif Des États-Unis." *Cycnos: Les Études Anglophones* 30 (January 2014): 3–22.

———. *Reigniting the Labor Movement: Restoring Means to Ends in a Democratic Labor Movement*. Abingdon, Oxon: Routledge, 2007.

———. *State-Making and Labor Movements: France and the United States, 1876-1914*. Ithaca: Cornell University Press, 1998.

———. "Success and Failure in Third-Party Politics: The Knights of Labor and the Union Labor Coalition in Massachusetts, 1884-1888." *International Labor and Working-Class History* 62, no. 1 (2002): 164–88.

———. "The Political Economy of Early Southern Unionism: Race, Politics, and Labor in the South, 1880-1953." *The Journal of Economic History* 60, no. 2 (2000): 384–413.

———. "The Sanctity of Property Rights in American History." ScholarWorks@UMass Amherst. http://scholarworks.umass.edu/peri_workingpapers/30.

Friedman, Milton. *Capitalism and Freedom*. Chicago: University of Chicago Press, 1962.

———. *Essays in Positive Economics*. Chicago ; London: University of Chicago Press, 1964.

———. *Free to Choose: A Personal Statement*. 1st ed. New York: Harcourt Brace Jovanovich, 1980.

———. *Price Theory, a Provisional Text*. Chicago: Aldine Pub. Co, 1962.

Geithner, Timothy F. *Stress Test: Reflections on Financial Crises*, 2014.

Genovese, Eugene D. *The World the Slaveholders Made: Two Essays in Interpretation*. Middletown, Conn.; Scranton, Pa: Wesleyan University Press; Distributed by Harper & Row, 1988.

Gilman, Charlotte Perkins. *Human Work*. New York: McClure, Phillips, 1904.

———. *Women and Economics: A Study of the Economic Relation Between Men and Women as a Factor in Social Evolution.* 9th ed. New York: Gordon Press, 1975.

Gladwell, Malcolm. *Blink: The Power of Thinking without Thinking.* New York: Little, Brown and Co., 2005.

Goldin, Claudia Dale. *Understanding the Gender Gap: An Economic History of American Women.* New York: Oxford University Press, 1990.

Goldin, Claudia Dale, and Lawrence F Katz. *The Race between Education and Technology.* Cambridge, Mass.: Belknap Press of Harvard University Press, 2008.

Goldin, Claudia Dale, and National Bureau of Economic Research. *Marriage Bars: Discrimination against Married Women Workers, 1920s to 1950s.* Cambridge, MA (1050 Massachusetts Avenue, Cambridge, Mass. 02138): National Bureau of Economic Research, 1988.

Goldstein, Robert Justin. *Political Repression in Modern America from 1870 to the Present.* Cambridge, Mass: Schenkman Pub. Co, 1978.

Gomez, Rafael, and Konstantinos Tzioumis. "What Do Unions Do to Executive Compensation?" CEP Discussion Paper. Centre for Economic Performance, LSE, 2006. http://ideas.repec.org/p/cep/cepdps/dp0720.html.

Gould, William. "Does the National Labor Board Work for Labor?" *WorkingUSA* 4, no. 4 (2001): 34–48.

Gould, William B, and IV. "The NLRB at Age 70: Some Reflections on the Clinton Board and the Bush II aftermath.(National Labor Relations Board)(Forum: At 70, Should the National Labor Relations Act Be Retired?)." *Berkeley Journal of Employment and Labor Law* 26, no. 2 (2005): 309–18.

Greenfield, Kent. *The Myth of Choice: Personal Responsibility in a World of Limits.* New Haven; London: Yale University Press, 2011.

Greenstone, J. David. *The Lincoln Persuasion: Remaking American Liberalism.* Princeton Studies in American Politics. Princeton, N.J: Princeton University Press, 1993.

Guy, Kolleen M. *When Champagne Became French: Wine and the Making of a National Identity.* Baltimore: Johns Hopkins University Press, 2003.

Hacker, Jacob S, and Paul Pierson. *Off Center: The Republican Revolution and the Erosion of American Democracy.* New Haven: Yale University Press, 2005.

———. *Winner-Take-All Politics: How Washington Made the Rich Richer-and Turned Its Back on the Middle Class.* New York: Simon & Schuster, 2010.

Hahnel, Robin. "The Case Against Markets." *Journal of Economic Issues* (Association for Evolutionary Economics) 41, no. 4 (2007).

Henretta, John C. "Uniformity and Diversity: Life Course Institutionalization and Late-Life Work Exit." *The Sociological Quarterly* 33, no. 2 (1992): 265–79.

Hirschman, Albert O. *Exit, Voice, and Loyalty: Responses to Decline in Firms, Organizations, and States.* Cambridge, Mass: Harvard University Press, 2004.

———. *Rival Views of Market Society and Other Recent Essays*. 1st Harvard University Press pbk. ed. Cambridge, Mass: Harvard University Press, 1992.

———. *The Passions and the Interests: Political Arguments for Capitalism Before Its Triumph*. Princeton, N.J: Princeton University Press, 1977.

Hodgskin, Thomas. *Labour Defended against the Claims of Capital; Or, The Unproductiveness of Capital Proved with Reference to the Present Combinations amongst Journeymen*. London: Hammersmith Bookshop, 1964.

Hodgskin, Thomas. *Popular Political Economy*. New York: A.M. Kelley, 1966.

Horwitz, Morton J. *The Transformation of American Law, 1780-1860*. Cambridge, Mass.: Harvard University Press, 1977.

Huang, Qianqian, Feng Jiang, Erik Lie, and Tingting Que. "The Effect of Labor Unions on CEO Compensation." SSRN Scholarly Paper. Rochester, NY: Social Science Research Network, March 1, 2014. http://papers.ssrn.com/abstract=1571811.

"IMF: Reducing Inequality With Transfers Increases Growth." *Demos*. Accessed March 30, 2014. http://www.demos.org/blog/2/27/14/imf-reducing-inequality-transfers-increases-growth.

Internal Revenue Service. *The 400 Individual Income Tax Returns Reporting the Highest Adjusted Gross Incomes Each Year, 1992-2007, 2012*. http://www.irs.gov/pub/irs-soi/07intop400.pdf.

Iyengar, Sheena. *The Art of Choosing*. New York: Twelve, 2010.

Jacobs, Jane. *The Death and Life of Great American Cities*, 1961.

Jacobs, Lawrence R, and Benjamin Page. *Class War?: What Americans Really Think About Economic Inequality*. Chicago: University of Chicago Press, 2009.

Jacquart, J. Scott Armstrong Philippe. "Business School Experts: High CEO Pay Hurts American Companies, Stockholders." Text.Article. FoxNews.com, April 15, 2014. http://www.foxnews.com/opinion/2014/04/15/business-school-experts-high-ceo-pay-hurts-american-companies/.

Jacquart, Philippe, and J. Scott Armstrong. "The Ombudsman: Are Top Executives Paid Enough? An Evidence-Based Review." *Interfaces* 43, no. 6 (December 1, 2013): 580–89. doi:10.1287/inte.2013.0705.

Jensen, Michael C., and Kevin J. Murphy. "Performance Pay and Top-Management Incentives." *Journal of Political Economy* 98, no. 2 (April 1, 1990): 225–64.

Jevons, William Stanley. *The Theory of Political Economy*. London; New York: Macmillan, 1871. http://catalog.hathitrust.org/api/volumes/oclc/3598082.html.

Johnston, David. *Perfectly Legal: The Covert Campaign to Rig Our Tax System to Benefit the Super Rich—and Cheat Everybody Else*. New York: Portfolio, 2003.

Jones, Geoffrey. *Beauty Imagined: A History of the Global Beauty Industry*. Oxford: Oxford University Press, 2010.

Jr, Henry M. Paulson. "Lessons for Climate Change in the 2008 Recession." *The New York Times*, June

21, 2014. http://www.nytimes.com/2014/06/22/opinion/sunday/lessons-for-climate-change-in-the-2008-recession.html.

Kahneman, Daniel, Ed Diener, and Norbert Schwarz, eds. *Well-Being: The Foundations of Hedonic Psychology*. New York: Russell Sage Foundation, 1999.

Katznelson, Ira. *Fear Itself: The New Deal and the Origins of Our Time*, 2013.

Kawachi, Ichirō. *The Health of Nations: Why Inequality Is Harmful to Your Health*. New York: New Press, 2002.

Kessler-Harris, Alice. *In Pursuit of Equity: Women, Men, and the Quest for Economic Citizenship in 20th Century America*. Oxford; New York: Oxford University Press, 2001.

Keynes, John Maynard. *Essays in Persuasion*. London: Macmillan, 1933.

———. *The Economic Consequences of Mr. Churchill*. London: L. and V. Woolf, 1925.

———. *The Economic Consequences of the Peace*. London: Macmillan, 1919.

———. *The General Theory of Employment, Interest and Money*. London: Macmillan and co., limited, 1936.

Kindleberger, Charles Poor. *Manias, Panics and Crashes a History of Financial Crises*. 5th ed. Hoboken, N.J: John Wiley & Sons, 2005.

Kolko, Gabriel. *Railroads and Regulation, 1877-1916*. Westport, Conn: Greenwood Press, 1976.

———. *The Triumph of Conservatism; a Re-Interpretation of American History, 1900-1916*. New York: Free Press of Glencoe, 1963.

Korpi, Walter. *The Democratic Class Struggle*. London; Boston: Routledge & K. Paul, 1983.

Kotz, David M., Terrence McDonough, and Michael Reich, eds. *Social Structures of Accumulation: The Political Economy of Growth and Crisis*. Cambridge ; New York: Cambridge University Press, 1994.

Krueger, Alan B, and Lawrence H Summers. "Efficiency Wages and the Inter-Industry Wage Structure." *Econometrica* 56, no. 2 (1988).

Kruse, Douglas, Richard B Freeman, and Joseph R Blasi, eds. *Shared Capitalism at Work: Employee Ownership, Profit and Gain Sharing, and Broad-Based Stock Options*. Chicago; London: The University of Chicago Press, 2010.

Kuhn, Thomas S. *The Structure of Scientific Revolutions*. 3rd ed. Chicago, IL: University of Chicago Press, 1996.

Kuznets, Simon. "Economic Growth and Income Inequality." *The American Economic Review* 45, no. 1 (1955): 1.

Lane, Robert Edwards. *The Loss of Happiness in Market Democracies*. New Haven: Yale University Press, 2000.

Lange, Oskar, Benjamin E Lippincott, and F. M Taylor. *On the Economic Theory of Socialism*. Minneapolis, Minn.: University of Minnesota Press, 1938.

Laurie, Bruce. *Beyond Garrison: Antislavery and Social Reform*. Cambridge: Cambridge University Press, 2005.

Layard, Richard. *Happiness: Lessons from a New Science*. New York: Penguin, 2006.

Leibenstein, Harvey. "Allocative Efficiency vs. 'X-Efficiency.'" *The American Economic Review* 56, no. 3 (1966): 392.

Lemieux, Thomas. "Increasing Residual Wage Inequality: Composition Effects, Noisy Data, or Rising Demand for Skill?" *The American Economic Review* 96, no. 3 (June 1, 2006): 461–98.

———. "Postsecondary Education and Increasing Wage Inequality." *The American Economic Review* 96, no. 2 (May 1, 2006): 195–99.

Levitt, Steven D. *An Economist Sells Bagels: A Case Study in Profit Maximization*. Working Paper. National Bureau of Economic Research, April 2006. http://www.nber.org/papers/w12152.

———. *Freakonomics: A Rogue Economist Explores the Hidden Side of Everything*. Rev. and expanded ed. New York, NY: William Morrow, 2006.

Lingard, C. Cecil, Fairbank, John King, Teng, Ssu-yü, Fairbank, John K. "Trade and Diplomacy on the China Coast: The Opening of the Treaty Ports, 1842-1854." *International Journal* 10, no. 2 (1955): 150.

Lino, Mark. *Expenditures on Children by Families*, 2011. Washington, D. C.: United States Department of Agriculture, Center for Nutrition Policy and Promotion, June 2012. http://www.cnpp.usda.gov/Publications/CRC/crc2011.pdf.

Lipsey, R. G, and Kelvin Lancaster. "The General Theory of Second Best." *The Review of Economic Studies* 24, no. 1 (1956): 11–32.

Mann, Charles C. *1491: New Revelations of the Americas before Columbus*. 2nd Vintage Books ed. New York: Vintage, 2011.

———. *1493: Uncovering the New World Columbus Created*. 1st ed. New York [N.Y.]: Alfred A. Knopf, 2011.

Mannheim, Karl. *Ideology and Utopia: An Introduction to the Sociology of Knowledge*. San Diego: Harcourt Brace Jovanovich, 1985.

Marglin, Stephen. "What Do Bosses Do? The Origins and Functions of Hierarchy in Capitalist Production." *Review of Radical Political Economy* 6, no. 2 (n.d.): 60–112.

Marmor, Theodore R. *Social Insurance: America's Neglected Heritage and Contested Future*. Public Affairs and Policy Administration Series. Thousand Oaks, California: SAGE/CQ Press, 2014.

Marshall, T. H. *Citizenship and Social Class, and Other Essays*. Cambridge [Eng.: University Press, 1950.

Marx, Karl. *Capital: A Critique of Political Economy*. London & Toronto: J. M. Dent & sons ltd,

1934.

———. *Wage-Labor and Capital*. Chicago: C. H. Kerr & company, 1935.

Meyer, Stephen. *The Five Dollar Day: Labor Management and Social Control in the Ford Motor Company, 1908-1921*. SUNY Series in American Social History. Albany: State University of New York Press, 1981.

Michael Jensen, and William Meckling. "Theory Of The Firm: Managerial Behavior, Agency Costs And Ownership Structure." *Journal of Financial Economics* 3 (1976): 305–60.

Mill, John Stuart. *On Liberty*. Indianapolis: Hackett Pub. Co, 1978.

———. *Utilitarianism*. Raleigh, N.C.: Alex Catalogue. http://search.ebscohost.com/login.aspx?direct=true&scope=site&db=nlebk&db=nlabk&AN=1085956.

Minchin, Timothy J. *Empty Mills: The Fight against Imports and the Decline of the U.S. Textile Industry*. Lanham: Rowman & Littlefield Publishers, 2013.

Mintz, Sidney Wilfred. *From Plantations to Peasantries in the Caribbean*. Focus Caribbean. Washington, D.C: Latin American Program, Woodrow Wilson International Center for Scholars, 1984.

———. *Sweetness and Power: The Place of Sugar in Modern History*. New York: Penguin Books, 1986.

Mitchell, Wesley C. "The Backward Art of Spending Money." *The American Economic Review* 2, no. 2 (1912): 269.

———. *The Backward Art of Spending Money*. New Brunswick, N.J., U.S.A: Transaction Publishers, 1999.

Montgomery, David. *Beyond Equality; Labor and the Radical Republicans, 1862-1872*. 1st ed. New York: Knopf, 1967.

Morin, Richard. "Study: More Men on the 'Daddy Track.'" Pew Research Center. Accessed June 18, 2014. http://www.pewresearch.org/fact-tank/2013/09/17/more-men-on-the-daddy-track/.

Moss, David A. *Socializing Security: Progressive-Era Economists and the Origins of American Social Policy*. Cambridge, Mass.: Harvard University Press, 1996.

———. *When All Else Fails: Government as the Ultimate Risk Manager*. Cambridge, Mass.: Harvard University Press, 2002.

Munnell, Alicia H., Steven A. Sass, Robert Hutchens, Joyce Manchester. "The Labor Supply of Older American Men/Comments on 'The Labor Supply of Older American Men' by Alicia H. Munnell and Steven A. Sass." Federal Reserve Bank of Boston. Conference Series, no. 52 (2007): 83–157,366,368–70.

North, Douglass Cecil. *The Rise of the Western World; a New Economic History*. Cambridge [Eng.]: University Press, 1973.

Norton, Michael, and Dan Ariely. "Building a Better America—One Wealth Quintile at a Time." *Perspectives on Psychological Science* 6, no. 1 (2011): 9–12.

Novak, William J. *The People's Welfare: Law and Regulation in Nineteenth-Century America*. Chapel Hill: University of North Carolina Press, 1996.

Novak, William J. *The People's Welfare: Law and Regulation in Nineteenth-Century America*. Studies in Legal History. Chapel Hill: University of North Carolina Press, 1996.

Okun, Arthur M. *Equality and Efficiency, the Big Tradeoff*. Washington: Brookings Institution, 1975.

Olson, Mancur. *The Logic of Collective Action; Public Goods and the Theory of Groups*. Harvard Economic Studies, v. 124. Cambridge, Mass: Harvard University Press, 1965.

———. *The Rise and Decline of Nations: Economic Growth, Stagflation, and Social Rigidities*. New Haven: Yale University Press, 1982.

Pareto, Vilfredo. *Manual of Political Economy*. New York: A.M. Kelley, 1971.

Paulson, Henry M. *On the Brink: Inside the Race to Stop the Collapse of the Global Financial System*. New York: Business Plus, 2010.

Peter, Laurence F, and Raymond Hull. *The Peter Principle*. Taiwan: [publisher not identified], 1969.

Peyrefitte, Alain. *The collision of two civilisations: the British expedition to China in 1792-4*. London: Harvill, 1993.

Phillips, Kevin. T*he Emerging Republican Majority*. New Rochelle, N.Y.: Arlington House, 1969.

Piketty, Thomas. *Capital in the Twenty-First Century,* 2014.

Pontusson, Jonas. *Inequality and Prosperity: Social Europe vs. Liberal America*. Ithaca, N.Y.: Cornell University Press, 2005.

Powell, Lewis. "The Powell Memo (also Known as the Powell Manifesto)." Reclaim Democracy! Accessed June 27, 2014. http://reclaimdemocracy.org/powell_memo_lewis/.

Production the Cause of Demand Being a Brief Analysis of a Work Entitled "The Social System, a Treatise on the Principle of Exchange," by John Gray: With a Short Illustration of the Principles of Equitable Labour Exchange. Birmingham: Published under the superintendence of an Association for the Dissemination of the Knowledge of the Principles of Equitable Labour Exchange, 1832. http://libproxy.smith.edu:2048/login?url=http://galenet.galegroup.com/servlet/MOME?af=RN&a e=U104840410&srchtp=a&ste=14&q=Mlin_w_smithcol.

Property Rights in American History: From the Colonial Era to the Present. New York: Garland Pub, 1997.

Putnam, Robert D. B*owling Alone: The Collapse and Revival of American Community*. New York: Simon & Schuster, 2000.

Quadagno, Jill S. *The Color of Welfare: How Racism Undermined the War on Poverty*. New York: Oxford University Press, 1994.

Radcliff, Benjamin. *The Political Economy of Human Happiness: How Voters' Choices Determine the Quality of Life*. Cambridge: Cambridge University Press, 2013.

Raff, Daniel M. G. "Wage Determination Theory and the Five-Dollar Day at Ford." *Journal of Economic History* 48, no. 2 (1988).

Ransom, Roger L, and Richard Sutch. "The Labor of Older Americans: Retirement of Men On and Off the Job, 1870-1937." *The Journal of Economic History* 46, no. 1 (1986): 1–30.

Rawls, John. *A Theory of Justice*. Cambridge, MA: Belknap Press of Harvard University Press, 1971.

Reich, Robert B. *Beyond Outrage: What Has Gone Wrong with Our Economy and Our Democracy, and How to Fix It*. New York: Vintage Books, 2012.

Reich, Robert B. *The Work of Nations: Preparing Ourselves for 21st Century Capitalism*. 1st Vintage Books ed. New York: Vintage Books, 1992.

Resnick, Stephen A. *Knowledge and Class: A Marxian Critique of Political Economy*. Chicago: University of Chicago Press, 1987.

Risen, Clay. *The Bill of the Century: The Epic Battle for the Civil Rights Act*, 2014.

Robinson, Joan, and John Eatwell. *An Introduction to Modern Economics*. Maidenhead: McGraw-Hill, 1973.

Roediger, David R. *The Wages of Whiteness: Race and the Making of the American Working Class*. Rev. ed. Haymarket Series. London ; New York: Verso, 2007.

Schneier, Bruce. *Liars and Outliers: Enabling the Trust That Society Needs to Thrive*. Indianapolis: Wiley, 2012.

Schor, Juliet. *The Overspent American: Why We Want What We Don't Need*. New York: HarperPerennial, 1999.

———. *The Overworked American: The Unexpected Decline of Leisure*. New York, N.Y.: Basic Books, 1991.

Schultze, Charles L. *The Public Use of Private Interest*. Washington, D.C.: Brookings Institution, 1977.

Senor, Dan, and Council on Foreign Relations. *Start-up Nation: The Story of Israel's Economic Miracle*. 1st ed. New York: Twelve, 2009.

Shattuck, Anne. "Older Americans Working More, Retiring Less." Issue Brief. Carsey Institute, Summer 2010. http://www.carseyinstitute.unh.edu/publications/IB_Shattuck_Older_Workers.pdf.

Shiller, Robert J. Irrational Exuberance. Princeton, NJ: Princeton University Press, 2000.

———. *Irrational Exuberance*. 2nd ed. Princeton, N.J: Princeton University Press, 2005.

Simon, Herbert A. *Models of Bounded Rationality*. Cambridge, Mass.: MIT Press, 1982.

Simon, Herbert A. *Models of Man: Social and Rational; Mathematical Essays on Rational Human Behavior in a Social Setting*. New York: Wiley, 1957.

Sivulka, Juliann. *Soap, Sex, and Cigarettes: A Cultural History of American Advertising*. 2 edition. Australia; Boston, MA: Cengage Learning, 2011.

Smith, Adam. *The Theory of Moral Sentiments; to Which Is Added, a Dissertation on the Origin of Languages.* New ed. Bohn's Standard Library. London, New York: G. Bell & Sons, 1892.

Smith, Vernon L. *Rationality in Economics: Constructivist and Ecological Forms.* Cambridge; New York: Cambridge University Press, 2008.

Social Science Research Council. *The Formation of National States in Western Europe.* Studies in Political Development 8. Princeton, N.J: Princeton University Press, 1975.

Steinbeck, John. *The Pearl.* New York: Viking Press, 1947.

Stephens, John D. *The Transition from Capitalism to Socialism.* London: Macmillan, 1979.

Steven H. Woolf and Laudan Aron, Editors; Panel on Understanding Cross-National Health Differences Among High-Income Countries; Committee on Population; Division of Behavioral and Social Sciences and Education; National Research Council; Board on Population Health and Public Health Practice; Institute of Medicine. U.S. Health in International Perspective: Shorter Lives, Poorer Health. Washington, D.C.: The National Academies Press, 2013.

Stevenson, Betsey, Wolfers, Justin. "Economic Growth and Subjective Well-Being: Reassessing the Easterlin Paradox." *Brookings Papers on Economic Activity* 2008 (2008): 1–87.

Stigler, George J. *Production and Distribution Theories, the Formative Period.* New York: Macmillan, 1941.

Stigler, George J. "The Theory of Economic Regulation." *The Bell Journal of Economics and Management Science* 2, no. 1 (April 1, 1971): 3–21. doi:10.2307/3003160.

———. "The Xistence of X-Efficiency." *The American Economic Review* 66, no. 1 (March 1, 1976): 213–16.

Summers, Lawrence H. "Relative Wages, Efficiency Wages, and Keynesian Unemployment." *The American Economic Review* 78, no. 2 (1988): 383–88.

Sweezy, Paul M. *The Theory of Capitalist Development: Principles of Marxian Political Economy.* New York: Oxford University Press, 1942.

Teles, Steven Michael. *The Rise of the Conservative Legal Movement the Battle for Control of the Law.* Princeton, N.J.: Princeton University Press, 2008. http://site.ebrary.com/id/10312554.

Thaler, Richard H. *Nudge: Improving Decisions about Health, Wealth, and Happiness.* New Haven: Yale University Press, 2008.

Thompson, E. P. *The Making of the English Working Class.* New York: Pantheon Books, 1964.

Thompson, William. *An Inquiry into the Principles of the Distribution of Wealth Most Conducive to Human Happiness,* 1824. New York: A.M. Kelley, Bookseller, 1963.

———. *An Inquiry into the Principles of the Distribution of Wealth Most Conducive to Human Happiness; Applied to the Newly Proposed System of Voluntary Equality of Wealth.* London: Printed for Longsman, Hurst, Ross, Orme, Brown and Green [etc.], 1824.

Tilly, Charles. *The Contentious French.* Cambridge, Mass: Belknap Press, 1986.

Tullock, Gordon, and Locke Institute. *Public Goods, Redistribution and Rent Seeking.* Cheltenham, UK; Northampton, MA, USA: E. Elgar Pub., 2005.

United States, and Financial Crisis Inquiry Commission. *The Financial Crisis Inquiry Report: Final Report of the National Commission on the Causes of the Financial and Economic Crisis in the United States.* Washington, DC: Financial Crisis Inquiry Commission : For sale by the Supt. of Docs., U.S. G.P.O., 2011.

United States, Miscellaneous Pamphlet Collection (Library of Congress), and Israel Thorndike Pamphlet Collection (Library of Congress). Alexander Hamilton's Report on the Subject of Manufactures. Edited by Alexander Hamilton and Mathew Carey. 6th ed. Philadelphia: Printed by W. Brown, 1827.

Van Horn, Robert, Philip Mirowski, and Thomas A. Stapleford, eds. *Building Chicago Economics: New Perspectives on the History of America's Most Powerful Economics Program.* Historical Perspectives on Modern Economics. Cambridge ; New York: Cambridge University Press, 2011.

Veblen, Thorstein. *The Theory of the Leisure Class; an Economic Study of Institutions.* New ed. New York: The Macmillan Company; [etc., etc.], 1912.

Viscusi, W. Kip. *Fatal Tradeoffs: Public and Private Responsibilities for Risk.* New York: Oxford University Press, 1992.

———. *The Value of Life: Estimates with Risks by Occupation and Industry.* Harvard Law School: Harvard: John M. Olin Center for Law, Economics, and Business, May 2003. http://www.law.harvard.edu/programs/olin_center/papers/pdf/422.pdf.

Walras, Léon. *Elements of Pure Economics, Or, The Theory of Social Wealth.* London: Published for the American Economic Association and the Royal Economic Association and the Royal Economic Society by Allen and Unwin, 1954.

Wilentz, Sean. *The Rise of American Democracy: Jefferson to Lincoln.* 1st ed. New York: Norton, 2005.

Wilkinson, Richard G. *The Spirit Level: Why Greater Equality Makes Societies Stronger.* New York: Bloomsbury Press, 2010.

Williams, Eric Eustace. *Capitalism & Slavery.* Chapel Hill: University of North Carolina Press, 1994.

Wills, Garry. *Lincoln at Gettysburg: The Words That Remade America.* New York: Simon & Schuster, 1992.

Wise, Steven M. *Though the Heavens May Fall: The Landmark Trial That Led to the End of Human Slavery.* Cambridge, Mass.: Da Capo Press, 2005.

Wollstonecraft, Mary, and Carol Poston. *A Vindication of the Rights of Woman: An Authoritative Text, Backgrounds, Criticism.* New York: Norton, 1975.

Zieger, Robert H. *American Workers, American Unions: The Twentieth and Early Twenty-First Centuries.* Fourth edition. The American Moment. Baltimore: Johns Hopkins University Press, 2014.

INDEX

IMAGE CREDITS

CHAPTER 1

p. 1: public domain

p. 2: Friedman Foundation for Educational Choice, Creative Commons CC0 1.0 Universal Public Domain Dedication

p. 3, Radiohead logo: Scmbg, GNU Free Documentation License Version 1.2

p. 3, Thom Yorke: Tim Cochrane, Creative Commons Attribution 2.0 Generic license

CHAPTER 2

p. 9, Rubik's Cube: Cbuckley, Wikimedia Commons, Creative Commons Attribution-Share Alike 3.0 Unported license

p. 9, Leibniz: public domain

p. 10, Leibniz Machine: public domain

p. 10, Candide: Creative Commons Public Domain Mark 1.0

p. 12: public domain

p. 13: public domain

p. 14, Wayland: public domain

p. 14, Ricardo: Creative Commons Public Domain Mark 1.0

p. 15, Labor protest: public domain

p. 15, Karl Marx: John Mayall. International Institute of Social History, public domain

p. 16, *Das Kapital*: public domain

p. 16, May Day in London: Ardfern, Creative Commons Attribution-Share Alike 3.0 Unported

p. 17, John Bates Clark: public domain

p. 17, Marie-Esprit-Léon Walrass: public domain

p. 19, John Maynard Keynes: International Monetary Fund, public domain

p. 20: public domain

p. 21: public domain

p. 22, Visiting a nail factory: Léonard Defrance (1735-1805), public domain

p. 22, Liberty ship construction: United States, Office of War Information, Overseas Picture Division, Washington Division, public domain

p. 23, Castaway Island: Shutterbuggery, Creative Commons Attribution-Share Alike 3.0 Unported license

p. 24: GNU Free Documentation License, Version 1.2

CHAPTER 3

p. 30: public domain

p. 31, Rev. Dr. Martin Luther King Jr.: National Archives and Records Administration

p. 31, Advertisement for slaves: John Addison, Printer, Government Office, East India Company, St. Helena, public domain

p. 32: GNU Free Documentation License

p. 33, Roman slave market: Jean-Léon Gérôme, public domain

p. 33, African slaves: public domain

p. 34: Edward S. Curtis, public domain

p. 35, Factory workers: Hugo Rydén, Gunnar Stenhag, Dick Widing: *Litteraturen genom tiderna. Kortfattad litteraturhistoria för gymnasieskolan*. Stockholm 1982, public domain

p. 35, Chinese railroad workers in the snow: public domain

p. 35, Women munitions workers: public domain

p. 35, Chinese women textile workers: Creative Commons Attribution-Share Alike 3.0 Unported

p. 37: public domain

p. 38: Ramon F. Velasquez, Creative Commons Attribution-Share Alike 3.0 Unported

p. 40: Jos. A. Beard, public domain

p. 42, Loaves of bread: Rob Qld, Creative Commons Attribution 2.0 Generic

p. 42, Richard Wolff: University of Massachusetts, used by permission

p. 42, Stephen Resnick: University of Massachusetts, used by permission

p. 42, David Kotz: Courtesy of David Kotz

p. 43, Salvadoran migrant workers: Holger Hubbs, Creative Commons Attribution 3.0 Unported

p. 43, Digital rights management: public domain

p. 46, Generic Drugs: LadyofProcrastination, Creative Commons Attribution-Share Alike 2.0 Generic

p. 46, Corn: public domain

p. 46, Kindle: Marco Ciampa, Creative Commons Attribution-Share Alike 3.0 Unported

p. 46, Shoes: Thomas Steiner, GNU Free Documentation License

CHAPTER 4

p. 51: Marlith, Creative Commons Attribution-Share Alike 3.0 Unported

p. 52, John Stuart Mill: public domain

p. 52, Ronald Coase: Ionel141, Creative Commons Attribution-Share Alike 3.0 Unported

p. 53, Alexis de Tocqueville: public domain

p. 54, Birthday party: Kitetails, Creative Commons Attribution-Share Alike 3.0 Unported

p. 56, Jacoby Ellsbury: Parker Harrington, Creative Commons Attribution 3.0 Unported

p. 56, Honesty box: David Hawgood, Creative Commons Attribution-Share Alike 2.0 Generic license Saudi

p. 57, Sarah Michelle Gellar: Saudi, Creative Commons Attribution 2.0 Generic license

p. 57, David Boreanaz: RavenU, Creative Commons Attribution 2.0 Generic license

p. 57, Grey's Anatomy: lukeford.net, Creative Commons Attribution-Share Alike 2.5 Generic license

p. 58, Swimming pool: Nevit Dilmen, GNU Free Documentation License

p. 59: public domain

p. 62: BU Interactive News, Creative Commons Attribution 2.0 Generic

p. 63, Microsoft Word: RRZEicons, Creative Commons Attribution-Share Alike 3.0 Unported

p. 63, Dakota Bison: National Park Service, public domain

CHAPTER 5

p. 98, Marianne Ferber: University of Illinois Archives, used by permission

p. 99, Arthur Okun: AP Images, used by permission

p. 99, John F. Kennedy: White House Press Office (WHPO), public domain

p. 99, Lyndon B. Johnson: Arnold Newman, White House Press Office (WHPO), public domain

CHAPTER 6

p. 103: NASA, public domain

p. 104: Tim McCabe, USDA Natural Resources Conservation Service, public domain

p. 105: Gerald Friedman

p. 106: Photographer's Mate 2nd Class Matthew Bash, U.S. Navy photo, public domain

p. 107: Jim Champion, Creative Commons Attribution-Share Alike 2.0 Generic license

p. 108, tree: Gerald Friedman

p. 108, mosaic, Gerald Friedman

p. 108, *The Transformation of American Law*

p. 109, Vinny Burgoo, GNU Free Documentation License

p. 112: Prolineserver, Creative Commons Attribution-Share Alike 3.0 Unported

p. 113, river cleanup: vastateparksstaff, Creative Commons Attribution 2.0 Generic

p. 113, Nuremberg rally: Scherl, Creative Commons Attribution-Share Alike 3.0 Germany

p. 116: John Messina, public domain

p. 117: Ionel141, Creative Commons Attribution-Share Alike 3.0 Unported

p. 118: University of Massachusetts News Office

p. 119, Arctic ice: Jesse Allen, NASA, public domain

p. 119, polar bear: Agrant141, Creative Commons Attribution-Share Alike 3.0 Unported

p. 124, opium pipe: Fotodienst Amsterdam Pipe Museum, Creative Commons Attribution 3.0 Unported

p. 124, wine bottle: Ile-de-re, GNU Free Documentation License Version 1.2

p. 124, beer mug: Scott A. Miller, Creative Commons Attribution 3.0 Unported

p. 1125 espresso: journeyscoffee, Creative Commons Attribution 2.0 Generic

CHAPTER 8

p. 148, Monopoly logo: Parker Brothers, public domain

p. 151, clockwise from top left: Dirk van der Made, Creative Commons Attribution 1.0 Generic license; Erik Christensen, GNU Free Documentation License Version 1.2; AEMoreira042281, Creative Commons Attribution-Share Alike 3.0 Unported license; Kyle Owen, Creative Commons Attribution-Share Alike 3.0 Unported license

p. 152: Downingsf, Creative Commons Attribution-Share Alike 3.0 Unported license

p. 153, OPEC map: Bourgeois, public domain

p. 153, Apple logo: Apple, fair use

p. 153, UMass logo: UMass Minutemen, public domain

p. 153, Disney logo: Disney, public domain

p. 153, Monopoly logo: Parker Brothers, public domain

p. 156, Levi's label: M62, GNU Free Documentation License Version 1.2

p. 156, runway model: Tiago Chediak, Creative Commons Attribution 2.5 Generic license

p. 156, women in jeans: Adam Jones, Creative Commons Attribution-Share Alike 3.0 Unported license

p. 157. MS Office logo: Microsoft, public domain

p. 157, Hunger Games logo: Diseñadores publicitarios, public domain

p. 157, Windows 8 logo: Microsoft, Creative Commons Attribution-Share Alike 3.0 Unported license

p. 159, iStockPhoto

p. 160: Argox, Creative Commons Attribution 1.0 Generic license

CHAPTER 9

p. 172: Lee Gillen, Creative Commons Attribution-Share Alike 2.0 Generic license

p. 175: Guest2625, Creative Commons Attribution-Share Alike 3.0 Unported license

p. 176, Sheena Iyengar: Columbia Business School, Creative Commons Attribution 3.0 License

p. 176, Laduree jams: Michal Osmenda, Creative Commons Attribution-Share Alike 2.0 Generic license

CHAPTER 10

p. 187, Beverly Hillbillies: CBS Television, Creative Clearance-Publicity photos

p. 234: Thomas Hedden, public domain

p. 235, Robert Pollin: University of Massachusetts, used by permission

p. 235, Robert Reich: U.S. Department of Labor, public domain

p. 235, Thomas Sowell: AP Images, used by permission

p. 239, Co-op Italia: Creative Commons Attribution-Share Alike 3.0 Unported license

p. 239, Mondragón logo (English): Creative Commons Attribution 3.0 Unported license

p. 239, Mondragón logo (Spanish): Creative Commons Attribution 3.0 Unported license

p. 240: Gan-Shmuel archive via the PikiWiki-Israel free image collection project, Creative Commons Attribution 2.5 Generic license

p. 242: Bob Sandberg, LOOK photographer, LOOK Magazine Photograph Collection at the Library of Congress, public domain

p. 243: Aido2002, Creative Commons Attribution-Share Alike 3.0 Unported license

p. 244, left to right: Creative Commons Attribution-Share Alike 3.0 Unported license; rick, Creative Commons Attribution 2.0 Generic license; Mark Wolfe, FEMA Photo Library, public domain; SSgt. Derrick C. Goode, U.S. Air Force, public domain

p. 246: University of Massachusetts, used by permission

CHAPTER 13

p. 251: public domain

p. 252, Abe Coleman: Jeffrey S. Meltzer, public domain

p. 252, Iran protest: Milad Avazbeigi, Creative Commons Attribution-Share Alike 2.0 Generic license

p. 252, Sid Vicious: Chicago Art Department c/o L. Schorr, Creative Commons Attribution 2.0 Generic license

p. 253, Irving Fisher: George Grantham Bain collection, United States Library of Congress's Prints and Photographs division

p. 253, dice: Niabot, Creative Commons CC0 1.0 Universal Public Domain Dedication

p. 255: Mass Communication Specialist 1st Class Michael Hight, USN, Public domain

p. 255: Imprimerie Royale, Creative Commons CC0 1.0 Universal Public Domain Dedication

p. 257, George Akerlof: Yan Chi Vinci Chow, Creative Commons Attribution 3.0 Unported license

p. 257, lemons: Paoletta S., Creative Commons Attribution 2.0 Generic license

CHAPTER 14

CPSIA information can be obtained at www.ICGtesting.com
Printed in the USA
BVOW09s2031070916

461323BV00004B/8/P

9 781939 402172